DATE DUE

			PRINTED IN U.S.A.

Children's
Literature
Review

Guide to Gale Literary Criticism Series

For criticism on	You need these Gale series
Authors now living or who died after December 31, 1959	*CONTEMPORARY LITERARY CRITICISM (CLC)*
Authors who died between 1900 and 1959	*TWENTIETH-CENTURY LITERARY CRITICISM (TCLC)*
Authors who died between 1800 and 1899	*NINETEENTH-CENTURY LITERATURE CRITICISM (NCLC)*
Authors who died between 1400 and 1799	*LITERATURE CRITICISM FROM 1400 TO 1800 (LC)* *SHAKESPEAREAN CRITICISM (SC)*
Authors who died before 1400	*CLASSICAL AND MEDIEVAL LITERATURE CRITICISM (CMLC)*
Authors of books for children and young adults	*CHILDREN'S LITERATURE REVIEW (CLR)*
Black writers of the past two hundred years	*BLACK LITERATURE CRITICISM (BLC)*
Short story writers	*SHORT STORY CRITICISM (SSC)*
Poets	*POETRY CRITICISM (PC)*
Dramatists	*DRAMA CRITICISM (DC)*
Major authors from the Renaissance to the present	*WORLD LITERATURE CRITICISM, 1500 TO THE PRESENT (WLC)*

For criticism on visual artists since 1850, see

MODERN ARTS CRITICISM (MAC)

ISSN 0362-4145

R

volume 30

Children's Literature Review

Excerpts from Reviews,
Criticism, and Commentary
on Books for Children
and Young People

Gerard J. Senick
Editor

Tina Grant
Sharon R. Gunton
Associate Editors

 **Gale Research Inc.** · *DETROIT · WASHINGTON, D.C. · LONDON*

STAFF

Gerard J. Senick, *Editor*

Tina Grant, Sharon R. Gunton, *Associate Editors*

James A. Edwards, Anna J. Sheets, Brian J. St. Germain, *Assistant Editors*

Jeanne A. Gough, *Permissions & Production Manager*
Linda M. Pugliese, *Production Supervisor*
Donna Craft, Paul Lewon, Maureen Puhl, Camille Robinson, Jennifer VanSickle, Sheila Walencewicz, *Editorial Associates*

Sandra C. Davis, *Permissions Supervisor (Text)*
Maria L. Franklin, Josephine M. Keene, Michele Lonoconus, Denise Singleton, Kimberly F. Smilay,
Permissions Associates
Jennifer A. Arnold, Brandy C. Merritt, Shalice Shah, *Permissions Assistants*

Margaret A. Chamberlain, *Permissions Supervisor (Pictures)*
Pamela A. Hayes, Keith Reed, *Permissions Associates*
Arlene Johnson, Barbara Wallace, *Permissions Assistants*

Victoria B. Cariappa, *Research Manager*
Maureen Richards, *Research Supervisor*
Robert S. Lazich, Mary Beth McElmeel, Tamara C. Nott, *Editorial Associates*
Kelly Hill, Daniel Jankowski, Donna Melnychenko, *Editorial Assistants*

Mary Beth Trimper, *Production Manager*
Catherine Kemp, *Production Assistant*

Cynthia Baldwin, *Art Director*
Nicholas Jakubiak, C. J. Jonik, Yolanda Y. Latham, *Desktop Publishers/Typesetters*

Library of Congress Catalog Card Number 86-645085
ISBN 0-8103-5703-8
ISSN 0883-9123

Printed in the United States of America
Published simultaneously in the United Kingdom
by Gale Research International Limited
(An affiliated company of Gale Research Inc.)
10 9 8 7 6 5 4 3 2 1

The trademark **ITP** is used under license.

Contents

Preface   vii

Acknowledgments   xi

Preface

Children's literature has evolved into both a respected branch of creative writing and a successful industry. Currently, books for young readers are considered the most popular segment of publishing, while criticism of juvenile literature is instrumental in recording the literary or artistic development of the creators of children's books as well as the trends and controversies that result from changing values or attitudes about young people and their literature. Designed to provide a permanent, accessible record of this ongoing scholarship, *Children's Literature Review (CLR)* presents parents, teachers, and librarians—those responsible for bringing together children and books—with the opportunity to make informed choices when selecting reading materials for the young. In addition, *CLR* provides researchers of children's literature with easy access to a wide variety of critical information from English-language sources in the field. Users will find balanced overviews of the careers of the authors and illustrators of the books that children and young adults are reading; these entries, which contain excerpts from published criticism in books and periodicals, assist users by sparking ideas for papers and assignments and suggesting supplementary and classroom reading. Ann L. Kalkhoff, president and editor of *Children's Book Review Service Inc.,* writes that "*CLR* has filled a gap in the field of children's books, and it is one series that will never lose its validity or importance."

Scope of the Series

Each volume of *CLR* profiles the careers of a selection of authors and illustrators of books for children and young adults from preschool through high school. Author lists in each volume reflect these elements:

- an international scope.

- approximately fifteen authors of all eras.

- a variety of genres covered by children's literature: picture books, fiction, nonfiction, poetry, folklore, and drama.

Although earlier volumes of *CLR* emphasized critical material published after 1960, successive volumes have expanded their coverage to encompass important criticism written before 1960. Since many of the authors included in *CLR* are living and continue to write, their entries are updated periodically. Future volumes will supplement the entries of selected authors covered in earlier volumes and will include criticism on the works of authors new to the series.

Organization of This Book

An author section consists of the following elements: author heading, author portrait, author introduction, excerpts of criticism (each followed by a bibliographical citation), and illustrations, when available.

- The **author heading** consists of the author's name followed by birth and death dates. The portion of the name outside the parentheses denotes the form under which the author is most frequently published. If the majority of the author's works for children were written under a pseudonym, the pseudonym will be listed in the author heading and the real name given on the first line of the author introduction. Also located at the beginning of the introduction are any other pseudonyms used by the author in writing for children and any name variations, including transliterated forms for authors whose languages use nonroman alphabets. Uncertainty as to a birth or death date is indicated by question marks.

■ An **author portrait** is included when available.

■ The **author introduction** contains information designed to introduce an author to *CLR* users by presenting an overview of the author's themes and styles, occasional biographical facts that relate to the author's literary career or critical responses to the author's works, and information about major awards and prizes the author has received. Introductions also list a group of representative titles for which the author or illustrator being profiled is best known; this section, which begins with the words "major works include," follows the genre line of the introduction. Where applicable, introductions conclude with references to additional entries in biographical and critical reference series published by Gale Research Inc. These sources include past volumes of *CLR* as well *Authors & Artists for Young Adults, Classical and Medieval Literature Criticism, Contemporary Authors, Contemporary Authors Autobiography Series, Contemporary Authors Bibliographical Series, Contemporary Literary Criticism, Dictionary of Literary Biography, Drama Criticism, Nineteenth-Century Literature Criticism, Poetry Criticism, Short Story Criticism, Something about the Author, Something about the Author Autobiography Series, Twentieth-Century Literary Criticism,* and *Yesterday's Authors of Books for Children.*

■ **Criticism** is located in three sections: **author's commentary** (when available), **general commentary** (when available), and **title commentary** (in which commentary on specific titles appears). Centered headings introduce each section, in which criticism is arranged chronologically. Titles by authors being profiled are highlighted in boldface type within the text for easier access by readers.

The **author's commentary** presents background material written by the author or by an interviewer. This commentary may cover a specific work or several works. Author's commentary on more than one work appears after the author introduction, while commentary on an individual book follows the title entry heading.

The **general commentary** consists of critical excerpts that consider more than one work by the author or illustrator being profiled. General commentary is preceded by the critic's name in boldface type or, in the case of unsigned criticism, by the title of the journal. Occasionally, *CLR* features entries that emphasize general criticism on the overall career of an author or illustrator. When appropriate, a selection of reviews is included to supplement the general commentary.

The **title commentary** begins with the title entry headings, which precede the criticism on a title and cite publication information on the work being reviewed. Title headings list the title of the work as it appeared in its first English-language edition. The first English-language publication date of each work is listed in parentheses following the title. Differing U. S. and British titles follow the publication date within the parentheses.

Entries in each title commentary section consist of critical excerpts on the author's individual works, arranged chronologically by publication date. The entries generally contain two to six reviews per title, depending on the stature of the book and the amount of criticism it has generated. The editors select titles that reflect the entire scope of the author's literary contribution, covering each genre and subject. An effort is made to reprint criticism that represents the full range of each title's reception, from the year of its initial publication to current assessments. Thus, the reader is provided with a record of the author's critical history. Publication information (such as publisher names and book prices) and parenthetical numerical references (such as footnotes or page and line references to specific editions of works) have been deleted at the editor's discretion to provide smother reading of the text.

■ Selected excerpted are preceded by **explanatory notes,** which provide information of the critic or work of criticism to enhance the reader's understanding of the excerpt.

■ A complete **bibliographical citation** designed to facilitate the location of the original book or article follows each piece of criticism.

■ Numerous **illustrations** are featured in *CLR*. For entries on illustrators, an effort has been made to include illustrations that reflect the characteristics discussed in the criticism. Entries on major authors who do not illustrate their own works may also include photographs and other illustrative material pertinent to the authors' careers.

Special Features

Entries on authors who are also illustrators will occasionally feature commentary on selected works illustrated but not written by the author being profiled. These works are strongly associated with the illustrator and have received critical acclaim for their art. By including critical comment on works of this type, the editors wish to provide a more complete representation of the author's total career. Criticism on these works has been chosen to stress artistic, rather than literary, contributions. Title entry headings for works illustrated by the author being profiled are arranged chronologically within the entry by date of publication and include notes identifying the author of the illustrated work. In order to provide easier access for users, all titles illustrated by the subject of the entry will be boldfaced.

CLR also includes entries on prominent illustrators who have contributed to the field of children's literature. These entries are designed to represent the development of the illustrator as an artist rather than as a literary stylist. The illustrator's section is organized like that of an author, with two exceptions: the introduction presents an overview of the illustrator's styles and techniques rather than outlining his or her literary background, and the commentary written by the illustrator on his or her works is called "illustrator's commentary" rather than "author's commentary." Title entry headings are followed by explanatory notes identifying the author of the illustrated work. All titles of books containing illustrations by the artist being profiled as well as individual illustrations from these books are highlighted in boldface type.

Other Features

■ The **acknowledgments,** which immediately follow the preface, list the sources from which material has been reprinted in the volume. It does not, however, list every book or periodical consulted for the volume.

■ The **cumulative index to authors** lists all of the authors who have appeared in *CLR* with cross-references to the various literary criticism series and the biographical and autobiographical series published by Gale Research Inc. A full listing of the series titles appears on the first page of the indexes of this volume.

■ The **cumulative nationality index** lists authors alphabetically under their respective nationalities. Author names are followed by the volume number(s) in which they appear. Authors who have changed citizenship or whose current citizenship is not reflected in biographical sources appear under both their original nationality and that of their current residence.

■ The **cumulative title index** lists titles covered in *CLR* followed by the volume and page number where criticism begins.

A Note to the Reader

CLR is one of several critical references sources in the Literature Criticism Series published by Gale Research Inc. When writing papers, students who quote directly from any volume in the Literature Criticism Series may use the following general forms to footnote reprinted criticism. The first example pertains to material drawn from periodicals, the second to material reprinted from books.

[1]T. S. Eliot, "John Donne," *The Nation and the Athenaeum,* 33 (9 June 1923), 321-32; excerpted and reprinted in *Literature Criticism from 1400 to 1800,* Vol. 10, ed. James E. Person, Jr. (Detroit: Gale Research, 1989), pp. 28-9.

[1]Henry Brooke, *Leslie Brooke and Johnny Crow* (Frederick Warne, 1982); excerpted and reprinted in *Children's Literature Review,* Vol. 20, ed. Gerard J. Senick (Detroit: Gale Research, 1990), p. 47.

Suggestions Are Welcome

In response to various suggestions, several features have been added to *CLR* since the series began, including author entries on retellers of traditional literature as well as those who have been the first to record oral tales and other folklore; entries on prominent illustrators featuring commentary on their styles and techniques; entries on authors whose works are considered controversial; occasional entries devoted to criticism on a single work or a series of works; sections in author introductions that list major works by the author or illustrator being profiled; explanatory notes that provide information on the critic or work of criticism to enhance the usefulness of the excerpt; more extensive illustrative material, such as holographs of manuscript pages and photographs of people and places pertinent to the authors' careers; a cumulative nationality index for easy access to authors by nationality; and occasional guest essays written specifically for *CLR* by prominent critics on subjects of their choice.

Readers who wish to suggest authors to appear in future volumes, or who have other suggestions, are cordially invited to write the editor.

Acknowledgements

The editors wish to thank the copyright holders of the excerpted criticism included in this volume, the permissions managers of many book and magazine publishing companies for assisting us in securing reprint rights, and Anthony Bogucki for assistance with copyright research. We are also grateful to the staffs of the Detroit Public Library, the Library of Congress, the University of Detroit Library, Wayne State University Purdy/Kresge Library Complex, and the University of Michigan Libraries for making their resources available to us. Following is a list of the copyright holders who have granted us permission to reprint material in this volume of *CLR*. Every effort has been made to trace copyright, but if omissions have been made, please let us know.

COPYRIGHTED EXCERPTS IN *CLR*, VOLUME 30, WERE REPRINTED FROM THE FOLLOWING PERIODICALS:

Appraisal: Children's Science Books, v. 4, Spring, 1971; v. 5, Fall, 1972; v. 7, Fall, 1974; v. 8, Spring, 1975; v. 9, Spring, 1976; v. 12, Spring, 1979; v. 13, Winter, 1980; v. 13, Fall, 1980. Copyright © 1971, 1972, 1974, 1975, 1976, 1979, 1980 by the Children's Science Book Review Committee. All reprinted by permission of the publisher.—*Appraisal: Science Books for Young People,* v. 14, Spring, 1981; v. 15, Fall, 1982; v. 16, Winter, 1983; v. 17, Spring-Summer, 1984; v. 18, Summer, 1985; v. 20, Summer, 1987; v. 21, Spring, 1988; v. 23, Winter, 1990. Copyright © 1981, 1982, 1983, 1984, 1985, 1987, 1988, 1990 by the Children's Science Book Review Committee. All reprinted by permission of the publisher.—*Australian Book Review,* n. 53, August, 1983 for "Self-Portraits 2" by Mavis Thorpe Clark. Reprinted by permission of the author.—*Best Sellers,* v. 37, October, 1977. Copyright © 1977 Helen Dwight Reid Educational Foundation. Reprinted by permission of the publisher.—*Book Week—The Sunday Herald Tribune,* May 9, 1965. © 1965, *The Washington Post.* Reprinted by permission of the publisher.—*Book Week—The Washington Post,* May 7, 1967. © 1967, *The Washington Post.* Reprinted by permission of the publisher.—*Book World—Chicago Tribune,* May 7, 1972. © 1972 Postrib Corp. Reprinted by permission of the *Chicago Tribune* and *The Washington Post.*—*Book World—The Washington Post,* May 5, 1968; May 4, 1969. © 1968, 1969 Postrib Corp. Both reprinted by courtesy of the *Chicago Tribune* and *The Washington Post.*/ November 5, 1972; February 10, 1974; November 7, 1976; March 12, 1978; May 12, 1985; May 13, 1990. © 1972, 1974, 1976, 1978, 1985, 1990, *The Washington Post.* All reprinted with permission of the publisher.—*Bookbird,* v. XV, September 15, 1977. Reprinted by permission of the publisher.—*Booklist,* v. 71, September, 1974; v. 73, November 15, 1976; v. 73, January 1, 1977; v. 73, January 15, 1977; v. 73, March 15, 1977; v. 73, June 1, 1977; v. 74, June 1, 1978; v. 76, November 15, 1979; v. 78, February 1, 1982; v. 79, October 1, 1982; v. 80, October 1, 1983; v. 81, October 1, 1984; v. 82, October 1, 1985; v. 82, June 15, 1986; v. 84, March 1, 1988; v. 85, April 1, 1989; v. 85, July, 1989; v. 86, March 1, 1990; v. 86, May 1, 1990; v. 86, June 1, 1990; v. 87, June 15, 1991; v. 87, August, 1991; v. 88, October 1, 1991; v. 87, February 1, 1991; v. 88, December 15, 1991. Copyright © 1974, 1976, 1977, 1978, 1979, 1982, 1983, 1984, 1985, 1986, 1988, 1989, 1990, 1991 by the American Library Association. All reprinted by permission of the publisher.—*The Booklist,* v. 66, September 1, 1969; v. 66, September 15, 1969; v. 67, May 15, 1971; v. 70, March 15, 1974. Copyright © 1969, 1971, 1974 by the American Library Association. All reprinted by permission of the publisher.—*The Booklist and Subscription Books Bulletin,* v. 64, January 15, 1968; v. 64, May 1, 1968; v. 64, June 1, 1968; v. 64, July 1, 1968; v. 65, January 1, 1969. Copyright © 1968, 1969 by the American Library Association. All reprinted by permission of the publisher.—*Books and Bookmen,* v. 24, November, 1978. © copyright Marie Peel 1978.—*Books for Keeps,* n. 47, November, 1987; n. 64, September, 1990. © School Bookshop Association 1987, 1990. Both reprinted by permission of the publisher.—*Books for Young People,* v. 1, October, 1987 for "Morgan, May, Melinda: New Heriones Offer Humour and Fantasy" by Bernie Goedhart; v. 3, April, 1989 for "Birthday Cake,

January, 1970; v. 17, September, 1970; v. 17, October, 1970; v. 17, November, 1970; v. 17, January, 1971; v. 17, March, 1971; v. 18, September, 1971; v. 18, September, 1971; v. 18, December, 1971; v. 18, February, 1972; v. 18, March, 1972; v. 19, April, 1973; v. 20, September, 1973; v. 20, December, 1973; v. 20, February, 1974; v. 20, March, 1974; v. 21, October, 1974; v. 22, October, 1975; v. 22, February, 1976; v. 23, November, 1976; v. 23, December, 1976; v. 23, January, 1977; v. 23, May, 1977; v. 24, September, 1977; v. 24, November, 1977; v. 25, September, 1978; v. 25, January, 1979; v. 25, February, 1979; v. 26, March, 1980; v. 23, November, 1980; v. 28, January, 1982; v. 28, May, 1982; v. 29, November, 1982; v. 29, February, 1983; v. 30, December, 1983; v. 30, March, 1984; v. 30, April, 1984; v. 30, August, 1984; v. 31, October, 1984; v. 31, November, 1984; v. 31, February, 1985; v. 31, April, 1985; v. 32, September, 1985; v. 32, August, 1986; v. 33, December, 1986; v. 33, February, 1987; v. 33, March, 1987; v. 34, September, 1987; v. 34, October, 1987; v. 35, June-July, 1988; v. 35, September, 1988; v. 35, November, 1988; v. 35, April, 1989; v. 35, September, 1989; v. 35, November, 1989; v. 36, February, 1990; v. 36, June, 1990; v. 37, March, 1991; v. 37, May, 1991; v. 37, September, 1991; v. 37, December, 1991; v. 38, January, 1992; v. 38, June, 1992; v. 38, October, 1992. Copyright © 1964, 1967, 1968, 1969, 1970, 1971, 1972, 1973, 1974, 1975, 1976, 1977, 1978, 1979, 1980, 1982, 1983, 1984, 1985, 1986, 1987, 1988, 1989, 1990, 1991, 1992. All reprinted from *School Library Journal,* a Cahners/ R.R. Bowker Publication, by permission.—*Science Books: A Quarterly Review,* v. 2, March, 1967; v. 3, December, 1967; v. 4, May, 1968; v. 4, September, 1968; v. 7, May, 1971; v. 7, March, 1972; v. 8, May, 1972; v. 8, March, 1973. Copyright 1967, 1968, 1971, 1972, 1973 by AAAS. All reprinted by permission of the publisher.—*Science Books & Films,* v. XII, December, 1976; v. XIV, September, 1978; v. XV, March, 1980; v. 16, November, 1980; v. 16, January-February, 1981; v. 17, November-December, 1981; v. 18, November-December, 1982; v. 21, November-December, 1985; v. 21, March-April, 1986; v. 22, March-April, 1987; v. 22, May-June, 1987; v. 25, September-October, 1989; v. 25, March-April, 1990; v. 25, May-June, 1990. Copyright 1976, 1978, 1980, 1981, 1982, 1985, 1986, 1987, 1989, 1990, by AAAS. All reprinted by permission of the publisher.—*Scientific American,* v. 227, December, 1972. Copyright © 1972 by Scientific American, Inc. All rights reserved. Reprinted by permission of the publisher.—*Signal,* n. 39, September, 1982 for "Magic in the Poetry of Charles Causley" by Neil Philip. Copyright © 1982 The Thimble Press. Reprinted by permission of the author./ n. 12, September, 1973; n. 18, September, 1975; n. 29, May, 1979; n. 41, May, 1983. Copyright © 1973, 1975, 1979, 1983 The Thimble Press. All reprinted by permission of The Thimble Press, Lockwood, Station Road, South Woodchester, Glos., GL5 5RQ, England.—*The Spectator,* v. 231, October 20, 1973. © 1973 by *The Spectator.* Reprinted by permission of *The Spectator.*—*Time,* **New York,** v. 112, December 4, 1978. Copyright 1978 Time Warner Inc. All rights reserved. Reprinted by permission from *Time.*—*The Times Educational Supplement,* n. 3308, November 24, 1978; n. 3445, July 9, 1982; n. 3448, July 30, 1982; n. 3462, November 5, 1982; n. 3685, February 13, 1987; n. 3806, June 9, 1989; n. 3932, November 8, 1991. © The Times Supplements Limited 1978, 1982, 1987, 1989, 1991. All reproduced from *The Times Educational Supplement* by permission.—*The Times Literary Supplement,* n. 3458, June 6, 1968; n. 3484, December 5, 1968; n. 3529, October 16, 1969; n. 3566, July 2, 1970; n. 3605, April 2, 1971; n. 3672, July 14, 1972; n. 3719, June 15, 1973; n. 3743, September 24, 1973; n. 3742, November 23, 1973; n. 3774, July 5, 1974; n. 3837, September 26, 1975; n. 3991, September 29, 1978; n. 4069, March 27, 1981; n. 4156, November 26, 1982; n. 4275, February 22, 1985; n. 4381, March 20, 1987; n. 4416, November 20-26, 1987; n. 4625, November 22, 1991. © The Times Supplements Limited 1968, 1969, 1970, 1971, 1972, 1973, 1974, 1975, 1978, 1981, 1982, 1985, 1987, 1991. All reproduced from *The Times Literary Supplement* by permission.—*Top of the News,* v. 31, April, 1975. Copyright © 1975 by the American Library Association. Reprinted by permission of the publisher.—*Virginia Kirkus' Service,* v. XXXII, February 1, 1964; v. XXXIII, April 15, 1965; v. XXXIV, February 1, 1966. Copyright © 1964, 1965, 1966 Virginia Kirkus' Service, Inc. All reprinted by permission of the publisher.—*Voice of Youth Advocates,* v. 7, February, 1985; v. 8, October, 1985; v. 8, December, 1985; v. 11, April, 1988; v. 14, February, 1992. Copyrighted 1985, 1988, 1992 by *Voice of Youth Advocates.* All reprinted by permission of the publisher.

COPYRIGHTED EXCERPTS IN *CLR,* VOLUME 30, WERE REPRINTED FROM THE FOLLOWING BOOKS:

PERMISSION TO REPRODUCE ILLUSTRATIONS APPEARING IN *CLR*, VOLUME 30, WAS RECEIVED FROM THE FOLLOWING SOURCES:

Illustration by Don Freeman from his *Mop Top*. The Viking Press, 1955. Copyright 1955 by Don Freeman. Used by permission of Viking Penguin, a division of Penguin Books USA./ Illustration by Don Freeman from his *The Guard Mouse*. The Viking Press, Inc., 1967. Copyright © 1967 by Don Freeman. Used by permission of Viking Penguin, a division of Penguin Books USA./ Illustration by Don Freeman from his *Norman the Doorman*. Copyright © 1959 by Don Freeman. Copyright renewed Lydia Freeman, 1987. Reprinted by permission of Penguin Books Ltd./ Illustration by Don Freeman from his *Corduroy*. Viking Penguin Inc., 1968. Copyright © 1968 by Don Freeman. Used by permission of Viking Penguin, a division of Penguin Books USA./ Illustration by Lydia and Don Freeman from their *Pet of the Met*. The Viking Press, 1953. Copyright 1953 by Lydia and Don Freeman. Used by permission of Viking Penguin, a division of Penguin Books USA./ Illustration by Susan Jeffers from *Stopping by Woods on a Snowy Evening*, by Robert Frost. Illustrations copyright © 1978 by Susan Jeffers. Reprinted by permission of E.P. Dutton, an imprint of New American Library, a division of Penguin Books USA Inc./ Illustration by Susan Jeffers from her *Three Jovial Huntsmen*. Copyright © 1973 by Susan Jeffers. Reprinted by permission of Bradbury Press./ Illustration by Susan Jeffers from *Brother Eagle, Sister Sky: A Message from Chief Seattle*. Copyright © 1991 by Susan Jeffers. Design by Atha Tehon. Reprinted by permission of the publisher, Dial Books for Young Readers./ Illustration by Dayal Kaur Khalsa from her *I Want A Dog*. Copyright © 1987 by Dayal Kaur Khalsa. Reprinted by permission of Clarkson N. Potter, published by Crown Publishers, a division of Random House, Inc./ Illustration by Dayal Kaur Khalsa from her *How Pizza Came to Queens*. Copyright © 1989 by Dayal Kaur Khalsa. Reprinted by permission of Clarkson N. Potter, published by Crown Publishers, a division of Random House, Inc./ Illustration by Dayal Kaur Khalsa from her *Julian*. Reprinted by permission of Tundra Books./ Illustration by Chiyoko Nakatani from her *The Day Chiro Was Lost*. The Bodley Head, 1969. English text copyright © 1969 The Bodley Head Ltd., London. Illustrations © 1965 Chiyoko Nakatani. Reprinted by permission of HarperCollins Publishers, Inc./ Illustration by Chiyoko Nakatani from *The Hippo Boat*, by Eriko Kishida. The Bodley Head, 1967. English text copyright © 1967 The Bodley Head Ltd., London. Illustrations © 1964 Chiyoko Nakatani. Reprinted by permission of HarperCollins Publishers, Inc./ Illustration by Faith Ringgold from her *Tar Beach*. Copyright © 1991 by Faith Ringgold. Reprinted by permission of Crown Publishers, a division of Random House, Inc./ Illustration by Faith Ringgold from her *Tar Beach*. Copyright © 1991 by Faith Ringgold. Reprinted by permission of the Solomon Guggenheim Museum, New York City.

PERMISSION TO REPRODUCE PHOTOGRAPHS APPEARING IN *CLR*, VOLUME 30, WAS RECEIVED FROM THE FOLLOWING SOURCES:

Courtesy of Macmillan Children's Book Group: **p. 1**; Photograph by Mark Gerson: **p. 18, 108**; © News Ltd.: **p. 46**; Courtesy of Mavis Thorpe Clark: **p. 50, 55**; © The Herald & Weekly Times Ltd.: **p. 60**; The Wichita Eagle: **p. 63**; Photograph by Jeannine L. Dickey, reproduced by permission of Roy A. Gallant: **p. 83**; Courtesy of Penguin USA: **p. 127**; Copyright © Karen Benzian: **p. 162, 164**; Courtesy of Marie Brown Associates: **p. 168**; © John Graves, courtesy of Theodore Taylor: **p. 172**.

Children's
Literature
Review

Carol Ryrie Brink

1895-1981

American author of fiction.

Major works include *Caddie Woodlawn* (1935), *Baby Island* (1937), *Magical Melons: More Stories about Caddie Woodlawn* (1944), *Family Grandstand* (1952), *Andy Buckram's Tin Men* (1966), *Two Are Better Than One* (1968), *The Bad Times of Irma Baumlein* (1972).

An author of historical and realistic fiction who is often praised for her understanding of childhood and family life as well as for her knowledge of history, Brink directed her works, which often feature orphaned or motherless girls and boys as protagonists, to readers in the elementary grades through junior high school. She is best remembered as the author of the Newbery Medal-winning *Caddie Woodlawn,* a novel based on her grandmother's recollections of childhood in pioneer Wisconsin. *Caddie Woodlawn* is widely regarded as a classic of juvenile literature and is often favorably compared with Louisa May Alcott's *Little Women* and Laura Ingalls Wilder's *Little House* books. Brink wrote seventeen children's novels, all of which are characterized by the author's gentle good humor and promotion of traditional values such as cooperation and respect for others. In the words of Mary E. Reed, "Brink's books for children are in the old-fashioned sense upright and uplifting, yet they escape a maudlin sentimentality or that flat unreality too often found in children's literature." While critics have occassionally pointed out that Brink's stories have weak and predictable plots, they commend the author's sense of fun and adventure, her vivid characterizations of children, and her detailed depictions of place and time.

Many of Brink's works were inspired by her background, experiences, and travels; she also drew on the experiences of her immediate family and relatives for the subjects of her books. Her first story for children, *Anything Can Happen on the River* (1934), was based in part on a boat trip the author's family took up the Siene; Brink later used European settings for several of her other books. With her next novel, *Caddie Woodlawn,* Brink created the popular story of an eleven-year-old girl growing up in a large Wisconsin family during the Civil War years, a period when that state was still part of the frontier. Basing her story on actual events related to her by her maternal grandmother, Brink introduced a lively and independent heroine to children's literature with Caddie, who has recently been considered a prototypical feminist by some critics. Brink later wrote a three-act play about Caddie as well as a second book about the Woodlawn family, *Magical Melons,* a collection of short stories. The town of Warsaw, Idaho, where Brink was raised, serves as the setting for *Two Are Better Than One* and *Louly* (1974), both of which include a character named Chrystal Banks who is believed to be modeled after the author as a child; *All Over Town* (1939) is set in a similar small town in the west, Warsaw Junction.

In two of her books, Brink experimented with lighthearted fantasy: *Baby Island* involves two girls shipwrecked on a tropical island with four babies for whom they provide in various inventive ways, and *Andy Buckram's Tin Men* tells the story of a young boy whose homemade robots, crafted from tin cans and salvaged machine parts, come to life after an electrical storm. Brink also wrote novels, poetry, and essays for adults. In addition to the 1937 Newbery Medal, *Caddie Woodlawn* won the Lewis Carroll Shelf Award in 1959. Brink's fiction was also honored by the National League of American Pen Women and the Southern California Council of Literature for Children.

(See also *Something about the Author,* Vols. 1, 27, 31; *Contemporary Authors New Revision Series,* Vol. 3; and *Contemporary Authors,* Vol. 104.)

AUTHOR'S COMMENTARY

[The following excerpt is from Brink's Newbery Medal acceptance speech for Caddie Woodlawn, *originally delivered on May 12, 1936.]*

This year's Newbery book began a very long time ago. It

began, I suppose, in 1857 when John Woodhouse left Boston with his wife and four children for the wilds of Wisconsin. He went to install and operate a sawmill for the Carson and Rand Company at Eau Galle in western Wisconsin.

When the family arrived there, the settlement consisted of a tribe of Indians and two or three white families. The settlement grew rapidly, and John Woodhouse soon established his lively and increasing family on a farm near Dunnville. Here Caddie grew from a delicate baby to a sturdy tomboy and later to a young girl on the verge of womanhood. To this child from the East everything in the pioneer life about her was wonderful and thrilling. Her eyes were wide open to observe and remember. She was extremely happy and enjoyed all of her adventures to the fullest. The fact that she left this wilderness home when she was thirteen or fourteen only served to crystallize her memories into a lasting record.

From Wisconsin the family moved to St. Louis, and Caddie married a young doctor who was as much of a pioneer as she was. Together they went to Idaho and settled there when it was still a territory. She has never returned to the old Wisconsin home, but her memories of it are so accurate, that seventy years later I was able to locate all of the geographical details from her descriptions. That is how the book of **Caddie Woodlawn** had its beginning.

My grandmother is a naturally gifted story-teller, but she is not at home with pen and paper. The adventures of Caddie would probably have remained unwritten, if I had not been a lonely little girl who adored stories. When I was eight years old I went to live with my grandmother and aunt. I had neither father, mother, brother, nor sister, and one of my greatest delights was to hear of the teeming family life of the numerous and adventurous Woodhouse children. I was quite a spoiled child, but I could be bribed to do almost anything if Gram would tell me about her childhood in Wisconsin. It was only a few years ago that the idea of setting these stories down for other children occurred to me. If I had liked them so much, why shouldn't other children like them, too?

I did not see my grandmother at all during the writing of the book, but many letters and questionnaires flew back and forth, and the writing of the book involved a good deal of research and a visit to Dunnville. I already knew northern Wisconsin very well, and loved it, so that it was not difficult to transfer my knowledge and affection to western Wisconsin as well.

I wanted to write a book which should be accurate in background and in the life of the times. I wanted to make a family record and to use real characters, places, and events. And yet I felt that all of this must combine to make a lively book with enough general appeal and plot to interest all children. This was rather a large order, and I often found myself sighing over the great profusion of material which had to be untangled. The difficulties lay in this large amount of true material which seemed to have little form or chronological order, and all of which seemed too interesting to discard. I did, however, have to discard a good deal which was just as interesting as some I kept, but

which seemed impossible to work in. I limited the time of action to one year, and worked in much material which undoubtedly happened either earlier or later. . . . Then I had to form some sort of coherent plot, and for the sake of plot I added the few imaginary incidents in the book. But even these grew out of real situations. The best test that these imaginary incidents have had is that my grandmother approves of them.

There were many things that obviously had no relation to the plot, such as the passenger pigeons and the story of PeeWee. But I felt that these things had a real place in the book, nevertheless. When a living person can remember the sky being darkened by the flight of thousands upon thousands of beautiful birds, which now after seventy years are absolutely extinct, it seems to me worth recording. The story of PeeWee was more doubtful. I am not even now sure that it was original with Tom as my grandmother believes that it was. It is very much like the Hans Andersen story of Big Claus and Little Claus, but I have never found the PeeWee version in any book. Perhaps some of you, who know so much more about children's books than I do, may have found it in some old book. If you have or if you ever do, please let me hear of it.

Curiously enough in our present-day adult world which has so few ideals, it seems that children still admire great deeds and noble endeavors and that they thrill to unselfish ideals. If children are disillusioned and have low aims today, it is only a reflection of our own weariness of the world. For they have their lives before them, and only a word from us is needed to encourage them. In the period that we like to call Victorian, the ordinary children's books were so full of ideals and moral precepts that there was very little room for any real life. They were dreadfully dull books. I don't think that our books can ever be so dull again, because we are aiming at real life even in our most ordinary stories. But let us not forget that our children need ideals, too.

Before I began writing **Caddie Woodlawn** I had not thought very much about the duty we owe our children in regard to the past. Particularly in the Middle West, the last seventy years have seen more sweeping changes than any other period that I can think of in history. In a single span of life we have passed from the most primitive struggle for existence to the most sophisticated and luxurious of urban life. I talked with a number of old pioneers while I was forming my background for the story, and the more I talked with them the more convinced I became that we are about to lose a most precious contact with something which has vanished.

The sturdy blood of these pioneers still flows in the veins of our children. They have the same bone and muscle, but they can have no conception of the hardships and struggles and dreams that built these bodies of theirs. They have all the ease which electricity and the various machines can give them, but our luxurious modern age is full of problems, too, which are more complicated than those our grandfathers faced. If we can just keep hold of some of the sturdy pioneer qualities of these grandparents to hand down to our children, perhaps our children will be better fitted to meet courageously the difficult problems of our modern world. It is an entirely different world, but after all the pioneer qualities of courage, willingness to go to meet the unknown, and steadfastness under difficulties are the things most needed today, as they were then. (pp. 248-50)

Carol Ryrie Brink, " 'Caddie Woodlawn', Newbery Medal Winner 1936: Her History," in The Horn Book Magazine, Vol. XII, No. 4, July-August, 1936, pp. 248-50.

GENERAL COMMENTARY

Naomi Buchheimer

Fortunately for all of us, Nora and David Brink came home from Sunday School—one day about twenty years ago—with a poorly written Bible newspaper. Their mother, looking it over, decided then and there that she could equal or excel the stories in that paper. So Carol Ryrie Brink began to write for her own youngsters—first short stories, then whole books. She soon found that other young people appreciated her work just as much as her own children did. The Macmillan Company published one book after another which flowed from her fluent pen. Today, her children are grown up, but now Mrs. Brink has three grandchildren who will soon be old enough to listen to grandmother's tales of adventure.

Although Carol Ryrie Brink sets her novels for children in far-off places and far-off times, we must remember that it is natural for her to do so. Her own interesting life has provided the basis for much of her writing. Born in Idaho, in what had so recently been frontier country, she was brought up by her maternal grandmother after her parents' untimely death. Her own grandmother's stories of her girlhood stuck with Carol Ryrie until years later when *Caddie Woodlawn* was born. In fact, Mrs. Brink recalls sending her grandmother questionnaires to answer so that she could fill in the gaps in her own knowledge of pioneer life. The girl, Carol Ryrie, married a young mathematician by the name of Raymond Brink. Professor Brink is now head of the mathematics department at the University of Minnesota. *Family Grandstand,* the latest Brink book, is certainly based on actual campus living. The Brinks and their two children have traveled extensively and frequently. *Mademoiselle Misfortune* and *Anything Can Happen on the River* were direct outgrowths of their trips to France during the early '30's. In fact, only one book, *Baby Island,* seems to be far afield from Mrs. Brink's own experience. And *Baby Island* is a fascinatingly imaginative book of a very original nature.

Carol Brink acknowledges her indebtedness to her family in dedicating her books. *Caddie Woodlawn,* of course, was dedicated to her grandmother, and *Magical Melons* includes a note saying that her grandmother, the original Caddie, had died four years before the publication of this book. *All Over Town* was dedicated to her Aunt Elsie, and *Lad with a Whistle,* to the memory of Alexander Ryrie, her father. *Mademoiselle Misfortune* bears an inscription to her daughter, Nora, and *Family Grandstand* is dedicated in part to Susan Carol Hunter, Nora's older child. Professor and Mrs. Brink and their son, David, were "the

crew of the Minnehaha" to whom *Anything Can Happen on the River* was dedicated. (The Minnehaha was the motorboat in which the Brink family navigated the Seine and Yonne Rivers.)

It would appear sensible to discuss the three pioneer-life books together. The two books about the Woodlawns, *Caddie Woodlawn* (1936) and *Magical Melons* (1944), are highly realistic. One feels that Mrs. Brink fully understands both children and pioneers. For instance, Hetty, Caddie's younger sister, is a little know-it-all and tell-it-all. But Mrs. Brink helps her young readers to understand Hetty by explaining that Hetty really had no close companionship within the family and that she found gossip the only way to make herself feel important. In *Magical Melons,* Mrs. Brink returns to the character of Hetty and shows how the child made herself useful to the doctor's wife who needed her friendship and help. There are countless examples of historically valid pioneer details such as the Indian uprising scare, the authentic songs sung by the hired man, the school which was in session for two months in summer and three in winter, the circuit rider, the description of the mail delivery, the discussion about the expense of sulphur matches, and the statement by Mr. Woodlawn that he had paid a man to fight for him in the Civil War.

A fine basic philosophy seems to shine through these stories as well as through all the Brink books. Stated succinctly, it is the belief that everyone is of some use in the world. Even Obediah, the bully, saves the schoolhouse from fire. Even Hetty, the tattler, helps the doctor's wife. This delicate undercurrent, coupled with a wise use of humor and a deep understanding of human emotions, makes the Brink books readable at any level. An adult revels in the antics of pre-adolescent Caddie as much as any child. This author never "talks down" to her audience in any sense of the word. Her vocabulary and her situations are aimed high enough so that anybody can enjoy her books. Who would not laugh at the scene in which the children discover Cousin Lucy's wig? Who would not think that Cousin Lucy's leave-taking, at which the children make themselves cry by smelling onions, was funny?

The other pioneer book, *All Over Town* (1939), is also somewhat autobiographical. Mrs. Brink asserts in the opening note that the scene of the book, a small western town called Warsaw Junction, is "something like" the town in which she grew up. Here, instead of Caddie, the central character is Ardeth Howard, the motherless child of a country doctor. Her playmates are the minister's sons who are forever getting into mischief. Here again, that gentle humor provides many good laughs for the reader. Nobody could possibly keep a straight face while reading about the tea party given by the boys and Ardeth for the good ladies of Warsaw Junction. Again, too, we have that understanding of child psychology which is shown when describing the manner in which Ardeth ate her ice-cream soda, and when explaining how Martin, the older son of the minister, got the neighborhood youngsters to envy his little brother Henry instead of ridiculing him for his "sissy part" in the town pageant. Excitement is kept at a high level in these books by the fire and dog poisonings in *All*

Over Town, and by the possible inheritance and Caddie's dramatic horseback ride to warn Indian Joe in *Caddie Woodlawn.* Mrs. Brink illustrates that the minister's sons have their function in life in general and in Warsaw Junction in particular when they solve the mystery of the fire and bring the village back-sliders into the church.

Mademoiselle Misfortune (1937) and *Anything Can Happen on the River* (1934), both inspired by the Brink family's sojourns in France, are again based on the theory of every person's usefulness to society. In *Mademoiselle Misfortune,* Alice Moreau, one of seven children (six of whom are girls), feels that she is a misfortune to her parents because there are so many female children, all of whom must be provided with dowries or "dots." Alice and two of her brothers and sisters prove their worth by easing the burden on their parents and fending for themselves, while they remain loyal to their family. The excitement in this book comes from the Peruvian gang who are trying to catch Miss Weatherwax, the American woman whom Alice is looking after. The humor is unbeatable. When Miss Weatherwax and an irate Frenchman have a minor automobile accident, Alice "interprets" in such a way that the two protagonists become friends. Speaking of interpreting, Mrs. Brink's use of French words adds color to the story, for she explains the words so subtly that the reader feels that he knew them all the time. The description of Alice's and Miss Weatherwax's journey through France is educational without being didactic. The way in which the Moreau girls used their vivid imaginations in dressing up and in role playing is indicative of Mrs. Brink's understanding of children. *Mademoiselle Misfortune,* dedicated to the author's daughter, is more suitable reading for girls than for boys.

On the other hand, *Anything Can Happen on the River* would probably interest boys more than girls. The hero is a fourteen year old orphan, Jacques Poirer—a boy hero for the first time. The scene is Paris, about ten years after World War I. Realism is introduced by Monsieur Bonnard, the victim of gassing in the war. Yet, it must be understood that M. Bonnard is never allowed to become a gruesome or frightening person, only a pitifully sick man. Mrs. Brink's descriptions of French food fairly make the mouth water. The reader enjoys traveling with the hero in the environs of Paris. The main plot of the story, the mysterious disappearance of the houseboat which had belonged to Jacques's family, is more highly developed than in any of her other books until *Lad with a Whistle.* The scene in which poor undersized Jacques tries to share a bed with the gigantic river man, Lulu, is highly amusing. One can easily visualize the mountains and valleys created by the fat Lulu and how Jacques must have been continually falling into the valleys or been pushed out of bed by his snoring friend. The central theme of usefulness is again demonstrated by Jacques's forlorn dependency which turns to self-assurance and maturity as he solves the family mystery and helps his benefactor to find his own missing boat.

Baby Island (1937), although fantastic and "Robinson Crusoeish," contains the basic elements of humor and essential usefulness of all human beings. Mary Wallace, age twelve, her younger sister, and several tiny babies, are set adrift in a life boat in the Pacific Ocean when their ocean liner is believed to be sinking. The two Wallace girls, who love babies, adapt themselves to the desert island on which they are cast ashore. In learning to adjust to their new way of living, they are surprised to find out that babies must be burped, that the ocean tide is something more significant than a lesson from a geography book. Their "Man Friday," a Cockney hermit, displays the goodness of his soul by falling in love with one of the babies and by making useful objects for the children until they are all rescued. Mixing up the "Pink" twin with the "Blue" twin and the final recognition of their difference because only one twin knew the word "crab" is one little incident which adds much humor to what could be a pathetic situation.

Lad with a Whistle (1941) is in many ways a child's version of *Wuthering Heights.* The bleak Scotch countryside and the dark ancestral home combine to create a mood of impending doom. The death of the Old Laird starts a series of events which end in happiness for all concerned only because this is a children's book. The mystery is carried forward by a secret panel hiding a secret room, several thefts, nightly wanderings, burned letters, and treacherous servants. There is a boy hero again, as in *Anything Can Happen,* and that hero, Rob McFarland, is an orphan like Jacques Poirer. (Both *Baby Island* and *All over Town* have motherless heroines. We may well wonder what connection there is between the choice of these circumstances and Mrs. Brink's own life.) In keeping with the themes of the other books is the ability of the orphaned beggar, Rob McFarland, to prove his worth by taking care of the Old Laird's grandchildren, at great sacrifice to himself. Sir Walter Scott figures briefly in this story, no doubt to help create a richer background for the readers of this historical novel for children.

Mrs. Brink's latest book, *Family Grandstand* (1952), published by Viking Press, deals with the Ridgeways, a faculty family at Midwest University. Mrs. Ridgeway is a writer of mystery stories and Professor Ridgeway teaches, not mathematics, but ancient history. There is no doubt, however, of the autobiographical elements involved here. The professor, an exceptionally realistic one, is very much interested in maintaining academic standards and "adechemic" dignity. This last is a new word coined by the youngest member of the Ridgeway family. In this book, Mrs. Brink employs a clever device to use adult expressions by having the literal-minded children "translate" everything that is said by their parents. For example, Mrs. Ridgeway insists that the near-by stadium is "in their laps" and she often maintains that their old faculty home was "built in the year one." But Susan or George, the older Ridgeway children, would explain that "the stadium isn't really in our laps. It's a block and a half down the street," and the children would know that although Mother said that the house was built in the year one, it was just her funny way of saying 1895! There are at least eight well-integrated threads of plot in *Family Grandstand,* and all of them work out satisfactorily. The children are finally allowed to use the yard as a parking lot on football days; their football hero passes chemistry and can stay on the team; they become the legal owners of an over-sized dog;

they win third prize for their home-coming decorations; little sister is discovered *not* to be a prodigy; the canary returns; the neighborhood terrors are squelched; and Dorothy, Mrs. Ridgeway's helper who is working her way through college, learns that life can be something more than one long study period. The "Terrible Torrences," the little boys whose mother "can't do a thing with them," make an about-face when they realize that outsiders expect them to act grown-up, even though their parents do not seem to expect anything of them. In addition to the "terrors" who prove themselves, Dorothy Sturm, too, shows that she is basically a sensitive person with normal emotions, despite her stated disdain for football and her contention that she came to college for an education, not to "waste time."

Mrs. Brink's only acknowledged formula for writing successful children's books is to "express what you want to say in the simplest possible fashion." That, indeed, seems to be a fairly accurate formula for writing any type of material. Furthermore, she feels that good writing should move the writer himself as he writes it as well as moving the reader. And, one can safely say that most sensitive adults who read her work will find themselves close to laughter or tears.

This author has a regular schedule for writing. When in St. Paul, she spends several hours in the morning at her desk. And if the writing is going exceptionally well she will keep right on into the afternoon. When she and her husband travel, they have no pre-arranged itinerary, but settle down in whatever place takes their fancy and Mrs. Brink continues her regular schedule. She writes her first draft in pencil so neatly that a typist can take it immediately and prepare it for the publisher.

In Mrs. Brink's comfortable home, just to the right of the fireplace, is a built-in bookcase. On the lower shelf is one book after the other bearing the name "Brink." Twelve of those volumes are the original copies of the children's and adults' books written by Carol Ryrie Brink. Others of them are translations into French, Japanese, Danish, and various other languages of her best-loved children's books. *Caddie Woodlawn,* especially, the Newbery Award book of 1937, has been adopted by the children of many nations. The bookshelf is completed by a number of books by Professor Raymond Brink on higher mathematics.

Thus Carol Ryrie Brink writes from the rich background of her own experience as well as from a mature personal philosophy. The influence of her grandmother, her extensive travels through Europe, and her life with her own family certainly provide most of the stimulation for her stories for children. Though perhaps unconsciously, her deep concern for humanity pervades each and every one of her writings. Her belief in the personal worth of all mankind, her conviction that there is some good even behind apparent evil leave her young readers with a feeling that they should come to sense the basic goodness of all people everywhere. Lois Lenski has expressed this very adequately [in her *Told under Spacious Skies,* 1952] when she points out what the reader should get from his exploration of literature:

He acquires new respect and reverence for life in all its various manifestations. He begins to look deeper than appearance, deeper than a spoken accent or a surface materialism, deeper than social castes and conventions, to a sounder appreciation of human character. Only as a person is judged in the light of his environment, and the economic pressures which it brings on his way of life, can he be understood for his own true worth.

(pp. 65-9)

Naomi Buchheimer, "Magical Caddie," in Elementary English, *Vol. XXX, No. 2, February, 1953, pp. 65-9.*

Mary E. Reed

Carol Brink's writings unquestionably qualify her as an important Idaho novelist and regional writer, yet unaccountably few inside Idaho know of her even though her Newbery Award-winning *Caddie Woodlawn* is a classic of children's literature. Unlike Idaho "authors" such as Ernest Hemingway and Ezra Pound, Brink was both a native of Idaho and a writer who wrote about her state. These facts alone should qualify her for serious attention from teachers, librarians, and historians. Her ranking as a regional writer rests on her skillful use of settings, characters, and plots unique to Northern Idaho and the surrounding area, and her ability to transcend the confinements of place and time with themes of universal interest and importance. Although we are aware that her settings are unmistakably drawn from the mountains and wheat fields of her Moscow childhood, her characters reveal the ambiguities and problems of the human race which touch us all. (pp. 142-43)

There are other reasons to embrace Carol Brink as an Idaho novelist. There is her insistence on the integrity of her works. When Macmillan urged her to continue writing books for a Caddie Woodlawn series like the highly profitable one by Laura Ingalls Wilder, Brink refused. Her readers knew that *Caddie* and its sequel, *Magical Melons,* were based on real people and events, and she would not betray this trust by inventing further adventure of the Woodlawn family. She also refused to ridicule, humiliate, or exploit anyone in her books, although her knowledge of small town Moscow provided her with ample material. Above all, Carol consistently maintained high literary standards in all her writing.

Brink's ability to write good fiction for both adults and children is remarkable if not unique. Other notable authors have written for both groups: Carl Sandburg (*Rootabaga Stories*) and E. B. White (*Charlotte's Web*) are two examples. Most authors, however, generally confine their talents to one audience. Brink believed that children's fiction demands equal seriousness and effort, if not more. In an article written for the *Horn Book* magazine in 1967, **"Keep the Bough Green,"** Carol described the writer's responsibility to a juvenile audience:

Let us try to help children to adjust to the everyday world they live in, neither by sentimentalizing nor brutalizing it, but by appreciating what is good in it and by making a courageous fight to better it . . . And let us try to inspire courage and a zest for good living and honest thinking in the young people who are growing up around us.

(p. 143)

Brink's writing talent was . . . nurtured by the natural storytelling gifts of her grandmother. Caroline Watkins' tales of her childhood in Wisconsin taught the young Carol the importance of cadence of speech, selecting significant details, emphasizing dramatic elements, and capturing small ironies which are important to oral as well as written literature.

Brink's books for children are in the old-fashioned sense upright and uplifting, yet they escape a maudlin sentimentality or that flat unreality too often found in children's literature. The appeal of *Caddie Woodlawn* lies in the struggles of the young heroine with sombre responsibilities of growing up. The author knows that Caddie, like the real Caroline Woodhouse and Carol herself, must come to terms with her womanhood. The tension between a girl's childhood and the restraint and prudence demanded of women is a problem which Brink well understood. It is Caddie's father who prepares the girl for this transition by explaining the qualities of a true woman:

> A woman's work is something fine and noble to grow up to, and it is just as important as a man's . . . I don't want you to be the silly, affected person with fine clothes and manners, whom folks sometimes call a lady . . . I want you to be a woman with a wise and understanding heart, healthy in body and honest in mind.

Brink's other works of juvenile fiction with Idaho settings follow this theme of exploration and growth. *All Over Town,* written in 1939, introduces the modern child to the full panoply of small town characters of the early 1900's. *Two Are Better Than One* (1968) and *Louly* (1974) are clearly autobiographical, centering on Carol as a school girl and her interest in becoming a writer. (p. 145)

Carol Brink's life after . . . her early years followed a tranquil course of a college education at the University of Idaho (capped by a senior year at Berkeley), marriage to a professor of mathematics, a long writing career punctuated by several honors, and a happy if somewhat uneventful life as faculty wife, mother, and traveling companion to her husband. All these parts of her life are included in her works, but the fiction with the greatest depth and power has its roots in the Idaho years. At the core of these Idaho memories is Moscow, the setting of a bittersweet childhood which gave her fearful yet joyful insights into human experience. Toward the end of her life she remarked on the privileges of a child growing up in a small town:

> All of the virtues and vices of the large world blossom in the small town with the most superb intensity. In this drop of water under a microscope you can observe all nature and become acquainted with people of all walks of life. Cities are too onesided and diffused. The section in which you live in a city may represent only one phase of life or activity. But the child who has

grown up with open eyes in a little town has inherited the earth.

That inheritance Carol Brink has passed along to us, her heirs. (pp. 146-47)

> *Mary E. Reed, "Carol Ryrie Brink: Legacy of An Idaho Childhood," in* The Idaho Librarian, *Vol. 34, No. 4, October, 1982, pp. 142-47.*

TITLE COMMENTARY

Anything Can Happen on the River (1934)

Mrs. Brink's choice of a title for her book is a happy one. There is something appealing and adventurous about rivers, and have we not the testimony of Kenneth Grahame's ever quotable Water Rat to the joy of "messing about in boats"?

The boy in the book, 14-year-old Jacques, had as a start in life a letter to Monsieur Desmoulins, the owner of a boat yard, two rusty keys and the memory of the barge "La Belle Oudinette" that had once belonged to his family. The girl, Janine, had a dog and a marionette show. With these she and her father made a scanty living, going from one village fair to another. M. Desmoulins, kind, though quick-tempered, had been a friend of Jacques's father and finds a place for the boy in his boat yard. Last but by no means least, there was "Lulu," the big river man, with whom Jacques is sent out to deliver a new motor boat, the Psyche. . . .

This is a first book that shows promise. Mrs. Brink's characters have individuality and her style is lively and direct. The interest is sustained without recourse to overdrawn and too highly colored incidents, and the setting and plot are fresh and unhackneyed. The author has succeeded in suggesting the atmosphere of French country. . . .

> *Anne T. Eaton, in a review of "Anything Can Happen on the River," in* The New York Times Book Review, *April 29, 1934, p. 11.*

A slow but exciting journey up the Seine from Paris is the setting of this story of present day France. Jacques, an orphan; Lulu, the boatman; Janine and Papa Max are all interesting characters. The book has humor, but the multiplicity of incidents tends to make the story drag somewhat.

> *Mary R. Lucas, in a review of "Anything Can Happen on the River," in* Library Journal, *Vol. 59, No. 17, October 1, 1934, p. 76.*

Exotic and charming foreign setting is one of the chief resources upon which Carol Ryrie Brink depends in *Anything Can Happen on the River.* Jacques and an old boatman set off down the Seine in the Psyche, a new motorboat which gets them into many difficulties but introduces them also to romantic environs. Everything comes out properly in the end, after more than enough complications. This is a useful book to give children whose duty it is to learn something about France. They will be "introduced" without quite realizing it.

> *George N. Shuster, in a review of "Anything*

Can Happen on the River," in The Commonwealth, *Vol. XXI, No. 3, November 16, 1934,
p. 98.*

Caddie Woodlawn (1935)

Those who enjoyed Carol Brink's promising first book,
Anything Can Happen on the River, will not be surprised
to find that in **Caddie Woodlawn** she has written an even
better story. There is again an abundance of lively incidents, while the characterization is deeper and the background filled in with a surer hand.

Twelve-year-old Caddie and her brothers and sisters—
there were six Woodlawn children—lived in Western Wisconsin during the Civil War, but so remote was the Wisconsin frontier of those days that their life reads like a pioneer tale. The story never seems overdrawn, but events
that will appeal to the imagination of boys and girls and
will help to give them a sense of the stirring qualities of
frontier life follow one another thick and fast. There is the
threat of an Indian massacre. Caddie's ride by night to the
Indian village and Indian John's pledge of friendship; a
frontier school, including a "speaking day," with songs
and recitations by the pupils. A real Indian scalp belt is
entrusted for a time to Caddie's keeping, and two fine dogs
play a part in the story.

The climax comes when a letter from England makes it
necessary for the Woodlawn family to decide whether they
will remain in America or go back to the English estate
which the father has unexpectedly inherited. The older
children are allowed to help make the decision and to vote
Go or Stay on a slip placed in the family Bible. The reader,
too, feels a moment of suspense as Caddie waits breathlessly until she learns the result. We leave her in her loved
Wisconsin, with the feeling that we have made the acquaintance of a genuine and endearing child.

> *Anne T. Eaton, in a review of "Caddie
> Woodlawn," in* The New York Times Book
> Review, *May 12, 1935, p. 10.*

What a lot has happened since last year when I
dropped the nuts all over the dining-room floor!
How far I've come! I'm the same girl and yet not
the same. I wonder if it's always like that? Folks
keep growing from one person into another all
their lives; and life is just a lot of everyday adventures. Well, whatever life is, I like it.

This is Caddie Woodlawn speaking, near the end of the
book which bears her name. Her words tell a good deal
about the latest John Newbery medal book, selected as
"the most distinguished contribution to American literature for children" published in 1935. A lot does happen
to Caddie and her brothers and sisters in this story of pioneer life in Wisconsin. And since Caddie likes life, her adventures are lively and make enjoyable reading. A seven-
year-old boy, too young to read **Caddie Woodlawn** for
himself, begged to have more and more of the story read
to him. An elderly couple remarked on hearing parts of
Caddie, "Isn't that just like children?" Their comment
was justified. Caddie; her brothers, Tom and Warren; her
sisters; Indian John; and all the others were real people.

Caddie is still living and 82 years old when **Caddie
Woodlawn** was written by her granddaughter, Mrs. Carol
Ryrie Brink of Minneapolis. Altho this prize book does
appeal to all ages, it will be of most interest to older boys
and girls, 10 to 15 years of age. Teachers who are looking
for material about the pioneer school which children can
use during American Education Week will find it in this
book. . . .

Only five of the 15 Newbery medal books have an American setting. **Caddie Woodlawn** is one of these five. This
characteristic is one of the great values of the book. First
of all, it is a jolly good story, full of humor, and written
in a most readable, inviting style. But its authentic historical background gives children a good picture of home life
in pioneer days of the Middlewest. The Woodlawn family
is typical of the many fine people who left our eastern
states to establish homes, schools, and stable communities
in the Middlewest. The ideals of the Woodlawn parents in
being good neighbors, in dealing fairly and kindly with the
Indians, but most of all in the democratic, wholesome upbringing of their children make this book an excellent contribution to American literature for young people. Children in the Middlewest, particularly, can be grateful to
Mrs. Brink for preserving some of the life of that section,
now gone. On this point, the author of **Caddie** says: "Before I began writing **Caddie Woodlawn** I had not thought
very much about the duty we owe our children in regard
to the past. . . . I talked with a number of old pioneers
when I was forming my background for the story, and the
more I talked with them the more convinced I became that
we are about to lose a most precious contact with something that has vanished."

> *Ethel Blake, " 'Caddie Woodlawn': The New-
> bery Medal Book," in* The Journal of the Na-
> tional Education Association of the United
> States, *Vol. 25, No. 8, November, 1936, p. 261.*

Caddie Woodlawn by Carol R. Brink is a Newbery winner.
Not a recent one, but still extremely popular. Caddie is a
young pioneer girl, allowed to run free with her brothers.
She is happy and strong in her so-called tomboy role.
Though her mother pressures her to become more of a
"lady," the reader feels serenely certain that Caddie will
remain her own person. Alas, as the book draws to a close,
Caddie's father pleads: "It's a strange thing, but somehow
we expect more of girls than of boys. It is the sisters and
wives and mothers, you know, Caddie, who keep the
world sweet and beautiful. . . ." Thus subdued, she joins
the insipidly depicted girls at the weaving loom. True, the
boys do ask her to teach them how to weave. Apparently
they may choose to join women at their work, but no longer may Caddie choose to run free in the woods. And we
are left feeling cheated. Why should it be the *right* choice
for her obediently to join the "sweet and beautiful"
women of the world on their pedestals? Why shouldn't she
continue to struggle for a life in which she might fulfill
some inner potential? (p. 254)

> *Feminists on Children's Media, "A Fem-
> inist Look at Children's Books," in* Sexism and
> Youth, *edited by Diane Gersoni-Stavn,
> R. R. Bowker Company, 1974, pp. 249-59.*

The western Wisconsin settlers in *Caddie Woodlawn* perceive a nearby village of docile Indians as a constant threat. Carol Ryrie Brink strikes an ambivalent chord. She allows Caddie's parents to disclaim the prevailing mentality toward the Indians, while at the same time their contrary actions speak louder than their words. Mr. Woodlawn declares he would stake his farm on the Indians' honor and friendliness, yet he encourages his nervous neighbors to huddle together to wait out a rumored "massacree." He never repudiates his wife's fiery remarks about "wicked redskins" and "savages." Caddie, unlike her father, backs her words with courageous action and warns Indian John that the settlers are scheming to strike first before the Indians have a chance to scalp them. Later, when Indian John comes to the Woodlawn home, Caddie's mother, "nearly frightened out of [her] wits," peeped "timidly at him from the dining-room door" until he "stalked out." Then she tells Caddie, "Why folks seem to hate the red men . . . I can't say." Indian John himself, the only Indian villager brought into focus, is given an Uncle Tom role as admirer of little "Missee Red Hair" and harmless contact for the white community.

Katharine Everett Bruner, in a review of "Caddie Woodlawn," in School Library Journal, *Vol. 35, No. 1, September, 1988, p. 125.*

Caddie Woodlawn, written by Carol Ryrie Brink in 1935, is an episodically structured historical novel based in large measure on the author's memories of her grandmother's accounts of her own experiences in western Wisconsin. Set in 1864 and 1865, the novel chronicles a series of events unified by its central character, Caddie Woodlawn, who turns twelve in the course of the year, whose seasonal pattern also gives coherence to the anecdotes and scenes which form the whole. The novel opens and concludes in the early fall and follows the "three adventurers" (Caddie and her brothers, thirteen-year-old Tom and nine-year-old Warren) as they visit the local Indians; enjoy visits from the circuit rider, their Uncle Edmund, and Cousin Annabelle; attend school; farm the land; celebrate the cycle of holidays; and affirm their identities as settlers on the western frontier.

Brink's tone is frequently humorous, but the reader is to take Caddie's character seriously throughout the work, for the novel finally depends on character and on Caddie's own developing awareness of herself as, on the one hand, a special child and, on the other, an American pioneer at the edge of womanhood.

As in other works in this genre, Caddie is her father's child and in many respects male-identified. The author introduces her as a "wild little tomboy, . . . the despair of her mother and of her elder sister Clara," but emphasizes that "her father watched her with a shine of pride in his eyes, and her brothers accepted her as one of themselves without question." Brink stresses the dichotomy between male and female worlds throughout the novel, and Caddie must eventually come to see the split as a difficulty for her. For most of the work, however, she enjoys the freedom of male prerogatives and resents the constraints of traditional female experience. Her relationship with her father is a constant comfort to her and an affirmation of her matur-

ing self. Caddie's red hair associates her for the reader with her brothers but particularly with her father, called "Red Beard" by the Indians, who remain throughout his and Caddie's particular friends. In fact, Caddie's character is attributable in the terms of the novel to her father, who declares to the circuit rider, " 'it is my fault that Caddie is running wild instead of making samplers and dipping candles'." Brink writes that "he had begged his wife to let him try an experiment with Caddie" to improve her initially weak health, and he pleads successfully with her to "let me have Caddie." The results are impressive: "She was brown and strong" in a way that causes her mother and sisters to look at her and sigh, but her father takes satisfaction at once in her independence and his achievement. Caddie, too, identifies herself with her father, feeling even in a political discussion she does not quite understand that "whatever Father said was true, and that she loved him better than anyone else on earth. She was glad that her hair was rough and red like his."

Others are aware of Caddie's tomboy nature. When her Uncle Edmund tries to frighten her with a toy snake, Tom laughs at him: " 'You'd ought to know you can't fool Caddie on snakes or clock springs. Try that on Hetty'." Even Mr. Woodlawn comes to acknowledge with pride that Caddie is capable of traditionally male attitudes and abilities that he did not suspect. For example, her interest and dexterity in taking apart clocks leads him to teach her to be his "partner" in fixing them, declaring, " 'I don't know why I never thought of you before!' " When her mother argues with her father about Caddie's upbringing, enumerating the traditionally female tasks she could perform at her daughter's age, the somewhat indignant Mrs. Woodlawn asks, " 'What does Caddie know how to do?' " Caddie humorously answers, " 'I can plow'."

But the young girl who can respond to Tom's declaration that he has an idea by saying with aplomb " 'Spit it out' " does not want to be male. While she enjoys the liberation from female social constriction that traditionally male behavior permits, she simultaneously wants to be female in a new way; she wants to become a woman in terms other than those offered by mid-nineteenth-century standards. Thus, as in other works of this genre, the young protagonist is frequently contrasted with other females, who offer her a range of models of womanly behavior. For example, her mother, frequently in contradistinction to her father, presents to Caddie traditional, ideal female behavior on the basis of her own relatively sophisticated experience of growing up in the urban East in the 1830s. But such a version of womanhood, whose true home "centered in the churches, the bookshops, the lecture rooms of Boston," Brink presents as inadequate, for it is Mr. Woodlawn whom we and Caddie admire, and he "was entirely happy on the outskirts of civilization . . . where he could breathe freely as he had never done in the narrow streets of Boston." Mrs. Woodlawn's ideal appears embodied in the figure of Cousin Annabelle Grey, who comes to visit with her fashionable dress with its "eight and eighty" buttons that "all the girls in Boston are wearing now." Her arch expressions and cultured insensitivity (she hurts seven-year-old Hetty Woodlawn's feelings by rejecting the little girl's welcoming nosegay, exclaiming, " 'I should hate to stain my mitts' ") make her a figure of fun for Caddie, Tom, and Warren.

If the Boston ideal is, on one level, easily rejected as hypocritical and unsuited to real life in the West, Caddie is uncomfortable with the idea of being typecast as a tomboy and wants to preserve her alternatives, for she is sensitive to the advantages that girlish girls have. For instance, she is quite impressed with the literary polish of Cousin Annabelle's letter accepting the Woodlawns' invitation to visit and wonders with anticipation and reservations, "What would a girl be like who could write such a letter?" She reflects further, "Caddie Woodlawn would never write a letter like that. Couldn't she or wouldn't she? She honestly did not know, but it made her a little ashamed and apprehensive to think about it." Similarly, while her older sister, Clara, wishes she might wear hoops everyday, Caddie vehemently disagrees, for she finds them awkward and silly. When Clara chides her, however, Caddie silently insists to herself, " 'I'm not really so much of a tomboy as they think. Perhaps I shall wear hoops someday, but only when I get good and ready'."

In fact, Brink and Mr. and Mrs. Woodlawn, as well as Caddie, clearly understand her freedom as limited by time; the question is merely what sort of womanhood will supplant it. An alternative to Caddie's cousin's rather hypocritical, pale, and uninteresting Boston belle appears in the character of Katie Hyman, the seamstress's daughter. Katie does not have the eastern panache Mrs. Woodlawn admires in Annabelle, nor does she embody the good breeding and class of the transplanted Woodlawn family, with their Boston and English ancestry, still—as her name suggests—she is worthy of courtship, and Tom himself, to Caddie's chagrin, has a crush on her. Katie is, the author implies, what Caddie might have become had she not been allowed to "run wild" for her health: Katie is delicate, even sometimes sickly, with "little pale fingers." When she receives from Tom "the best valentine in the Dunnville store," Caddie is rather hurt and perplexed, thinking:

> I do everything with Tom. I'm much more fun than Katie. Why she's afraid of horses and snakes, and she wouldn't cross the river for worlds. I don't believe she's spoken three words to Tom in her life. But she's what you call a little lady and I'm just what you call a little tomboy. Maybe there's something in this lady business after all.

Katie is interesting to Caddie as well because of her virtues: she is sweet-tempered, discreet, and gentle. Still Katie is too different in character from Caddie really to provide an alternative mode of being. For example, when the neighbors seek refuge with the Woodlawns during a rumored intended Indian massacre, Katie, like her mother, asks "nothing but protection," her eyes "round with alarm." She keeps her promise to Caddie about not revealing her departure to warn Indian John of the settlers' inclination to attack first, but when Caddie returns, "Katie, who had sat pale and silent in a corner . . . crumpled like a wilted flower, and had to be carried away to bed."

Frailty, affected or real, forms no part of Caddie's charac- ter, but experience has not prepared her to consider seriously as models either Hetty or Clara or even her mother. As frontier women, these three might be expected to suggest alternative female roles at least to some extent, but Clara and Mrs. Woodlawn, until just before the end of the novel, cling to eastern notions of status and class, implicitly rejecting frontier life, while Hetty is too young to be taken seriously by the others. In addition, Caddie has had no training in traditionally female tasks: when the neighbors seek shelter at the Woodlawns', "Mrs. Woodlawn was in her element," and Clara works beside her mother, "her thin cheeks red with excitement, her capable hands doing as much as a woman's." Caddie tries to help, but Brink points out that "after she had broken a dish and spilled applesauce over the kitchen floor, her mother told her she had better run and play, and Caddie ran."

The novel's central issue of Caddie's future identity as a woman is brought to the fore in the work's double climax: Caddie is, she feels unjustly, severely punished for her rude treatment of Annabelle, and Mr. Woodlawn receives a letter from England offering him a large inheritance and a title if he and his family will renounce their United States citizenship and move to Europe. In the first climax, Brink juxtaposes Caddie and her mother, addressing directly the crucial problem of Caddie's destiny as a female. Mrs. Woodlawn's outrage explicitly concerns Caddie's gender: when Tom tries to assume some of the blame, she responds:

> "I cannot blame *you* so much. But that a *daughter* of mine should so far forget herself in her hospitality to a guest—that she should be such a hoyden as to neglect her proper duties as a lady! Shame to her! Shame! No punishment that I can invent would be sufficient for her."

Brink's language is carefully chosen and raises with irony Caddie's chief difficulty: she has not "forgotten herself"; she does not know herself or have yet a self which is her own. Caddie resolves to run away; if what the Woodlawns want is a girl like Annabelle, she reflects, let them adopt her in Caddie's place. Caddie considers joining the Indians, who she feels would accept her as a special woman, for on moral as well as realistic grounds she consciously rejects her mother's notions of femaleness: if the Indians took her in

> then she would never have to grow into that hateful thing which Mother was always talking about—a lady. A lady with fine airs and mincing walk who was afraid to go out into the sun without a hat or a sunshade! A lady, who made samplers and wore stays and was falsely polite no matter how she felt!

Perhaps the reader should not be surprised that it is Mr. Woodlawn who finally provides Caddie with a vision of womanhood, however romanticized in his mind, that creates a real and admirable alternative for his favorite daughter. Coming to Caddie to explain his wife's behavior, he offers her the possibility of becoming what he calls "a splendid woman" in a significant speech:

> "It's a strange thing, but somehow we expect more of girls than of boys. It is the sisters and

wives and mothers . . . who keep the world sweet and beautiful. What a rough world it would be if there were only men and boys in it, doing things in their rough way. A woman's task is to teach them gentleness and courtesy and love and kindness. It's a big task, too, Caddie— harder than cutting trees or building mills or damming rivers. It takes nerve and courage and patience, but good women have those things. They have them just as much as the men who build bridges and carve roads through the wilderness. But no man could ever do it so well. I don't want you to be the silly, affected person with fine clothes and manners, whom folks sometimes call a lady. No, that is not what I want for you, my little girl. I want you to be a woman with a wise and understanding heart, healthy in body and honest in mind. Do you think you would like to be growing up into that woman now? How about it, Caddie; have we run with the colts long enough? . . . I'm sort of responsible for you, Honey. I was the one who urged Mother to let you run wild, because I thought it was the finest way to make a splendid woman of you. And I still believe that, Caddie."

Despite the stereotypes here, the vision Mr. Woodlawn offers Caddie seems a noble one, and it is out of the dual identification of father and daughter, the one with the other, that Caddie accepts it, saying merely, " 'Father, Father'." Brink stresses this point by commenting that "It was all she could say, and really there was nothing more that needed saying." Mr. Woodlawn, in the place of her mother, then prepares his daughter for bed—"with his big hands, which were so delicate with clockwork, he helped her to undress and straighten the tumbled bed." When Caddie awakes, Brink indicates her excitement with the new future:

> She knew that she need not be afraid of growing up. It was not just sewing and weaving and wearing stays. It was something more thrilling than that. It was a responsibility, but, as Father spoke of it, it was a beautiful and precious one, and Caddie was ready to go to meet it.

But several issues remain unresolved here (Caddie's relationship with her mother, for example, and with her brothers), and Brink's feminism needs further delineation. She understands that new roles for women imply simultaneously, if secondarily, new roles for men as a matter of justice as well as logic. Thus she reveals that Mr. Woodlawn, in the name of fairness, punishes both Tom and Warren for their shared rudeness to Annabelle, and when Caddie decides that she, whose hands, like her father's, are good with delicate clockwork, should be able to quilt as well, Brink has Tom and Warren join in the sewing project with enthusiasm, concluding, "So it turned out that, when Caddie began to learn to be a housewife, the boys became housewives, too."

Caddie's new vision of herself thus implies new relationships with the men and women in her world. Knowing that "her old, wild past was ended," Caddie must confront the novel's second climax, which will provide her with the community of relationships that will make her new self possible. Mr. Woodlawn presents the issue of rejecting

America for England as a family question on which each member will vote, considering " ' "What will be best for my future? Where shall I be most useful and happy?" ' " Caddie feels that her mother and sisters will vote to go abroad, while she and her brothers and father will vote to stay. Yet a new relationship with Hetty has slowly been developing in the last quarter of the novel, and as Hetty becomes less of a tattletale, Caddie begins to realize a deep sisterhood of femaleness with her. Alone on the hill near her sister Mary's grave, Caddie reflects on the bonds of sisterhood and, when Hetty joins her, agrees with her that " 'It's kind of nice to be just us two alone, too, isn't it? Without the boys'." Thus, to Caddie's mild surprise, Hetty vows to vote as she does, and Caddie affirms the growing bond, symbolized here in the shared desire "to be an American," by kissing her younger sister and saying, " 'no matter whether we go to England or stay in Wisconsin, let's be better chums'." When the votes are finally in, only one is marked "go," and Clara acknowledges that it is hers and she wants now to tear it up. Mr. Woodlawn is shocked that his wife has voted to stay and wonders if she has sacrificed her own desires for his. Calling him "Johnny," Mrs. Woodlawn declares, " 'I did it all for myself . . . I never knew how much I loved it here until I had to choose—better than England . . . better than Boston!' " Taking her in his arms, Mr. Woodlawn affirms her as part of him, as he is now part of her, by calling her " 'Hattie, Hattie'." Thus the children, "with gaping eyes and mouths," witness their mother's rejection of her former ideals in favor of the frontier lives of "splendid" man-and-woman-hood they have now each freely chosen for themselves.

The novel's conclusion is hence not merely sentimental, but symbolically just and feminist as Caddie returns to Indian John the nameless dog she has been keeping for him during his summer away, only to welcome home her own faithful dog, Nero (a precursor of Lassie), whom Mrs. Woodlawn ill-advisedly let her brother take to St. Louis. In the final scene, our female hero turns her face to the west, and Brink affirms Caddie's feminist future when she writes that her face "was always turned westward now, for Caddie Woodlawn was a pioneer and an American."

Feminism is alive and well in this American novel of 1935. Whether *Caddie Woodlawn* is evidence of feminism's persistence despite the fate of the movement after 1920 or evidence of one of the ways in which it went underground until the 1960s in a manner not yet fully acknowledged or understood by feminist scholars, I am not ready to say. But the novel is an important example of a genre of works by American women for a young female audience that present admirable girl heroes as feminist role models. (pp. 110-16)

Caroline Zilboorg, " 'Caddie Woodlawn': A Feminist Case Study," in Children's literature in education, *Vol. 21, No. 2, June, 1990, pp. 109-17.*

Mademoiselle Misfortune (1936)

The latest winner of the Newbery medal has responded

briskly to the confidence thereby declared in her powers as a writer for young folks with a truly refreshing new story for girls, harder to write than the other because it is contemporary, and uncommonly well written.

Five simultaneous French daughters may be a bonanza, but six successive sisters in a French family where the system of the dot still prevails may be considered by a cold-blooded outsider as a cumulative financial calamity. The first time that Alice, fourteen and oldest of the set, overheard them called by the head of the pension where they all boarded, "the six misfortunes," she took it out on the pension piano in her ensuing hour of practice. Nobody had ever brought that home before to any of the gentle, well educated, polite little steps of this feminine staircase, with their French schoolgirl clothes all alike and their English names all so different from those of French schoolgirls. Alice, both the imaginative and the practical one, the one on whom they all depended to organize and illuminate their work and their play, felt that something drastic must be done about this. Papa, however omniscient, was not omnipotent: he was a gentleman and a diplomat, not working now as the latter but retaining from it his preference for English names and determination that the girls should be linguists. Bringing up an adored only son and a lovely quiverful of daughters on an inconsiderable income takes some doing. Mama did what Papa said. Everybody really loved everybody else in the family. Edward the unique, who agreed with the general conviction that he ought always to come first, was so bearable a brother that when the girls were unaccountably asked to the opera instead of him all six put their money together and bought him a tennis ball because he was taking it so nobly. Moreover, Edward appreciated not only the ball but the spirit in which it was bestowed: he was a good brother. But nothing at the pension seemed to get the family anywhere.

Until, of course, an American spinster with a passion for ham-and-egg breakfasts and a manner of speech affrighting to foreigners, but due only to her not speaking any French, came with a letter of introduction to Papa. She had the sense to carry off Alice as traveling companion to the south of France, where, I may say, Edward, in a burst of protest against being brought up, joined them later and found a job. The traveling part is excellent, and any one will find it true who has so much as flitted through golden Provence, but the chief excellence of the book lies in a transition period when—in remoter corners—parents like Papa, with "presence" and convictions, can still hold out against the subversive individualism of the young. You can't help liking Papa: all his family love him perhaps the more because he also inspires awe. But two of them must make their personal fights and flights, discreetly but firmly going in another direction. The talk is lifelike, had the character of Big Sister, buoyant as it is, does not push out those of the little sisters of whom not so much is seen. There is, besides, a dash of mystery and a happy ending.

May Lamberton Becker, in a review of "Mademoiselle Misfortune," in New York Herald Tribune Books, *November 15, 1936, p. 26.*

This is a very readable story, written with charm and humor, but the melodrama on which the plot is based seems artificial and extraneous, and one looks in vain for the richness and substance which won the Newbery Medal for the author's *Caddie Woodlawn.* (p. 24)

Ellen Lewis Buell, in a review of "Mademoiselle Misfortune," in The New York Times Book Review, *November 15, 1936, pp. 13, 24.*

The author of *Caddie Woodlawn* has produced another book of distinction for girls, which is attractively illustrated by Kate Seredy. The heroine, fourteen-year-old Alice Moreau, is the eldest of the six daughters of a proud and impoverished French diplomat, and is as real and lovable as the brave and high-spirited Caddie herself. . . .

This is a sensitively written, imaginative and at times amusing story of modern France. Its character development is good. It is a welcome addition to the few good books for girls on the threshold of the teens.

A review of "Mademoiselle Misfortune," in The Junior Bookshelf, *Vol. I, No. 2, February, 1937, p. 37.*

Baby Island (1937)

For little girls (and there are many), whose fondest dream it is to borrow a real live baby to play with and take care of, Mrs. Brink's latest book is the perfect fantasy. When, on the night of Sept. 20, the S. S. Orminta on its way from San Francisco to Australia is struck by a tropical storm and badly disabled, Mary Wallace, 12 years old, and her younger sister, Jean, are saved through Mary's presence of mind. More than that, they manage to rescue all the babies on board, the 20-months-old Snodgrass twins, Elisha and Elijah; 4-months-old Jonah, and Ann Elizabeth, aged 1 year. After drifting about in a lifeboat they arrive at a tropical island, where the two girls set up housekeeping and take care of the babies.

One morning they discover large footprints on the beach. Fearing pirates or savages, they cautiously investigate, but the prints prove to be those of Mr. Peterkin, an Englishman who has come to the island to escape from his sister's children and the cares of home life. Though he is very gruff at first, the girls' quiet assumption that he will help them wins his friendship and before long he is sharing with the babies the milk that his goats provide. Mr. Peterkin has a parrot, and the children adopt a monkey. The babies approve of Mr. Peterkin, soon the two households are on the friendliest terms and when the children's tepee blows away in a storm he takes them all home to his shanty. There they have just time to celebrate Christmas when a ship arrives with the children's parents, and takes them all back to civilization.

The story is told with a gentle humor and the logic and realistic detail that children demand in a tale which combines the extraordinary and the everyday.

Anne T. Eaton, in a review of "Baby Island," in The New York Times Book Review, *October 3, 1937, p. 10.*

If fantasy and truth as little girls see it have been more simply and successfully combined, I have not seen it. The winner of one of the Newbery Medals has produced a winsome and lovable story that will appeal to almost any little girl.

This is told by the classic combination of "pictures and conversation"; the tale shines with affection and snaps with fun. [Illustrator] Helen Sewell is in her happiest vein. No small child will believe this "really happened," but any little girl who loves to borrow babies will wish, from her heart, that it could.

> *A review of "Baby Island," in* New York Herald Tribune Books, *November 14, 1937, p. 9.*

Small girls of nine, ten or eleven who have no babies in their families, will, I think, get some fun and enjoyment from this nonsensical tale. Two small girls who love babies and have always borrowed their neighbors' are shipwrecked on a tropical island with four babies. The ingenuity of Mary and Jean in providing food and shelter for all of them is worthy of *Swiss Family Robinson.* Mr. Peterkin, who has fled to this island to escape children and thinks he doesn't like them, in the end succumbs to the flattery of one of the babies. To the small girl, the story will be very real and wholly possible or it will be lots of fun and nonsense—all depending on the type of small girl she is. . . . Recommended.

> *Mary R. Lucas, in a review of "Baby Island," in* Library Journal, *Vol. 62, No. 20, November 15, 1937, p. 881.*

All Over Town   (1939)

Ardeth had always been a quiet, well-behaved child until the Reverend Mr. Dawlish and his two sons came to live next door and a friendship developed between the three children. Their well-intentioned adventures usually ended in disaster and the disapproval of some of the church members was felt to the extent that the Dawlishes feared they would have to leave this parish, as they had previous ones, because of the boys. The children's attempts to bring some of the town's backsliders into the fold in order to make the minister's position secure, make good reading for sixth and seventh grade boys and girls. The book has good humor and action and will be very popular. It is, however, not up to *Caddie Woodlawn.*

> *Marian Herr, in a review of "All Over Town," in* Library Journal, *Vol. 64, No. 20, November 15, 1939, p. 904.*

This is a lively tale of very real children told with a directness and a strict attention to the events of the story very acceptable to boys and girls from 8 to 12. The author permits her characters to speak for themselves, and because the reader becomes acquainted with them by what they say to one another and about one another and, above all, by what they do, he has somewhat the feeling that he is watching a play, for which the small town of Warsaw Junction provides the stage. . . .

The author knows children and the life of a small town and writes of both with humor and understanding. The book reads aloud well.

> *Anne T. Eaton, "Small Town Life," in* The New York Times Book Review, *December 7, 1939, p. 10.*

A reissue of a juvenile novel first published in 1939 which should prove enjoyable to children today. There are minor flaws—some odd coincidences, some unlikely opportunities for heroism—yet these can be forgiven in a story so convincing and high-spirited. The book tells of the adventures and misadventures of the doctor's daughter and the minister's sons in a small western town in the early 1900's—likable, very real children worthy of the creator of Caddie Woodlawn. The book also provides a valuable and entertaining glimpse into family life during the early part of this century.

> *Rachel Smith, in a review of "All Over Town," in* School Library Journal, *Vol. 15, No. 3, November, 1968, p. 83.*

Lad With a Whistle   (1941)

It's a gay story of wandering minstrels in the days of Sir Walter Scott and a mysterious one of a beggar boy given the guardianship of two children of wealth; it's of strangers coming by stealth at night, of a secret room in the great house, of a father gone to America and his intercepted letters, of servants full of trickery. And it's as readable as any this author has written. The plot may be improbable and some of the characters unconvincing as individuals, but the Scotland of a certain era is vividly portrayed. Particularly good use has been made of many Scotch phrases which add to the atmosphere and impede not at all the swift movement of the story.

> *Miriam Snow, in a review of "Lad with a Whistle," in* Library Journal, *Vol. 66, No. 17, October 1, 1941, p. 845.*

Rob McFarland earned the only living he had by playing his whistle and drum on Edinburgh street corners or, if he pleased, on the open road. Free as the wind and proud of it, this young Scotsman knew how to take care of himself. But a surprising circumstance one day made him the sole guardian of a boy and girl only slightly younger than himself, the grandchildren of the Laird of Kirkness.

Fast-moving in its easy, popular style, this is an obvious kind of story, relying upon all the usual sentimental values of its early nineteenth century setting.

> *Irene Smith, "Kirkness Castle," in* The New York Times Book Review, *November 9, 1941, p. 12.*

Magical Melons   (1944)

Another Caddie Woodlawn story in a series of rollicking episodes in which the highly individualized members of her family have a share. There's Caddie's adventure trying to bathe her pet sheep; there are Warren's reading difficulties at school; there are Hetty and Minnie finding their chicken pet; there's Tom's adventure at the Medicine Show; there's the uproarious discovery that Cousin Lucy wears a wig. Delicious dish to set before the king—the most entertaining of family books. . . . Carol Brink, in these stories of western Wisconsin around the 1860's, has captured an enthusiastic and loyal audience.

> *A review of "Magical Melons," in* Virginia Kirkus' Bookshop Service, *Vol. XII, No. 17, September 1, 1944, p. 402.*

Ten years ago Caddie Woodlawn dashed into children's literature from pioneer Wisconsin, romped away with a Newbery Medal, and gathering round her a crowd of admiring nine-year-olds, set off toward being a children's classic. News of "more stories about Caddie Woodlawn" comes to an audience eager to give her the same affection she aroused on her first appearance.

In some respects this book is more of an achievement than the other; there are some among the stories in this varied collection—such as the one about the circuit rider—that will come back in later years, revealing an understanding of human nature that a first reading could not as yet appreciate. The title tale, though story-tellers will welcome it as new material for this time of year, means less than several that follow, such as that in which Caddie adopts the aged ewe. The one in which Emma, only efficient member of her family, gets a day off to walk with other girls to a medicine show, will be ruefully recognized by middle-aged people, whose families, sitting comfortably after supper, used to wait till they moved two feet and then, chanting "now you're up, you may as well" . . . send them on errands from garret to cellar. Poetic justice rescues Emma, but the show had to come to her while she carried out commissions people insisted wouldn't take her a step out of her way. These are all well made stories; it is really harder to make stories, of what might be called magazine length, for children, than to write a book for them. A well made short story is neither an anecdote nor a chapter from a longer work; none of these are; they are scenes from the life of the same children and so they hold together, but each separately justifies its existence.

> *May Lamberton Becker, in a review of "Magical Melons," in* New York Herald Tribune Weekly Book Review, *November 12, 1944, p. 10.*

Delightful short stories of Caddie, her brothers, friends and neighbors. This pioneer Wisconsin community lives again through Caddie's whole-souled and eager adventures. Be it the tender story of Caddie's ewe or the highly amusing one of her purchase of a gift for her mother, all are skillfully handled. Two stories show family understanding and loyal respect for the individual.

> *Isabel McLaughlin, in a review of "Magical Melons," in* Library Journal, *Vol. 69, No. 22, December 15, 1944, p. 1106.*

Caddie Woodlawn: A Play   (1945)

Coming in time for Book Week celebrations, here to stay for a long time, this dramatization of one of the Newbery Medal winners most popular with children follows the story with a fidelity children will approve, and besides providing excellent entertainment in production, gives them, as reading matter, what may be their first intimation of the basic differences between writing plays and writing stories. For when they ask what has become of this or that old friend, the author makes it clear to them in a preface why he had to be left out; the outstanding episodes only have been left in, but enough of all the leading characters' qualities and conduct remains to make their appearances delightful. One seems to hear the applause that will greet the entrance of Cousin Annabelle from Boston with her eight-and-eighty buttons, or little Tom's recitation of "If at first you don't succeed, fry, fry a hen," while Caddie, who skips and storms through all three acts, will be like a dream come true.

> *May Lamberton Becker, in a review of "Caddie Woodlawn: A Play," in* New York Herald Tribune Weekly Book Review, *October 7, 1945, p. 6.*

Scenes taken from the well-liked story by Mrs. Brink are here made into a three-act play for elementary and junior high school children. While the story is, of necessity, greatly condensed, some twenty characters appear in the episodes laid in the Woodlawn home, in Wisconsin, in 1864. Besides the family, Indian John and the cousin from Boston are included, and the story of the little dancing clogs has its place. Mrs. Brink made her own dramatization, and so it is likely to prove very successful with school children.

> *Alice M. Jordan, in a review of "Caddie Woodlawn: A Play," in* The Horn Book Magazine, *Vol. XXI, No. 6, November-December, 1945, p. 465.*

Family Grandstand   (1952)

The special charm of this perceptively written story is the feeling it gives the reader of real acquaintance with Professor Ridgeway's likeable household. Each child is worth knowing: Susan, a wise and imaginative child-sitter at twelve; George, ten, who collects pets; and Dumpling, relieved at six to learn she is not a prodigy (which, she understands, means being "very, *very* good"). Lighthearted fun comes with new pets and with watching football from their own cupola "grandstand" and suspense in united efforts to get their football hero, Tommy Tucker, to pass his chemistry examination. The university town and its traditions are as real as these characters, whose naturalness proves again that the author, a Newbery Medal winner, has a deep understanding of children.

> *Virginia Haviland, in a review of "Family Grandstand," in* The Horn Book Magazine, *Vol. XXVIII, No. 6, December, 1952, p. 410.*

This is an unusually good book for the holidays—one to read aloud to the whole family at Christmas time. The Ridgeway family lived in a college town. Professor Ridgeway was on the faculty; Mrs. Ridgeway wrote mystery stories, was a marvelous cook, and possessed a lively sense of humor. Susan Ridgeway, who was twelve, had more than her share of charm and common sense. George, who was nine, loved and understood all animals, birds, and insects. Dumpling, who was six, was the most interesting of them all. A highly original child, she was regarded with great respect by the family. Their common hero was Tommy Tokarynski, called Tommy Tucker for short, who was the star player on the football team and was in a state of near-despair over his chemistry examinations. The things that happen to the Ridgeways might happen anywhere to any family, but by the time you have read a chapter or two you are so fond of the Ridgeways, so concerned in their affairs, that everything seems of vital importance. To share their adventures is the very nicest kind of a Christmas present.

> *A review of "Family Grandstand," in* The Saturday Review, *New York, Vol. XXXV, No. 50, December 13, 1952, p. 45.*

The Ridgeway children lived on College Avenue, and "had the football stadium in their laps." They also had a special football hero and a tower from which they could watch him with a spyglass at the games. They contrived to get help for him with his studies so he could stay on the team. The plot is slight, but the family is most engaging, from small Dumpling, with her high I. Q. and her spectacles, on up to the very real parents. It is a period family portrait of life in a Mid-West college town, done with great charm. Girls of about ten to twelve who like family stories will enjoy it.

The writer is author of the Newbery Medal book of 1936 the widely loved **Caddie Woodlawn.** Much of the humor and realism of her new book stem from experiences of her own children in the university town where she still lives.

> *Louise S. Bechtel, in a review of "Family Grandstand," in* New York Herald Tribune Book Review, *January 4, 1953, p. 8.*

The Highly Trained Dogs of Professor Petit (1953)

Even if you don't particularly care for dog stories, don't pass this one up. Set in Puddling Center in 1852 it's well-paced with excitement, mystery and suspense, plus a liberal dose of homey philosophy. Of course there are dogs too. But they are mighty unusual. The strength of Prince, the nimbleness of Liddy, the dexterity of Grushenka, the sagacity of Sancho and even the laziness of Tip make for a dog act that truly reflects the Professor's credo of "skill and kindness, gaiety and art."

A calamity puts the troupe out of business temporarily while a rival company that features a tiger threatens to make it permanent. Through Willie, a local boy-of-all-chores, the Professor's dogs find work tending sheep, pulling a baker's cart, catching mice for the miller and chasing balls of yarn for the weaver. When injustice follows misfortune, it's a thrill-a-chapter until the wrongs are righted.

> *Pat Clark, "A Dog's Life," in* The New York Times Book Review, *November 15, 1953, p. 22.*

There were not enough boys in Puddling Center in 1852 to do all the work boys usually have to do; so Postmaster

Scrivens sent for his sister's son, Willie, to come to help out. Nobody could foresee what a change this simple act would make in Puddling Center, in Willie's own life, and in the fortunes of Professor Petit and his five remarkable dogs who came to the village to give their performance. A good plot amusingly worked out and Mrs. Brink's ability to write with a kind of dry humor that fits the story perfectly make this an exceptionally good "funny" book. It does not need to be read aloud to capture the children's interest, but it would be a pity to miss sharing its laughter with them.

> *Jennie D. Lindquist, in a review of "The Highly Trained Dogs of Professor Petit," in* The Horn Book Magazine, *Vol. XXIX, No. 6, December, 1953, p. 455.*

Family Sabbatical (1956)

No one who has read **Family Grandstand** needs to be introduced to the Ridgeways, but they may be happily met for the first time in this book. Mrs. Brink makes you a part of the family immediately. The Professor and his wife, busy writing books, he a history, she a mystery story, have brought their children to France for six months. Susan, now twelve, is keeping a diary of their experiences; George, eleven, is still collecting stones but he learns quickly how to teach American slang to a long-suffering, Mademoiselle; and Dumpling, seven, is full of wise remarks and always sure that "home is best." The gay and natural children make friends with a charming, fairy-godmother Princess, have a "formidable" Halloween and Thanksgiving on the Riviera, see a few castles (quite anonymous until Dumpling has a sad experience in one) and then share some characteristic experiences in Paris. We gain a vague glimpse of France through the eyes of these children of a Mid-Western city. (Mrs. Brink has given us a splendid closer view in **Anything Can Happen on the River.**)

Like Susan, as we close the book, we should like to draw a heart surrounded by flowers and say "It has been educashunal and improving. At least I think so. Anyway, everything turned out for the best and it was fun. The End."

> *Margaret Sherwood Libby, in a review of "Family Sabbatical," in* New York Herald Tribune Book Review, *May 13, 1956, p. 24.*

In this warm, leisurely sequel to **Family Grandstand** all of the Ridgeways travel from their college town to France to spend father's sabbatical year. Professor Ridgeway is gathering material for a book; Mrs. Ridgeway is still writing her mysteries. Dumpling is now seven, George ten, and Susan thirteen. This pleasant account of the small catastrophes, discoveries and celebrations that fill their days in Paris and on the Riviera gives a real and happy picture of those places and, especially, of the fun children can have through such a travel experience. New acquaintances—a genuine princess, other boarding-house friends, and a devoted governess—appear as real as the children and their understanding parents. A satisfying longer-than-usual book for children who love family stories.

Virginia Haviland, in a review of "Family Sabbatical," in The Horn Book Magazine, *Vol. XXXII, No. 3, June, 1956, p. 189.*

The Ridgeways (of **Family Grandstand**) are in France for a six months sabbatical during which time Mr. Ridgeway plans to write a book. After a short stay in Cannes they move on to Paris, seeing the high spots of interest along the way. The author writes with the same zest that made the first book such fun, but unfortunately she has depended for humor in this book on situations that typify all that is most objectionable to Europeans in American tourist behavior. The French characters are all stereotypes and are exaggerated for purposes of ridicule.

A review of "Family Sabbatical," in Bulletin of the Children's Book Center, *Vol. X, No. 3, November, 1956, p. 35.*

The Pink Motel   (1959)

When the Mellen family inherited a motel, they promptly went down to Florida to see what it was like, deciding to run the place until it could be sold. Their guests were an odd lot: two men who seemed to be gangsters, a Miss P. DeGree and her valuable dogs, a magician and the fey Miss Ferry, an artist amongst them. On the trail of a treasure left by deceased Uncle Hiram, the Mellen children found that the motel itself and the happy life it provided were the real treasure. A mélange of humor (not always successful), adventure, and fantasy. Some of the odd characters are caricatured too heavily, and the overtones of magical events are awkwardly obtrusive, but the author's style is for the most part light and humorous. (pp. 110-11)

A review of "The Pink Motel," in Bulletin of the Center for Children's Books, *Vol. XIII, No. 7, March, 1960, pp. 110-11.*

A lighthearted combination of realism and imagination, different from anything Mrs. Brink has done, this story is set in an old-fashioned motel on a lovely Florida Beach. . . . With an obvious climax and unconvincing parents, this is not Mrs. Brink's best book, but the fanciful tongue-in-cheek fun has a decided appeal. Recommended.

May H. Edmonds, in a review of "The Pink Motel," in Junior Libraries, *Vol. 6, No. 7, March, 1960, p. 136.*

Andy Buckram's Tin Men   (1966)

Mrs. Brink writes with a kind of cheerful understatement, comfortably and sparely. Her twelve-year-old hero is an incurable tinkerer who babysits for his two-year-old cousin, Dot, under duress, and only to make money for "electrical cord, and solder, and hinges, and rivets and flashlight bulbs." The first robot Andy constructs is named Campbell, after the soup cans which constitute his legs and arms. The second one is much bigger. His name is Bucket and he can do a few of Andy's chores around the family place. Next, a girl robot with an old record player inside her. Last of all comes Andy's masterpiece, Super-

can, who besides complex motor abilities has an "obsolete" computer in his head for a brain.

The tin people work on batteries or cords plugged into house current, until one night when there is a terrible storm and flood. Lightning strikes in the best Frankenstein tradition, galvanizing the robots so that they function hereafter without external electrical power. The shift from the plausible to the fantastic is deft and lighthearted. Andy's behavior is beautifully illustrative of children's aesthetic criteria for the behavior of characters in fantasy. The proper question here is not "How could robots come to life?" but "How would you act if you were marooned on an island in a flood with four friendly, but unpredictable, tin men?"

Mary Nash, "Adventures of a Boy and His. . . ", in The Christian Science Monitor, *May 5, 1966, p. B4.*

Children fascinated with automation will enjoy this story of Andy and the four robots he builds. When a thunderstorm and flood separate Andy, his two-year-old cousin, and a neighbor girl from their parents, the tin men, electrified by lighting and guided by Andy, help them to safety. Not the usual fantasy with its aura of magic, this is, rather, the story of a resourceful boy, reminiscent of Henry Reed (but not nearly so well defined), who works his way out of situations of varying difficulty with humor, ingenuity, and luck. (pp. 3255-56)

Amy Kellman, in a review of "Andy Buckram's Tin Men," in Library Journal, *Vol. 91, No. 12, June 15, 1966, pp. 3255-56.*

Not science fiction but fantasy with a robot twist, this is an amusing book. It was when Andy was baby-sitting with his tiresome little cousin Dot that his mind wandered to the possibilities of building robots from tin cans, and he turned his day-dream into reality. Each robot is talented, each has a personality, and they all help Andy through a series of hair-raising experiences. Not for literal-minded boys, with a robot teacher possibly looming in the not-so-far-off future, but for imaginative boys and girls who will see the fun of it.

Alice Dalgliesh, in a review of "Andy Buckram's Tin Men," in The Saturday Review, *New York, Vol. XLIX, No. 26, June 25, 1966, p. 61.*

Two are Better than One   (1968)

In the year before they enter high school Cordelia and Chrystal play with dolls, write a "romantical" novel, and make a gentle transition from childhood to maturity. If the story, set in Idaho in the early 1900's, is old-fashioned, it is not sentimental; with quiet humor the author of **Caddie Woodlawn** reconstructs episodes from the comfortable lives of two small-town girls and evokes a sense of their friendship—their giggling fits, special language, secret projects, and the originality which sets them slightly apart from other classmates.

A review of "Two Are Better Than One," in

The Booklist and Subscription Books Bulletin, *Vol. 65, No. 9, January 1, 1969, p. 493.*

A pleasant period piece, set in the 1900's, the episodic structure smoothly knit together by the author's easy humorous style and by the interpolated chapters of a story written by the two protagonists. Cordy and Chrys are almost thirteen, best friends, the lonely home of one balancing the crowded, lively home of the other. Together the girls brave a teacher's wrath, succumb to Easter finery, suffer through a party with boys, and write their suffocatingly romantic adventure story. The story closes with the girls passing the high school entrance exams—and playing with their dolls, a key to one aspect of the book that may limit reader interest: Chrys and Cordy seem very young for their age in many ways.

Zena Sutherland, in a review of "Two Are Better Than One," in Bulletin of the Center for Children's Books, *Vol. 22, No. 91, May, 1969, p. 139.*

Lester and Lynette are two china dolls given by Chrystal to her friend Cordy at Christmas. These two symbolise the children's friendship. The plot covers about six months in this friendship during a vital time in the girls' development. Suddenly they grow up, learn to dance, go to parties and in the end the dolls are stored carefully and lovingly away with their childhood. What is so charming about this book is its sincerity and simplicity together with the beautiful illustrations by Fermin Rocker. Set in a small American town about sixty years ago the two little girls come through as real people, much more so than some of the contemporary characters. Though the pace of their life is more dignified they do have similar problems to today's teenagers. The story moves slowly and carefully and yet has a sharpness and clarity beautifully characterised in the illustrations.

Girls between ten and thirteen who have enjoyed the nineteenth century writers like Mrs. Molesworth and Frances Hodgson Burnett will find this a most attractive book.

A review of "Two Are Better Than One," in The Junior Bookshelf, *Vol. 34, No. 2, April, 1970, p. 94.*

Winter Cottage (1968)

Set during the Great Depression, this book shows the author's ability to tell a good story, imbue her tale with a sense of time and place, and develop strong and believable characterizations. . . . Minty, the older girl, troubled by the need for a more conventional and secure life, emerges as the clear-headed, lovable heroine of a story that girls will thoroughly enjoy.

Gertrude B. Herman, in a review of "Winter Cottage," in School Library Journal, *Vol. 14, No. 9, May, 1968, p. 78.*

An appealing heroine is presented in this rather placid story of the Depression period by the recipient of the 1935 Newbery Medal. Minty is thirteen, the sensible manager of her small family—a younger sister and an impractical father more inclined to quote poetry than to make plans. The three shelter in an unoccupied cottage and decide to winter there. They take in a runaway adolescent boy and two other people; one turns out to be the owner, investigating the squatters, but his daughter becomes Minty's chum. Parts of the story were published in magazines in 1939 and 1940. The story line is weakened by its dependence on coincidences at several points; however, the quiet woodland setting and the amicable family scenes are attractive.

A review of "Winter Cottage," in The Saturday Review, *New York, Vol. LI, No. 19, May 11, 1968, p. 40.*

It was the autumn of 1930, and widowed Pop Sparkes, with a passion for poetry but no skill at making a living even in the best of times, was feeling the deep hopelessness of the great depression. Pop with his two adoring daughters, eleven-year-old Eggs (short for Eglantine) and thirteen-year-old Minty, was traveling from Chicago to Minneapolis to accept the reluctant charity of a fussy, despised aunt. When their rickety automobile collapsed on a deserted road in northern Wisconsin, they were forced to take refuge for the night in an empty lakeside summer cottage. Of the three, only Minty was practical and realistic; but as they had neither funds nor transportation, she was persuaded that they should remain snugly in the cottage all winter, arranging some way to pay the rent later. The arrival of a lonely, runaway boy provided help in time of need; a trailer full of provisions (left from Pop's last business fiasco, a grocery store) assured a well-fed family; and the two girls, fresh from a drab city apartment, discovered the pure exhilaration of a winter in the country. Through their appreciative eyes, one perceives the beauty of the changing seasons; and although the mystery in the quiet, well-told story is rather transparent and the climax wholly predictable, the three main characters are individual and convincing. (pp. 418-19)

Ethel L. Heins, in a review of "Winter Cottage," in The Horn Book Magazine, *Vol. III, August, 1968, pp. 418-19.*

The Bad Times of Irma Baumlein (1972)

A casual fib generates farcical consequences as Irma Baumlein's face-saving boast of owning the largest doll in the world is taken up by her classmates who want a prize winning exhibit for the school's Harvest Home festival. In a moment of inspired bravado, the normally timid Irma makes off with one of the dummies from her grandfather's department store. The humor comes in hiding the contraband from the live-in couple, Mr. and Mrs. Dillingham, holding crosspurpose conversations with her nearly deaf Aunt Julia and hoping that no one will recognize the "doll" for what it is (incredibly, they don't). Both the mansion on the hill setting and the pat resolution (a nick of time confession that absolves all guilt) are as ersatz as Irma's oversized toy, but the Newbery prize winning author (for **Caddie Woodlawn**) dresses them up respectably, and younger readers can be expected to enjoy the escapade in spite of its threadbare plot.

A review of "The Bad Times of Irma Baumlein," in Kirkus Reviews, *Vol. XL, No. 13, July 1, 1972, p. 723.*

Hardly a child is now alive who hasn't at one time or another desperately blurted out a fib to gain status with his or her peers, and readers can sympathize with Irma, whose lie gave her a very bad time indeed. Her mother was at a health resort, her father very busy at the family department store, and her home life dominated by a fusty great-aunt and uncle and a crusty pair of caretakers. And she'd just moved to town. Irma's boast that she had the biggest doll in the world was tested when one of her classmates suggested that the doll should be part of a school exhibit. Driven to theft, Irma made off with a store dummy, concealed it at home, and with much trouble produced the "doll" at school. To this slim plot there is added a clean-slate denouement in which Irma makes a public confession, finds her mother is in the audience, and learns that she is there to stay, that everybody understands, that she and Mama and Daddy are moving into a house of their own, and that she now can have a longed-for pet. The characterization is adequate, the plot far-fetched here and there, but the story has plenty of action, humor, and the perennial appeal of a protagonist in a predicament with which readers can identify.

Zena Sutherland, in a review of "The Bad Times of Irma Baumlein," in Bulletin of the Center for Children's Books, *Vol. 26, No. 6, February, 1973, p. 87.*

The Bad Times of Irma Baumlein shows with humour and point how a self-conscious girl tries to impress her schoolfellows and how she learns from her mistakes. it was a mistake, undoubtedly, to insist that she had the Largest Doll in the World at home, for inevitably she was asked to bring it to the school festival and she was not likely to find the friends she so badly wanted when they realized that all she had was an ordinary-sized, though certainly ancient, wax doll. "Be sure your sins will find you out," my aunts used to tell me when I was Irma's age, but though Irma is found out, there is a happy ending for her all the same, with her artist mother rather moreaware of her and Irma herself more sensible than before. This agreeable domestic tale has the bright dialogue and oddball characters of so many American tales and makes excellent entertainment. (pp. 2168-69)

Margery Fisher, in a review of "The Bad Times of Irma Baumlein," in Growing Point, *Vol. 12, No. 1, May, 1973, pp. 2168-69.*

Louly   (1974)

A period piece set in Warsaw, Idaho, during 1908. "Professor" Tucker, the high-school principal, and his wife, off for a six-week vacation, leave responsible Louly, going on fifteen, sixteen-year-old Ko-Ko (Conrad), and ten-year-old Poo-Bah (Paula Belle) to manage the household and vegetable garden. . . . Vividly filled in and smoothly tied together by the author of **Caddie Woodlawn,** these are happy, sometimes humorous, recollections of a peaceful, secure era, but far less spicy and lively than those of Caddie's childhood.

Virginia Haviland, in a review of "Louly," in The Horn Book Magazine, *Vol. L, No. 5, October, 1974, p. 135.*

All the nostalgia of a turn-of-the-century summer in a small town is here along with mild flashes of humor and a clear growing up message. However, the episodic narrative with lengthy lapses between important events weakens the story. Louly, an obvious embodiment of the virtues of self-confidence, becomes one-dimensional, while her younger friend Chrys, less central to the story, is the more real character.

Jean Lambert, in a review of "Louly," in School Library Journal, *Vol. 21, No. 2, October, 1974, p. 110.*

Chrys and Cordy, the two friends of **Two Are Better Than One,** are thirteen now and very much impressed by the dramatic ingenuity of their friend Louly, who—although she is almost fifteen—takes the lead in directing the spontaneous plays the girls enjoy. Louly also takes the responsibility for a back yard campout, and Chrys (who is the author) envies her friend's composure and forthrightness; Chrys is shy, especially about the poem she's had published. While the characters are convincing, most of them are not drawn in depth; the book lacks a strong plot line, but it is full of lively incidents and very smoothly written, and it gives a realistic picture of the small adventures, the pleasures, and the problems of a group of children in a small town in 1908.

Zena Sutherland, in a review of "Louly," in Bulletin of the Center for Children's Books, *Vol. 28, No. 7, March, 1975, p. 107.*

Charles Causley

1917-

English poet, reteller, dramatist, and editor.

Major works include *Figgie Hobbin: Poems for Children* (1970), *The Tail of the Trinosaur* (1972), *The Puffin Book of Magic Verse* (editor, 1974), *The Sun, Dancing: Christian Verse* (editor, 1981), *Jack the Treacle Eater* (1987).

Celebrated as a major poet, Causley is considered a master of the ballad form whose works have helped to blur the distinction between poetry for children and adults. In his verse for young people, which encompasses both ballads and lyric poetry, he crafts dramatic, often humorous works featuring contemporary themes as well as topics from history and legend. Causely is praised for the power, richness, and imagistic quality of his poetry, which is also noted for its approachability and childlike vision. A quintessentially English poet, Causley, in the words of critic Michael Glover, "can make the Matter of Britain come alive for children in a way that is unmatched by any other poet of his generation." Causley's belief in Christianity and interest in magic and folklore inform his treatment of subjects that recur in his poetry: the beautiful but potentially destructive sea, the changeable nature of the author's native Cornwall, and the passage from innocence to experience. Owing to his contention that young readers possess the emotional capacity to understand and appreciate a wide range of feelings, his poems for children are not very different from his poems for adults, which are often favorably compared to those of such traditionalists of modern English poetry as Walter de la Mare and Philip Larkin. In addition to his original writings, Causley has assembled a number of extremely well-received anthologies of children's poetry. His selection for anthologies of other poets' work including *The Puffin Book of Magic Verse* and *The Puffin Book of Salt-Sea Verse* is regarded as consistently careful, original, and diverse.

Except for six years of service in the Royal Navy during World War II, Causley has lived all of his life in Launceston, a small Cornish town in England. The region of Cornwall is the setting for most of his stories and poems; the landscape, the customs and language of its people, and its proximity to the Atlantic Ocean are all prominent elements in his work, though he shuns the notion that he is merely a regional poet. For example, a reader from any background might relate to the poem "Who" from *Figgie Hobbin: Poems for Children*. The poem is narrated by an adult confronted by a phantom of the child he once was, and its progression from bewilderment to sadness and nostalgia has been called haunting. In *The Tail of the Trinosaur*, a long narrative poem, Dunborough—a town patterned after Launceston—is presented with a large vessel containing the remains of a three-pronged dinousaur which mysteriously comes to life. Distinguished by whimsical stylistic inventions and what Aidan Chambers calls "a compassion and belief in ordinary folk," the poem has

been compared to Robert Browning's poem "The Pied Piper of Hamelin." In 1975 Causley included his children's poetry along with his poems for adults in his *Collected Poems*, purposely not distinguishing between the two. This gesture was meant to underscore his belief that good poetry should appeal to any audience. Indeed, such children's poems as "Who," "What Has Happened to Lou" and "I Saw a Jolly Hunter" are considered some of the finest examples of Causley's work. *Jack the Treacle Eater*, Causley's collection of children's poetry from 1987, features ballad-type narratives as well as nonsense verse. Published in celebration of Causley's seventieth birthday, it is marked by the same concern for craft that distinguished his earlier work, and it addresses many of the same themes. "On St. Catherine's Day" is considered a moving account of the saint's life, and "Twelve O'clock Stone" retells an ancient Cornish legend. In "Fable," he creates a biography of the fabulist Aesop out of fact and myth. In addition to his poetry, Causley has written two plays for children and is the reteller of episodes from English folklore. *Early in the Morning: A Collection of New Poems* won the Signal Poetry Award in 1987 and was runner-up for the Kurt Maschler Award in 1986. *Jack the Treacle Eater* received the Maschler in 1987.

(See also *Something about the Author,* Vols. 3, 66; *Contemporary Literary Criticism,* Vol. 7; *Contemporary Authors,* rev. ed, Vols. 9-12; *Contemporary Authors New Revision Series,* Vols. 5, 35; *Dictionary of Literary Biography,* Vol. 27; and *Major 20th-Century Writers,* Vol. 1.)

AUTHOR'S COMMENTARY

[The following excerpt is from an interview by Brian Merrick.]

[Brian Merrick:]   Can you remember a point in your life when you began to think of yourself as a poet?

[Charles Causley:]   Oh no. No. I don't think that I do now, particularly. I think it's a kind of appellation that people should apply to themselves, maybe, not at all. It's for other people. Nothing is worse than a self-appointed poet.

Everybody thinks he can write poetry because it doesn't seem to require very many words and looks as if it can be done easily like the short story; but like the short story it is a profoundly difficult occupation. Who was it said to Mozart, "too many notes"? Trouble with poetry, "too many words." One has to slice away words all the time. I always wanted to write a book. I loved reading from the time when I was a tiny boy, and always wanted to write a book. To me, somebody who'd written a book would be the most interesting person in the world. I knew that I would rather meet somebody who'd written a book than meet the King or the Pope or the Tzar of Russia, or anybody like that. It seemed to me a wonderful kind of magical trick to be able to do it. And all through my teens I had this urge to write, and tried all kinds of forms, I mean plays, the novel, poetry and the short story, absolutely everything. And I was hampered by the fact that nobody had ever said to me that the material for poetry is what lies under your nose—you don't go and search for it. I felt that my own life was too constricted and restricted ever to produce anything interesting enough to put into a book. So as a child, and when I was still in my teens, I was writing plays about London, and I'd never been to London. I was trying to write terribly sophisticated stuff. One has to work through all that.

And then I found myself in the Navy—the war came along—I was called up. I was six years in the Navy. And I found myself in this totally new world with its marvellously Elizabethan language. The slang. Wonderfully exotic. Travelled the world. And couldn't get it down as a novel or a play—you can't write novels and plays on the lower deck of a destroyer, but you can write poems in your head while you are doing other occupations. That was what channelled me into writing what I hoped were poems, and that's mainly what I've gone on doing ever since. (pp. 123-24)

BM: Your fascination with the sea is very strong still isn't it?

CC: Yes. Oh yes. It's very alarming. I mean, it's very frightening. Although I've lived all my life in Cornwall and knew from tradition and from reading what the sea could do, I'd no conception of just what kind of an element it was until I found myself on a destroyer in mid-Atlantic. This terrifying, unresting, sleepless element. I absolutely loathe it, and I wouldn't set myself on it unless there was absolutely no alternative, nowadays. Certainly, not since I came out of the Navy in '46. I can remember reading an abridged version of *David Copperfield,* and there's a moment when young David is on the beach at Yarmouth with Little Em'ly—I think it must have been while Mrs. Copperfield is marrying the dreadful Mr. Murdstone, and David goes down to stay at Yarmouth—and David says "Oh, I love the sea. I think it's wonderful." And little Em'ly says, "Oh I don't! It's cruel and sleepless and I've seen it tear a boat as big as our house all to pieces." Something like that. That absolutely woke me up as to what the sea could do. And by God, little Em'ly was right. So I find it very alarming. And it creeps into you. If you live in Cornwall you're never more than 15 miles from the sea, wherever you live. I like looking at it—for limited periods—but it's in my consciousness quite enough without me wanting to add to it. The war was just an awful experience one had to get through. But the sea was much more alarming to me than the Germans or the Japanese in the Second World War. And now the very last thing I would do would be to hire a boat and put out from Boscastle to catch mackerel.

BM: I would like to talk about how you see yourself as a poet. Does that sound like an impossible question?

CC: Well. It's very difficult. I dislike being called a Cornish poet, for example. This is not because I don't want to be regionalised. Cornwall is very beautiful and is a great fund and fount of experience for me, but I don't see why one should be necessarily proud of an accident of birth. I don't think it matters where you were born or where you live—you simply make the most of wherever you are, what you see, and whatever your imagination prompts you into. I feel like a man who walks through a meadow in summer, perhaps, and you come out with all kinds of little things sticking to your clothes—little burrs, and little leaves, and little fragments of grass and all that—and that may be bits and pieces of Cornwall. But I'm unconscious of the fact that it's there. If I seem to write with a Cornish accent, fine, but I certainly don't want to go down the road of professional Cornishry, if you know what I mean.

BM: The immediate locality, on the other hand, has been very important to you.

CC: Oh yes. This goes back to the old business of teaching in a school: you write about what you know, or what you *think* you know. I've lived most of my life here in this town, where I was born, and I still try to write about it. But it's very difficult and dangerous because I have, all the time, to examine what I've written to make sure that I'm not writing about something, or an experience which I *think* looks like that, or *at one time* looked like that, but which maybe if I walked into the town or descended from Mars doesn't look or feel like that at all. Because places, like people, are organisms, and they change. So it's perpetually fascinating just to walk from one's own acre and try and identify just what's happening to the place, and just what's happening to me and the people who live here. But it's very difficult to keep a straight eye on it.

BM: A long time ago I asked you how many of the poems you start get thrown away, and you said none, every poem that you start eventually gets finished. Would you say that's still true?

CC: Yes. It's a kind of stubbornness in a way. I don't think that one should be defeated by one's material. I remember Roy Campbell—who is a great and very good friend of mine—saying to me once about writing poems that there's nothing more discouraging than seeing a poet in the grip of his material, rather like trying to wrestle with an octopus. You must always be the winner. But only just. Not ostentatiously. So you *have* to be in control of your material. . . . It takes me some time to embark on a poem—whether I really want to write it, how much I want to say it—but I think a lot of good poems haven't been written because poets have abandoned them for various reasons. Eliot said a poem is never finished but merely abandoned, and he was quite right. The great danger that I have always experienced is that I work too much on a poem. I beat the living daylights out of it. And one has to be very careful: you have to know when to stop, when the reader can exercise a kind of leap of imagination and intuition to grasp what it is that you're saying and what you're *not* saying, what you've missed out, and the reverberations and resonances that you've tried to exercise between the lines, the things unsaid. The reader has to do some work. It shouldn't be pap. But I would still struggle and finish it somehow or other.

BM: Does that mean that you're not necessarily satisfied?

CC: Absolutely. The poem as published, or as finished, would be the best I could make of it at the time. But I wouldn't care to go back over a lot of my early poems and rewrite them, do the sort of thing that Robert Graves, I think, did quite cheerfully. I think that a poem should represent you at a particular moment, saying whatever it is you want to say, as well as you can at that particular time. And instead of rewriting poems I think you should use that imaginative energy in writing something new, something fresh. (pp. 124-27)

BM: All of your poetry has got a sharp edge to it, and with much of it, as used in schools, the sharp edge perhaps doesn't reach the child. Does that bother you?

CC: No. It doesn't trouble me at all. I think that the wonderful thing about poetry is that you can read a poem all your life, and it is not until years later that it suddenly illuminates itself. Certainly that is true for me, and I am talking about my reading of the work of other poets, I'm not talking about my own. I think a poem should be a kind of magic stone that gives out signals . . . keeps on giving out signals. And because a poem is a living organism it is going to change. All the time. This is what makes a poem great. You can read it a thousand times and it gives out something different every time, no matter how familiar. So one just hopes that something will come through. I know what it is that I'm trying to do . . . I'm trying to say. So one just lives in hopes. I don't really mind what works. Po-

etry is an enormous forest or garden, and nobody is going to like everything in the garden or everything in the forest. The great thing about it is that there is something there for everybody. Absolutely everybody. And what works for one doesn't work for others. It's an entirely personal thing.

BM: To what extent do you see yourself as a children's poet separately from an adult poet?

CC: Oh I don't see these separately at all. What happened was that I didn't write a book of children's poems, or so-called children's poems, until 1970: until *Figgie Hobbin.* I'd written what I considered purely adult poems all my life until then, and I noticed that a lot of the poems up to that point were used in children's anthologies—as well as in adult anthologies. I'd just published *Underneath the Water,* a collection of adult poems, in 1968. At that particular time my mother fell ill, with whom I was sharing this house, and she talked a lot about her childhood. I had to be here because she was virtually incapable of movement, and she talked a lot about her childhood. And I turned a lot of this into poems which I thought I'd make into a book of children's verse. I've always been very much influenced by the idea that the only difference between an adult poem and a children's poem is the *range* of the audience. I mean a children's poem is a poem that has to work for the adult and the child as well—at the same time— that's the only difference.

BM: But there are poems which work for adults but not children?

CC: Absolutely. A child's experience would be incapable of encompassing some particular things. What I'm really saying is that I try to look at the poems with an absolutely straight eye, and not write down to children. Only when I'm asked for a poem for children by a publisher would I think about whether it was for adults or whether it was for children. If I have an idea for a poem I write it and decide afterwards whether I should put it in a book for children or a book for adults. I keep two absolutely distinct files. Sometimes it's impossible to decide, so I put 'em in both!

BM: At the time when you first produced *Figgie Hobbin,* had you read any of your poetry in school?

CC: No. You know that I was a teacher for well over 25 years? No, I felt my audience was a captive one and that it would be very unfair of me to read my own stuff. There was so much else that I wanted to do with children as far as poetry went, that I thought with a bit of luck they might come on to mine later. But whether or not they did was of no great concern to me.

You see, when I began teaching, or rather when I began being employed by the education authority—which is how I would describe it—in '48, I had absolutely no idea what to do when it came to reading poems or talking about poetry to children. We were in the Stone Age as far as that kind of experience was concerned, and I tried all kinds of different poems—the sort of thing that *I* thought was children's poetry, like A. A. Milne—which personally I had no feeling for at all; and I very rapidly made the discovery that the children in my classes hadn't very much feeling for it either, because it spoke of a world which was almost entirely divorced from their own. I tried all kinds of ways of doing poetry, and all the so-called children's poems didn't seem to work.

But round about that time, I had a double class of boys on Thursday afternoons. All the girls did needlework: in those days girls were supposed to be the only ones interested in needlework. And so I had about 80 boys on a Thursday afternoon, and I used to read them a story. One day I was making off into the classroom, and I picked up the wrong set of books and I found myself in there with them, *not* with the books that I intended bringing. I daren't go out . . . you don't go out and leave a class of 80 boys in a Primary school . . . and I had, as luck would have it, a book I had just bought. It was a selection by Robert Graves of English and Scottish traditional ballads, and I thought, "God, I must do something," and I just opened the book.

It opened at a poem called "Young Beichan," and I thought, well here goes, and I read:

> Young Beichan was a noble lord
> A lord of high degree
> He wente forth to Palestine
> Christes tomb for to see . . .

A little boy was sitting in the front row. I can see his face even now. I had to turn over—the first verse was at the bottom of the page—and I turned over two pages and was fumbling a bit, and this boy said, "Go on then!" And I made what was for me a major discovery: that very young children are quite capable of taking poetry, or literature or anything else, whatever one has the courage to give them. They know all about betrayal, seduction, sudden death, marital infidelity, murder, and God knows what, and they simply lapped up those ballads. I discovered that young children were a kind of medieval people. For this reason, whenever we did a Christmas play I tried always to do the medieval plays, from the Mysteries. They seemed to understand what was going on on the surface *and* underneath the poems as well. That was how I started on a very long road of discovery as to how or what one should offer to children.

I think another thing is that one should never use the word "poem." I used always to say to the children, or to anybody else for that matter, "What do you think of this?" or "I like this story. What do you think of it?" and I avoided using that dread word, which I think is terribly off-putting.

There are another couple of points I would like to make. One is that my schooldays were made absolutely miserable because I had no feeling whatever for any kind of sporting activity except swimming—which I've always loved. And I came across some fairly unsympathetic people as a child. Not entirely. But some. And I always vowed that I'd never do the same things as far as English Literature or History were concerned. I was an English and a History specialist, so called, although in a Primary school you had to teach everything from religious instruction to disorganised games. Everything. And if Miss Stansbury was away I had to take needlework—wonderful! That's all very good for

someone who's trying to be a poet. But I hoped that I would never put anybody off poetry, or literature, or reading—and always had this in the back of my mind.

BM: How regular a thing was reading in your normal teaching week? Would you read just when you felt like it?

CC: Well the nice thing about being a Primary teacher in those days, of course, was that nobody in the world except your little class, which was very like a little family, knew what was going on once the classroom door was closed. So if things weren't going very well in Maths, which they very often weren't, or some other boring activity, I used to pack it in and read. Or maybe, we'd sing. I became "A Music Specialist" because I am a pianist, and so we were always able to sing. I mean, in the event of national disasters and things which invaded the normally quiet life of the school, the headmaster would say "I'll deal with this. Mr. Causley will take singing in the hall." I was very popular with the rest of the staff because they all had an hour off.

No matter what inspectors said you were able to do it your own way. And the children knew that. I'm jumping about in my experience now over years, but I remember, not long before I left teaching, the children were writing poems. We published an anthology and I always used to give them lots of time to write their poem. I never said "I want it by twelve o'clock." *I* couldn't write a poem by twelve o'clock. It might take me three months. So I didn't mind if *they* took three months as well. (pp. 127-31)

And I found children had the most wonderful eye for the architecture of a poem. I don't think enough work has been done on the visual effect of poems. I mean, I don't know about you, but when I think of a poem I can see it on the page even before I can conjure up the actual words. And I found children have a very, very, good eye for just how a poem should look and just how long it should be and whether it should be a short thick one, as some of my children used to say, or a long thin one, which was their marvellous description of a ballad. But I was very, very careful not to interfere but just to make suggestions. And to encourage them. I never worried about misspelling. I think the only thing that the teacher, so-called, in this particular activity should do is get the spelling right if the thing is going to be printed and distributed amongst other people. Otherwise the poem becomes comic, and people are amused . . . especially semi-illiterates who are more interested in bad spelling than the feeling and the impulse in the poem itself. So I used to get the spelling right before the poem was printed, but apart from that, I interfered as little as possible.

And the other thing to be wary of was that literate children—such as I was, and such as most teachers are—tended to have that kind of facility, that kind of slickness in writing which made them produce poems which on the surface seemed good. But the most interesting poems for me were almost always written by children who could scarcely put two words together. But they had feeling, the real personal feeling: they hadn't read it in a book and they weren't trying to imitate something which they'd seen or read somewhere else. It was something which came absolutely from the well, the deep well, of their own experi- ence. I think one should beware of fluency. It's the same danger that adult writers have. You can be so fluent that everything bowls along easily, but there's no substance, there's no gristle in it: the thing has no guts to keep it going. (pp. 131-32)

BM: When a child had finished a stage of their poem, or thought they'd finished the poem completely, did you ever interfere?

CC: No. I would ask them if they thought it was fin- ished . . . and they usually knew. My only contribution to the anthology was to write an introduction just to make it clear what I thought a poem was—what it might be. Anything else was quite unnecessary. The thrilling thing was that everybody, but everybody, had something in the book. Nobody was missed out. My view wasn't a charita- ble one: it wasn't based on the fact that all parents must have something from their child. Not at all. Everybody was *capable* of rising to the occasion and by God, they did! . . .

BM: Did you write poetry at school?

CC: We did have a very enthusiastic and very standards- demanding Welsh teacher, who would occasionally set us a poem to write for homework. And write the poems we did. I think those were the first poems that ever I wrote. I would have been about 12 or 13 I suppose. And this chap was very demanding. Never gave high marks for anything. My social standing and all that was absolutely zero at grammar school, with all my wild inefficiency at every- thing. But I produced this poem, and I got 10 out of 10. And I remember the attitudes of my contemporaries changed, not because they thought it was a very good poem, but because the chap had given me all these marks for it. And I was quite pleased myself. It was terrible stuff of course, but that was how I began. (p. 133)

> *Charles Causley and Brian Merrick, in an in- terview in* Children's literature in education, *Vol. 19, No. 3, Fall, 1988, pp. 123-35.*

GENERAL COMMENTARY

Stanley Cook

Charles Causley's ballads are so much a pleasure in them- selves that it will not necessarily and may not easily occur to their admirer that they are a means of putting contem- porary poetry in perspective. It is like a recent appearance of his on television: it was so much a pleasure to hear him *sing* his work that only afterwards could one think of the social and critical implications of this. Clearly there is the probability that at some time in the near future the work of Causley and other contemporary writers in the ballad form may be brought in from the margin of literary criti- cism to the centre. At such a time it will be seen, I think, that Causley not only sustained a great traditional form but also made characteristic and valuable developments in it. In particular, his best ballads have that quality peculiar to first-rate examples of their kind: that you can first meet them at ten or eleven but never grow out of them. In fact,

though he has written some poems explicitly for children, it is usually when he is *not* writing for schools that he writes just the kind of poem that will succeed there.

The success of his ballads depends, irrespectively of his other powers, on a great gift. (My reader will guess I am going to name the silver spoon that all ballad poets have to be born to.) He is dramatic. For example, I feel that his masterpiece, **'The Song of Samuel Sweet'**, acts itself out in the mind's eye with beautifully managed fluctuations of story and interest and beautifully managed tension and is unforgettable. (p. 304)

I should say that the majority of Causley's ballads are on three classic ballad themes through the facts of each of which legend long since established a right of way: man's rejecting Christ, the sea's rejecting man and the unfairness of death. These themes he charges—with a pair of rich rhymes for spurs—with verve.

Between the confident rich rhymes (written in a time of free verse, pararhymes and assonance) Causley finds space for personal developments of his simple metre. I suggest that a poet writing fully rhymed verse is at his weakest or strongest not quite so much in his choice of rhymes as in his choice—when he already knows his rhymes—of what comes before them and fills out the line. Take for example the first verse of Causley's **'The Statue of William the Con- queror, Falaise'**:

> See him ride the roaring air
> In an iron moustache and emerald hair,
> Furious with flowers on a foundry cob
> The bastard son of the late Lord Bob.

'Bastard' and 'late' are accurate; 'roaring' and 'furious', 'iron' and 'foundry', and 'emerald' are Causley. (p. 305)

Causley says:

> The effect of a poem (but not necessarily its 'meaning', whatever that implies) should be in- stantaneous. At the same time, the poem should conceal certain properties that may only reveal themselves very gradually. The poem must have something in reserve; it must be capable of show- ing fresh aspects of its nature to reader as well as writer, perhaps over a period of years of read- ing and re-reading.

It is the unconventional adjectives and even more the un- conventional verbs that you notice in re-reading Causley: hardness and violence—sea on granite.

The other considerable addition that I think Causley has made to the traditional use of the ballad form is his culti- vated symbolism and, where he has scope, imagism. For example, everyday speech rhythm subtly highlights the symbolism of the last two lines of **'Ballad of the Bread Man'**. In longer poems he finds scope to demand re- reading at verse length. He is, at intervals, an imagist, as in **'The Song of Samuel Sweet'**:

> Rig the gallows, troopers!
>   Make the ship shine!
> Here's a likely cabin-boy
>   For the death or glory line!
> Give him a hempen collar

As he heavenward steers,
The clouds about his ankles,
The stars about his ears.

Is there any other poet who has written a verse like this in a ballad (and not impeded the narrative flow one jot)?

Causley is also a lyric poet. It seems to me that in lyric as in ballad he is at his best in realising a medieval tradition in contemporary terms. (pp. 305-06)

As far as school use is concerned, I have already said that Causley has a great deal to offer anyone aged about ten and over. In particular, I think that one good answer to anyone who says, 'Which poets can serve as a bridge from the Pop Poets to poetry that is more consciously literary and less limited emotionally?' is 'Charles Causley'. The very emphasis that he himself puts on re-reading and the genuine scope for it that he creates means he is not Pop: but he is related—a splendid uncle. When he writes explicitly for an audience aged ten and under, I think that in his earlier work he is less successful. His nonsense lacks the method of Lear and Milligan; or he tends to be theatrical rather than dramatic. At the same time, I must say that I feel his collections for children, *Figgie Hobbin* and *Figure of Eight,* do have a place in the junior school library: they enable children to meet him, who have only seen him passing in a crowd in anthologies. *The Tail of the Trinosaur* is, I think, a marked step forward in his work explicitly for children. It uses a well-tried situation, enhanced by adroit and lively versification. I should think its best audience would be nine-year-olds: some nine-year-olds will read it through but, even allowing for half the book's being (apt) illustration, this is a single story of 120 pages and I imagine its being read to children in instalments, when, I should think, Causley's craftmanship would be especially effective. This would be only right for someone who is above all a ballad poet. His latest children's book, *The Hill of the Fairy Calf,* seems to me his best, a successful attuning to children's needs towards which earlier work developed. It is, significantly, a ballad, an adaptation of an Irish fairy tale; and, like his ballads ostensibly for adults, has a simple, traditional story going on like a stream with pebbles of comparison or description on which his poetry sparkles. . . . I should think its best audience would be in the age range eight to ten.

Of the anthologies Causley has edited I would praise most *Dawn and Dusk,* a collection made in 1962 of 'poems of our time'. The choice is impeccable. It begins at infant level and comes up to secondary, but I think it is essentially a junior and middle school anthology. *Modern Folk Ballads . . .* is a good introduction, probably useful in the thirteen to sixteen age range. I think industrial folk song is least well represented, but that could be easily remedied by playing the class 'The Iron Muse'—a logical step since, among other material, it has 'Farewell to the Monty', which Causley also has. I am doubtful about *Rising Early* ('Story Poems and Ballads of the Twentieth Century'). In his introduction, Causley says

> When a poet writes a story poem or ballad he speaks without bias or sentimentality. He doesn't seek to moralize. He allows the incidents of his story to speak for themselves.

This is incidentally a good description of his own practice and it describes that of some poets in his collection, but others do not allow 'the incidents . . . to speak for themselves'. I don't think the two types of poem mix and Causley's introduction shows which ought to go. One might argue, perhaps, that the extension of story into impressionism is something worth demonstrating to more academic secondary pupils. His *Puffin Book of Magic Verse* seems too indeterminate to me. It goes from technically orthodox old spells to merely metaphorical magic in modern poets; the children, also, who are so young that they need to be warned in the introduction not to use the spells but to go to the doctor are not old enough for Milton and Osbert Sitwell. Beddoes's 'The Phantom-Lover' and Roy Fuller's 'The Start of a Memorable Holiday' would, however, be sickening, I should think, at any age. (pp. 306-07)

Causley without his ballads is still a notable poet and Larkin so represents him in *The Oxford Book of Twentieth-Century English Verse,* but I agree with Edwin Muir that his songs and ballads are his 'chief glory'. They are compelling and fresh and I can only regard with awe the poet who plucks them out of the air. (p. 308)

Stanley Cook, "Modern Authors: II, Charles Causley," in The School Librarian, *Vol. 24, No. 4, December, 1976, pp. 304-08.*

Michael Benton

Since the war the amount of poetry written and published for children has steadily increased, but the main tradition has been sustained principally by three poets: in the 1950s by James Reeves and in the last two decades by Charles Causley and Ted Hughes. (p. 120)

At first sight, Charles Causley and Ted Hughes seem to represent quite antithetical approaches in their poetry for children. Causley, a skilled ballad-writer, often on Christian themes, seems far distant from the hard, uncompromising images of Hughes's predominantly free-verse poems. Causley often celebrates creation and seems to compose his poems in neat patterns like reflected miniatures of some grander design. Hughes is always locked in struggle with creation, "mixing it" with the pain of birth and death and, in his recent anthologies, *Season Songs* and *Moon-Bells and Other Poems,* making few concessions to the child reader. The black voice of *Crow* is never far away: indeed, it appears once in the latter anthology to sing a sardonic death-chant, entitled "Horrible Song." Yet, for all their differences, there is a frequent sense of loss at the end of Causley's poems and often a feeling of hard-won achievement in Hughes's that suggest an ambivalence that is common to both. Two recent poems—each written in the characteristic style of its author—which catch this quality are Hughes's "March Morning Unlike Others" and Causley's **"The Forest of Tangle."** These pieces, along with Hughes's "Work and Play," "Leaves," "The Stag," "The Warm and the Cold," and Causley's **"The Animals' Carol"** and **"The Green Man in the Garden"** are the contemporary poems that are continuing the main tradition of children's poetry and, in doing so, blurring the borderline between adult and children's verse in just the same way that the work of Blake and de la Mare did in earlier periods. (pp. 120-21)

Michael Benton, "Poetry for Children: A Neglected Art," in Children's literature in education, *Vol. 9, No. 3, 1978, pp. 111-26.*

Aidan Chambers

Last autumn there appeared Charles Causley's **The Puffin Book of Salt-Sea Verse,** a companion to his already well-known and admired **Puffin Book of Magic Verse,** which came out in 1974. I can think of no recent anthologies for eight-year-olds and up that surpass these.

I have written before about Causley's own poetry . . . ; readers know of my admiration and respect for the man and his work. His personal generosity, his commitment to poetry and knowledge of it, his respect for children and their potentiality, his understanding of the ways poetry can best be brought to the young: All these combine to qualify him as an exceptional maker of poetry books for children.

He knows, to start with, that you have to get the code right. You have to know how to engage young minds, how to plug them into the most demanding poetry by enjoying with them their delight in matters often thought too frothy for serious adult and poetic attention. In **Magic Verse,** for example, everything is arranged under such happy titles as "Charms and Spells," "Curses," "Ghosts and Hauntings"—signals as catchy as firecrackers.

But Causley does not pull his punches; he does not, either, try to disguise his more serious purpose. "All poetry is magic," he begins his introduction, at one stroke releasing himself from any too-narrow selection his headings might force on him. The poets included range from Shakespeare to Brian Patten. He avoids the chocolate-box and Christmas-card hacks so many other anthologists seem unable to do without when compiling for children. His knowledge of the real McCoy is so detailed that all his needs can be satisfied from the worthwhile poets. In English poetry there is never any need to go to anything but the best; whatever one is looking for, there is so much to be found.

In this respect, then, Causley is a master from which other children's anthologists have much to learn. He does not suppose that if you leave pages of Great Poetry lying around for children to come across and read, they will turn overnight into avid poetry devotees. He knows they are far more likely to fold the pages into paper airplanes or use them to set the house on fire. You must see a pattern in the raw material which will gain children's attention; and you must know poetry so well that every shade you want, every change of pace, every shift of mood and point of view will play into that pattern and develop it beyond what the child expected.

[In] **Salt-Sea Verse,** the same talents are on display even more impressively than before. Nothing is more evocative to English minds than the sea. We love it, hate it, like to be beside it; ravage, plunder, and pollute it; speak to it and of it as having supernatural power; long to retire to some beetling cliff top overlooking its tumbling waves; and altogether regard it as essential to our happiness and well-being. (Look at how hard we have fought over the years against a road tunnel under the Channel, despite the

strong vested interests who want such a monstrosity.) When English people get too far from the sea they feel uneasy. And they cannot comprehend the vastness of the United States, because nowhere in England are you ever farther than eighty miles from the "wild and wasteful ocean." So when Americans talk of "coast to coast," we English see a comfortable embrace of land between two seas, not the endless stretches of continent you have in mind.

Causley was born on the leggy peninsula that kicks out into the Atlantic from the bottom left-hand corner of England, and which contains, stuffed into it like presents into a *matelot's* kit bag, the seagoing counties of Devon and Cornwall. "Here," he says in the introduction to **Salt-Sea Verse,** "it is impossible to be more than a score of miles from the sea. . . . Since childhood, then, my view of the sea has been respectful, but—of course—by no means an entirely sober and serious one." Very telling, that interjected "of course"; we'll be finding plenty of off-duty fun in the anthology as well as some hard hauling.

It is true that the sea has borne our poets at their best. Causley extracts "The Ancient Mariner;" he could not have done less. Children should hear it read at a sitting when they are about twelve years old; if they take it and enjoy it, they are ready for their heritage; if not, there's a tough job to be done before it is too late. Causley might also have used those universally-known lines, "Water, water, everywhere / Nor any drop to drink," as the best example of the remark he makes at the end of his introduction, where he ties together the salt-sea and all poets with these words: "The secret dream of every poet is to write a line that lasts forever, and the voice of Raphael Alberti is a subtle and prudent reminder of this ever-present hope: 'If my voice should die on land, / take it to sea-level / and leave it on the shore.' "

The subject, then, was a natural one to bring out the very best in Causley and a naturally appealing one to English children. But again, Causley gets the organizational code just right. Pennants flutter at mastheads: "Findings and Keepings"; "Wreckers, Invaders, Pirates and Prisoners"; "Shipwreck, Storm and Disaster." But properly, too, considering the subject, he mystifies with "Lovers False and Lovers True" (only an ex-sailor would have thought of that grouping: Causley had a lower-deck rating during the second World War); "Sea Changes"; "In Deep"; and "Dreamers, Solitaries and Survivors." It is all a matter of preparing young minds to join the poet in turning bare bones into something rich and strange. (pp. 113-14)

[Causley] offers us an anthology that tells us what all anthologies for children should be. (Forgive now the jumbling metaphors.) They are appetizers for tasting this and trying that. They are maps, and like all maps, they differ in kind: road maps for finding the way, topographical maps that give us a view across the country, geological maps that help us understand what lies beneath the surface, even globes that try to show us the whole world in a little orb. They are libraries for browsing and useful for quick reference. They are traveling companions, too, Baedekers of verse—and then it matters most what the anthologist's personality is like. They can be all of these things at once and more besides. (p. 114)

Aidan Chambers, "Letter from England: Something Rich and Strange," in The Horn Book Magazine, *Vol. LV, No. 1, February, 1979, pp. 111-15.*

Tony Bradman

"Salty" is a useful word to describe Causley's work. Causley himself, in his introduction to *The Puffin Book of Salt-Sea Verse* (a superb, un-put-downable anthology of sea poetry for children) says "It seems to me a happy accident that salt is . . . the ancient symbol of purity, vigour, wit, strong love and . . . incorruptibility and eternal life; all qualities associated with the best of poetry". He could not have summed up his own work more concisely. His first two books were filled (as were his subsequent ones) with a tang of salt. Mostly it is the sea itself which fills his work as it fills the air of his native Cornwall, which also forms both subject and background to many of his poems. But there is also purity of language and form, wit by the trawl-full and the salt of strong love, eternity and incorruptibility. There is also the sea change of death and decay, the salt taste that makes life so ineffably sweet. *Hands To Dance And Skylark* has been re-published recently . . . with an introduction and autobiographical essay by Causley, and deserves a place in any history course that takes in the War. The poems of Aggie Weston are mostly included in *Collected Poems 1951-1975,* as are the others mentioned in this article, and this magnificent book deserves a place on every bookshelf in the country, of both adult and child.

As for themes, Causley introduced in the third poem of *Aggie Weston* the particular subject which has been his constant—if sometimes implicit rather than explicit—concern. *Nursery Rhyme of Innocence and Experience* is, seemingly, a traditional story told in traditional ballad form. A boy asks a sailor who is about to go on a voyage to bring him back some exotic presents. The swinging rhythm and rhyme lead us on easily, but we are soon made to feel uneasy. There are disturbing echoes of that other great poem of innocence and experience, Coleridge's *Rhyme Of The Ancient Mariner* in the ship that returns "after three long summers" with "her flashing rigging" all shot away. It isn't the original sailor who runs to bring the boy his presents, and the child's words show that he is no longer a child and return us to a chilling, haunting reality of time past forever: "Why have you brought me children's toys?"

This painful turning of golden innocence into the ironic knowledge of experience—in short, the process we have all experienced and know more prosaically as growing up—is at the core of Causley's work. It is this which lies behind his writing of several excellent poems *about* children such as **"School At Four O'Clock"** and **"Conducting A Children's Choir,"** both of which express this theme perfectly (and also reveal that Causley has learned enough about real children in his many years as a Primary School teacher in his home town of Launceston, Cornwall, not to have any illusions about them). It must have been a natural progression for him to turn to writing *for* children,

therefore, which he has done with notable success, most eminently in *Figgie Hobbin.*

Causley says . . . that he went to three schools as a child, and was happiest at one: "possibly because most of the time I was there I was in a state of innocence. Lost innocence, of one form or another, is a strong thread in the work of many poets". He adds that he is not talking about a loss of "virtue", but of a state where "in those days, the world still seemed to me just made, Eden-fresh".

It is Causley's gift to have been able to retain some of this child-like vision, and one that he shares with many great poets. In the best of his poetry, and particularly the best of his poetry for children, he can still see the world as if it were new-minted, fresh, unseen before by anyone. It is this which makes his poetry so effective and affecting for both adult and child, for in every adult there is the child that once was, who saw connections in the strangest of things and kept his eyes open to all that happened around him. The adult who reads Causley can recapture something of what it was to be a child, and the child is fortunate who reads Causley and experiences what Causley offers in abundance—an understanding of how the child sees the world.

Causley has also revitalised English poetry—quietly, but nonetheless effectively. Because he has used traditional forms like the ballad, the long narrative poem (the best of his are collected in *Figure of 8,* eight wonderful stories in vigorous verse) and made a virtue of that seemingly old-fashioned craft, skill with words and verse forms, he has not received the critical acclaim that is undoubtedly his due. But the power and relevance of his vision works with and through the forms he uses so well that he puts an individual stamp on every form he touches. He has also turned his hand to refurbishing medieval drama and pageant. *The Gift Of A Lamb* is a retelling of the story of the three shepherds at Christ's Nativity and is a marvel of grace and simplicity which every child deserves to see or read. Just published is *The Ballad of Aucassin and Nicolette,* a marvellous combination of pageant, drama and ballad in which Aucassin, the young lover, finds his Nicolette again after many trials. In both the verse is a delight.

Wry humour with a very salty taste has also been a Causley hallmark. This is exemplified in his long narrative poem, *The Tail Of The Trinosaur* with marvellous illustrations by Jill Gardiner, and *Figgie Hobbin* (the title refers to a "Cornish pudding sweetened with raisins") is full of fun in poems like **"Colonel Fazackerley's Ghost"** and the delightful nonsense of *As I Went Down Zig Zag* (which has been made into a delightful, small picture book illustrated by John Astrop). Causley has also produced two marvellous picture books, *The Hill of the Fairy Calf,* a re-working of an Irish folk tale with pictures by Robine Clignett, and *The Animals' Carol,* in which he takes the story of the animals in the stable at the Nativity bursting into human speech and makes of it a haunting poem, exquisitely complemented by Judith Horwood's pictures. Causley's work as an anthologiser also deserves mention—*The Puffin Books of Salt-Sea* and *Magic Verse* are a must for every child (and every adult, come to that), as is the excellent ***Batsford Book of Stories in Verse*** which has illustrations by Charles Keeping as an added bonus.

Perhaps it is the very last poem in ***Figgie Hobbin*** that tells us most about innocence and experience, and about the strange sense of loss that growing up brings and that we sometimes remember as adults; and also that tells us most about the child in Charles Causley, the child in most of us. In this poem—called **"Who,"** Causley asks: "Who is that child I see wandering, wandering?" and ends on an eternal question:

> When I draw near him so that I may hear him,
> Why does he say that his name is my own?
>
>   (pp. 55-7)

Tony Bradman, "Charles Causley: Nursery Rhymes of Innocence and Experience," in The Junior Bookshelf, *Vol. 45, No. 2, April, 1981, pp. 55-7.*

Neil Philip

'All poetry is magic', writes Charles Causley in the introduction to his ***Puffin Book of Magic Verse.*** A poem is a spell; writing a poem is, says Thom Gunn, 'an act of trusting search for the correct incantation that will return to me certain feelings whenever I want them'. And what is the essential of a spell, asks Constantine the poet in Rebecca West's masterpiece *Black Lamb and Grey Falcon—That if one word is left out it is no longer a spell.*

'Words alone are certain good,' wrote Yeats. A partial, dangerous truth: but one we do well to ponder. Behind the phrase lies an affirmation of the importance of poetry, of measured utterance. Behind it, too, lies a recognition of the poet's task: to re-create language. Each of us, with our unique minds, creates a unique language; but our loyalty is to the common tongue. The poet owes no such loyalty. It is to the integrity of his inner, private language and its unique rhythms that his responsibility lies. He serves not his audience, his culture, his fame, but his words.

In some cases, and for some purposes, this service excludes the audience altogether. We are like the Grail knights who never understood what they were searching for, and got nowhere near it. Sometimes we are, like Lancelot outside the Grail chapel, vouchsafed a glimpse of the mystery. Sometimes—rare, precious times—we enter its heart. But in real poetry a mystery is enacted whether we perceive it or not.

Ted Hughes found it necessary at one time to invent a new language, Orghast, to say what he had to say. Luckily, most poets inhabit a language close to our own. We can learn their language, and—if we respond to the forces which shape it—use it to modify our own. And when our own language changes, we change, magically, in our most personal, intimate selves.

One can analyse a writer's themes, his ideas, his techniques, his career, his characters, his indebtedness to other writers, the interaction of his life and work, but in the end everything—shape, substance, worth—depends on the words. A writer's individuality, his claim to be a writer, is that he chose these particular words, put them in that particular order. He may not be aware of all the signifi-

cance which readers will find in this choice and arrangement of words; he merely chooses and arranges. When a writer subordinates this role, of choosing and arranging words, to that of preacher, or teacher, pays more attention to what he wants to say than to how he has to say it, he steps down from the plane of creation to that of communication. He may still write well, movingly, fittingly, but he will have to abandon, at least in part, his inner language, and use our common one instead.

By doing so, the writer steps out of the area he shares with the magician, forgoes his magic, which is the magic of naming, of discovering true names. This is more apparent, and sad, in the tawdry, patronizing jingles offered to children than anywhere else. 'Children's poets' all too often either deny, with a false jollity, that their craft is also a mystery, or, in grasping an imagined magic (the fey, wraithlike magic of bad de la Mare in 'Sleepyhead') leave hold of their real magic (the lean, intent magic of good de la Mare in 'The Silver Penny').

It is very rare to find poets who can hold steadily to their true magic, speak confidently in their own language, and yet remain accessible to children: more than that, can speak direct from heart to heart. At the moment we have two, the two greatest children's poets since Blake, Ted Hughes and Charles Causley. Significantly they are both, like Blake and Rossetti, primarily religious poets: men compelled to elucidate a vision. A betrayal of language for them would also be a betrayal of the vision.

A comparison of the two would serve little purpose, for they approach their subject from opposite ends: Causley is a poet of loss, Hughes a poet of repossession. Hughes, anyway, has been criticized frequently and well. But Causley remains one of the most neglected of our major poets. His work has meant a great deal to me since I first devoured his section of *Penguin Modern Poets 3* at the age of twelve or thirteen; I feel still the pleasure he gave me then, and draw on it here to celebrate his complex simplicities.

Causley's language, his secret tongue, is deceptively open. We may feel—a scattering of dialect words and sailors' slang apart—that it is already our own. But it is not, and it is the slight discrepancy between his words and ours which gives his poems their tense energy: their rhythms, easy and comforting, do not lull us, because the language spikes our senses. Throughout the thirties Causley tried to write and could not: his three published one-act plays had no force; the language had no spikes. In an article **'In the Angle of the Waters'** Causley tells us that he felt 'that my life in a small West Country town was too local, too parochial to be of interest'. The same was true, I guess, of the language. The Second World War both shocked Causley out of his bland linguistic competence and, by taking him away from it, gave him the perspective on his 'parochial' existence which enabled him to see its true value. He returned to Launceston, where he was born, and lives there still.

The first step, however, was not to relearn a language of his childhood—or rediscover or reinvent inside himself a language which corresponded to it—but to relearn what language is for at all. The sailors' lingo he relished was not only salty, vigorous, expressive, but was so for a purpose: 'life at sea demands an economy of language; often a great deal must be said in a short space' (Causley, **'Skylark'**). This enforced economy is shared by the ballads Causley had sung at primary school, and whose rhythms and narrative devices he was to adapt for his own uses. It is also shared by the speakers of the linguistic tradition to which Causley was heir: men and women like 'My Uncle Johnnie, known as Silent Jack,' who spoke little and to the point:

> Where all around his drystone speeches stand
> Printed across the strong page of the land
> **('Silent Jack')**

It is the mingling and refreshment of these three traditions in Causley which give him his distinctive note.

Because this language is filtered through a sophisticated literary consciousness, it has to fight to retain its bareness, its balance. The process forces Causley to think in first images, to strip back accretions of thought and experience to get at the bone. 'Returning to Cornwall after the war,' he writes in his contribution to Geoffrey Summerfield's *Worlds*, 'I saw its sights, heard its sounds and echoes, the forms of speech, as though I had been newly born.' And this is where language and theme interact: for the moment of first looking, of freshness, holds within it the awareness of its own passing, of loss:

> Their summer eyes anticipate the snow
> **('Conducting a Children's Choir')**

Innocence is a frequent word, and a key word, in Causley's poetry, but it is one which he uses with some subtlety. It is the word which has drawn him to write of and for childhood, for in children he found a natural conjunction of his twin themes, which are not, as in Blake, innocence and experience but innocence and death. They are opposites which to some extent are one and the same; the **'Sailors Asleep in a Cinema'** are caught 'in attitudes of innocence or death'. For the innocence of children—an innocence of eye and trust—carries the seeds of its own destruction. Without the knowledge that the child grows up, the concept of childish innocence has no emotional resonance. That, for Barrie, is the tragedy of Peter and Tommy: the refusal to grow up makes them less than children, not more than. The central question Causley asks is: is it possible to battle through from an innocence which is unknowing to an innocence which is all-knowing—an innocence one could retain even on the Cross?

> I saw my Son, naked as Eden, turning
> And on his head a bough of thorns was burning.
> **('At the Ruin of Bodmin Gaol')**

The story of Eden and the Fall is very important to Causley. But for him the Fall is a very particular knowledge, embodied not in the story of Adam and Eve but of Cain and Abel: the Fall truly happens when man learns how to kill.

> And on the land where seven stones stand
> He stretched his hand to me
> And on my brow of staring snow
> Printed a gallows-tree.

('Christ at the Cheesewring')

One would need a book to explore the multiple meanings of 'snow' in Causley's work. It is closely linked to his concepts of both innocence and death, but never rigidly, never in such a way that one could say: this is what it means.

The two reference points of the Fall and Cain naturally lead to a third: the Crucifixion, subject of several of Causley's most original and powerful poems—**'For an Ex-Far East Prisoner of War'**, *'Cristo de Bristol'*, **'Guy Fawkes Day'**, **'In Coventry'**, **'A Certain Man'**, the bitter **'After the Accident'**. The crucified Christ can mutate into Cain, Judas, the good Samaritan, or an ordinary man. All the biblical figures in Causley are seen more as elements of common personality than as individuals. The speaker of **'For an Ex-Far East Prisoner of War'** has become Christ through suffering; the speaker of **'Christ at the Cheesewring'** has become Cain through the shared guilt of a century in which such suffering has become a commonplace.

The figure of Christ crucified is given sharpness by a closer image: a generation 'hanging on the old barbed wire' in the trenches of the Great War. It was, indeed, the living presence of the terror of trench warfare in Causley's childhood—his father he remembers only as 'a gaunt and dying man' (**'Skylark'**)—which sent him into the Navy when war came to his generation. If one wants to understand Causley or Hughes, Paul Fussell's brilliant *The Great War and Modern Memory* is a useful starting point. Reading the Great War poets helped form Causley's style.

Causley's repeated use of the imagery of the Crucifixion underlies much of his verse. The Crucifixion is the archetypal betrayal of innocence, which is the subject, direct or indirect, of a very large number of Causley's poems. It was perhaps inevitable that his anthology of Christian verse, when it came, should centre on the Passion. But it also demonstrates a faith in the restoration of innocence, in its title, *The Sun, Dancing.* The reference is to the belief that the sun dances on Easter day, for those with eyes to see. (pp. 139-43)

This is the ability Causley admires in children (though it makes him 'afraid' [**'Conducting a Children's Choir'**]), the ability to feel wonder, to feel, as Myfanwy Thomas did in the incident described in her father's poem 'The Brook', that 'No one's been here before'. To see the world new, to see it, in a key Causley phrase, 'Eden-fresh', is for him the poet's task. In his best poems the effort to see the world anew brings not only freshness of language and springiness of rhythm but also a perception of the wonder of the transforming power of 'the white tiger / Imagination' (**'Demobilisation Leave'**), which elicits from him some marvellous metaphors; in his least successful poems it lures him into glib similes which have a shock effect but no lasting power, and worst of all into a heavy-handed allegorizing (for instance, at the end of **'Ballad of the Faithless Wife'**).

Two marvellous early poems about dead sailors, **'Convoy'** and **'Rattler Morgan,'** both draw on Ariel's 'Full fathom five' song to express this sense of wonder at the transformation of something ordinary into something 'rich and strange'. In **'Convoy'** the sombre, elegiac, liturgical note of the first five lines twists elegantly, mysteriously, movingly into wonder:

> Draw the blanket of ocean
> Over the frozen face.
> He lies, his eyes quarried by glittering fish,
> Staring through the green freezing sea-glass
> At the Northern Lights
>
> He is now a child in the land of Christmas

Causley achieves this sense of wonder by means of subtle verbal dislocations, effecting the sort of shift of sensibility which makes one believe, sitting in a moving train, that it is the world which is moving and the train alone which is still. Thus in **'Young Edgcumbe'** he writes,

> Down by the Tamar river
>   As young Edgcumbe walked by
> He heard from sleep the woodcock leap
>   Into the sudden sky.

The sudden sky. There is a magic phrase. Replace it with description rather than action—'into the cloudy sky', 'into the bright blue sky'—and the whole stanza crumbles into nothing. Rephrase it—'Suddenly to the sky'—and the feeling is completely lost. It is the sky moving not the birds.

If one word is left out, it is no longer a spell.

Spells, I said earlier, are to do with naming. . . .

Characters in quite a few Causley poems are searching for a name. In **'Grave by the Sea'**, the speaker kneels to decipher the name on a gravestone and reads his own. Edward Levy in his essay 'The Poetry of Charles Causley' points out the connection with **'Who?'**, also the last poem in a collection, in which the speaker sees the ghost of a child and asks

> 'Why does he say that his name is my own?'

'Who?' seems to me to overdo the wistfulness, but **'Grave by the Sea'**, despite the elusiveness of its narrative line, is Causley at his best. The first stanza reads:

> By the crunching, Cornish sea
> Walk the man and walk the lover,
> Innocent as fish that fare
> In the high and hooking air,
> And their deaths discover.

This is as simple and straightforward as could be: yet, like the rest of the poem, and like any good spell, impossible to parse. How right that threatening onomatopoeic 'crunching' is, for instance. The sea is never a tame thing in Causley's work; here it is a huge mouth, which spits a man out and then speaks his doom. The line 'Walk the man and walk the lover', by the simple repetition of a word, captures perfectly the rhythm of stepping by the sea. The whole piece is constructed with sly accuracy: one word, hooking, is enough to induce in the reader a peculiar sensation of being unable to breathe—the very air is set with traps. The deft alliteration in each line is a common feature in Causley's work.

The second stanza contains a line which aptly illustrates my point about each poet's special idiolect. It reads,

> His heart as candid as the clay.

All these words—heart, candid, clay—have special meanings for Causley, as part of a pattern of words expressing his concept of innocence, often with intimations of disaster. He uses 'candid' always in the archaic sense of 'pure': in **'Time like a Saucy Trooper'**, **'Autobiography'**, **'Nelson Gardens'**, **'Riley'**.

As for the clay, the emotional landscape of Causley's poetry is exactly the physical landscape of Cornwall; his poems the equivalent of Silent Jack's walls on 'the strong page of the land'. Clay is a protecting, nurturing substance; in **'Reservoir Street'** Causley and his brother sleep with

> Four walls round us pure as cloam.

Yet in **'At the British War Cemetery, Bayeux'**, clay proves insufficient. 'Syllables of clay' clog the speaker's mouth. It is not until the magnificent **'A Short Life of Nevil Northey Burnard'** that they are transformed by art into 'syllables of light'. Burnard's story, reminiscent of Clare's, is of a man who

> retraced the spoor
> Of innocence.

In doing so, he makes once and for all the equation of innocence and death. His grave is also a birthplace, though

> No cross marks the spot where he first saw day.

'A Wedding Portrait', the last poem in the *Collected Poems*, replays the transition from clay to light:

> I am a child again, and move
> Sunwards these images of clay,
> Listening for their first birth-cry
> And with the breath my parents gave
> I warm the cold words with my day:
> Will the dead weight to fly. To fly.

Very little of Causley's achievement is inaccessible to children. Even the poems whose meaning yields itself up reluctantly—**'To a Poet Who Has Never Travelled'**, **'Hymn for the Birth of a Royal Prince'**—retain a heady potency. There are the startling openings—'Oh mother my mouth is full of stars' (**'Song of the Dying Gunner AA1'**)—the fresh, vivid images—'crawling back to the docks as the dawn / Cracked on my head' (**'HMS *Glory* at Sydney'**)—the intoxicating bursts of rhetoric—'Night, on my truckle-bed your ease of slumber / Sleep in salt arms the steering night away' (**'The Prisoners of Love'**)—and always the words which strive to house a vision of the world new-minted. Many of the early poems—**'A Ballad for Katharine of Aragon'**, **'Nursery Rhyme of Innocence and Experience'**, **'The Seasons in North Cornwall'**, **'Timothy Winters'**—with their strong narrative lines, secure rhythms and simple diction, are as open to children as adults. So, too, are such fine recent poems as the free verse **'Ten Types of Hospital Visitor'**. But Causley has also written deliberately for children, bearing in mind his belief that 'The "adult" poet, particularly when writing for an audience he knows will be composed mainly of children, needs to remain resolutely aware of the fact—again—that a poem is a poem, or nothing' (foreword to T. Rogers *Those First Affections*).

Some of Causley's children's poems do suffer from uncertainty of tone—the humour of **'King Foo Foo'** and **'As I Went Down the Cat-walk'** is childish, which is all right *from* children, but not for them—but mostly they succeed, beyond any expectation. Even the simplest—and poems scarcely come simpler than **'I Saw a Jolly Hunter'**—offers the reader a genuine poetic experience, taking him into the emotional and linguistic realm of Causley's adult work with no bullying, false promises, cajolery or patronage.

As evidence of their effect on children's imaginative and expressive capacities, we have two volumes of splendid poems by Causley's own eight- to nine-year-old pupils (*In the Music I Hear* and *Oats and Beans and Barley*); in her essay 'One Class and Its Reading' in Grugeon and Walden's *Literature and Learning,* Margaret Walden testifies, 'Charles Causley's *Figgie Hobbin* and his collected poems were undeniable favourites, and his work was a source of inspiration for much of the children's writing'. It should be noted that Causley includes his children's poems in the body of his ***Collected Poems,*** not in a special section or a special volume 'for the children'. Some of them sit on the sidelines of his work, rather like children overawed at an adult party, but others seem to me the heart of his achievement: fluid children bringing grace to a formal adult gathering. Lyric poems such as **'Mary, Mary Magdalene'**, **'Figgie Hobbin'**, **'My Young Man's a Cornishman'** and **'Logs of Wood'** are among the best he has written for any audience. Likewise his other children's collection, *Figure of 8,* offers some of his best narrative verse. I would particularly draw attention to the beautifully modulated **'St Martha and the Dragon'**: a story Causley then plundered for its comic possibilities in the boisterous *The Tail of the Trinosaur,* in which, as in **'Stoker Rock's Baby'**, the influence of W. S. Gilbert can be felt. The other influence is, of course, Ted Hughes's *Nessie the Mannerless Monster,* about which Causley writes enthusiastically in his entry on Hughes in *Twentieth Century Children's Writers.*

It is in the recently published three-act musical play *The Ballad of Aucassin and Nicolette* that his narrative skill and his delight in humour most fruitfully merge. It is a tour de force, bringing the medieval French tale into vigorous twentieth-century life, without guying or abusing it. Aucassin and Nicolette's is the sort of story Voltaire parodied in *Candide:* lovers parted by parental decree flee by ship to topsy-turvy land, are captured by paynims, storm-blown to their separate homes, and reunited innocent and undamaged. It oddly mixes high romance and broad comedy; Causley captures both, in supple verse which celebrates both life and language. He turns the tale's ambivalence of tone into an advantage; that the heart makes fools of us all is his message.

The abrupt switches of mood are one of the play's delights. When the Ballad Singer gives us a comic picture of Aucassin in pursuit of Nicolette ('He rode the long brake at the pace of a shatter-pate'), a rollicking profusion of image and sound, it is immediately countered by Aucassin's own curt, taut

> Fall, dark.
> Light, die.
> Sink, heart.

> Swim, eye.
> Hunger and thirst,
> Body's clay;
> Love is here
> And far away;
> And far away.

The farcical scene in which Aucassin routs the King of Torelore from his feigned childbed also includes the play's most chilling line: 'the pain that first has its source in the mind burns both body *and* spirit the more fiercely. This you shall know in good time.'

There is bawdry (Nicolette 'Be she living, be she dead, / Is of every maiden, head'), music-hall double-entendre (Martin Oxboy in his exuberant self-introduction produces his great club with the cry, 'And this, my accoutrement'), word-play ('Sir Viscount, are you not my vassal, town captain, satellite, sizar, pensioner, dependant and creature?'), physical humour (when Aucassin captures Bougars, after a splendid 'elimination song-and-dance', it is by the nose, not the nose-piece of his helmet). Alongside these is a lyric strand of aching purity. Nicolette's

> Tell me, mariner,
> As you draw
> Your anchor deep
> From the ocean's maw

recasts the plangency of **'Nursery Rhyme of Innocence and Experience'** into a message of hope. On the comic side, Martin Oxboy's account of his biblical ancestry ('My great-great-grandaddy lived in Genesis Street') is as bouncy and funny as any of its predecessors. The scene in which the three shepherds find Aucassin on the beach contains perhaps the best single song: a wreckers' hymn which sets the action firmly in Cornwall.

The Ballad of Aucassin and Nicolette is typically varied in technique, employing ballad, jazz and popular song rhythms to brilliant effect. One of the things Causley has learned from traditional ballads is how to tell a story cleanly and economically, retaining only what is absolutely necessary. His fondness for narrative verse—he has edited two anthologies of 'story poems', *Rising Early* and *The Batsford Book of Stories in Verse,* and a collection of *Modern Folk Ballads*—is one of the elements which distinguishes him from his contemporaries. Few of his poems are without a narrative thread. He also takes over the anonymous 'I' from the ballads: the 'I' of his poems is never the confessional 'I', and when he wishes to adopt that mode in the very moving **'Ward 14'**, he moves into the third person:

> *Weep on, mother!*
> It is your right.
> It is your due.
> Helpless at the foot of your crucifixion
> He is not going to deny you that.

Causley seems to me to have learned how to make use of the forms and flavour of traditional verse from two sources. First, and foremost, from Hardy, another poet of loss. But second, surely, from Auden: much of early Causley resonates to such thirties Auden poems as 'O what is that sound that so thrills the ear' and 'As I walked out one evening'. It was reading poetry such as that, I suspect, which enabled Causley to devote his considerable literary skills to producing verse as outwardly simple and inwardly rich as, say, the folk songs collected in Ruth Tongue's *The Chime Child.* Look, for instance, at Old Shepherd's **'Tending the Sheep'** and **'Babel Tower'**, or at the fisherman's love song **'The Lazy Wave'**:

> The lazy wave slides over the sand,
> My love and I were hand in hand.
> It ran till it came where we did stand,
> And faded away in the Severn sand.

The underlying purpose of it all is that which also sustains the work of John Clare, a poet of prime importance for Causley: by seeing everything new, and discovering and pronouncing its true name, to construct a spell which will re-establish a primal innocence. Just as Thom Gunn writes, 'Of course I have never completely succeeded in finding the correct incantations', so Causley's is a labour of trust rather than hope. Whereas Clare's attention in his obsessive programme of poetic recovery is focused on the landscape of the unenclosed Helpstone of his youth, on the betrayal of nature, Causley's poems centre on the betrayal of man. They are about our debt to the dead—the debt we owe them as 'survivors'. In the end what we can bring them is not much, but we must hope it is enough: 'Only a loving heart'. That is what the dove in Causley's ***Animals' Carol*** tells us to bring the infant Jesus—who comes as a redeemer, but who in Causley's more tortured poems seems almost a destroyer. In **'Death of a Pupil'** (originally **'Now'**), death, 'that other friend', has a 'gospel face' and a 'thorned kiss'. In an earlier nativity poem, the minatory **'The Sheep on Blackening Fields'**, the birth brings not joy but a resigned dismay. The eucharist is an empty ritual, not a celebration:

> A star of bitter red
> Above the mountain crest
> Writes on the squalling dark,
> *Christus natus est.*
> Silently we renew
> The ruined bread and wine;
> Take the huge-bellied child
> Whose flesh is yours, is mine.

The thaw the poem describes is a cruel one, like Eliot's April 'breeding / Lilacs out of the dead land'. As for 'huge-bellied', whether it signifies pregnancy or malnutrition, who can tell? Causley's reaction to loss is as complex as Hardy's; it can accommodate alongside **'The Sheep on Blackening Fields'** the lively and sustaining nativity play *The Gift of a Lamb.*

In *Signal 30,* September 1979, Stephen Corrin wrote criticizing the selection of Ted Hughes's *Moon-bells* for the Signal Poetry Award. He concluded his argument by saying that if he were teaching English to children he would avoid 'anything that I couldn't explain to myself or to my pupils.' He has a point; but I would use the example of Causley to argue the opposite case: only those poems one cannot 'explain' are worth our attention. This is not an argument for the wilfully obscure or the clever-clever: Causley is neither of these. It is an argument for mystery, and for magic. I would be hard put to 'explain' a single Causley poem, even **'I Saw a Jolly Hunter'**, and it is the element

I cannot explain which makes me return to them again and again, and which makes me want children to have the opportunity to engage with them. For Causley's, like Hughes's, are real poems, full of transforming magic; real spells, in which the omission of a word would be fatal. His own comment on Frances Bellerby (from his introduction to her *Selected Poems*) applies equally to himself: 'By exact observation, and the most delicately organized reverberations of rhythm and sense and sound, the world is re-created. We see, as if for the first time, what is most precious, and what has unwittingly been lost sight of.' (pp. 143-51)

> Neil Philip, "Magic in the Poetry of Charles Causley," in Signal, No. 39, September, 1982, pp. 139-51.

Margaret Meek

[Charles Causley] never makes [the] mistake of thinking that because they are not yet adult, the young have small emotions. He knows that their feelings outstrip everything else, so he trusts them with important poems, as his . . . anthologies, ***The Puffin Book of Magic Verse*** and ***The Puffin Book of Salt-Sea Verse,*** make plain. The myriad magic of poetry, its spellbinding qualities, its Protean shapes and just-over-the-horizon awareness and intuitions that are made by language alone are all part of his own work and his presentation of the work of others. He arranges verses into new groupings, especially in the ***Salt-Sea Verse*** collection, that are as shifting and patterning as the sea itself. He has a masterly grasp of how to make the voices of long dead poets into metaphors for the late twentieth century.

This is specially true of the anthology, ***The Sun, Dancing,*** which I admire very much. The collection is an extension of his own awareness; it is an event for the poet-editor as well as for his readers; a celebration of poetry on the special theme that the young, for well or ill, associate with poetry from quite early in their lives. In the presentational symbolism of the book as a whole, Charles Keeping's line drawings are an essential part, organically conceived, forging their own expressive force within the theme of the collection.

Causley says, 'I see the poems I have chosen to have been written basically from a Christian point of view.' As a privileged insider of the viewpoint, I think this is the case; the strongest effect is not narrowly Christian, however, but that of *religio,* the sense that Elizabeth Cook says children may easily miss 'of the strange, the numinous, the totally Other, of what lies quite beyond human possibility and cannot be found in any human relationships. This kind of "religion" is an indestructible part of many human minds, even though the temper of a secular society does not encourage it'. Studies of adolescents' responses to literature show the actual experience of the numinous to be widespread. It is this feeling which Causley structures in his book with skill and reticence and releases within it a special readerly kind of joy that is both Good Friday and the 'Dancing Easter Day'. (pp. 62-3)

Most young children in school meet formal poetry as hymns or the ways of celebrating whatever prose is not fit for. This early impression remains beyond later attempts to demythologize it and to acknowledge the force of 'popular' verse. Causley takes all that they know of ritual and extends it to meet the seasons of the soul with his passionate regard for what deceptively simple language can do. Look at his own **'On All Souls' Day'** and Ted Hughes's 'Birth of a Rainbow' in the section called 'Comings and Goings'; Gavin Ewart's 'Prayer' alongside Christopher Smart's 'Hymn for Saturday', and save for a special moment, as I do, Karen Gershon's 'Lot's Wife', a poem that links every human catastrophe with the earliest refugees.

The Sun, Dancing is a beautiful, moving book, from which I shall continue to create meanings beyond this year's Easter, that has been both pilgrimage and protest. But I know I am an insider, in Kermode's terms, and for the young this will be a special event in coming to know about poetry; spare, perhaps, and for most outsiders, strange. (pp. 63-4)

> *Margaret Meek, "The Signal Poetry Award,"*
> *in* Signal, *No. 41, May, 1983, pp. 59-66.*

Morag Styles

[Charles Causley] is a delightful man, even more fascinating and entertaining than his poetry promised. Any sense of a poet limited by living in a quiet backwater should be dismissed at once. (He has, of course, travelled widely.) The many books covering every possible surface of the Causley study reveal an intellectual with a breadth of interests. He is also modest, down to earth, laughs a lot and doesn't believe in taking himself too seriously, even though he is now Causley, CBE.

Causley attended the local primary school in Launceston of which he was later to be teacher himself for twenty-five years. He was a keen reader from a young age, but he didn't remember much exposure to poetry in his early years of schooling except 'a faint-hearted attempt to interest us in Christopher Robin . . . he didn't go down terribly well with me or anybody else in the National school in the late 1920s—he might as well have come from outer space!' Later at Grammar school Causley showed obvious promise as a writer and was introduced to the Georgian poets whom he found boring, preferring the resonances of 'Young Lochinvar' and 'Ozymandias'. 'Great stuff!'

What Causley did remember with affection was his old headteacher (soon to figure prominently in his forthcoming *The Young Man of Cury*), a fine musician, pumping away furiously on the harmonium as he took the whole school for mass singing lessons through the entire repertoire of Cecil Sharp's extensive collection of English folk songs. Causley has always been drawn to the musical side of poetry and he is much admired for his own body of wonderful ballads. He has also devoted a lot of time to writing for Music Theatre, often composing between books of poetry.

As a teenager in the thirties, Causley and his contemporaries involved themselves in the usual activities of that age group, drinking, dancing and, in his case, playing for the local dance band. But they were well aware of events in Europe and the inevitability of war. What made Caus-

ley angry then and still does today is that 'if you had any intelligence at all it was perfectly clear what was happening to the Jews in Europe . . .'

It was the fact that poets like Auden, Spender and MacNeice were prepared to speak the truth that attracted Causley as a young man to poetry and he has never moved away from that position. 'The interesting thing about the poem . . . for me . . . is that there's always a sub-text . . . the skin of the poem is never what it's really about . . .'

Causley writes for both an adult and juvenile readership and doesn't discriminate seriously between the two. His *Collected Poems* contains much of the body of work on the children's list, as well as his adult books. Causley does *not* believe that writing for a younger audience is light relief. He offers them challenges and mystery like the poem **'Why?'**, based on a childhood memory. . . .

Readers of Causley are drawn to his work because of its musicality and because the poetry feels so rich and deep, although it is often an apparently simple tale on the surface. 'The great problem (in writing poetry) is to achieve these resonances and hints and suggestions and reverberations and it's an endlessly difficult and endlessly fascinating task to get the thing to work somehow or other . . .' And, of course, he succeeds wonderfully. Causley is now seventy-three, clearly at the height of his power, and there are several new collections in the pipeline.

Causley produced one of the earliest anthologies of contemporary poetry for children, *Dawn and Dusk,* in 1962. Since then he has compiled three of the finest anthologies of the twentieth century for the young. (p. 16)

The main influences on Causley as a poet have been the circumstances of his own life. Living in Cornwall, the feel for the natural world and the sea; the folklore associated with that part of the world; his partiality for music including all kinds of songs; his compassion for the underdog, partly stemming from his working-class roots, his humane beliefs and his hatred of Auden's twentieth-century ogres, particularly intolerance. Then there was Causley's family and his deep attachment to his parents. His father died quite a young man in 1924 from the effects of the First World War. The pain of this experience is suggested in some of Causley's poetry. . . .

Causley's mother was a great fund of stories and memories, one of the most celebrated of which is **'My Mother Saw a Dancing Bear'**. It is typical Causley—a good story, simply told, with a strong, understated message.

> They paid a penny for the dance,
> But what they saw was not the show;
> Only, in bruin's aching eyes,
> Far-distant forests, and the snow.

One of the most remarkable things about Causley is how closely in touch he remains with himself as a child. Perhaps that is one of the reasons why he is such a good writer for children. (p. 17)

> *Morag Styles, "Autograph No. 64: Charles*
> *Causley," in* Books for Keeps, *No. 64, September,*
> *1990, pp. 16-17.*

TITLE COMMENTARY

Dawn and Dusk: Poems of Our Time (1962)

[Dawn and Dusk *was edited by Causley.*]

Charles Causley, the editor of **Dawn and Dusk,** has had the good fortune (not often allowed to anthologists for the young) of being able to choose his book of poetry entirely from new and recent material. Ninety-one poems are here, as he tells us, from the work of fifty modern poets. The hazard is, when judgment has not had time to settle, that so much hangs on the compiler's personal bias. Mr. Causley himself is a poet, a balladeer, a rough romantic with a slightly sinister tinge. One might easily guess which of the two directions of modern taste he is likely to follow: one might guess, for instance, that poems by Dylan Thomas would be in this book, and by Dame Edith Sitwell too. And indeed, they are. Yet the choice on the whole seems curiously careful and just, within the range of his likings; the real misfires are few ("Wild Wilbur" is surely one of the worst of these); many of the poems will be new to almost everybody; in fact, the book ought to give something of pleasure and value to anyone who reads, particularly the young for whom it is designed.

> *"Fine Excess: Verse for All Tastes," in* The Times Literary Supplement, *No. 3168, November 23, 1962, p. 893.*

[Dawn and Dusk] is the sort of book which England does well, the man-of-letters honoring letters. One section is called "Occasions, Seasons, and Festivals." In it Dylan Thomas writes of "A springful of larks in a rolling / Cloud and the roadside bushes brimming with whistling / Blackbirds and the sun of October." Here also is T. S. Eliot on a winter evening: "A lonely cab-horse steams and stamps. And then the lighting of the lamps."

Mr. Causley has brightened his selections with random and casual notes, sometimes of his own devising, sometimes quotations from the poets. These may be geographical or historical explanations, or a scrap of fact about an animal. Ruth Pitter comments on her fanciful poem, "The Hut": "Remember you are looking through the tiny window at the tree outside, and at the same time seeing the reflection of the fire in it, as though the Dryad (the spirit of the tree) actually had a home with a fire burning, up there among the leaves." Her note is as curious and attractive as anything in the poem.

Although Mr. Causley's taste in verse seems to prefer the quiet, the meditative, the occasionally slight, he has put together a book of much variety including names little known in this country (the contributors seem all to be like the editor himself, English).

> *Paul Engle, in a review of "Dawn and Dusk," in* The New York Times Book Review, *Part II, November 10, 1963, p. 2.*

[A] pleasant anthology of poems by contemporary authors; the text is divided into five sections: "Songs and Ballads," "The Other World," "Carnival of Animals," "People and Places," and "Occasions, Seasons, and Festivals." Some of the poetry is lovely and none of it is of poor quality, although the book has a range in literary quality as it does in mood and subject. Author and first-line indexes are appended, as is a series of brief notes on the authors—especially useful because it cites titles of some of their published books.

> *Zena Sutherland, in a review of "Dawn and Dusk," in* Bulletin of the Center for Children's Books, *Vol. XVIII, No. 4, December, 1964, p. 51.*

Rising Early: Story Poems and Ballads of the Twentieth Century (1964; U.S. edition as Modern Ballads and Story Poems)

[Rising Early *was edited by Causley.*]

The Story-Poem's reputation is a little uneasy; some confused promoters of anthologies of narrative in verse seem to have worked on the principle that children dislike poetry: children do not dislike stories; therefore, narrative can make verse-form palatable. This shoddy nonsense belittles poetry, children and logic. Mr. Causley's new collection of modern ballads and story-poems is a vigorous and refreshing refutation. His criteria, as he has already shown in **Dawn and Dusk,** are stringent and sensitive, and he does not patronize poet or child. **Rising Early** ranges very widely; Mr. Causley's introduction reminds us that 'to most of us, a story is irresistible. As he tells it, we notice how the poet preserves the ancient virtues of this particular kind of writing'. These poems touch most of human experience; the poets speak directly and forcefully—today's idiom, and the young reader's imagination is stretched without being teased. Not only young people will find the book fresh and exhilarating.

It is edited with a meticulous concern; the black-and-white drawings [by Anne Netherwood] like the occasional notes and introduction) illuminate what the poet has to say without intrusion or distortion.

> *Sheila Brennan, in a review of "Rising Early: Story Poems and Ballads of the Twentieth Century," in* The School Librarian, *Vol. 13, No. 1, March, 1965, p. 77.*

The mood of this new anthology by Charles Causley is stark. The poems are full of terror, cruelty, suffering, mystery, and weird and ghostly happenings. A parent might well flinch from buying it; a teenager might flinch from reading it. "Horrible," was the reaction of a 13-year old to Bertolt Brecht's "Children's Crusade, 1939"—a valid judgment since the subject of the poem is horrible. Nevertheless, this volume is a fine one and strongly recommended. Among other things, it teaches the youngster that poetry need not be "pretty" or "beautiful," that there is no "poetic" subject. Thus he will encounter an esthetic paradox: that a poem can be beautiful when the subject matter is not. It is a fact that will teach worlds about the shaping power of art.

These poems are narrative poems, some in ballad form. Though the story element will carry the reader along, he will soon discover that they cry out for additional meanings, that there is something above and beyond the tale that is told. It will be surprising if a youngster doesn't sense something more than the irony and bite in Auden's "James Honeyman." Some poems like Elinor Wylie's "Peter and John," and Dorothy Howard's "Birkett's Eagle" may take a little working out. Others such as Thom Gunn's "St. Martin and the Beggar" may seem inconclusive and unresolved. That too is good. For the young person should learn that not every poem is neatly tied nor every line squared away. These ambiguities will drive him back to the poem.

In addition, he will come upon poetry that is cool, objective, even remote in contrast to verse that is romantic and subjective. A poem like John Manifold's "The Griesly Wife" has the same kick at the end as the centuries-old ballad "Edward, Edward," and thus he will learn that it is possible to put new wine into old bottles. But the purpose of the book is not to teach but to provide pleasure, and there are any number of poems that do so.

> *Thomas Lask, in a review of "Modern Ballads and Story Poems," in* The New York Times Book Review, *March 7, 1965, p. 26.*

Modern Ballads and Story Poems takes its tone from Bertold Brecht. It has a strong universal element. It is for winter's child; its magic is of the shadows and the storm. It is for the child mature beyond his years. It pits him against the sterner stuff of life, yet is somehow confident that he is a match for life.

> *Peter J. Henniker-Heaton, in a review of "Modern Ballads and Story Poems," in* The Christian Science Monitor, *May 6, 1965, p. B8.*

Figure of 8: Narrative Poems   (1969)

Charles Causley's new book of narrative poems is his first to appear in the guise of a children's book, though his poems have for many years been appearing in anthologies of poems for children and he is well known as the compiler of those two excellent collections, *Dawn and Dusk* and *Rising Early.* Causley's poetry has always been considered suitable for children in the way that nursery rhymes and ballads are considered suitable, for their surfaces, though strange, are accessible, their rhythms and rhymes strong and encouraging. Underneath the surfaces, of course, there lie not children's toys but, in the phrase of Picasso's which Causley has himself quoted approvingly "weapons of war against brutality and darkness".

Figure of 8 has six entirely new poems, one (**"Balaam"**) which has already been heard in the Jupiter recorded anthology, and the eighth cut version of **"The Song of Samuel Sweet,"** which first appeared in *Survivor's Leave* in 1953. The cuts in this seem to be mainly on the grounds of excessive length rather than of style. This story of a 17th-century farm lad, who is hanged for unwittingly harbouring a rebel soldier, is much the better for being cut by a quarter. But it is still marred by some purple passages and images not worth the carrying, such as one rarely finds in Causley's more recent work. Describing the wounded soldier, he does not know where to stop.

Causley does not make such mistakes in **"Young Edgecumbe"**, a splendid ballad about a young man who refuses to acknowledge Richard the Third as king. The king hears his treachery and condemns him to death. ("He is alive, the cold King , But is already dead!") Again we have the wounded soldier, but it is handled much more crisply. . . .

This particular poem could be called pastiche. It is none the worse for that, but one is rather sorry that Causley does not make more use in this collection of his ability to surprise with anachronism, to use old and new material and idioms side by side. There is nothing here quite so good as his poem about Herod. **"The Innocents' Song"**, which asks so directly and deceptively:

> What are all those presents
> Lying on the kitchen floor?

There is nothing quite so good, either, as his **"By St. Thomas Water"**, the poem about two children playing in a country churchyard and thinking the dead may wake. There are, indeed, no children in *Figure of 8,* unless one counts Stoker Rock's baby, a most unlikely infant, which coos and crows for hours without so much as a drop of milk and very satisfactorily causes the cancellation of a battle. This rollicking naval yarn, with a W. S. Gilbert flavour, is the only one with a really modern setting, though Causley does slip in a nice, surprising reference to the County Council in the Obby Oss poem and Balaam's ass has become a contemporary animal with comments like: "Watch it or we'll take a spill."

Two more impressive poems must be mentioned—the story of the kidnapping of John Polruddon, with its short lines and tight rhymes, a splendidly mysterious happening; and the longer, more complex poem about the power of love, **"St. Martha and the Dragon"**.

It is sad, but probably inevitable, that the illustrations [by Peter Whiteman] are not really right. They are overdecorated, too exotic. But at least they don't attempt to hold the poem frozen, immobile. For, as Causley himself has said: "Like a chameleon, a poem will often most wonderfully change while one is still looking at it." If only Peter Whiteman had given that dragon its six and thirty bear's claws on six human feet.

It is good to hear that Causley is hoping to produce a companion volume for rather younger children. One hopes that in that he will use more material from his own experience. Legend and history are fine, but children need to be reminded that poetry is not only to do with far-off things and battles long ago. One would like to meet some of Timothy Winters's friends.

> *"Causley Stories," in* The Times Literary Supplement, *No. 3529, October 16, 1969, p. 1189.*

Charles Causley's style is alert, swift and absolutely in tune with our times; rhythm, humour, variety, a spice of word and idiom and a strong sense of form—these are qualities to appeal directly to the young . . . The poet takes ballad-metres in his stride, from the recognisable form of:

"King Balak sat on his gaudy throne
His eyes like bits of glass
At the sight of the children of Is-ra-el
Camped on the river grass."

to the less orthodox form of **"John Polruddon"** or the agitated lines of **"The Obby Oss:"**

"Early one morning Second of May
Up jumped the Obby Oss, Said, 'I'm away!' "
With his tall dunce-head And his canvas gown
He tiptoed the street Of Padstow town."

There is the broader stanza form of the rollicking comedy of **"Stoker Rock's baby"** and the multiple verse forms of the long and touching poem **"St. Martha and the dragon,"** based on a legend of Tarascon. Each poem has what one might call a folk-lore basis—even the tale of Balaam and the ass—and each one has teasing suggestions of meaning beyond the story. The readership of a book as intriguing and sensitive as this needs no definition but I will suggest that primary teachers might consider themselves well served by it, as a downward limit.

> *Margery Fisher, in a review of "Figure of Eight Narrative Poems," in* Growing Point, *Vol. 8, No. 5, November, 1969, p. 1431.*

Mr. Causley clearly has some reputation as a poet and as a writer of narrative verse which, the present collection, modest though it is in extent, does much to support. If we are to continue to interest modern children in modern verse a good proportion must be in story form and too few examples which are appealing as well as competent seem to come our way. As a teacher, the author has no doubt found more than once that the necessary material has to be supplied by himself if he is not to wait ages for a suitable selection to appear at a price which a school can afford. Perhaps his example may encourage more practising teachers to follow suit. While he has clearly profited from wide knowledge of traditional and modern ballads his style is still his own and, like Wordsworth before him, he experiments with verse forms in an essential effort to provide variety and, again like Wordsworth, much of his content is based on local incidents and personalities. Thus, Mr. Causley celebrates the fate of a Somerset farmhand caught up in the aftermath of Sedgemoor; young Richard Edgcumbe's escape from Cotehele House in the reign of Richard III; and the saga of Stoker Ross's cut-price baby. This makes for vital verse and human appeal.

> *A review of "Figure of 8: Narrative Poems," in* The Junior Bookshelf, *Vol. 34, No. 1, February, 1970, p. 30.*

Figgie Hobbin: Poems for Children (1970)

Charles Causley's adult verse, which is mostly in ballad form, turns the rhythms and the imagery of children's rhymes in a peculiarly sophisticated, sometimes ominous, way: a queer blend of the very simple and the very knowing. Touches of the adult manner turn up in *Figgie Hobbin*—in the lurking menace of 'Tom Bone' and 'Green Man, Blue Man', and some straight, very good ballads like 'My Young Man's a Cornishman' and 'Mary, Mary Mag-

dalene'—but writing directly for children has elsewhere had a loosening effect on Causley's style, producing a mixture of successes and near-misses (but nothing actually *bad*) with their forebears in other practitioners of balladry and fantasy. He is de la Mare-ish in **'Miller's End'** and in his tale of Lulu who disappeared:

What has happened to Lulu, mother?
What has happened to Lu?
There's nothing in her bed but an old rag doll
And by its side a shoe . . .

and even Housman-like in **'Caistor Town'**:

If you should go to Caistor town
Where my true-love has gone,
Ask her why she went away
And left me here alone.

On the whole, with a few ingenious exceptions, the lighter verse is least good; his perennial territory—love, death, the point where reality reassembles itself in shapes of mystery or alarm—is worked better here than the realm of pure extravaganza; as one would expect.

> *Alan Brownjohn, "Balladry," in* New Statesman, *Vol. 81, No. 2085, March 5, 1971, p. 316.*

Figgie Hobbin consists of ballads (and no one writing in English today handles this form more adroitly than Charles Causley), slightly wistful lyrics about the turn of the seasons, and youth and age, and a number of exuberant nonsense poems. The best of the ballads, **"Eagle One, Eagle Two"** and **"Mary, Mary, Magdalene"**, are a delight; they are catchy and they are forthright, yet they successfully invest the inanimate—two lead eagles and a granite figure of a saint—with the most mysterious undertones. One or two of the lyrics are outstanding, too: the ominous **"Tom Bone"**. . . . and **"Who?"**, an utterly haunting poem about childhood which ends

Why does he move like a wraith by
the water,
Soft as the thistledown on the breeze
blown?
When I draw near him so that I may
hear him
Why does he say that his name is my
own?

But was this written for children? The paradox is that all the best poems in *Figgie Hobbin* would fit just as easily into Mr. Causley's adult canon, as many of the poems in that canon would fit into *Figgie Hobbin.* The blurb's claim that this is a poet "whose particular gift lies luckily within the compass of the young" is roundly true, and it is when Mr. Causley neglects this rare gift and aims specifically for children that his work is least successful. This applies above all to the nonsense poems that often strain too hard for effect, use worn imagery, and generally lack the fine precision of thought and language that inform the best poems. May Charles Causley long continue seriously to explore the areas that have always exercised him—youth, death, the war, the sea, Cornish history and folklore—for it is with more of these poems, so subtle and yet a fresh and accessible, that he is likely to reward not only adults but as often as not, children as well.

"Two Modern Poets," in The Times Literary
Supplement, *No. 3605, April 2, 1971, p. 382.*

Charles Causley's lovely volume tempts one to excesses of
praise. Is it the most successful, and the most delightful,
book of verse for children since *Thomas and the Sparrow?*
Reading and re-reading it, my thoughts kept going back
beyond Ian Serraillier's to an older and more exalted book.
In their individual quality, their variety and their ageless
assuredness, which makes the reader think that he has
known them all his life, these verses recall *Peacock Pie.*
This is some measure of their excellence. Mr Causley is a
poet in the de la Mare mould, although he is in no wise
derivative but always magnificently himself. He ranges
wide in subject and mood, he is funny and sad and grim,
and always, whether he is being flippant or lyrical or stern,
his is the authentic voice of a real poet and a real person.

> *Marcus Crouch, in a review of "Figgie Hob-*
> *bin," in* The School Librarian, *Vol. 19, No. 3,*
> *September, 1971, p. 283.*

Causley is a master of the ballad form . . . , and although
the poems in **Figgie Hobbin** are short, the ring of the
story-teller's voice can be heard in them. They are tough,
vigorous, concrete (surely no poet could possibly use fewer
abstract nouns than Charles Causley does) and set firmly
into their Cornish contexts. They sound out loud and
clear; but as the sound dies away, sometimes the echo
steals back.

> Mother I hear the water
>   Beneath the headland pinned,
> And I can see the sea-gull
>   Sliding down the wind.
> I taste the salt upon my tongue
>   As sweet as sweet can be.
>
> *Tell me, my dear, whose voice you hear?*
>
>   It is the sea, the sea.
>
> (p. 303)

> *John Rowe Townsend, "Virtuosity in Verse,"*
> *in his* Written for Children: An Outline of En-
> glish-Language Children's Literature, *third*
> *revised edition, J. B. Lippincott, 1987, pp. 296-*
> *303.*

The Tail of the Trinosaur   (1972)

Charles Causley has written a long funny narrative poem,
"a story in rhyme told in 24 shakes". Teachers may regret
that **The Tail of the Trinosaur** is not another **Figgie Hobbin,** that favourite of the classroom. Reviewers may regret,
when so few poets write stories for children, that Causley
has visited territory where Ted Hughes has been before
with his Mannerless Monster. The Trinosaur is in fact a
characterless creature compared with Nessie. But children
will quite rightly not be concerned with these adult regrets. Their concern is enjoyment and **The Tail of the
Trinosaur** is enormously enjoyable. The verse forms Causley uses are endlessly variable, his rhyming marvellous, his
invention and humour a delight. The Trinosaur arrives in
the small town of Dunborough in an enormous container.

It is a present to his home town from an explorer in South
America. Unfortunately

> The rather special clay
> Of the jungle where it lay
> Had preserved it
> Ninety million years alive.

When the central heating in the new Museum goes wrong,
the three-pronged beast wakes up and causes more than
a hundred pages of chaos. . . . Have we at last found England's answer to Dr Seuss?

> *"Verse and Worse," in* The Times Literary
> Supplement, *No. 3719, June 15, 1973, p. 679.*

Of our few totally convincing poets writing for children,
the two most entertaining (and most popular with children), Charles Causley and Spike Milligan, have in common their attention to form and their humour. Causley's
The Tail of the Trinosaur is a splendidly inventive long
comic narrative poem . . . , quite exceptionally carefully
designed and produced. It bowls along joyously, easy to
read, with just that twist to the line every now and then
that marks the difference between a poet and a versifier in
this kind of writing. What has there been in this class since
The Pied Piper of Hamelin? Children will find themselves
able to read a poem as long as a whole book, and apart
from the enjoyment, will be delighted with their own
achievement. What would be a wonderful sight to see
would be a long poem from Causley, readable by children,
about a human character. He has the genius and the
craftsmanship. His **"Ballad of the Bread Man"** comes in
an adult collection, *Underneath the Water,* by the way,
and shouldn't be missed. (p. xxiv)

> *Alan Tucker, "Poetry for Children," in* The
> Spectator, *Vol. 231, No. 7582, October 20,*
> *1973, pp. xxiv-xxv, xxvii.*

> To cure the sickness of the heart, ah—
>   Bring me some figgie hobbin!

Figgie Hobbin, for those not in the know, is a Cornish
plum duff, made with raisins and eaten either as a savory
or, garnished with sugar and figs, as a sweet pudding. That
Charles Causley chose to write a poem about the spiritual-
ly uplifting qualities of such a humble dish, that he titled
his second book of verse for children after it, and that I
instinctively used its lines to help me begin this letter
about England's foremost living poet whose work is especially associated with the young isn't at all surprising.

Causley is a Cornishman, an accident of birth which put
him in a corner of England that's as uneasily English as
Wales. Nearly all his life he has lived in Launceston, a hig-
gledy-piggledy small town covering a hill topped by a ruined two-circled tower, which was originally erected as a
fortification by the Romans. Now he teaches in the same
school he went to as a child and lives in a small cottage
with two cats, a quartet of ancient clocks, and a collection
of curiosities of a kind that grows only in a household
that's been rooted to one place for a long time. This very
rootedness gives Causley great pleasure; as you tour the
town with him, he radiates his satisfaction. And the results
are there for all to see in his poetry. (p. 406)

Just across the valley from Launceston is the village where Causley's mother saw the chained bear dancing and gawped with her friends at the prancing beast, though

> what they saw was not the show;
> Only, in bruin's aching eyes,
> Far distant forests, and the snow.

Climb back into town, and you can go into the churchyard where there's a church whose walls are covered with carvings like sculptured tattoos. Among them is the bas-relief of

> Mary, Mary Magdalene
> Lying on the wall,
> I throw a pebble on your back
> Will it lie or fall?

And, superstitious or not, like me and everyone else who visits there—having read the legend revived by Causley's telling of it—you'll pick up a pebble for yourself and lob it onto Mary's already loaded back and wish a wish as you do. (p. 407)

Mary Magdalene and figgie hobbin tell us everything about Causley as a poet. Both have been around for a long time. Both belong very particularly to one place, one small corner of Britain; they're local, even parochial. But in Causley's hands they've become universal, have been given freshness, new life. And Causley *is* a poet of refreshment, a cure for souls, a man who pares away the blinkers.

He is no innovator; he hasn't expanded the forms of verse. But he can make the forms come to life in a way that's wholly contemporary. It isn't surprising, therefore, that he talks about the craft of writing poetry, that he admires technical discipline, knowing your job, being able to operate the old rules of the art. If a poem sings well, he says, you know you've got it right.

That's a creative philosophy which places Causley squarely in the mainstream of the best of English verse, a tradition that feels most at home with song and ballad and narrative. Its sources of inspiration and its subjects are solid things, routine day-to-day experiences, real people, anecdotes. Many poets nowadays would feel uncomfortable and restricted working in such a vein. And truly the sugared lines on cheap greeting cards are often mistaken for poetry of this sort. But Causley, like the laureate John Betjeman, sees it differently. They find opportunity in the old rules, not suffocation. And both possess a special quality that saves them from falling into the trap of banality: a sense of ironic humor, which in Causley has as many stops as an English organ—everything from the wit and the delicacy of the flutey baroque to the slapstick of the rude and rumbling open diapason.

All of this came together in one work for children published here in 1972—to my mind one of the most significant children's books since 1945. With some astonishment I discovered only recently that it has yet to appear in the United States. . . . Causley's *The Tail of the Trinosaur* is undoubtedly something you should know about. Properly described as a long narrative poem, it might better be called a comic novel in verse, told not in chapters but "in twenty-four shakes."

The story itself is simple enough. One day a large truck drives into Dunborough town (Launceston, of course, with a few minor alterations), bearing a gift for the Mayor and people from a grateful ex-citizen. Straight from the steamy Amazon jungle he has sent a "truly remarkable creature," apparently a fossil the size of a circus tent, its "stem and stern . . . infinitely slender," and down its back a single row of dragon-like bumps "denoting that it was of female gender. . . . But the most astounding feature of this antiquated creature was its *most amazing mode of locomotion*" for it propels itself by two huge-clawed legs in front, while propping itself up with one steadying tail behind.

Having recovered from the shock of such a unique if daunting present, the townsfolk set about building a Suitable Home for their new possession, making it as carefully reminiscent of the jungle's overgrown and sticky interior as they can. Indeed, so diligently does Boiler Bill stoke his gutsy furnace in a conscientious effort to reproduce tropical temperatures that he somewhat overdoes matters. The unexpected result is that the trino wakes from its primitive sleep and sets out on a good-natured if nonetheless disastrous slow-motion rampage through the panic-stricken town.

Thereafter each shake of the tale tells of the various methods, all calamitous, employed by the afflicted people as they try to subdue the misbehaving monster before their town is entirely destroyed. In the end, all is well. The trino is not at all as fearsome as his size and age and strangeness lead everyone to believe. Even the Mayor must finally admit that

> "Although it broke up floors and doors
> And sheds and beds and ceilings,
> It's clearer now—one should allow
> For the trino's FINER FEELINGS."

If a moral *must* be drawn, I guess we could say that the whole point of this enchanting story is that things are frightening only when they're strange.

The trino itself isn't the hero of this tale. That role is a corporate one, shared by the scampering, scatty people of Dunborough. Humanity is the hero. And that includes everyone from grumbling Grannie Penney . . . right down to little Sammy Smother, who first had intimations that all was not well with the fossil. (pp. 407-09)

Causley's precise observation of people's personal tic, their weaknesses and strengths, their unthinking acts of selfishness and courage, their goofy stupidities and sublime inspirations enliven this tale. The obvious parallel, and I can't think of another to match it, is Browning's *Pied Piper of Hamelin*. But if Browning is technically more sophisticated than Causley, then Causley has Browning beaten with his unflagging humor, his invention, and, most of all (the thing I feel is a serious lack in *Pied Piper*), a compassion and belief in ordinary folk. Not just that, a love of them, despite their petty flaws and dire failures.

Maybe this is why Causley, all unplanned on his part, is such a fine and successful poet for children. He knows how to make the young laugh—and they respond at once; and he knows how to transmit through his verse the world as he sees it, feels it, understands it, loves it. And that's what makes him for anyone, not only children, a poet who—like figgie hobbin and Mary Magdalene—cures the sickness of the human heart.

The Tail of the Trinosaur, like most of Causley's work, is deceptive in its approachability, its ease on the eye, the ear, the tongue. Nowadays people, even poetically educated people, think contemporary poetry has to be difficult, obtuse, oblique before it can be profound and worth attention. Causley and the trinosaur give the lie to all that. Like Carroll's verses in *Alice,* which also come trippingly off the tongue, there's a lot more in it than meets the lazy eye. (pp. 409-10)

> *Aidan Chambers, "Letter from England: Charles Causley and 'The Tail of the Trinosaur'," in* The Horn Book Magazine, *Vol. LI, No. 4, August, 1975, pp. 406-10.*

The Puffin Book of Magic Verse   (1974)

[The Puffin Book of Magic Verse *was edited by Causley.*]

'All poetry is magic', says Charles Causley at the start of his Introduction—a sweeping pronouncement which looks at first as though it might be an excuse for putting any whim or fancy into his book of magic verse. Instead, it forms the first stroke in a simple sketch of the mysterious way in which 'a good poem "works" on a reader'. Poetry, as Mr. Causley sees it, has its origins in magical incantation—even down to wordless prehistoric 'rhythmic grunts and cries'—and he thereby gives room to an unspoken suggestion that our enjoyment of any poetry is rooted in a recognition of that primal force which, in Robert Graves's words, causes our hairs to stand on end, our eyes to water, our throat to be constricted and our skin to crawl. Poetry as such partakes of no literary syllabus. It is a conjuring with experience in what may prove to be ever more sophisticated forms, so that a subtle chain of subliminary reactions may connect the direct appeal of magic in lovers' charms and curing songs to the high art of 'My Mistres eyes are nothing like the Sunne' or 'A Dialogue between the Soul and the Body'.

The anthologist who adopts such an attitude towards his raw material is a powerful figure by any standard—and, in the compilation of collections for children he is near enough ideal. . . . All the traditional text-book notions of 'suitability' or 'representation of classics' are subordinated to the creation of a book that will speak *for* the poet and proffer *his* responses rather than those of the schoolmaster or the critic. And children, whose natural inclination for poetry is too often blunted or even annihilated by an excess of either wet gush or dry formalism should be quick to see the strength and authenticity of such representation.

Mr. Causley's anthology is thus no mere handbook of quaint spells or the versification of strange events (even though it contains a share of such things—which, thank heaven, may be funny as well as mysterious). Alongside Graves's rescension of 'Amergin's Charm' therefore, or

Thomas Hood's account of 'Sally Simpkin's Lament' there are poems like Blake's 'Long John Brown and Little Mary Bell', or Kipling's 'The Egg-Shell', or Brian Patten's 'A Small Dragon', which take the reader through mystery to a highly concrete human situation. One may quibble perhaps at the occasional bleeding chunks—gobbets from Shakespeare and Tennyson seem to me to be pointing back towards the faults of the old anthologies—but, in its total impact, Charles Causley's book will do nothing but good, for it leads direct from the magic of some spells to the magic of all real poetry. (pp. 111-12)

> *Brian W. Alderson, in a review of "The Puffin Book of Magic Verse," in* Children's Book Review, *Vol. IV, No. 3, Autumn, 1974, pp. 111-12.*

As a poet, Charles Causley's sense of magic is strong, and his anthology, *Magic Verse,* shows that he also perceives the enchantment of words when it appears in the work of others. From a vast variety of sources he presents the reader with an array of supernatural beings, charms and wishes, as well as the ordinary phenomena of nature seen through changed eyes. Besides some obvious choices, there are a good many American Indian pieces; and he adds bits of creepy fun from Gilbert, and Roy Fuller. It is good to see that Mr Causley was not too modest to include himself. A lovely book.

> *Christopher Wordsworth, "Broken Boughs," in* New Statesman, *Vol. 89, No. 2305, May 23, 1975, p. 698.*

This is the world of the spunky, the ghost, the goblin, the witch; the world of the enchanted forest and haunted glen, the powerful spell, the sorcerer, the occult. YOUR world! And you're not likely to forget that once you've read this wide-ranging, brilliantly organized, . . . anthology of poems of magic. Shivery throughout? No, but all the more shivery in its general impact because of the occasional contrasting sunny, funny ghost—like John Betjeman's grandfather "toddling along from the Barbican". A magnificent anthology which not only introduces the reader to a huge range of poets and experiences but surely casts the spell of poetry addiction over him for life. (p. 84)

> *Elaine Moss, "The Arts: Architecture, Theatre, Music, Poetry, Painting," in her* Children's Books of the Year: 1974, *Hamish Hamilton, 1975, pp. 81-90.*

Collected Poems, 1951-1975   (1975)

It is splendid to have available again a number of Causley's poems which originally appeared in volumes now out-of-print; and having a collection covering all his work to date (including twenty-three new poems) is a kind of ritual acknowledgement of the fact that he has become a major English writer. No other writer is more approachable—hence his success with children—and yet, as this book demonstrates, he touches the profoundest of thoughts and feelings.

One of the many things I enjoy about him is his use of colloquial words and phrases, especially those drawn from the messdeck language of the Royal Navy, that verbal well from which our language has constantly been refreshed down the years. Causley has always used his experience in the R.N., but I hadn't fully realized how much he has also drawn on the Christian religion, though in the Cornish rather than the Home Counties Anglican form. There are some deeply touching poems about death and the approach of death which are new to me, and indeed belong to the last few years, and there are others in which Causley lets loose his sharp and slicing wit. One of the most telling of these is **"On Being Asked to Write a School Hymn"**, set to the tune of Buckland—"Loving Shepherd of Thy Sheep".

The publishers describe Causley's book as "a milestone in the literature of our time". For once a blurb has got it right and without exaggeration. The *Collected Poems* is an absolutely necessary addition to the library of anyone who claims even a passing interest in and value for English literature today.

> *Pelorus, in a review of "Collected Poems, 1951-1975," in* Signal, *No. 18, September, 1975, p. 148.*

For most of his career, Charles Causley has dealt boldly with that most tricky of inherited forms, the ballad. Its attraction is understandable, since it is associated with so much that in any case appeals to him: drama and colour; the preservation of local traditons and oddities of custom and speech; the accommodation of the Christian story to a timeless literary or mythical landscape or to the quaint byways of history; simple violence and simple compassion.

A poet launching his career in the late 1940s might be forgiven in these circumstances for sounding like Thomas or Treece, or (in the case of the poems which recapture his experience as a naval rating in the Mediterranean or in Ceylon) for producing the usual travelogue. Indeed, the early poems sometimes begin predictably: "O spring has set off her green fuses"; "Under the willow the willow"; "I met her by the Rifle Range"; "Now that my sea-going self-possession wavers" (Thomas, Auden, Betjeman, Eliot—all the authoritative voices). But Mr Causley proceeds with great assurance, and it is never long before his own particular sense of the lurid, the magnificent or the absurd is effortlessly brought into play.

For instance, the first stanza of **"Song of the Dying Gunner AA1"** is high-pitched and somewhat derivative in manner, though packed with sensuous implications that make the reader retreat in horror from his understanding of them. The lines may be dangerously musical, but the reality is in view:

> Oh mother my mouth is full of
> > stars
> As cartridges in the tray
> My blood is a twin-branched scarlet
> > tree
> And it runs all runs away.

Mr Causley ballasts the rest of this short poem with all the pathetic details of the sailor's small comforts and childish argot. The strategy seems absolutely right, and touchingly

supplies a more human elevation in the memorable final stanza:

> Farewell, Aggie Weston, the
> > Barracks at Guz,
> Hang my tiddley suit on the door
> I'm sewn up neat in a canvas sheet
> And I shan't be home no more.

Much of Mr Causley's later work contrives a similar conflation of the exalted and the mundane. In the increasingly religious flavour of the poems, this sometimes issues in a Christian sentimentalism that is not much to my taste. The poet is a holy fool; tinkers and outcasts are unfallen innocents; the Apostles are Cornish fishermen; and we are on familiar terms with such Merrie England stage-props as Jack O'Lent, gallows-trees, the Galilee man, dancing bears and Captain Jesus. It is a world where three gypsies become the Magi, and even a November guy has its side slit by the speared sky. It is a world too habitually "terrible" or "wicked", a world at the edge of apocalypse. When this scenario is fleshed out with close observation of the mundane or vulgar (as it is, for instance, in **"Demolition Order"** or in **"Timothy Winters"**, with its *Beano*-like descriptions) then the tenderness, the wish to redeem a bleak world, is movingly achieved and we really feel the myth of the underprivileged being saintly. There are a number of poems of experience and memory, particularly about childhood, at the heart of the collection, which quietly validate Mr Causley's fancy elsewhere, his metaphorical bravura firmly in control. . . .

The predominant tone of the collection remains, however, that of the rapt storyteller. It is significant that some of the longest of the narrative poems were written for children (**"St Martha and the Dragon"** seems rather *too* long) but are not here distinguished as such. Fair enough. There is no clear dividing line in Mr Causley's work between his adult and juvenile ballads. The irony of a Plomer, an Auden or a Durrell is unknown here, and we are back in a world of oddities, picture-book history, village anecdotes, explanation of place-names, hauntings, betrayals. The account of Nelson's body popping up out of its cask of brandy could have been written by Masefield (compliment intended) while some of the shorter charms and love lyrics have an authentically Gravesian or de la Mareish nursery air. The biblical emphasis is still observable, but the insistently Cornish setting overrides it in the end: every other saint is a sailor.

There are, it should be said, twenty-three new poems at the end of the collection, on the whole a vintage cross-section of Mr Causley's range and capability. A poem like his **"Ten Types of Hospital Visitor"**, with its angular, witty, unusually free verse, does however point up by its rarity the contrasting smoothness of the balladeering style where (among many dangers) the sense of easy choice of epithet is often too evident, onward movement being the prime concern. Mr Causley's epithets can be colourful, grotesque, idiomatic, but we can quickly learn to recognize his palette. I think it is all to his credit that he has stuck for so long and so successfully to his last, but it may be that the quieter, sharper, elegiac note of some of the new poems represents a change of direction for the future.

But, however he develops, this book stands as a tribute to his attention to an essential function of verse: the power to enchant.

John Fuller, "Exalted Mundanities," in The Times Literary Supplement, *No. 3837, September 26, 1975, p. 1080.*

Causley's tradition is not much practiced these days: he employs rhyme, regular measure, a narrative base (many of these poems are ballads, some quite long), tactics considered out-of-date by some. But his tradition—British first, as he is, and including such mentors as Housman, Blake, Rupert Brooke, and Auden—is never *passé:* the problem is that few poets are up to its demands. Causley is, and then some. This book is first-class poetry through and through, full of marvelous accuracy both physical and psychological, abounding with various characters and situations, involved with history yet making it. As a craftsman Causley is diverse, a true professional who exercises himself in the forms available to him, modulating those into new and able instances. The poems are dense and calculating and can't be read in bunches: they are poems for a long life.

Dabney Stuart, in a review of "Charles Causley 1951-1975: Collected Poems," in Library Journal, *Vol. 100, No. 2, December 1, 1975, p. 2252.*

When Dad Felt Bad   (1975)

The "Little Nippers" are designed for the child whose reading practice needs encouragement in the really early stages, through simple words, lively pictures and a complete but very brief story. Dad's hangover is hardly improved when the cat jumps on his bed and lays a live mole on his head, but the dash into the garden with the unwelcome gift works an instant cure. Splendidly disrespectful in both words and [Richard Rose's] hilarious coloured pictures, this miniature rhymed drama is enough to shock anyone into reading.

Margery Fisher, in a review of "When Dad Felt Bad," in Growing Point, *Vol. 14, No. 7, January, 1976, p. 2808.*

The Hill of the Fairy Calf: The Legend of Knockshogowna (1976)

Verse of a very different calibre, ballad-like, felicitous and economical, tells the legend of Larry Hoolihan the piper of Knockshogowna, who ventured on fairy ground at night for a wager and by his courage (and, it must be added, a natural curiosity) withstood the shape-changing of the angry Queen and a strange aerial journey over Ireland. The artfully artless tale has its own verisimilitude and so do the pictures [by Robine Clignett], which in surrealist style take up literal points, representing the apparitions ("a sea-painted fish . . . That danced in scarf and boots" and "a black and quizzing cat" among them) in a weird landscape under a starry sky. A truly impressive book.

Margery Fisher, in a review of "The Hill of the Fairy Calf," in Growing Point, *Vol. 15, No. 4, October, 1976, p. 2973.*

Of all the traditional poetic forms, narrative verse has changed the least. It continues to attract poets, primarily British, who use it in various ways. Ian Serraillier, in re-telling such medieval ballads and romances as *The Challenge of the Green Knight* (1966) and *Robin in the Greenwood* (1967), retains a vigorous pace, and with dramatic character and costume captures an authentic medieval tone in modern diction.

Also writing with a contemporary nakedness of speech is Charles Causley, whose incantatory literary ballad **The Hill of the Fairy Calf** is a piece of modern folk art:

> And when the harvest moon was white
> Above the heavy hill,
> The sky a-quake with beating stars,
> The night-herd soft and still,
> The herdsman laid aside his staff,
> And leaned upon a stone,
> And smiled and said, 'The moon and stars
> Are mine and mine alone.'

Causley's rich diction, clean imagery, tight rhyme scheme, and meter are underpinned in this and other works by more metaphor at the heart of the story than in earlier narrative verse for children. And his herdsman's quest for power over the faery queen is, of course, humanity's search for meaning in life. The poetry's magical, fairy-tale quality is matched by the primitive, dreamlike illustrations of Robine Clignett which recall the paintings of Chagall. (pp. 232-33)

Sheila A. Egoff, "Poetry: 'The Hill of the Fairy Calf'," in her Thursday's Child: Trends and Patterns in Contemporary Children's Literature, *American Library Association, 1981, pp. 232-33.*

The Puffin Book of Salt-Sea Verse   (1978)

[The Puffin Book of Salt-Sea Verse *was edited by Causley.*]

[Here] there is subject matter of inexhaustible variety and interest and power and the book does this justice. In the hard-back edition especially it is a sturdy satisfying book to have, with bold print and finely detailed, imaginative black-and-white drawings by Anthony Maitland. The sections are well chosen and immediately evocative in a distinct way—The Sea Itself, Creatures of Sea and Land, Findings and Keepings, Fishing and Fisherfolk, these are only four of some sixteen or eighteen. As most readers probably know, Charles Causley was in the Navy during the war and has always lived and worked in Cornwall, so there is a strong affinity between the poetry and the actuality for him. My only surprise is that he has not produced the anthology earlier; my only regret that he has not included a few sea shanties, for instance, "What Shall We Do With a Drunken Sailor," as originally sung, instead of only a parody arising from it by Noel Coward. This small criticism aside, though, this is a book I am very glad to have. (p. 56)

Marie Peel, "A Sense of Tradition," in Books and Bookmen, *Vol. 24, No. 2, November, 1978, pp. 56, 58.*

Before I had looked far into Charles Causley's anthology . . . , I paused for a few minutes just to think about what I had expected. Tennyson's 'Kraken', Eliot's 'Marina' ('And the scent of pine and the woodthrush singing through the fog')? 'Full fathom five', of course; some lines from Whitman's 'Sea Drift'; and perhaps Michael Alexander's fine translation of 'The Seafarer' from his Penguin collection, *The Earliest English Poems:* 'there was no sound there but the slam of waves / along an icy sea. The swan's blare . . . ; or Ezra Pound's more famous translation of the same piece. 'Sea Fever' is a likely choice. Really I didn't need to look any further . . . except that none of these pieces is in the book, and I found Causley's selection much less predictable and far more interesting than I could have hoped. Perhaps poetry about the sea is as various and interconnected and huge as the sea itself, wine-dark, or the sun glinting on it, or

> so flat and glassy
> that if you breathed on it, it would mist.

This is from 'Fishing' by Alasdair Maclean, a masterly poem that Causley includes among innumerable discoveries and rescues, all within a context of famous set pieces and much loved favourites: Viola's 'What country, friends, is this? This is Illyria, lady' from *Twelfth Night;* Kate from *The Tempest;* 'Rule, Britannia'; 'Drake's Drum' and 'I do like to be beside the seaside'. Just one piece of prose, Hesiod, translated by Samuel Butler. . . . (p. 67)

Children read poems because of what they are about. They are as bad as newspaper readers for demanding more of what they like and nothing at all of anything else. They immediately made Charles Causley's earlier companion anthology, **Magic Verse,** one of the best-selling Puffins. The idea of the sea as a subject is almost as good, and the choice of poems is perhaps even better.

Good subject, superb poetry, with exactly the right man to present them: quite obviously this is the best anthology to be published for children this year. (pp. 67-9)

Alan Tucker, "The Runners-up," in Signal, *No. 29, May, 1979, pp. 67-73.*

The Gift of a Lamb: A Shepherd's Tale of the First Christmas Told as a Verse-Play   (1978)

Charles Causley has re-created sensitively, in modern circumstances and imaginative poetry, the mediaeval Towneley *Second Shepherds Play.* The three shepherds, three generations of the same family, like their ancestors readily burst into song. Vera Gray's music is best in the instrumental episodes, pleasingly modal and reminiscent of old carol and folksong, but the more repetitive songs should prove easily remembered by child actors. Appropriately the shepherds celebrate the birthday of the youn-

gest, Thieving Jack takes the audience into his confidence as he steals a lamb, the angel host transforms the play with lyric verse bursting with light on the midnight hill, and the shepherds take gifts to Bethlehem, where Jack is converted. The style skilfully keeps the sense of traditional Biblical speech without sounding archaic. This should be a useful addition in an area where piety is often stronger than literary excellence.

M. Hobbs, in a review of "The Gift of a Lamb," in The Junior Bookshelf, *Vol. 43, No. 1, February, 1979, p. 27.*

Three Heads Made of Gold   (1978)

Charles Causley retells this sad and slightly macabre English folk tale rather as Walter de la Mare did in *Told again,* and it is a method which can be approved only for poets. In the process the story becomes longer and more detailed, but the ore with which Mr Causley fills every rift is the genuine precious metal. Pat Marriott keeps the haunting tale firmly down to earth in her admirable designs.

Marcus Crouch, in a review of "Three Heads Made of Gold," in The School Librarian, *Vol. 27, No. 1, March, 1979, p. 35.*

The Animals' Carol   (1978)

On the wall of the prior's chamber in Shulbrede Priory in the far west of Sussex is painted one of the very earliest of strip cartoons. The subject is the Nativity. All the beasts are there with balloons coming out of their mouths, on which the dialogue appears in good medieval Latin. Charles Causley has taken his cue for this book from a later version of the same theme, and out of it has conjured an enchanting poem. "Christus natus est" catches the very rhythm of the cock's crow, and the ox bellows "Ubi?" "Bethlehem" is the voice of the lamb—just lengthen the first syllable into a bleat. The rest is Mr. Causley's invention in Latin and English and both good. The poem cries out for music, and with the right composer it could take its rightful place in the annual carol repertory.

M. Crouch, in a review of "The Animals' Carol," in The Junior Bookshelf, *Vol. 43, No. 2, April, 1979, p. 93.*

The Last King of Cornwall   (1978)

[Charles Causley] seems to be using **The Last King of Cornwall** as a way of enumerating for "foreigners" his country's treasures of tin, copper, china clay and fish, though this conclusion is suitably reached through the traditional process of magic riddles, set by the witch Nimue for a poverty-stricken and ineffectual ruler who has to be helped to understand their meaning. Taking an easy, nonchalant way with folk-lore, Causley extends the tale by elaborating the humour of King Mark 99th and Giant Brown Willy, to make a pleasant, small book for readers from nine or so, who should enjoy his exuberant style. . . .

Margery Fisher, in a review of "The Last King of Cornwall," in Growing Point, *Vol. 18, No. 1, May, 1979, p. 3509.*

Narrated with the polished ease of a distinguished poet, **The Last King of Cornwall** is forged from the essential materials of the folk tale: wizardry and villainy, riddles and secrets, giants and supernatural beings, the weak made strong, failure transformed to success and defeat to triumph. Krystyna Turska's illustrations, from broad spread to small details, decorate every page and crystallise the mood, characters and situations of an imaginative story.

G. Bott, in a review of "The Last King of Cornwall," in The Junior Bookshelf, *Vol. 43, No. 4, August, 1979, p. 204.*

The Ballad of Aucassin and Nicolette　(1981)

Charles Causley has turned the medieval Provençal romance of Aucassin and Nicolette into a most versatile play. It was produced originally with a cast of six, and subsequently broadcast with a rather larger team, but it would be equally effective as a pageant play with plenty of extras and lots of colour. Much of the text is designed for singing, and this edition includes a sample of the music composed by Stephen McNeff which makes only modest demands on the voice. A useful addition, therefore, to the very small repertoire of worthwhile pieces for young players or mixed companies of adults and children.

This is not the acting edition but a book designed to be read. It hardly needs me to say that Mr. Causley writes with rare wit and grace and with a fine mixture of fun and sentiment. The story is told mainly by a ballad singer, his narrative interrupted by action as the passage of the tale calls for it. Mr. Causley keeps some of the unique atmosphere of the original but does not hesitate to bring in his own characteristic humour and sense of the ridiculous. He has great fun with the episode in the topsy-turvy kingdom of Torelore where the Queen goes to war while her royal husband lies at home suffering labour pains, tended by his midhusband. The original tale was rather repetitive and the modern poet does not hesitate to invent some delightful incidents to lend variety to the story. . . .

There are some useful notes on production and music. Altogether a highly pleasing and valuable book.

M. Crouch, in a review of "The Ballad of Aucassin and Nicolette," in The Junior Bookshelf, *Vol. 45, No. 4, August, 1981, p. 156.*

The Sun, Dancing: Christian Verse　(1981)

[The Sun, Dancing *was edited by Causley.*]

Aficionados of **Dawn and Dusk, Rising Early** and **The Puffin Book of Magic Verse**—they are very many and I am one of them—reckon that Charles Causley is probably the best anthologist for children in the country. So the appearance of **The Sun, Dancing** is a matter of excitement

and considerable curiosity. Has Causley rung the changes between fervour and piety and innocence and longing and mystery and ecstasy in such a way that the anthology echoes all the octaves of the Christian faith?

The short introduction is a little unsettling. While one welcomes the suggestion that "all creative activity in the arts is essentially religious in origin", some readers may raise an eyebrow at the cursory dismissal of the idea of an anthology representing no one specific religion but religion in general on the grounds that it would "promise nothing more than dilution of effect". What about Victor Gollancz's quite superb *A Year of Grace*? It is not impossible to visualize a counterpart for children. Then again, one may demur at the claims made for certain poems / poets and fail to see that in these rather poor flat lines D J Enright writes "with a devastatingly clear eye of his childhood":

> Yet we were sent to Sunday school.
> Perhaps in the spirit that others
> Were sent to public schools. It
> Might come in useful later on.

The anthology is divided into short sections—"Creatures and the Kingdom," "Christmas", "The Childhood of Christ", "Saints and Prophets" and so on, each prefaced by a half-title and a virile illustration by Charles Keeping—and one of its strengths is the amount of good and unfamiliar poetry, especially contemporary poetry, to be found in it. Ranged alongside the great masters, Milton and Herbert and Hopkins, are ninety poets represented by 150 poems. It is unthinkable that any imaginative child, confronted with this book, should fail to find flashpoints, poems that lead to a fuller understanding of the Christian faith.

That said, and bearing in mind that it is always easy to field a substitute team, what is missing? Why are there no Old English poems, not even "Caedmon's Hymn"? Why no early Irish and Welsh lyrics, some of them captivatingly fresh narratives? These omissions are odd in so far as there are translations here from German, Polish, Spanish and Portuguese and specially commissioned translations—effectively colloquial they are—from *Piers Plowman*. Why so very little from the Miracle Plays and so few of the superb, singing and simple medieval lyrics? Above all, why are there virtually no Marian poems? This is a real shortcoming, speaking from literary, representative and ecumenical viewpoints. I cannot conceal some disappointment in this anthology, perhaps exaggerated because my expectation was so great.

Kevin Crossley-Holland, "Echoing All the Octaves," in The Times Educational Supplement, *No. 3448, July 30, 1982, p. 21.*

In his introduction to this magnificent anthology Charles Causley explains that he has chosen poems 'written basically from a Christian standpoint, or to embody a Christian point of view' but he also offers a definition of religion as 'that which represents the link between man and God, or the gods' and the creative activity celebrated in the poems chosen is of the widest application. The title reflects a medieval legend of Easter which in itself evokes the warm intimacy and homeliness of the anonymous songs and carols of that time, and surely dancing is a more universal and natural expression of the best in man than the fervid evangelism and sickly sensual imagery of the received doctrines that drive so many away from organised religion. Here are no dogmas, no sentimentality, but personal statements, agonised or contented, philosophical or practical, each demanding and deserving proper and leisurely attention. In the sixteen thoughtfully planned sections every reader will find poems that strike home; for me, Causley's piercing **'Ballad of the Bread Man'** and the Harrowing of Hell from Piers Plowman are supreme. A book not only for believers but for the interested of any beliefs; a book to be kept and savoured for its content, for Keeping's dignified, powerful embellishments, and for the fine authority of the whole production.

> *Margery Fisher, in a review of "The Sun, Dancing," in* Growing Point, *Vol. 21, No. 3, September, 1982, p. 3957.*

Anthologising is a natural activity for a poet, and Charles Causley is a master in both spheres. **The Puffin book of magic verse** and **The Puffin book of salt sea verse** have already shown how a collector can bring forth a new element—the essence of a theme—by the way he links the poems together. For this he needs editorial support. The poems in this collection are a *parure,* more than a jointure of jewels. They are selected because they 'reflect the Christian experience', so they need not be orthodox in belief if only they 'represent the link between man and God, or the gods'. Causley believes that 'all creative ability in the arts' is essentially religious in origin. In this he agrees with Elizabeth Cook who stresses the importance of *religio* 'the sense of the strange, the luminous, the totally Other', but he also wants to make religious verse take part in the here and now, the unjustness of things linked to the redeemable way of the world.

Thus the spectrum of the poems is shot through with the colour and quality of mode and feeling: grim, glorious, obsessive, released, sombre, fantastical, homely. There are love songs, and songs of good life; verses from Lapland and new ones. Here I met Karen Gershon for the first time; her poem about Lot's wife haunts my days. Some of the subtlety of the collection lies in the subheadings (e.g. in *Starting points* is 'Flower in the crannied wall'). The sheer variety and variability of the experience is stunning. I like best the groups called *To Easter and beyond* and *Comings and goings* (where I found again Edwin Muir's 'The border'). All of this will be gloriously ransacked for assemblies, but when individual readers in quiet places meet Langland next to 'Early morning feed' and, as they turn the pages, contemplate the restrained involvement of Keeping's powerful symbol drawing, something else will happen that only words can bring about. It is a lovely book, and a lift to the heart in sombre times.

> *Margaret Meek, in a review of "The Sun, Dancing," in* The School Librarian, *Vol. 30, No. 3, September, 1982, p. 282.*

Charles Causley, lovely poet and master anthologist, has put together a rich and imaginative collection of poems inspired, very broadly, by the Christian theme. Not much of it is what we might think of as 'religious' verse, but it is, in one way or another, enlightened by a spiritual quality or prompted by an aspect of the message of Christ. There are no easy comforts here; for Causley and his poets Christianity is no soft option but a hard choice, typified by R. S. Thomas' stark picture of the empty manger. This is not to say that these are gloomy poems. The centrepiece of Mr Causley's anthology is Easter Day when the sun dances. Significantly the few poems chosen for Christmas are sadder.

The editor ranges wide for his poems, with some emphasis on the seventeenth century (Herrick, Vaughan and others), and embracing Spain, Poland and Ronald Tamplin's marvellously colloquial rendering of the Middle English of Langland. The choice is always personal but by no means quirky. It is always stimulating, surprising and unexpected. Even the most widely read adult will find many unfamiliar and delightful things here; for the receptive child the book will be a voyage of discovery, not least of self-discovery.

> *M. Crouch, in a review of "The Sun, Dancing," in* The Junior Bookshelf, *Vol. 46, No. 6, December, 1982, p. 228.*

Early in the Morning: A Collection of New Poems (1986)

The long wait for a new volume of Causley's matchless children's poems has proved fully worthwhile. His writing here is full of joy and exuberance, as well as the familiar plangent note of loss and longing. Some of them really are as the blurb describes them, new nursery rhymes, telling stories of hectic compression which are entirely dependent on the logic of rhythm and rhyme. Others strike a more personal note, while never straying far from the demands of narrative. **"John, John the Baptist"**, **"One for the Man"**, **"Stone in the Water"**, **"Tell, Tell the Bees"**: the emphatic simplicity of the titles prepares us for something special.

Causley's words themselves draw wonderful pictures in the head: of Tommy Hyde, for instance, writing a love letter on the strand, and "watching for the water to rub it off the shore / And take it to my true love in Baltimore." . . .

Twenty of the poems have also been set to tunes by Anthony Castro, and are clearly printed with full piano accompaniment and guitar chords. The music is straightforward and uncluttered, and, like the equally simple poetry, far from dull. The instructions at the beginning of each piece set the tone: "nice and bouncy", "sadly", "slow and gentle".

> *Neil Philip, "Picture Poems," in* The Times Educational Supplement, *No. 3685, February 13, 1987, p. 46.*

It must be eight years, or thereabouts, since we had a set of Charles Causley's children's verse; far too long, but now our patience is richly rewarded.

For these new poems Mr. Causley has looked to the loose

verse forms and the blended inconsequence and earthy wisdom of the nursery rhyme. The subjects are universal; their application very much that of today, with nail varnish, ukuleles and tractors among the matters under discussion. The mood changes quickly from tenderness to ribald absurdity, and there is literally never a dull moment.

Of the forty poems in the book twenty have been provided with musical settings by Anthony Castro, with piano accompaniment and guitar chords indicated. The keys may be unadventurous and the tunes sometimes trite, but Mr. Castro makes up for this (and he has no doubt limited himself in order to make the music accessible to young singers) with some delightfully astringent harmonies. A charming carol should attract many performers. **'Johnny Come over the Water'** is expressively tender, and an account of the family band—**'The Money Came in'**—is cheerfully rumbustious. My personal favourite, in which words and music come most happily together, is **'I Love My Darling Tractor'**, in which the farmer's joyful celebration of his new machine is punctuated by perky discords in the left hand.

> *M. Crouch, in a review of "Early in the Morning," in* The Junior Bookshelf, *Vol. 51, No. 3, June, 1987, p. 125.*

Some years have passed since the publication of **Figgie Hobbin,** a stunning example of excellence in poetry for children. Now an even younger audience can find delight in Causley's remarkable compositions—an unerring blend of sound and sense, humor and nostalgia, poignancy and joy. By combining remembered rhythms from traditional nursery rhymes with his own fluid poetic vision, the poet has created a lilting collection of forty poems, notable for their originality, their aesthetic quality, and their undeniable appeal. . . . As in the old nursery rhymes, there are some wonderfully idiosyncratic characters, like the "old woman of Chesterle-Street / Who chased a policeman all over his beat." There's a counting rhyme, which is also a miniature story in verse, for it describes how one nature lover outwits the fox hunters. The lyrical **"Take Me to the Water Fair,"** for which the score suggests a "slow blues" pacing, has the insistent, wistful charm of "Scarborough Fair," particularly in the concluding quatrain: "As high above the chestnut burns / Its candles on the sky / You say that summer cannot end—/ And you will never lie." Like the "silent sun" mentioned in the title poem, the collection explodes in a brilliant burst of light, illuminating the goals toward which all who write for children should strive. (pp. 751-52)

> *Mary M. Burns, in a review of "Early in the Morning: A Collection of New Poems," in* The Horn Book Magazine, *Vol. LXIII, No. 6, November-December, 1987, pp. 751-52.*

Jack the Treacle Eater   (1987)

Here are all the qualities that make Causley such a special poet for children: the way he uses and extends familiar, traditional rhyme forms, his humour, a voice that never condescends or patronises. There is a strong sense of real places and real people and, running through all the poems (they are arranged in six sections), a powerful sense of time passing, days and seasons turning, the thread that holds generations.

> *Pat Triggs, in a review of "Jack the Treacle Eater," in* Books for Keeps, *No. 47, November, 1987, p. 5.*

Children's verse tends towards the riddle, the ballad, the mystery down the dark alley, the remoteness of all that is beyond a child's immediate grasp, and who is better qualified in this territory than Charles Causley? . . . [In **Jack the Treacle Eater**] there is a tang of particularity: 'Such joys we knew with those dinners *à deux* / At the bottom of the parking lot / On roasted gnu and buffalo stew / And Tandoori chicken in a pot' (**'When I was a Hundred and Twenty-six'**). In his adult verse Causley writes in a timeless, universal mode, unaffected by literary fashion, and his style adapts effortlessly to the demands of a young audience. He's good at amiable nonsense, as in **'The Elephant and the Butterfly'**—'You could make yourself wings out of palms and things / With the aid of the creeper and vine'—but can go much deeper: **'Teignmouth'** is the end of the Edwardian garden party, finely described in terse lines: 'Sand-artist crimping / the crocodile: / Quartz for a yellow eye / Shells for a smile'. The illustrations by Charles Keeping are unobtrusive rather than striking but **Jack the Treacle Eater** is a fine celebratory volume to mark Causley's 70th birthday.

> *"A Happy Hunting Ground," in* The Listener, *Vol. 118, No. 3038, November 19, 1987, p. 40.*

[This] superb collection is a reason for celebration, offering all the imagination and originality sadly lacking in much banal verse labelled 'for children'. Causley knows better than to write condescendingly for readers of seven years upwards. These poems with their haunting rhythms and subtle rhymes, wit and mystery, richness of vocabulary and variety of subject, will appeal to adults too.

Several poems are based on fact and clear notes at the back enhance their meaning: the charming **'On St Catherine's Day'** reminds us of the saint commemorated when catherine wheels whirl on November the fifth; **'Twelve O'clock Stone'** tells a legend of Causley's home county, Cornwall. . . .

Old Maggie Dooley feeding her stray cats, Susanna's fears on bonfire night, thoughts on the milkman (or milklady?), Mawgan Porth—the superior cat: all these remain with me and take their place in what promises to be a rare and timeless collection.

> *Anne Harvey, in a review of "Jack the Treacle Eater," in* British Book News Children's Books, *Winter, 1987, p. 26.*

'In the days when you called me your own Rich
   Tea
And you were my Custard Cream.'

So sings Charles Causley's lively and still loving centenarian-plus in one of the many delightful, bubbling and exquisitely crafted poems of his new collection. He ranges wide for his subject-matter around the West Country, in legend and history, and in his fertile imagination, creating a string of entrancing eccentrics from Aesop to Aunt Leonora and Maggie Dooley (who feeds stray cats in the park). All these poems show a total mastery of traditional forms and rhythms, but the reader seldom stops to discover how superbly it is all done, being swept along on the flood of the poet's fantasy and humour. It is not all just fun either. There is a rock-hard note in **'The Twelve-o'clock Stone'** which treats of a Cornish tradition, a gentle nostalgia in **'Summer was Always Sun'**, and a spare economy in **'Morwenstow'**. Those who tell stories to young (and old) listeners should add **'The Apple-Tree Man'** to their repertoire; this is a version of a Somerset folk-tale which, in balance and perfection of timing, is as good in its way as Eleanor Farjeon's 'Mrs. Malone'. . . .

This is a book which is going to give much pleasure now and for a long time to come. The blend of a fine text, superb illustrations and excellent format also make it an obvious choice for the collector.

> *M. Crouch, in a review of "Jack the Treacle Eater," in* The Junior Bookshelf, *Vol. 52, No. 1, February, 1988, p. 42.*

Anything new by Charles Causley is likely to be a fine and lasting treat. Many poems from his earlier *Figgie Hobbin* are already longstanding anthologers' favourites: this collection can be guaranteed a similar following. Charles Causley loves to tell a tale and he does this with masterly simplicity. His language rings sufficiently to draw younger listeners along with its music yet remains infinitely readable even for an adult. People, places, tradition, legend. . . . It would be pointless to choose one particular area of favourites. These are all Causley strongholds from the echoing sea in **"Morwentow"** . . . to the treacle-stained Jack (a famous message-runner from Somerset), or **"Fable"** where he gathers together poignantly some of the supposed facts about Aesop's life. One poem hauntingly captures the life of Lady Jane Grey in just four simple verses. King George V and his pet parrot Charlotte are woven into another based on some of the phrases the bird was said to have been taught . . .

A perfect book to share with any child from about 9 years to old age!

> *Judith Nichols, in a review of "Jack the Treacle Eater," Books for Your Children, Vol. 23, No. 1, Spring, 1988, p. 27.*

The Young Man of Cury and Other Poems (1991)

For some, perhaps, there may be too much pathos in Charles Causley's new collection. The plangent note of loss and regret which sounds so strongly in poems such as **"Quarterjacks"** and **"Jack Swallow"** forms an underswell even in the nonsense poems. Like Lear, you often cannot tell whether Causley is being funny or sad; in truth, the two feelings are inextricably mixed. Suffice it to say that this is Causley's best and most varied book for children since *Figgie Hobbin.* Many of these poems will soon become firm favourites, and some of them, such as **"Pepper and Salt"** and **"Dream Poem"** are as good as anything he has written so far. There is no one writing today who can so surely recall how the child's eye creates its own wonders.

> *Neil Philip, "The Versifier and the Poet," in* The Times Educational Supplement, *No. 3932, November 8, 1991, p. 40.*

It takes a particular gift to write poems so traditional in form and language as to seem less like poems newly made than poems discovered, imprisoned in the rock of tradition. It is a question of freeing the poem from the clutter of expectation and formulaic phrase, polishing up lines here and there, until there it is—something as natural as sitting or talking. This has been Charles Causley's way: indeed he has made himself so much a part of that rock, it is sometimes hard to say whether a poem reminds us of something genuinely old or of something else by Causley. There is no appearance of striving or struggle, little of the glossy nowness and hereness of life, little of the paraphernalia with which determinedly relevant writers determinedly stuff their work. There are no high-rise blocks, no broken families, no dope or dole, no identity crisis—but the poems are not poorer for the fact that they live on the edges of yesterday, dipping their toes, so to speak, in the timeless past where all things shine equally brightly before disappearing under the waves.

The Young Man of Cury is, in this respect, no different from Charles Causley's other books for children. The poems are rooted in Cornwall, in the presence of the sea and in the magic of names: Old Billy Ricky, Lord Hazey, Mrs Malarkey, Solomon Fingergreen, Sam Groom, Danny Grout, Mother Cardle, Miss Pennyluney, Tamasine Long and Jeremy Peep, names which are as queer and commonplace as pebbles, and equally at home with King Neptune, Trim-and-Tall and the White Witch as with the town council and Inter-City trains. It is a country rather than a town world, a world combining the remote with the immediate past: the Obby Oss is danced round Padstow, the young man mourns for his rescued mermaid near Lizard Point, steam trains smudge the sky, there are coalmen coming up the drive and sextons ringing the curfew bell.

Behind all the poems lurks the ballad from with its choruses and parallelism:

> The water came in at the window,
> It came in at the door,
> It swallowed up the cellar
> It came up through the floor
> > **("Riverside")**
> > > . . .

Michael Foreman's watercolour illustrations are lyrical and witty: some, like the eccentric castle for **"Don't Wake Up Lord Hazey"**, delight in fantasy, others, like the frontispiece for the "At Sea" section, have a romantic depth and richness. The generally light colours and skipping lines make for a pretty, but not at all twee book, which has its successes but also some means and averages where the poetic mannerisms can appear a little tired. At least half the poems make excellent reading and a few are ready to enter the permanent canon which is their natural home. These include poems such as **"What Happened"**, **"Venton**

Ham" and **"Tam Snow",** in which Causley's gifts for revitalizing the verities and raising individual lines through the specific into the energy field of imagination are especially evident.

The great virtue of the best of these poems is that they talk neither up nor down to children—nor do they set out to endear themselves with a false complicity. They haven't done their market research. They don't pretend to address children's immediate interests. They roll to their own rhythm, and weave their way into the experience of childhood which is indifferent to ideas about itself.

> *George Szirtes, in a review of "The Young Man of Cury and Other Poems," in* The Times Literary Supplement, *No. 4625, November 22, 1991, p. 22.*

Mavis Thorpe Clark

1912-

(Also writes as M. R. Clark and Mavis Latham) Australian author of fiction and nonfiction and scriptwriter.

Major works include *The Brown Land Was Green* (1956), *The Min-Min* (1967), *Blue above the Trees* (1968), *The Boy from Cumeroogunga: The Story of Sir Douglas Nicholls, Aboriginal Leader* (1979), *Solomon's Child* (1981).

One of Australia's major writers of historical and contemporary realistic fiction for young people, Clark is acknowledged as among the first authors to introduce a cultural and environmental consciousness to juvenile literature about her country and its people. Her writings focus on many different aspects of life in Australia, drawing on experiences from her extensive travels and exploring the country's history, people, and problems with patriotism and compassion. Scrupulous about the accuracy of the material she presents, Clark researches each of her works for several months and submits her manuscripts to an expert in the field before publication, commenting that "detail, awareness, is so important to today's youth . . . that I can see no reason for withholding a relevant fact." While some critics have suggested that she presents an excessive amount of facts which might bore or overwhelm young readers, others maintain that Clark tempers her scholarly approach with appealing characters, a deep concern for nature, and an optimistic outlook on Australia's future. Furthermore, Clark is known for her sensitive depictions of Australia's Aboriginal community. Sir Douglas Ralph Nicholls, the first Aborigine to achieve knighthood, became the subject of two of Clark's best known works: a biography for adults, *Pastor Doug,* and *The Boy from Cumeroogunga,* an examination for children of Nicholls's lifelong struggle to improve the conditions for Aborigines in Australia.

Clark's books generally either chronicle an episode from Australian history or address a modern social problem. Walter McVitty has praised her for contributing "interesting, entertaining and properly researched historical fiction with Australian settings for children." One of Clark's first works, *The Brown Land was Green,* has been heralded as particularly progressive. The story of a pioneering English family settling in the western district of Australia in 1844, it contains Clark's sympathetic portrayal of the Aborigines as well as her characterization of Henrietta, the twelve-year-old female protagonist, as intelligent, aggressive, and resourceful are considered unique for their time. Another historical novel, *The Blue above the Trees,* realistically recounts the events surrounding the destruction of the Australian rainforest by English settlers in the 1870s. Clark's approach to this subject is notably objective; she laments the loss of natural beauty and recounts the plight of the lyrebird and the koala bear while offering a sympathetic and realistic portrayal of a family's struggles to overcome hardship and live off the land.

In *The Min-Min,* which is often considered her best book, Clark turned to comtemporary issues, examining inequality and poverty in the Australian outback. In this novel, Sylvie, a sensitive and impoverished girl, runs away with her brother Reg in search of the flickering lights, known as min-min, said to be an omen of good fortune. Similarly, many of Clark's subsequent works focused on contemporary issues, including problematic family relationships and the country's need to be ecologically aware. *Iron Mountain* (1970), for example, presents seventeen-year-old Joey's struggle to establish his autonomy and find acceptance in an iron mining town in western Australia. In *The Hundred Islands* (1976), Clark called attention to the dwindling mutton-bird population in the Bass Strait in a story of a teenager confronting his father on the ecological soundness of the family's land. Clark's work has become known for providing thorough and captivating portrayals of Australia life as well as for challenging young people to seek solutions to the country's problems. *The Min-Min* was chosen Book of the Year by the Australian Children's Book Council in 1967. The Council also offered commendations to *The Brown Land was Green* and *Blue above the Trees.*

(See also *Something about the Author,* Vol. 8; *Something about the Author Autobiography Series,* Vol. 5; *Contemporary Authors,* Vols. 57-60; and *Contemporary Authors New Revision Series,* Vol. 8.)

AUTHOR'S COMMENTARY

In my early years as a writer, I wrote because I had discovered the intoxication of working with words; the discovery that words were a fluid raw material, adaptable, obedient, subservient, pliable, powerful. They allowed me to reconstruct and hold forever, sights, sounds, colours, thoughts, emotions, landscapes. I found great joy in experimenting with outline and colour, until I achieved what I considered a satisfying likeness. Which meant, simply, that I enjoyed the physical and mental activity of writing. . . .

However, being young when I began, not only in years but in life experience, I wasn't particularly aware, and certainly not fired or excited, by the world's joys and sorrows. Without taking a conscious decision on the matter, I wrote stories that offered little but entertainment.

It was my period of apprenticeship. By actual and loving practise, I was learning structure, framework, individual style, and the mechanics of my tools. I was also putting into that practice what I had already learned of the craft, from an early age, as a compulsive reader. Any skill I have is derived from that early reading and that faithful early practice. Not that we ever cease to learn, to develop, or to change our tone, our ideas or our approach.

And then the world's joys and sorrows presented themselves to me; in an offering that I was almost afraid to accept, yet from which I couldn't turn away. With that presentation came an irresistible motivation to go out and experience, to know, to be excited. Since then, I've never willingly turned down an experience, or lost the ability to be excited. And by excited I mean not only a euphoria of spirit, but emotional involvement.

I have worked in most of the various forms of written expression; biography, novels, factual works, some poetry, adult short stories and articles, radio plays. I have scripted serials of my own children's novels—which are for the older reader—and now television. While I regard my adult biography of Sir Douglas Ralph Nicholls, entitled ***Pastor Doug,*** as my most important single work, the main body of my writing has been for young people. *I am a children's writer.* It is with gratitude and a sense of distinction that I make that statement.

Children's literature is part of the enduring, universal and classic literature of the centuries; beginning, perhaps, with *Aesop's Fables* written circa 600 BC.

Australian children's literature has already achieved universal appeal and international acceptance; reaching farther, I believe, than our adult works. (p. 4)

The next decade or so could be crucial to the survival of Earth and its people. Never before has Earth stood so close to the brink. The minds of the elders who will shape and decide that destiny—to plunge over or to draw back—

belong to the children of today. No other generation has been faced with the ultimate choice.

To write for today's child is to write for the most important generation of people ever born. This is a humbling thought.

What leads a writer into this particular form of written expression? He may come to it by various routes, and at any time of life. All of them legitimate, provided he takes to this road only because he *must*.

Literary expression comes in many forms—poet, playwright, novelist, historian—different yet the same, all endowed with the ability to define and express with the tool of words. Many writers work in more than one medium but most of them will have one forte in which they excel.

It is not enough, however, to look over the field of literary choice and thrust in a red pin. To say "I'll be a poet" won't make that person a poet, unless he already has the rhythm of poetry flowing through mind and body. The one who says "I'll write a children's book", believing it to be an easy form of writing, or because he thinks it more lucrative than the adult novel, will not write a good book for the young. The writer of children's books, for whatever age group, must be drawn to this medium as inexorably as the poet is drawn to his music in words.

My route to this track? There were no writers in my family, but the house was ever full of books. Born with it? Probably, though there were other things I might have done. If I had been a man, I feel I would have worked in wood, in some form or another. I admire, envy, those who can create fine furniture, fine buildings. I may have worked in wood by day, and written at night. If I were starting out today, though female, I'm certain I would also include wood.

I started to write when I was very young, as soon as words had graduated from the flight of speech to be snared on paper. Even in those early pieces, I wrote mainly about the things I knew, the happenings I experienced, the trappings of my environment. Which probably explains my leaning still towards the factual. I wrote about children because, still being a child, these were the kinds of people I knew about. I had my first acceptance with children's material. This was a setting of direction, on an already prescribed course. Later, the writing of those adult short stories, radio plays, biography, did not seduce me away from writing for children. So this is my life's rhythm of writing.

I am still surprised to find that a news item, a place, a story told to me, a meeting with someone, will trigger off a story for the young, yet seldom offer me the ingredients for an adult work. Yet I am not unaware that the ingredients in many cases would make an adult novel. From this, I deduce, with much satisfaction, that there is no accident in my being a writer for children. Nor do I sidestep the issue by saying, well, I'm probably still a child myself. I am a child only in the sense that I retain the ability to be surprised, excited, jolted, by some discovery, good or ill; and that is not a trait confined to the writer.

We are all aware that technology—the media, instant communication, fast travel—has changed society general-

Clark as a young girl with her family: clockwise from left, brothers Alec and John, Aunt Martha, Mavis, and her mother Rose. Aunt Martha inspired Clark's award-winning novel The Brown Land was Green *(1956).*

ly. Our children have reacted, too. They have not changed in the basic qualities of loving, hating, being jealous, kindly, envious, violent, gentle, but in knowledge. What I learned slowly, over years and in snippets, the youngster now acquires in a few nights of television. This knowledgeable child allows an author to range wide.

Does it release him from responsibility? I don't think so. Knowledge cannot be equated with experience, and therefore understanding. Recognition of this will impose its own restraints on the author. And yet . . . when I start a book . . . my conscious sense of responsibility drops away from me. I write what I want to write. (We all claim this! It's as hoary a claim as the 1000 words a day syndrome!) But this one is true. If it were not so, there would be no spontaneity, no free-flow in the text. I write my book because my subject has excited me, involved me; and because it excites, involves, demands to be written.

In particular, my own country excites me. The red earth, a few pudding-shaped saltbush, a mill on the skyline, dusty, red, long-legged sheep, an emu pacing my vehicle, the etchings drawn by the tail of a kangaroo . . . all excite me. In *The Min-Min,* I was not only excited by my country but moved deeply when I observed the child growing up in the squalor of a siding on the east-west line. In *Blue Above the Trees* I was saddened and motivated by the tearing-down and burning of the mountain ash forest of South Gippsland. I was so afraid for the possible destruction of the mutton bird and the Cape Barren goose of Bass Strait that I wrote *The Hundred Islands.* The abandonment of a child on the doorstep of a Babies' Home disturbed my nights, resulting in *The Sky is Free.* I felt so strongly about the child of separating parents, who had to choose to live with one or the other of the two people she

loved, that I wrote *Solomon's Child,* even though it took me into research of the legal maze of law.

But then I have followed some maze of factual research in every novel I have written since the days of my apprenticeship. It is the reason why the writing of a book occupies me for a year or more. It is an extra workload on a novel, but work I enjoy. I appreciate gaining for myself a knowledge of and insight into a hitherto unexplored area. And no doubt this is why my didactic pieces, so-called, are there in my work. Detail, awareness, is so important to today's youth—and the detailed life unfolding ahead of them—that I can see no reason for withholding a relevant fact.

In using a factual background or backdrop—mining town, destruction of a forest, Aborigines, law—accuracy of detail is all-important. When the novel is complete, after carefully checking my own study and understanding, I pass the manuscript to an expert in the particular subject matter for further checking. Our children are entitled to accuracy; and their keen knowledge demands it. This is a responsibility that the author cannot leave to his subconscious.

My own understanding of the responsibility of the author—as separate from factual accuracy—is to present truth as he sees it. The picture will vary from author to author because we each see the truth of our world—the reality—with different eyes. The truth—as human eyes see it—is both beautiful and ugly. We should not be afraid to raise the ecstasy of seeing, understanding, and appreciating beauty; or to sicken with the picture of ugliness.

Then there is the projection of ideas. I once heard one of our leading children's writers say in a radio interview that a writer for children should *not* project his ideas on his readers. I could only take that statement to mean that a writer for children should not project ideas in the form of any kind of propaganda, and with this I agree. Propaganda is ideas, but only from one narrow angle. When this particular writer (the one on the radio) presents his theme he says, in effect, to the child—or so I presume—these are the facts of the matter, now work it out for yourself.

Or this is what he thinks he does, believes he does. I don't agree. I think he does project himself. He is a man of ideals and integrity; those ideals and integrity come through. We are all creatures of ideas, of varying value; the projection—of varying value—is inevitable.

Another hoary aspect that writers for children talk about is hope—not leaving a child reader without hope. It is a statement that gives a self-satisfying glow; but is also true. Perhaps one of the factors that has brought this Earth and its men to the brink of the ultimate is that writers of adult works have wallowed so long in the hopeless. They've presented a gloomy analysis and a gloomier prognosis, seemingly unaware of joyful anticipation. Yet hope—joyous anticipation—is a basic quality of the human being. It is the diamond glow in the eyes of a baby, anticipating the excitement of a seventy-year journey of living. Those children who are going to decide Earth's and their own future need to approach that ultimate decision with the light still brilliant. Otherwise, they'll find relief in jumping over.

The writer without hope, himself, should keep his mind off words for children.

The writing of a children's novel involves no less labour, physical and mental, than in an adult work. Characterization and structure are equally important, yet the children's book demands the tightness and economy of the short story. A child, while aware of the rhythm of words, is not interested in words as such, but in the pictures they create for him. The clarity and simplicity of a good children's book—especially for the younger age groups—is deceptive.

While the author is writing for people with all the basic qualities, traits and emotions of the adult, he can't be diffuse as he can in an adult work. He has to ensnare the attention of a reader who is not yet an established reader. He may have to labour over a sentence, a phrase, with the same patience and skill as a poet. Yet his writer's tools are not as many nor as sophisticated. That simple style has to offer a variety of words and imagery—with original metaphors and similes—but not too-difficult words. Which all means that writing for children is a discipline in itself. (pp. 4-6)

> *Mavis Thorpe Clark, "Self-Portraits 2," in* Australian Book Review, *No. 53, August, 1983, pp. 4-6.*

GENERAL COMMENTARY

Walter McVitty

Mavis Thorpe Clark has the distinction of having had her first book, a boys' school story called **Hatherley's First Fifteen,** published when she was only eighteen. She has continued to write steadily and well since that time, and is equally at home writing biography, educational books or children's fiction.

In the historical context of Australian children's literature, Mavis Thorpe Clark has been a trend-setter in certain respects. With her early successes **The Brown Land was Green** (1956) and **Gully of Gold** (1958) she was one of the first contemporary writers to produce interesting, entertaining and properly-researched historical fiction with Australian settings for children. **The Min Min** was a comparatively early venture into the social and psychological realism of the 'teenage' (or young adult) novel. She also wrote with genuine sympathy for Aboriginals at a time when this would have been unusual. And, long before the feminist movement began clamouring for it, Mavis Thorpe Clark was unselfconsciously filling her novels with heroines who, without apology, and at the expense of nobody else, eschewed passive sex-stereotyped roles in order to live adventurous lives in which they were responsible for their own cheerful and courageous initiatives. As with Henrietta in **The Brown Land was Green,** they were sparkling personalities in their own right.

To understand Mavis Thorpe Clark's achievement as a writer and to appreciate her books on their own terms, one needs to understand something of the person. Mavis Thorpe Clark is quietly and deeply devoted to her own country, to an extent which might be called spiritual. She has probably come as close as a European realistically can come to an affinity with the land itself. She has travelled extensively throughout Australia, not as a tourist nor even necessarily to gain background for stories, but from a love of her country and a need to get closer to it, to renew herself constantly. She appears to be perfectly at home in whatever environment she chooses to experience.

It would be most unusual, as a consequence, if her books did not reflect the author's responses to and experience of her *milieu,* however varied. She records with regret what little chance natural life has against man's technology, ambition and potential to 'develop' anything profitable. Obviously she hopes her work will play a part in moulding the greater sensibilities of the young, the future 'developers'. Combined with this notion is a didactic intent to supply, within the framework of a story, lots of accurate factual information. At times, especially in the more recent books such as **Iron Mountain** (iron-ore mining setting at Mount Tom Price in the Pilbara region of Western Australia), **The Sky is Free** (opal mining, as at Coober Pedy) or **The Hundred Islands** (the fate of mutton-birds and the Bass Strait eco-system generally), the impulsive reciting of statistics and the emphasis on passing on of 'educational' facts comes close to overwhelming the novel's storytelling function. The creative transformation of life-experience into literature is not helped by the arbitrary inclusion of mere statistics and mundane facts in the drama.

This is not to say that encyclopaedic information is of no interest to children—on the contrary, curiosity about the world is one of the hallmarks of childhood. The problem is rather one of literary aesthetics, of the difficulty of reconciling the informative function with the dramatic, of integrating the two in such a way that the teacher does not intrude too much on the storyteller, the preacher on the poet. **The Min Min** succeeds, and deserves its acclaim, because of the fine balance of the author's creative impulses, the drama being fixed firmly where it belongs, not in a treatise on the flora, fauna and geology of its unusual Nullarbor Plain setting (which the author knows well), but in the lives of the people who live there. The story is never lost sight of: what happens in it, and the working out of its theme, is always determined by the nature of both its characters and the setting. This confident, natural approach makes **The Min Min** a more integrated, compelling and believable story than, say, **The Sky is Free,** which is pedantic by comparison.

Didacticism has gradually become the most distinctive (and unfortunate) characteristic of Mavis Thorpe Clark's writing for children. The impulse to impart information was more controlled in this author's earlier work, whereas in some of her later books there is an imbalance which is serious enough to interfere with the enjoyment of what, for children, is the whole point of reading—the *story* itself.

Mavis Thorpe Clark's earliest children's books are out of print and probably now would be regarded as being too slight to warrant reissue. They do, however, typify the general standards of their time, being lightweight formula-stories with interest resting solely in plot. **The Twins from Timber Creek** (1949), for instance, is little more than a pleasant yarn about the trouble the twins Peter and Liz have when, without their parents' knowing, they smuggle their pet dog along with them on the family beach-holiday. Of course they fall foul of the beach inspector but manage to win him over when they rescue him from shark attack. It is a story for and of an era which regarded the state of childhood as one of innocence.

One early novel which has survived, due to the insatiable appetites of horse-story fanatics, is *Pony from Tarella*. What sets it apart and makes it acceptably 'modern' is its teenage characters and strong thematic interest. While on holidays from his orphanage home, fourteen-year-old Sandy, staying with the head stockman on Tarella Station, becomes firmly attached to a spirited golden-brown mare, bestowing on it the stored-up love which he has always had inside him. When he returns to Tarella for his next holidays Sandy is dismayed to find that the pony has been promised to another boy who is, in every respect, the opposite of himself. The arrogant usurper tries to bully the pony into submission but finally comes to see that the pony is indeed a one-man horse—Sandy's. *Pony from Tarella* deserves its longevity. There's nothing original about its plot, but the writing has an admirable economy and warmth, and has stood the test of time well.

The rest of Mavis Thorpe Clark's books can be divided into two convenient groups: on the one hand, the novels which can be classed as historical fiction, being set in nineteenth-century colonial Victoria, and, on the other, the modern 'problem' novels with their precisely defined regional settings. The historical novels have an air of adventure and excitement whereas the 'problem' novels of experience are fittingly darker and heavier (*Blue Above the Trees* marks a transition from one into the other). *The Brown Land was Green* is Mavis Thorpe Clark's first substantial achievement in writing for children after her first five 'songs of innocence'. It is the earliest title still in print and widely known, enjoying a status not accorded its predecessors. *The Brown Land was Green* has, indeed, outlived two of its earlier publishers.

The early 1950s saw the beginnings of recent Australian historical fiction but it was all centred on the first settlement of Sydney, with books such as Ruth Williams's *Verity of Sydney Town* (1950), Eve Pownall's *Cousins-Come-Lately* (1952) and Doris Chadwick's *John of the 'Sirius'* (1955). Mavis Thorpe Clark chose to write about the early days of pastoral settlement in the western district of her home state Victoria. Set in 1844, just ten years after the founding of the capital Melbourne, and thus during the comparative calm before the phenomenal gold rush of the 1850s, *The Brown Land was Green* is similar to Australian children's books actually written *in* the Victorian era, in that it is about the arrival, as settlers, of an English family

Clark with Harold Darwin, "The Library Man," who took his mobile library throughout Australia. Clark traveled with Darwin on several journeys, the first of which inspired The Min-Min. *On subsequent trips, Darwin introduced Clark to Coober Pedy, the Australian opal field, which became the subject of several of her books.*

and their resulting adventures as pioneers. The Webster family consists of an impoverished ex-builder from London, his four children and, as matriarchal overseer and mother-substitute, his sister Belinda, the epitome of staid Victorian respectability. She has insisted on accompanying her bereaved brother and his children in their quest for a new life and a fresh chance in the raw colony. Belinda can be seen as an example of a stock pantomime figure (she is indeed a maiden aunt if not a grand dame) or else as typical of this author's wish always to portray women in vital roles—although her role is a negative one for she has no intention of staying in what she is determined will be a wretched, uncivilised wilderness and intends to hurry the family back to England as soon as they have seen the folly of it all.

The only girl in the family is twelve-year-old Henrietta, who is a figure to gladden the hearts of those looking for positive female roles in children's books—she is wise, resourceful and strong-willed, prepared to take initiatives and determined to tackle the new adventure with great gusto and to make a success of it. As an Irish sailor says of her at the start of the book, 'There's a girl for ye, a girl for a new land'. The book ends by confirming the truth of his prophesy.

The Brown Land was Green starts with the family arrival at the embryo settlement of Portland. Honest and trusty John Webster is immediately offered a job as a carpenter and general station-hand by Benjamin Jones, the devious manager of a large property owned by a wealthy absentee landlord. The plot concerns itself with Jones's chicanery and the way in which the children finally bring him to justice.

It is a standard plot with bushfires, snakebites, broken legs and villains, but some aspects of the book do lift it above the ordinary. For instance, its sympathetic attitude towards Aboriginals, and its concern for them, would have been most unusual in 1956 when *The Brown Land was Green* was first published. The author's stance is in no way paternalistic but arises from a commitment to the native people who were forced off their religious sites and out of their tribal lands in the most callous fashion, and ill treated by people like Jones.

It is interesting to note the brevity of each episode in *The Brown Land was Green,* for this reflects the style of children's book prevalent at the time and during the previous decades in which things usually moved at rattling pace with so much happening all the time that the young reader was kept racing along to see what would happen next. In just over two hundred pages *The Brown Land was Green* contains twenty-nine chapters. This is quite a contrast to today's slower-moving, inward-turning peregrinations in which nothing very active, at least of a physical nature, might be happening. Writing styles have changed in the past two decades and perhaps the assumptions we now make about children themselves are not quite fair: we seem to downgrade the importance of entertainment and fun in children's literature. Certainly, *The Brown Land was Green* offers far more action and excitement than do this author's more recent novels.

Gully of Gold is a shorter book but it has even more chapters. One can reasonably infer from this that it is fairly light reading with lots of interesting things happening all the time, setbacks for the villains, and a happy ending. This sounds like a description of an enjoyable children's book and, with Mavis Thorpe Clark, one knows it will be clearly child-centred and well researched. Its contrived nature, stock characters and melodramatic plot are obvious weaknesses, but this is essentially escapist, undemanding—yet informative—reading which seems somehow forgivably appropriate considering the era it describes. Its setting is the gold diggings around Buninyong, near Ballarat, in 1851. Like the previous book, it starts with a family of four children arriving by ship, this time with neither mother nor father. The orphans have set out from England with their Uncle Harry, determined to prosper in the manner of the Websters from *The Brown Land was Green,* but the uncle dies on the voyage and the eldest child (Jane Ellen, seventeen) tries to persuade the others to abandon the venture and return to the comfort and security of England and their mother. In this respect she is a counterpart of Aunt Belinda in the earlier book and, in turn, a forerunner of Leah Rose in *Iron Mountain*—each plays the same strategic role as a negative force acting on the aspirations of the rest, but always losing out to the power of the country itself.

The description of the arrival at Melbourne, and the transfer from the moored ship to the small lighters which will take the passengers and their goods to the shore, is a particularly lively one:

> Soon all manner of goods were being tossed to the bobbing decking far below, often to the accompaniment of the frenzied anxiety of the owner. Bedding, boxes, cedar chairs, even a bird-cage leapt from one deck to the other.
>
> Tension and excitement grew in the disembarking passengers. It hissed like the steam from the lighter's engine. Children screamed as favourite doll or fire-cart seemed about to disappear into the deep. Sailors shouted, a bell clanged incessantly, and people rushed hither and thither in a last minute search for some nearly forgotten article.

While such a bustling style appears to be a bit breathless, it does demonstrate the vitality which gives freshness and strength to the earlier books of Mavis Thorpe Clark.

On arrival in Melbourne, the children discover that gold fever has struck, and they are soon caught up in it, setting off, after a period of crude domesticity in Melbourne, and against the inclinations of Jane Ellen, to walk to the gold fields of Buninyong, sixty miles away, accompanied by a boy named Peter, who has been a stowaway on board the ship—he seems to have some secret mission driving him ever onwards. After many vicissitudes, gold is discovered, and Peter finds his father, in a somewhat contrived literary convention of coincidences.

Less successful is *They Came South* (1963). It is the story of an English lad's escape, as a cabin boy, to Australia after accidentally setting fire to the squire's haystack. As in the other books, he eventually makes good through his own efforts in the new land, repays the squire and arranges for his sister to come to Australia to join him. *Blue Above the Trees* is the last of Mavis Thorpe Clark's historical novels, and is her most highly regarded, probably because it eschews formulae, is about a clearly perceived time and place ignored by other writers and centres on genuine personal conflicts (including the 'generation gap' problem much discussed at the time the book was written). Its setting has a unique flavour, powerful and pervasive—the mountain rain-forest of Gippsland in the Victoria of 1877.

Gippsland had been traversed by Strzelecki in 1840 but for thirty years it remained an unknown and mysterious region. Its great forests of mountain ash, with their towering canopies, constantly shrouded in a humid atmosphere of dripping clouds, with an understory of myrtle, beech and blackwood, and ground plants such as musk, hazel, tecoma, tree ferns, sassafras, wattles and wiregrass formed an almost impenetrable mass of vegetation, making the topography unknowable. With its own perfectly balanced ecology and self-created micro-climate, the South Gippsland hills defied easy settlement.

Blue Above the Trees is the chronicle of a pioneering family's attempt to subdue a patch of forested hill-country, twenty-seven miles south of Drouin, in 1877. The Whitburn family consists of a stern, authoritarian father, a patient, long-suffering mother, seventeen-year-old Clarissa who hates the bush and runs away to Melbourne, and Simon, the sensitive boy who deeply loves his new environment and its inhabitants. Because his father must first destroy this environment in order to farm the land, a conflict with the son is inevitable. The boy takes an interest in a pair of lyrebirds and becomes attached to them. He eventually determines to become a surveyor which is, in itself, intentionally or not, symbolic of the dilemma of settlement—the conflict between development and conservation, the one negating the other. (This conflict seems to be resolved, to the author's satisfaction, in the rather proud attitude she seems to take later on in *Iron Mountain* towards controlled mineral exploitation.)

It is easy to sympathise with Clarissa in *Blue Above the Trees.* Hemmed in by huge forest walls, able to get to the outside world only through tunnels hacked through dense, dark forest, Clarissa's need for human contact and her feelings of claustrophobia are understandable: 'When are we going to see people, other faces, hear other voices than our own! These forest walls are prison walls!' Indeed, one could imagine a very 'modern' novel, in our age of experience, being written about Clarissa's mental state rather than Simon's idealism.

It is a feeling for the ethos of Gippsland pioneering life, rather than exact details of day-to-day existence, which is the special strength of *Blue Above the Trees.* The characters quite definitely are subordinate to setting. Even Simon, the main interest in the book, and an uncommonly affectionate portrayal by this author, is never wholly convincing (he is perhaps too idealised to be true) but this is understandable, given the overwhelming nature of the massive primeval forest which dominates the telling just as surely as it dominated the life of the early settlers. . . . (pp. 8-17)

That the setting of *Blue Above the Trees* is always described by specifying its features, allowing it then to speak for itself, as it were, shows commendable restraint on the part of the author, who might have been tempted to produce passages of belaboured purple prose. Her observation and reporting remain precise and uncluttered throughout.

Mavis Thorpe Clark's historical novels are as good as anything in the field but her present reputation rests more on the contemporary realism of the modern 'problem' novels of her recent period. Of these, *The Min Min* is far and away the most accomplished. It is the story of the adolescent Sylvie, living an unhappy and depressing life in a tiny settlement along the railway line which crosses the vast Nullarbor Plain of South and Western Australia. Her father is an uncouth drunkard with a shadowy past, her mother constantly ill, her brother inclined to destructive delinquency. Her physical environment is one of overwhelming nothingness. She is at the point of searching for alternatives—there must be more to life than this, she feels.

For Sylvie, the school teacher represents or embodies the outside world—and the promise of the future. In his presence she experiences the vision of the min-min lights, the Jack O'Lantern phenomenon named by the Aboriginals. . . . Sylvie knows that the min-min is an equivocal image, but she takes it for her own symbol of hope for a future that *must* hold more promise than that offered by the barrenness of her real-life situation.

Sylvie's brother Reg, with his gang, wrecks the local school in an act of frustration, boredom and vandalism which is symptomatic of the settlement's brutalising effects on its inhabitants. The resulting castigations by the crestfallen young teacher make Sylvie decide to run away from home, taking Reg with her. But in the wilderness of the Nullarbor, where is there to run? She knows one family, the Tuckers, living on an isolated out-station of a large property and she decides to head there for refuge—to distance herself for the time being in order to clarify her ideas of the future. The sojourn with the friendly Tuckers helps Sylvie see herself in a more positive light, and the errant Reg is miraculously reformed under their influence.

The Min Min, with its strange element of pessimism, or

"Digging that hole": Clark at Coober Pedy.

at least its unromanticised view of the aspect of Australian life it portrays, establishes, in the very first pages, the kind of people who inhabit the single row of fettlers' huts at a lonely railway siding: 'They were noisy, some of them not very clean, and if any of them were young, the youth was hidden under the lines of hard living'. . . . As in a Russell Drysdale painting, the prose presents man, his buildings and his belongings as having taken on something of the harsh landscape:

> The houses had recently been painted in pastel shades of pink, blue, beige and green, and the roofs silver-frosted. But this sign of care didn't off-set the litter of parts of old cars, cardboard cartons, broken toys, bottles; while the first layer of red dust, blown in by the filthy wind from across the Nullarbor, had already settled.

Where Sylvie's father, and the other men, reflect the dreary and shabby desolation of barren surroundings, Sylvie, as viewed by the author, embodies its crushing loneliness and wastrel neglect: 'She was tall for her age and thin, but taking shape, with thin arms and legs. Her cotton dress was faded, the waist line far too high, her feet bare. Her face showed that she had not had enough sleep.'

The opening pages of *The Min Min* show the author at her best, describing, and interpreting, for us, a precise and real experience, closely observed, understood and transformed. Sylvie is a real person in the way that her counterparts in other Mavis Thorpe Clark novels are not—she has obviously touched the author and fired her imagination—and thereby hangs an interesting tale. Mavis Thorpe Clark once made a number of trips through the Nullarbor region as the companion of a book-mobile driver. During a brief stop at a remote settlement the author saw, at the edge of the group of people clustered round about, a lonely, dispirited-looking girl. No actual contact was made but a short period of observation was enough to raise a score of questions in the mind of the imaginative watcher. What must life be like for this girl?

What are her problems? Her hopes? Her fears? These questions were eventually taken up and explored in *The Min Min,* through the character of Sylvie, clandestine surmising (all the more intriguing because the encounter was never actually made) being transformed into universal literary terms. The essential point is that Sylvie's hopes, fears, doubts, yearnings do not depend on her particular geographical location. Her brother Reg's vandalism is not unique to the South Australian inland, and there are girls in many isolated parts of the world who would share Sylvie's uncertainties. More to the point, her feelings are very well known to adolescents living in the largest of cities.

The use of the symbol of the elusive min-min lights helps the author, as it does her heroine, to determine where she is going. It gives shape and purpose to the novel as a whole, keeping the focus fixed on thematic developments. If the image seems at all unconvincing or even confusing, perhaps this is fitting, simply because for Sylvie vagueness is the whole point of the min-min lights. The clearest use of the min-min as symbol comes when the fugitive children observe a satellite traversing the night sky, the author being helpfully explicit through this related, yet contrasting image:

> Sylvie stared at the small winking star, moving determinedly across the tremendous space. It certainly wasn't a min-min. A min-min wasn't so exact; so sure of its direction—a min-min beckoned, and receded, and when you went after it, taunted you by dousing its glow. This light travelled high, with knowledge and purpose.

The book ends with Sylvie living in the steel and ship-building town of Whyalla (hardly the place for her to realise her yearnings for a contented and rewarding life): 'And she would stay in this town which was on the edge of the min-min country, and perhaps, some day, she would return and learn what it was that beckoned from afar'.

Freshness and vitality and an intense interest in the varied life of Australia have continued to shape all Mavis Thorpe Clark's novels but, after *The Min Min,* there has been a tendency for the background information to become too intrusive. Such details find it hard to stay in their place, being so eager to claim attention that they come right onto the stage, interfering with the action, slowing it down, shouting to be noticed. The *raisons d'être* of some of this author's more recent books, such as *Iron Mountain* or *The Hundred Islands,* seem to be to impart messages, like long television commercials but not as entertaining.

Didacticism was evident in the earlier books when information thought to be useful was included, as, for example, with this small detail of arrival in Portland, at the start of *The Brown Land was Green:*

> Henrietta knew that this must be Richmond House, the fairly new home of Stephen Henty. The original Henty home, built by Edward and Frank, and where the first white male child of the Colony was born to Stephen and Jane Henty in 1837, had been pulled down to make way for town planning and the formation of Bentickt Street.

(pp. 17-22)

This sort of intrusion is harmless enough—indeed when it comes to describing the methods of mining and panning for gold, or the Miner's Right issue, it is most helpful in understanding aspects of the narrative, as well as having intrinsic interest—but only when properly incorporated into the fabric of the novel. The risk is that the story might become subordinate to the background information.

The Sky is Free, a novel which is really an extension of the identity crisis theme which made *The Min Min* so compelling, tells of two runaway boys hoping both to 'find themselves' in a small opal-mining settlement. It is difficult to develop much sympathy for the characters and themes when the telling is so preoccupied with geography. The incessant listing of details—exact heights above sea-level, lengths in metres, capacities in litres and depths of mine shafts, all recorded with the zeal of company prospectuses, travel brochures or government reports—have nothing to do with the state of mind or aspirations of the protagonists. Within seven paragraphs, halfway through the novel, fourteen lots of statistics are interpolated, none being of any dramatic significance. Tony, on his furtive and clandestine visit down a mine-shaft, actually discovers a real piece of opal but in what ought to be a dramatic high point in the story the reader is coolly informed of its thickness in centimetres. At the very moment when one cries out to know what the exotic treasure is *like,* and what Tony's feelings are, with the deeply-desired object there in his hand, the reader is confronted with arithmetic.

For the boys in *The Sky is Free* (as with Sylvie in *The Min Min*) the self-discovery theme *is* a serious and universal one, but it is too blatantly stated, if not declaimed, pregnant pauses and all: 'I don't know—who—I am', bemoans Tony, and he keeps saying it. . . . He wears it like a badge, and is too conscious of it.

Crisis of identity is a recurrent theme in Mavis Thorpe Clark's novels. Usually the interest is in an underprivileged adolescent outsider, often with a secret past, but always striving to discover himself, to find his own place, and acceptance, in the world. Peter, the stowaway in search of an unknown and wronged father in *Gully of Gold,* Angus McIvor, the runaway shepherd boy of *They Came South,* the poor orphan Sandy in *Pony from Tarella,* Sylvie in *The Min Min* (her father has the criminal past), both boys in *The Sky is Free* and the parole-breaking Joey Simpson of *Iron Mountain*—each is a variation on the other. The identity-quest theme is at least as old and as universal now as it was when Oepidus cried, 'I *will* know who I am!' Its variations are endless and will remain so.

By contrast, it is difficult to accept the unfortunate character who is created not to embody universal themes but as an excuse for propagandising, albeit in a good cause. It is difficult for a character to come alive in any convincing way if he seems only to represent an altruistic ideal and to parrot particular arguments. In certain books one keeps encountering spokesmen for Conservation, always posturing and protesting too much. Roger in *Nowhere to Hide* (1969) feels 'hatred of the man on the beach who had robbed the big grey possum of life, to sell his skin in the city, where some day it would hang in some woman's wardrobe'. It would be more effective, in terms of the desired result, if the prose were somehow to make the reader *feel* this emotion for himself instead of being *told* what is worthy. The gentle Steven in *Wildfire* identifies strongly with an eagle he calls Wedgee, while his friend Bill's passion for fire-fighting comes from memory of having once had to kill a singed koala to end its agony; he'd 'rather see humans get hurt, than animals'. Simon fights for the retention of the forest sanctuary for his beloved lyrebird family in *Blue Above the Trees.* He pleads with his father, who is determined to transform the land and, while one can applaud the sentiments of his appeal, it comes across unfortunately, as the speech of a prig. . . . (pp. 22-4)

All these earnest and concerned children, passionately devoted to the preservation of wildlife, are the *one* person culminating in the unlikely Greg of *The Hundred Islands* who, like Simon, shouts at his father, like a character from Victorian melodrama (one arm outstretched, the other over his eyes?): 'Not the swamp patch! You can't take the swamp! That has to be saved. At whatever cost!' Yet, strangely enough, the author seems finally to be aware that

in this book she has taken the pedantry too far—Greg's father looks at his son, 'as though he was some kind of apparition. A schoolboy—spouting all this!' This understandable reaction, shared by the reader, comes after a typical speech by Greg:

> 'I've got to do the new uni course—Environmental Science. Takes in the whole concept of man and everything around him. We have to learn—get ideas—how man and his sheep and his cows can adapt to living, sharing the habitat . . . with all the wild things of the world. *That's* the problem. To save man we have to learn to save everything else. I have to do this course, Dad!'

Greg tells his girlfriend, 'Jenny . . . you know as well as I do that all I'm interested in is animals—the land—wild things'. It is to be hoped that, like Fern in *Charlotte's Web,* his passions will eventually encompass other things, but any teenager who talks (as opposed to *thinks*) like this has already lost much credibility anyway. This boy, who is 'shocked' at the thought of a gambling casino proposed for his island, is yet said to have a face so young 'that a woman on the bus on the way to the air-terminal had offered him one of her sweets, a licorice allsort'. I must say that he is unlike anybody I have ever encountered in real life. He represents genuine and serious concerns but has no more reality than his identikit counterparts in other similar books. While one sympathises with the feelings of these admirable ecologists, one regrets the turgid sermonising which is their literary lot. (pp. 24-5)

It's not just the environmentalist children who talk like this. Many adult characters are given passages of correct officialese—there seems no way of keeping the eager teacher in her place. The American in *Nowhere to Hide* tells the Brewster family:

> 'Your Australian authorities treat their prisoners very well . . . Their rations are the same, in quantity and quality, as their Australian guards . . . They are paid a shilling a day for working . . . This money is credited to the British Government—whose prisoners they are—to help defray the cost of their keep.'

In talking about his homeland, he is just as encyclopaedic: 'Hurricanes are indigenous to that Atlantic coast', he says. He talks like the outback warden in *The Sky is Free,* who even while struggling with the steering wheel 'as his vehicle lurched down the pot-holed hill', describes the jolting terrain, in a geological lecture which ends: 'Levelled to this peneplain that covers almost the entire area of Central Australia'. When adults talk like this in these books, it is no wonder that the children copy them. In *Wildfire* Bill says things like, 'No forces could be deployed to help you'. Even eight-year-old Fizzer, in the same book, speaks in public-service jargon: 'It's a two thousand dollar fine or two years in gaol, or both, if you start a fire'.

Iron Mountain demonstrates most tellingly the unfortunate effects of didacticism, for here is a novel with a real problem to explore (of a youth exiling himself in the Pilbara after being charged for culpable driving in Melbourne—he has a past to forget, a future to discover and

Clark writes of this photo, "These Aborigines, far out in the bush, became part of The Min-Min *story."*

responsibilities to confront) but what chance has this when page after page 'booms' with statistical superlatives to match the 'booming' north-west itself and when its characters, even in moments of supposed crisis, speak as though they are reading prepared scripts for patriotic film commentaries, or else have memorised whole sections of government yearbooks and are unable to keep the information to themselves? C. S. Lewis once said: 'I will not say that a good story for children could never be written by someone in the Ministry of Education, for all things are possible. But I should lay very long odds against it.' What he had in mind, no doubt, was something like *Iron Mountain.* It gets top marks for accuracy, effort and enthusiasm but fails on imaginative inspiration. For all its worthiness, it is a geography lesson rather than a literary experience.

Yet the finest single passages of this author's writing come from one of the didactic books, *Wildfire,* especially when she forgets to belabour its theme of peer-group rivalry for two central chapters of pure narrative. In describing the arrival of the bushfire in the settlement of Murton she is obviously very close to the whole terrible disaster itself, knowing what it is *like* to be in such a dreadful holocaust. The writing is excellent. It has conviction, authority, concentration. The author is moved to alter the swing and balance of her sentences: 'Old and drear, too, looked the men and women who reeled back from the fire to grab a drink of water'. Or again, with feeling for the resigned tragedy

of it all: 'Tom went into his house and got his rifle, and walked across the black paddock to put an end to the creatures' suffering, and their red blood seeped into the charred earth'. Her style here is simple and direct, her observation fresh, her imagery precise and vivid. Here is Mavis Thorpe Clark at her best, a fusion of reporter and interpreter, heightening the reader's awareness of an extreme experience, in writing which is simple enough to be handled by quite young readers:

> The houses were left like an island in a flat black sea except for one narrow, unburned exit patch on the east that led away to the line of forest. Many of the houses had eaves burning where sparks had lodged and caught alight. Only urgent action saved these dwellings. Old Tommy's white hens, which he had let out of the fowl-house, were strung out across his yard like a white paper-chase. Dead. They hadn't burned; the forty hens had died of fright and smoke. And the fowl-house was smouldering ashes. Pratt's wood-heap was ablaze and the back fence gone. Apricots had roasted on the apricot tree; nearly all the sheds on the western flank of the fire had been destroyed. Every house was filthy with ash and burnt debris. Paint had lost its lustre and looked suddenly old and drear.

Could there be an image to fix itself more firmly on one's consciousness than that of the dead chickens, now so much farmyard litter, reduced to a 'white paper-chase'? It must be something the writer has seen, here recollected in tranquility.

When Mavis Thorpe Clark creates characters who are real people in their own right, existing independently of messages, her compassion becomes less objective and she moves us most. She once said that for all authors there is at least one children's story to be told, that being the author's own. It is this story which has yet to come from Mavis Thorpe Clark and if and when it does come, *sans* didacticism and with the inside involvement it will have with its chief character, in a setting which can be taken for granted, we can expect, given her strong sense of story, thematic persistence, and artistic integrity, that it will be her finest contribution to children's literature. She has produced a formidable range of books over a number of years, and her professional approach, coupled with an active, stimulating and adventurous lifestyle, gives the observer confidence that she still has much to offer in writing exciting, adventurous and informative books for children. One hopes that any future movement in the balance between storyteller and teacher will be decidedly in the favour of the former. (pp. 26-9)

Walter McVitty, "Mavis Thorpe Clark," in his Innocence and Experience: Essays on Contemporary Australian Children's Writers, *Thomas Nelson, 1981, pp. 7-35.*

TITLE COMMENTARY

Pony from Tarella (1959)

An orphan returns to an Australian cattle-station where in the previous year he had struck up a friendship with a fine but nervous mare Sunflower, to find that he now has a rival, pot-hunting middle-class Phil Dickens, friend of the family, who plans to buy the horse for competitions. Sandy's plot to tire the mare with long dawn exercises might have injured her if conscience, and a timely act of heroism, had not changed his life, with the prospect of adoption into the Reid family and the gift of Sunflower. The fairy-tale rags-to-riches plot will be redeemed for some readers, though not for all, by the precise topography and agreeable open-air atmosphere of this Australian story.

Margery Fisher, in a review of "Pony from Tarella," in Growing Point, *Vol. 16, No. 4, October, 1977, p. 3190.*

The Min-Min (1966)

AUTHOR'S COMMENTARY

[*The following excerpt is from Clark's speech upon accepting the Australian Children's Book of the Year Award.*]

A writer can never anticipate what moment, what contact, will yield for him the pearl of great price. But when it happens, he recognises it immediately. Excitement lifts his being, and his feet grow light. In return, it becomes his in-

sistent privilege to communicate this moment of experience.

The background of **The Min-Min** was absorbed over a period of time, but it did not become a background until, by chance, a girl—whom I called Sylvie in the book—paused for a few brief moments while she attended to some affair of her own, and we shared, with others, a rocky hill. I can't remember whether I spoke to her, but I think not. Yet her face remained . . . and the excitement.

The Min-Min was written first as an adult short story. In that form it was called *Sylvie*. It won a short story competition but was not published. For several years, Sylvie continued to visit my consciousness. When this happens to an author, he knows he has an unfulfilled commitment.

I started to write **The Min-Min** about two years after I had written the short story. But I had not progressed beyond the first three chapters when I was asked to write the biography of the Aboriginal leader, Pastor Doug Nicholls. This was not the kind of work that could be combined with any other. So reluctantly I laid aside the story of Sylvie.

Pastor Doug took nearly two years to write. During that time I was wholly concerned in gathering factual material, and examining the character of this exceedingly lovable Aborigine. It was a period of working long hours, one which gave no freedom for imaginative impulses. Yet Sylvie never ceased to come to me. Sometimes, bits of her story would unfold in the still hours of a wakeful night. But I made no notes. My whole allegiance was given to Pastor Doug. The writing of this biography was a very rewarding experience, mostly in revealing the material differences, yet the spiritual universality, of man.

With the completion of **Pastor Doug,** I returned to the story of this girl, as though there had been no break, but certainly with the greater understanding derived from a broadened horizon.

The Min-Min was written very quickly—the first draft in a few weeks, and the complete book in a few months. But this was not surprising, for the whole family had been part of my life for so long. I knew them all so well.

More than one reviewer has pointed out that in this book I have stepped into realism and each has welcomed the trend. This was not done deliberately, nor did I consciously claim realism as I wrote. Certainly I was aware that I was on a different course from my other children's books, but there was no other course for me to follow. This was Sylvie's story, not mine. And it demanded honesty, as I saw it.

The writing of this book, and there was satisfaction and joy and excitement in the task, has taught me that an author has more to offer a child than just entertainment, or education. He may offer a view of life in which the child may recognise a problem similar to his own, and be heartened. But if an author offers realism to the young merely to excite, then he has lost sight of values and shed his own responsibility. (pp. 29-30)

Mavis Thorpe Clark, "On Accepting the Aus-

tralian Children's Book of the Year Award," in Bookbird, *Vol. 1, No. 4, December 15, 1967, pp. 29-30.*

In Britain it is hard to imagine a land where it hardly ever rains, where the sun blazes down day after day, and where it is possible to go for miles without seeing any sign of life or habitation. Mavis Thorpe Clark has chosen this setting for her story and made it possible to realise that such conditions do exist. Her characters are real people, so that along with them one can feel the heat and the thirst and wonder if one will die a lingering death out in the Australian desert. She has given her children problems too—Reg is a young scamp, not really naughty, but his parents do not control him and so he runs wild. Sylvia, his elder sister, is a far more gentle character trying to cope with the problems of adolescence but finding it very hard without any adult help or guidance. Children of all ages will appreciate this story because it will mirror their own lives, to a certain extent, and yet give them a glimpse into a completely different way of life at the same time.

A review of "The Min-Min," in The Junior Bookshelf, *Vol. 31, No. 3, June, 1967, p. 179.*

When Sylvie runs away with her younger brother Reg, it's not just that he's in trouble or that her father hit her or that their teacher, Mr. Scott, is going to leave their Australian outback community. She's looking for something beyond the graceless confining life of a railroad siding, and that same sensibility responds to the idea of the min-min, outback "lights" that beckon and retreat. Both Sylvie and Reg notice the fuller lives of the Tucker family they run to, and both undergo significant changes: Reg gives up his plans for escaping to Sydney, and Sylvie—after a new dress, grooming hints, and subtle ego boosts from mothering Mary—finds her perceptions altered. "P'rhaps it's just making something of our lives," suggests Mary, nudging the young girl's self-respect into open expression. The texture of life in South Australia's frontier twist in and out of the story, as do Sylvie's thoughts about the teacher (a somewhat familiar "inspirational" figure), about her parents, about what a family can be—and what she can be, and Reg's younger, less abstract observations are an artful complement. Further, the negligence of the parents is not skirted—her father acknowledges his shortsightedness and *asks* her to return. At once genial and penetrating, with an unmistakable pull. (pp. 678-79)

A review of "The Min-Min," in Kirkus Reviews, *Vol. XXXVII, No. 13, July 1, 1969, pp. 678-79.*

With powerfully simple understatement Mavis Clark paints the harsh land down under and the people and wild things which survive there. Her strong, terse prose is reminiscent of Mary Patchett's *Cry of the Heart* and evokes tears. Her images are pragmatic and original: the rising moon looks like the "round full yoke of a yellow egg," and an approaching train sounds like "wind in the earth's stomach."

Jane Manthorne, in a review of "The Min-

Min," in The New York Times Book Review, *January 25, 1970, p. 26.*

Blue above the Trees (1967)

Perhaps it is because opportunities of pioneering anywhere on the earth's surface have now almost vanished that so many good stories are being written about homesteading in the American West, or making farms and homes in the Australian forest. It was always, in any case, one of the most imaginatively exciting of all themes: the family beginning again, in ferociously exacting and exotic circumstances. **Blue Above the Trees** is a brilliantly fresh example. In the 1870s the Whitburns have come from Devon to cultivate 600 acres of infinitely ancient forest in Victoria, Australia. Father is a severe, narrow man, glad that his accounting business failed, because he had always longed to be a farmer and sought hardship. His wife is resigned and sad; two of his sons, being like him, are in their element; his elder daughter is angry, bitter.

His younger son, Simon, has a quality his father cannot understand at all, and that makes the boy conceive a passionate love of the forest they must destroy, and especially of the wild life in it. Tensions enough there to keep any story going, and the author makes the most of them: very subtly, too, for the way of life of the family of lyrebirds that Simon observes year after year is ironically but unobtrusively contrasted with the dissatisfactions and strains within the human family. All is well in the end, but not until after real excitements—of achievement or setback. The story gives one a haunting familiarity with the forest, the paths through it, the growing areas of cultivation.

"Making a Fresh Start," in The Times Literary Supplement, *No. 3458, June 6, 1968, p. 583.*

How pleasant it is to come upon a book like this. The plot is gripping, the characterization strong and the background authentic. The Whitburn family come out from England in the middle of the nineteenth century to retrieve their fortunes in the great virgin forest of Victoria. Individually they come to terms with the new world and in the end the dream of returning to the old country fades gently away and they are Australians. Simon, the link man, is thirteen when the story opens and most of their adventures are seen through his eyes. The blue above the trees of the title is symbolic of the clearing of the vast forest and also one feels of the clearing of their way of life. In the raw, problems are stripped to their basic conceptions. The period is a part of the development of the Commonwealth that we in Britain know very little about and this book will be a good introduction for teenage readers, both boys and girls. The descriptions of life in early cabins, both domestic and social, are interesting and those of the primitive jungle are magnificent, one can almost smell it. Thirteen to fifteen year olds will be fascinated by it and in a strange way will possibly identify themselves, subconsciously, with their Whitburn comtemporaries in their struggle for freedom, parental and otherwise. Perhaps even today there are times when it is difficult to see the

Clark, at lower left, at the cliffs at the head of the Great Australian Bight.

blue above the roof tops of our great industrial cities. (pp. 235-36)

A review of "Blue above the Trees," in The Junior Bookshelf, *Vol. 32, No. 4, August, 1968, pp. 235-36.*

This is a rather plodding description of the family's struggle to clear land and to have a comfortable life in the wilderness; it is also the story of a Victorian martinet whose family must accede to his every desire, however unreasonable. The setting is entrancing, although the recurrent scenes in which one of the children watches a family of lyrebirds in the rain forest become tedious. The plot is quite patterned, the writing style occasionally awkward, and the characterization flat.

Zena Sutherland, in a review of "Blue above the Trees," in Bulletin of the Center for Children's Books, *Vol. 23, No. 3, November, 1969, p. 40.*

Spark of Opal (1968)

The interplay of action and character in **Spark of opal** marks this as a book which has something to say to the 'teens; boys and girls may recognise problems of their own in its pages, even if it is unlikely that many of them will find themselves in exactly comparable situations. The Watsons live in an opal-mining town and the children—

sixteen-year-old Liz and her brother Bill—have no particular wish to move, but their mother is determined that Liz shall go to college and enjoy the benefits of city life. Following a hunch, Mike takes up a claim near his own worked-out mine, only to find that newcomers have somehow got wind of his enterprise and have leased land all round him. As he feared, it is one of these newcomers who makes the spectacular strike only inches from his boundary; but his children tenaciously explore an apparently exhausted seam in the old mine and, after an accident that could have been fatal, the coveted piece of precious rock is discovered. With the thrills of opal-mining to dominate the plot, the growing pains of the young people and their friends provide a second theme of absorbing interest. Liz has to face her responsibility for her aboriginal friend Kathy and eventually to accept that other people can find a better future for the girl than she can: Bill has problems in his relations with Greek Nikos and with the aboriginal boy Steve, who is steadily determined to train as a policeman. The author makes her points forcibly in the context of a community with its own customs and prejudices, and the background of the story is as fascinating as its events.

Margery Fisher, in a review of "Spark of Opal," in Growing Point, *Vol. 9, No. 9, April, 1971, p. 1709.*

Mavis Clark explores several sets of relationships skilfully—within the Watson family, between the aborigines and the settlers, between the various groups of opal-mad miners. The conflicts, friendships and enmities are deftly traced and interwoven, and the unusual, lonely setting gives a lively impression of pioneer days and ways with modern trimmings. (p. 240)

> *G. Bott, in a review of "Spark of Opal," in* The Junior Bookshelf, *Vol. 35, No. 4, August, 1971, pp. 239-40.*

The rough, desolate ambience of an isolated Australian mining town is the story's only distinguishing feature, though Liz' attitudes toward the aborigine children she befriends (she hopes to take one, Kathy, to live with her in Adelaide) are sometimes as paternalistic as they are altruistic. The opposition between the visionary, adventurous menfolk and the cautious, guilty women (at one point, Liz decides to purposely fail her exam so the family won't have to leave) is infuriatingly banal typecasting, but the unusual locale and background on opal mining methods should hold most readers' attention. (p. 1432)

> *A review of "Spark of Opal," in* Kirkus Reviews, *Vol. XL, No. 24, December 15, 1972, pp. 1431-32.*

Iron Mountain (1970)

Joey, a troubled boy on probation for reckless driving in Melbourne, leaves his cheerless home and is fortunate in hitching a two-thousand-mile ride to a mining community in western Australia. His journey with Leah, Susan, Woodie, and Amanda (who are on their way with their grandfather to join their miner-father) brings trials. Joey's unsuccessful attempt to hide his past, and the problems of the individuals in Leah's family fill an engrossing, well-told story. The exaggerated geographical conditions heighten tensions; and the hot, dust-filled iron-mining country, where workers receive hardship bonuses and air-conditioned company houses, even becomes a protagonist. One can easily envision the mining operations, the dangers of the trackless mountain terrain and the cyclones, and Joey's and Woodie's follies. Joey, who could become excited because of the impressiveness and the beauty of the mountain colors, makes a strong central figure; and his decisions from first to last are convincing.

> *Virginia Haviland, in a review of "Iron Mountain," in* The Horn Book Magazine, *Vol. XLVIII, No. 1, February, 1972, p. 56.*

The current Australian novel for children has a sense of purpose, of didacticism even, which belongs to a developing art; this country's freedom from it is perhaps a sign of incipient decadence. *Iron Mountain,* for all its contemporary technology, is a moral tale and a remarkably good one. The action becomes suspended from time to time while the actors listen to a lecture on geology or metallurgy. None of the information is gratuitous, for everyone in the story is caught up in some way with the adventure of Tom Price Mine and the terrible, beautiful deserts of Western Australia.

The mine and the mountain help Joey to discover himself, after he has run away from Melbourne and his own delinquent image. The mountains, too, strengthen his resolve

to abandon new-found security and friendship to face his past. The awkward, confused product of the slums has something in common with Leah, eldest and most beautiful of the Rose family, with whom he throws in his lot on the hike across Australia. The reader scents romance, but there are no easy solutions to the dilemmas of this tough, honest, rather slow-moving tale.

> *"Rites of Initiation," in* The Times Literary Supplement, *No. 3672, July 14, 1972, p. 803.*

The book is aptly named, for the iron ore mountain in Western Australia plays the leading role; to it come a family from the east, together with a lad from a city slum whom they have picked up on the way. On this new western frontier everything is biggest and best, and the author is full of enthusiasm for the whole set-up notwithstanding dust and flies, and in her eagerness to involve the reader she is far too prone to slip in lumps of undigested information about mines and mining with its brash new towns springing up in what was hitherto desert. The reader from an older civilisation is likely, however, to have doubts for the future of the miners when he reads of company stores, company houses and other symptoms of an out-of-date paternalism. This sort of thing will not worry the young reader as long as the book is readable, which it undoubtedly is, and it seems to give a very fair likeness of life in such a town at the present day. But the older reader may also question the advisability of making the chief human character a boy on the run from the police who seems likely to get away with breaking his parole and even to benefit from it. The glossary of Australian terms at the end would be better omitted unless it could be enlarged, for in it I could find none of the words I looked up. (pp. 240-41)

> *C. Martin, in a review of "Iron Mountain," in* The Junior Bookshelf, *Vol. 36, No. 4, August, 1972, pp. 240-41.*

A first-class author working with great skill. . . . Mavis Thorpe Clark evokes her locale and creates her characters with the same expertise she showed in *Spark of Opal* and *Blue Above the Trees.* While one is concerned about Woodie Rose's escapade on the loading wharf at Dampier, or with Amanda Rose's getting lost in the bush, one does not realise how much technical and topographical detail the author is using to sustain her narrative. An exciting and informative book for thirteen and on.

> *C. E. J. Smith, in a review of "Iron Mountain," in* Children's Book Review, *Vol. II, No. 4, September, 1972, p. 113.*

Wildfire (1973)

The wildfire that periodically ravages Victoria, Australia is the villain and chief protagonist here, and ranged against it are the Mob, a predictably varied lot of local children who find themselves trapped together in an old wooden cabin behind the fire lines. The fire grows inexorably closer and hotter, and its real and projected horrors—burned sheep, the death of a pet dog, the explosion of the nearby mill, the prospect of boiling alive in the house's water supply tanks—are vivid enough to rivet the atten-

Clark at her desk.

tion of the most blasé bystanders. In contrast, the children's reactions are pretty much straight out of their leader Bill's volunteer Book of Operations and the final discovery that the fire was started—not by gentle, absent-minded Steven—but by churlish farmer Brown cuts the fragile threads of human guilt and irony that held the Mob to the fire as more than casual victims. Plenty of large-scale danger and excitement, but not the equal of Southall's very similar *Ash Road.* (pp. 633-34)

> *A review of "Wildfire," in* Kirkus Reviews, *Vol. XLII, No. 12, June 15, 1974, pp. 633-34.*

In *Wildfire* there is a deliberate, vital contrast between two boys of fourteen—Bill, whose sense of responsibility has led him to join a voluntary fire-fighting unit, and Peter Lawson, a newcomer to the town of Oceanside and its environs, who has with airy confidence assumed leadership of the local lads, as a townee among rustics. Because he resents Bill's preoccupation with his training, Peter sees fit to criticise him as a prig, and their hostility to one another becomes serious when a runaway bushfire threatens the district. The subject of bushfires may be common enough in stories from Australia, but this one commands attention for the vivacity and force of the author's descrip-

tions and narrative technique, and above all for her manipulation of her characters.

> *Margery Fisher, in a review of "Wildfire," in* Growing Point, *Vol. 13, No. 2, July, 1974, p. 2428.*

This author's account of the ravages of forest fire in Victoria (Australia) would have been exciting enough as a documentary. The fact that she has moulded it into a shapely piece of fiction with controlled inter-connections of plot and personality has naturally intensified the elements of suspense and disaster which must be present year after year in this part of the world, and on which she bases the urgency of action and survival techniques. In 1851, Victoria "burned from end to end"; in 1939, seventy-one people died; in 1969, twenty-one. With statistics such as these the author need fear no accusations of sensationalism, which her style certainly does not suggest. She adds a confident handling of events and dialogue, the result of long practice and first-hand experience of her native environment and of more remote areas where man is so much at the mercy of nature and his own carelessness or indifference to the safety of others. In "the Mob", consisting of Bill, Jan, Pete, Steve and Shane, not always co-existing in perfect harmony, we have a band of convincing characters sufficiently varied to strike the necessary sparks from human relationships as well as to carry out the exploits which are illustrative of the theme.

> *A. R. Williams, in a review of "Wildfire," in* The Junior Bookshelf, *Vol. 38, No. 5, October, 1974, p. 291.*

The Sky Is Free   (1974)

Even if the structure and plot of ***The Sky is Free*** were less effective, Mavis Clark's picture of an opal mining town and its Australian environment almost deserves the epithet "devastating". Her gift for atmosphere is enough to make one feel breathing is difficult and it is dangerous to touch any sheet metal, and food does not get a chance to melt in your mouth. She plants within this climatic maelstrom the runaways, Sam and Tony, and sets them to work while a charge of burglary hangs over their uncertain heads. There is a harmless element of girl-interest which both helps to soften the work-obsessive atmosphere and establishes contact with a more normal world. Both boys achieve regeneration of a kind. Above all, they decide to give home another try. ***The Sky is Free*** is altogether well composed.

> *A. R. Williams, in a review of "The Sky Is Free," in* The Junior Bookshelf, *Vol. 39, No. 4, August, 1975, p. 262.*

Opal Town, a locale Mavis Clark has mined successfully before . . . , is as convincingly drab as ever and rather more contemporary as the destination of two runaways— middle-class Sam and enigmatic Tony—who agree to work free for a down-and-out miner as an alternative to jail when they're caught in the act of stealing food from the town store. Sam, who narrates most of this, is primarily a follower, attracted to Tony's courage but suspicious about his role in another, unexplained petty theft and, later, paralyzed by the knowledge that Tony is wearing a stolen opal around his neck. Tony, whose behavior is a mixture of calculating self-preservation and passionate gestures, is less convincing on his own than as a foil for Sam's lack of commitment, and it is Tony's final rebellion, when he releases some penned camels before running away to avoid being sent to reform school, that gives Sam, destined for release to his family in any case, a chance to express his loyalty by taking the blame. At bottom, there's little to distinguish Sam from other confused teenagers, but Opal Town offers uncommon scope for both foolish mistakes and freewheeling dreams . . . and seen here, less encumbered by plot than it has been in previous visits, the lure is stronger than ever.

> *A review of "The Sky Is Free," in* Kirkus Reviews, *Vol. XLIV, No. 14, July 15, 1976, p. 798.*

As in her previous novels, the geography of the Australian Outback plays an important role in Clark's story and, though her teenage characters are more cognizant of local flora and fauna than seems believable, it adds an interesting dimension to the book. She is also fond of adding some unsuspected sidelights, for example, the fact that Afghans once were plentiful in the Outback and that their abandoned camels still run wild there. The character of Tony is handled well—readers will readily accept his confusion and bitterness about his life—and the ending, while not conclusive, is satisfying. Sam, unfortunately, is less credible. Close to his upper middle class family, he seems to suffer only minor regrets over leaving home. But then this is basically Tony's story. While readers will have some difficulty with Australian terminology (spoon drains, claypans, gibbers, utes), they'll stick with it and enjoy this very well-written adventure story.

> *Robert Unsworth, in a review of "The Sky Is Free," in* School Library Journal, *Vol. 23, No. 3, November, 1976, p. 67.*

If the Earth Falls In   (1975)

> [If the Earth Falls In *was originally published in Australia in 1973 as* New Golden Mountain.]

When a gift of hand-me-down dresses convinces Louise that she had better leave Aunt Eva and her shabby home in an old Australian mining town, she decides to sell Aunt Eva's only treasure—an old Chinese painting on glass—to raise the fare. Somehow—guiltily?—she cracks the picture and then accepts an offer of money from the shopkeeper's son, Johnathan . . . without bothering to wonder where the cash is coming from, or whether it's somehow connected to Johnathan's run-ins with Bruce, the local bully. It all comes together when she and Bruce discover Johnathan's underground cache of antique bottles and cause a landslide that traps all three of them in an old mine shaft. At this point, and none too soon, Louise begins to exhibit the admirable qualities we've had to take for granted all along; the ordeal is perfectly timed to teach responsibility and reunite her with Eva, who after all has sacrificed everything in her behalf. Well crafted, though only Clark's

familiarity with towns like Louise's—where old bottles and souvenirs of departed Chinese laborers are all that remains of a booming past—distinguishes this from so many other times of testing.

> *A review of "If the Earth Falls In," in* Kirkus Reviews, *Vol. XLIII, No. 21, November 1, 1975, p. 1227.*

Although the evocation of the dreariness of the strip-mined land is well done, the lore of the Chinese immigrants who worked the mines interesting, and the description of the near disaster in the tunnel excellent, there are problems. The opening chapters, abounding with characters and characterization, are slow going; Louise is unusually introspective for her young years; and many readers will be stumped by the Australian jargon (e.g., "tucker," "fossicker") for which there is no glossary. This is an intelligent novel; however, there are too few tenacious readers who will see it through to its exciting finish.

> *Robert Unsworth, in a review of "If the Earth Falls In," in* School Library Journal, *Vol. 22, No. 6, February, 1976, p. 50.*

[This] is a rather stark and intense story set in a depressed mining town where three young people are trapped by falling debris in an old mine. . . . The writing style is smooth, the characters convincing and the changes in them believable, but the book may be somewhat limited in appeal because it moves rather slowly until the final episode, and that—for all its drama and suspense—is much like other accounts of being trapped below ground.

> *Zena Sutherland, in a review of "If the Earth Falls In," in* Bulletin of the Center for Children's Books, *Vol. 29, No. 8, April, 1976, p. 123.*

The Hundred Islands   (1976)

This takes place on an island off Australia where Greg, Jenny, and Darryl have grown up together and where Greg, dead serious about the island's ecology, now confronts his hard-working sheep farmer father, who thinks feeding people is more important than saving wildlife. Greg is willing to help Dad on the farm if it's run his way (no poison, a vermin-proof fence), but when Dad sticks to *his* terms Greg leaves home—to dive for abalone with Darryl and save money for an environmental science course at the university. Pretty Jenny, who studies birds, sustains Greg throughout ("It was very wonderful to be one of two people who could communicate") and Dad maintains that "it's that girl" who is luring Greg to the uni. But a break with Jenny when Greg decides to go "birding" for money—he wants to conserve but is also willing to "harvest"—makes him all the surer that his motives are pure. The problem though is not that Greg, like many his age, thinks in self-righteous black and white, but that Clark's presentation of the issues and actors is just as heavyhanded.

> *A review of "The Hundred Islands," in* Kirkus Reviews, *Vol. XLV, No. 13, July 1, 1977, p. 672.*

The author's concern about endangered Australian wild-life certainly comes across; however, the pages and pages describing birds' migrating, mating, and behavior patterns swamp this story of a young man's struggle to go to college. . . . Some of the characters are overdone and don't ring true—Jenny's too dedicated to her cause, Greg's mother is so timid she feigns a toothache to get out of the house—and the plot with its plethora of puzzling words (not defined in context) is forced and melodramatic.

> *Susan Sprague, in a review of "The Hundred Islands," in* School Library Journal, *Vol. 24, No. 1, September, 1977, p. 123.*

A totally unusual geographical setting gives freshness to the novel which treats both ecological and adolescent problems. . . . If the information sometimes seems over-abundant, the story is not without high drama, for a storm strikes while the young people are in a boat returning from the island research grounds. Their personalities and that of Greg's father are well drawn and the tensions of adolescence sensitively projected within the conflict between science and economics.

> *Virginia Haviland, in a review of "The Hundred Islands," in* The Horn Book Magazine, *Vol. LIII, No. 6, December, 1977, p. 667.*

The Boy from Cumeroogunga: The Story of Sir Douglas Nicholls, Aboriginal Leader (1979)

A certain stiffness is almost inevitable when an adult book is re-written for younger readers, but if this is apparent in Mavis Thorpe Clark's account of Sir Douglas Ralph Nicholls, based on her earlier book **Pastor Doug,** it soon wears off and the human touch reasserts itself without descending to the sentimental. Sir Douglas was appointed the first aboriginal Governor of South Australia in 1976, towards the end of a long life devoted to the cause of the Christian religion, sport and the improvement of the lot and status of the aborigine in the white-dominated continent. Despite the almost fairy-tale aspects of the story the reader's feet are kept on the ground, though there is no gainsaying the romance of the tale of such a man. The upshot is a biography which should find a place in the junior section of every library.

> *A. R. Williams, in a review of "The Boy from Cumeroogunga," in* The Junior Bookshelf, *Vol. 44, No. 5, October, 1980, p. 245.*

Solomon's Child (1981)

The heroine of **Solomon's Child** displays a bright, Aussie resilience through a series of experiences which might have led Job to call it a day. Her unmarried parents have lived together in Melbourne throughout her 13 years, only for her father to return to his pommy wife. After the break-up, Jude is caught shoplifting, assaults another girl in a jealous struggle over a boy, tangles with the law again when she wrecks a car borrowed without permission, and is tempted by a drug pusher; and her Mum drinks. Rites of passage aren't getting any easier. Perhaps sated with Narnia or Kirrin Island, readers often relish this kind of world: "Just like real life," they say, and ask for more. *The Pigman* was the trendsetter here: and like Zindel's protagonists, Jude and her friends are not altogether sympathetic characters. The dilemma facing Jude's parents is strongly drawn—both care for her and their concern engages a reader's interest in how things work out for Jude. Mavis Thorpe Clark takes on some tricky issues—rather too many, perhaps—but there is a sense of authorial integrity throughout the novel.

> *Geoff Fox, "Finding Fathers," in* The Times Educational Supplement, *No. 3445, July 9, 1982, p. 26.*

Here we go again, with a main character who is reacting to parental parting by shoplifting. Judith's story contains the variations that her father and mother have never been married and her law breaking escalates. By the time she and her friends Tricia and Rosemary stand before the magistrate in the suburb of Melbourne where they live Judith, the ringleader, is accused not only of stealing from the shop but also of assault, and of taking a car and driving it carelessly.

This piling up of wrongdoing tends to be counter-productive. Although the incidents are, individually, understandable and the author treats Judith sympathetically such a succession of misdemeanours diverts an adult reader's sympathy to her unhappy mother and the understandably antagonistic parents of her friends. Possibly an adolescent would more easily identify with Judith, though readers in this age group must surely be becoming satiated with accounts of domestic trauma.

> *R. Baines, in a review of "Solomon's Child," in* The Junior Bookshelf, *Vol. 46, No. 5, October, 1982, p. 196.*

Don Freeman

1908-1978

American author and illustrator of picture books.

Major works include *Pet of the Met* (with Lydia Freeman, 1953), *Fly High, Fly Low* (1957), *Dandelion* (1964), *Corduroy* (1968), *A Pocket for Corduroy* (1978).

One of the most beloved creators of American picture books for children, Freeman is remembered for creating deceptively casual stories and pictures that often feature anthropomorphic animals and toys in exotic settings. Immensely popular with young children, his works are characterized by their simplicity, honesty, charm, and sensitivity. Freeman's approach, while unpretentious, allows for the inclusion of a variety of information as well as an occasional moral: through their experiences, his endearing, often humorous characters gain insights about themselves and learn to help others. Freeman's work is also informed by his love for New York City's theaters, and he once compared theatergoing with producing children's books, commenting that "I can create my own theatre in picture books. I love the flow of turning the pages, the suspense of what's next." Freeman wrote and illustrated dozens of children's stories, many of which are still in print and remain favorites, particularly among children between the ages of four and eight; his best-known book, the story of a stuffed bear named Corduroy, has become a classic of children's literature. Since much of the storylines in Freeman's works are conveyed through his illustrations, done most frequently in crayon and line, he worked for hours on revising each of his sketches in order to achieve the level of detail and visual humor that would prove engaging to children. As critic Linda Zuckerman describes, "Don's approach to a story was . . . expansive, generous, and not a little corny. He went out of his way for a pun or a rhyme or a bit of visual slapstick that would make children laugh and adults groan. Don had an absolutely accurate instinct for what would appeal to children . . . he could be silly, the way a child can be silly."

After relocating from New York City to California in the late 1940s, Freeman collaborated with his wife, Lydia Cooley, on his first two stories: *Chuggy and the Blue Caboose,* published in 1951, and *Pet of the Met* published two years later. *Pet of the Met* was inspired by Freeman's experience producing drawings for the theater sections of New York newspapers, and features a mouse who resides in the attic of the Metropolitan Opera House and his nemesis, a cat who lives in the basement. Charmed by the music of Mozart's opera *The Magic Flute,* the cat and mouse eventually become friends. The story was well-received by reviewers, who remarked on the economical text and stimulating artwork and praised the Freemans for exposing young children to opera. Similarly, *Norman the Doorman* and *Guard Mouse* feature mice who reside in culturally inspiring places, such as an art museum and Buckingham Palace; Freeman's illustrations were again praised for ef-

fectively providing educational material through pictures. Over the next twenty years Freeman produced such popular tales as *Mop Top*—in which a reluctant little boy is sent to the barbershop but instead hides in a hardware store until he is mistaken for a mop—and *Fly High, Fly Low*—in which a pigeon named Sid temporarily loses his home and family when the billboard on which he built his nest is moved to another part of the city. In 1968 Freeman published *Corduroy,* the story of a stuffed bear on a department store shelf who searches after hours for the button missing from his overalls. The bear is eventually purchased by a little black girl, who repairs his clothing and gives him a good home. Freeman completed a sequel, *A Pocket for Corduroy,* just before his death. Although the demand for more stories of Corduroy remained, and several books were subsequently published, none were as successful as Freeman's. His children's books have been translated into several languages and have been adapted for filmstrip and film. *Fly High, Fly Low* was a runner-up for the Caldecott Medal in 1957.

(See also *Something about the Author,* Vol. 17; *Contemporary Authors,* Vol. 77-80.)

GENERAL COMMENTARY

Barbara Bader

A determined steam shovel, a brave tugboat, a curious monkey anyone can understand; but a mouse who turns the pages for the prompter at the Metropolitan Opera House and, for kicks, plays Papageno in *The Magic Flute*—who would conceive of such a story? what child would put up with it?

Lydia and Don Freeman's *Pet of the Met,* a perennial favorite, bears out the unconventional wisdom that there are no good or bad subjects, only good or bad treatments. Freeman, who describes himself as "backstage struck," sketched the Broadway scene for newspapers and magazines for many years; on his own, he put out a very irregular periodical, *Newsstand,* consisting of lithographs and short write-ups of New York life on all fronts. The tribute to Heywood Broun, theater critic and people's champion, typifies Freeman's manner and point of view, his combination of theatrics and social criticism. A fine bit of bravura John Sloan, it shows the same eye for incident, a like skill in handling light and dark. Even closer in spirit to Sloan, with whom he studied at the Art Students League, are Freeman's side-street vignettes of battered lives, their pathos offset by signs of pride.

From drawing on stone for small editions (per *Newsstand*), Freeman proceeded to drawing on zinc for offset reproduction and, for *Pet of the Met,* to drawing on Dynabase, the thin plastic medium whose use Morris Colman advanced at Viking. 'Its slightly grained surface takes a pencil, prismacolor, the way litho pencil takes to stone (almost),' Freeman writes; and, as Colman explains, "the drawing is exposed by direct contact with the film in a vacuum base," bypassing the camera (and the half-tone screen) and retaining "every minute element of each stroke of the artist" (almost). The autographic quality of *Pet of the Met*—the illusion that one could run one's fingers over the paper and feel the crayon, the sense that the artist has just stroked in those streaked layers of color, that he has just dashed off those broken black outlines—has much to do with its visual impact. That and the color itself, the four colors used throughout becoming, to the average eye, full color.

Not gratuitous color, which is why even today, when full-color printing has become commonplace, the scene during the performance of *The Magic Flute* dazzles: it is preceded (in reverse order) by a spreading glow as the Opera House fills, by the pink-accented black and white elegance of the Petrinis, by the shadowed depths of their attic home. Color is used with calculation, for a colorful story.

During his stint in the prompter's box, Maestro Petrini forgets himself and springs on stage, only to be interrupted during his dance by Mefisto the cat, terrible from his red cape to his outstretched claws. But even Mefisto is not immune to music's charms (by now the Freemans can get away with anything), and the two pirouette together "until the curtain had to be brought down."

That wasn't the last of the Petrinis. In *Norman the Doorman* they venture into the thinly veiled 'Majestic' Museum where cousin Norman's mouse-trap sculpture, entered in a contest anonymously, takes first prize—a spoof of both the pretensions of the cognoscenti and the pretentiousness of modern art. *The Guard Mouse* takes them around London, of all places, in the company of cousin Clyde who, stiff-backed and fur-hatted, guards the cracks in the walls of Buckingham Palace, a natural role for an upstanding mouse.

What more natural, too, than for a toy bear to want a pillow when he resettles in a cave? Besides the picaresque/picturesque adventures of the mouse clan, Freeman did many other books—single books and sorts of books in a variety of mediums. *Beady Bear,* a slip of a story for small children done in scratchboard drawings, is a neat conjunction of ends and means. Left behind by his boy, Beady reads that "B is for Bear, an animal brave who lives in a cave," and takes off. He can't seem to get settled and, worse, he muffs his chance to be brave—becoming unwound, he topples over on the ground. He needs his boy with a key, and his boy . . . ? "I need Beady!" The kickoff and the comeback are devices (that work) but the sight of that desolate little bear trudging back and forth—for a pillow, a flashlight, the newspapers—and discovering that the comforts don't make home, that's the simple truth in black and white.

Among storytellers, Freeman is unusual in his involvement with the vagaries of life. A boy dispatched to the barber drags his feet; by a kind of crazy logic that Freeman sets up, he takes everything floppy and fuzzy, in need of shearing or clipping, as an okay for his own unruly mop. Then, the kill—a woman shopping mistakes his crouching head for a real mop, and he's off with a bound to the barber chair. It couldn't happen, hardly, but it touches a common chord and sheer graphic energy—some of Freeman's best on-the-spot drawing—puts it over the top.

Nothing that Freeman has done, though, is more deft than *Dandelion*—in the spirit of the title, Mop Top as a fop. . . . [After much primping, Dandelion shows up at a party and no one recognizes him. When he is drenched] in a downpour, curls and cap gone, divested of his jacket, Dandelion is welcomed to the party by Jennifer Giraffe. That silly-looking lion who came to the door earlier was he, he confesses to his friends, but "from now on I'll always be just plain me."

Appropriately plain-spoken and free of rinkydink rhyme, held to two colors and spared extraneous background, *Dandelion* is all Dandelion's show, and all the funnier because it's played straight. (pp. 206-09)

> *Barbara Bader, "The Storytellers: Don Freeman," in her* American Picturebooks from Noah's Ark to the Beast Within, *Macmillan Publishing Co., Inc., 1976, pp. 206-09.*

Barbara Bader

Don Freeman died in February, when his latest picture book, *A Pocket for Corduroy,* was on press. Of the 24 he'd written and illustrated for Viking, his principal publisher, 22 were in print. Jaunty, casual, artless-seeming books, they didn't garner prizes. Not that it mattered—artists and children knew his worth.

Corduroy, first met in a 1968 picture book of that name, is a stuffed bear in green corduroy overalls. Otherwise, he has no distinguishing mark, no costume props or crotchets. He is Freeman's creature, the product of the artist's hand—with one proviso: in **Corduroy** he is manifestly lacking a shoulder-strap button, and *A Pocket for Corduroy* speaks for itself. Character + quandary = story. That is, when both are authentic.

Freeman came to New York in the late 20's "to live and look around," as he tells it in his memoir, **Come One, Come All!** He kept himself afloat, precariously, by playing the trumpet, he sketched surreptitiously in dime-store drawing pads, studied painting with John Sloan, picked up lithography, and, night after night, went "Broadwaying." When he didn't have the price of a seat, he looked for lost ticket stubs; when he couldn't get into a show, he watched the audience arrive. He hung around stage doors with his sketchpad until a friendly popsicle seller introduced him to Shubert Alley at intermission—and his drawing of the scene made the front page of The Herald Tribune drama section. . . .

During the following years Freeman became an annex of the theater, like his good friend, the artist Al Hirschfeld. He contributed regularly to The New York Times, The Herald Tribune, PM, Theater Magazine, Stage; designed show cards and illustrated programs; and put out a very irregular periodical, Newsstand, containing lithographs and short write-ups of New York life on all fronts—"the light and not-so-light fantastic goings on." That slapdash style concealed a triple-threat talent for theatrics, pathos and social criticism. (p. 26)

During World War II, Freeman, serving in the Army, put out an issue of Newsstand based on what he called "my war with Oklahoma," which grew into a cartoon book entitled *It Shouldn't Happen—*. But Freeman was not a cartoonist in either the Punch/New Yorker or the editorial-page sense, not a wit or a rager—he was an artist-reporter in the line of Daumier, John Sloan, William Gropper; and by the 50's opportunities on the New York newspapers had dwindled almost to nothing. For some years linear artists, confronted with the decline in book and magazine illustration, had turned to two new, growing markets, advertising and children's books. Freeman, who had something to say and his own way of saying it, was clearly no advertising man; but he was now a father.

The Freemans returned to their native California, settled into a house near the Santa Barbara railroad tracks and, with their small son, took a fancy to the signalman's house nearby. Freeman, as usual, was sketching; and out of the coming and going of the trains came a picture book, *Chuggy and the Blue Caboose* that passed muster with the redoubtable May Massee, children's book editor at The Viking Press. There, against much-garlanded competition, Freeman's ostensibly lightweight books were to become (according to the late editor Velma Varner) the publisher's best-selling juveniles.

Pet of the Met, the auspicious second (and first in the hearts of many), concerns a family of backstage mice at the old Metropolitan Opera House who—counter to what-do-children-care logic—put on their own performance of "The Magic Flute." The Petrinis are unabashed opera-lovers, but, mouselike, they have a dread enemy in Mefisto the cat; and the two strands fuse in the excitement of preparing for a performance, the pomp and ceremony of operagoing—Freeman's pre-eminent domain.

Like Newsstand's lithographs, **Pet of the Met**'s crayon drawings (technically, lithographs) have an unbookish spontaneity and verve. It's as if Freeman had just dashed off those black bounding lines, just streaked in those layers of color—which, to the untutored eye, resemble full color: the dim recesses and bright lights of the opera.

Later, in black-and-white scratchboard and watercolor, he achieved a similarly close fit between means and ends. Like his best-beloved Newsstand, picture books afforded him freedom as an artist: "No one tells me what sort of stories to write or how to draw." And, even more than Newsstand, they gave him access to a wide—indeed, worldwide—audience.

The spiffy, self-possessed Petrinis made two return appearances. In **Norman the Doorman** they venture into the "Majestic" Museum, where cousin Norman's mousetrap sculpture, entered in a contest anonymously, wins first prize. *The Guard Mouse* finds them seeing the sights of London in the company of cousin Clyde, who, in regulation red jacket and fur hat, guards the cracks in the walls of Buckingham Palace.

But Freeman didn't need out-of-the-way settings; he was attuned to the drama of everyday life.

His version of *Tom Sawyer* was **Mop Top** "the story of a boy who never wanted to have his hair cut." By the kind of crazy logic that kids find perfectly natural, Moppy interprets everything in need of a trimming—dog, lawn, trees—as justification for his own unruly mop. The drawings are in two colors, carrot-red for you-know-what, and crayon black; and they leave lots of white space for Moppy to zoom around in (this is Freeman at his sketchiest best) until, shaken by a lady shopper who takes his head for a mop, he makes a last flying leap into the barber's chair.

But no Freeman book is more cherished, especially by the smaller children to whom it is scaled, than the intimate, wistful story **Beady Bear,** kin to the two about Corduroy. Beady is a wind-up bear who, left behind by his boy, sets out to live in a cave: "B is for Bear / An animal brave," he's read in an alphabet book. But pillow, flashlight, evening papers don't add up to the real, intangible comforts of home.

There will be one more Freeman book, coming out next fall: *Dinosaur, My Darling,* written by Edith Thacher Hurd. Freeman, busy with his own projects, seldom illustrated the work of others, but he took to this story of a city boy's tender affection for a long-buried dinosaur (who is really a dragon). For her part, Mrs. Hurd remembered Freeman's Herald Tribune drawings to be, like her story, crowded with people, and funny and sad.

His sketches are character sketches, his lines express feeling. His work is slow to date because, individual and unchanging, it was never fashionable. Children will continue

But look! Can it be? Yes, it is!
Maestro Petrini, completely carried away
by the music, has leaped out of his box
before the Prompter can
stop him!

From Pet of the Met, *written and illustrated by Lydia and Don Freeman.*

to be touched by his picture books—and adults will return to his city scenes—insofar as they were, as he once wrote, "drawn from life." (pp. 26, 34, 36)

> *Barbara Bader, "Child of the Theater, Artist to Children," in* The New York Times Book Review, *April 30, 1978, pp. 26, 34, 36.*

Linda Zuckerman

[*The following excerpt is taken from an essay based on a speech originally delivered on July 13, 1978 by Freeman's editor at the Viking Press*]

Don Freeman was one of the most loving, generous, and kind men I have ever known. He loved people, found them fascinating, and never seemed to make judgments about them. He loved life and was an incurable optimist. He often said, "I am nostalgic for the future." His enthusiasm was boundless. And he had a concern for *my* well-being, for whether I was working properly or showing signs of distress, needing support or staunch defense. He helped me as if our roles had been reversed.

Don and his wife Lydia lived in Santa Barbara, but Don would make periodic jaunts to New York to see us at Vi-

king, visit old friends, go to the theater, and breathe the air of the big city. (p. 274)

[Don would sit down in my office and] hand me a manila envelope and produce a dummy of his new book. Without taking his eyes off me for a second, he would watch me go through it as I sat reading, looking, and always smiling.

That first look at a picture book dummy is intensely exciting for an editor. A dummy is not just a series of preliminary drawings; it is a picture of an idea—albeit a somewhat undeveloped idea—which has been cooking in the author's mind for a long time and which has already gone through many changes. Still, the newness of the idea, the freshness, and often the spontaneity of the sketches themselves are all unique. Looking at a dummy is one of an editor's rewards.

Every time Don handed me a dummy for the first time, he said, "It's perfect. I just know it's perfect." He did this, I think, on purpose; partly to let me know that he would only show me something he was pleased with and that he felt was his best, partly to remind me to be careful of his feelings, and partly to make it as difficult as possible for me to be critical. It worked. But I tried to be as honest as I could, and often it was the easiest thing in the world to be honestly enthusiastic. So I would sit with the new dummy in my hands, opening each page slowly, savoring it, loving it, and being fully prepared to tell him so, while at the same time my mind was going at top speed, trying to figure out what the problems were (if any), how they could be fixed (if they could), and how to present them to this wonderful man sitting there with his eyes riveted to my face, having just happily told me, "It's perfect."

From then on it would be work. Every day Don would come in to talk about the book; each time we would go through it again, page by page, talking about where it worked best, where it didn't. Don's approach to a story was characteristic of him—it was expansive, generous, and not a little corny. He went out of his way for a pun or a rhyme or a bit of visual slapstick that would make children laugh and adults groan. Don had an absolutely accurate instinct for what would appeal to children, and he often followed that instinct in spite of his editor's advice—which was fortunate. He was a man of great dignity, yet he was secure enough to allow himself to be silly, the way a child can be silly. He could allow himself to think and feel like a child without fearing he would lose his way and never get back. My instincts and experience are pointed toward organization and order; I tend to get complex and analytical, so I learned a great deal from Don about children's books.

It is easy to think that his books are simple, that they were executed quickly by a man who worked by instinct rather than by reason; yet nothing could be further from the truth. Don Freeman was a meticulous craftsman, who often drove me crazy making changes. The files are crammed with fourth and fifth versions of a manuscript, each one a little better than its predecessor. Just when I would think we were ready to go, another letter with another series of changes would come. And it was not only the manuscript that got this kind of attention. The artwork would be changed and modified in subtle ways again and again until it felt, looked, and read exactly right. Then when the production process began, there were galleys, proofs, and more proofs. Through the months of corrections and changes that produce a book Don would be critical and demanding about the quality of reproduction he expected and about the final result. Working through a manuscript or a dummy with an author can be painful, depending on the state of the thing to begin with. This process of refining, sharpening, making sure of every word, every picture, and every character can only take place over a period of time, during which the editor is probably doing most of the suggesting and criticizing, and the author is listening, arguing, or defending.

Don was a complete professional at his work. He knew, as all professional writers and illustrators know, that revision and refinement are as much a part of the creative process as the original writing or sketching; he appreciated the fact that both author and editor served specific functions in the ultimate evolution of a book and that we both had to do our best, even when that might mean disappointment or disagreement. He relished the process of working out a picture book as much as I did and was always grateful for criticism and suggestions. Even so, it wasn't easy for me, especially when he showed me something I didn't like. One day, I remember, we discussed a new book at great length. I had tried my best to explain with clarity and tact why I thought something important was missing in the story he proposed. I'm afraid I went on at great length, sensing that I was belaboring the point but helpless to do anything about it and convinced that I had been discouraging, that I was making him depressed and unhappy. I was certain he would hate me. After I finished, Don leaned back in his chair, shook his head, and said, "I love the way your mind works." Of course, he wasn't sure he agreed with me, but he would think about it. And when I saw him later that afternoon, he said, "I don't want you to be concerned about hurting my feelings. I'm worried about you being worried about me."

Don's response to editorial suggestions were, for the most part, positive. And every single line of every story was carefully thought through for its implications—every word counted. *Bearymore,* a charming story about a performing bear who must try to think of a new act for the spring season and get his hibernating done at the same time, was the subject of many a lively discussion between us. First it was important to find things for Bearymore to try for his new act. Then we needed to find something that would put him to sleep. At first Don wanted Beary to fall asleep reading a boring book. In defense of publishers, I resisted the suggestion that a book could be boring. Don countered, suggesting a cookbook. He wrote in the margin of one version of the manuscript, "I hope the idea of a book being boring will dissolve in your mind [when I make] it clear that Beary picked up a cookbook. This is [obviously not] a regular book, and understandably it could easily bore a bear." He wanted to call it *Sara Bear's Cookbook* and tactfully ignored my suggestions of *Julia, James,* or *Craig Bear's Cookbook.* We finally decided to let Beary fall asleep out of sheer exhaustion—his and ours.

Then there was the problem of getting Beary to ride his unicycle on the clothesline carrying an umbrella. Beary went to sleep, setting his alarm for April. He awoke to find it raining (thus he would need his umbrella to venture outdoors). So far, so good. But why in the world, we asked ourselves, would a bear want to take his unicycle outside in the rain—even with an umbrella—and ride it across a clothesline? Then, during an elegant lunch in a New York restaurant Don had an absolutely brilliant idea: If at the beginning of winter, Beary accidentally left the unicycle outside, he would surely have to go out in the rain to get it. We could get him up on the clothesline by having him decide to avoid the puddles. We were jubilant.

I don't mean to suggest that Don was always delighted with everything we did at Viking. Going through the files, I found evidence enough of painful disappointments—proofs of artwork that were poorly done and mistakes that could be corrected only at great expense and with much turmoil. Don, for all his good nature, could be tough and plain-spoken. About one printing he wrote, "The results are an artistic atrocity. This has to be the worst printing job I've ever seen. . . . If someone wanted to conspire to ruin my reputation—these printers couldn't have done a better job." Unfortunately, it was not a good printing, and there was not much we could say to defend it. We flew Don to New York to have him watch a second printing on the press; ultimately, we were able to produce a book that pleased us all.

Don's last book, *A Pocket for Corduroy,* had a happier history. It was a sequel to Don's most popular book and was published exactly ten years after *Corduroy.* For a long time I had thought a sequel would be a good idea, which I never felt it would be appropriate for me to suggest. The conception of a book should normally be the author's, and the editor should not usurp the author's prerogative. But finally I took a deep breath and mentioned to Don over the phone that I had an idea for a book, and would he mind if I told it to him? He said no, so a few days later I timidly wrote, "Perhaps it's not a new idea, and perhaps it has already occurred to you, and you've rejected it. But I think it would be wonderful to have a sequel to *Corduroy.* I think you can do it. For some reason or other the title *Corduroy's Pocket* keeps coming back to me. I don't know what this means or what kind of story it would be. I guess I just like the title and would like to see a book attached to it." That was on March 25, 1977.

On April 26 a dummy arrived in the mail. Don wrote, "Your suggestion hit a responsive chord. As you know I don't usually take ideas for books that are flung at me, but this was such a natural I set right to work on it. I like to think that this new story doesn't lean or depend on Corduroy's first story, [but] that it has a life of its own." And in a later letter—"Unlike my other stories, *Corduroy* number one hasn't a thick plot, as I'm sure you know. It has a theme, and in creating this sequel I've had to hold to the form and nature of the original. In other words, a book is a world of its own [and] in this new story I've had to keep within the bounds of that world.

"Just possible you would like to hear something of the background of *Corduroy* as I first came upon it," he went on. "Of course I can't remember exactly how it started, but I do recall wanting to do a story about a department store in which a character wanders around at night after the doors close. Then I also wanted the story to show the vast difference between the luxury of a department store [and] the simple life [most people live]. The idea of simple basic values was another theme that was running around in the back of my head. I don't remember how or when a toy bear came into my life, but he must have come from way out of my past. You know, I could just see a bear wearing corduroy overalls with one button missing . . . the minute I settled on Corduroy and Lisa, everything came together.

"Now we switch to the laundromat," Don continued. "I've always wanted to do a picture book about a laundromat. I had a studio right next door to one, and I loved the whole scene. It seemed to me that this is one of the few places where people come together naturally and on their own go about their chores . . . however, the instant you mentioned *Corduroy's Pocket* everything fell into place. I knew the laundromat was a perfect setting for this story. Even the underlying theme came clear . . . looking for a pocket amongst all the laundry objects. The less self-conscious I am about how and why the laundromat seems

a perfect setting, the better; nevertheless I believe our pocket story evolves out of the good feeling of people getting together."

The apparent simplicity and spontaneity that are the hallmarks of Don's style came from a complex, sophisticated man. I finally became fully aware of Don's dual nature for the first time a few years ago when the Margo Feiden Gallery in New York had a one-man show of his early paintings, drawings, and lithographs of New York and the theatre scene in the thirties and forties. Many of his pictures were prominently featured on the opening pages of the drama sections of *The New York Times* and *The New York Herald Tribune.* The remarkable work was filled with exuberance, gentle satire, and acute observations of the frailties of men and women in all walks of life; it was sentimental, witty, even romantic and could not possibly be the work of the man who thought up *Dandelion*—or could it? That these two separate bodies of work could come from the same man in the course of one productive lifetime is a tribute to Don's versatility and an indication of the contradictions that seemed to exist quite happily within him. This shift back and forth from a worldly sophisticate to an ingenuous optimist made Don an intensely attractive and interesting man.

Don Freeman was an unusually successful creator of children's books, which have appeared all over the world in hardcover and paperback, in foreign languages, and on filmstrips and films. Through his appearances at conferences, conventions, local schools, and libraries he met thousands of readers, librarians, and teachers. The enormous popularity of his books meant a great deal to him. Yet, although he had one Caldecott Honor Book—*Fly High, Fly Low*—he never received a formal acknowledgment of his contribution to the world of children's books. I think I know why.

Don's approach to a picture book never really changed with the design trends of the time. His pictures were always free, spontaneous, and sometimes a little sketchy. We tried occasionally to put them into a frame, to suggest borders, to design the book so that the type and the art were consistently related to each other in terms of space, size, and placement on the page. But Don's unpretentious, down-to-earth, old-fashioned approach never varied. His books are not glamorous, and by some standards perhaps they are not consistently beautiful. But they are honest. And they will remind us by their worn bindings and their smudged pages that the child is the final judge and that the children of the world have given Don Freeman the highest award—their loyalty and their love. (pp. 274-81)

Linda Zuckerman, "Don Freeman: An Editor's View," in The Horn Book Magazine, *Vol. LV, No. 3, June, 1979, pp. 273-81.*

TITLE COMMENTARY

Chuggy and the Blue Caboose (with Lydia Freeman, 1951)

A new train story is always an event for a large portion of the picture book public. This one is distinguished by some fine pictures, vigorous, full of action and brilliantly colored. These enliven the durable theme of an outmoded machine saved from ignominy by its own virtue. Here there are *two* old relics: Chuggy, the engine and the retired Blue Caboose for which Chuggy cherishes a special tenderness. Chuggy proves his usefulness when a blizzard blocks the tracks and then goes happily with the Blue Caboose to join a circus train. This romantic note seems coy and out of place in a story of mechanical characters, especially in one for so young an audience, but the clever use of assonance and repetition of words appeals to children as do the pictures.

> *Ellen Lewis Buell, "Clear Track!" in* The New York Times Book Review, *April 29, 1951, p. 30.*

The unsual pair of friends found in this stunning picture-story book should tickle the fancy of all small train enthusiasts. They are Lucy, a little Blue Caboose, who once was part of a circus and now stands alone on a siding near a busy railroad yard, and the equally lonely Chuggy, a little old out-of-date engine who works hard all night and flashes his headlight at Lucy as he chugs by. How Lucy gets all dressed up to be the switchmen's club car, and how Chuggy saves the day when a big blizzard comes and the slick silver streamliner gets stuck, and how together they face a happy future—all this is told and pictured in the gayest possible manner.

> *Polly Goodwin, in a review of "Chuggy and the Blue Caboose," in* Chicago Sunday Tribune, *June 3, 1951, p. 10.*

From Mop Top, *written and illustrated by Don Freeman.*

Pet of the Met   (with Lydia Freeman, 1953)

It is an exciting day when the Met offers *The Magic Flute* at the children's matinee. Down from his cosy attic harp case comes Maestri Petrini, a mouse who earns his daily cheese as the prompter's page-turner; and up from his fiddle case in the basement creeps Mefisto, a cat whose appearance fits his name. What happens when each is bewitched by the *Magic Flute* music is sheer fun. Bright drawings conveying the elegant festivity and bustle of the occasion make an original and distinguished book that contains much to surprise and delight both children and adults.

> *Virginia Haviland, in a review of "Pet of the Met," in* The Horn Book Magazine, *Vol. XXIX, No. 2, April, 1953, p. 116.*

We have often heard of singing mice, but never have we met such a musical mouse as Maestro Petrini, who lived in a forgotten harp case, high up in the attic of the Metropolitan Opera House. Next to his family, Maestro Petrini loved the opera more than anything else in the world and happily earned his daily cheese as page-turner for the prompter. Down in the cellar (in an empty violin case) lived the cat Mefisto, who loathed mice *and* music. How these two meet on the stage, right in the middle of a matinee performance, and how the strains of "The Magic Flute" work their legendary spell in the savage breast of Mefisto make one of the merriest picture books of the season. The economical prose (scarcely more than captions) is perfectly integrated with the pictures. In the latter the intensity of color, the vigor of line heighten the theatrical effect of both setting and plot.

> *Ellen Lewis Buell, "Musical Mouse," in* The New York Times Book Review, *April 12, 1953, p. 28.*

As merry a tale of a mouse, a cat, and music, as ever was invented, this gay picture book will amuse a wide audience. Here is a mouse family living in the attic of the Metropolitan Opera House. Their father, Maestro Petrini, assists in the prompter's box. Their favorite game is to perform "The Magic Flute." So, when it is given especially for children, Madame Petrini and the children attend, hidden behind a white glove.

What they see is hilarious, for their papa and the cat, music-hating Mefisto, get tangled in the act in which Papageno charms the forest beasts. The happy ending is all one could desire: cat and mouse are friends, through the magic of music. The text is brief and dramatic; the big, bold, full-color pictures are dashing, humorous and full of the spirit of the beloved old Met. What a laugh it would have given Mozart!

The book is 10 inches long by 8 high, clothbound. You may be interested to know that a book this big, with such excellent full-color on every page, at this price, was achieved by the artist making four drawings for each picture. Thus. Mr. Freeman made actually 240 drawings plus the plates for the delightful end papers and irresistible jacket. He was originally inspired to start the book when he was doing back-stage drawings for the music and theater sections of the "Times". It was his wife who invented the mouse family and it all was told and retold to their small son.

> *Louise S. Bechtel, "The Three 1953 Prize Books," in* New York Herald Tribune Book Review, *May 17, 1953, p. 6.*

Beady Bear (1954)

Beady's a rare toy bear owned by appreciative Thayer, but one night he's all wound up, gets his bearings and goes out to live in a cave. Oddly enough he can't sleep a wink. He keeps going back home to get things—flashlight, newspapers, pillow—until he's all unwound and quite relieved when Thayer comes to fetch him. A happy comment on the overly adventurous, with especially humorous block prints by the author.

> *A review of "Beady Bear," in* Virginia Kirkus' Bookshop Service, *Vol. XXII, No. 15, August 1, 1954, p. 479.*

The ABC book said "B is for Bear—an animal brave who lives in a cave." But when Beady, a wind-up toy bear, tries to live according to the book, he quickly discovers it takes more than a cave to satisfy him. His several trips from cave to home and back again to fetch the comforts of civilization add up to a series of amusing situations. Beady finally realizes that only his master has the real key to his happiness.

There is wholesome emotional satisfaction here for those pre-schoolers who have similar toy attachments. With simple page-by-page black and white scratchboard illustrations for each rhythmic sentence, this is the kind of book small children will delight in "reading" to themselves after a couple of out-loud readings by mother.

> *Pat Clark, "Cave Dweller," in* The New York Times Book Review, *November 14, 1954, p. 42.*

Mop Top (1955)

Almost 6 and never been clipped—that was Moppy. He didn't care if his head did look like a floppy red mop. All he wanted was to stay home playing things like eagle (definitely not bald) and lion (that was easy). Mother, however, sent him off to the barber shop the day before his birthday party. Moppy moped and dawdled along the way, discovering lots of things that needed a trimming more than his head. But when he hid behind a barrel of brooms and brushes and a near-sighted lady grabbed his red thatch as a mop for her kitchen floor—that settled it!

If there is any indecision among moppets about the first trip to the barber there's help here and a few chuckles besides. Mr. Freeman's breezy dialogue and crisp, lively illustrations should break down even the most stubborn resistance.

> *George A. Woods, "First Haircut," in* The New York Times Book Review, *August 13, 1955, p. 48.*

Fly High, Fly Low (1957)

Few young children have the chance to take an aerial tour of San Francisco, but Don Freeman's sweeping crayon drawings are a good substitute, delighting their eyes and widening their world.

Although the story begins slowly and lacks the originality and verve of Mr. and Mrs. Freeman's enchanting *Pet of the Met,* it has a gentle quality, a feeling of a friendly world. And young listeners will be intrigued as to the reason for Sid's choice of the letter B—revealed on the last page.

> *Alice Low, "Home Was Letter B," in* The New York Times Book Review, *October 6, 1957, p. 40.*

A big, flat picture book with end papers showing the fine blue sweep of San Francisco Bay from a pigeon's-eye-view among the clouds, and many inviting glimpses of the city and the Golden Gate bridge, relates an incident in the lives of Midge and Sid, two clever pigeons who realized the wisdom of nesting in an electric sign. . . . Kindly Mr. Hi Lee, friendly wreckers and a, perhaps, far-fetched bit of luck provide a satisfying ending. These simple ingredients fascinated a group of five to eight year olds who heard it in a summer reading group. They were breathlessly anxious for the nest to be saved and for Sid and Midge to be reunited. They delighted in Sid's mishaps, stalling traffic by obscuring the green light on a traffic signal as he fluffed his fog-dampened feathers, and being knocked over by the clapper of a cable-car bell. To our mind this has the most attractive pictures Don Freeman has done. Big, boldly drawn, with lovely coloring, they tell the pigeons' story clearly while giving a wonderful sense of the beauty of San Francisco. This book is simpler and more suitable for young listeners with a short span of attention than our favorite *Pet of the Met* that hilariously original introduction to the "Magic Flute" on which Mr. and Mrs. Freeman collaborated.

> *Margaret Sherwood Libby, in a review of "Fly High, Fly Low," in* New York Herald Tribune Book Review, *November 17, 1957, p. 4.*

The illustrations are almost breath-taking in their color and sweep as they give a bird's eye view of San Francisco. Unhappily the story plods along, bogged down by awkward writing that is in no way comparable to the superb quality of the pictures.

> *Zena Sutherland, in a review of "Fly High, Fly Low," in* Bulletin of the Children's Book Center, *Vol. XI, No. 5, January, 1958, p. 53.*

The red, yellow, and blue illustrations . . . are defined by black lines and often have the effect of those works by Taro Yashima. Though not as dark and heavy as Yashima's, these illustrations also contain quick, expressive lines which give minimal detail to the blended, blurred shapes of color.

The actual pencil strokes, at times, assimilate the strokes of a brush and lend the pictures an Oriental style, which is also evident in the architecture of the streets of San Francisco and in the character of Mr. Hi Lee.

Freeman's text, a bit melodramatic at times, is aided considerably by his energetic illustrations which are full of diagonals and eye-catching lines and color. The book stands as an example of the wide variety of styles that are beginning to develop in the late 1950s—a trend that will continue in full force into the 1960s.

> *Linda Kauffman Peterson "The Caldecott Medal and Honor Books, 1938-1981: 'Fly High, Fly Low',*" in Newbery and Caldecott Medal and Honor Books: An Annotated Bibliography, *by Linda Kauffman Peterson and Marilyn Leathers Solt, G. K. Hall & Co., 1982, p. 313.*

The Night the Lights Went Out   (1958)

Thacher is a little boy with a problem. He cannot decide what he wants to be when he grows up—a fireman, an engineer, or a pioneer. But the night of the big blizzard when all the lights go out and nothing works, not the television, the clocks, or Thacher's electric train, the problem is solved. Thacher wants to be an "electricianeer" so that when the lights go out, he can fix them. The author's bold black and yellow illustrations are particularly successful in the feeling of light and dark which they convey, and the experience of one night by candlelight should stack up to a real-life adventure in the mind of the young reader.

> *A review of "The Night the Lights Went Out,"* in Virginia Kirkus' Service, *Vol. XXVI, No. 14, July 15, 1958, p. 499.*

A picture book that is as striking visually as it is appealing in narrative for a small boy. . . . Brilliant and effective use of scratchboard, with yellow wash, highlights figures moving in the near-darkness of blowing snow, candle- and firelight. Thacher, usually seen with his cat, is a sturdy boy in coonskin cap or train engineer's hat, and very real, both in story and drawings.

> *Virginia Haviland, in a review of "The Night the Lights Went Out,"* in The Horn Book Magazine, *Vol. XXXIV, No. 5, October, 1958, p. 377.*

This simple story and picture book has captured the spirit of a family "pioneering" when the lights go off one night and the stove, the oil burner, the clocks, the television, and Thatcher's train won't work. Illustrations in black, white, and soft candlelight are very different from those of *Fly High, Fly Low* and *Mop Top,* but equally as delightful. (pp. 48, 50)

> *Nancy Jane Day, in a review of "The Night the Lights Went Out,"* in Saturday Review, *Vol. XLI, No. 44, November 1, 1958, pp. 48, 50.*

Norman the Doorman   (1959)

Norman is a doorman. He is also a mouse. Most important of all, he is a sculptor, particularly gifted in his manipulation of mousetraps into mobiles. This story, set in a museum, . . . boasts illustrations of rare charm and quality. And the world of art lovers, exhibit openings, and mousedom, portrayed in Don Freeman's delicious pastels, will enchant children and delight the most sophisticated of parents.

> *A review of "Norman the Doorman,"* in Virginia Kirkus' Service, *Vol. XXVII, No. 6, March 15, 1959, p. 224.*

Norman the doorman lived in an old armored knight's helmet in the basement of the art museum; his job was to tend the well-hidden hole around in back. Norman was a bachelor mouse, and his passion was art. Night after night up in his helmet, with the visor as a skylight, Norman tried to create something pleasing or beautiful—perhaps a painting of Swiss cheese and crackers, or a statue. One bitter cold day he made a little beautiful something out of an old mouse-trap and odd scraps of wire. It looked for all the world like a mouse on a trapeze. Norman was so proud of it that he carefully crept upstairs and placed it in the sculpture contest, with a result that was amazing. It certainly proved, as one young reader commented, that size does not gauge greatness. Norman is an endearing little mouse, but he lacks the verve and dash of his cousin Maestro Petrini, hero of the author's *Pet of the Met.* Though less lustrous, *Norman The Doorman,* still is invaluable in introducing the very young to the splendor and majesty of an art museum in a most charming and painless fashion.

> *Olga Hoyt, "Bachelor Mouse,"* in The New York Times Book Review, *May 3, 1959, p. 32.*

Norman, the doorman at the mousehole in the Majestic Museum of Art (obviously the Metropolitan) is as fond of art as his cousin, Father Petrini, the *Pet of the Met,* (by The Don Freemans) is of music. He shows all art-loving mice the treasures in the basement just as Father Petrini explains the operas to his family. Norman's great desire is to see in safety the paintings in the main part of the museum but, alas, there is a trapsetting, sharp-eyed guard upstairs. His artistic tastes result in a most astounding adventure, rather more improbable than that of the pet of the Met who owed his life to the effect of the soothing strains of Mozart's "Magic Flute" on his enemy, the cat. Norman's adventure occurred because of a most original wire mobile he made and entered in the upstairs sculpture contest, a mobile constructed of materials that gave the sharp-eyed guard a clew to the artist's nature and led to his capture! Children under eight should have great fun with Norman and thoroughly enjoy the amusing situation when the fierce guard finds that he had won a prize. The wealth of pictures are the gayest of crayon drawings filled with hilarious detail of which Don Freeman is a master.

> *Margaret Sherwood Libby, in a review of "Norman the Doorman,"* in New York Herald Tribune Book Review, *May 10, 1959, p. 20.*

Space Witch (1959)

In plenty of time for Halloween, Mr. Freeman supplies a kindergarten equivalent for Madison Avenue's soft sell, namely the soft scare. His witch, Tilly Ipswitch, flies across the title page looking about as malevolent as round-eyed Jimmy Savo, and by page seven she has won all hearts except that of her cat (a sour puss who drinks sour milk) by asking, "Kit, how would you like to spend Halloween frightening creatures on other planets?" It takes the promise of visiting the Milky Way to persuade Kit, but the rest of us should be willing passengers on the Zoom Broom, a space ship powered by jet-black magic and lacking only a sense of direction as it sails through Mr. Freeman's blue-black outer space. Perhaps it knows, as he does, that "there's no space like home." Perhaps a witch who has a television set and wears her hair in a pony tail is just too human to leave the world behind. But no surprise endings are going to be revealed here. Good night, Tilly Ipswitch, wherever you are.

> *R. N., in a review of "Space Witch," in* The Christian Science Monitor, *October 15, 1959, p. 14.*

Tilly Ipswitch, Queen of Halloween, decides to make a space ship, called the "Zoom Broom," in which she and her cat can go off to frighten inhabitants on other planets. This amusing picture book will be useful for Halloween storytelling and popular with our younger space men. The fantastic and exuberant humor and the neat play on words are somewhat reminiscent of Dr. Seuss.

> *Miriam S. Mathes, in a review of "Space Witch," in* Junior Libraries, *Vol. 6, No. 2, October, 1959, p. 151.*

Cyrano the Crow (1960)

Don Freeman's Cyrano, a crow with a distinct *panache*, is shown clothed in cloak and ruff and feathered hat on the title page of this sprightly picture book. His story, while likely to fascinate the picture book age, is more a slight anecdote than a completely rounded tale, like his earlier **Norman the Doorman,** or **Pet of the Met,** and is less important than the pictures. It tells of a mocking crow who could imitate all sorts of bird calls (ten types to be exact), enjoyed watching television and even entered a TV contest because he thought he could do better bird calls than the man imitator already on the program. The only trouble was that Cyrano, as his old friend a scarecrow had long ago told him, knew how to be every kind of bird but a crow. When Cyrano learned to "be himself," he may have looked less like his eloquent namesake of the long nose and colorful costumes but he was far happier.

> *Margaret Sherwood Libby, in a review of "Cyrano the Crow," in* New York Herald Tribune Book Review, *September 4, 1960, p. 4.*

A rather disappointing picture book, verging on the slapdash and garish, from this promising author-illustrator. The plot is a confused blend of whimsy and realism as Cyrano wins an opportunity to appear on TV to imitate birds, but cannot imitate a crow! The choice illustration in the

story has him flying disconsolately home through the rain. There is a feeling of haste rather than vigor throughout the book. Not recommended.

> *Peggy Sullivan, in a review of "Cyrano the Crow," in* Junior Libraries, *Vol. 7, No. 2, October, 1960, p. 165.*

Crayon, solid color, and line are resourcefully combined in the big, bursting-with-energy pictures with which Mr. Freeman illustrates his latest book for the 4-8's. If they have a touch more brashness, a touch less warmth than some he has done before, they are eminently suited to his fable of a crow who goes on television to imitate birdcalls. Mr. Freeman seems equally at home in a cornfield and among the planes, antennae, and harlequin eyeglasses of modern life, and his sense of fun is accompanied by a sense of value. Sometimes even a crow needs to be reminded to "know thyself."

> *Rod Nordell, in a review of "Cyrano the Crow," in* The Christian Science Monitor, *November 3, 1960, p. 2B.*

Come Again, Pelican (1961)

Author and illustrator of many delightful books here presents one of the most lucid pictures of the ocean's tidal movements and their effect on one little fisherman. In the company of a friendly pelican who demonstrates his own skill as a fisherman, Ty parks his boots on shore and himself on a pole and waits for a bite. As the tide rolls in, it carries the red boots out and Ty with hook, line and sinker retrieves one, enclosing a perfect fish. But the trick of the day is performed by the pelican, for as the tide rolls out and Ty walks back to his trailer, the delightful bird perched on a dune opens its mouth and returns to him the other boot. Evocative illustrations in sublime color evoke the full panorama of sea, dunes and a perfect day.

> *A review of "Come Again, Pelican," in* Virginia Kirkus' Service, *Vol. XXIX, No. 13, July 1, 1961, p. 536.*

This new picture book, by the author-artist of **Fly High, Fly Low, Beady Bear,** and **Mop Top,** will delight every child who ever has observed the tides.

Don Freeman's stunning illustrations fill each page with the beauty and color of sky and water and the fun a little boy has on his first fishing expedition alone. Before the story ends, Ty has a present for the pelican and, best of all, the pelican has a surprise for him.

> *Hope H. Evans, in a review of "Come Again, Pelican," in* Chicago Sunday Tribune—Books, *November 12, 1961, p. 10.*

A long beach with no one on it but a file of jaunty sandpipers, their wet shadows and a small intent boy, the sea all white and curved on the beach, all green purple and level on the horizon—Don Freeman's pictures are full of space, peace and gentle color. There is humor, too, in curled, bare toes and in the very shape of a pelican, coziness in a family supper enclosed against the darkness. And the artist has a story too for the 4-8's about Ty, the boy in red

From Norman the Doorman, *written and illustrated by Don Freeman.*

wading boots who goes fishing, watches a pelican and learns the surprising thing about tides.

Pamela Marsh, in a review of "Come Again, Pelican," in The Christian Science Monitor, *December 21, 1961, p. 7.*

Ski Pup (1963)

Hugo, a trained St. Bernard, grew restless in his lonely dog house on the mountain where he watched for skiers in trouble. His droopy eyes droop lower, until one day he sees a small boy lose his comrades. Hugo rushes to his aid, and, shortly the mortified dog finds himself in goggles and ski-cap, going down hill on one ski. In the full color illustrations, Mr. Freeman has not used his palette very artistically. And, although the pictures do have some appeal, Hugo looks like any old, lumbering St. Bernard; he has not been given a personality of his own. This tale does not live up to some of the author's earlier works, such as *Fly High, Fly Low.*

A review of "Ski Pup," in Virginia Kirkus' Service, *Vol. XXXI, No. 3, February 1, 1963, p. 106.*

Hugo, a comical looking St. Bernard, trained to carry a thermos of hot chocolate tied to his collar and to rescue people lost in the snow, fulfills his destiny in Don Freeman's new picture book but only after being rescued himself. The cause of Hugo's humiliation and triumph was a small boy separated from the other members of his ski class who decided, when he met the great dog on the upper slopes, to rest for a moment. Idly he amused himself dressing Hugo up in his cap and goggles, whereupon the dog, accidentally stepping on a ski, found himself hurtling down the mountain and plunging into a deep drift. The ensuing double rescue will tickle the sense of humor of the picturebook age although the large, boldly sweeping and brightly colored mountain scenes do not seem to us among Mr. Freeman's best.

Margaret Sherwood Libby, in a review of "Ski Pup," in Books, *June 16, 1963, p. 9.*

Botts, the Naughty Otter (1963)

What happens when busy beavers drop their work and try to frolic like otters and one otter is forced to take over the tiring work of beavers *could* have tickled young onlookers.

But black and white pictures are cartoonish to an undesirable degree; a coldness pervades which leaves Botts a bug-eyed, characterless bundle of wet fur.

> *A review of "Botts the Naughty Otter," in* Virginia Kirkus' Service, *Vol. XXXI, No. 16, August 15, 1963, p. 793.*

The Turtle and the Dove   (1964)

The artist has created a distant world of misted ocean and island by using soft blue greens and greys in the clear, serene pictures. Mr. Freeman proves that he is equally at ease with words: the descriptions are terse and startling; the brief dialogue blends into the text. Listeners will enjoy the leisurely, drifting friendship of Dove and Turtle, the interlude of family-raising, and the eventual multi-Dove-Turtle reunion. The book is a fine example of an artist at work without strong color.

> *A review of "The Turtle and the Dove," in* Virginia Kirkus' Service, *Vol. XXXII, No. 3, February 1, 1964, p. 105.*

A gentle, rambling story about a tired dove who finds rest on a turtle far out at sea. A storm separates them but after other adventures they are reunited on a tropical island. Adult readers may find the story pleasantly allegorical. Be that as it may, it is still a delightful tale for very young children, done with the gentle Don Freeman touch. His quiet, reassuring, blue-gray drawings are delicately excellent, and readers will close the book with a wistful sigh.

> *G. L. P., "Turtle-Dove Friendship," in* The Christian Science Monitor, *May 7, 1964, p. 3B.*

Most children will enjoy this story. . . . It is a pretty, imaginative book, which must be taken entirely as romantic fancy. However, I sometimes wonder how far we are going with animal picture books. This story ends with young doves swimming on young turtles' backs as the young turtles follow their parent. (Mother turtles are in fact not noticeably good parents; after the eggs are laid they cast off responsibility.)

> *Alice Dalgliesh, in a review of "The Turtle and the Dove," in* Saturday Review, *Vol. XLVII, No. 30, July 25, 1964, p. 34.*

Dandelion   (1964)

Dandelion receives an invitation to tea and taffy at Jennifer Giraffe's. His elaborate preparations render him unrecognizable. Rejected, he paces back and forth near Jennifer's house, and a sudden storm ruins his clothes and coiffure. He is then welcomed by his old friends and resolves never to become a dandy again. The humor of the story is solely in the very funny pictures of the lion as he is transformed into an elegant gentleman. Children may have a sense of disappointment at the rather weak ending, but the comical pictures make it worth the purchase.

> *A review of "Dandelion," in* School Library

Journal, *Vol. 11, No. 1, September, 1964, p. 108.*

Don Freeman's books for children are so beguilingly simple that they are almost unique. In many books one feels the heavy hand of child psychiatry and a happy-go-lucky story about a lion trying to look like a dandy in order to go to a giraffe's party is a refreshing experience. If you find a moral in a Don Freeman book, it is always gentle and acceptable—like an extra sugar doughnut in an old-fashioned baker's dozen.

> *Guernsey Le Pelley, "Social Pigeons, Lonely Penguins," in* The Christian Science Monitor, *November 5, 1964, p. 3B.*

Humor for young children must be simple and spontaneous. Most children chuckle at Don Freeman's **Dandelion,** the story of a lion who dresses up so much for a party that his hostess fails to recognize him and refuses to let him in. The story and the cartoon-style illustrations are indeed humorous, and yet the theme, that one should be true to one's nature, comes out "loud and clear." Since it is presented in this delightfully humorous manner rather than in a didactic manner, the young reader is more likely to accept this message as being a worthy one. (p. 98)

> *Patricia Cianciolo, "Using Illustrations in the School," in her* Illustrations in Children's Books, *second edition, Wm. C. Brown Company Publishers, 1976, pp. 94-123.*

A Rainbow of My Own   (1966)

The little boy, all decked out in mackintosh, rain hat and boots, looks prepared for something tougher than this fragile fantasy about his search for a rainbow and the games he would play with it if he found it. The full-size, water color and pastel illustrations are bright and attractive. Especially well done is the coloring of the sky and landscape during the heavy thundershower, and the turbulence they suggest helps to balance the sweetness of the story for the boy returns home to find the rainbow in his room and the scenery becomes flooded with inspirational-looking sunbeams.

> *A review of "A Rainbow of My Own," in* Virginia Kirkus' Service, *Vol. XXXIV, No. 3, February 1, 1966, p. 105.*

On a showery day, a little boy vainly chases an elusive rainbow. Childlike, he plays games with an imaginary one until finally, back at home, he finds that the sun, shining through the water in his goldfish bowl, gives him a dancing rainbow all his own. The simple text—as artless as the spontaneous joy of a small child—is reflected and amplified in the beautiful pictures suffused with iridescent light and color against stormy, gray-blue backgrounds.

> *Ethel L. Heins, in a review of "A Rainbow of My Own," in* The Horn Book Magazine, *Vol. XLII, No. 3, June, 1966, p. 299.*

Simply, sensitively, Don Freeman's newest picture book reflects some enchanting moments of a young child's fancy and delight in rainbows. A sentimental ending dilutes some of the charm and naturalness. Even so, the water-color illustrations glitter in lovely arcs of color and effectively hold the luminous mood of a glistening summer garden.

Margaret F. O'Connell, in a review of "A Rainbow of My Own," in The New York Times Book Review, *July 10, 1966, p. 38.*

The Guard Mouse (1967)

Henceforth all mice had better look to their laurels. They will have to step lively to be as appealing and proper, hospitable and friendly as Clyde, the tiny mouse guard at Buckingham Palace. On duty in the full regalia of a Grenadier Guard, he sees to it that no wee creatures slip through the openings in the Wall. Off duty he settles the tired children of his visiting New York cousins in his bearskin hat, places it gently alongside his sentry-box, and takes off with the parents on a whirlwind tour of London. It's breakfast at Covent Garden, then up to the roof tops to see London Bridge; an unexpected slide down the slippery slates onto a gentleman's umbrella, a few leaps in the rain from one umbrella to another down to Whitehall, a fast run down Big Ben, then a rush back for the Changing of the Guard, only to discover Clyde's fur hat has disappeared. The commotion brings the Queen, who calls Scotland Yard, who finds the hat. Good hilarious fun, full of color and zip.

Mary Silva Cosgrave, in a review of "The Guard Mouse," in The Horn Book Magazine, *Vol. XLIII, No. 2, April, 1967, p. 195.*

Chin up, shoulders back, tail smartly curled, Clyde the Guard Mouse stands on duty outside the walls of Buckingham Palace. . . . When Clyde has an unexpected visit from American relatives, he gallantly escorts them on a quick trip around London, thereby affording Don Freeman an opportunity to paint some delightful London scenes. The story ends with a minor, easily surmounted crisis. . . . The illustrations are awash with color, movement, humorous details, and a splendid feeling of amused affection for Londoners.

Zena Sutherland, in a review of "The Guard Mouse," in Saturday Review, *Vol. L, No. 16, April 22, 1967, p. 99.*

The Guard Mouse is an amusing story and picture book by one of our most durable illustrators, whose quality has not diminished over a period of several decades. Don Freeman is a man of many gifts—he published his own *New Yorker* magazine 30-odd years ago, did theater drawings for the old *Tribune,* and kept his artistic and agile fingers in many pies without losing his identity in the asphalt jungle. He has a special affinity for mice, it seems—witness his previous **Pet of the Met**—and this present production shows his old skill in spinning a yarn and incidentally providing a reporter's wealth of information in his drawings.

Although **The Guard Mouse** is the story of Clyde, mouse Grenadier guard at Buckingham Palace, the plot also conveys a sweeping mouse's-eye view of the Queen's London. Through the courtesy of visiting kin, the Petrinis from

New York, we are taken around in a double-decker bus to see with them Piccadilly Circus, the Covent Garden Market, London Bridge, Westminster Abbey, with some harrowing experiences on the hour hand of Big Ben. Under Don Freeman's benign hands all ends well—as usual—and the only thing left to wish for would be better reproduction of the nice color wash-drawings. (pp. 5, 20)

Fritz Eichenberg, "Treasure Hunt," in Book Week—The Washington Post, *May 7, 1967, pp. 5, 20.*

Don Freeman has a splendid time illustrating the progress of the tiny creatures atop a city umbrella, coveting the pigeons' corn in Trafalgar Square, or clinging to the hour hand of Big Ben. The large, colour washed pictures are at their best when they give a panoramic view of well known parts of London. Since the book boasts of being authentic, the excessive excitement of the human guardsmen which forms its climax is strikingly unlikely.

R. Baines, in a review of "The Guard Mouse," in The Junior Bookshelf, *Vol. 40, No. 2, April, 1976, p. 81.*

Corduroy (1968)

A bear missing a button looks shopworn, so Corduroy sets out after the department store closes to find his. Up an escalator ("I think I've always wanted to climb a mountain") onto a floor filled with tables and chairs and rows and rows of beds ("I guess I've always wanted to live in a palace") where he finds a mattress button that pulls off with a POP, tumbling him into a table lamp. The crash brings the night watchman who returns Corduroy to his shelf, still unbuttoned. But a little girl wants him badly enough to empty her piggy bank and he goes home to a bed just the right size and, to make him more comfortable, a button to fasten his shoulder strap. Corduroy and Lisa break the spell by talking to each other but otherwise it's the sort of predicament that children recognize, made more poignant by the plea in Corduroy's eyes. (In case you care, Lisa has warm brown skin.)

A review of "Corduroy," in Kirkus Reviews, *Vol. XXXVI, No. 3, February 1, 1968, p. 109.*

A winning, completely childlike picture book in which a stuffed bear waiting hopefully in a toy department finds a home with a little Negro girl who wants Corduroy so much that, when her mother refuses to buy him, she comes back the next day with her own money. Endearing, brightly colored pictures together with the text affectionately recount Corduroy's adventures in the big store one night as he hunts for a button missing from his overalls and his happiness at being taken home to live with Lisa.

A review of "Corduroy," in The Booklist and Subscription Books Bulletin, *Vol. 64, No. 17, May 1, 1968, p. 1042.*

As Don Freeman shows, any bear self-respecting enough to embark on a store-wide hunt for a button off his overalls deserves a good home. And Corduroy gets one. The very best kind of home—with a little girl who wants him so much she empties her piggy bank to buy him. And—evidence of another kind of home-coming—the little girl is Negro.

P. M. D., in a review of "Corduroy," in The Christian Science Monitor, *May 2, 1968, p. B2.*

Toys, as fictional characters, can help to define a child's world as well as offering an illusion of escape into something wider. Scale is all-important. The child can either imagine himself smaller, a happy interloper in the doll's world, or he can imagine toys as his equals, in size as in enterprise. In either case illustration seems crucial, to establish the direction of the fancy. In **Corduroy,** for example, we have a very simple tale in which a toy translated from lonely melancholy to domestic joy is in one way a stand-in for a child: the book is almost therapeutic in its emphasis on the gentle happiness of home, as it follows a teddy bear in his search through the deserted store for the lost button which has made a prospective customer reject him, and builds up to the dénouement when the eager little girl is at last able to buy him. The size of the toy as he peers round enormous pieces of furniture and blunders into a towering standard-lamp provides a visual comment on the helplessness of toys and so deepens the mood of the happy ending. (pp. 3403-04)

Margery Fisher, in a review of "Corduroy," in Growing Point, *Vol. 17, No. 4, November, 1978, pp. 3403-04.*

Add-a-Line Alphabet   (1968)

Chalk talk trickery. Turning each letter into an animal ("B becomes a big brown bear busily going somewhere") makes a good performance but it has little application to learning; the illustrations are oversized sketches that don't bear a second glance.

A review of "Add-a-Line Alphabet," in Kirkus Reviews, *Vol. XXXVI, No. 5, March 1, 1968, p. 254.*

One of Don Freeman's popular chalk talks, an A to Z zoo of animals built with a few quick strokes upon the basic lines of the 26 letters, has long been appreciated by audiences of all ages fortunate enough to see and hear him. Now, in the form of a gay oversize (9" x 11½") picture book, the fun can be shared with children everywhere, who not only will enjoy the lightning sketches and cheerful captions ("L is a Lion's nose, good for snores and sneezes; M is a Mouse's nose, good for snuffing cheeses") but will need little urging to follow the artist's suggestion, "to draw your own zoo, using animals and birds of your own choosing." The book's final send-off, "Happy Alphabeting!," provides a suitable two-word annotation in itself.

Della Thomas, in a review of "Add-a-Line Alphabet," in School Library Journal, *Vol. 15, No. 1, September, 1968, p. 181.*

Quiet! There's a Canary in the Library   (1969)

Daydreaming, a little girl welcomes all manner of animals to the library but openhouse becomes a madhouse when

From The Guard Mouse, *written and illustrated by Don Freeman.*

mice scurry in; then it's only thanks to the canary ("she's telling them it's time to go") that order is restored. A little weak word play ("I'm so proud to see you, Peacock"), a very minor diversion. Say horsing around.

> *A review of "Quiet! There's a Canary in the Library," in* Kirkus Reviews, *Vol. XXXVII, No. 7, April 1, 1969, p. 368.*

An easy to read daydream that has elements to please both librarians and the youngest would-be librarians. The setting is a children's library, where Cary goes every Saturday morning. She reads a book about a zoo, then begins imagining herself as librarian and how she'd have a special visiting day just for birds and animals. Top-knot and all, Cary graciously welcomes many awkward and unaccustomed browsers (canary, lion, elephant, cow, etc.) until the scampering mice come in and upset the erst-while librarian's dream which ends with a blush of embarrassment as she returns to reality—aloud. The pastel-colored cartoon pictures tell most of the story, supported by a minimum of text. Appropriate to this girl's story, they are light and feminine, in contrast to Freeman's previous success, *Mop Top,* with its positive masculine approach. (pp. 74-5)

> *Alice Guss, in a review of "Quiet! There's a Canary in the Library," in* School Library Journal, *Vol. 15, No. 9, May, 1969, pp. 74-5.*

Tilly Witch (1969)

To get back to being wicked, Tilly—who's been frolicking like Queen of the May—mounts her surfbroom (yes, a surfboard with a whisk broom for a skeg) and visits Doctor Weegee the (pure white) witch doctor who prescribes a refresher course at Miss Fitch's Finishing School for Witches. There she's worse (i.e. better) than ever until she realizes that children will lose their faith in Halloween unless she reforms (i.e. reverts to type). When last seen she's astride her broomstick on her way to make mischief. As slapsticky as a squashed pumpkin but then backsliding witches can't go wrong.

> *A review of "Tilly Witch," in* Kirkus Reviews, *Vol. XXXVII, No. 18, September 15, 1969, p. 991.*

Forever Laughter (1970)

Most of the humor is in the unaccompanied pictures—and unaccompanied pictures are not the usual choice of children old enough to enjoy the joke. "Make me laugh, Fool, or I shall banish thee!" the very sad King threatens the very dejected Jester. 'Delving' into his bag of tricks, the Jester finds a mirror . . . and the King makes faces until he's making whoopee . . . and playing the Fool himself. While the other, putting on the discarded crown, sits glumly on the throne . . . and banishes the quondam King . . . until proffered the mirror, he perks up . . . "And they lived with love and laughter / forever after." Funny enough if you'll settle for a story in facial expressions.

> *A review of "Forever Laughter," in* Kirkus Reviews, *Vol. XXXVIII, No. 6, March 15, 1970, p. 316.*

This is a bridge between completely wordless picture-books and books that can be read easily. A court Jester must cheer up a "very sad King"; the trick that he uses, and the way the tables are turned when the Jester sits on the throne and demands cheering from the King, are shown in full by the amusing illustrations. The small amount of text, printed in large, clear, decorative, easy-to-read type, serves for the most part as an introduction to the story. The vocabulary is advanced for beginning readers, but they could easily learn the few words from hearing the story. This humorous book will also be appreciated by remedial reading specialists who are working on sequence skills. (pp. 3038-39)

> *Sybilla A. Cook, in a review of "Forever Laughter," in* Library Journal, *Vol. 95, No. 16, September 15, 1970, pp. 3038-39.*

Hattie the Backstage Bat (1970)

Hattie the backstage bat becomes the star of the show by first scaring everyone stiff . . . or by hook or by crook which is all this hangs on. But then *Pet of the Met* was no masterpiece of plotting and look how that perseveres; probably a winsome, behatted bat casting a monstrous shadow across the stage will get her share of handclaps.

> *A review of "Hattie the Backstage Bat," in* Kirkus Reviews, *Vol. XXXVIII, No. 16, August 15, 1970, p. 866.*

[*Hattie the Backstage Bat* is] a letdown. In format, style and oddly antique subject matter, it looks and sounds like a 1930's picture book. Hattie's fly-on role in a creeky horror drama induces nothing more exciting than an eerie sense of *déjà vu.*

> *Selma G. Lanes, in a review of "Hattie the Backstage Bat," in* The New York Times Book Review, *Part II, November 8, 1970, p. 53.*

Penguins, of All People! (1971)

That resemblance which has not escaped notice here wafts Peary Byrd Penguin to the U.N. as the new ambassador from Antarctica—whereupon, momentarily at a loss for words, he remembers son Pengo's "aark aark," which, translated into "Have fun!" by the one interpreter who understands Penguinese, reduces tensions and induces friendship all around. "If penguins can live together peaceably, so can we" might not strike you as the best of sense but Mr. Freeman doesn't belabor the point or, on the other hand, work at being funny. Actually he puts it almost all into pictures, and the scenic watercolors of the Antarctic, New York harbor and the U.N. (a double-page sweep of flags with "a snowy white flag, which they knew must be theirs," at the end) have a breadth and luminosity that makes the subjects impressive. Perhaps respect rather than raillery is the secret of the book's modest success.

A review of "Penguins, of All People," in
Kirkus Reviews, *Vol. XXXIX, No. 7, April 1,
1971, p. 355.*

Don Freeman has written and illustrated a full shelf of picture books for very young readers. The best of the books use an exotic or dramatic setting and with wit and gaiety give considerable information about it—as his *Pet of the Met* does about Mozart's magic flute and the opera house, or his *The Guard Mouse* does about London and the Queen's home.

The formula has betrayed Mr. Freeman here; he uses it without inventiveness or verve. The Emperor Penguin is invited to explain to the United Nations how penguins (of all people!) manage to live together peacefully. Neat idea with good possibilities, but what is the Emperor Penguin's message? Have fun, he shrieks, as he slips and slides in front of the delegates. Returning home triumphant, he describes the delegates: "Oh, they're friendly creatures just like us, only they talk more than we do, and they look funny when they walk."

Though Mr. Freeman's imagination and story-telling sense have failed him, his artist's hand hasn't. His colors are as clear, his washes as gleaming and lucid as ever, with some beautiful pages of cool icebergs floating across a mint-green sea under a crisp blue sky. Maybe that's what keeps penguins so amiable.

Adele Z. Silver, in a review of "Penguins, of All
People!" in The New York Times Book Review, *May 2, 1971, p. 45.*

Fragile fun is here weighted down by a massive message: Nations that play together stay at peace together. Ambassador Peary Byrd Penguin is called to the United Nations from Antarctica to help the people of the world solve their problems. His little boy, Pengo, tells him to have fun, but he insists that he is on an important, serious mission. After a long journey by helicopter and freighter, the penguin delegation reaches the UN where Peary is to speak. Confronted by the serious, troubled faces of the other world delegates, Peary is at a loss for words until he remembers Pengo's message. He and the other penguins begin sliding and slipping on a large, glass table which is similar to the ice at home. His Penguinese squawks are translated as "Have fun! Work together! Play together! Be one family!'" After watching themselves on the late news and riding in a ticker-tape parade, the penguins journey back home. Asked what people are like, Peary replies, "'. . . they talk more than we do, and they look funny when they walk.'" This isn't Freeman anywhere near the top of his storytelling form (as in *Fly High, Fly Low, Mop Top,*) but his color cartoons are as lightly amusing and as distinctive as ever.

Jean Coleman, in a review of "Penguins, Of All
People!" in School Library Journal, *Vol. 18,
No. 1, September, 1971, p. 103.*

Inspector Peckit   (1972)

The redoubtable inspector is a pigeon, a suave French bird. When he sees Annette crying by her window, he flies to her aid. Poor Annette has lost her fluffy new white bag, a cherished gift, in the Luxembourg Gardens. The brave private eye promises to scour all Paris in search of the lost treasure. After days of frustration as he suspects a small boy, a squirrel, and Annette's pet cat, Peckit is victorious. But he has very good reasons for not telling the girl where he has found the bag. Both pictures and story are sophisticated and an unqualified delight.

A review of "Inspector Peckit," in Publishers
Weekly, *Vol. 202, No. 9, August 28, 1972, p.
263.*

Over the years, Don Freeman has created some of juvenile literature's most enchanting characters, from Dandelion and Mop Top to Hattie the Backstage Bat. The newest member of the club is a suave Parisian detective, *Inspector Peckit,* who also happens to be a pigeon. He speaks impeccable French and, naturally, pigeon English, and always gets his man. The object in point is a missing knit bag, a young girl's birthday present. Despite his numerous *faux pas,* the ending is rewarding, in more than one way. (p. 2)

Michael J. Bandler, ". . . then to Read," in
Book World—The Washington Post, *November 5, 1972, pp. 2-3.*

Peckit, the Parisian pigeon who is also a private eye, has much in common with Inspector Clouzot, the inept French detective immortalized by Peter Sellers. When he magnanimously undertakes to retrieve a girl's lost bag he gets side-tracked on to one false trail after another, and it is pure luck that ultimately enables him to complete his assignment. Don Freeman's pictures, soft blue and dove grey, bring in all the right props to indicate the Parisian background, and the artist invests his hero with a range of expression and emotion of which one would never have thought the pigeon physique capable.

A review of "Inspector Peckit," in The Times
Literary Supplement, *No. 3742, November 23,
1973, p. 1441.*

Flash the Dash   (1973)

An amusing tale about two dachshunds, Flash and Sashay. Sashay, the female, industriously runs errands around town for which she receives food. When Sashay decides it's time for lazy Flash to do his share, Flash gets a job as a messenger for a telegraph office. He is well suited to the work and, except for a brief bout of spring fever, all ends happily with Flash the father of Sashay's three pups. The lighthearted, charming drawings in soft mustard and brown add to this endearing dog story that will appeal to young readers and listeners alike. (pp. 56-7)

Eleanor Glaser, in a review of "Flash the
Dash," in School Library Journal, *Vol. 20, No.
1, September, 1973, pp. 56-7.*

Two dachshunds, Sashay and Flash, live in a comfortable dog house; Sashay urges her mate, who is lazy, to share the financial burden, since she has been earning food by delivering flowers and newspapers. Flash gets a job delivering telegrams, is zealous and reliable until hit by spring fever. He lets a telegram escape in the breeze, it is caught by a woman, she reads it to him, he discovers Sashay is in the Hot Diggety Dog Hospital with a litter of three. How did he know? "I got the message," the story ends, the drawings are deft, but the colors are humdrum; the story is weak in construction, with little sequence or focus, and with several weak spots: for example, Flash begs (by standing on his hind legs) that the telegram be read to him, yet the text states that he found a telegram under the office door and "without looking to see to whom the telegram was addressed" he went off.

> *Zena Sutherland, in a review of "Flash the Dash," in* Bulletin of the Center for Children's Books, *Vol. 27, No. 4, December, 1973, p. 63.*

The Paper Party   (1974)

Sitting alone and watching his favorite television program, the Dinky Donk Show, small Jory is enchanted when a puppet clown leans out to beckon him in. The clown puts down a small ladder, and Jory climbs in to join the cast in a paper party: confetti snow, papier mâché cake, etc. Invited to remain, Jory remembers his dog Peetz, and leaves. En route to his room and his pet, Jory turns to look at the set and the ladder is gone. The fanciful idea of entering the set has been used before, but it is one that appeals to children; the plot is, however, not substantial, being more an extended situation than a story, and the separation of fantasy and realism at the close is weak. The illustrations of the party scenes, with gay paper streamers and puppet characters, should prove attractive to the read-aloud audience. (pp. 146-47)

> *Zena Sutherland, in a review of "The Paper Party," in* Bulletin of the Center for Children's Books, *Vol. 28, No. 9, May, 1975, pp. 146-47.*

An exuberant gay little story about the land of puppets and the characters who live there. Young children whose watching of the television screen goes on all night might learn from Jory that however exciting the fantasy world of show-business his own familiar room and his pet dog have a great deal to offer too.

> *J. Russell, in a review of "The Paper Party," in* The Junior Bookshelf, *Vol. 41, No. 5, October, 1977, p. 275.*

The Seal and the Slick   (1974; British edition as *The Sea Lion and the Slick*)

The soft, romantic water color washes and sweetly childlike drawings of the seal and its young rescuers are inadequate for the technological tragedy which nearly drowns the seal incapacitated by an oil spill. And because only one foolhardy "young explorer" is caught in the slick while the older, wiser sea lions avoid the danger, Freeman inadvertently suggests that the pup is partly to blame for his own troubles. A smoothed out, toned down ecology lesson for the very youngest—provided the message doesn't slide right over their heads.

> *A review of "The Seal and the Slick," in* Kirkus Reviews, *Vol. XLII, No. 3, February 1, 1974, p. 105.*

Don Freeman is at his best in ***The Seal and the Slick.*** A beautiful new style and vigor in his painting is an added bonus: His watercolor pictures of seals, foggy rocks, the sea and the sky will make art lovers out of nature lovers and vice versa.

> *Guernsey Le Pelley, "Stories to Share with Grandpa," in* The Christian Science Monitor, *May 1, 1974, p. F2.*

Although the format suggests a picture book for very young children, this story points a moral for readers of any age concerning the dangers of oil pollution, especially to wildlife. The text makes no concession in vocabulary, but the double-spread pictures make the danger readily understood. When the youngest and friskiest pup gets into difficulties because the oil rig has had a blow-out, two children do all they can to save his oil-covered body, and succeed.

> *B. Clark, in a review of "The Sea Lion and the Slick," in* The Junior Bookshelf, *Vol. 40, No. 5, October, 1976, p. 261.*

Will's Quill   (1975)

The idea of a country goose being buffeted about on the streets of London is probably as old as Freeman's "Merrie Olde England" setting, and the language of the young actor-playwright that Willoughby Waddle meets in the lane is downright hokey. "Forsooth, it does seem life is full of woe, e'en for a lowly goose," says the stranger as he brushes garbage from Willoughby's wings. The grateful goose follows his rescuer, causing hilarity by nipping his on-stage duel opponent in the breeches, and later hears the young man (called Will) answer his companions' plea with "poetic lines": "I can but try. This very night I intend to finish the play I have been working on for lo, these many moons." Thus Willoughby gets his chance to return Will's kindness, for when the playwright that night throws feathers from his window, grumbling "Curse these quills! How can I write with such wretched pens?" the goose donates some of his own long, strong ones and becomes the writer's boon companion. Freeman bathes the encounter in a soft, affectionate glow that invites participation—but if this sentimental dolt can be proved to be William Shakespeare, Bacon's stock is sure to rise.

> *A review of "Will's Quill," in* Kirkus Reviews, *Vol. XLIII, No. 13, July 1, 1975, p. 708.*

William Shakespeare as a supporting character in an animal fantasy for children? You betcha. . . . The humorous story of this unusual alliance is perked up by Freeman's vivid, pastel watercolor illustrations which catch the hubbub and vitality of Renaissance London. Because of the Elizabethan jargon—lots of "forsooth's" and "methinks"—this is best suited to storytelling sessions. (pp. 89-90)

> *Ilene F. Rockman, in a review of "Will's*

From Corduroy, *written and illustrated by Don Freeman.*

Quill," in School Library Journal, *Vol. 22, No. 2, October, 1975, pp. 89-90.*

The story of Willoughby Waddle, a country goose who goes to Elizabethan London, is one of the nicest Freeman books in a long time. Soft, bright paintings have intriguing details of costume and architecture, and they are full of action. . . . The dialogue is a bit heavy with "Gadzooks" and "Forsooths" but the plot is adequately structured, and both text and illustrations have plenty of humor and action.

*Zena Sutherland, in a review of "Will's Quill,"
in* Bulletin of the Center for Children's Books,
Vol. 29, No. 9, May, 1976, p. 143.

Bearymore (1976)

You'll like Bearymore, the unicycling circus bear, even though his problem—working up a new act before next season—is as old hat as the ringmaster says his performance is, and the not so novel solution, riding his unicycle on a tightrope, presents itself in a most contrived and unlikely manner: Waking from his winter's sleep on a rainy April day, Bearymore notices his cycle hitched to the tele-

phone/laundry pole, and so as not to get wet himself he travels across the clothesline to fetch it inside. But Freeman tells it with disarming innocence, and his yellow-shaded pencil drawings have a quiet glow that is equally becoming to the bustling de-camping circus and the bear's lonely trailer. And nightshirt-clad Bearymore, dripping wet and grinning away after the sheer force of his idea has knocked him from the clothesline into a puddle, is a sight to applaud.

A review of "Bearymore," in Kirkus Reviews,
Vol. XLIV, No. 20, October 15, 1976, p. 1132.

When the rest of the circus moves to its Florida winter quarters, Bearymore, a unicycle-riding bear, must work up a new act or lose his job. Before he knows it he drops off to sleep for the winter. In April, when he wakes, he realizes he left his unicycle outside. To avoid spring mud, he walks the clothesline to reach it and, since he can't ride in the mud, he ventures halfway back on the clothesline. Voilà! The new act! Freeman's huggable bear in gold pastel and charcoal will appeal to the picture-book crowd, as usual. The text does not talk down but gives children interesting words like "hibernate" and "roustabout" as well as some background on circus life. (pp. 48-9)

Helen Gregory, in a review of "Bearymore," in School Library Journal, *Vol. 23, No. 4, December, 1976, pp. 48-9.*

The Chalk Box Story (1976)

This nicely understressed demonstration of creativity in process begins with a box of colored chalk and a blank sheet of paper. Then one by one the eight chalk sticks emerge—first, to make a picture (Blue draws sky and sea, Yellow sun and sand, Brown a little boy and two trees, Green palm leaves and a turtle, and Purple gives the boy a stick); and then, with no perceptible shift in gears, they tell a story. White puts a flag on the stick and Red writes HELP ME on it, Black makes a boat in the distance. Finally, with all eight colors used and the boys' plea still unheeded, the creation takes over. The turtle begins to move, invites the boy onto his back, and paddles him out to the boat. Thus the story grows on you, as you read it.

A review of "The Chalk Box Story," in Kirkus Reviews, *Vol. XLIV, No. 21, November 1, 1976, p. 1167.*

A small picture book in the tradition of Crockett Johnson's *Harold and the Purple Crayon* and Martha Alexander's *Blackboard Bear*. Confronted by a piece of paper tacked on a board, eight sticks of chalk—six colors as well as black and white—decide to make a picture. Beginning with blue, which draws the sky and the ocean, the various colors contribute their share until they all create an island at sea—with a boy, two palm trees, and a turtle. When the little castaway is not able to attract a ship on the horizon, the turtle brings about his rescue. Each of the colors not only adds to the cumulative series of pictures but sets the background and tells the story; as the turtle returns to her sandy island, the last page of the book glows with mingled sunset hues. In a natural, unforced way the book could conceivably inspire a stimulated viewer to invent a similar kind of pictorial narrative.

Paul Heins, in a review of "The Chalk Box Story," in The Horn Book Magazine, *Vol. LIII, No. 2, April, 1977, p. 149.*

A Pocket for Corduroy (1978)

Don Freeman took his editor's advice last year: that he create a sequel to *Corduroy,* and bring back his overall-clad little teddy bear after a decade. *A Pocket for Corduroy,* published last week, turned out to be his final work.

His death on February 1 of a heart attack at 69 ended a productive career as creator of a gallery of anthropomorphic heroes—including Dandelion, Pet of the Met, Inspector Peckit, Norman the Doorman and Hattie the Backstage Bat—in a couple dozen affectionate, sensitive, often funny and occasionally moralistic children's stories.

What are the forces that inspire an artist to create—in one lifetime—backstage ping-pong players in Elizabethan garb, riveters inside a bomber's nose and (in *Penguins, Of All People!*) a sash-bedecked penguin envoy to the United Nations? What sparks a writer to describe a love affair with a city and (in *Will's Quill*) the pastoral adventures of a goose who provides young Will Shakespeare with a fine quill to overcome a nagging case of writer's block? What emotions and compassions lurk in the background of a sketch of night-shift workers on a wartime assembly line, and between the lines of a story (*The Seal and the Slick*) about a seal pup entrapped in a perilous offshore oil slick?

Some of the answers may be found in *Come One, Come All,* his memoir of the pre-World War II period; the backstage drawings that appeared in newspaper drama sections in the 1930s; the scenes of bomber plants and boot camps published in *The New York Times Magazine* in the early 1940s; three decades' output of children's books; and the recollections of friends and associates.

Cartoonist Al Hirschfeld was one of those friends. Together with William Saroyan (who wrote young trumpeter Freeman into one of his plays), scene designer Boris Aronson, theater critic John Beaufort, raconteur Alexander King and humorist S. J. Perelman, he was part of a scruffier, less formal version of the legendary Algonquin Round Table during the '30s. Freeman's self-published newspaper *Newsstand,* 30 or 40 pages of gossip, news and literature, was a staple of theatrical and literary circles in those days.

"He was 69 going on 30," Hirschfeld remarked a recent interview. "He always had the spirit of a young kid, a boyishness, a great love of life. There never was anything introverted about him. He was completely open."

Linda Zuckerman, the Viking editor who suggested the Corduroy sequel, recalls that he created, in his books and illustrations, "a childlike, spontaneous, unpretentious and apparently ingenuous world," yet actually prepared and paced his books meticulously. He never wrote down to kids, either. Designed for ages four to eight, his texts contained such words as *raucous, reproving, solemnly, reluctant* and *inspired*—to cite just a few.

His last book, regrettably, is not his best. Delicate, simply drawn in water colors and India ink, it carries Corduroy through a series of mishaps in a laundromat as he searches for material out of which a pocket can be made for his overalls. Typically unpretentious, it nonetheless lacks the bustling exuberance of *Will's Quill,* the high comedy of *Dandelion* or *Penguins, Of All People!* and the sensitivity of *The Seal and the Slick.*

Michael J. Bandler, "The Warm World of Don Freeman," in Book World—The Washington Post, *March 12, 1978, p. E6.*

The lovable hero of the popular *Corduroy* accompanies his friend Lisa and her mother to the laundromat, where he discovers that his favorite green pants lack a pocket. While searching to remedy the situation, Corduroy is left behind when Lisa's mother hurries her away. He meets a happy artist, nearly gets put in the dryer, makes a snowslide out of a tipped-over box of soap chips, and falls asleep. The next day he's rescued by Lisa and given the pocket he longs for. A somewhat pallid story further marred by an unsympathetic mother, but fans of the first

Corduroy tale will find the same stalwart bear appealingly portrayed here in similarly styled full-color illustrations.

> *Barbara Elleman, in a review of "A Pocket for Corduroy," in* Booklist, *Vol. 74, No. 19, June 1, 1978, p. 1551.*

Children have loved **Corduroy,** a shopworn teddy bear who finds love and happiness despite a missing button. Whether his many fans will find this second story about him as satisfying is debatable. . . . While the two stories have a number of parallels, there is a universality in **Corduroy** which is missing from the sequel. Black and Spanish children may respond to the inner-city setting, but neither the search for the pocket nor Corduroy's apparent loss generates much concern. Children may well read the present book on the strength of the first; for the uninitiated, it will have little appeal.

> *Janet French, in a review of "A Pocket for Corduroy," in* School Library Journal, *Vol. 25, No. 1, September, 1978, p. 108.*

Corduroy's Party   (1985)

[Corduroy's Party, *illustrated by Lisa McCue, features Freeman's original character.*]

Corduroy, the stuffed bear, was the hero of praised and popular picture books by the late artist Don Freeman. Although his sensitive touch is missing here, McCue's full-color, quaintly detailed pictures illustrate the simple story appealingly. Clad in his familiar green corduroy overalls with the patch pocket, the bear writes invitations to all his friends, who arrive at his gaily decorated house to help celebrate his birthday. The gang, bearing gifts, have a good time feasting and playing games for which they thank Corduroy politely before going home. The little book is meant for the very youngest tykes, who will meet the likable bear again when they are a bit older, in Freeman's creations.

> *A review of "Corduroy's Party," in* Publishers Weekly, *Vol. 227, No. 4, January 25, 1985, p. 93.*

The watercolor illustrations in this board book are colorful and have cheery details. However, little of the charm, warmth and personality of Freeman's **Corduroy** are retained. This Corduroy is a flat character with cute, stuffed friends. And where is Lisa or the friendship they shared? Illustrations are bright and might appeal to preschoolers—but why not give them the real thing? This is a sad imitation.

> *Marion B. Hanes, in a review of "Corduroy's Party," in* School Library Journal, *Vol. 32, No. 1, September, 1985, p. 116.*

Corduroy's Christmas   (1992)

[Corduroy's Christmas, *illustrated by Lisa McCue, features Freeman's original character.*]

Corduroy is getting ready for Christmas, and young listeners will love watching him decorate the tree, make cookies, wrap presents, sing carols, etc., etc. On each page, children are invited to lift the flap of a present, or wrapping paper, or a scarf to find a hidden object. And even if it's not the genuine Corduroy, the book will make a nice gift. It won't last long on library shelves, however, as eager little fingers lift and peek. Fun idea, but nothing beats the original "Corduroy." (pp. 39-40)

> *Jane Marino, in a review of "Corduroy's Christmas," in* School Library Journal, *Vol. 38, No. 10, October, 1992, pp. 39-40.*

Roy A(rthur) Gallant

1924-

American author of nonfiction.

Major works include *Exploring the Universe* (1956), *Man the Measurer: Our Units of Measure and How They Grew* (1972), *How Life Began: Creation versus Evolution* (1975), *Earth's Vanishing Forests* (1991).

One of the most distinguished and prolific authors of scientific works for both children and adults, Gallant is known for his thorough and accessible examinations of complex subjects and his engaging prose style. His works not only encourage young people to acquire an interest in science, but also to consider learning an important and enjoyable lifelong pursuit. Gallant's best-known work, *Exploring the Universe,* promotes critical thinking in its readers. One in a series of eight "Exploring Books" by Gallant, *Exploring the Universe* presents the history of astronomy from its origins in ancient Egypt up through its applications during the Enlightenment and in the modern world. While including discussions of the solar system and other galaxies, Gallant presents advanced and conflicting theories in unbiased and understandable terms. The book received a Thomas Alva Edison Foundation Award for best children's science book in 1957 and was revised in 1968 to include a discussion of the Russian satellite *Sputnik.* While the many attractive illustrations and simple graphs in Gallant's works draw an elementary school audience, many critics note that the text is best directed toward middle school and, particularly, high school students.

Gallant has written several books on astronomy and other topics for which he has received National Science Teachers Association awards for outstanding science books. His *Memory: How it Works and How to Improve it,* which won the award in 1980, describes the memory process and the chemistry of the brain as well as suggesting activities for improving the memory. In *101 Questions and Answers about the Universe,* Gallant fields actual questions asked by children visiting the Southworth Planetarium in Maine, where he serves as director. Identifying the name of the child and his or her school, Gallant answers such questions as "why is the sky blue?" and "how many stars are there?" The winner of the Children's Book Council's Outstanding Science Trade Book for Children Award in 1987, Gallant's *Rainbows, Mirages, and Sundogs* provides insights on natural atmospheric phenomenon and includes suggestions for experiments as well as tips for observing and photographing natural wonders.

Gallant has also authored biographies for young people including a study of Charles Darwin and a work entitled *Explorers of the Atom,* which includes several biographical essays and provides an overview of the field of physics. In his most recent works, however, Gallant has focused on popular environmental issues, addressing young people's concerns for the future of the earth and humankind. In *The Peopling of Planet Earth,* Gallant discusses the popu-

lation explosion and the rapid growth of cities as well as such results of expansion as famine and epidemics. In *Earth's Vanishing Forests,* he explores the destruction of rain forests, suggesting some causes, ramifications, and methods of preservation. In these and other works, Gallant continues to provide, in the words of one reviewer, "unusual material of a provocative and exciting nature," conveying his fascination with science and prompting his young readers to ask questions and consider a wide variety of answers in their attempts to comprehend the universe.

(See also *Contemporary Literary Criticism,* Vol. 17; *Something about the Author,* Vol. 4; *Contemporary Authors New Revision Series,* Vols. 4, 29; and *Contemporary Authors,* Vols. 5-8, revised edition.)

TITLE COMMENTARY

Exploring the Moon (1955; revised edition as *Exploring the Moon: A Revised Edition of the Science Classic*)

An interesting account of lunar history and exploration by remote control covers theories of origin and the various interpretations of lunar formations we can see through strong telescopes today. Two opposing theories of origin are George Darwin's which maintains that the moon was a big blob of lava that broke from the earth, and Von Weizsacker's, which holds that it is a collection of travelling space particles. This absorbing kind of controversy continues through the discussion of the formation of seas, craters, mountains and seas. An imaginary trip to the moon tops it off.

> *A review of "Exploring the Moon," in* Virginia Kirkus' Service, *Vol. XXIII, No. 18, September 15, 1955, p. 703.*

This is an extremely handsome and worthwhile book. Gallant's text is sensible, authentic, and exciting. [Lowell] Hess' large drawings, many in color, are not only explanatory but also beautiful and striking.

Exploring the Moon relates clearly many of the known facts about the moon. More important, it emphasizes the many mysteries still remaining. And, for once, the trip to the moon is made without aid of rocket ship or space suit. The author merely asks the child to imagine himself there, and that the temperature and atmospheric conditions bother him not. Saves a lot of fuss with space gear.

> *John Lewellen, "Moon and Astronomy," in* Chicago Tribune—Books, *Part 4, November 13, 1955, p. 42.*

[*The following excerpt is from a review of* Exploring the Moon: A Revised Edition of the Science Classic, *published in 1966.*]

Since the publication of the original edition in 1955, considerable new information on the moon has been developed through astronomic and astronautic research. Every page of this revised edition bears evidence of meticulous updating. Outstanding new features are the end papers that present a chronology of events and discoveries relative to the moon and to the earth, and two full-page photographs from the Lick Observatory showing moon craters. The work discusses the various theories of the creation of the moon, the formation of craters; its mountains and seas, and other features; as well as the phenomena of eclipses and tides. Excellent factual reading for children.

> *A review of "Exploring the Moon," in* Science Books: A Quarterly Review, *Vol. 2, No. 4, March, 1967, p. 262.*

Exploring Mars (1956)

A good general description of Mars by an established science writer for young people arranges its information in an orderly manner. After starting with a general description of the planet, the material moves on into the history of its discovery by early astronomers, then to contemporary theories about the canals or channels (Schiaparelli's and Lowell's) and possibilities for life. More general data on Mars' origin, place in the solar system, physical characteristics, future exploration and so forth, follow. There are exact color pictures by Lowell Hess. Very good for those interested and more of a picture book than other studies of Mars have been.

> *A review of "Exploring Mars," in* Virginia Kirkus' Service, *Vol. XXIV, No. 15, August 1, 1956, p. 521.*

This survey of the planet Mars includes most current information and thought about the red planet. Written in straightforward, uncomplicated language, it is a companion to Gallant's **The Moon**. . . . Simpler and less detailed than Branley's *Mars* but more appealing to the average reader. Needs index. Highly recommended. For all libraries.

> *Albert Monheit, in a review of "Exploring Mars," in* Junior Libraries, *Vol. 81, No. 18, October 15, 1956, p. 131.*

[*The following excerpt is from a review of the revised edition published in 1968.*]

[**Exploring Mars** makes] use of Mariner IV information, though it appeared too early to profit from Mariner VI and VII. It is written, I judge, for junior-high or younger students; it describes briefly, though quite adequately, our ideas about the planet. . . . One sentence may force chemistry teachers to take corrective steps in later years: on page 47 is the statement, "Since Mars has a very thin atmosphere, it cannot hold much water vapor." This is incorrect. The possible concentration of water vapor depends on temperature alone; the presence of other gases, unless they react with water like ammonia or hydrogen chloride, has no effect.

> *Harry C. Stubbs, in a review of "Exploring Mars," in* The Horn Book Magazine, *Vol. XLV, No. 6, December, 1969, p. 696.*

Exploring the Universe (1956)

The author of **Exploring the Moon** and **Exploring Mars** takes a look with a wider sweep at the whole of the universe as we know it, and efficiently relays basic information in a way that captures one's interest immediately. The most striking aspect of the book is the colored spreads and diagrams, by Lowell Hess, of the heavens as the ancients thought of them and as we know them today. Yet the real color and excitement lies in the text. Organized chronologically, it comments on the history of astronomical thought from the days when Egyptians used it for political purposes to the dawn of enlightenment with Copernicus and Galileo. Traditional but apt presentation brings the science up to the present, in which the most advanced and controversial theories—for instance of whether the universe is expanding away to nothingness or whether it will eventually contract—are understandably discussed. These, along with profiles of our own planetary system, the stars and the other galaxies, blend to bring on the heady fascination and the more ultimate implications of the subject.

> *A review of "Exploring the Universe," in* Virginia Kirkus' Service, *Vol. XXIV, No. 21, November 1, 1956, p. 806.*

A rapid survey of the universe similar in style and format to the author's **Exploring the Moon** and **Exploring Mars.** Contains less factual information than many standard texts on astronomy, e.g. Zim's *The Stars,* but easier to read and comprehend by the average reader. Gallant's style is entertaining and informal.

> *Albert Monheit, in a review of "Exploring the Universe," in* Junior Libraries, *Vol. 82, No. 4, February 15, 1957, p. 592.*

[*The following excerpts are from reviews of the revised edition published in 1968; the illustrations in both the original edition and revised edition are by Lowell Hess.*]

Revised to conform to post-Sputnik observations, this now includes more precise characterizations of galaxies, specific mention of both Bessel and parallax and Shapley and RR Lyrae, expanded entries on "Visitors from Outer Space" (asteroids, meteorite showers, etc.) and a brief consideration of quasars. Some necessary corrections (e.g. the Mizar as an optical binary) have been made, and there is the about-face suggestion to think of constellations as straight lines rather than mythological figures. Several of the illustrations have been improved, especially photographs of nebulae, although the Constellation Chart has been relegated to the front end papers. Minor style changes contribute to the newer sound.

> *A review of "Exploring the Universe," in* Kirkus Service, *Vol. XXXVI, No. 12, June 15, 1968, p. 653.*

[The first edition] traces the progress of man's knowledge of the Universe from the ancient Chinese up to the present time and explores such topics as the types of stars, novae, meteors, comets, quasars, and the expanding universe. The 1968 revision has been completely revised and updated with some new illustrations. Although very condensed, it still is one of the best and most attractive introductory books on the subject. The new edition has an index, which was absent in the first edition.

> *A review of "Exploring the Universe," in* Science Books: A Quarterly Review, *Vol. 4, No. 2, September, 1968, p. 98.*

Exploring the Universe, tries to get its readers to be critical. It presents the history of astronomy as a struggle with error and dogma. It describes what we know of the universe today as a challenge to find out what's wrong with the picture and to extend human knowledge. It does give a thoughtful reader a good deal of that knowledge.

It also knocks the printed word off its pedestal. What the author describes is not just knowledge, but the process of knowing, the great adventure in which mankind will never run out of challenges. The essence of science, the author says, is "a lot of people trying to ask the right questions, finding and comparing answers, and then being able to give up old ideas when those ideas are shown to be wrong." It's an important attitude for young readers to acquire as they shape their view of the world. This book would help them do it.

> *Robert C. Cowen, "Stellar Attraction: Magnetic Pull," in* The Christian Science Monitor, *November 7, 1968, p. B9.*

Exploring the Weather (1957)

The latest addition to the series of big flat dramatically illustrated picture-texts on science by Roy A. Gallant and [illustrator] Lowell Hess is a clear, succinct, dramatically illustrated essay on the weather. It is fine to have this gifted team working a bit nearer home. Their former explorations were of the Universe, Mars and the Moon, and interesting as those subjects are, a concrete study of "our ocean of air" and "weather in the making" is even more helpful in building up important concepts of the world we live in. Just at present the children of ten or over, who will pore over the vivid explanatory diagrams, are especially anxious for just this sort of information because of sputnik.

Particularly useful are instructions on reading the weather map, and a Beaufort scale with map symbols, speed, description of wind and familiar changes at certain speeds—the action of branches and flags, for instance. The authors have also given a well-selected short list of other fairly simple books on weather published in the last few years. It was wise of them to include George Stewart's novel *Storm,* which would be most stimulating for a bright student of twelve or so. Another that occurs to us is Conrad's *Typhoon* which deeply impressed us long before we could understand the forces that form hurricanes.

> *A review of "Exploring the Weather," in* New York Herald Tribune Book Review, *November 17, 1957, p. 28.*

With the aid of Lowell Hess' excellent diagrams, Roy Gallant concisely presents the fundamentals of meteorology, the science of weather. He explains what makes weather good and bad; why it is difficult, because of little understood influences, to predict it accurately very far ahead, and suggests how exploration of the atmosphere and space will help in forecasting. This introduction for 10-to-14-year-olds is detailed enough to stimulate more than casual interest.

> *Robert K. Plumb, "Earth, Sea and Stars," in* The New York Times Book Review, *November 17, 1957, p. 6.*

[*The following excerpts are from reviews of the revised edition published in 1969.*]

This revised edition of a reputable 1957 title features some minor updating and corrected information—but retains outdated illustrations, provides no significant coverage of interim technological advances, and includes some additional errors. An old-style radiator and a bathtub with legs are still depicted; hardly any space is devoted to the modern computer, hurricane seeding, and weather satellites; and, whereas in the last edition the earth was said to rotate on its axis at 16 miles a minute, in this edition its rotating speed is given as 160 m.p.m. . . . There are better choices on the topic for the age group, among them Schneider's *Everyday Weather and How It Works* (McGraw, rev. ed. 1961) and Ross's more advanced *Weather* (Lothrop, 1965).

> *Ralph J. Folcarelli, in a review of "Exploring the Weather," in* School Library Journal, *Vol. 16, No. 2, October 1969, p. 3820.*

Exploring Chemistry; Exploring the Planets; Exploring the Sun (1958)

[*Exploring the Sun* is] a beautifully packaged job. No youngster (or grown-up, either) can fail to be fascinated by the large, clear, and attractively-colored illustrations [by Lee Ames]. And if the youngster is enticed by these into reading the book, he will be rewarded, for he will find in a few pages an extraordinary wealth of information, from man's early observations of the Sun in primitive temples such as Stonehenge to the recent startling theories of astronomer Fred Hoyle concerning the majestic birth and the catastrophic death-to-come of the star that gives us life.

> *Isaac Asimov, in a review of "Exploring the Sun," in* The Horn Book Magazine, *Vol. XXXIV, No. 5, October, 1958, p. 394.*

Science has grown through the experimentation and speculation of many men who from the dawn of history have searched sky and earth for the truth about the universe. They are the explorers in each of these attractive books, which will appeal particularly to young people who have some knowledge of the subjects treated, and who are asking, "How were these discoveries made?"

In *Exploring the Planets,* young astronomers will find essential facts about the members of the sun's family, and much more. They will learn about the investigations and theories of scientists about such puzzling features as the rings of Saturn, the "red spot" of Jupiter, the "canals" of Mars and the clouds of Venus. What is known is carefully distinguished by the author from what is speculative.

Somewhat more specialized is *Exploring the Sun,* the first half of which is devoted to a history of theories about solar origin and conditions. The balance of the book describes the sun's structure, the source of its energy, its "storms," and its radiations. There is a dramatic final section on "the day the sun goes out."

Exploring Chemistry tells how that science had its beginnings in the control and use of fire by ancient man, in the search of the Greeks for an explanation of what matter was and how it changed, and in the attempts of the alchemists to make gold. Fundamental principles of modern chemistry are then developed through the work of scientists such as Priestley, Lavoisier and Dalton.

These books, which provide both information and inspiration, merit a place on the teenager shelf.

> *Julius Schwartz, "Universal Quest," in* The New York Times Book Review, *Part II, November 2, 1958, p. 16.*

These latest of the author's **"Exploring"** series are, if anything, more informative, better organized, and more spectacularly packaged and illustrated than the previous ones. In *Exploring the Planets,* each planet (including our Earth) is taken up singly and the latest information available on each is presented in a clear and forthright manner. The whole is preceded by an able description of the various theories of the formation of the Solar System. Some of the illustrations [by John Polgreen] are worth framing.

In *Exploring Chemistry,* Gallant abandons astronomy for the first time in the series but maintains his high quality of presentation with enviable ease. Actually, this is Chemistry Past and Future, rather than Chemistry Present. The first two-thirds of the book tells the dramatic story of how our present knowledge of chemistry slowly developed through Greek speculation, alchemical groping, and the experimentation of the early chemists. The last third tells the even more dramatic story of how chemistry may serve to give the world's growing population new food, new water, and new minerals. (pp. 483-84)

> *Isaac Asimov, in a review of "Exploring the Planets" and "Exploring Chemistry," in* The Horn Book Magazine, *Vol. XXXIV, No. 6, December, 1958, pp. 483-84.*

[*Exploring the Sun* and *Exploring the Planets* are from] the "**Exploring**" series—the big, shiny flats, written clearly and interestingly by Roy A. Gallant and illustrated by various artists with sensational, bright-colored pictures. Lee Ames has used diagrams chiefly for the new one on the sun, arranged in an eye-catching way. Half of the text is a brief survey of the steps by which man has come to understand the nature of the sun, the rest is about its atmosphere, its interior and its rays.

The second book on the planets is nearly three times as long, with diagrams and brilliantly colored, imaginary landscapes by John Polgreen. Mr. Gallant, after a general introduction about man's gradual discovery of the solar system, gives an interesting discussion of various theories about its origin. There is a chapter for each of the nine planets as well as one for the moon and asteroids. He appends two very useful charts from Fred L. Whipple's *Earth, Moon and Planets.*

> *Margaret Sherwood Libby, in a review of "Exploring the Sun," "Exploring the Planets," and "The Nine Planets," in* New York Herald Tribune Book Review, *February 1, 1959, p. 7.*

[In *Exploring Chemistry,* the] great stages in the development of chemistry are all delightfully reviewed. From the early technicians of 4000 B.C. and the Greek philosophers, through the alchemists and the earlier and more important chemists to present developments, the reader is fascinatingly led. Current problems, whose solution lies in the future, are also described. The profusion of excellent illustrations [by Lee Ames] illuminate, illustrate, and amplify the text which teaches much sound chemistry incidentally. This is the best book of this kind I have yet seen; one that should be in all school libraries.

> *J. D. Bloom, in a review of "Exploring Chemistry," in* The School Librarian and School Library Review, *Vol. 10, No. 2, July, 1960, p. 173.*

[*The following excerpt is from a review of the revised edition of* Exploring the Planets *published in 1967.*]

The 1958 edition of Gallant's introductory book on the planets has been enjoyed by a great many readers of all ages. This updated version therefore is timely. The book begins with a review of the basics of astronomy and various theories concerning the origin of the Solar System. Then follow a series of chapters, one for each planet, that discuss the principal features, which have been brought up to date by the inclusion of new knowledge obtained from astronomical and astronautical research. Mr. [John] Polgreen has supplied many dramatic and colorful new illustrations, and reproductions of photographs obtained from NASA have been inserted where they are helpful in understanding the accompanying text. There is an adequate index and a useful table of comparative data on the nine planets. Although its format suggests a juvenile book, many adults who lack and desire to acquire an elementary astronomical background will enjoy it. All public and school libraries need this book; those owning the old edition should replace it.

> *A review of "Exploring the Planets," in* Science Books: A Quarterly Review, *Vol. 4, No. 1, May, 1968, p. 19.*

Man's Reach into Space (1959)

Scientists in the fields of aircraft engineering and space medicine are working toward manned space flight. This book describes the progress made to date and experiments being conducted toward this end. After explaining what is already known about how the human body reacts to extremes of atmospheric pressure, temperature, and speed, the author goes on to describe tests and devices for determining effects of stress, noise, confinement, and monotony on human beings. Final section is devoted to supersonic aircraft and problems of designing space ships. Many useful diagrams and illustrations [by Lee J. Ames], although some of the latter are too garish and sensational to appeal to the serious reader. These and the oversize make-up of the book may prejudice older high school students and adults against it, but text is more suitable for them than for younger ages. Timely subject, well presented by an authority in the field. Recommended. (pp. 41-2)

> *Dorothy Schumacher, in a review of "Man's Reach into Space," in* Junior Libraries, *Vol. 85, No. 2, January 15, 1960, pp. 41-2.*

Typical of the author's **"Exploring"** books, this is large, well made, well written, full of information, and generally beautiful. It is longer than the others, and more unusual in that it deals with a new subject—the gaining of knowledge that will help us to send men safely out into space. What can the human body endure in the way of unearthly environments, sudden extreme decelerations, exposure to heat or to low air pressure, or just to endless boredom and enclosure? I have seen no discussion of the human side of space flight, written for *any* age level, that is as interesting and informative as this.

> *Isaac Asimov, in a review of "Man's Reach into Space," in* The Horn Book Magazine, *Vol. XXXVI, No. 2, April, 1960, p. 146.*

Exploring under the Earth: The Story of Geology and Geophysics (1960)

Roy Gallant has successfully synthesized science for eight to eleven year olds (and up) in a succession of books. This latest is the story of geology and geophysics, and covers a range that is perhaps beyond what one might expect. He goes back to the formation of the earth, the atmosphere, the oceans; then on to the development of geology as a science. The new findings of the under-ocean world are given their place; the formation of continents, the facts about earthquakes, about volcanoes, the building of mountains, the significance of magnetism and the poles—all this is brought together in readable, concise form. . . .

> *A review of "Exploring under the Earth," in* Virginia Kirkus' Service, *Vol. XXVIII, No. 22, November 15, 1960, p. 962.*

Reviewing first some of the theories that have been held about the formation of the earth and its atmosphere, and describing the evolution of geology as a science, the author then discusses the ocean floor, the formation of continents and theories of continental change, earthquakes, volcanoes, mountain systems, and magnetism. An index is appended; endpapers—in two double-page spreads—give a time-chart of world history. One paragraph on undersea trenches is printed on a background so dark as to be almost illegible. A good introduction, but not an extensive treatment of any of the areas examined.

> *Zena Sutherland, in a review of "Exploring under the Earth," in* Bulletin of the Center for Children's Books, *Vol. XV, No. 4, December, 1961, p. 59.*

The ABC's of Astronomy: An Illustrated Dictionary (1962)

This book is for would-be amateur astronomers, and it combines a dictionary of the astronomical language and a handbook for those who desire firsthand acquaintance, by naked-eye observation or the use of a small telescope, with the heavens always spread out above us. . . . [*The ABC's of Astronomy*] is really a collaborative work with John Polgreen, whose drawings, diagrams, and selections of astronomical photographs are an essential part of the presentation. . . .

I find [the book] a bit disappointing. The writing is direct, simple, and clear, the illustrations excellent, and the format attractive. As dictionary definitions go, these are pretty good, with a few exceptions ("centrifugal force" is one); the art of definition is a very difficult one, and it is much easier to find fault than to contrive a better definition in as few words. Some of the diagrams and charts are very good. But to the amateur learning how (and how *not*) to get the most out of a small telescope, this book tells little of value, nor does it provide enough sky lore to make naked-eye star study very inviting. Perhaps, as a professional teacher, I have some bias against the scrappy assembly of unsystematized facts presented in a dictionary. But I have seen many such books that were not as good as this one.

Bancroft W. Sitterly, "Astronomy for Laymen," in Science, Vol. 139, No. 3549, January 4, 1963, p. 31.

Rather a potpourri, this book is, in the first half, an astronomical dictionary, with most of the definitions accompanied by clear diagrams that explain what would otherwise be too cryptic for the young reader. The second half is devoted to photographs of astronomical objects, to star maps with directions for use, to interesting tables of astronomic data—even to the Greek alphabet.

On the whole, this book did not please me as much as [Leonard de Vries' *The Book of Telecommunication*], for astronomy has become a comparatively overwritten subject. Yet Gallant's book is so pleasing to the eye that it was difficult even for me to make a fair comparison. (pp. 192-93)

Isaac Asimov, in a review of "The ABC's of Astronomy: An Illustrated Dictionary," in The Horn Book Magazine, Vol. XXXIX, No. 2, April, 1963, pp. 192-93.

The ABC's of Chemistry: An Illustrated Dictionary (1963)

Everything has its place though it is difficult to find one for this book. It will be of only minimum help to those who have not yet had high-school chemistry, because it requires knowledge of specific terminology and language. And for those already studying chemistry, the book offers little extra dimension or freshness of approach to complement the course. The definitions read as though they came from a chemistry text, and this the public schools already provide free of charge. DDT, for example is defined as "An insecticide made from coal tar." Billions of bugs have been silenced by DDT; it and the other chlorinated hydrocarbons have been loudly condemned for silencing the birds of spring, yet DDT and the entire, heavily researched field of insecticides receive six words. Other topics get more—the inert gases get seven full lines and two cross references. The author carefully explains why some gases cannot combine with any other element, apparently unaware that this theory came down with a crash in 1962 when xenon tetrafluoride was created with embarrassing ease.

Henry W. Hubbard, in a review of "The ABC's of Chemistry: An Illustrated Dictionary," in The New York Times Book Review, January 12, 1964, p. 20.

Two rather elaborate dictionaries are on my desk. One is **The ABC's of Chemistry**. . . . This contains the usual definitions that would be expected to be of help to anyone taking a first course in general science; it is clear, concise, and accurate. However, the most useful feature of the book is the numerous tables that are to be found through the body of the list of definitions and in the special section at the end. Under "hardness," for instance, is an excellent table of the hardness of minerals—a much better one, in fact, than is to be found in the usual textbook. The periodic table . . . is an unusually clear and attractive one.

Isaac Asimov, in a review of "The ABC's of Chemistry," in The Horn Book Magazine, Vol. XL, No. 1, February, 1964, p. 80.

Discovering Rocks and Minerals: A Nature and Science Guide to Their Collection and Identification (with Christopher J. Schuberth, 1967)

Children's science books, like most things in modern life, are rifling in on specialties. Not many books come out now talking about anything so broad as "Science Through the Ages," or "A Child's Guide to the Sciences." Instead it's "Magnets and Magnetism," or a whole book on what floats and what doesn't and why, or in-depth tomes on steel, or stargazing, or navigation. This tightening trend to specialization filters through strikingly in this fall's sampling of science books.

Out of a group of 10 fall volumes, no two really zero in on the same subject—and none is very general. Given this continuing turn to specialization the criteria then become: How much do they tell the young reader about their specialities and how well do they tell it? By this yardstick four of the new books stand out; two come off reasonably well; four others fall short.

One of the four best is **Discovering Rocks and Minerals**. . . . It is a comprehensive guide to collecting and identifying rocks and minerals. It also tells how they became what they are. A well-illustrated book full of helpful tables ranging from the family tree to common minerals, to the geological ages, this is an excellent buy for the preteen rock hound.

John C. Waugh, "The Lens Narrows," in The Christian Science Monitor, November 2, 1967, p. B8.

This pretty book is designed for the instruction of amateur collectors of geological objects. It treats in cursory fashion of rocks, minerals, and fossils—where to find specimens and how to collect and catalog them. Keys are included for identification of common rocks and minerals. The work is fleshed out with summary accounts of earth structure, physiographic provinces of the United States, topographic and geologic maps, geochemical dating and geologic time. Bibliographic sections at the end offer guides to geological information agencies in the U.S.A., Mexico, and Central America; geological publications of interest to the collector; special collecting areas; and popular journals on rocks and minerals. At the end is a short glossary of geological terms. . . . The book should be useful as collateral reading in general science or earth science.

A review of "Discovering Rocks and Minerals: A Nature and Science Guide to Their Collection and Identification," in Science Books: A Quarterly Review, Vol. 3, No. 3, December, 1967, p. 216.

A concise, lucid text, supplemented by a wealth of tables, charts, diagrams, maps, and photographs, explains what rocks and minerals are, how to identify them, and where and how to collect them. There is information on the physiographic provinces of the U.S. and on reading topographic and geologic maps, collecting fossils, and telling geologic time. Listings of books, pamphlets, and magazines about rocks, minerals, and fossils are included along with a glossary of geologic terms. An excellent guide for the more than casual beginner or seasoned collector, by a geologist and a well-known writer on scientific subjects. (pp. 587-88)

> *Sally C. Estes, in a review of "Discovering Rocks and Minerals: A Nature and Science Guide to Their Collection and Identification," in* The Booklist and Subscription Books Bulletin, *Vol. 64, No. 10, January 15, 1968, pp. 587-88.*

Man Must Speak: The Story of Language and How We Use It (1969)

Language as a distinctly human phenomenon, in a brisk, bright explication. This begins with a fairly extensive survey of forms of animal communication—courtship patterns, chemical signals, sounds and gestures, stimulus-response behaviors—and the author is careful to distinguish action from "thought"; in fact, an early point, and one returned to strategically, is the error of anthropomorphism (as per Walt Disney *et al.*). Gallant's primary differential: an animal acts not because of thought but in response to an environment; man, on the other hand, has the *habit of speech* built into his biological system. The section on language growth ("From Ugh! to Ungulate"), which summarily traces English on the Indo-European language tree, is quite abbreviated but not overly simplified; the discussion of the development of writing is more extensive (several decipherments) and, ending with a few pages on "Playing with Language" (palindromes, alliteration), leads into some examples of how words color experience (sesquipedalian words, jargon and genteelisms) and how vocabulary (and, implicitly, structure) reflects world views. He does not consider the more subtle aspects of human communication (as in Chase's recent *Danger— Men Talking*) but he does mention the comparative appeals of various mass media. Further, the illustrations are apt (a Yamashiro silk screen reproduction and a dictionary extract listing 34 definitions for the word "fowl" as well as the more expectable hieroglyphs) and the idiom is animated and current. (pp. 1158-59)

> *A review of "Man Must Speak: The Story of Language and How We Use It," in* Kirkus Reviews, *Vol. XXXVII, No. 21, November 1, 1969, pp. 1158-59.*

An excellent overview of linguistic theory, this presents some very accurate, current views of the subject. Just about anything school children of this age should know is enjoyably presented here. While there are several other books that do much the same thing—Pei's *All About Language* (Lippincott, 1954) for instance—Gallant's book is eminently more readable. The sections on playing with language and mass media are particularly good, as is the material on communication among animals. This book and the Bell Telephone film *Alphabet Conspiracy* would make a great package in school media centers.

> *Robert S. Tapply, in a review of "Man Must Speak: The Story of Language and How We Use It," in* Library Journal, *Vol. 95, No. 13, July, 1970, p. 2539.*

Man's Reach for the Stars (1971)

A description of the importance of one of man's major feats, getting to the moon, sets the scene for a well-planned development of some of the questions associated with our progress in exploring space. Case studies for a sequence of events that has led to space travel are presented with emphasis on the adjustments that man has had to make from his customary environment to new extremes imposed by space travel. Skillful blending of current information is apparent. This arrangement seems to have an underlying objective to show the necessity and use of an orderly approach to problems having long-term solutions. The author's choice of problems and answers to consider contributes to the value of the book by helping the reader understand some of the judgments and decisions that have been required. The enthusiasm of a few of the outstanding scientists and administrators of our time is successfully captured in the presentation; this demonstrates to the reader that real people exist to make decisions, to offer new ideas, and to be responsible for leadership in their particular specialties. The reader is left thinking.

> *A review of "Man's Reach for the Stars," in* Science Books: A Quarterly Review, *Vol. 7, No. 4, March, 1972, p. 328.*

The extraordinary information contained in this second glance at the importance of Apollo 11 can best be explained by a look at chapter headings: "The Moon:" many misconceptions corrected; "Higher and Faster:" what happens to humans as they move astronomically; "Torture Chambers:" the agonies of the tests for outer space survival; "Speed, Speed:" how time slows down as the speed of light is approached; "A Home in Space." At this point one is not surprised to read that explorers who journey to the world of outer space may choose not to return. This book is exciting and thought-provoking as it introduces the human changes, physical and psychological, that crowd in upon us as man conquers space travel. The organization of the material could be more systematic and thus eliminate the need to return to earlier chapters to follow the author's thought.

> *Sister Mary E. Rock, in a review of "Man's Reach for the Stars," in* Appraisal: Children's Science Books, *Vol. 5, No. 3, Fall, 1972, p. 19.*

In the large view, this book is well organized and full of interesting facts about man's tolerance to aircraft and spacecraft environments, and the history and prognosis of these technologies. In detail, however, the descriptions are often marred by strained analogies, by simplistic and erroneous science, and by a tendency to wander off the subject. Nevertheless, for interesting reading, this volume is a success and includes unusual material of a provocative and exciting nature. However, the danger of corrupting an uncritical student's repertoire of knowledge is ever present, unnecessary, and unfortunate.

David G. Hoag, in a review of "Man's Reach for the Stars," in Appraisal: Children's Science Books, *Vol. 5, No. 3, Fall, 1972, p. 20.*

Me and My Bones (1971)

If the skull under the skin is not too fearful to examine for its beauty and meaning, this cleverly made book of brief text and many photographs charts a high road to comparative anatomy and evolution. Engaging Cirsten Carle acts as the living counterpart of a child's skeleton in many close-ups and set positions. Other bones come on the scene, from cat and chimpanzee, horse and elephant. The skeleton walks, runs, jumps. The main bones are given their Latin names and diagrammed on the bony specimen, while Cirsten poses obligingly across the page to flesh out our own mineralized frame. Gallant goes pretty far toward cuteness in maintaining the lightheartedness such a *memento mori* seems to need. Apart from a few excesses— "Grownups have up to 32 teeth (for snapping at children with)"—he has made a book of value and delight for fifth-graders and up.

> *Philip Morrison and Phylis Morrison, in a review of "Me and My Bones," in* Scientific American, *Vol. 227, No. 6, December, 1972, p. 112.*

Unlikely as it may seem, this American book about the skeleton is one of the liveliest information books of the season, with matching pictures of attractive Cirsten and a skeleton friend, chapter headings like "The Point of a Pelvis", snappy questions, easy to assimilate text. We not only take in the facts given, but are left wanting to know more.

> *A review of "Me and My Bones," in* The Times Literary Supplement, *No. 3719, June 15, 1973, p. 689.*

Not everyone has a sense of humour, and those who do agree that it varies tremendously from person to person. Even taking that into consideration there is no doubt that this book has been written by someone whose sense of humour is painful in the extreme. His jokes are too pathetic even to appeal to children and his style of writing is irritating. All this might have been forgiven had not illustrations of various bones been shown throughout the pages and, instead of being informed what they were, the reader was asked "Whose ribs are these? Hint: Ever hear of Jumbo?" and then had to turn to the end of the book to find out the answer. The concept behind the book is excellent, to show children a little bit about evolution by comparing their bones with those of various animals, but the writing has taken much appeal away from the excellent photographs and the knowledge which could have been gained.

> *G. L. Hughes, in a review of "Me and My Bones," in* The Junior Bookshelf, *Vol. 37, No. 4, August, 1973, p. 254.*

Charles Darwin: The Making of a Scientist (1972)

[*The following excerpt is from an advance review of* Charles Darwin: The Making of a Scientist.]

Though it offers little that is new, this relaxed and intimate portrait of Darwin the man is a pleasing addition to the abundant biographical literature. Drawing heavily on Darwin's own writings, Gallant traces his intellectual development from reluctant student to amateur naturalist to theoretician and describes the prevailing intellectual climate (science was considered an appropriate avocation for clergymen) which caused better trained men to ignore the evidence of evolution. Darwin's ideas are introduced gradually as he himself developed them: his observations of Galapagos finches provide the occasion for an explanation of evolution; the light and dark-winged moths of Manchester demonstrate survival of the fittest. But the chief value lies in the sharp delineation of personalities, particularly with regard to the uneasy friendship of Darwin and Captain Fitzroy (men who embodied two contrasting aspects of the Victorian temper). The Horizon *Charles Darwin and the Origin of the Species* (1968) better elucidates the Darwinian theory, but Gallant makes the historical Darwin unusually accessible.

> *A review of "Charles Darwin: The Making of a Scientist," in* Kirkus Reviews, *Vol. XXXIX, No. 22, November 15, 1971, p. 1219.*

As the subtitle indicates, the emphasis here is on the process by which Darwin came to his conclusions. About half of the account is devoted to Darwin's early years; the rest to his work on the H.M.S. *Beagle.* The importance of his theories is viewed in light of his times, and Gallant insightfully describes those factors—e.g., the close tie between religion and science; the state of geology and of biology; etc.—that made *The Origin of Species* a cause célèbre. Similar information about the naturalist's life and work is stimulatingly presented in Gregor's *Charles Darwin* (Dutton, 1966) and in *Charles Darwin and the Origin of the Species* (American Heritage, dist. by Harper, 1968), but the lucid account of the growth of Darwin's ideas here justifies purchase of this title where additional material on Darwin or evolution is needed.

> *Brooke Anson, in a review of "Charles Darwin: The Making of a Scientist," in* School Library Journal, *Vol. 18, No. 7, March, 1972, p. 134.*

Are creative geniuses born or made? Even though the pretentious subtitle might lead a potential reader to believe that the author might have some fresh insights on this classic conflict, nowhere in the book is the subject broached in depth. Gallant has essentially written an abbreviated, light biography with substantially the same viewpoint as Sir Gavin de Beer's *Charles Darwin: A Scientific Biography.* Although de Beer is certainly a recognized Darwin scholar, Gallant has apparently not perused more current biographical literature on Darwin. For instance, he continues to perpetuate the myth of Darwin as dull school boy unfit for the position as naturalist aboard the H.M.S. *Beagle* despite evidence to the contrary. The saving feature of Gallant's book is the frequent use of quotes from Darwin's books, letters, and autobiography. Perhaps no young scientist should miss being introduced to the idiom of the 19th-century naturalists; in this vein, Gallant's book will suffice.

A review of "Charles Darwin: The Making of a Scientist," in Science Books: A Quarterly Review, *Vol. 8, No. 1, May, 1972, p. 15.*

Man the Measurer: Our Units of Measure and How They Grew (1972)

Familiar but still productive games such as inventing a personal unit of measure, graphing the results of a series of coin tosses and estimating the number of hairs on a person's head help demonstrate that a standard measurement can be any agreed upon quantity, that the precision of a measurement should be appropriate to its intended use, and that a more precise measurement is not necessarily a more accurate one. Gallant's breezy history shifts a little abruptly from Egypt to England, but he does give many examples of the variety of measurements used by modern scientists—from the tiny fermi to the 93 million miles which constitute one astronomical unit, and the appended tables reveal the complexity and unwieldiness of the British/American weights and measures in contrast to the logic of the metric system. An open-ended, undemanding introduction to the use of measurement as a scientific tool.

A review of "Man the Measurer," in Kirkus Reviews, *Vol. XL, No. 15, August 1, 1972, p. 862.*

I greeted this title with glee, having based my eighth-grade general science course on the measuring concept for a good many years. Actually, the book turned out to have fewer laboratory ideas than I had hoped, though a fair number are to be found in the Things You Can Do sections at the end of each of the three major parts of the book. Any disappointment I might have felt was more than offset by the fine supply of historical and descriptive material. Perhaps one of the most useful parts of the book, to a pro-metric person like myself, is the frightening list of British-American weight and measure units at the end of the book, accompanied by the oh-so-straightforward metric ones. (pp. 71-2)

Harry C. Stubbs, in a review of "Man the Measurer: Our Units of Measure and How They Grew," in The Horn Book Magazine, *Vol. XLIX, No. 1, February, 1973, pp. 71-2.*

This interesting book is intended for eighth graders, but it has value for students both above and below that level. The contents fit neatly into three parts: a selective history of measurement units, measuring, and the metric system. Each section includes several experiments that students can carry out. Mr. Gallant obviously has a command of his subject and can make his ideas clear to his readers. Although he steers clear of some of the subtle problems associated with measurement, the book has value for teachers too: they can get a better feeling for the arbitrary choice of measurement units and the need for simplified standards. Of particular interest is the binary nature of the ancient Egyptian system in which liquid measurement units

double in size: mouthful, jigger, jack, jill, cup, pint, quart, pottle, gallon, pail, peck, bushel, strike, coomb, cask, barrel, hogshead, pipe and tun. The book is free of errors with two very minor exceptions: A pace is given as "heel of one foot to toe of the same foot" instead of heel to heel or toe to toe, and the ruler is not marked as indicated in the text. . . .

A review of "Man the Measurer: Our Units of Measure and How They Grew," in Science Books: A Quarterly Review, *Vol. 8, No. 4, March, 1973, p. 308.*

Explorers of the Atom (1973)

Gallant's brief, efficient historical survey begins refreshingly with a quotation from physicist Alfred Romer: "Do not think for a moment that you know the real atom. The atom is an idea, a theory, a hypothesis. . . . An idea in science, remember, lasts only as long as it is useful." Assuming the tentative nature of scientific investigation and progress he reviews the development of atomic theory from Democritus, especially the chain of discoveries beginning with J. J. Thompson's study of the electron's "puzzling glow" in a vacuum tube and the investigations of "mysterious rays" by Roentgen, Becquerel and Marie Curie, then on to Chadwick and Heisenberg and the "weighing of atoms" leading to the production of radioactive isotopes. Thus prepared, readers can better appreciate both Gallant's discussion of atomic energy from Fermi's early experiments to the promise of fusion reactors and his sober concluding chapter on the dangers of radioactive wastes—none of which are "clean" or unconditionally "safe." Non-mathematical and undemanding but admirably free of hand-waving leaps and misleading simplification, this provides a valuable orientation and a timely warning.

A review of "Explorers of the Atom," in Kirkus Reviews, *Vol. XLII, No. 5, March 1, 1974, p. 254.*

This book is a very pleasant, concise review of man's developing knowledge of the atom, told through the lives of the men and women who made the basic discoveries. The author handles some fairly difficult concepts as well as I have seen them done, with the aid of some excellent illustrations (except for three mysteriously untitled photographs early in the text). I'm particularly pleased that the author makes a point of commenting on some basic features of the way science "works" (the role of serendipity, the importance of publication, confirmation, and the like). Recommended for senior, and possibly junior, high school students.

David E. Newton, in a review of "Explorers of the Atom," in Appraisal: Children's Science Books, *Vol. 7, No. 3, Fall, 1974, p. 23.*

Explorers of the Atom includes a most lucid introduction to what the atom really is, the development of the atomic theory from Democritus to Heisenberg, and a particularly engrossing account of the uses and misuses of atomic energy today. Succinct, clear, full of well-placed explanatory diagrams, this book provides a valuable introduction to the knowledge about atoms. Detailed index.

> *Virginia A. Tashjian, in a review of "Explorers of the Atom," in* Appraisal: Children's Science Books, *Vol. 7, No. 3, Fall, 1974, p. 23.*

Astrology: Sense or Nonsense? (1974)

A responsible, intelligent treatment of astrology, rare enough in adult books, is unprecedented in juveniles. Gallant doesn't hesitate to draw the obvious conclusions from his demonstrations that today's astrology is based on Ptolemy's discredited astronomy and on observed motions of the stars and planets now known to be illusions and that a study of the precession of the equinoxes shows even the dates used to classify a Gemini, Taurus or whatever are incorrect. Yet none of this has the air of a put-down or a polemic, and Gallant tells readers more about signs and houses, the schemes relating planets, gods, days and organs, the history of astrological theory and practice, and the casting of a horoscope (as samples, JFK's birth and death charts) than do the teasingly equivocal or gushingly promotional rip-offs that the subject usually inspires. In addition Gallant introduces a number of provocative side issues such as the speed-of-light factor in calculating influences and the extensive phenomena of biological clocks which are evidence that heavenly bodies do affect our lives after all. Annotated reading list, glossary, and numerous well chosen old prints and diagrams included. (pp. 1015-16)

> *A review of "Astrology: Sense or Nonsense?" in* Kirkus Reviews, *Vol. XLII, No. 18, September 15, 1974, pp. 1015-16.*

Why has astrology gained in popularity and what does it offer are questions central to the author's extensive covering of his topic. Mr. Gallant begins with two conflicting schools of thought within astrology: astrological predictions can be proven by statistics; or astrology involves more than science, and the astrologer possesses secret knowledge. To document these thoughts the author traces astrology from its Babylonian beginnings and the creation of the Zodiac by the early Greeks through the historical, religious, scientific, and philosophical growth of Western civilization to the present. . . . The prose is clear, highly readable, lively, and interesting; illustrated with a variety of black and white charts, photographs, woodcuts and prints. A bibliography of astrology titles, glossary of terms, and index complete the tight organization of the book. The author's point of view is expressed by the last word of the title.

> *Debbie Robinson, in a review of "Astrology: Sense or Nonsense?" in* Appraisal: Children's Science Books, *Vol. 8, No. 2, Spring, 1975, p. 19.*

Gallant's writing abilities are by this time well established, and this book will do nothing to harm that reputation. He provides a thorough and a thoroughly enjoyable introduction to the complex subject of astrology. To my delight, he asks some penetrating questions about what it is that astrology can and cannot do. A fascinating book, although what it is doing in this review publication is not clear, since, as Gallant points out a number of times, astrology is NOT (whatever else it may be) a science.

> *David E. Newton, in a review of "Astrology: Sense or Nonsense?" in* Appraisal: Children's Science Books, *Vol. 8, No. 2, Spring, 1975, p. 20.*

How Life Began: Creation versus Evolution (1975)

It's hard to know how to react to this purportedly impartial review of the creation/evolution controversy. First of all, though Gallant claims that he is not taking sides, and though he does allot considerable if not equal time to biochemist Duane Gish's creationist argument, he doesn't hesitate to give evolutionists the last word (represented by lengthy excerpts from Richard P. Aulie's critique of the Creation Research Society's high-school biology text and from geneticist Theodosius Dobzhansky's more far reaching arguments). He also characterizes the politically powerful CRS as "ultraconservative" and points out that "the vast majority of scientists today regard evolution through natural selection not as theory but as fact." (In fact, Gallant often seems to be playing the creationists' own game, citing the number of advanced degrees and Nobel prizes on his side in answer to their pathetic roster of hydraulic engineers and such.) But even without the pretense of objectivity, doesn't a pro-Darwin argument at this point take his opponents more seriously than their case and status warrants? There's also an Antigravity Society in America—why not a YA book pro and con gravity? The answer of course is that same political power which Gallant notes has been sufficient to change a number of state laws. And it's on political terms that this has to be judged—depending on whether you interpret his "on the other hand" approach as giving in to the pressure or the best way to resist it . . . or maybe simply on your degree of pessimism.

> *A review of "How Life Began: Creation versus Evolution," in* Kirkus Reviews, *Vol. XLIII, No. 21, November 1, 1975, p. 1242.*

Gallant discusses why people tend to create myths as explanations for things they do not know enough about and why "man the myth maker" has throughout the ages needed these myths to explain such things as the origin of the universe. But Gallant does not hide the fact that his own prejudice is for the scientific view, which is constantly producing, according to his presentation, better and truer knowledge about the world. The same attitude is expressed in Gallant's chapters on evolution and opponents to it, where he states that he is going to present both sides of the question (which he does quite well), but where his own bias clearly comes through against the opponents. His final chapter is devoted to the study of life on other planets, which represents for Gallant, the next step forward in the triumph of science over mythical and superstitious beliefs about the universe. My own bias would be in favor of presenting this fascinating subject less as a steady "march toward the present" than as a study in alternative world views. Yet Gallant has done a fine job, and the result is an exciting and thought-provoking book.

Shirley Roe, in a review of "How Life Began: Creation versus Evolution," in Appraisal: Children's Science Books, *Vol. 9, No. 2, Spring, 1976, p. 21.*

The Scopes Trial in 1924 marked the beginning of public awareness of the debate between those who hold the special creation theory of man (as described in the Book of Genesis) and those who hold the evolutionary theory. The trial did not resolve anything, but rather intensified the conflict. The recent increase in publicity on this issue has demonstrated again the need for a clear presentation of the merits and demerits of both sides. Roy Gallant gives such a presentation in **How Life Began.** He does not gloss over the gaps in the current evolutionary theory (such as missing links) nor does he ridicule the opinion of the creationists, although he supports the evolutionists. His account is precise, clear and concise. He discusses the historical development of the problem and the gradual acceptance of evolutionary theory. This book would be very interesting to anyone concerned about this problem. It is written for all levels of readers; the language is nontechnical, but the discussion is not superficial. There are further references. At times, the author does not make clear the possibility of a combination of the two theories, but that is not his purpose. There are few books on this subject that are as easy to follow as this one, and it is highly recommended.

Peter Arvedson, "How Life Began: Creation versus Evolution," in Science Books & Films, *Vol. XII, No. 3, December, 1976, p. 142.*

Beyond Earth: The Search for Extraterrestrial Life (1977)

While there is no concrete evidence that alien life forms exist, Gallant argues that earthlings are not the only intelligent beings in the universe. Chronicling scientific discoveries concerning creation and human evolution, he convincingly hypothesizes that the same natural causes that made life on earth possible can operate anywhere in the universe. The text also includes sci fi speculations about possible alien anatomies and descriptions of communication with other worlds. Though this topic has been treated similarly by other writers—notably Ben Bova, Alvin Silverstein, Thomas Aylesworth, and Sylvia Engdahl—Gallant's study is the most up-to-date and diverse.

Anne C. Raymer, in a review of "Beyond Earth: The Search for Extraterrestrial Life," in School Library Journal, *Vol. 24, No. 3, November, 1977, p. 70.*

Roy Gallant's book naturally interested me very much in view of my forty-odd years as a science fiction fan. It is good, these days, to see the question of extraterrestrial life being discussed soberly and seriously by competent scientists. Dr. Gallant is a little more conservative than I in setting criteria for the shapes and chemistries of possible life, but he does quote with apparent sympathy from some of the old classics of science fiction, such as Stanley Wein-

baum's *A Martian Odyssey* and E. E. Smith's *Galactic Patrol.* He describes in detail some of the suggested techniques for communicating with beings from other worlds; and the various bases for estimating the possible number of life- and intelligence-bearing worlds are well covered. If you have already read Sagan and Shklovsky's *Intelligent Life in the Universe,* the book will add little to your information; but for younger readers who might find the other work too heavy, this one is fine.

Harry C. Stubbs, in a review of "Beyond Earth: The Search for Extraterrestrial Life," in The Horn Book Magazine, *Vol. LIV, No. 2, May, 1978, p. 189.*

Most of this book deals with the essential topics in a scientific estimation of the possibility of life elsewhere: the origin and history of the universe and of stars, the commonness of planets, and the origin and diversification of life. The rest of the book is a consideration of the possibility of contact and of space travel. The technical material is interspersed with selections from early thoughts on the possibility of extraterrestrial life and some science fiction passages. Among the latter is a delightful collection of speculations on forms of extraterrestrial life. This elementary book is written for people with no scientific background, and most should find it easy to follow. It is probably best suited to a juvenile audience, but it should be informative to anyone who has not previously been exposed to scientific inquiry into life elsewhere. Serious errors or misleading statements are relatively few and do not inhibit the flow of major ideas. The illustrations, consisting of black-and-white photographs, line drawings and charts, are helpful. Also useful are an annotated bibliography and a glossary.

James L. Goatley, "Beyond Earth: The Search for Extraterrestrial Life," in Science Books & Films, *Vol. XIV, No. 2, September, 1978, p. 93.*

Fires in the Sky: The Birth and Death of Stars (1978)

History of our knowledge of the nature of stars and their life cycles, emphasizing the sun and giving a few experiments readers can try to make their own solar observations. The development is clear and well planned, showing that Gallant has frequently used and carefully refined the lecture notes on which the book is based. He does oversimplify some points, but this may be necessary to keep it accessible to young readers. Both Franklyn Branley's excellent *Black Holes, White Dwarfs, and Super Stars* (Crowell, 1976), which gives more detail on different kinds of stars, and Isaac Asimov's *Alpha Centauri, the Nearest Star* (Lothrop, 1976), which spends more time on star names and constellations, really need at least a seventh grade background. Gallant provides a solid grounding and avoids making controversial statements that may be proved wrong tomorrow.

Margaret L. Chatham, in a review of "Fires in the Sky: The Birth and Death of Stars," in School Library Journal, *Vol. 25, No. 5, January, 1979, p. 53.*

This book on astronomy is excellent in some aspects and poor in others. It's excellent in its authoritative treatment of many of the astronomic phenomena: supernova, neutron stars, pulsars, black holes, etc. Its attempt to give the young reader some experiments to try in measuring some of the physical properties of the solar system is admirable. Its step-by-step use of arithmetic calculations to give a feeling of method of quantitative astronomy is very good. However, the author curiously converts the earth-sun distance to millimeters in calculating the sun's diameter from its subtended angle and then finally has to convert the result in millimeters back to kilometers. He argues erroneously that if the sun's mass were different, the earth's orbital speed and distance would both have to change for a stable orbit. Early in the book he identifies gases as being "made up of a collection of atoms," and then later in the book recognizes four molecules which are present in air. . . . A section describing nebulae identifies them by their accepted names but does not point out the valuable fact that photographs of each of them are included later on. Reference to these would have been difficult, however, because they lack figure numbers and appear all together in a group of unnumbered pages. In describing stellar luminosities, Pollux is used as an example, but Pollux is missing from the table on the same page listing the luminosities of some nine other stars. There are other problems. However, a special glossary and appendix are excellent, as is the index.

David G. Hoag, in a review of "Fires in the Sky: The Birth and Death of Stars," in Appraisal: Children's Science Books, Vol. 12, No. 2, Spring, 1979, p. 22.

Mr. Gallant's work is historical in nature, and he goes deeply into the reasoning which connects observation with opinion. As a rule his statements are cautiously qualified, but occasionally he states as fact things which are still very dubious. Epsilon Aurigae's invisible companion may actually be, for example, an infrared giant star larger than the orbit of Saturn; but as long ago as 1960 there were at least two other published explanations for the eclipse data, and I doubt very much that at this moment any astronomer would care to risk his reputation with a definite choice among these or even claim that one of them is probably right. A few errors appear on the galleys, which are not merely typographical. The Crab Nebula's width is about 4.2 light years, not 42 (though accompanying data would let the reader catch this slip for himself). Less obvious is the half-life of Rubidium 87, given in one of the appendixes as six million years. It is actually about 10,000 times as long. Even if these mistakes appear in the finished book, it will be well worth reading—a good, clear summary of current astronomical thought.

Harry C. Stubbs, in a review of "Fires in the Sky: The Birth and Death of Stars," in The Horn Book Magazine, Vol. LV, No. 2, April, 1979, p. 214.

Earth's Changing Climate (1978)

Of the many books published recently on this subject, this is by far the best. It is well organized and very clearly written; anecdotes, examples, diagrams and photographs help to make this a lively presentation. Gallant explains the concept of climate change, defines climate and discusses the factors that cause it. He reviews the history of the earth's climate, and the effects of different climates in the past. Final chapters discuss the causes for climate change, the possible climates of the future, and the complex problems of technological climate control. This is aimed at the same age group as Cohen's *What's Happening to our Climate?* (Evans, 1979) and Gilfond's *The New Ice Age* (Watts, 1978). . . . But of the three, this is the clearest and the most appealing. The text is smooth and easy to understand. Subjects are arranged in a logical progression, and different concepts are explained separately within a larger topic. Chapter and topic headings add to the book's clarity. There is a selected reading list, glossary, index and table of contents.

Christine McDonnell, in a review of "Earth's Changing Climate," in Appraisal: Children's Science Books, Vol. 13, No. 1, Winter, 1980, p. 18.

Gallant is one of the premier science writers of our time, and he has done a superb job on the topic of the earth's climate. As usual, he demonstrates a real mastery of nearly every possible aspect of the subject on which he has chosen to write. There is scarcely an aspect of climatology on which he does not appear to be knowledgeable. There are some small errors of fact . . . but these are minor distractions from an otherwise admirable text. The reading level is fairly high, and the book is probably accessible only to junior high students of better-than-average reading abilities or to senior high students.

David E. Newton, in a review of "Earth's Changing Climate," in Appraisal: Children's Science Books, Vol. 13, No. 1, Winter, 1980, p. 18.

A black dwarf star passes through our solar system and disturbs the earth's orbit slightly. How would the passage of this wandering, burned-out star change our lives? What steps would you take to ensure survival? These and other interesting questions are examined in **Earth's Changing Climate.** This book is a readable exploration of the earth's climates: past, present and future. Gallant combines carefully developed examples with basic meteorological and climatological facts to capture the reader's attention. His lucid writing makes a complex topic easy to grasp. His treatment of the unresolved ice age question presents three perspectives to this controversy without forcing the reader to a conclusion. Inadvertent climate modification and direct climate control are carefully considered. These are problems of current and future concern to the general public as well as to scientists and will determine the future lifestyles of all of us. This book is suitable for the general reader and as collateral reading in a survey meteorology course at the college level. Assign **Earth's Changing Climate** to advanced high school students to heighten their interest in geophysical studies.

William S. Irvine, Jr., in a review of "Earth's

Changing Climate," *in* Science Books & Films, *Vol. XV, No. 4, March, 1980, p. 208.*

The Constellations: How They Came to Be (1979)

A welter of myths from all over the world is combined with guidance on what amateur astronomers should look for where with eye, binoculars, or small telescopes in 44 northern hemisphere constellations. Each constellation appears in an area star map which indicates star magnitudes and again in its own diagram with the imaginary figure laid over the stars and at least its two brightest stars named. There is a wealth of information here: more myths than in Limburg's *What's in the Names of Stars and Constellations?* (Coward, 1976), more approachable star guides that in Menzel's *Field Guide to the Stars and Planets* (Houghton, 1964); but it isn't always well digested. The text has choppy spots and there are some discrepancies between text and diagrams. Still, this is an appealing guide, . . . with open format and many black-and-white photos of what those spots and blurs would look like if one had a 200 inch telescope in one's backyard. (pp. 130-31)

> *Margaret L. Chatham, in a review of "The Constellations: How They Came to Be," in* School Library Journal, *Vol. 26, No. 7, March, 1980, pp. 130-31.*

This book by Gallant leaves much to be desired. Although classified as juvenile literature, the reader would have to be at least marginally formal operational in a Piagetian sense of cognitive development to comprehend the space-time relationships, anthropomorphism, and the multicultural stories of mythology offered by the writer. A graphic error is presented on page 15 of the book. The author has attempted to depict the reason for our seasons on Earth and illustrates this phenomenon with a diagram that is scientifically incorrect. Gallant refers to the Earth's obliquity (a formal concept unto itself) as being the primary cause of our seasons. The lower portion of the diagram tilts the Earth inaccurately to illustrate the summer and winter solstices. On June 22, the Northern Hemisphere should be angled toward the Sun, not away from it. During the winter, our inclination is just the opposite. In addition, the upper portion of the drawing portrays the Sun's rays originating from the center of the picture. The bottom sketch alters this perspective so that the luminescence radiates from the sides. This permutation tends to conceptually confuse the diagram even further. Whenever the author uses an astronomical term in the text that he deems to require additional clarification, he refers the reader to the glossary. The problem here is that the glossary appears not to be edited or modified to enable the neophyte astronomer to comprehend it. For example, the author mentions doublestars in his writing. Gallant's glossary defines the physical pairing as: "Also called 'binary stars;' two stars held in gravitational association with each other and revolving around a common center of mass." This certainly is a higher-order answer for a person with limited, if any, background on the subject. Gallant also launches headlong into a mythological explanation for the origins of constellations without any reference to the properties, stature, and rank of the specific gods and goddesses. Un-

less one is familiar with Greek and Roman mythology, the legends unfurled by the author hold limited value. A prefatory explanation would certainly be in order at this juncture. A chart of the deities is presented on page 182 albeit out of sequence with its own utility. The diagram on page 47 that orients the stargazer toward many noteworthy constellations by extending lines through the Big Dipper is definitely beneficial and advantageous. However, the major star charts in the text lack lines of right ascension and declination which are the guidelines, the "longitude and latitude," for navigation in the heavens. In short, the book has several major deficiencies. If used as a mythological reference *The Constellations: How They Came To Be* could be a useful tool. (pp. 23-4)

> *James E. Palmer, in a review of "The Constellations: How They Came To Be," in* Appraisal: Children's Science Books, *Vol. 13, No. 3, Fall, 1980, pp. 23-4.*

There is a mysterious drama in the night sky that has fascinated people since the first sentient beings turned their eyes skyward. For some inexplicable reason, the ancients populated the sky with their heroes, divinities, animals and artifacts. What we must realize is that they did not see the figures in the sky—rather they dedicated areas of the sky to those creatures. However, we are a literal society and if someone points out a lion in the sky, we expect to find every star fitting a strategic part of the lion's anatomy. This obviously cannot be so. Thus we have difficulty associating the individual stars with a constellation figure. In *The Constellations,* Gallant is aware of this feature. To set the stage for the description and the constellation stories, he provides the historical background of the constellations. He then introduces them and outlines the creature it is supposed to represent. To provide orientation, the author also includes quarterly star maps drawn as a mercator projection. A map of the polar sky is also provided. One meritorious feature of the book is that the author has carefully researched the constellation stories and has included some little known and obscure ones. The Indian legends are particularly well presented. *The Constellations* is well written and represents one more popular guide to the stars suitable for the general public and high school students.

> *I. M. Levitt, in a review of "The Constellations: How They Came to Be," in* Science Books & Films, *Vol. 16, No. 2, November, 1980, p. 71.*

Memory: How It Works and How to Improve It (1980)

[The author] not only covers the memory question from a structural and chemical viewpoint but dwells at some length on the analogies between the brain and the computer. The field is still open, of course; as with gravity, we do not know what memory fundamentally is or why it works. But the author gives an excellent description of the observed behaviors, similarities, and differences among the various kinds of memory, suggests where the problems still lie, describes nicely some of the experimental work in the field and the reasoning which has followed from it, and finishes the book with what appears to be some practical exercises for improving one's memory. I found the book both interesting and informative—although I'll have to read it again, probably several times, before all of its essence is properly in *my* memory. Index.

> *Harry C. Stubbs, in a review of "Memory: How It Works and How to Improve It," in* The Horn Book Magazine, *Vol. LVI, No. 6, December, 1980, p. 670.*

This short book contains a potpourri of information. Following a brief discussion of some early memory systems, Gallant mentions some of the pioneering work relating brain function to memory (e.g., Lashley and Penfield). Memory is said to consist of sensory information storage, short-term memory, and long-term memory in which encoding, rehearsal and retrieval are critical processes. Implications of the research on "split-brains" (e.g., Sperry; Gazzaniga) are discussed in one chapter, and another chapter outlines some basic facts about digital computers and how they have influenced the conceptualization of human memory. A final section covers several suggestions on how to improve one's memory, including the methods of chunking, loci, rhyming, imagery and association. In general, the material is accurate and the writing style is adequate, but not scintillating. This book might be useful as a cursory introduction for the general reader, but Kenneth L. Higbee's *Your Memory: How It Works And How To Improve It* (Englewood Cliffs, NJ: Prentice-Hall, 1977) is preferred. The latter is more comprehensive, more closely related to the appropriate empirical evidence, and almost as easy to read.

> *Charles L. Brewer, in a review of "Memory: How It Works and How to Improve It," in* Science Books & Films, *Vol. 16, No. 3, January-February, 1981, p. 119.*

Roy Gallant almost always delivers more than he promises. His books on science for children provide benchmarks for the rest of us in science writing in the clarity, accuracy, and motivation they embody. This book is no less admirable than its many predecessors in that respect. Gallant reviews just about everything that is known or suspected about human and machine memory. His suggestions for student activities along the way (although somewhat modest in number) are likely to motivate students and help them understand concepts more completely.

> *David E. Newton, in a review of "Memory: How It Works and How to Improve It," in* Appraisal: Science Books for Young People, *Vol. 14, No. 2, Spring, 1981, p. 17.*

National Geographic Picture Atlas of Our Universe (1980)

Fantastic! Our whole family flipped over this book and the "Our Universe Space Kit" that came with it. The book is lavishly illustrated with the splendid color photographs, paintings, and diagrams one expects from the National Geographic Society. It should serve from a youngsters' flipbook to a coffee-table showpiece, with lots of good reading for those in between. Content is heavy on the solar system, with an up-to-date accent on space exploration, but lean on the rest of the universe. The space kit includes an LP stereo record with an exciting range of space-related sounds. The kit also contains a star and constellation finder of very good quality. Finally, there is a "Space Scope," a realistic telescope kit you assemble yourself that is really a filmstrip viewer. Vivid fields of view on six strips illustrate stars, moon phases, views of Earth from space, space fantasies, a voyage into space, and the evolution of the universe. The book and kit have been done with outstanding skill and imagination. They will make users enthusiastic partners in the amazing scientific adventures of our time.

> *Arthur A. Hoag, in a review of "National Geographic Picture Atlas of Our Universe," in* Science Books & Films, *Vol. 17, No. 2, November-December, 1981, p. 92.*

The word "atlas" hardly describes the exciting quality of this blend of fine science writing and superb graphics. The latter—all in color—dominate the book: space photos, planetscapes by Pesek, planet maps by Jay Inge, and other art by well-known science fiction illustrator Michael Whelan, space artist Ron Miller, and others. The text in no way fails the art; Mr. Gallant has done an outstanding job of covering a mind-bogglingly vast subject. Although there is not as much specific detail as in Patrick Moore's *The Rand McNally New Concise Atlas of the Universe* (Rand McNally, 1978 . . .), the format here is more open, colorful, and attractive, and the text has more narrative drive and flow. *Our Universe* occupies a middle ground in difficulty and in style between *The New Challenge of the Stars* by Patrick Moore and David Hardy (Rand McNally, 1978) and Moore's *Atlas of the Universe,* having the factual approach of the latter and the visual and imaginative impact of the former, plus its own unique qualities. It also reads surprisingly fast for its size. Besides an index, there are a list of space age highlights, a glossary, a selected list of planetariums, observatories, and space or science museums, and an explanation of measurements used in astronomy. A vinyl disc, "Space Sounds," is also included in a separate pocket. This book will be an outstanding addition to any astronomy collection, grade school through adult; very highly recommended. (pp. 24-5)

> *Daphne Ann Hamilton, in a review of "National Geographic Picture Atlas of Our Universe," in* Appraisal: Science Books for Young People, *Vol. 15, No. 3, Fall, 1982, pp. 24-5.*

As usual with the National Geographic publications, this is a beautifully illustrated volume. The text is just about as good. Inevitably, it became slightly dated during the process of manufacture—we now know that Saturn's moon Titan is slightly smaller than Jupiter's Ganymede, and some forty degrees Celsius colder at the surface than the estimate given here; but this is part of the game, which should bother nobody and probably gladdens the hearts of anti-scientists who like to gloat over the constantly changing "facts" of "establishment" science.

The suggested extra-terrestrial life forms are interesting and amusing, though a hard-line science fiction enthusiast would criticize some of them. The Titanian stove-belly doesn't seem to have enough intake capacity for either ice or methane—the latter is at rather low concentration in the atmosphere—to permit reaction rates high enough for flame (unless it stores over long periods and fires up only occasionally), and it seems unlikely that even skate-shaped feet would let the European being apply pressure enough to make ice slippery at that satellite's gravity and temperature. However, it's thought-provoking and fun.

> *Harry C. Stubbs, in a review of "National Geographic Picture Atlas of Our Universe," in* Appraisal: Science Books for Young People, *Vol. 15, No. 3, Fall, 1982, p. 25.*

The Planets: Exploring the Solar System   (1982)

It is a most propitious time, now that the exploration of the solar system by space probes is at an apparent lull, to bring forth a book for young people that describes our current understandings of the many diverse objects found in our solar system. *The Planets: Exploring the Solar System* does, in a somewhat satisfactory way, bring together the wealth of new observational information and the current physical interpretations deduced from all these data. After a brief historical introduction relating primarily to the origin and age of the solar system, Gallant discusses the sun, its energy production and its structure; the inner planets of the system, including the moon; and the asteroids and meteoroids. He also describes the giant outer planets, Pluto, and finally, the comets of our planetary system. The book concludes with a valuable glossary. There are unfortunately a number of places throughout the book where Gallant's interpretations would be better considered as current high speculation. All in all, after reading this book, young readers would be able to have a fairly sound understanding of how and what we have learned about much of the solar system.

> *A. M. Heiser, in a review of "The Planets: Exploring the Solar System," in* Science Books & Films, *Vol. 18, No. 2, November-December, 1982, p. 90.*

A clearly written, information packed, comprehensive book on our solar system for older readers. More than the planets are described in detail: moving in logical order from the sun to Pluto, Gallant discusses the theories of formation of this solar system, the sun itself, planets, asteroids, meteors and comets. Each chapter on the planets is introduced with a page of statistical information—size, speed of rotation and revolution, number of moons, mythological name reference, etc. The numerous fine photographs, artists' drawings, and diagrams are well integrated into the text.

This is for an older reader than Branley's *Nine Planets* (Crowell, rev. 1978) and McGowen's *Album of Astronomy* (Rand McNally, 1979), and includes more up-to-date information than those titles (it includes the results of the 1981 Voyager probes).

> *Arlene Bernstein, in a review of "The Planets: Exploring the Solar System," in* Appraisal:

Science Books for Young People, *Vol. 16, No. 1, Winter, 1983, p. 25.*

The Planets gives a marvellous overview of the major bodies in our solar system: our sun, planets, moons, asteroids, and comets. If you are looking for one, authoritative source which contains all the latest information on our solar system, including an up-to-date moon count, this is the book, It even encompasses the Voyager II flyby of Saturn. The text is very concise, covering the entire solar system in about 175 pages. Mr. Gallant has masterfully distilled gobs of data into an easily assimilated and very accurate synthesis of our present knowledge of the solar system.

My criticisms of the book are relatively minor. There are a few typos; for example, *plane* is misspelled *plain* on page 135 and *wispy* is *whispy* on page 127. The right and left designations on the caption for a sketch on page 40 are reversed. The artist's conception of Uranus on page 134 should be rotated counter-clockwise about 90° to be more realistic in terms of an earth-based observer. Further, the tilt in Uranus' axis (angle between the rotational and orbital planes) is 98°, not 80° as stated on page 133. Better editing could have cleaned up some of these minor errors.

Since Mr. Gallant was obviously restricted in the amount of material he could present in his book, he had to pick and choose from among many theories and interesting astronomical details. For the most part, I agree with his judgements. In the near future when the data from the Voyagers have been more thoroughly analyzed and interpretations tested in earth-based laboratories, better theories will evolve. However, for today, Mr. Gallant's interpretations are sound and are a good starting point for young readers. Teachers will find the book one of the best resources presently available on the solar system. An appendix with metric conversion factors, an index, and a glossary are included. Other features such as charts summarizing basic statistics on all the planets, special sections on temperature scales and the Voyager spacecraft, and historical highlights of major astronomical discoveries add to the value of the book. (pp. 25-6)

> *Martha T. Kane, in a review of "The Planets: Exploring the Solar System," in* Appraisal: Science Books for Young People, *Vol. 16, No. 1, Winter, 1983, pp. 25-6.*

Roy Gallant, one of the deans of American science writing for children, has written an impressive guide to our solar system, using the latest information from the Voyager spacecraft to give up-to-date views of the planets. This book's accuracy and descriptive qualities will make it a standard children's work on the planets until major new discoveries are made. Gallant follows a logical sequence of topics. The chapters refer to each other, maintaining a good sense of overall perspective, but hampering those students who are writing short reports about individual planets. They read like lectures given at a planetarium show—accessible language, popular style, clear explanations. Illustrations are primarily black-and-white photos, mainly from NASA space missions. More diagrams would help clarify the text. With the exception of the exciting findings of Voyager 2 about Saturn's rings, the same information is given with much more colorful and effective illustrations in **The National Geographic Picture Atlas of Our Universe,** for which Gallant wrote the text. Gallant's previous book **Exploring the Planets** is now out of date. **The Planets** requires the reader to understand basic science concepts such as the basic states of matter (solid, liquid, gas) and chemical reactions.

> *Jonathan R. Betz-Zall, in a review of "The Planets: Exploring the Solar System," in* School Library Journal, *Vol. 29, No. 6, February, 1983, p. 88.*

Once around the Galaxy   (1983)

Gallant assembles much material available elsewhere into a convenient volume. His concise history of astronomy explains the nature of the Milky Way along with the people and the methods that assembled our knowledge of our galaxy. By tracing the development of theories concerning the heavens from the heliocentric/geocentric debate through the discovery that our galaxy is only one in a universe of countless galaxies, Gallant describes how scientists' understanding of the universe has changed over the years and provides a clear description of current astronomical thinking. The great names—Aristotle, Copernicus, Kepler, Galileo and Newton—appear here, as do other, less celebrated but influential thinkers, such as Eratosthenes and Hipparchus, who, in the second and third centuries B.C., measured with amazing accuracy the sizes of the Earth and moon, respectively. Wayward theories, such as Ptolemy's epicycles, are included and demonstrate that bad ideas can explain puzzles but are always subject to revision and replacement by more accurate work. Clear black-and-white photos and diagrams support the readable text, as do a thorough glossary and index. A striking cover photo of the Great Nebula in Orion should attract browsers.

> *Jeffrey A. French, in a review of "Once Around the Galaxy," in* School Library Journal, *Vol. 30, No. 7, March, 1984, p. 172.*

This is a first-class addition to any astronomy collection. According to the author, it is based on a course in "the dynamics of the galaxy within a historical context"—in less intimidating terms, it is about the structure of the galaxy and how we found out about it. The book is therefore a brief history of astronomy, albeit from a special viewpoint, as well as a description of galaxies, especially the Milky Way.

The text has a fine flow to it and leads the reader smoothly into increasingly complex views of the universe. Explanations are clear and succinct, and the organization is outstanding. Illustrations are attractive and perfectly integrated with the text; in fact, the format as a whole is a perfect complement to the outstanding writing. It should draw both the beginner and the more experienced reader in the field. An excellent glossary and an index are included. This is highly recommended for all children's and young adults' collections.

> *Daphne Ann Hamilton, in a review of "Once*

Around the Galaxy," in Appraisal: Science Books for Young People, *Vol. 17, No. 2, Spring-Summer, 1984, p. 21.*

This is a book which is remarkable for its clarity. Explanations actually explain rather than obscure, and the text has a smooth, inviting flow to it. For the interested high school student, this book will provide a great deal of astronomical information and understanding, with a minimum of reader struggle and effort. It should definitely be made available to high school students and others of similar reading ability.

The reader soon realizes that this book is quite "meaty." It presents a great deal of information in a highly readable form, but it requires some concentration and effort on the part of the reader. The author does not waste the reader's time.

Overall, this is a high-quality presentation of some of the history of astronomy and astronomical thinking. Beyond that, the author presents some of the current thinking about cosmology, and suggests the probable course of some future research.

Unfortunately, the book is occasionally weak when it attempts to deal with quantitative and geometric concepts. On page 10, for example, the geometry required to understand how Eratosthenes determined the size of the earth is not at all clear from the diagram. Apparently the artist had not the slightest idea of how to present the most important geometric features, so the angle at the center of the earth is not even included. The naive student simply cannot get a clear and complete explanation from the diagram.

A diagram on page 31 does not seem to clarify the associated text, and it should be redrawn because the concept is important. On page 36, the author uses "a giant powder puff" as an analogy to help describe the shape of our galaxy. I had few students who found that analogy helpful, primarily because they were not familiar with powder puffs.

Page 38 displays two diagrams which should supplement each other to clarify the concept of parallax. Unfortunately, the bottom diagram does not continue in the same orientation as the top one, and this weakens the explanatory effects of both. Confusion is compounded on page 39, where ambiguous reference is made to "our circle" and "the circle."

Although there are minor, irritating editorial oversights, such as a few unclear and inadequate diagrams, and some pages which are not numbered, the book is vastly superior to many of the others available on the same topics. It is too bad that the author did not include a bibliography, because some students will be motivated to read further. (pp. 21-2)

> *Clarence C. Truesdell, in a review of "Once Around the Galaxy," in* Appraisal: Science Books for Young People, *Vol. 17, No. 2, Spring-Summer, 1984, pp. 21-2.*

101 Questions and Answers about the Universe (1984)

This miscellaneous information about astronomy and space exploration answers questions that children have asked at the Southworth Planetarium in Maine. The question and answer format leads to repetition on some subjects and gaps in others. It is especially annoying when answers are incomplete. For example, the answer to "Where do the stars go during the day?" correctly says they don't go anywhere, but the fact that the light scattering by the atmosphere hides them during the day isn't mentioned until 52 questions later. There are some cross references between questions, but not always the most relevant ones. The scattering of illustrations range from sharp black-and-white photographs to a diagram of relative sizes of stars that is badly out of scale. This book is not very useful for answering the questions kids ask most often in libraries ("Where are the quickest answers to these questions my teacher gave me?"). Yet it may be of some interest as a browsing book for odd tidbits such as a theory about why the inner planets are smaller than the outer ones or explanations other sources may omit as obvious, such as why a balloon can't float up to the moon.

> *Margaret L. Chatham, in a review of "101 Questions and Answers about the Universe," in* School Library Journal, *Vol. 31, No. 6, February, 1985, p. 84.*

Roy Gallant applies himself in ***101 Questions and Answers about the Universe,*** to demystifying the secrets overhead, in the heavens. As director of the Southworth Planetarium in Maine, Gallant explains, he has been asked every question in the book "one or more times by elementary school groups."

Doubtless this experience accounts for the refinement of his answers to such questions as: "Why is the sky blue?" (because the atmosphere scatters the sun's blue light most of all); "What planets have the biggest moons?" (Jupiter, Saturn and Neptune); and "What makes the stars twinkle?" (the movement of air currents in the atmosphere). My hunch is that many parents and teachers, as well as youngsters, will find their curiosity sated by Gallant's clearly—and deftly—written explanations.

It is less certain, I regret to say, whether they will have their imaginations challenged in the process. My concern is that Gallant's answers are so refined and close-ended that they do not encourage the reader to contemplate the subtleties or uncertainties of speculative questions, such as "How was earth made?" or "What's infinity, and how big is it?" Because of this, I fear, Gallant's otherwise excellent book is likely to invite the unwarranted impression among many of his younger readers that science has all the answers. (p. 19)

> *Michael Guillen, "Adventures for Young Scientists," in* Book World—The Washington Post, *May 12, 1985, pp. 13, 19.*

The best possible childrens' science book, it seems to me, is one that answers questions or covers topics that are of great interest to children, and is written by someone who can supply the answers with great skill and accuracy. This is such a book.

The "101 Questions . . . " are actual questions posed repeatedly by young visitors to the Southworth Planetarium at the University of Southern Maine. They are solid, basic, important questions.

The author of the book is the director of the planetarium, who knows both his subject and how to talk to children. His answers are impeccable, as are the helpful diagrams found among the many excellent photographic illustrations.

This book should be well received by a wide range of young people who want to know more about the universe, space, and astronomy.

> *Norman F. Smith, in a review of "101 Questions and Answers about the Universe," in* Appraisal: Science Books for Young People, *Vol. 18, No. 3, Summer, 1985, p. 19.*

This question-and-answer book contains a tremendous amount of accurate astronomic information well illustrated with a diversity of black-and-white photographs and line drawings. Unfortunately, the question-and-answer format works poorly here. One problem is unevenness. Selection of questions actually asked at a planetarium results in questions of vastly different scope and importance. (What's a supernova and a nova? Why did Pluto cross Neptune's orbit? Can earth have many explosions like the sun? Is there a difference between astronomy and astrology?) An even greater problem is organization. Some subjects (such as the sun) may be splintered into 10 or 11 questions, while other topics with ramifications may be compressed into one (supernovae and neutron stars). The index is helpful but incomplete as is the cross-referencing between questions. The best description of Io is indexed, but another description with a photograph of this interesting Jovian satellite is neither indexed nor cross-referenced. Although the reader can understand the sentences one by one, and terms are defined (albeit sometimes after they are used), new concepts are introduced too quickly for novices. Still, the book piques interest and is informative for young readers with prior knowledge. One diagram, claiming to show relative star sizes by using our sun and planets as the scale of distance, fails for lack of proportion. Certain concepts are handled vividly and imaginatively. A village is photographed at dusk, showing street lights winding up a hill, as well as close and distant lighted windows. The same scene at night showing the formation of lights of greater and lesser magnitude becomes a metaphor for the flattened, two-dimensional constellations seen by humans throughout time. Editing would have helped the occasional, poor sentence structure that sometimes results from an attempt to include too much detail in a limited space. I commend the author for acknowledging, by name and school, the students who submitted the questions.

> *Joanne D. Denko, in a review of "101 Questions and Answers about the Universe," in* Science Books & Films, *Vol. 21, No. 2, November-December, 1985, p. 86.*

Fossils; The Ice Ages   (1985)

Two useful additions to library collections. Gallant explains what **Fossils** are, how they are formed and their importance to science. He also includes encouragement for beginning collectors by furnishing sources of information about collecting, safety tips in the field, care of fossils, labeling instructions and advice on laws and regulations concerning fossil and rock collecting on public lands. This information plus the book's readability make it more useful than *Rocks and Fossils* (EDC, 1983) by Cork and Bramwell and a good complement to Frank Rhodes' *Fossils* (Western, 1962), which is helpful for identification. Unfortunately, some of the black-and-white photographs are too dark to show details clearly. **Ice Ages** is a straightforward account of how and why they occur and what geological changes are made by the movement of glaciers. *The Story of the Ice Age* (Harper, 1956) by Gerald Ames and Rose Wyler complements this book because it concentrates on early studies done by Agassiz and Charpentier on glacier trails. One error appears in the Gallant book: the caption beneath a photograph of the Yosemite Valley states that the floor of the valley "lies buried beneath up to 1,800 feet of ice," yet the text on the next page says that the valley is under "1,800 feet of clay and sand." Diagrams rather than photographs illustrate the land formations created by moving glaciers, and they are not totally clear, but otherwise, this is a lucid account of ices ages. Not only are these books informative reading, but they will encourage students to read and explore these subjects further.

> *Cynthia M. Sturgis, in a review of "Fossils" and "The Ice Ages," in* School Library Journal, *Vol. 32, No. 1, September, 1985, p. 132.*

Almost anything a junior high student might want to know about glaciation is presented concisely in [**The Ice Ages,** an] attractive illustrated, smoothly written short book. The author gives immediacy to what usually seems a distant subject by describing the "Little Ice Age" that chilled Europe from about 1400 to 1850. Photos of mountain glaciers, too, convey the message that massive ice is very much a part of our world today, and only small drops in temperature could—indeed, probably will—produce another ice age in the distant future. The possible causes of major glacial periods are discussed, along with the many geological reminders of the continental glacier that can be seen in this country. Good features are a brief description of methods of dating; a section of U.S. National Parks where glaciers may be visited; and a glossary.

I feel the book should have included a more detailed explanation of the effect of the last ice age in temporarily joining Asia and North America, which made possible the first migration of human beings to this continent. By omitting the Bering land bridge, moreover, the global map showing the peak of glaciation around 18,000 years ago could be confusing to a young reader.

Gallant's writing is admirably clear, lively, and varied. The book definitely belongs on school and library shelves, and should make interesting casual reading for a young person with a scientific bent.

> *Elsa Marston, in a review of "The Ice Ages," in* Voice of Youth Advocates, *Vol. 8, No. 4, October, 1985, p. 274.*

Fossils concentrates not on the plants and animals preserved in fossil remains but on the fossils' importance to geologic study. The author discusses the formation of different types of sedimentary rock and thus of different types of fossils, then describes the use of fossils in relative dating of rock formations. A section on "The Ages of the Earth" summarizes geologic eras and the fossils typical to each. Short chapters discuss starting a personal fossil collection, early fossil hunters, and the Dinosaur National Monument. Important terms are highlighted in the text and defined in a glossary; an index is also provided.

Unfortunately, the reader may be sufficiently confused by the first three pages to give up on the rest of the book. Two typographical errors on the first page—a misprint in a date and an unintelligible phrase—make a correct picture caption on the third page appear wrong. In a later chapter, a photograph cited directly in the text is misplaced. These difficulties aside, **Fossils** may be a useful companion to books on dinosaurs and early animals, because of its stress on the geologic side of paleontology.

> *Margaret Miles, in a review of "Fossils," in* Voice of Youth Advocates, *Vol. 8, No. 4, October, 1985, p. 274.*

As the author says [in **Fossils**], his main interest "has been to explore what fossils are, how they were formed, and their importance to science." Had he concentrated here on these particular interests, the product might have been better. However, this book's excursions into sedimentology, stratigraphy, radiometric dating, and plate tectonics results in an overall superficial treatment. Contrary to statements in the text, fossils do not have to be 10,000 years old; sedimentary rocks are not necessarily "soft and crumbly" and made of "bits and pieces of other kinds of rock"; organisms without hard parts may be preserved as fossils; chalk is not a synonym of gypsum; and geologic maps do not necessarily show "the slope of the land." These oversights are not likely to be perceived by the young readers for whom the book is intended, less so because of the engaging and stylish writing in which they are couched. However, even beginners will find at least a third of the illustrations so muddy as to be unintelligible.

> *Claude Albritton, in a review of "Fossils," in* Science Books & Films, *Vol. 21, No. 4, March-April, 1986, p. 214.*

The author's main aim—to examine the nature, origin, and scientific importance of fossils—is largely realized [in **Fossils**] as well as presented in an interesting and intelligible fashion. Illustrations generally show what they are supposed to show, and although some of the photographs are a bit dark, they will probably deliver the appropriate message to the interested reader. The book includes a number of defects that could have been avoided. In addition to errors of fact, as listed by the first reviewer, interpretations are presented in the same language as fact, and the untrained reader will not be able to distinguish between the two categories. Some interpretations, such as the implication that preservation of footprints required hundreds of years, do not reflect the evidence. Each footprint layer was probably impressed, dried, and covered within a year at most and perhaps as quickly as a few days following a downpour. Nor is the frequent reference to seas drying up acceptable. In most cases, the withdrawal of continental seas is due more to tectonic uplift than to climatic change. Omission of these details causes a loss not only of accuracy but also of some of the drama intrinsic to the story. To have included these details would have lengthened the text only a little. In short, however, I feel I can recommend this book despite its errors and deficiencies.

> *Nicholas Hotton III, in a review of "Fossils,"* in Science Books & Films, *Vol. 21, No. 4, March-April, 1986, p. 214.*

Lost Cities (1985)

The rediscoveries of five ancient cities—Crete, Mycenae, Troy, Pompeii and Chichen Itza—are highlighted in this outstanding introduction to archaeology. Gallant's emphasis is on the various information and methods used by the archaeologists to pinpoint the sites, rather than an attempt to explain why the civilizations disappeared or to provide technical information on the mechanics of a dig. The book is visually appealing with bold type, clear maps and high quality black-and-white photographs and reproductions. An objective, well-researched overview which brings alive the romance and serendipity of archaeology.

> *Marguerite F. Raybould, in a review of "Lost Cities,"* in School Library Journal, *Vol. 32, No. 1, September, 1985, p. 132.*

Private Lives of the Stars (1986)

In reasonably simple, readable language, the author explains the most generally accepted theories about the universe, the stars, and many of its other components. Differences among various classes of stars as well as the reasons for the differences are elucidated. Black holes may be old hat to the astronomy buff, but few readers will have previously learned about "goblins". This volume presents what should be a valuable updating of theories and information about astronomy.

> *Elliot H. Blaustein, in a review of "Private Lives of the Stars,"* in Children's Book Review Service, *Vol. 15, No. 1, September, 1986, p. 8.*

The amount of material covered here is impressive, from scientific explanations of the Big Bang theory to detailed descriptions of different kinds of stars, their origin, development, and eventual demise. The style is somewhat uneven. At his best Gallant is straightforward and lucid, as in his very good sections on dwarf and neutron stars, but sometimes he digresses into wordy historical background, analogies, or comments, and these obscure his points. One does sense, however, that such peregrinations stem from his enthusiasm, which happily he manages to communi-

cate to the reader. An extensive glossary buttresses the information in the text. . . . (pp. 47-8)

> *Betsy Hearne, in a review of "Private Lives of Stars,"* in Bulletin of the Center for Children's Books, *Vol. 40, No. 3, November, 1986, pp. 47-8.*

Behind this catchy title are descriptions of the many different types of stars in the universe, including our sun. Each type is represented by a description of the most important member stars or star-groups. In addition to describing stars from dwarfs to super-giants, Gallant extends the discussion to nebulae, variable stars, novae, pulsars, and black holes. *Private Lives* . . . is similiar in grade level to Branley's *Black Holes, White Dwarfs, and Superstars* (Crowell, 1976; o.p.), but takes a more descriptive approach. Both titles should be in library collections, as they are complementary. (pp. 115-16)

> *Margaret M. Hagel, in a review of "Private Lives of the Stars,"* in School Library Journal, *Vol. 33, No. 4, December, 1986, pp. 115-16.*

From Living Cells to Dinosaurs; Our Restless Earth (1986)

Each book takes a comprehensive first look at its subject in a clear, concise, readable text. The chapters have black-and-white captioned photographs, illustrations [by Anne Canevari Green], and diagrams that elucidate the text. The glossaries are adequate, but the lack of a pronunciation guide is unfortunate. Gallant makes it clear that the theories presented (gathered from the evidence of rocks and fossil records and knowledge of how chemicals of life form) are what scientists believe happened. *From Living Cells to Dinosaurs* is not just another dinosaur book, but rather a discussion of the evolution of the earth and its plants and animals from the Precambrian to the Mesozoic eras. Darwin's main ideas about evolution are included. The scope is broader and the reading level slightly higher than Elting's *Macmillan Book of Dinosaurs and Other Prehistoric Creatures* (Macmillan, 1984) and Greene's *Before the Dinosaurs* (Bobbs-Merrill, 1970; o.p.). *Our Restless Earth* discusses the theories geologists have formulated about the formation of the earth and the continual changes that have taken place. More comprehensive than Lambert's *The Active Earth* (Morrow, 1982), this should be a hit with young geologists. Interesting reading that will also be useful for reports because of the easy accessibility of facts through the index and chapter headings. (pp. 89-90)

> *Alice R. Arnett, in a review of "From Living Cells to Dinosaurs,"* in School Library Journal, *Vol. 33, No. 6, February, 1987, pp. 89-90.*

The increased interest in geology spawned by plate tectonics and continental drift has created a market for books such as [*Our Restless Earth*]. Gallant, an experienced author of children's books, has put together a generally competent introductory presentation for youngsters. The book is wide ranging, beginning with the origin of the earth and its crust and moving on to such standard topics as rock origins, geologic time, plate tectonics, volcanoes and earthquakes, mountains, oceans, and glaciation. Ten line drawings and 26 photographs accompany the text. These black-and-white illustrations are not numbered and are best described as adequate but uninspired. One legend for a photograph of Hawaiian lava describes it as "dried" lava, an unforgivably erroneous choice of adjectives. One line drawing defines sedimentary rocks as "rocks formed by pressure," a rather inadequate way to characterize them. Another line drawing depicting how continents move locates convection currents incorrectly and mistakenly identifies the earth's crust where the mantle should be. A typographical error dubs the late, great oceanographer Maurice Ewing as "Maurcie". . . . These mistakes aside, the book appears to be generally free of major errors and flows smoothly.

> *Joaquin Rodriguez, in a review of "Our Restless Earth," in* Science Books & Films, *Vol. 22, No. 4, March-April, 1987, p. 232.*

As its title implies, **From Living Cells to Dinosaurs** is an overview of early life on earth. This relatively small volume is packed with information on the origin of life, the rise of living cells, and the evolution of early cell life into highly advanced plants and organisms. Each of the seven chapters covers significant advances, beginning with pre-biotic life and ending with the fall of the dinosaurs some 70 million years ago. This book does an excellent job of covering such a vast area of knowledge without avoiding details. The text and illustrations overflow with simple yet accurate information of earth's historical past. Particularly impressive is the author's ability to explain some advanced biological concepts in a simple, straightforward, and interesting way. The book reads more like a story than a dry textbook. Although the illustrations are primarily black-and-white pictures, they are appropriate and supplement the text material well. In all, the entire work is well presented. As a supplement to class work or as just a good science book to read for information and fun, **From Living Cells to Dinosaurs** would make sound, educational reading for young people. (pp. 239-40)

> *Michael Jury, in a review of "From Living Cells to Dinosaurs," in* Science Books & Films, *Vol. 22, No. 4, March-April, 1987, pp. 239-40.*

The Macmillan Book of Astronomy (1986)

A clear, up-to-date introduction to the solar system, and a "hello" to the rest of the universe in an attractive oversized volume. Gallant gives a balanced presentation of the known and the postulated, describing several of the newer ideas astronomers are considering these days, but pointing out which ones are unproven. The illustrations are gorgeous, whether full-color photos or artists' visualizations from vantages that no camera has yet visited. The diagrams are also in full color and beautiful, but in the one that shows the relative sizes of the sun and the planets, the labels for Venus and Mars are reversed, Pluto is missing, and the moons, as so often happens, are not shown to scale. This is about half of the book that Richard Muarer's

fine *Nova Space Explorer's Guide* (Crown, 1985) is, covering only the things learned about space and not how they were learned, but it is just as appealing and better organized for assignments.

> *Margaret L. Chatham, in a review of "The Macmillan Book of Astronomy," in* School Library Journal, *Vol. 33, No. 6, February, 1987, p. 79.*

The title is a little misleading. Roy Gallant's book focuses mostly on our solar system, with some information at the end about comets, other stars in the universe besides our sun, and the probable origin of the universe.

The lively, informative text, coupled with superb illustrations that include color drawings, photographs, and computer graphics, more than make up for that minor discrepancy, however.

Because the subject is such an enduringly popular one, there are many other good books on the subject. One of the best is *The Grand Tour: A Traveler's Guide to the Solar System,* by Ron Miller and W. K. Hartmann (Workman, c. 1981). Aimed at an older audience, it can also be enjoyed by any intellectually curious child of about eight or older who also loves breathtakingly beautiful drawings.

Other good books include *Astronomy Today: Planets, Stars, Space Exploration,* by D. L. Moche (Random House, c. 1982), which combines a broader perspective on astronomy with excellent color drawings and diagrams. Another broad overview, for a slightly older age group, is *Astronomy,* by P. L. Brown (Facts On File, Inc., 1984).

> *Lee Jeffers Brami, in a review of "The Macmillan Book of Astronomy," in* Appraisal: Science Books for Young People, *Vol. 20, No. 3, Summer, 1987, p. 36.*

This softbound book arrived for review just as I began to plan doing some astronomy with my young grandchildren. It appears to be well suited for this use.

The book deals in depth with what is known about the planets, their moons, the sun, comets, stars, and the Big-Bang Theory of how it all began. A handy table of sizes, distances, and other statistics is shown for each planet.

I could not help but wonder why greater use was not made of photos and information from the remarkable visits to some of the planets by the "Voyager" spacecraft. Also, it is not stated whether some of the illustrations included are photos from these missions or man-made "paintings". One drawing, showing why seasons occur, is not at all clear.

The text does not have the crisp, authoritative ring of *Astronomy Today,* by astronomer D. L. Moche, reviewed several years ago, but the text is well done and packed with information. Spot checks (with an astronomy textbook) of a number of items about which I was uncertain showed no discrepancies.

> *Norman F. Smith, in a review of "The Macmillan Book of Astronomy," in* Appraisal: Science Books for Young People, *Vol. 20, No. 3, Summer, 1987, p. 37.*

The Rise of Mammals (1986)

Gallant traces the development of mammal species during the Cenozoic era. Both geological and biological history is explained alongside the evolution of mammals, thus providing important and relevant contextual information. However, there is so much information that readers will need to have some familiarity with the subject in order to find this volume accessible. The concept of evolution is explained by inference, not by a clearly stated definition and discussion. Certain terms (e.g., mollusk, marsupial) are defined neither in the text nor in the brief glossary. Species after species is introduced but rarely described. The text is divided into four chapters (presenting background information, geologic periods, and the development of Man), and is supplemented by black-and-white reproductions from natural history museum illustrations and dioramas. A heavily pro-science appendix discusses the controversy between Creationism and Evolution. Cramped typeface and page design do little to help readers pause to digest the sophisticated information being presented, and the index is not thorough. (pp. 156, 158)

> *Cathy Wood, in a review of "The Rise of Mammals," in* School Library Journal, *Vol. 33, No. 7, March, 1987, pp. 156, 158.*

This book summarizes what is known about the age of mammals, the geologic era spanning the last 65 million years called the Cenozoic. Earth history during the two periods comprising the Cenozoic—the Tertiary and Quaternary—is accurately described. The emphasis is on evolving mammals, shown against a backdrop of drifting continents, massive ice sheets, and erupting volcanoes. One of the four chapters is devoted to human evolution—about 35 percent of the total text—and provides an account that is both more accurate and complete than that found in the best-selling high school biology textbook. The chapter concludes with a discussion of human population growth. An appendix provides a succinct comparison of evolution and creation science, with the religious nature of the latter clearly identified. A good glossary and index complete the book. Black-and-white photographs and drawings effectively illustrate the text. Unfortunately, while the author presents the conclusions of science, he conveys nothing of the methods and logic used to reach these conclusions. For example, what evidence supports the concept of continental drift? How do we know that a given fossil belonged in fact to a mammal and not a reptile or dinosaur? This failure to discuss evidence restricts **The Rise of Mammals** to just the "recommended" category.

> *Wayne A. Moyer, in a review of "The Rise of Mammals," in* Science Books & Films, *Vol. 22, No. 5, May-June, 1987, p. 314.*

Rainbows, Mirages, and Sundogs: The Sky as a Source of Wonder (1987)

The sky is full of signs and wonders, not all of them astronomical; here Gallant stays close to home, surveying the special effects visible in our own atmosphere and slightly beyond: rainbows (single, double, and circular), mirages; auroras; zodiacal lights; eclipses; and less common phenomena (ever heard of *Gegenschein?*). Along the way he explains why the sky is blue—or white, or red—why stars twinkle, and why clouds appear to have silver linings. Young researchers who are willing to fiddle will find several hastily-described but simple and inexpensive experiments, as well as advice on observing (safely) and photographing eclipses or star trails. A scattering of serviceable drawings and diagrams clarify descriptions, but subtler optical effects don't come across in the murky black-and-white photographs. This is less detailed than Heuer's *Rainbows, Halos and Other Wonders* (Dodd, 1978), but covers some different ground (so to speak). (p. 188)

> *John Peters, in a review of "Rainbows, Mirages, and Sundogs: The Sky as a Source of Wonder," in* School Library Journal, *Vol. 34, No. 1, September, 1987, pp. 187-88.*

Why is the sky blue? How blue is it? What causes stars to twinkle? Gallant's premise is that there are many beautiful, and even mysterious, things to be seen in the sky which most of us fail to notice. He explains the manifestations of light and atmosphere which cause such visual phenomena as mirages, eclipses, auroras, star trails, sun storms, and the Northern Lights. The lucid, thorough text raises questions, provides considerable scientific detail, and includes instructions for conducting intriguing and relatively simple demonstrations. The reader is told how to actually photograph lunar eclipses without expensive equipment, how to recreate the colors of raindrops in a wineglass, and how to measure the height of a rainbow. There are captioned diagrams to illustrate many of the explanations, and several of the photographs have an almost surreal look as they capture instances of light that are indeed unearthly. Gallant's enjoyment of his subject and his substantial explanations are certain to inspire heightened awareness and curiosity about day and night skies. Index.

> *Mary A. Bush, in a review of "Rainbows, Mirages and Sundogs: The Sky as a Source of Wonder," in* The Horn Book Magazine, *Vol. LXIII, No. 6, November-December, 1987, p. 758.*

Besides the fascinating "events" and explanations, Mr. Gallant provides a number of experiments associated with some of them. Whether one simply finds the sky as interesting as the author does or whether an unusual science project is needed, this book is a most satisfactory aid.

The final chapter, about a city which can view the sky for only one night and one day every ten years, owes something to several well-known science fiction stories and is quite unnecessary to drive home the author's point; it is, however, a minor flaw in an otherwise successful book. (p. 14)

> *Daphne Ann Hamilton, in a review of "Rainbows, Mirages and Sundogs: The Sky as a Source of Wonder," in* Appraisal: Science Books for Young People, *Vol. 21, No. 2, Spring, 1988, pp. 13-14.*

This is an accounting of the things you can see all around you if you look up at the sky at the right time and the right place. Look up during the day and you may see rainbows, mirages, blue (or another color) sky, halos, sundogs, eclipses or flashes of color where you least expect them. Look up at night (sometimes with the help of a telescope or a camera) and you might see scintillating stars (at least you will if you live further out in the country than I do), auroras, gegenschein, noctilucent clouds, or star trails.

All of these phenomena, and others, are reasonably clearly and correctly explained with good illustrations and a very good text. What is very helpful are the suggestions for details to look for—small (or not very bright) things that you might overlook if it were not for the book's coaching.

Something that I wish could have been done a little better was the illustration of mirages—the light ray tracing sketches try to combine both what the observer sees and how things really are, to the detriment of both.

A very welcome addition to the book is a collection of interspersed experiments and measurements that most anyone can undertake—they are good pedagogical learning experiments, too, not mere cookbook trivia.

> *John D. Stackpole, in a review of "Rainbows, Mirages and Sundogs: The Sky as a Source of Wonder," in* Appraisal: Science Books for Young People, *Vol. 21, No. 2, Spring, 1988, p. 14.*

Ancient Indians: The First Americans (1989)

The origins of the native American races which populated the continents of the New World are shrouded in mystery. Modern scientific methods have provided enlightening clues to this enigma, while at the same time serving to deepen it. In his wide-ranging survey, Gallant makes an admirable attempt to deal with the ambiguities that are unearthed along with artifacts of stone and bone. Coverage of the sites and artifacts examined should pique interest in readers to learn more about archaeological and anthropological research methods and the lives of prehistoric native Americans. In the second half of the book, an attempt is made to survey all of the major native American cultures. Marked by broad generalizations, oversimplifications, and questionable assertions, the latter chapters fail by attempting to cover far too much. Specific books on various native American peoples are preferable, and some are included in the bibliography. A helpful section describes important sites in North America, such as Mesa Verde National Park, which can be visited by the public. The small black-and-white photographs are uninspired, and range in quality from fair to poor. (pp. 111-12)

> *David N. Pauli, in a review of "Ancient Indians: The First Americans," in* School Library Journal, *Vol. 35, No. 8, April, 1989, pp. 111-12.*

Of the many archaeology books available for the novice, this advanced volume will be most helpful to those who are already interested in the subject. Gallant's coverage is comprehensive, and his use of language is sophisticated. Although the book's format—smallish print and unexciting pictures—may deter readers, those who persevere will

find the theories discussed quite fascinating. Gallant describes ways the first Indians may have arrived from Asia, the development and spread of different native American societies, and the life-styles of various tribes. Treating his readers with respect, the author eschews pat answers and offers various explanations for the when, where, how, and why of Indian culture. Appended are a list of North American Indian ruins that can be visited, a glossary, and a lengthy bibliography.

> *Ilene Cooper, in a review of "Ancient Indians: The First Americans," in* Booklist, *Vol. 85, No. 21, July, 1989, p. 1902.*

This book is padded with disorganized and uncivil material. A quarter of it is not ancient archeology at all but a summary of the conquest of the Americas. Gallant gives brief sketches of many groups and, for no discernable reason, considers Eskimo and Southwest peoples together. Gallant mentions "miserable" slaves in Tlingit communities but not professional artists. He is quick to describe blood sacrifice by the Aztecs, but doesn't mention contemporaneous torture by the Europeans. In short, Gallant does not demonstrate respect for the people he is trying to describe. Too often, the words selected and the details presented are not favorable to the Native Americans. "Strange" is a prejorative word in the phrase, "a strange cultural group known as the Chimu." "Indian" evokes stereotypes. Scientific usage could justify the term paleoIndian, but the title isn't quite correct. Gallant does clearly convey the techniques of archeology and the development of theories. He also shows contrasting hypotheses regarding arrival of people on this continent. If Gallant had discussed cultural change or language classification as clearly as he discussed arrival, this would have been a valuable book.

> *Anne C. Fuller and William O. Autry, in a review of "Ancient Indians: The First Americans," in* Science Books & Films, *Vol. 25, No. 1, September-October, 1989, p. 31.*

Before the Sun Dies: The Story of Evolution (1989)

An outline of the history of evolution, relying heavily on fossil evidence for the depictions of life in earlier ages. Beginning with a well-thought-out description of the scientific definition of living processes, Gallant proceeds to cover the formation and evolution of the universe, the galaxies, and the physical Earth, and presents early and current ideas of how life began here. Darwin's initial development of evolutionary theory is well summarized, and the famous battle at Oxford between scientists and theologians is particularly well presented. Gallant describes fossils and how scientists use them to "read" the records of the earth, and genetic theory and how it is used to describe how animals and plants change over time. He then puts these ideas to good use in a description of animals evolving over many millions of years. Finally, he speculates on the possible future of evolution. Most other books for this age group concentrate on describing the evolution of life from a less theoretical viewpoint, giving less attention to how theories are developed and applied. A notable example is David

Attenborough's *Life on Earth* (Little, 1979), which features gorgeous photographs and a more urbane writing style. Nicholas Hotton's *The Evidence of Evolution* (Hale, 1968; o.p.) presents the theories as they were developed, but in a drier, less attractive style. Michael Benton's *The Story of Life on Earth* (Warwick, 1986) is aimed at a slightly lower age group and relies heavily on illustrations rather than the verbal descriptions that Gallant presents so masterfully. Gallant does the best job of presenting the scientific processes of how the major discoveries were made. (pp. 279-80)

> *Jonathan Betz-Zall, in a review of "Before the Sun Dies: The Story of Evolution," in* School Library Journal, *Vol. 35, No. 13, September, 1989, pp. 279-80.*

This is a good little book, well written and clear. It makes the topic of evolution palatable to even the most scientifically phobic individual—an important consideration given the woeful condition of scientific literacy in the United States today. Even in the organization of his book, Gallant follows the pattern that he so admirably describes with regard to the process of evolution. That is, the book begins very basically, with a discussion of the definition of life, and proceeds to build on that foundation with exemplary treatments of the Big Bang, fossils, genes, and past, present, and future human evolution. The glossary contains very clear and concise definitions, and the index is fairly complete. The illustrations, though black and white, convey needed information to the reader and are of good quality. If the book has a shortcoming, it is that not enough illustrations were included, particularly tables, as they would have helped to summarize some of the more pertinent material. These are minor criticisms, however. I recommend the book as a way to introduce the very difficult and important scientific concepts it deals with.

> *Craig Howard Kinsley, in a review of "Before the Sun Dies: The Story of Evolution," in* Science Books & Films, *Vol. 25, No. 5, May-June, 1990, p. 258.*

The whole notion of creativity in children's books is often part and parcel of a rebellion against disciplined instruction, which is somehow regarded as a repression of the latent potentialities inherent in the juvenile reader. These beliefs so dominate our educational establishment, our media, and even parents that Roy Gallant's **Before the Sun Dies** seems almost startling in its adherence to a cogent, disciplined description of the subject of evolution in its full gamut, from the big bang theory through geological, biological, human, and cultural evolution.

To accomplish this feat in 159 pages of text requires a sifting of such a mountain of information that only someone with seventy prior books to his credit, mostly for the young, would attempt this. The scope of this book is such that vast libraries could be assembled from the information in *each* of the thirteen chapters. In light of recent debate, statements in some cases seem too simple (the formation of galaxies from huge clouds in the early universe; or the role of RNA in chemical evolution), but such things rarely deter a good science writer.

An excellent glossary, suggestions for further reading, black and white photographs and an index enhance this nicely laid-out book, intended for anyone ten or over who seeks a comprehensive overview of the basics. Some of the titles on the reading list, such as Niles Eldredge's *Time Frames,* are clearly not introductory in any sense. For a one-volume overview which steers clear of the romanticizing of evolutionary trends, this sober book is more than adequate. (pp. 30-1)

> *Sarah Greenleaf, in a review of "Before the Sun Dies—The Story of Evolution," in* Appraisal: Science Books for Young People, *Vol. 23, No. 1, Winter, 1990, pp. 30-1.*

I feel that this is a very good book to have on the subject of classical evolutionary theory—its basics and its history. If the students are doing a report on this area of science, this is a valuable resource they'll want to use. If they are doing a report on contrasting the many theories of origin, this is also a good resource. If they are doing a report on contemporary evolutionary theory, one resource won't do—not even this one, good as it is.

Be aware that the book (1) will have the appearance of being an authoritative piece on the general subject of "evolution" which the students will discover is very hard to define and (2) presents many of the classical arguments as if no one, of late, has been suggesting alternatives. S. J. Gould, et al., are given a mention, but it is back to the classics, lickety-split. In other words, the students may come into class asking about the "new views" on origins not addressed in this book. Maybe the book would have been too long or too watered down if these had been included.

The book is up to date (on classical evolution, remember) and quite well written. Mr. Gallant does a very thorough job in discussing the work done to dispel spontaneous generation, covering more than most other authors do. His knowledge of cosmology, biology and geology make for a "desirable purchase."

There are some areas of dispute subtle enough as to postpone "trauma" for the children when the day that they discover the "whole truth" arrives. For example, I don't recall Darwin's receiving Wallace's letter as positively as Gallant says he did. Also, the two major factors of change and time are correctly identified as the cornerstones of evolution, but current discussions and debates indicate that both have equally viable alternative explanations. Let's hope Professor Gallant will examine these in another volume.

> *D. R. Freeman, in a review of "Before the Sun Dies—The Story of Evolution," in* Appraisal: Science Books for Young People, *Vol. 23, No. 1, Winter, 1990, p. 31.*

The Peopling of Planet Earth: Human Population Growth through the Ages (1990)

Gallant considers both evolution and demographics as he cuts across the globe to explore population growth as a function of human history. He begins with a kind of short course in anthropology, following traditional scientific theories about evolution from cell reproduction on a virgin earth to the proliferation of modern human beings. He explains geological, cultural, and economic factors; considers the growth of cities as a global phenomenon; and takes a look at famines, epidemics, and other crucial events that have had an impact on population growth over time. He devotes the last third of his text to the tenuous relationship between continuing population growth and world resources, painting a rather grim scenario of the future that involves some extremely hard and unquestionably controversial choices. Gallant's writing is polished and clear, and his use of questions within the narrative forces the reader to confront some difficult and intriguing issues head on. (pp. 1270-71)

> *Stephanie Zvirin, in a review of "The Peopling of Planet Earth: Human Population Growth through the Ages," in* Booklist, *Vol. 86, No. 13, March 1, 1990, pp. 1270-71.*

The Peopling of Planet Earth: Human Population Growth Through the Ages, a thorough, well-organized book by an experienced science writer, takes the young reader on a long evolutionary journey. It begins some 33 million years ago, the age of the oldest known hominid, and continues through various stages until modern human beings emerged about 100,000 years ago. We travel onward to the time, approximately 10,000 years ago, when perhaps five million people inhabited the earth, then on again until today, when the human population has grown a thousand-fold to over five *billion.* A look at the future of unchecked population growth (a projected world population of eight billion by the year 2020) completes the time journey.

Roy Gallant discusses the origin of human races, the role of agriculture and urbanization in human population growth and the differences in population growth on the various parts of planet Earth. His main concern, however, is to examine the relationship between man and his environment and to show how that relationship is affected by numbers of people. In the final chapter, "Population and the Quality of Life," Gallant discusses the search for optimum population size and the touchy, much-debated subject of world population control. His own point of view is summarized near the end of the book: "Every year that the world population continues to increase, the risks of widespread and frequent famines, disease, and long-lived ecological disaster also increase. We can only hope that a rational population policy will become a worldwide reality before any such event spells doom on a global scale."

Although he offers much scientific evidence, not everyone will agree with Gallant's conclusions about the dangers of unchecked population growth. Nevertheless, **The Peopling of Planet Earth** makes thought-provoking reading at a time when many people have forgotten—or are not aware of—the great concern that developed about world population growth in the 1960s and 1970s.

> *Brent Ashabranner, "How It Happened," in* Book World—The Washington Post, *May 13, 1990, p. 17.*

Gallant, a noted science writer, has ventured into the realm of social science to tackle this ambitious and timely topic. Adopting an interdisciplinary approach, he discusses a little bit of everything: spontaneous generation, evolution, earth's vanishing resources, world climate, acid rain—much that is interesting but extraneous to the book's main topic. Gallant's scientific bias does not always stand him in good stead. His view that myths "provided a kind of counterfeit experience that masqueraded as reality" may explain the awkward job he does in retelling the Enuma Elish and other myths about human origins. He incorrectly states that "Evolution is an established fact" rather than an established theory, and vastly underestimates the number of civilian casualties caused by World War II: "Nearly 17 million [troops] or 20 million including civilians." More disturbing is Gallant's oblivious-to-argument suggestion that it is better to let people in drought-afflicted areas starve because feeding them only encourages them to reproduce: "millions may survive to produce an even larger population that will require even more food." The material covering the rise of cities and spread of humankind to other continents is poorly organized and confusing. Gallant begins a section halfway through chapter 5 with "In Chapter 3 we left Cro-Magnon hunter-gatherers living in southern central Europe at the base of the glaciers of the last ice age." Further on, he asks, "What happened back on the European continent from the time Julius Caesar's legions had marched from Rome . . . ?" This globe-trotting, millennium-hopping approach is often confusing and at times ludicrous. While Gallant adequately explains the mathematics of population curves and birth and death rates, he shows a peculiar naïveté in holding China up as an example of family planning. Trying to cover too much material, the book offers, at best, a shallow treatment.

> *Ruth Ann Smith, in a review of "The Peopling of Planet Earth: Human Population through the Ages," in* Bulletin of the Center for Children's Books, *Vol. 43, No. 10, June, 1990, p. 238.*

Earth's Vanishing Forests (1991)

Gallant offers a thoroughly researched examination of the destruction of rain forests. In a clear, nonhysterical manner, he discusses how and why rain forests are being destroyed; the value, diversity, and interdependence of systems in tropical forests; the implications of their loss; and the current efforts to preserve remaining forests. Gallant is not shy about laying blame for the destruction of rain forests on rapacious lumber companies, the Japanese government, the World Bank, and Third World nations eager to trade their resources for progress and profit. In an ironic postscript, Gallant recounts the fate of "Fordlandia," Henry Ford's disastrous attempt to "manage" a Brazilian forest. After spending $9 million, Ford bailed out, selling the land back to Brazil for $500,000. "Over the 19-year period Ford had failed to produce enough rubber to make a pencil eraser." Unfortunately, we haven't learned from Ford's mistakes. Explanations of population momentum and photosynthesis, a glossary, and a comprehensive bibliography are appended.

> *Chris Sherman, in a review of "Earth's Van-*

ishing Forests," in Booklist, *Vol. 88, No. 3, Oc-tober 1, 1991, p. 314.*

Rosemary Harris

1923-

English author of fiction, picture books, and retellings.

Major works include *The Moon in the Cloud* (1968), *The Seal-Singing* (1971), *A Quest for Orion* (1978), *Green Finger House* (1980), *Zed* (1982).

Praised as an especially original writer whose works are set in the past, present, and future and reflect her insight into human nature, Harris is the author of unusually sophisticated literature for children and young adults. Insisting that young readers are capable of comprehending more than is usually expected of them, she writes books known for their complex plots, undiluted presentation of good and evil, and intricate prose style; as a stylist, critic Marcus Crouch calls her "one of the modern masters. . . ." Harris often draws from biblical and legendary sources, interweaving these traditional elements with her own observations on history and humanity to create thoughtful and often comical visions of the ancient world. She is best known for her "Egyptian Trilogy"— also called the "Nile Trilogy"—in which she creates memorable and convincing animal and human characters, colorful settings, and fast-paced romance. Harris has also written two works of futuristic science fiction, *A Quest for Orion* and its sequel *Tower of the Stars* (1980), which involve teenage resistance groups struggling against foreign domination of Europe aided by a Christian talisman that once belonged to the medieval emperor Charlemagne. Although reminiscent of the "Egyptian Trilogy" in that they feature an abundant cast of characters and a highly detailed setting, they are notably bleaker in tone. In addition, Harris is the author of young adult books on political subjects, including *Zed* and *Summers of the Wild Roses* (1987) and has authored retellings of *Beauty and the Beast* (1979) and *Heidi* (1983).

The daughter of a Royal Air Force pilot, Harris as a child moved frequently with her family around the British Isles. She cites her parents' divorce when she was eleven years old and World War II during her teenage years as important influences on her development. After receiving training in painting and sculpture at the Chelsea School of Art, Harris began a career as a picture restorer. During a bout with influenza, she began the "Egyptian Trilogy" with *The Moon in the Cloud,* an unusual reworking of the Noah's Ark story focusing on Reuben's animal-collecting journey to Egypt with his cat Cefalu, his dog Benoni, and his camel Anak. The second book in the trilogy, *The Shadow on the Sun* (1970), relates the story of Reuben's return with his wife Thamar to Egypt after the flood waters have receded, and *The Bright and Morning Star* (1972) focuses on Reuben and Thamar's foibles as Prince and Princess of Canaan. Throughout the trilogy, animals converse with each other and with the human characters, offering insights on the political intrigue surrounding them. Cats, particularly the wise and personable Cefalu, are essential

to the rapidly shifting complexities of the books' plots. Of the trilogy, critic Robert Bell notes that they "are undoubtedly among the most outstanding contributions to children's literature of recent years." Harris's skill at reworking legendary material is apparent in many of her most prominent works. *The Seal-Singing,* for example, is derived from a seventeenth-century legend of a woman whose actions cause the death of all the seals on an island off the Scottish coast impinges on the lives of two cousins. *The Child in the Bamboo Grove* (1971) is based on the Japanese legend of a bamboo cutter's discovery of a baby girl who brings him wealth and happiness, but who eventually must return to her origin, the sun. In *The Flying Ship* (1975), a novel based on a Russian folktale, a young man wins the hand of the czar's daughter with the help of three travelers, despite the czar's attempts to forestall the triumph. Harris has written of the extensive research that is required to bring the legends back to life, and the result of these investigations is evident in the convincing characterizations and thoroughness of detail in her description of settings. Furthermore, she imitates the tone and rhythm of the legends' original languages, and in many cases, illustrator Errol Le Cain supplies vivid images that capture the look of the country where the legends developed. Harris received the Carnegie Medal in 1968 for *The Moon in the Cloud,* and her *Green Finger House* won the 1981 Mother Goose Award.

(See also *Something about the Author,* Vol. 4; *Something about the Author Autobiography Series,* Vol. 7; *Contemporary Authors New Revision Series,* Vol. 13, 30; and *Contemporary Authors,* Vol. 33-36.)

GENERAL COMMENTARY

Nancy J. Schmidt

The only volume of historical fiction about Africa to receive the special acclaim which accompanies a children's literature award was a story about Egypt. Rosemary Harris received the Carnegie Medal for her first children's novel, **The Moon in the Cloud.** Harris had previously written novels for adults and subsequently has written other children's novels about Egypt. The Carnegie Medal is an award of excellence given to authors whose books are published in Britain. Works of fiction are judged on their plot, style and characterization. Apparently characterization and vocabulary need not correspond with the time period of the plot, for although the story takes place in ancient Egypt, it includes an animal trainer whose speech throughout is twentieth-century colloquial.

Harris owes a debt to the Bible, as well as to the sources on Egypt which she cites in her author's note, since the story takes place at the time of the flood, which she places during the time of the Old Kingdom with a fictional sixth dynasty king on the throne. The story is about Noah and the Ark as much as about royalty of the sixth dynasty. Harris admits that there may be inconsistencies in the Egyptian background, but excuses herself by saying that writers about ancient Egypt disagree on details. Certainly this is a historical novel that does not present a serious view of ancient Egypt nor does it attempt to take an Egyptian perspective. The approach to Egyptian religion is highly irreverent throughout, though it is not derogatory as were nineteenth- and early twentieth-century references to African religion. Surely the talking animals are not to be taken as serious historical representations, nor is the jaunty tone of the entire story. Although Harris treats them very lightly in her novel, neither the flood nor the religious issues of the sixth dynasty are matters for less than serious consideration.

The Moon in the Cloud is the first novel in a trilogy about Egypt. *The Shadow on the Sun* takes place in Egypt after the flood. Again the author acknowledges the use of historical sources, but indicates that her placement of Punt beyond the Blue Nile is imaginary and that much of what exists in Punt is fantasy. She pleads tolerance for this fantasy because the ancient Egyptians might have found it credible. This depiction of Punt is not entirely original on her part; rather, it is the reiteration of stereotypes about Africa which have frequently appeared in children's fiction. The "savage prince from the strange land of Punt" has a bone stuck in his nose, is dressed in skins and ivory anklets, and has "eyes wild as a panther's and as cruel." The Prince of Punt lives in a grass and mud compound

and at least some of his subjects, including young girls, are "naked." The religion of Punt is based on "magic" and some people can take souls from men's bodies. Again there are talking animals in the story, although the author does not acknowledge this as fantasy, and the language is twentieth-century colloquial, although the author does not plead tolerance for this historical deviation.

Harris admits that **The Bright and the Morning Star,** a story about a plot against King Merenkere by No-Hotep, is not factual. Claims, however, are made for the historical accuracy of the background. There is explicit mention in this novel that the people from Punt are black, whereas this was only implied in the preceding novel. As a whole, the tone of this novel is more serious than of the first two in the trilogy. But one still has the impression that Harris is writing more to be enjoyed than to re-create a historical period. Admittedly it is difficult to re-create the temper of the times in an era so distant from our own as ancient Egypt. However, Harris' novels are so full of improbabilities that [as John Rowe Townsend has written] "it seems safe to say [that she] created an Ancient Egypt . . . that never was." (pp. 157-58)

> *Nancy J. Schmidt, "Historical Fiction," in her* Children's Fiction about Africa in English, *Conch Magazine Limited (Publishers), 1981, pp. 155-70.*

D. J. Stroud

Twenty years ago saw the completion of a trilogy of outstanding books which are as delightful to read today as they were then, and which have since become classics in their own right. In 1968 Rosemary Harris, already a writer for adults, produced **The Moon in the Cloud,** the award-winning first book of what might be called her Egyptian or Nile trilogy, a splendid recreation of a distant period and of a story which she has declared "always had a hold on my imagination".

It may seem there is a certain incongruity between the Book of Genesis and a shabby travelling circus, but that is how **The Moon in the Cloud** opens. We are in the time of Noah, a somewhat pompous, oracular Noah, newly informed of the coming of a Flood, and camped close beside him is the gentle animal-tamer Reuben and his beautiful, spirited, young wife, Thamar. Reuben has been told about the coming disaster by Noah's cruel and cunning son, Ham, who has been given the, to him, highly unwelcome task of travelling to the black land of Kemi, its buildings "reared on the bones of slaves", to collect two sacred cats and a brace of lions. Ham prevails upon Reuben to go in his place in return for the promise that Thamar will be allowed into the Ark when the time comes, and the young man sets off accompanied by the faithful, golden-eyed herd dog Benoni, his indignant black cat Cefalu, and the grumpy camel Anak.

Not surprisingly, he runs into trouble when he encounters the caravan of the High Priest of Sekhmet returning to Egypt from a tax-gathering expedition, and he finishes up imprisoned in the great city of Men-nofer. The animals go to different owners, only Cefalu falling on his feet when he enters the Temple of Sekhmet and meets Meluseth, the disdainful feline of the establishment, with a high opinion of her own superiority. In the prison Reuben experiences the kindness of Tahlevi, a condemned tomb robber, and turns for consolation to playing his pipe. When the High Priest, newly disgraced because of his attempt to cheat the young King, hears of his talent, he has Reuben brought before the music-loving monarch. The King, bored and cynical despite his youth, is intrigued by Reuben's ingenuous nature, and welcomes him to his court, but despite the ruler's favour, Reuben longs to return home. He little dreams that during his absence Thamar has had to flee from the unwelcome attentions of Ham.

On the day of Tahlevi's execution, Reuben is given a chance to get away when there is a successful attempt to rescue his friend, and he sets off across the desert with his animals, Cefalu now accompanied by Meluseth. On the way they also collect a magnificent lion, but the cowardly Ham proceeds to take all the credit, conveniently forgetting the bargain he has made. His own viciousness, however, brings about his destruction, when one of Reuben's two elephants squashes him, enabling Reuben to take his place, together with Thamar, as the rain begins to fall.

In *The Shadow on the Sun,* published in 1970, the Flood is over, but Reuben is haunted by concern as to whether the deluge was only localised or whether the Land of Kemi was also submerged. He has never been completely accepted by Noah, who suggests that the young couple become Prince and Princess of Canaan, and with these titles they travel South. Kemi has, of course, survived, and the King warmly welcomes them, but he is preoccupied by his pursuit of the lovely sixteen year old Meri-Mekhmet, daughter of his Court Chamberlain, who calls him Menkere, not knowing who he really is, and enthralling him by her frankness and freshness. When she discovers his true identity, she rejects him, aware that he already has a sister/wife and many concubines. The young autocrat at first accepts her state of shock, but unaccustomed to having his proud will thwarted, grows increasingly impatient, particularly when his Vizier warns that such defiance is a bad example to others. He becomes harsh and tyrannical in his misery, finally falling dangerously ill. Now Thamar takes a hand in the matter, and brings a remorseful Meri-Mekhmet to the dying man's bedside. From that moment Menkere's condition begins to improve as he hears her promise never to leave him again, but his sickness has been shared by his wife and delicate son. The child recovers, but Menkere's consort dies leaving him free to marry his beloved Meri-Mekhmet.

Reuben in the meantime is warned by Cefalu that a sinister visitor to the Court, the Prince of the savage Southern Land of Punt, is acting suspiciously, but the warning is not taken seriously until Meri-Mekhmet suddenly disappears from the Palace. It is Reuben's cat, however, that discovers the Prince has had her abducted, and that she is already in a boat floating far up the Nile. Secretly Reuben, accompanied by Cefalu, sets out to follow on a royal ship, and later learns there is another passenger on board, Kenamaut, an old enemy from his first visit to Egypt. Eventually Reuben and Cefalu, now riding the faithful elephant M'Tuska, and guided by the untrustworthy Ken-

maut, reach Punt. Meri-Mekhmet has arrived before them, and in the country's most sacred place, has been rendered helpless by the magic of a terrible Wise Woman, M'bu, but when she uses her witchcraft against Reuben, he is protected by the power of the One God to whom he has prayed. Then, led to a tree of snakes, each with human eyes, Reuben is attacked by the greatest of these serpents, and in killing it, sets Meri-Mekhmet free. At almost the same time the Prince of Punt is drowned and M'bu slain by one of the unfortunates she has enslaved. When Reuben arrives, triumphantly riding M'Tuska, it is a simple matter to rescue Meri-Mekhmet from the shaken tribesmen. He also survives an attempt by Kenmaut to murder him, but in attempting this, Kenmaut falls into the jaws of a waiting crocodile.

There is a very joyous reunion when Reuben and Meri-Mekhmet return at last, overshadowed for Cefalu by the death of Meluseth during his absence, but at last the time comes for Reuben and Thamar to depart to take up their duties as guardians of Canaan. As they wave their farewells to Menkere and Meri-Mekhmet a hawk hovers overhead, the Horus of Gold, a sign to Reuben of the everlasting friendship between himself and the ruler of Egypt.

In the final book *The Bright and Morning Star* several years have gone by. In Canaan, which has become a happy land of "fruit and flowers and children", Reuben and Thamar have a family of five, but their happiness is marred by the plight of their second son Misraim, called Sadhi, now eleven, who is dumb and unhearing after a childish illness. His condition has made him often frantic and unmanageable, and in despair Thamar believes he will only be cured if she takes him down to Kemi. With them go her youngest son, Cefalu, now a very old cat, and one of his offspring, the kitten named Casper. In Kemi, Menkere and Meri-Mekhmet have a charming lively daughter, Ta-Thata, secretly dreading the traditional incestuous marriage she must make to her half-brother Sinhue, Menkere's weakling son by his first wife. Her greatest friend, for whom she feels a childish first love, after her beloved parents, is Hekhti, physician and Chief Royal Architect, and to whom she confides her fears about Sinhue, who is dominated by his tutor No-Hotep, an ambitious priest. She is, however, officially pledged to Sinhue, despite her own shrinking. Thamar is welcomed in Kemi, and reluctantly hands over her afflicted child to Hekhti. He quickly realises the boy's deafness is unlikely to be remedied, but by methods reminiscent of Annie Sullivan's treatment of young Helen Keller, sets about curing Sadhi's frustrations by teaching him how to communicate.

There is, however, black treachery afoot in Kemi, and during a conspiracy instigated by No-Hotep, abetted by forces from the Land of Shinar, Menkere and his wife are imprisoned in the royal tomb, while Ta-Thata and Sinhue become puppet rulers in the hands of the treacherous priest. Only Hekhti escapes No-Hotep's assassins when Tahlevi's young son brings a warning. Cefalu and three of his descendants escape from the Palace at the same time. At this desperate moment Reuben secretly arrives in the city, and there is a race against time to counteract the machinations of the sadistic No-Hotep (who intends to be

King) before Menkere is murdered. It is a close-run thing, and everyone, cats as well as humans, bravely plays a part. Menkere is rescued in the nick of time in true cliff-hanging fashion, but both his degenerate son and Hekhti perish. The physician's dying words to Ta-Thata are that Sadhi should be taken to the tomb of Hekhti's own great predecessor, Imhoptep. Reuben does this, and during an all-night vigil, shared by his old friend Tahlevi, sees in the dark sky overhead a brilliant star in the East. In the quietly happy conclusion of the book, with all past sorrows put to one side, Ta-Thata and Reuben's oldest son Joshua see a loving and mutual future before them, and this joy is completed when Sadhi utters his first word—his brother's name.

The three books are utterly delightful and highly original. Much of their charm lies in the animal characters, which although able to communicate with the human beings closest to them, are not impossibly anthropomorphic. There must at times have been some danger of the cats in particular, insidiously taking over, as indeed cats have a habit of doing in real life. Cefalu is an immense personality in himself.

The stories are full of delicious, unforced humour. The very adult themes inherent in the various relationships and situations are handled with great skill, and there is no attempt to gloss over the dark side of life in Kemi, and the cruelty and unpleasantness endemic then. After all Rosemary Harris has stated her objection to "writing down" for children, who are individuals very much in touch with reality. The final book in particular has a sombre feel to it, with a very real and chilling sense of evil and the powerlessness of its victims before the final denouement. Then all is well, good triumphs, but at a cost, for it is not only the villains who pay the price.

There is also the aspect of man's belief—the ancient story of Noah, compounded with race-memories of a Flood (not necessarily universal), have an extremely long-lasting quality. Perhaps Rosemary Harris' early recollections of sewing coloured animals on a counterpane, and drawing pictures of the Ark, have something to do with the inspiration which led to the writing of *The Moon in the Cloud.* Later we see the contrast between the primitive black magic of Punt, the superstitions of Ancient Egypt with its pantheon of deities, and the simple trust and faith of Reuben in the one true God.

Considerable scholarship is involved in this trilogy with strict attention to careful and most telling details. Rosemary Harris has modestly said there may be mistakes, but her recreation of life beside the Nile is superbly brought into existence, and her characters are of the order of those who stick in the mind—cats and all! (pp. 91-4)

> *D. J. Stroud, "Nile Trilogy," in* The Junior Bookshelf, *Vol. 56, No. 3, June, 1992, pp. 91-4.*

TITLE COMMENTARY

The Moon in the Cloud   **(1968)**

AUTHOR'S COMMENTARY

The ancient story of Noah and his Ark is as compelling for adults as for children. It is a marvellous story, and the fact that every toy shop, thousands of years after it was written, stocks a Noah's Ark, shows its extraordinary power over the human heart. It is also an extremely magical story, with its Ark as a place of safety in a turbulent, evil world; its animals symbolizing perhaps the various powers and instincts of man; and ending with God's moving covenant with Noah by the setting of a rainbow in the sky. Perhaps the story has always had a hold on my imagination, without my altogether realizing it till I wrote *The Moon in the Cloud.*

I remember sewing a counterpane with the animals when I was a child, and making drawings of the Ark later on; but I only thought of writing a book which included the legend when I was living in Hampshire, some years ago, and had influenza, and a framework of the story surfaced from my mind: perhaps fever had something to do with it—certainly my writing was so feverish that I had dreadful trouble deciphering it when I was completing the book. Why Reuben, Thamar, and their animals, and the King of Kemi too, in connection with Noah is hard to explain. Most people who do any form of creative writing will admit that what makes a collection of characters, scenes, dialogue, spring fully-armed to imaginative life, and refuse to leave till written down—often causing inconvenience— is a mystery: the whole process can probably best be compared with deep trance mediumship. People have asked me whether so much research was necessary on something like the Egyptian part of the story's background, for what is plainly fantasy. Yes, I think so: fantasy must be rooted in reality, otherwise it blows away into the sky, a balloon with too much gas in it. I don't think you can write, even lightly, of an historical period without this sort of attention to detail, though only one-sixteenth of what you do appears in the finished book. But if you put yourself in the position of seeing, as far as possible, as people of that time saw: this isn't very far, of course, as one must admit. But if, while writing, I can see in my mind's eye the flowers on trees the King of Kemi saw, know the sort of furniture he used, how his court officials would address him—then he moves in my mind, in space, as well as time, as much a real person as I can make him. It's a difficult far-off period to write of, and in spite of everything there were probably mistakes; I hope not too many. At least no one can correct me on Reuben and Thamar—and no one can really say they know much about Noah, and his family, and his Ark.

> *Rosemary Harris "The Moon in the Cloud,"   in* Chosen for Children: An Account of the Books Which Have Been Awarded the Library Association Carnegie Medal, 1936-1975, *edited by Marcus Crouch and Alec Ellis, third edition, The Library Association, 1977, p. 148.*

Sometimes a book appears of such individuality that it strikes one with a shock, as if there were suddenly a new note in the musical scale. We call it originality: such a book was, perhaps, *The Sword in the Stone*. Rosemary Harris's *The Moon in the Cloud* feels rather like another. Yet behind T. H. White's story was the whole, much-used matter of Arthurian myth. And behind *The Moon in the Cloud* lies another undefined immensity, the Egyptian Old Kingdom, and the chronologically parallel story of Noah and his Ark. So it is not subject matter but the fresh vision and use of it that makes the new flavour. Rosemary Harris tells how Ham, Noah's black sheep of a second son, is deputed to go down into Egypt and fetch two sacred cats and two lions for the Ark, while his more industrious brothers labour at the gopher wood. Ham, coward and pleasure-lover, passes this task on to Reuben, a gentle young musician and animal-tamer, blackmailing him into it by promising him, for his beloved, enchanting wife, Thamar, a passage on the Ark. Reuben sets off with Cefalu his black cat, and Benoni his herd dog, upon Anak his camel: endures the hardships of the desert, comforted by the conversation of these intelligent, but quarrelsome animals: falls in with an evil High Priest of an Egyptian god, and becomes his prisoner and slave. But his musical gift saves him, for the High Priest uses it to restore himself into the young King's graces; who, being passionately musical, takes Reuben into his household.

Reuben gains his freedom, and that of a friendly condemned tomb-robber, by a concatenation of dramatic events. Cefalu gains a sacred (albeit stupidly fluffy) mate, and also a lion, whom he speaks fair on the way home. Meanwhile poor Thamar has fled the attentions of lustful Ham, and is in the desert with the rest of their animals and a convenient female lion cub she has nursed. They return rejoicing: Ham over-reaches himself, and Reuben and Thamar take his place in the Ark. The tale is told with humorous assurance, wit, and charm, in sparkling narrative: the beast fable element—for all these animals show distinguishable animal-hood, according to their kind—is blended perfectly with that Old Testament simplicity which describes the Lord God's grumbles, as well as his instructions, to faithful Noah (himself rather the Noah of medieval Mystery plays). There is a sharp difference between the superstitious terrors and evil ways of the many-godded, cynical Egyptians and the lucid faith and uprightness of Noah's folk, which rings very true to the biblical viewpoint.

"Down into Egypt," in The Times Literary Supplement, *No. 3484, December 5, 1968, p. 1367.*

For sheer entertainment value this book is a winner, and I suspect that the author would be the last person to make a claim for it as a serious work of literature. There are all too few books of this kind on the market—unpretentious, inventive, slightly disrespectful to hallowed tradition, lively but unsubtle characterization—the sort of book one immediately enjoys and wishes were twice as long.

Colin Field, in a review of "The Moon in the Cloud," in The School Librarian and School Library Review, *Vol. 17, No. 1, March, 1969, p. 110.*

A teasing, knockabout version of the building of Noah's

ark that has surprising vitality . . . One objectionable manipulation: to get around a final Ham/Reuben impasse, Ham dies and Noah suggests that Reuben take his name—a fact unknown to history and somewhat unsatisfying after such resourceful operations. The rapidfire interplay of Biblical, Egyptian, and traditional elements with a quiet wit (e.g. a parenthetical seraph shrugs four of his six wings) is quite arresting: neither reverent nor irreverent, this reflects a wonderfully idiosyncratic creative energy. For the word- and worldly-wise, a prediluvian groove.

A review of "The Moon in the Cloud," in Kirkus Reviews, *Vol. XXXVIII, No. 1, January 1, 1970, p. 7.*

The style is simple, crisp, and direct; precise in imagery; and unabashedly frank and humorous: "And the female elephant rumbled her stomach ferociously in disgust, like the sound of distant thunder on a summer's dawn." The characters are richly varied: Noah, a bumbling prophet with disobedient sons; Tahlevi, although a thief, the kindest of men; the King, lonely, but generous and humane beneath his hieratic trappings; the High Priest and the Vizier, each constantly embroiled in political schemes; Reuben's animals, especially Cefalu; and Reuben himself, not only an animal-tamer and musician, but a stubborn monotheist and a loving husband, who undertook his quest for the sake of his wife. Subjecting both the myth-making faculty of the ancient world and the foibles of human—and animal—nature to an implacable scrutiny, the book successfully blends fantasy with comedy. (p. 168)

Paul Heins, in a review of "The Moon in the Cloud," in The Horn Book Magazine, *Vol. XLVI, No. 2, April, 1970, pp. 167-68.*

Reuben's quest is the centerpiece, yet Miss Harris has also woven a background of history, myth and Biblical lore. Without editorializing, she scores a strong point for monotheism by indicating the sheer nuisance of idolatry: with so many fickle gods to placate, the people of Kemi found it hard to remember all their names.

The pace of the narrative is brisk and Miss Harris's style is sprightly. Her humor at times seems a bit precious (in portraying the Lord as somewhat gruff and grumbly and Noah as rather dotty), but that may not bother younger readers.

Oona Sullivan, in a review of "The Moon in the Cloud," in The New York Times Book Review, *April 20, 1970, p. 26.*

The Shadow on the Sun (1970)

One could hardly dare hope for more of the story of Reuben and Thamar, that candid, enchanting couple from the days of Noah's Flood whom Rosemary Harris introduced to us in *The Moon in the Cloud.* But it was a rich vein, still workable: and here they are returning to Egypt, after the waters have retreated, to find the appealing young King Merenkere in the throes of a dreadful conflict. He has fallen, direly, in love with a court chamberlain's daughter whose unspoilt sincerity contrasts so sharply with the tired convolutions of the cynical courtiers. Meri-

Harris, at left, with her brother Anthony and sister Marigold.

Mekhmet has responded, not recognizing her King, a figure who, as she tells him, she thinks "must be absolutely disgusting". (In fact, who could fail to fall in love with *this*, unofficial, Merenkere, so full of gentleness, perception and charm, and apparently uncorrupted by his power?) Brought unwillingly to court by the priestess, her Aunt Tut (whose apt name is a good example of the humorous lightness with which the author wears her Egyptology), poor Meri-Mekhmet recognizes in the King her unknown lover. At the same shocking audience, Merenkere recognizes (behind a beard) his court musician Reuben, whom he receives back with joy. Meri-Mekhmet's decision is instant and unequivocal: she will have nothing more to do with the King. He pleads, pines, grows angry, and harshly tyrannical and, "unbalanced from sheer unhappiness" (as Thamar says), finally succumbs to the prevailing fever. Thamar, full of warmth and anger, knows what to do, and fetches Meri-Mekhmet (who must be weaned from her prudish exclusiveness and her horror at the large official number of concubines) to his bedside. However, the death of the Great Royal Wife from the fever saves her face and the King's honour, for their love is obviously the lasting passion of like for like. Then, when all seems plain sailing, Meri-Mekhmet, searching for her kitten, disappears. . . .

Then the noble cat Cefalu plays his part, investigating among the bandit cats at the waterfront: and he and his master Reuben and the elephant M'tuska set off to the outlandish region of Punt (into which the author injects all the symbolical terrors of Africa when still "dark"). Here a sorceress mesmerizes away the eyes of her victims and puts them into the heads of myriads of snakes, forming a hateful tree. Reuben, encouraged by the still, small voice of his lord God, must confront the tree. (One trembles to think how all English literature will manage without the "still, small voice" of the Authorized Version.)

It is, once more, an exciting, compelling story, full of tenderness and humour. Noah himself is complacent at being delivered from the Flood: Mrs. Noah, horribly fascinated by the wickedness of Egypt, comes to investigate, buys an almost transparent linen dress, and then makes herself indispensable in the wicked Vizier's kitchen, feeding him so well that, as the King says, "his teeth are drawn" and he

can quietly retire. A reformed tomb-robber, Tahlevi is now the King's jeweller. And once more the animals take their part, characterizing themselves and their species in their aptly translated talk; for (says the author) "their language is so well understood by Reuben and Thamar that it's here given as human speech".

> *"Romance in Ancient Egypt," in* The Times Literary Supplement, *No. 3566, July 2, 1970, p. 711.*

A successful sequel to **The Moon in the Cloud** . . . As in the previous book, the events are briskly related, and the protocol-loving Egyptians are presented as exemplars of a huge human comedy. . . . As in **The Moon in the Cloud,** the style is simple, concrete, and humorous and, on occasion, rises to moments of serious horror. "He [Reuben] raised his eyes, and had a shock. All the branches and creepers [on the tree] were alive with snakes. They coiled or writhed, or lay there watching him. Their eyes were human eyes." But the predominating mood of the book is humor, and it is found even in moments of great solemnity: "Reuben wished he felt himself as courageous as the still small voice expected of him. He would have given much to be elsewhere."

> *Paul Heins, in a review of "The Shadow on the Sun," in* The Horn Book Magazine, *Vol. XLVI, No. 5, October, 1970, p. 481.*

The pleasant but perhaps too hastily written book suffers from a contrived plot—its basic premises are improbable, and the problems it poses, too easily solved. For example, the death of the cat, Meluseth, seems unnecessary, structurally, as does the reintroduction of the villain, Kenamut; the Pharaoh's First Wife dies as conveniently as the Vizier Senusmet is tamed. This aside, the characterization is superb, the creation of mood and atmosphere, excellent, and the author's prose, a joy. Though not at potential classic level like **The Moon in the Cloud,** the book is a pleasant entertainment; that in itself is enough, for there's no abundance of those.

> *Michael Cart, in a review of "The Shadow on the Sun," in* School Library Journal, *Vol. 17, No. 3, November, 1970, p. 108.*

The Seal-Singing (1971)

[**The Seal-Singing**] is a rich, many-faceted novel for teenagers that has a haunting beauty. Laid in Scotland, it tells of 17-year-old Toby Carrigon, and his cousins, Catriona and Miranda, who spend a disturbing summer together on a remote island, the ancient home of the Carrigon family. They have been brought up on legends of St. Cuthbert, who made a pact of friendship with the island seals, and of their ancestor, the lovely but troubled Lucy, whom tragedy turned to witchcraft. Singing a strange lament, Lucy lured the seals to their death; now Miranda, not sure who she is at times or in which century, almost does the same. Famous until now for her stories of Old Testament Days, Rosemary Harris includes a fascinating account of a pet seal, and a sensitive portrait of two young people in love, in this original and outstanding novel. (p. 180)

Elizabeth Minot Graves, "The Year of the Witch," in Commonweal, *Vol. XCV, No. 8, November 19, 1971, pp. 179-82.*

A disappointing offering by the author of the well-received **The Moon in the Cloud** and **The Shadow on the Sun**. . . . This is basically an ordinary history-intrudes-on-the-present story, well-told but slow-moving, with appealing characterizations, detailed descriptions of island life, and an affectionate account of Toby's raising a baby seal. Though neither a gripping psychological fantasy nor an atmospheric mood piece, it's still an adequate addition to the teen-age romance shelf.

Margaret A. Dorsey, in a review of "The Seal-Singing," in School Library Journal, *Vol. 18, No. 4, December, 1971, p. 64.*

Totally different from the author's notable, witty story about Noah and the Flood in **The Moon in the Cloud** . . . and its sequel **The Shadow on the Sun,** this book is a compelling piece of contemporary fiction. . . . The author creates both excitement and humor by her skillful juxtaposition of strange and haunting elements. Especially dramatic is the impingement of the past on the present as in Alan Garner's *The Owl Service.* The successful conveying of the island atmosphere strengthens the story, and the love relationship between the two cousins is skillfully treated. A delightful reading experience for an able, sophisticated young person.

Virginia Haviland, in a review of "The Seal-Singing," in The Horn Book Magazine, *Vol. XLVIII, No. 1, February, 1972, p. 57.*

The Child in the Bamboo Grove   (1971)

The infant hidden in a bamboo stem grows up to great beauty, sends her suitors on impossible quests but is woman enough to explain to the favoured one, the Emperor himself, that as a daughter of the Sun she may not stay long on earth. The author fills out the touching Eastern legend by sharply characterising the suitors—greedy, lazy and cowardly as they are—and by balancing wit and mystery in her elegant prose.

Margery Fisher, in a review of "The Child in the Bamboo Grove," in Growing Point, *Vol. 10, No. 6, December, 1971, p. 1854.*

First a word of warning. Despite the format this is not a picture book. It has pictures by that outstanding master of the stylised drawing, Errol Le Cain, but these are only an accompaniment to Miss Harris' long-short story. The theme is a well-known one in fairy-tales, that of the child discovered by a poor man who grows up to bring her foster parent wealth and happiness. To this is added another, that of the suitors set tasks in order to win a bride. The conclusion contains an unexpected and deeply moving twist. The story is told with great beauty and in calm, timeless words. The text is literally flawless. . . . (pp. 377-78)

M. Crouch, in a review of "The Child in the

Bamboo Grove," in The Junior Bookshelf, *Vol. 35, No. 6, December, 1971, pp. 377-78.*

An old Japanese legend tells of a bamboo cutter who finds a baby girl in the forest and raises her lovingly and lavishly with the gold that mysteriously appears as well. When the girl grows up her surpassing beauty attracts all manner of suitors, but she evades even the five most persistent by setting them impossible tasks—until at last a visit from the smitten emperor himself precipitates her return to her real father, the sun, leaving behind an undying elixir which burns still on the summit of Fuji-yama. [Errol] Le Cain's decorative pictures, made to resemble old Japanese screens and scroll paintings (even to the predominantly ocher backgrounds), suit Rosemary Harris' respectful retelling, but the remote tone, and unfocused viewpoint, obscure motivation are likely to make this an elegant shelf sitter. (pp. 1144-45)

A review of "The Child in the Bamboo Grove," in Kirkus Reviews, *Vol. XL, No. 19, October 1, 1972, pp. 1144-45.*

The Bright and Morning Star   (1972)

Rosemary Harris deftly finishes her Egyptian trilogy in the year of what we have affectionately if irreligiously come to call "Tut's tomb", thereby greatly adding to its interest, and moreover setting a central scene of high drama in the future Great Eternal House of King Merenkere himself, the enlightened and gentle pharaoh whom readers of the earlier books have come to love.

The Bright and Morning Star begins, as usual, with Reuben and Thamar, now Prince and Princess of Canaan by Merenkere's generosity, and their family. Only one thing spoils their happiness; Sadhi, the second boy, has suffered an illness when small which has left him speechless and deaf, and furiously frustrated and therefore tyrannical and hating. He is the first cause of this new story. In fact, the tale begins with the old wise cat Cefalu, dreaming of his youth and teased by his many descendant kittens. Cefalu's tart commentary on events, and his offspring's use as spies and messengers are happily still evident, and one feels that age alone may have prevented him from playing the leading part he took in former times.

Thamar, endlessly distressed about Sadhi but ever hopeful, understands the chance word of a beggar and the sight of some falling stars to mean that she must take him down to Kemi, to seek help at the court of Merenkere. Her arrival coincides with an important event at Kemi: the ceremonial betrothal of King Merenkere's weak and ambitious son, Sinuhe, with his step-sister Ta-Thata. This beautiful and spirited princess is the daughter of Merenkere's beloved Great Royal Wife, Meri-Mekhmet, whose love story we heard in **The Shadow on the Sun,** and she is like her mother: both wish that the Custom did not force her to marry Sinuhe, a bully because he is weak (he is rather a stock character) and an easy prey for the ambitions of the sinister priest of Set, No-Hotep, who has been made his tutor. Indeed, various people at court are uneasily aware of evil forces and intentions, particularly Hekhti, Chief Royal Architect, a physician, and a philosopher, as well as a devoted friend to Ta-Thata. It is he who sets about first taming Sadhi and then teaching him a language of hand signs, an invention of his own, to let him out of the prison of his frustration.

Meanwhile, wicked No-Hotep has fabricated a precarious series of steps upwards to the Throne itself, in the accomplishment of which he intends to discard each innocent below who has served his purpose: only Ta-Thata, the heiress, whom he must marry to be accepted by the people, will be saved.

The story of how, finally, Hekhti sets in motion just as intricate, delicate and satisfying a plot for the rescue of the king and the eventual crocodiling of No-Hotep is, if anything, more breathlessly exciting than before; but do the characters of the Egyptian scene have an artificiality; their conversation a somehow contrived brittleness, which contrasts with the sure sense of inevitability in the two earlier tales? This applies more to the bad characters, and may simply illustrate the well-known truth that it is extremely difficult to draw convincing villains. Also, the truly brilliant convolutions of plot and counterplot leave less time for the gentler art of realizing the considerable number of new characters. All the same, Ta-Thata and Hekhti are fully-drawn, lovable people; the (very modern) study of Sadhi is interesting; and a new one is added to the speaking animals, the crocodile Hikupptah (the force of whose name may evade one on a first reading) who even holds out hope for No-Hotep, as he says: "There was a lot of good somewhere in that young man . . . Some criminals are very sour, you could say their criminality was pervasive. A pity he used his dark side instead of his light. . . ."

These entrancing stories, exotic and yet homely, humorous yet intensely dramatic, deserve to last long and bind many.

> *"Intrigue in Ancient Egypt," in* The Times Literary Supplement, *No. 3672, July 14, 1972, p. 810.*

This concluding volume in Rosemary Harris's uniquely flavoured Egyptian trilogy moves still further in the direction already signalled by **The Shadow on the Sun.** The plot becomes a stronger and more important ingredient, with swift moving events following each other thick and fast and all pervaded by a spicing of romance. However, the sophisticated verbal wit which was such a feature of the opening volume, is rather less in evidence.

The melodrama and romance both stem from the central situation in which the young princess Ta-Thata becomes the object of ruthless political intrigue, since the man who marries her will become the eventual ruler of the kingdom. The fact that both the legitimate and usurping claimants for her hand range from the mildly distasteful to the utterly repellent serves to create the sort of piquant situations more familiar to the readers of the romantic novels of the early years of this century, in which young English maidens are carried off by lustful sheiks. From which it may be inferred that girls (and boys too?) will find plenty here to feed their adolescent fantasies . . . and they certainly

won't complain at the somewhat uncharacteristic writing which has occasionally crept into the book:

> 'He twisted his right hand in her heavy hair to turn her face toward him . . . kissed her slowly and thoroughly, and then released her and stood up. If she had had a dagger she would have tried to kill him, whatever the result. He read it in her eyes, and smiled again. "I have you cornered, pretty panther, so keep those royal claws sheathed. Any violent action against me—or against yourself—and the Queen will suffer for it. . . ." '

In many ways this is the most straightforward of the trilogy and perhaps the story with the widest appeal. Although those who have not read the previous two volumes may be confused by the vast collection of characters with their unfamiliar names, they will soon be swept along by the action-packed plot, full of suspense, with kidnappings and brutal assassinations.

Rosemary Harris is one of the outstanding writers for children today. In this trilogy she has successfully combined the elements which characterise the best-seller: full-blooded plot, pace, action, romance, colourful settings and characters (including some splendid villains)—and served them up with a wit and elegance that lend her stories a unique and distinctive flavour.

> *Eleanor von Schweinitz, in a review of "The Bright and Morning Star," in* Children's Book Review, *Vol. II, No. 4, September, 1972, p. 114.*

The original characters are older now, but the new young people (including the great-great-great-great-great grandchildren of Cefalu) are just as enchanting and memorable, and the original magic, wit and sparkle are still there in full measure. There is even an added depth, poignancy and beauty in this book, and all three volumes are undoubtedly among the most outstanding contributions to children's literature of recent years. (p. 257)

> *Robert Bell, in a review of "The Bright and Morning Star," in* The School Librarian, *Vol. 20, No. 3, September, 1972, pp. 254, 257.*

The King's White Elephant   (1973)

Elephants seldom fail to please. Their star quality and almost universal appeal are well known. **The King's White Elephant** is no exception, though it is his more mundane grey fellows who figure largest in this book. The less common beast of the title, who will restore the luck of the King of Siam as well as resolving the problems of lesser mortals, becomes the object of the greatest quest that never was. His abrupt and timely arrival—literally his Materialization—comes as something of a shock to Western minds, but all is triumphantly carried off by the cool Miss Harris. A deceptive lightness of touch, combined with the oblique humour and verbal wit which distinguish all her work, makes this a real delight, to which is added the enjoyment of the "Siamese" pictures [by Errol Le Cain] in which elephants and their servants—never masters—perform against a lush background of exotic greenery, minarets and palaces, all set with butterflies and flowers.

> *"Aladdin's Caves," in* The Times Literary Supplement, *No. 3742, November 23, 1973, p. 1431.*

This may look like a picture book but is not. Rosemary Harris is one of the modern masters of elegant sophisticated prose, but she has no need of an artist to comment on her work and no wish to confine herself within the disciplines of the picture book form. What she has done here is to write a long-short story, as artificial and formally ornamented as the art and society of Siam in which it is set. She leaves Errol Le Cain little to do except to indulge his eclecticism in producing a series of most gorgeous designs in which fun breaks through the formal beauty. The result is a book for which the word "distinguished" is ready to hand, but it is by no means clear for which children it will have something to say. (pp. 23-4)

> *M. Crouch, in a review of "The King's White Elephant," in* The Junior Bookshelf, *Vol. 38, No. 1, February, 1974, pp. 23-4.*

In her previous collaboration with Errol Le Cain, *The Child in the Bamboo Grove,* Rosemary Harris based her text on a Japanese folk tale and Errol Le Cain drew on the traditions of Japanese art for his illustrations. *The King's White Elephant* is an original story with a strong oriental folk flavour that seems at odds with the facetious tone of the text, in which the author appears to be sending up not only the main characters but the whole society which forms the background to her story. Now this has always been a characteristic of Rosemary Harris's writing (remember the opening encounter between God and Noah in *The Moon in the Cloud*?) but a sophisticated approach which is effective (not to say dazzling) in a full-length novel for older readers, may be quite inappropriate in a picture story book for young children—especially one which draws so directly on traditional roots.

The stylistic uncertainties of the text seem to have communicated themselves to Errol Le Cain whose illustrations combine an uneasy mixture of broad caricature together with meticulous ornamental detailing in background and landscape. Neither text nor illustration seem sure of the note they wish to strike and this has resulted in a blunting of the highly individual style which both author and artist have exhibited in the best of their work for children.

> *Eleanor von Schweinitz, in a review of "The King's White Elephant," in* Children's Book Review, *Vol. IV, No. 1, Spring, 1974, p. 11.*

The Lotus and the Grail: Legends from East to West
(1974; abridged edition published in U.S. as *Sea Magic and Other Stories of Enchantment*)

Ten intoxicating stories, each based on a legend from a different country and involving superstitions, monsters, gods, or spirits. From France comes **"The castle of Ker Glas,"** a hero tale of a peasant boy's journey through the Forest of Illusion and a Sea of Dragons for the prizes of a magic lance and healing goblet. From Egypt is **"Bata,"** about a young man who loves his faithless wife so much that, to follow her after his death, he takes on the form of a bull, a tree, and finally her child. Each tale is more haunting than the last as the author skillfully transforms old and sometimes familiar yarns, filling them with character and mystery. The flavors in every story invite the reader to pace himself and rest often, savoring and thinking; they linger in the mind.

> *A review of "Sea Magic and Other Stories of Enchantment," in* The Booklist, *Vol. 70, No. 14, March 15, 1974, p. 819.*

The Lotus and the Grail, subtitled "Legends from East to West", is something more than re-telling. The author has taken a number of familiar tales and has turned them into what could be called reflective novellas. For each one she has chosen a style that will reflect the atmosphere of a particular country. Occasionally the local colour seems to me overdone—in **"The Guardian Snake"** from Hispaniola, for instance, with its hectic piling up of obeah incantations and bastard French phrases, or in **"The Cockleshell,"** a Maori legend whose re-telling lacks the characteristic breadth of emotion in which laughter and thought go together. There is also a curious coarseness and even a facetious note now and again that jars on the feelings—especially in **"King Solomon's Throne,"** a free expansion of one of the many legends from Persia of Solomon and Sheba; the author seems to have made an unwarranted attempt here to bring the royal and legendary lovers down to everyday human dimensions.

The most satisfying stories are those which are most truly part of our own heritage—tales from Greece, Romania, Russia, Germany and, above all, that most mysterious tale of all, the Breton "Peronnik," here called **"The Castle of Ker Glas"**; this story magnificently rounds off a volume concerned with folk and fairy tale in a most original and personal way. The volume has been sumptuously produced and has full-page illustrations by Errol Le Cain, who has taken his own way of looking at primitive tales that have gathered an accretion of later feelings. The design, composition and decorative detail of, for instance, his picture of the strange twins in the West African tale **"The Ten-year Child,"** or for the Greek tale of **"The stolen Prince,"** makes comments that are complete in themselves and yet fit with Rosemary Harris's exploration of the motifs and themes which she mentions in a Foreword. I doubt whether one should take too strictly her listing of "the swallowing of someone else's father to make strong magic" or "the finding or bestowing of gold as a reward", as examples of what has moved her to choose these particular tales. We can be content to accept her choice and accept that something in each of the tales has inspired a very personal and provocative version.

> *Margery Fisher, in a review of "The Lotus and the Grail," in* Growing Point, *Vol. 13, No. 2, July, 1974, p. 2422.*

In her foreword to *The Lotus and the Grail* Rosemary Harris describes her search for a theme for the book. Finding a general heading—such as "The Search"—unsatisfactory because such legends tended to be either repetitive or else nonexistent in some parts of the world, she finished by taking her choice from different groups: but

> in all of them something, someone; wholeness; wisdom; blessing; another person . . . or even the swallowing of someone else's father to make strong magic, is the goal. The finding or bestowing of gold as a reward is a common ingredient in quite a number. . . .

Which is simply to say that each one has a plot and that in many cases aspiration reaps a material reward.

In fact, the thread is tenuous in the extreme. The eighteen stories are links in a chain which puts a meandering girdle round the earth and each one has really been chosen for some wholeness in itself which appealed to the author's turn of mind. This is entirely as it should be, especially since Miss Harris's other avowed aim has been to give fresh interpretations of old tales rather than "correct folklore versions". No arbitrary similarities of theme could be half as telling as the strongest connecting thread of all, which is the writer's own identity.

They are good stories and Miss Harris tells them well. Her feeling for the provenance of each one is sure. Less so, perhaps, was the instinct which has led her to fall, now and then, into the local accent. Dialogue in pidgin Chinee has the effect of distancing, and at worst belittling, a touching story of a husband's devotion; where the same trick is used in narrative—as in the West Indian tale—it sits uneasily because the writer is not consistent. She drops it like a hot brick whenever it becomes inconvenient.

Only **"The Castle of Ker Glas"** (Peronik: France) and **"The Small Red Ox"** (Iceland, but widespread in northern Europe) are at all well known outside their countries of origin—or possibly even within them. Many contain a strong element of violence—murder, ritual sacrifice, battle and rape—but the values which emerge are those of love, gentleness and compassion. Even the saddest story, **"Trandafir"**, in which the hero-prince, born of a rose-tree, returns at last, disillusioned with the world of men, to become a rose in his turn, ends on a note of quiet resignation. And yet it is not altogether easy to picture the reader whom Rosemary Harris had in mind as she wrote.

Unlike the lyric poet whose words are an expression of his own mood, a storyteller must be talking to someone. Tales are not wasted on the ambient air: even "Midas has asses' ears" was whispered to the reeds. But these are not tales for young children, who are the usual consumers of legends. They are difficult in two ways. First, in the alien attitudes which inform them and which the writer has been at pains not to obscure. Secondly, in the degree of sophistication, both mental and physical, which robs them of the traditional, blunt innocence of folklore. This, while it ultimately brings a greater depth of understanding, also makes the traditional ingredients of sex and violence more immediately perplexing and horrific.

It is possible—although one hopes not—that this is a book which will fail to reach its true readership: going over the heads of some and not attracting those to whom it would have something important to say. The beauty of Errol Le

Cain's illustrations, which have a sophistication matching that of the text, should help to prevent this happening.

The Lotus and the Grail is an unusually rich production. . . .

> *"Fishing up the Murex," in* The Times Literary Supplement, *No. 3774, July 5, 1974, p. 716.*

There have been many collections of folk tales and there will be many more, but it will be difficult to equal this one for interest. It is a highly individual and fascinating assembly of eighteen stories from as many countries. Rosemary Harris has kept the national style of narration so skilfully that it needs only a few sentences to establish the country of origin in the reader's mind. So **"Irani and the Cuckoos"** could be only Indian, **"The Ten Year Child"** African, **"Bata"** Egyptian.

The author says that she has completed the stories where links are missing and interpreted the tales afresh, but this has been done so skilfully that the joins and interpolations defy detection and the "interpretation" is an imaginative re-creation which convinces.

To compile a collection of this scope entails a formidable amount of research, but the retelling is never academic but very much alive, with touches of the ironic humour which made ***The Moon in the Cloud*** so entertaining. The stories range from the sophisticated humour of **"King Solomon's Throne"** to the macabre **"The Graveyard Rose."**

While scarcely an anthology for "children", it could well appeal to "young people" (whatever age range this term means). Adults will appreciate its irony and the glimpses of other ways of thinking about life so evident in "the people's literature" folklore, which has such deep roots in religion and history.

The illustrations are splendid in design and execution and the perfect complement to the varied contents of the stories. A book of distinction in style and production. (pp. 229-30)

> *E. Colwell, in a review of "The Lotus and the Grail: Legends from East to West," in* The Junior Bookshelf, *Vol. 38, No. 4, August, 1974, pp. 229-30.*

The Flying Ship (1975)

Rosemary Harris has turned a familiar Russian folk-tale into a stylish novel, with extensive use of dialogue and with some personality attached to the spoilt Grand Duchess Annushka, her quavering old nurse, the noisy, bullying Czar and the "young man in a shrunken black smock" who wins his royal bride with the help of three travellers conveniently endowed with unusual talents. This is a story that lends itself to elaboration in words, and Errol Le Cain's pictures, gorgeous in colour and intricate in style, add a sophisticated gloss to it. He uses decorative borders to enclose scenes in which satire and humour complement one another; the magical aspect of the story is shown mainly in the interpretation of the ship itself, which is seen always in the distance, small, floating, gay and very evidently enchanted.

Margery Fisher, in a review of "The Flying Ship," in Growing Point, *Vol. 13, No. 9, April, 1975, p. 2612.*

This is a delightfully authentic-seeming fairy tale about a bad-tempered ruler who offers his daughter in marriage to anyone who can collect her in a flying ship. He tries to back out when a mere peasant boy, aided by the white magic of a wandering staretz, fulfils his condition, but his further impossible demands are met by the oddly assorted passengers the kind-hearted boy has picked up on his journey. The delight of this amusingly-told story is increased a hundredfold by the clever setting in a Russia which is at once fairy tale and an authentic picture of life under the Little Father of All the Russias, attended by faithful Boyars and devout Eastern Orthodox womenfolk, and giving vent when annoyed to unexpectedly daring "swears". Events and rescues fall so pat that there is an interesting effect of parody of the fairy tale form itself. The attractiveness is further increased by the fantasy-illustrations, with their Tolkien-like landscapes, compact humorous figures and folk-art borders. (pp. 175-76)

M. Hobbs, in a review of "The Flying Ship," in The Junior Bookshelf, *Vol. 39, No. 3, June, 1975, pp. 175-76.*

The retelling of an old folk tale achieves success in this case through the joint abilities of the author and illustrator. The fairy-tale atmosphere is admirably created by the combination of rich sounding words and gloriously detailed illustrations. The simplicity of the peasant lad who sets out to win the czar's haughty daughter is in sharp contrast to the opulence of the royal court. Peter's triumph over the czar's wily schemes is achieved with the help of the interesting characters he befriends, and their exploits are described with great charm and wit. A fresh approach to an old story.

Elizabeth Weir, in a review of "The Flying Ship," in The School Librarian, *Vol. 23, No. 4, December, 1975, p. 317.*

The Little Dog of Fo (1976)

Rosemary Harris has gone to the East for several legends and folktales on which to exercise her opulent style, and **The Little Dog of Fo** may have the same origin, though no source is stated anywhere in the book. She tells of a land where under Buddha's orders the animals live in peace and of a small lion who, unable to suppress his instincts, unlawfully kills a gazelle. As a punishment he is forbidden to join in a temple ceremony but, overhearing a plot to steal the treasures inside, he disobeys the Buddha and as a reward for his courage becomes official guard to the building. The story has called forth some very attractive decorative effects from [illustrator] Errol Le Cain, who excels especially in the way he uses leaves and branches formally to integrate jungle scenes; the pictures are also united through a colour scheme in which Chinese red and shades of brown predominate richly. However,

Harris with Anthony and their maternal grandmother, Alexandra Gruinard Battye Money, in 1941. Harris writes that her grandmother "was my first introduction to the born storyteller."

the strain of archness in the treatment of the little sleeve-Peke, which is treated with almost sentimental jocosity both by author and artist, has spoilt my enjoyment.

> *Margery Fisher, in a review of "The Little Dog of Fo," in* Growing Point, *Vol. 15, No. 5, November, 1976, p. 2994.*

Presumably the quaint figures to be seen at the entrance to temples and shrines in China and Japan, figures which seem to be uncertain whether to be lions or dogs, are the inspiration of this invented legend of Buddha. Buddha forbids all animals to kill and all obey, much against their natural instincts. Only the little lion is tempted and kills. Condemned to be an outcast, he wins forgiveness by killing a thief at the temple—hardly a logical solution. This is fantasy but fantasy too must have its logic.

> *E. Colwell, in a review of "The Little Dog of Fo," in* The Junior Bookshelf, *Vol. 41, No. 2, April, 1977, p. 78.*

A Quest for Orion (1978)

Nineteen ninety-nine. Western Europe is largely occupied by a "neo-Stalinist" regime; there are slave-labour camps and resistance cells. London is a no-go area run by street gangs; America, curiously, is neutral. And in this uncheerful setting, we find a potentially excellent book. Rosemary Harris's *A Quest for Orion* seems at first to be just a well-written adventure story, sharply paced and well-plotted. A group of middle-class adolescents joins up with a gang of London toughs, fights the occupation forces, and takes to the Northumberland hills. Matt escapes from a Bavarian slave gang, passes through the hands of German resistance groups, and finds his way back to England. The fact that he carries Charlemagne's crown and talisman with him may seem out of key with this bald summary; in the context of the book, it is both natural and inevitable.

These protective symbols are one of the ways in which Rosemary Harris escapes that most paradoxical failing of writers of books set in the future, that of not convincing us that their characters inhabit a complete world. Here they exist in the more profound continuum of space and time. Underlying the action, and often justifying the coincidences which hold it together, is a rich texture of symbol and allusion, an awareness of historic recurrence, of the re-enactment of legend, and an implication of cosmic intervention. It is an ambitious mixture, but, as with some of her earlier books, Miss Harris more or less brings it off by using skilful settings and characterizations, and by avoiding overt explanations. Thus the characters carry their multiple roles with surprising ease. Alastair may have the insight of a Sage, but he remains a puzzled, sad, spastic boy: Wolf takes on a tragic-heroic role, but he is still at root a shrewd wide-boy.

As the first of two linked books, *A Quest for Orion* has no real resolution, and it will be interesting to see whether the author solves her major problem, that of the mystic or magic clashing with the realistic and scientific. So far, partly because she has wisely avoided too much futuristic

hardware, the trick works. Although not flawless, this book deserves a good deal of attention.

> *Peter Hunt, "The Future Shook Us," in* The Times Literary Supplement, *No. 3991, September 29, 1978, p. 1089.*

A Quest for Orion takes an Orwellian look at 1999. Neo-Stalinist Freaks have conquered Western Europe; soft civilization is a burnt out wreck. But the Freaks are less efficient than the Thought Police—and pockets of Resistance fight on.

Ms Harris has her eye on the Charlemagne legend, where heroes do and die against impossible odds. The spark glimmers fitfully; the first of these two volumes ends with the balance well in favour of the night. The hard-edged style bears its own bitter realism (shots of a blackened London where survivors roam like wolves). There are also patches of escapist fantasy, impossible adventures and re-unions.

The style makes linguistic assumptions well beyond the level of the content; and for all its yobbery the middle class tone reminds one of a toughened up *Swallows and Amazons*. That apart, this epic tale grips the imagination. I look forward to reading the second volume after being left stranded in the dark before the dawn.

> *Peter Fanning, "Out of This World," in* The Times Educational Supplement, *No. 3308, November 24, 1978, p. 50.*

[*A Quest for Orion*] is an intrepid saga set in the final year of the twentieth century, when Britain and Western Europe are in the iron grip of a neo-Stalinist organization of technological, militaristic dictatorships, known to their enemies as the "Freaks." (p. 152)

The novel is more than just a fast-paced science fiction adventure. Any comparison with John Christopher's *The White Mountains* trilogy fails, because its mythic, romantic, and fantasy strains are more reminiscent of William Mayne's *Earthfasts* or Susan Cooper's *The Dark Is Rising* quintet. The power of the ancient hero-myths and legends resonates throughout the book. The mythical protectors of Europe—the Matter of Britain and France—hover in the air:

> "Plague, sword, exodus," said Bill abruptly. "Book of Revelation come to life, that's what it is. Sword: that's what *we* need, though—where's Arthur's, or whatsisname's. Roland's?"
>
> "What Europe needed was another Charlemagne, Matt said," murmured Jan, rousing herself to speak of him.

The novel is the legends come to life: the sleeping kings, Arthur and Charlemagne, who are in some way returning in symbol or spirit to aid their desperate people.

There are many characters in *A Quest for Orion,* and they are vividly sketched, leaving a taste of authentically delineated individuals. For although this is a story of plot and adventure, it is also one of character growth and formation. The characters are teenagers in a tale of survival and defeat, and the effects of struggle and suffering on the individual young people are made manifest in their character development. But even in character development, Harris maintains a mystic quality. Alastair, like Fiver in *Watership Down,* is a physically weak, psychically powerful person, half victim, half prophet, who becomes a kind of priest-king to a tribe of teenage boys led by his wild protector, Wolf, a slum kid whose natural survival skills and uncanny sense of leadership inspire fervent allegiance.

Wolf and Alastair are in some sense the two parts of the Arthur legend—the rough but honorable chieftain and the visionary king. One may also see in them a kind of restatement of Launcelot-Merlin-Arthur. However aligned, they do embody the essential legend of Britain. There is a harsh loyalty and emotional link between the two boys that sparks the insane jealousy of Alastair's brother, Tom, an embittered, Mordred-figure, who ultimately betrays the entire clan.

The novel's science fiction elements are observable only at the beginning (future time) and toward the end of this first book when Alastair and Walther, another of the protagonists, receive a song-chant-message from what appears to be the constellation Orion. Walther, in an astronomical observatory with his captors, notices the image of the northern hemisphere constellations beginning to circle:

> The giddy dance went on. He saw Orion's familiar belt of stars, closer and closer . . . he grew conscious of sound waves beating against his eardrums, growing in volume, high, hypnotic, meaning somehow conveyed through the rhythms of a wordless song.

> "You are still too far away—You must hold to the Great King's treasure. Hidden are the ways— . . . "Not flinch before . . . Deliverance . . . do you understand?"

As in all "high fantasy," the primeval struggle of good and evil is here engaged, and the striking presence of unknown, extraterrestrial powers from the constellation Orion and of the mythic legendary kings is akin to Susan Cooper's forces of Light. In this mesh of science fiction, fantasy, and psychic phenomena, the unknown beings from Orion seem to be communicating through "mind touch" rather than advanced technology. *A Quest for Orion* may be breaking new ground or it may turn out to be what Brian Aldiss called "a shining but unsubstantial wonder." Since the trilogy is not complete, judgment must be suspended.

Yet it is clear that Rosemary Harris . . . has enriched science fiction by her emphasis on character development, so lacking in children's science fiction until the 1970s. (pp. 152-53)

> *Sheila A. Egoff, "Science Fiction: 'A Quest for Orion',"* in her *Thursday's Child: Trends and Patterns in Contemporary Children's Literature, American Library Association, 1981, pp. 152-53.*

Beauty and the Beast (1979)

Only those who see some merit in Errol Le Cain's minute-

ly particularized, metallic illustration will see any value in this ornate dumb-show—with every character posturing, every curlicue vying for attention. Harris' retelling is geared to the double-page format, but not especially to reading aloud ("So she cajoled him till she forced his hand, and won his sorrowful consent—while her sisters inwardly rejoiced, but wept like crocodiles at the farewell"); apart from being shorter, in fact, it's inferior to the Lang version for any purpose. So that leaves the pictures—which themselves leave nothing to anyone's imagination, thereby constricting rather than expanding the story.

> *A review of "Beauty and the Beast," in* Kirkus Reviews, *Vol. XLVIII, No. 9, May 1, 1980, p. 576.*

Beauty and the Beast begins marvelously, with a grand illustration of the merchant and his daughters while still wealthy. The merchant saying farewell to his daughters in the woods is almost as good, but after that the effects are increasingly mannered and out of touch with the tale. And, unfortunately, Rosemary Harris, who tells the tale, is given to having Beauty say things like "Why should I weep? I shall die joyfully for our dear father." This badly disqualifies Beauty for anything except martyrdom in Beast's palace. Mr. Le Cain then tries out a half-dozen ways to render Beast because he seems to know it would be best, but extremely difficult, to settle for one way and stick to it.

> *Roger Sale, in a review of "Beauty and the Beast," in* The New York Times Book Review, *May 11, 1980, p. 25.*

In this retelling of ***Beauty and the beast*** Ms Harris makes no concessions to the reading competence of small children. Her style retains the formality and rhythmic form of the tradition and reads aloud well. Mr Le Cain provides exquisite full-page paintings, each showing in detail, in sombre rich colours, an event which is described on the accompanying page of text, the latter bordered by stylised flowers and fantastical birds. A delightfully pretty book, and much to be recommended, it meets the reader where he is and leads him outwards. (p. 142)

> *Gabrielle Maunder, in a review of "Beauty and the Beast," in* The School Librarian, *Vol. 28, No. 2, June, 1980, p. 142.*

Green Finger House (1980)

When her brother gets measles, Minna is sent not to young Cousin Cathy but to 'old Aunt Stubbs', who is prim and strict, but has an interesting way with plants. Inspired by her, Minna retires to the beach to construct a pebble ground-plan which she hopes will grow into a house. Before she is weary of her game, Cousin Cathy arrives to fetch her to stay in the new cottage across the bay, which seems oddly familiar. A rather bland text with a plea for imagination. . . .

> *Margery Fisher, in a review of "Green Finger House," in* Growing Point, *Vol. 19, No. 1, May, 1980, p. 3710.*

This is a lovely book, sensitive in its story. . . . It is the tale of a dream born out of loneliness, and centres upon a small energetic child sent to stay with a severe, precise maiden aunt. Trapped inside an unbearably over-neat house and garden, and forbidden the normal activities of a young child, Minna daydreams a house of her own, and furnishes it in her mind, the only unmessy way she can manage it. When the time comes for her to return to her family, it is to a new house which is, of course, her fantasy come true. This is all contrived with gentle simplicity, a quality demonstrable in the accompanying pictures by Juan Wijngaard. My first glance recalled *Ameliaranne and the green umbrella,* and indeed the two books have much in common. Both make something significant and satisfying out of a tiny event. Most warmly recommended.

> *Gabrielle Maunder, in a review of "Green Finger House," in* The School Librarian, *Vol. 28, No. 4, December, 1980, p. 370.*

Tower of the Stars (1980)

Fantasy has given many writers scope to deal with basic human struggles in a more direct way than realism permits. But, because of its lack of limits, it carries far greater dangers and temptations than realism ever can.

In *Tower of the Stars,* Rosemary Harris falls victim to some of the temptations. The book concludes the story, begun in *A Quest for Orion,* of the domination of Western Europe by the Free Association of Kindred States and Nations—the totalitarian Freaks. In the earlier book, the groups of teenagers who resisted the invaders in Britain and Germany met with a sizeable defeat, some of them being killed and some captured. In the sequel, the remains of the resistance rally, drawing on the powers of Charlemagne's Crown and his Talisman, which holds a piece of the True Cross. Guided by voices from the stars, which are channelled through the psychic Alastair, they take these symbolic relics to opposite ends of a ley line, one at Glastonbury and the other in the City in the Sea, which the Freaks have built to house their slaves. Once the Talisman has been brought, through great danger, to Glastonbury, the Freaks and their man-made island collapse into ruins.

Exciting and well told though the story is, it lacks real depth. The Freaks play a more direct part in the second book than in the earlier one, but remain crudely-defined enemies, their lack of solidity being epitomized by their ruling Praesidium, made up of masked members whose individual identity is irrelevant. This reduces the story to a simplistic struggle between good and evil, in which the main virtue is courage. But the forces of good are supported by the supernatural powers of the stars, while the forces of evil have only high technology to draw upon. With the scales so unevenly weighted, courage becomes less praiseworthy and the final victory seems too easy. It is significant that, at the end of the book, time turns backwards, wiping out not only the pains and costs of the struggle, but also the development which the characters have undergone.

Nevertheless, in spite of these limitations, both books are well worth reading for the richness and diversity of the characters, from Charlie, the cheeky younger girl who carries the Talisman, to the austere Walther, leader of the German resistance, who must seem to collaborate with the Freaks. All are totally credible, and the skill with which Rosemary Harris manages a large cast of characters split into scattered groups reinforces her claim to be an important children's writer. It is, indeed, the stature of the characters which makes the soft core of the story so obvious. Without that, the book would be a competent but ultimately insignificant piece of science fantasy. Because the author has reached beyond that, for something of greater importance, she has failed and the failure is disappointing. But it is also exciting, because it suggests what she may achieve.

> *Gillian Cross, "On the Astral Plain," in* The Times Literary Supplement, *No. 4069, March 27, 1981, p. 339.*

[In *Tower of the Stars,*] captured dissidents are taken to the Sea City, a kind of super ocean platform in the North Sea. There they are treated according to their potential usefulness to the master race, some enslaved, others experimented on, Walther, with his superior intellect, directed to the great observatory. But a few have been overlooked, notably the teenage gamine Charlie. It is part of the strength of Rosemary Harris' invention that she can show such a pathetic urchin as the instrument of destiny and make us believe it too, at least temporarily. While most of the youngsters do their bit on Sea City, a small party makes its way across England to Glastonbury where they link up with cosmic forces and blow the Freaks to Kingdom Come.

Although the Freaks are only too believable, especially the ruling oligarchy of nameless and faceless party bosses, it takes all of Miss Harris' formidable talents to persuade us to accept that the New Order can be destroyed by these means. No wonder the Americans put out a story about their President's brisk finger on the atomic button. There is a brilliant 'Postlude-Prelude' in which most of the freedom fighters find it easier to pretend that it never happened.

Most of the best science-fiction survives not on its science but on its psychology, and Miss Harris knows how to get us involved with her characters, an admirably mixed bag of skinheads, middle-class 'nice' people, and a variety of others. We really care, if not too deeply, that they should come out on top. In the event, amid all the catastrophic blood-letting, only one of our party is killed, and that is the professional killer, Hans, and he has hardly emerged as an individual person, having spent most of the book 'programmed' as a slave. Miss Harris' mastery of detail is impressive, and she handles her big scenes with tremendous gusto. It is a pity that the plot leans so heavily on leys, centres of power and other esoteric nonsense.

> *M. Crouch, in a review of "Tower of the Stars," in* The Junior Bookshelf, *Vol. 45, No. 2, April, 1981, p. 80.*

Sadly, very little of children's fantasy about the future

seems to hold out very much immediate hope. Rosemary Harris postulates a totalitarian tyranny in *Tower of the Stars,* which is a sequel to *A Quest for Orion.* It is set in England and Sea City in the North Sea, and tells of resistance in the last years of this century to the evil regime. There is a good deal of futuristic science as well as violence—some of it gratuitous—and a little politics. The style of writing is lacking in modesty, moving almost as jerkily as the events from description to action to interior monologue to sharp, expletive dialogue. It is a higher sort of Alistair Maclean. The idea of an ancient power emanating from leylines has significance; but the characters remain largely ciphers and are not individually imagined. (p. 145)

> *Ralph Lavender, "Other Worlds: Myth and Fantasy, 1970-1980," in* Children's literature in education, *Vol. 12, No. 3, Autumn, 1981, pp. 140-50.*

The Enchanted Horse   (1981)

A greedy Rajah sells his two sons to the Devil in return for a black opal but he gets little good of his bargain and his sons escape ill fortune through the magic of a steed of hidden identity. . . . Rosemary Harris's version of the tale is elaborate, somewhat novelistic in tone, and now and then a little whimsical; the book may settle in the nine-up age-range, at least for children who read this not as a nursery tale but as a fable of human nature.

> *Margery Fisher, in a review of "The Enchanted Horse," in* Growing Point, *Vol. 20, No. 3, September, 1981, p. 3948.*

Rosemary Harris' new story has an Indian setting. It is a most successful variant and extension of a folk-tale, told with great subtlety and beauty of language. It is very long for picture-book treatment and so detailed and explicit that it does not really need the help of pictures, even those as lovely and precise as Pauline Baynes'. Each of the elements in the book—word and picture—is as good as care and talent can make it—but the two together make an uneasy partnership.

> *M. Crouch, in a review of "The Enchanted Horse," in* The Junior Bookshelf, *Vol. 45, No. 6, December, 1981, p. 243.*

Zed   (1982)

In *Zed* Rosemary Harris has added to her distinguished works for small children, adults and teenagers. Over the years, her books for teenagers have become more coldly realistic, less warmly comforting. From the perhaps oversweet diluvian trilogy, starting with *The Moon in the Cloud,* in which all the evil or inadequate characters kindly die or are unmasked to allow the nice guys to live happily ever after, through the grimmer realism of her two-part science fiction novels, *A Quest for Orion* and *Tower of the Stars,* set at the end of the twentieth century, Ms Harris has come firmly to the present time and to horrific contemporary events. Thomas Z. Amsterel, eponymous hero,

was a timorous, insecure child of eight years when he, his loved uncle and rejecting father were all caught up, with many other adults randomly present at an office, in a siege there by the "Free Army of United Arabia". Lots were drawn for the first hostage to be murdered; loved uncle heroically substituted himself for, and was shot in place of, Zed's father, who cravenly permitted it. Despite his fear and misery, Zed nevertheless received comfort from Arabi, one of the terrorists. Eventually the hostages were rescued in an SAS type raid in which most of the terrorists were killed, including Arabi. This vividly real flashback is elicited from fifteen-year-old Zed by his school teachers, and as a result of his new insight he and his now orphaned cousin make contact, and eventually friends, with the son of the kindly terrorist.

Rosemary Harris has great sureness of touch, both in the delineation of character—with particularly cogent portraits of the superficial and self-centred charm of Zed's Lebanese Christian mother, and of his Saudi Turkish uncle's gentle and courageous maturity—and in her ability to evoke atmosphere, especially in her depiction of the abject fear of the hostages. From looseness of bowels to grovelling loss of reason, every symptom of the degradation that is wrought in people by terror is described with a clarity that is as ruthless as the terrorists themselves. The reader is left with no room to ignore the squalid realities. Indeed, it is not until Ms Harris tries to carry us through into the developing relationship between Zed, his cousin and the terrorist's son that she fails to convince, because she subordinates the credibility of the plot to her desire to illustrate a philosophy. But on the whole *Zed* is a courageous, and largely successful, effort to face with honesty the many aspects of violence, including some which are necessary and healthy. . . . [*Zed*] is tough, hard, realistic stuff for the mature teenager who can take the brutalities of life.

> *Jennifer Moody, "Aspects of Violence," in* The Times Literary Supplement, *No. 4156, November 26, 1982, p. 1302.*

When he was eight years old Thomas Z. Amsterel was among the hostages held in a London office complex by terrorists: in his last year at school his English teacher, inspired by a retrospective newspaper feature, persuades him to set down his memories of the event. Winding her way into the story of *Zed* in this indirect way, Rosemary Harris is able to introduce her characters obliquely and gradually, as the small boy saw them. His first impressions of the terrorists, and the way those impressions changed, provide one kind of emotional tension and argument; there is an equally compelling change in the boy when the respective fates of his much-loved father and uncle shatter his childish dependence on them and his innocent view of them as individuals. Like Peter Dickinson in *The Seventh Raven,* Rosemary Harris has taken one of the most alarming social dangers of our time and has scrutinised it from many points of view; dual attitudes reinforce one another, as the boy of seventeen thinks back to those earlier days of terror, curiosity and bewilderment. The mixture of races and beliefs (in Zed's own family alone, Syrian, Saudi, American, English and Turkish: Catholic, Anglican and Muslim) adds to the density of the novel and the implications of the situation. To do justice to this complex piece of work, the author uses a direct but concentrated style. Her dialogue is sharp and selective, full of overtones and individual idiom. She sets her scenes with the utmost economy but with a strong visual sense. . . . The close attention to physical movement and emotional states of mind continues when the physical danger is over and the families of victims and terrorists face the stresses of the future. In this way the child Zed is linked with the mature schoolboy he became and we can see, as he does himself, the extent of the damage which the incident has done to him and the way he has assimilated the experience. The tight but unconstricting shape of the novel, the firm direction of events and people, result in an outstanding piece of fiction. (pp. 4029-30)

> *Margery Fisher, in a review of "Zed," in* Growing Point, *Vol. 21, No. 6, March, 1983, pp. 4029-30.*

In the course of the four days in captivity, Zed learns that there are few absolutes in life and that men are a curious mixture of good and evil, of courage and cowardice. Harris eschews simplistic characterizations: courage and compassion as well as cruelty and cowardice are found among both the captured and the captors. The action sequences are fast-paced and riveting; the dialogue crackles, yet is laced with significant postulations of the nature of goodness and heroism; and the hero's coming of age—and his coming to grips with the fundamental truths of his life—is powerfully and realistically revealed. (p. 84)

> *Jerry Flack, in a review of "Zed," in* School Library Journal, *Vol. 30, No. 10, August, 1984, pp. 83-4.*

Janni's Stork   (1982)

The burgomaster of Janni's village refuses to allow storks for fear they might spoil the roofs, but Janni firmly believes the birds bring luck to any house they will nest on; when he finds a wounded stork, he smuggles it on to his grandmother's house and nurses it back to health. The poor boy's luck changes indeed and so does the burgomaster's surly mood, and the tale of a Dutch village in the past ends with folk-tale happiness, while the accuracy of bird and village life, as well as domestic history, are attested equally well in the quiet prose and the jewel colours and precise shapes of [Juan Wijngaard's] illustrations.

> *Margery Fisher, in a review of "Janni's Stork," in* Growing Point, *Vol. 21, No. 6, March, 1983, p. 4044.*

Rosemary Harris tells, with great charm, a nice little story about a Dutch boy who wins friends and influences people by attracting a stork to the roof of his house. . . . Miss Harris writes so eloquently and in such detail that her story hardly needs the addition of pictures. Juan Wijngaard has no need to reinforce the text, and contents himself with presenting the landscape, the architecture and the homely delights of Dutch life, and this he does with great relish. His very precise little pictures are as clean and closely detailed as a Vermeer. A very nice little book with

excellent colour and most carefully designed throughout. But I must emphasize that, despite the format, this is not a picture-book but a story with pictures. (pp. 67-8)

> *M. Crouch, in a review of "Janni's Stork," in* The Junior Bookshelf, *Vol. 47, No. 2, April, 1983, pp. 67-8.*

Although the lengthy text is quite British, details of Janni's life are well told, and children will cheer when his luck finally changes for the better. The story may be unrealistic, but it has an old-fashioned charm and is satisfyingly optimistic. Opening with a lovely silhouette of rooftops with storks against a pale pink background, Wijngaard's realistic muted full-color pictures are remarkable for their beauty, their authenticity and their spirit.

> *Catherine Blanton, in a review of "Janni's Stork," in* School Library Journal, *Vol. 30, No. 10, August, 1984, p. 60.*

Heidi   (1983)

In undertaking the abridgment of a classic, the usually

Harris with a picture by illustrator Errol LeCain from The Lotus and the Grail: Legends from East to West (1974), *which was published in an abridged edition in the United States as* Sea Magic and Other Stories of Enchantment *in the same year.*

gifted Rosemary Harris has tried to preserve the main outlines and original language. Her success is indifferent: the remaining story is choppy and oversimplified, motivations and causal relationships badly stated rather than evolving from accumulated detail—in short, a typical abridgment. Large collections may consider purchase for the sake of the illustrations. [Tomi] Ungerer's propensity for humor and caricature might be more appropriate to Pippi Longstocking than to Heidi, who has been traditionally portrayed in sentimental style, yet his emphasis on the lively side of the story and Heidi's character is refreshing. His virtuosity as draftsman and observer would find a worthier setting in an unabridged edition. (pp. 79-80)

> *Joanna Rudge Long, in a review of "Heidi,"*
> in School Library Journal, *Vol. 31, No. 6, February, 1985, pp. 79-80.*

Summers of the Wild Rose   (1987)

"Personally, I feel music overrides all differences, crosses all frontiers, and is invariably an influence for good." So speaks Nell Dobell's singing teacher, who is taking her choir to an international music competition at Innsbruck. And Nell (the choir's soloist) cannot wait to see this country of the mind, to meet Lotte Lehmann, Strauss, von Karajan. But it is 1937 and just before the *Anschluss:* Hitler visits the opera house; Fürtwangler conducts while jack-booted lads commit small-time atrocities; the competition itself is an occasion for political show. Like the ambivalent pastoral of its title, **Summers of the Wild Rose** is a story of innocent notions and their nightmarish evolutions, where escape from society results in political chaos. When Nell steps off the train and falls on top of and immediately in love with an Austrian Jew, Franz, the idyll she had imagined becomes a war-torn romance, and Miss Armstrong's naive words part of a larger debate about civilization itself.

If music is an ideal dimension it is so only in the way those Fairylands are whose enchanted grounds conceal dragons and other monsters. As Nell becomes increasingly aware of charmed surfaces and their sinister pitfalls, the Arcadian Austria with its pepperpot turrets turns into a gothic underworld—likened, with musical bravura, to Wagner's dragonland. On one occasion Nell goes to meet Hitler—called "Wolf" or "Wolfkin" by his friends—dressed in a pink extravagance bought for her by an aged princess who refers to herself as a fairy godmother. It is a worrying parody. For, although Harris assembles all the basic properties of fairy tales and folk traditions, they are always set in the frightening realistic context of history. What merely threatens in the fairy tale is here unable to reach a simple fictional resolution: the princess reminds Nell that wolves always gobble one in the end.

The parts of Harris's narrative arrange themselves like a nest of boxes. Stories invade other stories. Wagner's *Ring* crosses over into the triangular affair between Nell and Franz and the seductive Herr Graff; *Romeo and Juliet, The Hound of the Baskervilles,* or the tale of Count Dracula infiltrate other scenes; and the whole, like a true eclogue, is interspersed with songs from Goethe, Schubert

and Mahler. The main story itself has interrupted the book's opening tale of the grown-up Nell's niece, Clare (who, in love with a black boy and battling with her parents' prejudices, finds herself actively involved in her aunt's past), in an extended flashback. The novel is infected with the fear of invasion or interruption. Nell and Franz only spend fractured moments together and much of the narrative is spent anticipating the nearby dangers, the next step of the plot always precipitated by a threat. Just as the whole book too, waits, with controlled and effective symmetry, for the final reconciliation between Nell and Franz after thirty years apart.

The story's happy ending is the only place where Rosemary Harris allows a fairy-tale structure to override her ironic devices. But she is still reluctant to rest on a single level of events and continues to manipulate past and present when she takes Nell back to Innsbruck on a return train journey all those years after the beginning of the story. The motivation however, is realistic, and justified by the meticulous attention paid to character and historical detail. Told in the first person by the older Nell who looks analytically and seriously at her childish self, **Summers of the Wild Rose** is very much a grown-up book in disguise.

> *Anna Vaux, "Eclogue and Idyll," in* The
> Times Literary Supplement, *No. 4381, March
> 20, 1987, p. 304.*

Rosemary Harris is an expert craftswoman who knows how to clothe the bare bones of her plot in living flesh. She captures the perilous calm of Austria in its last days of independence and its menacing undercurrents. The music festival too, with its rivalries and its comradeship, is done very well. The personal and political problems are presented honestly. What is perhaps not fully engaged is the reader's sympathy. We understand Nell's dilemma, but we may not care much because neither she nor Franz comes out of the page as a real person. Nell is an actor in a play, not a human being from whose personality and actions the play springs.

That being said, it must be added that **Summers of the Wild Rose** is compellingly readable. Teenage girls will love it, and many responsible adults will respect the book's motives and its choice of subject. In fact, while it is in essence a superior romance, it may also be seen as a social document. (p. 132)

> *M. Crouch, in a review of "Summers of the
> Wild Rose," in* The Junior Bookshelf, *Vol. 51,
> No. 3, June, 1987, pp. 131-32.*

While the novel's first-love theme and its wartime background generally ensure a built-in audience, Harris has energetically punctuated the goings-on with musical allusions and foreign phrases, and her characters have a cosmopolitan aura about them—all of which sets her book out of reach for many. Yet the convoluted character relationships tantalize as does Harris' strong evocation of history and convention in times gone by, and the storybook conclusion that melds past and present is a true romantic's delight.

> *Stephanie Zvirin, in a review of "Summers of*

the Wild Rose," in Booklist, *Vol. 84, No. 13, March 1, 1988, p. 1131.*

Love and the Merry-Go-Round   (1988)

[Love and the Merry-Go-Round *was edited by Harris.*]

This is a splendid anthology of poems of love, life, war, death and renewal, for those who already enjoy poetry— some of those selected by Rosemary Harris are difficult to understand even for an experienced adult reader, but none the worse for that, if one is willing to surrender to their spell. (One hesitates to confine the collection within the 10-14 age range, however.) The oldest poets represented are Hardy, Kipling, Yeats and A. E. Housman and there are a number of translations from other languages (among them African, Arabic, Japanese—a touching letter from a mother to her distant daughter, and one of Helen Waddell's mediaeval Latin lyrics). There are little-known poems by well-known poets (an unpublished piece of Eliot, by way of *Cats*) and a number of less heavily-anthologised poets. Seamus Heaney, William Plomer, Sylvia Plath and C. P. Cavafy. In the space of some 70 poems, Elizabeth Jennings gets a good share, as well as Rainer Maria Rilke (from whom the second half of the title comes), Stevie Smith, Robert Graves, Housman and Yeats. If one says that Dylan Thomas' 'Fern Hill' is among the easiest to grasp, the quality of the collection should be clear. It is mind-stretching, thought-provoking and imaginatively arranged, following a pattern, humanly speaking, from youth to age. Rosemary Harris uses the word "ominous" of her poets, but also "fortifying"—this is a book to return to.

M. Hobbs, in a review of "Love and the Merry-Go-Round," in The Junior Bookshelf, *Vol. 52, No. 6, December, 1988, p. 303.*

Anthologies of often well-known verse, linked thematically, are thick on the ground these days. To make an impact becomes correspondingly difficult, but Rosemary Harris's **Love & The Merry-Go-Round** gets off to an arresting start with Sylvia Plath's wonderful 'Morning Song': 'Love set you going like a fat gold watch. / The midwife slapped your footsoles, and your bald cry / took its place among the elements.' Two poems by Rilke follow, and its clear that this won't be a conventional anthology. There's a fair bit of Georgian verse interleaved, but Seamus Heaney's 'The Skunk' will give an idea of the age-range this book will appeal to; it ends '. . . Your head-down, tail-up hunt in a bottom drawer—For the black plunge-line nightdress'.

Peter Forbes, in a review of "Love & the Merry-Go-Round," in The Listener, *Vol. 120, No. 3092, December 8, 1988, p. 40.*

Poets are 'more uncomfortably and constantly aware than we are of the merry-go-round we ride and from which we eventually dismount' but poetry is also 'fortifying'. With this basic brief for her very personal selection Rosemary Harris has arranged poems in a continuous unwinding progress from birth to death through many relationships and alliances. Here is Betjeman's wincingly black comedy

'Mortality' about 'The first-class brains of a senior civil servant' spread over the road like sweetbreads. Graves's sparse love-poems and some stern lines by Hardy; there is a superb pair of descriptive pieces by Rilke on statues of Adam and Eve in a cathedral; terse words from Housman and enigmatic lines from Stevie Smith add to the variegated texture of the book, in which each poem strikes a unique note, whether Chinese, rural Victorian, contemporary industrial or stateless. A remarkable collection, not to be missed. (pp. 5106-07)

Margery Fisher, in a review of "Love and the Merry-Go-Round," in Growing Point, *Vol. 27, No. 5, January, 1989, pp. 5106-07.*

Colm of the Islands   (1989)

Rosemary Harris's **Colm** seems to be neither myth nor folk-tale but an invented fairy story which holds elements of both. Set in the Hebrides it has to do with a turf-cutter whose sweetheart is stolen by giants and who rescues her through the familiar agency of animal helpers. . . . [The] book has a highly wrought text, but one which veers disconcertingly between formal and colloquial. As illustrator though, Pauline Baynes is . . . sensitive to her role . . . and she brings enough of a Birrer-like feeling for design to stabilize the wayward movements of the story. Her natural penchant has always been towards cool patterning and that suits Rosemary Harris's penchant for verbal effects, while Baynes's fine sense of colour and her pleasure in playing about with framing devices supply the character that is needed to give life to the picture book.

Brian Alderson, "Lives of the Saints," in The Times Educational Supplement, *No. 3806, June 9, 1989, p. B12.*

Humans who help animals in trouble may expect a reward in due time. This familiar folk-tale motif is central to **Colm of the Islands,** a neo-folk-tale about a young Hebridean farmer who has secretly freed a netted salmon, hidden a hunted otter and frustrated boys after an eagle's brood— all in spite of the scorn of his less sensitive neighbours. Generous in his attitude to the animals on his island, Colm rashly gibes at superstitions about the Little People underground and the giants whose power depends on the magical strength of nettle-thread. When his beloved Selva is snatched and forced to spin nettles into thread he is driven to believe the tales and to call on eagle, otter and salmon to help in a rescue that takes him into the giant's stronghold and under the sea. In this beautifully produced book artist and author are on equal terms, collaborating to produce enchantment in two media. Words convey the hideous power of the giant's greedy wife and contrast the luxurious appearance of the King of the Sea with his 'coral and cornelian crown, his cloak held by oyster shells', with the under-sea world where a nettle ring woven by Selva and borne to him by the salmon breaks the spell:

> The Sea Princesses were mermaids, sea-creatures with fish-tails and seaweed hair; even the lovely face of his bride was sea green. There was a sound like thundering hooves as everything about him fled away—the king and courtiers and

his foam-horses. All around Colm was nothing but a city of slimy rock dressed in shifting weed, and near by him lay a long-submerged rotting wreck.

The tale of kindness rewarded is duplicated in jewelled scenes where a craggy ruin and a brightly coloured undersea world are filled with figures dancing, threatening, inviting, among whom the prescriptive garments of the lad and his girl, homely and practical, emphasise the contrast between simple humans and enchanted folk. Full page scenes, friezes and vignettes have the same quality of decorated narrative as the text in a book notable for its unity of tone and atmosphere. (pp. 5181-82)

> *Margery Fisher, in a review of "Colm of the Islands," in* Growing Point, *Vol. 28, No. 2, July, 1989, pp. 5181-82.*

Ticket to Freedom   (1991)

Lallie's psychiatrist diagnoses her as suffering from depression, but the medical team tend to lose interest when they discover her father is not sexually abusing her. More positive support is offered by social worker Sue, old Miss Mimmie with whom Lallie discharges the hours of her community care order, a friendly neighbour and boyfriend Paul.

However, Paul's anxiety to collect enough money to buy a fresh start for himself and Lallie leads him, too, into trouble with the law.

Rosemary Harris is honest enough to show how awkward and difficult to help Lallie and Paul can be. Nevertheless her characters arouse the reader's sympathy, inspiring the hope that there may sometime be a settled future together for the two of them.

> *R. Baines, in a review of "Ticket to Freedom," in* The Junior Bookshelf, *Vol. 56, No. 1, February, 1992, p. 36.*

In Miss Mimmie we have a sympathetic but totally authentic presentation of the confused elderly. And she is only one of a host of interesting fringe characters who range from the yuppie horseriders on the common to the 'residents' of the common surveying the world from their cardboard boxes. An exciting story underpinned by valuable insights into life, death and human nature. (p. 31)

> *Elizabeth Finlayson, in a review of "Ticket to Freedom," in* The School Librarian, *Vol. 40, No. 1, February, 1992, pp. 30-1.*

This is a most unusual novel about a teenage thief called Lallie who lives with a violent father and stepmother. Sadly, Lallie seems to let down everyone who tries to help her: the probation officer, friends, kindly old lady and, unforgivably, her really caring boyfriend.

Uncomfortably, it reminds one of that very self-centred teenage period when promises and good intentions are cheerfully abandoned in pursuit of any offer of a good time, anywhere. Lallie usually intends well, it's just that appointments and responsibilities are boring, trying and involve loss of face.

Rosemary Harris' skill is in getting the reader really involved with the central character by giving her highlighted faults of the kind most of us have been guilty of at some time, and a really cheeky insouciance.

She has to come to terms with herself at the end, but even then it's a last-minute, unplanned let-down for people she's involved with. A fascinating character and a riveting read. . . .

> *T. Massey, in a review of "Ticket to Freedom," in* Books for Your Children, *Vol. 27, No. 1, Spring, 1992, p. 24.*

Susan Jeffers

1942-

American author and illustrator of picture books and re-teller.

Major works include *Three Jovial Huntsmen* (1973), *All the Pretty Horses* (1974), *Wild Robin* (1976), *Stopping by Woods on a Snowy Evening* (written by Robert Frost, 1978), *Brother Eagle, Sister Sky: A Message from Chief Seattle* (1991).

Considered a leading illustrator of contemporary American picture books, Jeffers is perhaps best known for making folklore and poetry accessible to young children through her works. She is often commended for providing visual retellings of familiar verse and tales that delight both readers and nonreaders. Producing illustrations for such poetic classics as Henry Wadsworth Longfellow's "Hiawatha" and Robert Frost's "Stopping by Woods on a Snowy Evening," she also adapts and illustrates stories from a variety of national and international sources; for example, in *Wild Robin* she retells the story of Tamlane, based on the Scottish ballad, in modern language. Called "an unusually gifted illustrator" by critic Harold C. K, Rice, Jeffers is often commended for her draftsmanship and sense of color and design. She characteristically uses subtle tones and delicate line to create her paintings, which are most often detailed double-page spreads.

After graduating from art school, Jeffers began her career as an illustrator by providing the pictures for such authors as Robert W. Service, Joseph Jacobs, and Mary Q. Steele. *Three Jovial Huntsmen* was the first book she both wrote and illustrated. Derived from the Mother Goose rhyme "Three Jolly Welshmen," the story focuses on the actions of three dimwitted men hunting in a forest and oblivious to the plentiful game around them. Jeffers spent three years creating this book, halting the production of her first version when she saw it in print, and producing a second version that met both her own and critical approval. Although some reviewers found her prose awkward, her illustrations were acclaimed for their subtle humor and delicate colors. Jeffers's next book, *All the Pretty Horses,* was inspired by the bedtime talks she and her sister had when they were children drifting off to sleep. This book features text adapted from the chorus of an old Southern lullaby and illustrations of a young girl's colorful dreams of horses as she sleeps soundly beneath her quilt. *Wild Robin* was similarly praised for its rich, double-paged illustrations of a fairyland of brilliant orchids and icy jewels, from which a farm girl rescues her naughty, lazy brother after he is abducted by fairies.

Critics cite Jeffers's artwork as particularly faithful to the meaning of the stories she depicts. She began introducing children to classic poetry in the late 1970s with *Stopping by Woods on a Snowy Evening*. Described by reviewer Stefan Kanfer as having a "tactile quality," the pictures ac-

companying this poem allow the nonreader to sense the warmth of the sleigh driver's flannel shirt and feel the biting chill in the air. Similarly, her large format illustrations for *Hiawatha* realistically depict a young Indian boy's life and natural surroundings through vivid colors and meticulous detail. Considered somewhat less effective were Jeffers's illustrations for *If Wishes were Horses,* a collection of Mother Goose nursery rhymes that some of Jeffers's critics found pleasing but frequently silly. In addition to illustrating several famous fairy tales and lullabies by such authors as the Hans Christian Andersen and the Brothers Grimm, Jeffers has also produced illustrations for Reeve Lindbergh's books *The Midnight Farm* and *Benjamin's Barn,* which personify the animals found on a farm and describe a child's interaction with them. Jeffers's most recent work is based on a speech delivered by Chief Seattle when the U. S. Government appropriated his tribe's land. *Brother Eagle, Sister Sky: A Message from Chief Seattle* adapts Chief Seattle's speech and depicts both sadness and hope in careful and powerful illustrations of the Native American struggle to live in harmony with nature in the face of adversity. Jeffers was awarded New Jersey Institute of Technology Awards for her illustrations in *Hiawatha* and *If Wishes Were Horses and Other Rhymes; Three Jo-*

vial Huntsmen received a Caldecott Honor Book citation in 1974 and the Golden Apple Award from the Biennalle of Illustrations Bratislava in 1975.

(See also *Something about the Author,* Vol. 17 and *Contemporary Authors,* Vol. 97-100.)

AUTHOR'S COMMENTARY

My career as an artist began in a tiny school in Oakland, New Jersey, when I was chosen to paint a history mural with the usual Egyptians harvesting in muddy tempera fields. I suspect that I was selected as much for my ability to keep poster paint from running—no mean feat—as for my drawing talent. Yet, I was on my way. I went on to Valentine Day calendars, fire prevention posters, and Easter Bunnies.

Happily for me, I have a very kind mother. She spent hours teaching me how to look at things. She showed me how to make objects appear round or flat and how to mix paint. Best of all, she gave me a feeling of immense joy in my work.

Early in my senior year of high school, I chose Pratt Institute for my art education. There I was associated with dedicated artists for the first time in my life. I remember slipping into Richard Lindner's illustration class twenty minutes late one day, hoping to be unobserved. He stopped the class and with great deliberation turned to me and said reproachfully, "Young woman, art is a love affair." I had never thought of art in quite those terms before, but that is how I have thought of it since.

After graduation in 1964, I worked in three publishing houses beginning with the simplest jobs: repairing type, pasting up illustrations, and designing books and jackets. I developed a concrete knowledge of children's books there and began to feel again the love I had for them as a child. As I worked with other artists' books, I became more and more impatient to do my own. That was my way of telling myself the time had come to get on with my own work.

It was rather frightening to think of working freelance, but it was the only alternative. I needed the freedom of my own time. I managed to make enough to live on and soon began my first book in 1968, ***The Buried Moon.*** At about this time, I also began a studio with Rosemary Wells. Together we worked on jackets and books, pooling our talents and ideas. It was wonderful for inspiration and encouragement, and especially for laughter.

My next book was ***The Three Jovial Huntsmen,*** which took three years to complete. I actually did the book from start to finish twice. The first version was a terrible disappointment on press, and the decision was made not to publish it. I took the next year off to mull things over and teach art at the Wiltwyck School for Boys. There was something compelling to me about that book, however, that I could not forget and I decided to begin again. The second version was a success and was wonderfully rewarded with a Caldecott Honor Book citation in 1974 and the

Golden Apple Award from the Biennial of Illustrations Bratislava, 1974.

All the Pretty Horses followed. Surely, the most effortless book I may ever do. It flowed directly from the talks I used to have with my sister when we were very young just before we dropped off to sleep. (pp. 59-60)

I live and work in Westchester County, New York, in a small house on a lake. Around me are woods and animals that I love to draw, including a Siberian Husky named Sitka, who is a hilarious model for my dogs, and a fat, sweet horse called Little Fox. (p. 60)

> *Susan Jeffers, in an excerpt in* Bookbird, *Vol. XV, No. 3, September 15, 1977, pp. 59-60.*

TITLE COMMENTARY

Three Jovial Huntsmen   (1973)

"There were three jovial huntsmen, / As I have heard men say, / And they would go a-hunting / Upon St. David's Day . . . ". Jeffers' text is shorter and—without the archaic British colloquialisms—more immediately accessible than the version used by Caldecott, but her pictures are far less direct and their humor sly instead of hearty. Instead of impelling readers from one mobile page to the next, she compels them to pause, drawing the eye into each double-page scene where variously hidden fine-line animals blend into the predominantly gray-toned backgrounds. There are ducks in the rushes, rabbits nestled among gnarled tree roots, owls and possums and raccoons in the night branches, and even deer among the birch trees; but none of them are observed by the hunters who see only a sailing-ship in the wind, the moon a-gliding, a hedgehog in a bramble bush, and a hare in a turnip—all of which they leave behind for reasons that the pictures tell. Beneath the chilly, subtly-colored surface loveliness there's more foxy play than substance in Jeffers' hidden pictures, but lovely they surely are, and foxy fun as well.

> *A review of "Three Jovial Huntsmen," in* Kirkus Reviews, *Vol. XLI, No. 22, November 15, 1973, p. 1258.*

Although superbly illustrated by Susan Jeffers, this version of the old rhyme "Three Jolly Welshmen" drops three stanzas (a repetitive refrain which young children enjoy) and ends too abruptly. The story involves three dimwits who hunt through a forest full of game without ever seeing any. However, viewers will have the pleasure of spotting all the nearly hidden animals the huntsmen either fail to see or mistake for something else. Meticulously executed, subtly colored illustrations, go a long way toward compensating for the flawed, awkward rhyme. The visual humor, without cartoon exaggeration, will be appreciated by children.

> *Bertha M. Chearham, in review of "Three Jovial Huntsmen," in* School Library Journal, *Vol. 20, No. 4, December, 1973, p. 43.*

The three huntsmen in this version of the Mother Goose rhyme are certainly not jovial, but since the artist has shifted attention away from them to the forest animals, the hunters' lack of gaiety may reflect awareness of their fall from grace. These proper British gentlemen—one portly, one bespectacled, and one tweed-capped—wander aimlessly through woods containing all manner of succulent dinners. Still, "All the day they hunted, And Nothing could they find." Although the obvious allurement of the book comes from the reader's locating the mysterious and wispy raccoons, ducks, opossums, squirrels, and turtles unnoticed by the hunters, its main attraction lies in the book's physical beauty: The subdued tones of the illustrations—created by yellow, red, blue, and black overlays on pen-and-ink drawings—have been masterfully blended and differentiated. In some of the night scenes, the twisted branches and muted blues are reminiscent of Arthur Rackham's work. The bouncy, spontaneous joviality of the Randolph Caldecott version of the rhyme may be more appealing, for his rendition glorifies the convivial humor of the verse. But this book has its own charm—it has been spun from the stuff that dreams are made of. (pp. 37-8)

> *Anita Silvey, in a review of "Three Jovial Huntsmen," in* The Horn Book Magazine, *Vol. L, No. 1, February, 1974, pp. 37-8.*

Of the two Caldecott runner-up titles [for 1974, **Three Jovial Huntsmen** and David Macaulay's *Cathedral*] Susan Jeffers's **Three Jovial Huntsmen** is another adaptation of traditional material, here a nursery rhyme about an unsuccessful trio (whether foolish, drunk or nearsighted remains properly unexplored) who disagree as to what they do see on their outing but remain unanimously oblivious to the ducks, rabbits, deer and other animals that the artist has cannily hidden in her chilly, subtly toned landscapes. The pictures are lovely and the book beautifully produced, but a comparison with [Margot] Zemach's gusto [in *Duffy and the Devil*]—not to mention the vigor and mobility of Randolph Caldecott's own *Three Jovial Huntsmen*—gives the impression that instead of vitalizing the old rhyme Jeffers makes it the showcase for an overrefined and ultimately static performance.

> *Sada Fretz, "Pinning the Tale," in* Book World—The Washington Post, *February 10, 1974, p. 4.*

To say of a book as elegant and clever as [**Three Jovial Huntsmen**] that it goes off at half-cock may sound like an attempt at a cheap jest, but the more one examines it, the more one gets a feeling that, at a vital stage of its growth the artist ran out of stamina and the publisher ran out of paper. For sure, there is good precedent for converting this traditional ballad into a picture book—after all, a Lancashire version of it was one of Caldecott's happiest inspirations—Susan Jeffers's idea for emphasising the foolishness of the huntsmen is a good one. (Actually, to make sense of 'St. David's Day' they should be Welshmen, but she is probably being deferential to contemporary nationalist sensibilities.) What she has done is to depict her huntsmen and their braggadocio dog questing about—but

And that they left behind.

From Three Jovial Huntsmen, *written and illustrated by Susan Jeffers.*

without much joviality—while their quarry lurks beyond their vision in branches or behind tree-trunks. The ghostly sketching in of these birds and animals and the whole of Miss Jeffers's handling of the hunting landscape is very deftly done and is enhanced by some beautiful colour printing.

Unfortunately though, the artist is not entirely consistent in her picturing of the story: on the one hand, backtracking, and modifying her play with the hidden animals in the second half of the book, and, on the other, jumbling her interpretations of what the huntsmen find and what they think they find. Certainly there is a moon—but it doesn't look much like a cheese; certainly there is a hedgehog—but not much like a pin-cushion. With another item though: the ship 'a-sailing with the wind' there is neither ship nor house 'with the chimney blown away', but only what looks like an outcrop of rock, and by the time that we get to the fourth item, the hare in the turnip field, everyone seems to be getting tired of the whole show and the ballad is brought to a hasty conclusion without any interpretation of the hare at all, and without the last three stanzas. What a pity that so much skill and devotion were not allowed more time and space to develop.

> *Brian W. Alderson, in a review of "Three Jovial Huntsmen," in* Children's Book Review, *Vol. IV, No. 3, Autumn, 1974, p. 114.*

Three Jovial Huntsmen is based on a rhyme of traditional dreamlike dottiness, yet not without poetry. Jeffers catches all of these elements. The zany three go forth upon St David's day with gun and dog, but go back as they went.

> All the day they hunted,
>   And nothing could they find
> But the moon a-gliding,
>   A-gliding with the wind.
> One said it was the moon,
>   The other he said, Nay,
> The third said it was a cheese
>   With half of it cut away.

Since they can't see what they see, the ninnies, they find nothing, but we see hare and bear, owl and ptarmigan, deer and porcupine. The expressive dog, who despairs of his idiot masters, sees them too. All the Jeffers skill goes into the delicately drawn creatures (the droll dog too) and foreground lifesize flowers and grasses, in the washes of mysterious woodland blues and greens and browns. In violent contrast are the human hunters, gross and oafish comics, even their clothes a garish intrusion of colour. Without stepping out of the bounds of the rhyme it's as good a comment on the interior theme as any.

> *Naomi Lewis, "The Hunter De-Romanticized," in* The Times Educational Supplement, *No. 3462, November 5, 1982, p. 27.*

When the three jovial huntsmen set out on St. David's day, they anticipate an excursion rich with the rewards of the sport. As they amble through woods full of deer, opposum, raccoons, ducks, and foxes, all that the simple men see, in their near-sighted vision, are objects appearing to be what they are not.

A ship, upon closer inspection, is only a rock; a porcupine,

merely a pincushion holding pins inserted backwards. The two fuzzy ears of a hare are more properly identified in the illustrations as the tails of skunks by the white stripe covering the back of the bodies and by the clouds of an odorous protection emitted in the direction of the hunters. Thus ends the expedition for the three jovial huntsmen.

The humor of this Mother Goose rhyme is appropriately captured in Jeffers's fine line drawings, which resemble puzzles with hidden objects; the illustrations reveal the animals that go unseen by the unattending sportsmen; woven into the lines that define roots, weeds, flowers, and undergrowth, animals peer out at the audience and at the hunters, in silent mockery.

There careful studies of nature and the natural habitats of the forest provide the backgrounds from which the animals emerge. Their presence, obvious to the undoubtedly delighted audience, goes unnoticed by the men, who are more intent on conjuring up their own visions than taking note of the opportunities before their noses.

The illustration on the jacket, which accompanies some copies of the book, succinctly captures the essence of the tale's humor as the three men gaze across the terrain from a rock ledge; a plethora of bear, quail, fox, rabbit, groundhog, and squirrel peer out from the rock formations below; the animals are unquestionably unthreatened by the presence of the huntsmen.

Jeffers's style capitalizes on the tale's humor by providing the appropriate natural environments from which her animals emerge, unseen by their human predators. (pp. 356-57)

> *Linda Kauffman Peterson, "The Caldecott Medal and Honor Books; Three Jovial Huntsmen," in* Newbery and Caldecott Medal and Honor Books: An Annotated Bibliography, *by Linda Kauffman Peterson and Marilyn Leathers Solt, G. K. Hall & Co., 1982, pp. 356-57.*

All the Pretty Horses (1974)

The short chorus of an old Southern lullaby provides an outlet for Jeffers to conceive a romantic, floral dreamland where all the pretty horses wander and cavort with the now dreaming heroine. The densely penned shadows that suggested forms in **The Three Jovial Huntsmen** are here, but mixed with sparely sketched, open-faced flowers; and orange, yellow, and blue washes bestow a springlike glow over the whole. Not so artistically solid in conception and execution as **Huntsmen,** but very pretty.

> *A review of "All the Pretty Horses," in* Booklist, *Vol. 71, No. 2, September 15, 1974, p. 100.*

Far more than the sprightly **Three Jovial Huntsmen;** this 40-word lullaby was made for Jeffers' sort of reverie. The floral bedspread covering her little girl at the beginning and end becomes a field where she romps on the backs of "blacks and bays, dapples and grays," all of them standing, prancing and resting on the flower tops in a dreamlike revision of natural scale. Jeffers seems to take her mugging child less seriously than she does the lovingly cross-hatched horses and foliage, for which pretty is surely the word—a characterization that pinpoints both the pictures' "classy" appeal and their limitations.

A review of "All the Pretty Horses," in Kirkus Reviews, *Vol. XLII, No. 19, October 1, 1974, p. 1058.*

Tucked in at night under her flowered quilt, a small girl dreams of horses. The words are those of the familiar lullaby, the pictures imaginative drawings, softly colored, of the child riding and playing with her dream horses among the flowers of the quilt, now huge. The pictures are beautifully detailed and the horses impeccably drawn, but the book may be limited in appeal because of the lack of story line or even incident, all of the action being variations on the girl-horse theme.

Zena Sutherland, in a review of "All the Pretty Horses," in Bulletin of the Center for Children's Books, *Vol. 28, No. 5, January, 1975, p. 79.*

Wild Robin (1976)

A naughty boy stolen away by fairies and later rescued by his sister is the subject of [*Wild Robin*], [a] familiar tale derived from Scottish folklore. Wild Robin, bad and lazy, runs off to the hills one day when even indulgent sister Janet loses patience with him and he ends up in a dazzling fairyland where "there is nothing to do but play and eat to your heart's content." But the easy life becomes lonely; a pitying elf advises Janet; and that night when the fairies parade in the greenwood she wrestles with a changing shape (frog / snake / swan) until, triumphant, she finds herself hugging "her own dear brother." Jeffers' paintings play up the contrast between the family's plain, sunny kitchen and barn (where a thick-legged Janet shovels cow dung) and the purplish fairyland of sensuous orchids and icy jewels. Despite an excess of billowing gossamer there is cleverness in the double page of Robin drowsing in a field of pearl or jewel-centered flowers, and visual impact in the next one of Robin lonely on a dreamlike staircase. More involving, the two worlds clash effectively in the pictures of Janet's climactic struggle. Still, we have the feeling throughout that the adventure interests Jeffers more as a showcase than as a story.

A review of "Wild Robin," in Kirkus Reviews, *Vol. XLIV, No. 23, December 1, 1976, p. 1261.*

[*Wild Robin*] is based on a tale in a 19th century publication, "Little Prudy's Fairy Book" by R. S. Clarke. In the gifted imagination and hands of Jeffers, the story of an errant boy and his good sister comes to glorious life. Robin is so wild and tricky that he finally alienates Janet who has been covering up his misdeeds and saving him from the wrath of their parents. In the face of universal disapproval at home, Robin runs away instead of shaping up and becomes a prisoner of the fairies and elves. The artist's magical paintings of fairyland and of everyday farm life are fine accompaniments to the story which takes many turns and ends when brave Janet risks dark forces to rescue Robin.

The book will surely add to the laurels Jeffers has won—a Caldecott Honor and a Golden Apple Award from the Biennale of Illustrations in Bratislava for *Three Jovial Huntsmen.*

A review of "Wild Robin," in Publishers Weekly, *Vol. 210, No. 23, December 6, 1976, p. 62.*

The text [of *Wild Robin*] is short. The story is stated and not over-explained. The illustrations are big, graphically rendered, beautifully colored double-page spreads that catch, hold, and bring the eyes back to discover small details and to re-examine and interpret facial expressions. Based on a Scottish ballad, "Tamlane," this is the story of Robin, an appealing bad boy who shirks his chores, wastes his food, and, when even his protective older sister Janet becomes irked with him, runs away. He falls asleep on the fairies' territory and they whisk him away. Janet pines for him and he for her until a spying elf's "little stone heart was touched" and the elf tells Janet how to release Robin from the fairies' power. She has to risk her neck to accomplish this, but she does and Wild Robin returns safely to his family forever. This "return of the prodigal brother" tale exerts the same centuries' old power as the biblical parable of the prodigal son. It reverberates with unspoken implications about family love, loyalty, sacrifice, and forgiveness. The illustrations tell the story for nonreaders and match the power of the story. (pp. 82-3)

Lillian N. Gerhardt, in a review of "Wild Robin," in School Library Journal, *Vol. 23, No. 5, January, 1977, pp. 82-3.*

The Scottish ballad of "Tamlane" (or Tam Lin) spawned Ipcar's romantic fantasy *The Queen of Spells;* now it helps give shape to [*Wild Robin*], a picture book in which good-hearted Janet—a young farm girl—rescues her wayward brother Robin from the fairies. Jeffers' strength lies in her sure draftsmanship: the most satisfying spreads are those in which her linework provides soft, sufficient detail; where occasionally color is called upon to stand in its stead, the clarity suffers. Yet the eye will easily follow the flowing spreads of rural beauty that give way to a darkly pastel fairyland; the vistas are at once hushed and ambitiously commanding.

Denise M. Wilms, in a review of "Wild Robin," in Booklist, *Vol. 73, No. 10, January 15, 1977, p. 719.*

[Susan Jeffers in *Wild Robin*] has retold a story from *Little Prudy's Fairy Book* by Sophie May, a story which was loosely based on the well-known folk tale "Tamlane." A sly, disobedient boy ran away from home when even his loving sister Janet lost patience with his wild ways. He was captured by the fairies and, although he led a carefree life, he became lonely and homesick. Finally, from an elf whose "little stone heart was touched," Janet learned the spell which would free him, and she bravely rescued him. The familiar story is distinguished by brilliant illustrations. Homely, everyday, but remarkably expressive animals and the open moors of Scotland are tellingly contrasted with the dazzling fairyland built upon motifs of glittering jewels and stiff, unbending flowers. The cold, unearthly beauty of the gossamer-winged fairies and of their aloof and mocking queen is clearly shown in a shimmering double-page spread of the fairy cavalcade with its elf lights and attendant creatures. A stunning feat of illustration. (pp. 150-51)

> *Ann A. Flowers, in a review of "Wild Robin," in* The Horn Book Magazine, *Vol. LIII, No. 2, April, 1977, pp. 150-51.*

Close Your Eyes   (1978)

[Close Your Eyes *was written by Jean Marzollo.*]

This is the most interesting and original picture book to be published in some time. . . . [The] illustrations by Susan Jeffers—whose impressive, if over-elaborate hide-and-seek animal pictures won her a Caldecott Honor Book award in 1974 for *The Three Jovial Huntsmen*—are a brilliant hide-and-seek montage of animals, fields, sky, water, a little boy and, in a parallel sub-plot, the humorous hide-and-seek of that little boy and his father, who's trying to put him to bed.

The rather too sweet and easy charm of the verse is more than balanced by the clear-eyed details of the drawings, with every fang and feather and blade of grass in sharp but never over-aggressive or self-indulgent detail. And this strong draftsmanship is tactfully softened by the warm pastel colors that wash over the images and by the deliberately more humorous and cartoonlike style of the sub-plot of father and son at bedtime.

There is a remarkable profusion of images in this short book—we see dozens of creatures and bits of trees, birds' nests, fur, insects' wings, feathers—and a subtle interpenetration of the world of the sleepy little boy's imagination, following the rhyme, and the world of the story of him and his father. Daddy lifts up a corner of the bedspread, which is also the sky above a field of rye, to discover the boy asleep with his arm around three pet dogs, with his rabbit-eared slippers next to a large rabbit, and with a lion cub in the foreground, as the field turns into a veldt.

So these subtle and intricate pictures are designed to be read as a sleepy boy's mental associations to the text: As we puzzle out the shapes on the page we are following his thoughts, even as we are also keeping an eye on the more objective (though paradoxically less clearly and vividly rendered) consciousness of his father. The balance between fact and fancy is truly charming, and this is a most unusual book for children.

> *Harold C. K. Rice, "Dreamers, Hunters, Schemers," in* The New York Times Book Review, *July 9, 1978, p. 32.*

The text is interpreted in magnificent full-color pastel-toned illustrations, remarkable for their clarity, meticulous detail, and delicate line. Another dimension is added through the artist's juxtaposition of two interpretations—one delineating dream fantasies in lush oversized images, the other depicting a weary father cajoling his child into bed in a contrapuntal series of smaller vignettes. Although

at one point text and pictures seem out of synchronization—the words "imagine drowsy geese at dawn" accompany an illustration in which the geese are subordinated to a gathering of liquid-eyed deer—the book is a charming production in the old-fashioned tradition of a warm and reassuring bedtime story.

> *Mary M. Burns, in a review of, "Close Your Eyes," in* The Horn Book Magazine, *Vol. LIV, No. 4, August, 1978, p. 388.*

Stopping by Woods on a Snowy Evening   (1978)

[Stopping by Woods on a Snowy Evening *was written by Robert Frost.*]

Robert Frost's *Stopping by Woods on a Snowy Evening* is one of the last poems Americans learned by heart. "The woods are lovely, dark, and deep, / But I have promises to keep" has resonances that go far beyond the ice-glazed trees and horse-drawn carriage of this nostalgic volume. With a minimum of color and some gentle line drawings, Susan Jeffers gives her suite of illustrations a tactile quality: the driver's flannel seems as warm as cloth, and the swirling flakes bring a wintry chill and a welcome Frost to every page. (p. 101)

> *Stefan Kanfer, "A Rainbow of Colorful Reading," in* Time, *New York, Vol. 112, No. 23, December 4, 1978, pp. 100-101, 103-04.*

Scale could have been a problem in *Stopping by Woods on a Snowy Evening* by Robert Frost, illustrated by Susan Jeffers. There is such delicate strength to this famous poem that stretching it to book size might easily have become a heavy-handed venture. Fortunately the artist has taken great care to love, honor and faithfully follow the words. Her drawing, which tends at times to prettification, is for the most part softly restrained. You can almost hear the silence of the woods in it. An old man in a plaid jacket stops his sleigh among snowy trees. His horse waits as he leaves seed for winter birds, dried grasses for the deer. The horse and old man proceed, stopping once to greet a friend and continuing on into the depth and whirl of flakes. The last spread is almost as lovely as the last line. Considering the last line, that's no mean accomplishment.

> *Karla Kuskin, in a review of "Stopping by Woods on a Snowy Evening," in* The New York Times Book Review, *December 10, 1978, p. 76.*

Jeffers is comfortable with [Robert] Frost's lyric. In soft pencil and pen washed with light orange, blue, and green, a man comes out of the snow, gets bigger and fades back into the swirling light grey storm. He is chubby, with a white beard, allusions to Santa unmistakable and regrettable. With comic spirit he rummages in the sleigh, rear sticking out and arms buried under the quilt; he falls down to make a snow angel and the forest animals flee his exuberance. Jeffers divides the lines, one and two per page, the way the poem might be read aloud. She speaks, with Frost, of the wonder of the woods, where just for a quiet moment, things are the way they seem. But in making the poem more accessible to younger children, she limits the

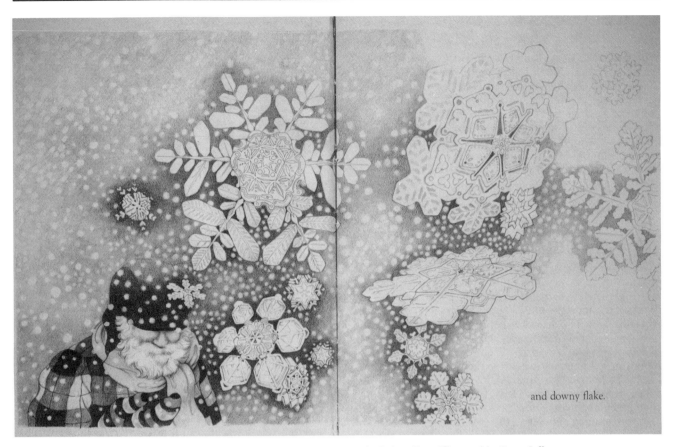

and downy flake.

From Stopping by Woods on a Snowy Evening, *written by Robert Frost. Illustrated by Susan Jeffers.*

traveler by giving him a reason to stop and a reason to go on—he leaves seed and hay for wild animals; his "promises" are to a family; perhaps he has other bundles to deliver. "Sleep" is not death here or the end of artistic struggle, but only itself, rest. And yet whatever dismay one feels at such definition, Jeffers does offer youngsters a fine first reading of Frost.

> *Sharon Elswit, in a review of "Stopping by Woods on a Snowy Evening," in* School Library Journal, *Vol. 25, No. 6, February, 1979, p. 40.*

A beautiful picture book, handsomely designed, which is obviously an inspired creation. [Susan Jeffers], working with artistry and skill and reflecting both the wintry atmosphere and the natural serenity of the poem, has made double-page spreads in which intricate patterning is balanced by an elegant plainness of coloration: shades of gray upon white with only occasional touches of pale green, yellowish brown, and blue. An illustrator, like a composer, librettist, or choreographer, has the right, of course, to produce a highly personal interpretation of a literary work. But it is often questioned whether an explicit line-by-line pictorial representation of a lyrical—not a narrative—poem may constrain a child's imagination and interfere with his or her response to poetic ambiguity—the spontaneous formation of images in the mind. Moreover, a spare but suggestive simplicity characterizes the famous poem; in [Robert] Frost's volume *New Hampshire* it is one

of a group of verses called Grace Notes, which contain some of his most haunting and quietly eloquent writing. The picture-book jacket states that a "kindly rotund figure . . . lends both humor and a Christmas feeling that should greatly enhance the enjoyment of the book." And it is precisely these additional elements—as well as a certain homely sentimentality—that seem incongruous with the poet's essential reticence.

> *Ethel L. Heins, in a review of "Stopping by Woods on a Snowy Evening," in* The Horn Book Magazine, *Vol. LV, No. 2, April, 1979, p. 182.*

If Wishes Were Horses and Other Rhymes from Mother Goose   (1979)

In *If Wishes Were Horses and Other Rhymes From Mother Goose,* illustrated by Susan Jeffers, an unusually gifted illustrator whose previous work (such as *Close Your Eyes*) I've admired, pulls off the hitherto impossible feat of stopping Mother Goose rhymes dead in their tracks. Moreover, she has taken her gift for visual whimsy and used it to produce pictures of a frenzied cuteness. Miss Jeffers should have scrapped the whole project and done herself justice.

> *Harold C. K. Rice, in a review of "If Wishes Were Horses and Other Rhymes from Mother*

Goose," in The New York Times Book Review, *November 11, 1979, p. 66.*

Words to these horse-centered Mother Goose rhymes sit sparely to the side, while Jeffers' softly penned and colored visions take over the pages. A not-quite-cloying sweetness pervades the drawings; most of the horses have a Shetland pony cuteness to them, while surrounding children and adults are comfortably benign or frolicsome. This is a quick take, a light confection that's enjoyable in lieu of more substantial Mother Goose fare. It's not Jeffers at her best, but it's certainly pleasing enough to capture a browser's lingering look. Ages 4-7.

> *Denise M. Wilms, in a review of "If Wishes Were Horses and Other Rhymes from Mother Goose," in* Booklist, *Vol. 76, No. 6, November 15, 1979, p. 508.*

Eight Mother Goose rhymes involving horses have been expansively illustrated with full-page, double-page, or multiple-paneled pictures. Seven of the poems are variants of verses found in the Opies' *Oxford Dictionary of Nursery Rhymes.* . . . The artist has captured a variety of equine positions—placid or dynamic, according to the exigencies of the poems—and portrayed happy children or stolidly humorous characters which suggest figures drawn by Helen Oxenbury. The clean-cut drawings with their added pastel coloring combine elegant coolness with nursery rhyme geniality; and on occasion they break forth with vigorous bounce and verve. (pp. 654-55)

> *Paul Heins, in a review of "If Wishes Were Horses and Other Rhymes from Mother Goose," in* The Horn Book Magazine, *Vol. LV, No. 6, December, 1979, pp. 654-55.*

Jeffers has chosen nursery rhymes about horses to illustrate with softly colored but strongly composed pictures in mixed media: line drawings in ink, colored by ink and pastel pencils. The result is effective, combining black and white people, slightly comic, with nicely textured and modeled animals.

> *Zena Sutherland, in a review of "If Wishes Were Horses and Other Rhymes from Mother Goose," in* Bulletin of the Center for Children's Books, *Vol. 33, No. 7, March, 1980, p. 139.*

Hansel and Gretel   (1980)

[Hansel and Gretel *was written by Jacob and Wilhelm Grimm.*]

Do we need another *Hansel and Gretel*? There are already a dozen in print, besides those in fairy-tale anthologies and collections. Both the light and dark sides of the tale are important, but it is the light side—the portrayal of the children's resourcefulness, gratification, and escape—that is featured here. The darker side of the tale—deprivation, rejection, abandonment and real evil—is downplayed. The text is the 1902 Lucas translation. The illustrations are enticingly pretty: the protagonists live in photogenic poverty; the stepmother looks cross but not

wicked; the witch is a plump, grandmotherly figure (her meaty grasp belies the text's "bony hand"). The children are so lovely it's hard to imagine anyone wishing them ill—though they do look good enough to eat. Cute animals, flowers, and a cake house thick with icing also soften the atmosphere of the tale. Countless minute circles are used to suggest light and shadow, beads of dew on branches or the shimmer of leaves, giving the pictures a lacy quality. The fineness of the drawing and the absence of borders make for an airy, clean look, though there is enough detail to satisfy the searching eye. The most powerful pictures show the children wandering in the woods—only here do we glimpse the dark underside of this potentially disturbing tale. (pp. 62-3)

> *Patricia Dooley, in a review of "Hansel and Gretel," in* School Library Journal, *Vol. 27, No. 3, November, 1980, pp. 62-3.*

A large, handsomely designed picture book version of the favorite tale by [Susan Jeffers] who draws and paints with equal artistry and skill. With superb use of color the dramatic action is shown chiefly in half-page pictures, while the serene forest scenes overspread two pages and give the book a definitive atmosphere that almost transcends the occasional touches of sentimentality. The book states that the translation of the story is from the work of Mrs. Edgar Lucas, published in 1902, and it notes: "The language has been altered only as necessary to avoid archaic references." One must wonder why the children's natural, spontaneous references to God were considered "archaic"; for changing such statements as " 'God will not forsake us' " and " 'the good Lord will surely help us' " to " 'we will not perish in the forest' " and " 'there is nothing to fear' " seems unnecessarily squeamish and, more important, completely unfaithful to the ethos of the tale. Moreover, the German text and the reliable translations clearly indicate that the witch's house was made of bread, the roof of cake, and the windows of clear sugar. The present version states that the house was made of cake. But the double-page spread showing the cottage prettily covered with confections and a row of smiling gingerbread children standing nearby among the trees and shrubbery deplorably follows the modern sentimental tradition; the picture goes even beyond the text and adds a note of incongruous banality to a book of considerable beauty.

> *Ethel L. Heins, in a review of "Hansel and Gretel," in* The Horn Book Magazine, *Vol. LVI, No. 6, December, 1980, p. 634.*

Susan Jeffers, who last year provided stunningly polished illustrations for an outsize picture-book rendition of *Thumbelina,* has now done likewise for the Grimm Brothers, *Hansel and Gretel.* But, where her "Thumbelina" pictures loomed almost larger than life, here the generous format seems as much an accommodation to a lengthy text, enabling it to be set within pleasingly wide margins. Even in two double-page illustrations, Miss Jeffers, curiously, keeps her viewers at panoramic distance. The single dramatic close-up is the jacket portrait of wide-eyed brother and sister in the woods. Nowhere do the pictures help us make sense of the bleak fact that the children's father agrees—albeit reluctantly—to lose his offspring in "the thickest part of the forest." The family's poverty and suffering from a "terrible famine" are not graphically convincing. There are picturesque patches on clothing, and one neat hole in the sole of an overturned slipper. True, father and children go barefoot (only the villains of the piece—stepmother and witch—are shod); but still, the indigence is too prettified to move us. And surely the entire family is overly plump and rosy-cheeked to convey desperation. Perhaps young listeners, caught up in the words, will supply their own mind's-eye adjustments. Yet there are other graphic failings as well. When Hansel and Gretel begin their moonlit walk home "guided by the pebbles that glittered like bits of silver," Miss Jeffers's entire forest is inexplicably aglitter. Her deep woods resemble Park Avenue at Christmastime—more festive than fearsome. Even her witch could pass for a benign Mother Hubbard. In sum, despite the high craft of Miss Jeffers's illustrations, there is an overdose of sweetness, at odds with the text's bitter truths.

> Selma G. Lanes, in a review of "Hansel and Gretel," in The New York Times Book Review, January 4, 1981, p. 25.

Oversize pictures afford the artist an opportunity for impressive large-scale pictures filled with intriguing detail: forest creatures amid the crowded tree-trunks of the forest, the succulent cake and candy details of the witch's house. The colors are soft and bright, the draughtsmanship skilled for this simplified version of one of the best-known Grimm tales.

> Zena Sutherland, in a review of "Hansel and Gretel," in Bulletin of the Center for Children's Books, Vol. 34, No. 6, February, 1981, p. 111.

The Wild Swans (1981)

[The Wild Swans was written by Hans Christian Andersen.]

Susan Jeffers's outsized picture-book rendition of Andersen's **The Wild Swans** might prove awkward to tuck under a pillow, but many a small fairy-tale aficionado will be mesmerized by the airy land of enchantment its elegantly designed and lovingly illustrated pages unfold. Certainly Miss Jeffers has been influenced by the grand conception of Nancy Eckholm Burkert's 1972 "Snow-White and the Seven Dwarfs," but her delicately tinted, full-color pictures—from a breathtaking double page of the heroine, Elise, being wafted through the clouds by 11 swans (her bewitched brothers) to the chillingly Gothic graveyard scene in which Elise gathers the nettles necessary to break her stepmother's evil spell—are distinctly Miss Jeffers's own in style and meticulous execution. The artist's mastery of design is surer here than in either her **Thumbelina** or her **Hansel and Gretel** of seasons past; occasionally Miss Jeffers's illustrations seem almost to embrace the type, so felicitously do her compositions flow from one side of a page to the other.

> Selma G. Lanes, "The Dane Doesn't Wane,"

in The New York Times Book Review, November 15, 1981, p. 66.

This highly abridged version of the wonderfully complex Andersen tale suffers from its own economy. In aiming at linguistic simplicity, layers of lovely imagery are lost. Ehrlich's translation describes the seaside landing as "eleven swans . . . flying toward the shore," while Erik Haugaard reveals them "like a white ribbon being pulled across the sky. . . . " Also lost are layers of meaning. When the wicked stepmother drops three toads in the bath, no mention is made of each one's intent, thus destroying the significance of their coming to rest on different parts of Elise's body. Gone, too, are the subtle gradations of power, the careful calibrations of good and evil embodied in the original queen and virgin. Unlike the language, the illustrations—at least those of the natural world—shimmer and glisten in true fairy-tale fashion. The finely textured drawings, steeped in pale luminous shades, are at once ethereal, magical and rich. But the people are unfortunate: uniformly heart-shaped faces—pale, pretty and sentimentalized—are posed atop vaguely draped (and one undraped) bodies. Even the horrible lamias—better left, in any event, to the imagination—fail to horrify.

> Kristi L. Thomas, in a review of "The Wild Swans," in School Library Journal, Vol. 28, No. 5, January, 1982, p. 58.

Hiawatha (1983)

[Hiawatha was written by Henry Wadsworth Longfellow.]

With large pastel paintings detailing the young Indian boy's life and his natural surroundings, Jeffers has illustrated part of the childhood section of the poem **Hiawatha** starting with, "By the shores of Gitche Gumee" and ending with the stanza, "Of all beasts he learned the language. . . . " She has beautifully illuminated the stanzas with details based on the poem. In the painting illustrating the animal stanza she portrays Hiawatha and Nokomis in a field surrounded by deer, rabbits, beavers and squirrels, some partially hidden by the tall grasses and trees. "When he heard the owls at midnight . . . " is illustrated by three large snowy owls on one page while on the facing page an obviously frightened Hiawatha sits listening to Nokomis tell him what he has heard. These are only two examples of how well Jeffers has captured the essence of this brief section from the classic poem. As in her other works, the pale tints of the pictures are in complete harmony with nature and with the text and show in detail how Hiawatha might have seen his world. A fine first exposure to the poem for children and a beautiful artistic experience.

> Margaret C. Howell, in a review of "Hiawatha," in School Library Journal, Vol. 30, No. 4, December, 1983, p. 58.

Jeffers has chosen part of Longfellow's poem to illustrate, and the oversize pages offer a splendid opportunity for beautifully detailed paintings of the small boy and his grandmother, Nokomis. The technique, which includes minute hatchings and parallel lines, soft colors, misty reflections, and richly vernal scenes, is well suited to the romantic quality of the poetry. (p. 92)

> *Zena Sutherland, in a review of "Hiawatha," in* Bulletin of the Center for Children's Books, *Vol. 37, No. 5, January, 1984, pp. 91-2.*

Silent Night (1984)

[Silent Night *was written by Joseph Mohr.*]

Intricate, oversized full-color paintings bring to life the lyrics of three verses of this favorite Christmas hymn. Deep blues, soft grays and startling purples are used to color the realistic outdoor scenes of Mary and Joseph on the plodding donkey and the guiding star that lights the wise men's way to the stable. Beams of light illuminate the stone cobbles of a courtyard as well as the faces of a small shepherd boy, the Holy family, the townspeople and the sheep and camels. The illustration of the shepherds quaking at their vision of the heavenly hosts is appropriately mystical, with the night sky's clouds and stars appearing as angels holding candles. Jeffers' paintings of animals and landscapes are far superior to those of people, but her vision of this favorite carol is still respectful and majestic.

> *Elizabeth M. Simmons, in a review of "Silent Night," in* School Library Journal, *Vol. 31, No. 2, October, 1984, p. 174.*

In an oversize book, Jeffers uses the space to full advantage for striking paintings of the town, the manger, the Holy Family, and the worshippers at the Nativity scene. The text consists of the words of the familiar carol, for which musical notation is appended. The first scenes: Mary and Joseph travelling through the starry night, and the silent streets of Bethlehem, are particularly effective in cool blues and greens, but the composition and use of color are almost as dramatic in the interior scenes, in which the tender faces and the play of light and shadow are outstanding.

> *Zena Sutherland, in a review of "Silent Night," in* Bulletin of the Center for Children's Books, *Vol. 38, No. 3, November, 1984, p. 52.*

The Midnight Farm (1987)

[The Midnight Farm *was written by Reeve Lindbergh.*]

A mother and her young son take a quiet tour of their farm in "the heart of the dark," counting out the animals they see—one dog, two cats, three raccoons—in loosely rhyming quatrains. . . . The illustrations carry the book: they're large, full-color pen-and-ink and gouache double-page spreads with strikingly pretty settings. The smiling human faces lack the detail of the animal faces, and all the compositions have a static flat quality, but the closeness of mother and son and the positive approach to the night should please young children. A quibble: when it's this dark in the country, how can anybody see all those animals? The illustrations portray an evening dark rather than a midnight farm.

> *Leda Schubert, in a review of "The Midnight Farm," in* School Library Journal, *Vol. 34, No. 2, October, 1987, p. 115.*

Through Susan Jeffers's powers of interpretation, **The Midnight Farm** is a gentle progression from disturbed waking to sleeping worlds, as well as a counting book. A bedroom curtain flutters, and a mother describes to her child what they would see if they went for a walk around the farm. Time and creatures move naturally. Late day turns to midnight, the story-child becomes increasingly tired and has to be carried. A cat wanders from one place and page to another; the owl is poised, the mice scamper. When the story ends, both worlds have merged, the child sleeps contentedly. The overall sense of design is admirable. Spaciousness and drama are treated with restraint. Unworked areas balance intricate passages, and the hatching models the images and settles the picture on the page. Colour is warm and dusky within doors, silvered without.

> *Jane Doonan, "Penned and Painted," in* The Times Literary Supplement, *No. 4416, November 20-26, 1987, p. 1284.*

Benjamin's Barn (1990)

[Benjamin's Barn *was written by Reeve Lindbergh.*]

One rainy spring day, a small boy named Benjamin sets off for his big red barn, where he spends hours with the flesh-and-blood animals of the farm and the exotic creatures of his imagination. Thus, an elephant and a newborn lamb share shelter from the storm, while a rhinoceros and a billy goat cavort in the hay. When sunlight breaks through the clouds and Benjamin's father comes to take him home, all that is left along with the barnyard animals is a princess' golden crown. . . . Jeffers' lifelike illustrations enhance the theme, lending as much reality to the leathery texture of a pterodactyl's wing as to the downy softness of goose feathers. Literal-minded children may question the undifferentiated juxtaposition of the fantastic with the real, but most will understand an imagination as big and wide as a barn, with room enough for pachyderms and pirates as well as pigeons.

> *Anna DeWind, in a review of "Benjamin's Barn," in* School Library Journal, *Vol. 36, No. 6, June, 1990, p. 103.*

Benjamin's imagination plays round the possibilities of the barn, which in his view is warm enough for an elephant, wide enough for pterodactyls to perch in, clean enough for a royal ball and grand enough for a whole brass band; opposite the scenes that he envisages we see more believable inmates like a new lamb, an old piebald horse, a flock of pigeons and a herd of cows with their milking machine. Opposing pictures neatly establish the contrast between reality and fancy while deep, rich paint and forcefully drawn figures expand a text arranged in rough, rhymed lines.

The bear, the deer, the great eagle, these are our brothers.

From Brother Eagle, Sister Sky: A Message from Chief Seattle, *written and illustrated by Susan Jeffers.*

Margery Fisher, in a review of "Benjamin's Barn," in Growing Point, *Vol. 29, No. 5, January, 1991, p. 5458.*

Brother Eagle, Sister Sky: A Message from Chief Seattle (1991)

[Chief Seattle's] message, as presented by Susan Jeffers in *Brother Eagle, Sister Sky* is remarkably timely. Jeffers uses the pages as sweeping canvases for her delicate but powerful images, and her artwork creates a visual counterpoint to Seattle's words, showing the pristine forests, rivers, and plains of an earlier time when people lived in harmony with their surroundings, and the gradual devastating transformation that accompanied westward expansion. The final image is a triumphant, and hopeful one, with children replanting a hillside stripped of timber as the spirits of a American Indian family look on in approval. Well-suited for either home or classroom use, the book would be a good springboard for discussing the importance of caring for the environment.

Heather Volgel Frederick, in a review of "Brother Eagle, Sister Sky," in The Christian Science Monitor, *November 1, 1991, p. 10.*

Chief Seattle's original speech—delivered at the signing over of his tribes' lands to the U.S. government and dealing mainly with his hopes for peace and the eventual vindication of Native-American rights—bears little resemblance to the text here presented. The speech, frequently rewritten and augmented over the years to be a testimony to the supposed belief of Native Americans in the unity of man and nature, now rings as warning and prophecy in modern ears. The words illustrated by Susan Jeffers are resonant with far-seeing wisdom: "The destiny of your people is a mystery to us. . . . What will happen when the secret corners of the forest are heavy with the scent of many men? . . . Where will the eagle be? Gone!" Jeffers's delicate yet strong illustrations offer a combination of sadness and hope. Glorious, almost spiritual, pictures of Native Americans living at peace with animals, flowers, and streams are followed by desolate depictions of endless fields of tree stumps. But even as we see the destruction of the forests, we see a family with children replanting seedlings. Although the text has been heavily adapted, the combination of message and illustration is potent and timely.

Ann A. Flowers, in a review of "Brother Eagle, Sister Sky: A Message from Chief Seattle," in The Horn Book Magazine, *Vol. LXVII, No. 6, November-December, 1991, p. 755.*

Dayal Kaur Khalsa

1943-1989

(Born Marcia Schoenfeld) American-born Canadian author and illustrator of picture books.

Major works include *The Baabee Books* (1983-84), *Tales of a Gambling Grandma* (1986), *I Want a Dog* (1987), *How Pizza Came to Queens* (1989), *Cowboy Dreams* (1990).

Considered one of Canada's most promising creators of picture books before her death, Khalsa is often lauded for the mastery of the genre she developed in her six-year career. Inspired by vivd memories of her girlhood in Queens, New York, she created works that reflect—and gently satirize—American culture of the 1950s while evoking with tenderness the thoughts and emotions of children. Critic Sarah Ellis commends Khalsa's "great gift for turning ordinary childhood events into joyous celebrations of family and community warmth." Khalsa's recollections of her grandmother in *Tales of a Gambling Grandma* and a trip by car to Florida in *My Family Vacation* (1988) are, like her other works, filled with a child's awe of such everyday items from the adult world as false teeth and motel soaps. As these observations accumulate, an original and compelling depiction of American society emerges, and the unique character of May—the determined, red-haired protagonist of several of the works—becomes apparent. Critics point out that the books might be enjoyable to parents who share the author's nostalgia as well as to children who identify with May's pluck and imagination. Khalsa maintained these qualities in her works even after being diagnosed with breast cancer. Her death came before she could complete illustrations for the text of her last work, *The Snow Cat.*

A self-taught writer and artist, Khalsa, who changed her name in the 1970s when she joined a Sikh Ashram in Montreal, turned to memories of her youth as the source of her works after producing three installments of the wordless *Baabee Books,* concept books for children under the age of one. *Tales of a Gambling Grandma* features anecdotes about and advice from May's spirited, loving grandmother, demonstrating the close relationship between the two. The title character, a survivor of Cossack brutality in Russia, insists on keeping the refrigerator stocked with borscht in case the Cossacks ever come back. Grandma cheated at cards to support the family during the hard times she encountered after immigrating to the United States, a practice she keeps up now for considerably lower stakes in poker games with other grandmothers. The story ends with the grandmother's death, and critics note that Khalsa's rendition of May's bereavement is moving without being maudlin. The next work, *I Want a Dog,* tells of May's unyielding quest to convince her parents that she is responsible enough to own a pet. May's tactics include buying a salami so that strays will follow her home and pulling a rollerskate along on a leash to prove her serious-

ness. The illustrations of *I Want a Dog* are often considered the best feature of the book. Rendered in a flat, geometric style reminiscent of American folk art, the pictures contain abundant detail and whimsy, features of all of Khalsa's books. The cover is a canine parody of Georges Seurat's painting *Sunday at the Park;* another illustration depicts all of May's classmates with dogs' heads as evidence of the depth of May's obsession. *My Family Vacation* follows May as she spars with her teasing older brother during a car trip to Florida, and in *How Pizza Came to Queens* (published in Canada as *How Pizza Came to Our Town*) she helps gather the ingredients for a mysterious dish for Mrs. Pellegrino, a visitor from Italy. The text and illustrations of both works present 1950s America as an enchanting, carefree landscape abounding in roadside diners, swimming pools, miniature golf courses, and amusing characters. Although Khalsa published only a small number of books during her lifetime, she made a distinct impression on children's literature in Canada; reviewer Marjorie Gann notes that Khalsa's "completed body of work is an enduring legacy to Canada's, and the world's, children." Khalsa received several awards for her books: *Tales of a Gambling Grandma* won a Children's Literature Prize Honorable Mention for Illustration from the

Canada Council and was a finalist for both the Ruth Schwartz Award and the Amelia Frances Howard-Gibbon Award in 1987, while *Sleepers* won the Parents' Choice Award in 1988 and was a finalist for the Governor General's Literature Award for Children's Illustration in the same year. In addition, Khalsa's books were frequently selected as notable children's books in their years of publication by American libraries and children's literature reviewing sources.

(See also *Something about the Author,* Vol. 62.)

GENERAL COMMENTARY

Sarah Ellis

In a biographical introduction for her child audience, author and illustrator Dayal Kaur Khalsa has written: "When I was a young teenager and wanted to be a writer and couldn't wait to leave home and go on the road in search of adventure to write about my mother said, 'There are stories right in your own back yard.' Hah!, I said. So I left home, went on the road, had lots of adventures, and eventually 25 years later, the first book I published took place in my back yard of childhood. Hah!"

In four recent picture books Khalsa plays with this dual perspective. The adult looks inward and back to re-create in pictures the clearly-remembered details of a suburban neighborhood of the early fifties, a landscape of saddle shoes, tinker toys, and pole lamps, a world of the fat, rounded curves of cars, refrigerators, toasters, and mothers. But in contrast to this backward look the heroine of all four books, a sturdy russet-haired child called May, looks forward and out, to new adventures. The stories the words tell are not rooted in any particular period but grow out of simple universal childhood experiences.

In *I Want a Dog,* for example, Khalsa takes a gorgeously simple idea. May wants a dog. Her sensible parents feel she is too young for the responsibility. After trying every persuasive tactic she can invent, May finally makes do with a roller skate which she pulls around on a leash, tying it up outside "no dogs" establishments and giving it a bath. Pictures and text work in juxtaposition. The words tell us how much May wants a dog, but only the pictures show the full extent of her obsession, as in a scene in May's classroom where all the children have dog faces. The text reassures us that May did eventually get a dog, yet the final picture shows only that all the children in the neighborhood now lead their roller skates around on leashes— so forceful is May's personality. Much of the gentle humor of the book lies in the pictures, but it is through the text that we really get to know May, a spunky, resilient protagonist whose personality is summed up in the line, "May was disappointed but not discouraged."

May broadens her horizons even further in *My Family Vacation.* In the story of a family driving vacation from the snowy north to Florida the pictures again place us firmly in the fifties. But we are also reminded of the timeless quality of highway travel. Gas stations, car trouble, miniature golf, motel soap—May relishes them equally. Her naive delight in counting cars and collecting souvenirs

exasperates her older brother, but she finally earns his respect by bravely jumping off a high diving board. From then on they share the pleasures of tourism. As in *I Want a Dog* the pictures have a folk art quality in which all objects seem to be given equal weight and importance. This style perfectly matches the text which straightforwardly describes objects and events and leaves us to draw our own conclusions about emotions and shifting family dynamics. The adult author uses carefully chosen details to re-create a child's viewpoint while showing a perspective on changing family relationships that only the distance of years can provide.

In *Tales of a Gambling Grandma,* a third perspective is provided by the reminiscences of the narrator's colorful, eccentric, Russian-born grandmother. This book has an explicit storytelling frame, opening with the words, "My grandma was a gambler. This is the story of her life as she told it to me and as I remember it." The format is set up for a historical document, a memoir.

But two elements give the book an added dimension. The first is that the grandmother's stories are presented through the filter of a young child's understanding and experience. Again, text and pictures work in tandem. The child quotes her grandmother's two pieces of advice, "One: Never, ever go into the woods alone because the gypsies will get you or, should you escape that cruel fate, you'll fall down a hole. Two: Just in case the Cossacks come to Queens, learn to say '*Da*' and always keep plenty of borscht in the refrigerator." In the pictures that accompany these words we see the child's vision of these scenes. In the first a group of stage-lit, operatic gypsies cavort in a landscape of perfectly symmetrical black holes, observed by the narrator in her cowboy outfit. In the second a group of tidy Cossacks sit on chrome and vinyl kitchen chairs and are served bright pink borscht by a small girl in a Brownie uniform. Both pictures are the perfect overlay of child vision on adult words. . . .

Plucky and self-contained, she is definite about her preference for a Ping Pong Pow gun over a Betsy-Wetsy doll, and she learns to take her losses at poker. At the end of the story the grandmother dies, and, again, Khalsa tells us nothing about how the child feels. She simply describes what she does. "I opened her closet door and stepped inside. I closed the door behind me and hugged and smelled all my grandma's great big dresses."

In a coda the narrator describes how as an adult she inherited her grandmother's ring. The adult remembers; the child experiences; and the grandmother makes her memories into stories—these points of view mingle and play in words and pictures.

A younger May is featured in the small book, *Sleepers.* In rhythms and variations reminiscent of Mary Ann Hoberman's *A House Is a House for Me* the unsleepy narrator describes how various people and animals sleep, "My father sleeps on the living room couch. / My mom in a hammock that swings. / Uncle Teddy sleeps in the bathtub and he snores as loud as he sings." But she ends each stanza with the declaration, "But I never sleep."

The illustrations here are simpler than in the other books.

Khalsa seems to take particular pleasure in blocky one-color silhouettes, palm trees against the tropical sunset, a big black baby grand piano, and a shiny white claw-footed bathtub. Likewise, the narrative point of view is more straightforward as even the youngest reader will see the child sink down under the covers as she valiantly insists, "But I never sleep." *Sleepers* shares with many classic picture books for the very young the technique of collusion between writer and audience who see through the ruses of the protagonist.

Of her work in progress Khalsa says she is writing a story in which May discovers pizza. From another artist this subject might seem slim, but given Khalsa's mastery of the picture book form and her feel for the details of childhood one looks forward to it with great anticipation. Khalsa's back yard has turned out to be fertile indeed. (pp. 393-95)

> Sarah Ellis, "News from the North," in The Horn Book Magazine, *Vol. LXV, No. 3, May-June, 1989, pp. 393-95.*

Linda Granfield

Dayal Kaur Khalsa was 46 when she died last summer after a four-year struggle with cancer. She left a legacy of joy for children, a picture-book world filled with the vivid sights, sounds, smells, and colours of her own childhood territory. . . .

Khalsa was born Marcia Schoenfeld in Queens, New York City. Her earliest ambition was to be an artist. Like the parents of the unnamed little girl in *Tales of a Gambling Grandma,* Dayal's parents both worked, and she spent her days with her grandmother, who became the greatest influence in the child's life. When Dayal was eight, her grandmother—her protector and friend—died. The loss was traumatic; at that point, Khalsa considered, her emotional life was over. She channelled all her energies into observation and learning. She read through the local library shelves, subject by subject, acquiring a vast knowledge of geography and art history.

She also paid close attention to her surroundings, and her detailed recollections of the social and cultural mores of the 1950s are powerfully evident in her books. A close friend and fellow artist, Yvonne Lammerich, has spoken of her "phenomenal memory. She remembered the slightest details from her childhood. All her stories are true, although they are a bit exaggerated. The houses, interiors, and streets are exactly as they were in the '50s and '60s. The books on the shelves are the titles Dayal loved, the art on the walls is the same."

After university, Khalsa became a social worker in New York City, then worked as a copywriter in advertising. Some of her early writing was for literary magazines. She studied art in New York, and although she was attracted to large-scale abstract painting, Dayal found herself doing small drawings, the work that would eventually illustrate her children's books.

The pictures for her books were always completed before she began writing the story. *My Family Vacation* captured the kitsch of Florida, then and now. Plastic flamingoes, the orange HoJo roof, the used-car dealerships, and the tacky motel rooms are portrayed in all their full-blown splendour. Her drawings could be as witty as her conversation, and she liked to poke fun at revered icons: her cover illustration for *I Want a Dog* is a send-up of George Seurat's "Sunday Afternoon on the Isle of La Grande Jatte," filled with heavenly hounds at rest on a lazy day. "Dayal Kaur Khalsa obviously remembered what really matters to children," observed Debbie Rogosin, executive director of the Canadian Children's Book Centre. "She had a child's-eye view of what happens in a child's world. Her texts are filled with a warmth that touches both children and adults."

In the mid-1970s Marcia Schoenfeld joined a Sikh ashram and became Dayal Kaur Khalsa. Although she had no children of her own, she tended the babies and young children during many summers spent in a Sikh women's camp in New Mexico. Her understanding of early childhood and her desire to rediscover her own family led her at last to writing and painting for children, and the list of Khalsa titles, once begun, grew quickly. . . .

To the many admirers of her work, Khalsa was a mysterious, gentle, white-turbaned figure, an author about whom they knew little; to those who knew her well Dayal was a humorous, contemplative, introspective person who sought the positive influences in life. She loved country music, rock 'n roll, Italian food, and cowboys. "Dayal was inspired by the American cowboy's free spirit and his style," says Lammerich. In the spring of 1990 Dayal Kaur Khalsa's *Cowboy Dreams* will be published . . . as a fitting tribute to Khalsa's passion for the joy of childhood.

During the final months of Dayal's illness, a friend read to her nightly from her favourite book, *The Wind in the Willows.* "She identified with Toad," recalls Lammerich. "He's the rebel who does what he wants, but at the same time he's the sweet, kind one who helps others, and he's honest: Dayal's perfect match."

> Linda Granfield, "Dayal Kaur Khalsa: 1943-1989," in Books in Canada, *Vol. 18, No. 8, November, 1989, p. 6.*

May Cutler

[Cutler was Khalsa's publisher at Tundra Books, Canada.]

Dayal—during the last four years of her life while she underwent operations, treatments and recurrent pain, battered by the alternate hope and despair that cancer inflicts—managed to write and illustrate seven books and write an eighth. They shine with joy, humour, and the fun of life. The five published before she died moved her to the ranks of those rare and precious creators of children's books who can both tell a good story and illustrate it spectacularly. You can count on two hands their number throughout the world. But it was not the success of her books that was so important to Dayal, although of course the accolades pleased. It was the actual work of making them; she admitted to laughing frequently as she put in the mischievous detail. I don't think she'd have traded any of it for a quick and easy death. (p. 258)

I met her in 1982 when she brought illustrations to show

us. They did not impress for idea, content, or technical proficiency, but they had one quality that is less common than you would think: strong colour sense. She could mix garish colours together—rather like the Berber women of Morocco—and come up with a vibrant and united whole.

The discovery was just being made at that time that babies don't like pastel colors; they can't even see the pale pinks and blues that parents have long adored. Dayal's colours led me to suggest a series of object recognition pictures and the twelve **Baabee** board books resulted. Babies loved them but adults didn't like their crude simplicity, the big-eared baby who came in skin shades of pink, yellow, brown, and blue. Dayal developed the images and colours, testing them on babies at a Sikh camp in New Mexico where she summered. They were indeed an experiment and an exercise, and they gave no hint of what was to come.

Dayal talked about the **Grandma** book long before she showed it to us. I remember staring, incredulous, at the first illustrations, at grandma taking an orange-juice bath on a train, at the fridge filled with borsch in case the Cossacks came back. Here was a unique talent.

Her illustrations are full of in-jokes, many of them take-offs or take-outs from some of the most famous art in the world. We recognize easily the cover of *I Want a Dog* as a fun variation of Seurat's *Sunday Afternoon on the Island of La Grande Jatte:* his park becomes a paradise for dog-walkers while dogless little May sits with her substitute roller skates. Do we also recognize the girl's bedroom in *Grandma* is designed after Van Gogh's? Art detectives can search out other fun borrowings.

She was a self-taught artist. She started art lessons once in New York, but gave up after seeing an Edward Hopper exhibition because "I could never paint that well." Yet she was in the mainstream of several modern art movements. Her illustrations are pop art without the sterility and magic realism without the sentimentality.

She was extremely generous with her art. Her books have as many as twenty-five paintings—in contrast to half that in many children's books—plus endleaves that are as caringly crafted as the interiors. I asked her once where she got the energy and time to develop the stories and do fifty or sixty illustrations a year. (This was between operations, hospital visits, chemotherapy, and all the accompanying discomfort.) She grinned: "It's easy, May, I've got a deadline."

Shortly before her death she phoned from Vancouver. "I want to say goodbye, and thank you." As if it wasn't us who should be doing the thanking. I have had a few honours in my life, but I think the one I shall always be proudest of is that she named the spunky, irrepressible heroine of so many of her books "May," after me. (p. 259)

May Cutler, "Dayal Kaur Khalsa (1943-1989): A Publisher's Tribute," in CM: Canadian Materials for Schools and Libraries, *Vol. XVII, No. 6, December, 1989, pp. 258-59.*

Robin Baird Lewis

Sleepers by Dayal Kaur Khalsa is a small compact delight that puts the lie to the publisher's maxim that a rhymed story or poem does not have wide appeal. Khalsa's speaker is a blissfully chatty youngster (a preschooler?) whose gender is not significant, but whose tone of voice is so true to that age which knows it all because they drove everyone mad the previous year asking questions.

As author/illustrator, Khalsa has balanced her text and visuals with admirable simplicity. In her solid tempera and strong colours, Khalsa's illustrations shine on the page. The text is brief but steady, as the speaker pronounces upon the sleepers known in the family and neighbourhood. Within the rhymed itemization, is the repeated assertion, "I never sleep" which eventually creates an even lulling mood ideal for bedtime when capitulation seems acceptable and welcome.

Longer in text and with a more challenging vocabulary, *I want a dog* is a slightly off-centre little story of childish persistence (and apparent success) in the face of adult pragmatism. Wrapped in a cover that is surely a deliberate homage to Georges Seurat, the greater portion of this tale (if you'll pardon the pun) is devoted to May's pitch to her parents for a dog and her eventual disciplined (if eccentric) demonstration that she can care for one. The fact that she uses a roller skate as her canine stand-in adds a fillip of whimsy, which Khalsa's appreciative public has come to expect and enjoy.

Although the actual success of May's campaign is mentioned as if an afterthought within the last thirty words, the punch line gently matches an illustration which is a perfect example of how the humourous, visual completion of a tale can be the most illuminating one.

Any review of Khalsa's work would be remiss if a word was not said about her visual style. In *I want a dog* especially, there is an arresting mix of boldly coloured tempera and pastel or chalk. The views of May's world are right out of the 'forties and 'fifties by way of Khalsa's remarkable memory for detail. Anyone sympathetic to the tiny visual minutiae which identify our cultural history will enjoy themselves immensely as they appreciate the cheap spotted kitchen lino, the vinyl and chrome dinette set, the frigidaire, the taxi interior as well as the other cars, the sparse "rec" room where May sets up her training course (the titles on her prop books are a hoot!), the decor in Sam's luncheonette—even the clothing style, fabric choice and colour combinations, speak of the corduroy and flannelette age before this poly-cotton era.

While only a cad would criticise Khalsa's flat, thick brush style of tempera, one might quibble with her renditions of the various dog breeds which seem to be too often in show-dog profile, as if an Illustrated Encyclopedia of Dogs was too close to hand. Her natural poses are far more fun. Certainly her work overall is simply delightful. (pp. 86-7)

Robin Baird Lewis, "Delicate Solidity and Whimsy . . . A Winning Mix," in Canadian Children's Literature, *Vol. 53, 1989, pp. 86-7.*

From I Want a Dog, *written and illustrated by Dayal Kaur Khalsa.*

Terri L. Lyons

One of Canada's leading illustrator/authors of children's books, Dayal Kaur Khalsa, died in July 1989 at the age of 46 after a long battle with cancer. Her publishing career spanned only three years but during that time she won numerous major awards in both Canada and the United States.

Generally speaking, art critics and reviewers examine an artist's whole body of work to detect patterns and growth over a lifetime. Unfortunately, Khalsa's oeuvre consists entirely of seven completed books and one text without illustrations. Despite the sparsity of finished works, Khalsa's work demonstrated definite growth and development. Patterns were beginning to emerge in her illustrations and stories. We can only speculate on what might have been, but there is little doubt in my mind that Dayal Kaur Khalsa would have become a leading international artist.

Khalsa was published exclusively in Canada by Tundra Books. Their writer's biographical data states that she was born in Queens, New York, in 1943. She attended City College and then wandered the United States and Mexico as a flower child before emigrating to Canada in 1970. She first lived in Toronto and then, in the late 70's, moved to Montreal to be a member of a Sikh ashram. Later she moved to an ashram in Vancouver to be closer to old friends.

As a completely self-taught artist and writer, Khalsa's accomplishments have been impressive (p. 70)

Khalsa was well known for her personal trademarks—her vivid flat illustrations and her whimsical sense of humour. By the time the author had completed *Julian,* certain other trends had emerged—the endpapers were illustrated and Khalsa had now clearly perfected her painting technique.

The first two books, ***Tales of a gambling grandma*** and ***I want a dog,*** had plain endleaves (the paper that covers the inside cover board and also serves as the first blank page). The following four books have delightfully illustrated endpapers. Khalsa, with her usual gentle humour, chose an identifiable motif from each story and decorated the leaves in a manner similar to wrapping paper. ***My family vacation*** has its endpapers covered with post card-like images and ***How pizza came to our town*** is decorated with wheels and slices of pizza floating through a cloud filled blue sky.

It is in ***Julian,*** however, that this treatment became something more. The brown dogs appear to be cut-out stencils on a rich green background. A reviewer, writing about ***I want a dog,*** said that " . . . one might quibble with her renditions of the various dog breeds which seem to be too often in show-dog profile, as if an Illustrated Encyclopedia of Dogs was too close to hand." . . . That may have been true for ***I want a dog*** but in ***Julian*** the format is perfect!

The dogs point in the same direction, all lined up in neat rows. Khalsa's unique vision is epitomized by the corresponding yellow dog in the lower right corner of both endleaves. Julian, the large boisterous dog, is depicted in mid-bound. Legs gathered together under him, ears flying out, Julian gallops wildly across the page. The mere juxtaposition of this mad lovable dog with the show-dog profile of the other animals exemplifies the author's humour and joy in life.

In addition to having a strong love of life, Dayal Kaur Khalsa had the unique ability to speak directly to *both* children and adults. What child wouldn't love May, the heroine of three books (*I want a dog, My family vacation,* and *How pizza came to our town*)? And every parent is sure to smile at the young girl's antics and then relate them to their own children as well as their *own* childhood memories. May, clearly based on the author's childhood, is universal and timeless. The girl's persistent determination to convince her parents that she is capable of taking care of a dog is, I am sure, something we have all experienced. Khalsa, however, took the theme one step further—she had May adopt a rollerskate as a surrogate dog. Anyone who ever had to pretend that an egg was a baby during Family Studies is going to smile in wry sympathy at May's gambits.

The knowledge that an adult brings to these books adds a deeper level of enjoyment. A child would certainly derive pleasure out of the vivid cover of *I want a dog* but an adult would further relish it for its play on George Seurat's *A Sunday afternoon on the Island of La Grande Jatte.* . . . In addition, Khalsa's settings are from the fifties. Robin Lewis wrote: "Anyone sympathetic to the tiny visual minutiae which identify our cultural history will enjoy themselves immensely as they appreciate the cheap spotted kitchen lino, the vinyl and chrome dinette set, the frigidaire . . . ".

The reader can also get a clear indication of the author's reading taste. In one scene in *I want a dog,* May creates an obstacle course for her rollerskate/dog. Piled up books serve as props for the boards doubling as sidewalks. The titles are as much fun to read as the text. In another book, *How pizza came to our town,* May and her friends take a trip to the library to try to find the meaning of the word "pizza". The main shelves are full of past classics, such as Tolstoy, and contemporary authors, such as Nadine Gordimer, but it is in the Little Readers section that Khalsa pokes fun (and perhaps displays a well-justified pride) in herself—cheek-by-jowl with classic children's books, e.g. Grimm's Fairy Tales, Mother Goose, etc.—sits the author's books, even those yet to be published.

It is with the use of these carefully chosen motifs that Khalsa touched and still touches the minds and hearts of her adult readers as well as their children.

Significant change, if not actual growth, can be seen in the artist's illustrations. An examination of the six books' three year span shows definite development in Khalsa's technique. Again, we can only speculate as to the outcome but her paintings are tighter, more cohesive and more polished in *Julian* than in *Tales of a gambling grandma.*

In the latter, published in 1986, Khalsa apparently used a combination of chalk/pastel and acrylic/tempera. Each illustration is a mixture of soft textured lines contrasted with bold flat colours. The paintings in this book tend to be gentler and quieter than the later ones.

In *I want a dog,* published one year later, Khalsa was using less chalk and more paint. The lines are sharper and more clearly defined. She was beginning to master the use of colour and detail. In *Sleepers* and *My family vacation,* published the next year, 1988, there are only a couple of indications of the softer medium—in both cases to indicate red brick walls!

In the spring of 1989, Tundra Books released *How pizza came to our town* and in the fall *Julian* was published posthumously. In both books, the author has used the same technique of flat untextured brushstrokes of rich vivid colours. The end result is, however, somewhat different. This slight difference could be attributed to an insightful author or an artist who was still exploring her medium. In the former books, the illustrations and the people within them are from a distant point of view. Is this distance supposed to indicate the smaller scale of a child's vision? Khalsa apparently sacrificed intimacy for a background of rich detail suitable for a child's exploration.

The illustrations in *Julian,* on the other hand, are larger in scale and more immediate. Instead of trying to include all elements of a scene, such as a whole room, Khalsa concentrated on fragments. These fragments, like family snapshots, welcome us into the farmhouse and into the story. The rich colourful details are still there—the vines and the flowers still adorn the wallpaper in riotous profusion and the landscapes still appear to be Japanese block prints, but the illustrations are warmer. By the time the author had completed this book she had apparently learned that two or three main elements can often create a more vital force than that of many.

In the spring of 1990, the author's seventh complete book, *Cowboy dreams,* was published, once again by Tundra Books. Dayal Kaur Khalsa had also written the text for an eighth book, *The snow cat,* just before she died. *Cowboy dreams* is the cumulation of a life-time of work and it will be interesting to see where her growth as a storyteller and as an artist had taken her.

May Cutler, of Tundra Books, said of Khalsa's books that "they are her affirmation of the joy of life. They are her monuments." Having spent these last few weeks studying and reading her books, I too have had great joy in sharing Khalsa's vision of reality. In the very process of dying, the author wrote eloquently of life and, as a result, assured her own immortality. Her readers, whatever their age, can be thankful for the legacy that Dayal Kaur Khalsa left for us to all share. (pp. 71-3)

> *Terri Lyons, "Dayal Kaur Khalsa," in* Canadian Children's Literature, *No. 59, 1990, pp. 70-4.*

TITLE COMMENTARY

The Baabee Books, Series I (Here's Baabee, Baabee's Things, Baabee Gets Dressed, Baabee's Home, 1983)

[*The Baabee Books*] are four interesting books intended for children under one year of age. Each has 12 laminated pages accordion-folded so the book can stand up. On each page is a picture, reminiscent of those in the Dutch Dick Bruna books, of objects that should be part of the baby's world. With each set of books comes a sheet of suggestions for ways an adult can use the books to play games with the baby, connecting the pictures to the actual objects.

I gave these books to some babies of my acquaintance and found that the bright colours did appeal to them, and that they enjoyed the way the books could be manipulated. In publicity material accompanying their release, Tundra says: "It seems that the earlier a baby recognizes that a two-dimensional picture stands for a three-dimensional object, the sooner that child will read and the higher its IQ is likely to be." Whether or not this is the case, the *Baabee Books* would make a more stimulating gift for a baby than yet another terrycloth sleeper.

> *Mary Ainslie Smith, in a review of "The Baabee Books," in* Books in Canada, *Vol. 12, No. 10, December, 1983, p. 14.*

The baabee books, created by Dayal Kaur Khalsa for children up to twelve months and published by Tundra Books, is actually a boxed set of four accordion-folding books, each with twelve brightly-coloured plates. These are pre-word books: there is nothing on the plates except simple, stylized drawings of faces, toys, articles of clothing, and household objects. The colours have been selected for maximum contrast: blue, yellow, pink, red, green, and brown.

We asked our four-month-old daughter, Stephanne, to field test *The baabee books,* and they performed admirably. At first, we were a bit disconcerted by the brown faces, blue babies, and yellow feet, but Stephanne smiled at them all. It is impossible to know whether she responded to the images or the colours or the fact that her parents were also interested in these *things,* but she did have fun looking at the images, folding the plates, and kicking them over. After twenty minutes of pointing and cooing, the inevitable mouth test proved another practicality of these books: they're virtually waterproof!

The sheet of instructions enclosed with the books suggests that "Baabee is a symbolic baby of either sex and any race," and that the different books are meant to reflect a baby's growing familiarity with his or her new environment. The four books are titled *Here's baabee, Baabee's things, Baabee gets dressed,* and *Baabee's home.* The books themselves are the result of research involving the early association of two-dimensional symbols and awareness-development of three-dimensional objects, and are the first of a projected series of twelve books. These four are bound accordion style; the remaining eight will be bound along one edge, as they are intended for the baby to hold.

Not that *The baabee books* aren't for holding—not at all!

You can hold them, stand them up on the floor or on a dresser, pin them on a wall, string them across a crib, tie them into a rotating shade, or simply sandwich them onto a bookshelf. Each book is made of sturdy cardboard with plastic lamination over the printed images, and has mounting holes on the top of each plate and at either end. They can be mounted individually or as a set, and the number of ways that you and your child can play with them is limited only by your collective imagination.

It would be hard to find fault with a design that is so simple and universal that its appeal is based on playing with colourful shapes. *The baabee books* series is well made, easy to store or mail, and comes with instructions. Our one concern was with the subtle suggestion in those instructions that a baby's intelligence will depend upon his or her earliest development, that play *is* child's work. "The primary aim of *The baabee books* is to give Your Baby pleasure," the instructions admit, but they carefully direct this play based on the suggestion that "there seems a close correlation between the early recognition of symbols or pictures and awareness-development. The sooner a baby understands that a two-dimensional pictograph stands for a three-dimensional object, the earlier that child will read and the higher will be its I.Q." that may be true. Certainly, no parent wishes to inhibit such early development, but undermining the outright pleasure of using *The baabee books* with such value-laden goals as obtaining a higher intelligence quotient is, at best, unnecessary. (pp. 75-6)

> *Peter Taylor, Nancy Taylor, and Stephanne Taylor, "From Baabees to Brownstones," in* Canadian Children's Literature, *No. 37, 1985, pp. 75-7.*

The Baabee Books, Series III (Bon Voyage, Baabee; Happy Birthday, Baabee; Merry Christmas, Baabee; Welcome, Twins, 1984)

Tundra has had great success with its series of Baabee books, created by Dayal Kaur Khalsa. They provide vivid, colourful symbols that babies as young as two months can enjoy and identify. The first Baabee books were mounted on stiff paper and could be opened out in strips to form frescoes or be folded into cube-like forms. The latest four books are bound in the ordinary way and intended for babies now at least one year old, presumably able to manipulate and turn pages. The range of experiences dealt with in the images now is wider. While the first books showed pictures of toys and familiar objects around the home, the titles of the latest four are: *Bon Voyage, Baabee*; *Happy Birthday, Baabee*; *Merry Christmas, Baabee*; *Welcome, Twins.*

> *Mary Ainslie Smith, in a review of "Bon Voyage, Baabee" and others, in* Books in Canada, *Vol. 13, No. 10, December, 1984, p. 11.*

Baabee, that many-coloured tot, was introduced in Tundra's accordion books; now, he/she reappears in standard board format. The signature design of bold colour edged with black has been retained in each title, and the attractiveness of the concept may give Dick Bruna fans pause.

In this third series, Dayal Kaur Khalsa's bald Baabee hosts a first birthday party, takes a trip, celebrates Christmas, and appears as twins. The practicality of these board books, with their washable covers and rounded corners, will further endear Baabee to parents of toddlers.

> *Linda Granfield, in a review of "Bon Voyage, Baabee" and others in* Quill and Quire, *Vol. 51, No. 3, March, 1985, p. 74.*

Cartoon-type illustrations peopled by what appear to be infants from another planet present various events in this series of board books. Garish colors outlined in black and identical babies of unlikely hues do little to enhance the appeal of the books. ***Merry Christmas, Baabee*** and ***Happy Birthday, Baabee*** consist of familiar objects and scenes from these celebrations, while ***Bon Voyage, Baabee*** is a wordless account of a trip by car and plane. ***Welcome, Twins*** shows pairs of pink, blue, yellow and orange children engaged in everyday activities, such as eating and playing. The sequence of events is confusing or nonexistent; in ***Bon Voyage, . . . ,*** for instance, a fire truck and an ambulance incongruously appear among the various modes of transportation. Quality books for babies and toddlers abound. Better choices include the "Chubby Board Books" and Eric Hill's "Baby Bear Books".

> *Lucy Young Clem, in a review of "Bon Voyage, Baabee" and others, in* School Library Journal, *Vol. 31, No. 8, April, 1985, p. 80.*

Tales of a Gambling Grandma　(1986)

[Dayal Kaur Khalsa], whose previous contribution to children's literature includes the Baabee Book series for infants, seems to have come into her own with this story. Written in the first person, it is the tale of her grandmother and is a fine example of the wisdom in that advice often given to and by writers, that one should write from one's own experience, about the things one knows best.

Tales of a Gambling Grandma is a loving, warm testimony to life, to family, to ties that bind, to the old enriching the young. The text, which offers humour as well as affection, is wonderfully written. Khalsa says just enough and never too much. She brings us to the brink of our own emotions without letting her subject-matter deteriorate into maudlin soppiness. Instead we're left wishing we could have met her caring, resourceful, opinionated, and quick-witted grandma. (Incidentally, for those who think the Baabee books are peopled with unattractive, bizarre little figures, never fear. In this book the artist offers paintings in a naive style full of colour, humour, and joy.)

> *Bernie Goedhart, "Colourful Books for Kids Illustrate a Fine Range of Talent," in* Quill and Quire, *Vol. 52, No. 6, June, 1986, p. 28.*

Since reading ***Tales of a Gambling Grandma,*** I've been wondering whether, if I were a child again, I would choose it for myself. Would I fall in love with the picture of the little girl in blue pants on the cover, playing cards with a white-haired older woman who looks like she knows a thing or two? The answer, undoubtedly, is yes. I would

have loved this book as much at any time in my life, and I can easily imagine most children will agree with me.

Grandma, who became a gambler, was born in Russia. She came to America wearing one black shoe, because the other shoe got lost on the night the Cossacks rode into her village. When she was older, she borrowed a balalaika and sat down on the steps of her building to catch a husband. She caught Louis the plumber. And then, because good jobs were hard to find, grandma learned how to play poker.

This is a beautiful book, filled with charm and wit and wisdom, certain to be read over and over again. Both Dayar Kaur Khalsa's text and her illustrations have a clear freshness, as if the granddaughter had just sat down to tell her grandmother's story. But it is not only the story of a remarkable grandmother; it is also, and above all, the story of the friendship between the old woman and the little girl who grows up to tell the story her grandma told. It is about a little girl whose parents work and who is therefore free to spend her days with Grandma under the weeping willow tree while the older woman knits and tells her tales.

There is so much tenderness here, such fine and loving sense of detail, such mastery of storytelling, that it seems the perfect antidote to a world in which children rarely feel safe enough or sufficiently protected. Everyone deserves a gambling grandmother, who lets you stay in her bed when you have a cold, makes the bed into a tent, sits all day next to you polishing pennies. You should have a grandmother who then, if you have hurried up and got better fast, takes you to see Rosie, the Beer-Drinking Hippopotamus, at the vaudeville show. Everyone needs a grandmother who gives advice about what to do if Cossacks should ever come to Queens ("say '*Da*' and always keep plenty of borscht in the refrigerator"), who knows how to exaggerate in the name of a good story, who teaches her granddaughter about life by beating her at cards and winning her allowance and who becomes in time her granddaughter's inspiration.

Few children will be fortunate enough to find a tutelary spirit of this kind, but who knows? Maybe this beautifully illustrated book about a wise old woman will serve as compensation.

> *Kim Chernin, in a review of "Tales of a Gambling Grandma," in* The New York Times Book Review, *September 28, 1986, p. 36.*

[This is a] warm and appreciative reminiscence. . . . Grandma is a real character and a storyteller. The twenty-two gorgeous full colour paintings in the book wonderfully depict both the settings of Grandma's life and the stories she tells her young granddaughter. Especially moving is the recounting of Grandma's death and the young girl's reaction to it.

Canadian children will have some difficulty in relating to the settings of this story and will require help with such concepts as "balalaika," "Cossacks," and "borscht," but the book can certainly find a place in a unit on multiculturalism or as a stimulus for children's own reminiscences about loved relatives. (p. 33)

Robert W. Bruinsma, in a review of "Tales of a Gambling Grandma," in CM: Canadian Materials for Schools and Libraries, *Vol. XV, No. 1, January, 1987, pp. 32-3.*

There are two things I really like about this book. The first is that it's funny almost by accident. The second is that the tone is so majestically irreverent. Humour and irreverence: what more can you ask for? No wonder, then, that readers feel the full force of a tragic ending. Not for a long time have I cried twice while reading a kids' book.

Tales of a gambling grandma is a schoolgirl's recollection of her grandmother, a Russian-born woman now living is Queens, New York. We know that the girl's parents work all day, and that Grandma lives with them. Grandma takes good care of her treasured grandchild, but, considering she's a grandmother, she has an uncommon skill. She's a "sharp-eyed" gambling card-player (initially, "to help make extra money"). The tragedy is that Grandma gets sick one day and dies.

I really felt like I was there. I was hugging and smelling those beautiful oversized multi-coloured dresses in my grandma's closet. I was collecting all those dirty old pennies in the corner of her drawer. I savoured the scent of the stale Evening in Paris cologne in its blue bottle. That anomalous breed of "old Country" woman, headstrong and self-reliant, curiously disapproves of non-sexist play patterns (Grandma insists that her granddaughter buy a doll and not a Ping-Pong-Pow Gun). At the same time, however, loving Grandma can't wait to teach her granddaughter how to play "real" cards—straight poker, five-card stud, three-card monte, chicago, and blackjack. The problem is Grandma always wins.

But Grandma isn't all kinky. She can knit, and she makes wholesome lunches. She also has a sense of social responsibility; she gets all the neighbourhood grandmas together to gamble for "trifles." The Sunshine Ladies Card Club meets in the backyard between the lawn mower and the umbrella clothes line. And this I know from the exquisite, brightly coloured illustration, naive yet exacting.

The book is convincingly written from the point of view of the little girl until the last paragraph (where she has supposedly, but not convincingly, grown up). When the storyteller's grandma dies, she says what other people say: "Oh, I'm sorry to hear that." Then she goes upstairs to her grandma's room, and mourns in a child's way. She hugs the dresses and checks the drawer. Khalsa's images, carefully repeated in the right places, both in joy and in sadness, are shared only by grandma and granddaughter, and they continue to be part of the repertoire of all grandmothers and their precious grandchildren. (pp. 91-2)

Marlene Kadar, "Convincing and Colourful," in Canadian Children's Literature, *Vol. 47, 1987, pp. 91-2.*

I Want a Dog (1987)

It's one of life's great ironies that children spend much of their childhood longing for the day they'll be grown up, while adults spend *their* time reminiscing about those

hey pooled all their allowances and took her out to eat at their favorite restaurant.

When she walked in, Mrs. Pelligrino sniffed in deeply and actually smiled. May and Linda and Judy and Peggy were so relieved. But when the waitress brought their grilled cheese sandwiches, Mrs. Pelligrino looked down at the little toasted squares and shook her head mournfully. "No pizza."

From How Pizza Came to Queens, *written and illustrated by Dayal Kaur Khalsa.*

blissfully innocent, carefree days of youth. Reality rarely lives up to either the anticipation or the recollection. As any adult can—and often will—tell a child, being grown up isn't all it's cracked up to be. . . . Likewise, any child can tell an adult that being young isn't all *it's* cracked up to be.

The central characters in three new picture-books—*I Want a Dog,* [Ian Wallace's] *Morgan the Magnificent,* and [Eugenie Fernandes's] *A Difficult Day*—are good examples. These girls are intelligent, resourceful heroines who take initiative. But they're still children, their lives ruled in part by the adults around them. No matter how loving those adults might be, each child feels the frustration of being dependent.

Of the three, the girl in Dayal Kaur Khalsa's *I Want a Dog* handles that frustration with the most aplomb. May tries every trick in the book to persuade her parents to allow her to have a dog. She strolls up and down the street with a slice of salami, luring the neighbourhood dogs to her home so that her parents will see what wonderful rapport she has with these animals. When that doesn't work, May buys her mother a puppy as a birthday present. "Nice try," says her mother. Her parents lecture May on the hard work and commitment having a pet entails; May only wants a dog all the more. Finally, her parents issue an order: "No, not now," they say. "You can have a dog when you're older."

May responds in a typically childlike fashion: she throws a tantrum, kicking her toys around her room. A roller-skate goes flying, bumps its way down the stairs, and gives May a wonderful idea.

At this point the book takes a quirky turn, and it is testimony to the author-illustrator's talents that the tale doesn't deteriorate into nonsensical drivel. In fact, Khalsa's flat, colourful, naive-style paintings are ideally suited to the humorous plot twist. In a move reminiscent of those school projects in which students are told to care for an egg as if it were a baby, May turns her roller-skate into a surrogate puppy and practises caring for the real dog she hopes will one day arrive. Her friends laugh at her, but her parents are impressed by her commitment, and May ultimately gets her wish. The final comic illustration is a double-page spread showing hordes of neighbourhood children with roller-skates in tow.

Khalsa first gave us a taste of her wit and whimsy last year, when she published *Tales of a Gambling Grandma. . . . I Want a Dog,* offering crisp, clean design with stylized capital letters launching each page's text, is a worthy successor.

> *Bernie Goedhart, "Morgan, May, Melinda: New Heroines Offer Humour and Fantasy," in* Books for Young People, *Vol. 1, No. 5, October, 1987, p. 24.*

This is the story of a little girl who desperately wants a dog. Her parents are not too thrilled about the idea, and as a result she pretends that her roller skate is a dog instead.

This premise is very original and whimsical, and I like the book's understated humor. There is a scene in the beginning where May, the little girl, gets all the dogs in the neighborhood to follow her home by leading them there with a slice of salami. She tells her mother, "Dogs just seem to want to be with me." However, a whimsical premise alone does not equal a plot, even if the author really really wants it to be one.

May pretends the skate is a dog, training it, taking it on a walk, taking it out sledding. Her friends inexplicably copy her. She loses the skate, gets it back, and at the very end the author lets us know that eventually, a couple of years down the line, her parents do, indeed, buy her a dog. Maybe this is what some people feel is all little children want to have happen in a story, but I don't think so.

If the plot seems minimal and somewhat static, however, the illustrations are anything but. They are beautiful, inspired, detailed, naïvely drawn and painted and extremely colorful. They place the book specifically in the 1950's in a suburb. Dayal Kaur Khalsa . . . has a style that is a sort of cross between a Persian miniaturist and a 19th-century American folk artist. The color is flat, bright and wonderfully varied. The indoor scenes have a real "indoor-ness" to them, a feeling of being lit by electric light, and the outdoor scenes seem to take place under an open sky.

Each painting contains lots of things to look at. There is a scene in May's parents' basement where she has set up an arrangement of boards and books on which to train the roller skate to walk. The books, however, are not random, generic objects. They are all titled: *The Good Earth, The Last Tycoon, Daisy Miller.* The laundry hanging in the background of the same panel isn't just blah little squares of color but specifically patterned sheets, towels, etc. There is a similar richness of detail in all the illustrations—the pink, cobalt and gray checked linoleum of a luncheonette, the chintz covering an easy chair, the cream-colored lilac-flowered wallpaper of a foyer in a trick-or-treat scene. These are the parts of *I Want a Dog* in which Ms. Khalsa is most successful in creating a mood and making this particular little girl come alive.

> *Roz Chast, "A Girl's Best Friend Is Her Skate," in* The New York Times Book Review, *November 8, 1987, p. 32.*

Children will love the way May solves her problem in *I Want a Dog.* She uses her imagination! Although the story is entertaining, there is a practical lesson on the responsibilities of dog ownership. The full-color artwork is a wonderful mix of fantasy and droll humor. The illustrations have a primitive look, but it is apparent that Khalsa is a top-notch painter. I also like the subtle references to contemporary art in the illustrations. The humans and dogs are both painted with equal skill, but, being a dog lover myself, I felt that the dogs were the definite stars of the book. *I Want a Dog* is one of my favorites of the year.

> *Nancy Carlson, in a review of "I Want a Dog," in* The Five Owls, *Vol. 2, No. 3, January-February, 1988, p. 42.*

Anyone who has ever been obsessed with longing—or who has dealt with a single-minded child—will immediately understand and appreciate this off-beat, gently humorous story of May, who "wanted a dog more than anything else in the world." Despite her pleadings, her assertions, complete with examples of how a dog would bring innumerable benefits to the entire family, her parents remain firmly opposed, always citing that far distant time when she would be older. Someday, however, is not in May's plans; consequently, she tries a number of clever schemes: carrying salami so that ten dogs follow her home; buying a puppy as a surprise birthday present for her mother; remaining obdurate to all adult descriptions of the difficulties which beset dog owners. Nothing works, but, undaunted, May develops a satisfying solution, suggested by watching her roller skate skitter down a flight of stairs. Amazed by the skate's resemblance to a frisky puppy, she begins walking it like a dog, taking it everywhere she goes—indoors and out, through good weather and bad—convincing her doubting friends that such unusual behavior is a necessary, even a desirable, prelude to the realities of pet ownership. Her parents, although similarly impressed with her newly exhibited responsibility, remain firm in their decision—for a couple of years. "Meanwhile, though, May, and all her friends, kept on practicing." While the text is strong enough to stand as a story on its own, May's plight and the ingenuity of her solution are given additional emphasis through striking, brilliantly colored illustrations, varying in size and design to complement stages of plot development. Although at first reminiscent of varied schools of painting—such as the composition of the pointillists—the illustrations are fresh, vigorous interpretations, true to the child's perspective and thoroughly engaging. (pp. 342-43)

> *Mary M. Burns, in a review of "I Want a Dog," in* The Horn Book Magazine, *Vol. LXIV, No. 3, May-June, 1988, pp. 342-43.*

Sleepers (1988)

In **Sleepers,** her third book, the author and illustrator Dayal Kaur Khalsa takes the incantatory tack typical of classics such as *Goodnight Moon,* using blank verse sprinkled with simple rhymes and lots of internal repetition—in this case, of a child's transparently false assertion that "I never sleep." Where Margaret Wise Brown composed a low-wattage litany of ordinary objects, Ms. Khalsa seems intent on spotlighting oddities: "twin aunts," for instance, "who can sleep sitting up," or an uncle who sleeps in the bathtub and "snores as loud as he sings."

Many parents might hesitate to introduce into a young child's hypnotic reveries the notion, however cheerily painted, of "a man in the park who sleeps on his back on a bench all day and only gets up when it's dark." Even the very first image, of a father who sleeps on the living room couch, would seem to presage divorce rather than a secure night's rest. And the picture over said sofa—an adaptation of Edward Hopper's painting "Nighthawks"—provides a tip-off to the sensibility being addressed: it's an adult in-joke. Children, even sleepy ones, are apt to pick up on the slight sneer implicit in the conceit of the *soi-disant* insomniac.

> *Sandy MacDonald, "Things That Go Baa in the Night," in* The New York Times Book Review, *May 8, 1988, p. 35.*

In a rhyme reminiscent of Hoberman's *A House Is a House for Me* (Viking, 1978) Khalsa has written a delightful bedtime book. A small girl narrates the sleeping habits of family, animals, and others (fireman, cowboy, clown) with the refrain, "But I never sleep." Humor is provided by the variety of places and styles preferred by these sleepers (twin aunts who sleep sitting up, grandma who sleeps in the car, etc.). With each refrain, the child sinks further into the bed until she finally says, "But I never sleep./ Instead I count sheep." Then counting begins, and she is asleep by number 11 (as are the sheep). Illustrations in this small square book are bright and colorful and impishly humorous, matching perfectly a child's conception of the sleeping habits of others. (pp. 91-2)

> *John Philbrook, in a review of "Sleepers," in* School Library Journal, *Vol. 35, No. 9, June-July, 1988, pp. 91-2.*

Bedtime stories, never in short supply, are seldom as beguiling and as original as the diminutive new book by a Canadian author-artist. . . . Careful, interesting composition, definitive images, and the juxtaposition of brilliant, flat shapes and patterns are all enclosed within the star-studded deep-blue end-papers. Although the miniature well-ordered pages sparkle with color, they create exactly the right impression of serene, reassuring simplicity.

> *Ethel L. Heins, in a review of "Sleepers," in* The Horn Book Magazine, *Vol. LXIV, No. 5, September-October, 1988, p. 616.*

Sleepers is intended to be read aloud. The rhyming text flows naturally, in vocabulary suitable for beginning readers. Adults will enjoy the sly humour and recognize the tendency to fall asleep in cars, on park benches and in bath tubs.

Writer-illustrator Khalsa of Montreal plans the outline for her books and as she paints the illustrations she develops and refines the text, thinking visually and literally at the same time. . . . The bold, vivid illustrations have a jewel-like Far Eastern flavour.

> *Hazel Birt, in a review of "Sleepers," in* CM: Canadian Materials for Schools and Libraries, *Vol. XVI, No. 6, November, 1988, p. 228.*

My Family Vacation (1988)

By combining two clichés—the nuclear family and its seasonal trip to Florida by car—Khalsa has produced a book that playfully reflects on American images.

On the one hand, we have May, a spindly and responsive little girl, alert to her brother's deprecations. ("You're such a baby," he accuses; and even more scathingly, "Don't be stupid.") Their rivalry serves as a source of suspense in the episodic story. In addition, children can emphathize with May's persistence at gathering miniature soaps wherever she goes. No tourist was ever more acquisitive.

On the other hand, the pictures, which exult in 1950s consumer kitsch, affectionately recreate a particular place and time. Khalsa's compositions are so strong, moreover, with perpendicular lines and flat, prominent patches of color, that they transcend the tacky setting. In one climactic illustration of May, she jumps from the high board to the hotel pool below. Almost instantly, this riveting picture achieves the author's goals of telling a story, creating a scene, and imposing a highly structured image on the viewer.

Finally, in all that Khalsa tells and shows of paradise, she gently satirizes trips on which families advance from one contrived, expensive diversion to another. On this particular trip, May seems an improbable target indeed for birds at Parrot Jungle who scream, "Hiya, Baby!" and "Hello, Joe." From *her* point of view, the snow, as it fell on her own backyard the day her family left home, was just as entrancing as any well-appointed beach.

Yet May enjoys her trip, her souvenirs, her moment of vindication with her brother. She is endearingly receptive to whatever comes her way. I think that readers, remembering trips of their own, will be happy to travel with her though this poised and funny book.

> *Mary Lou Burket, in a review of "My Family Vacation," in* The Five Owls, *Vol. 3, No. 1, September-October, 1988, p. 9.*

Vivid memories and vivid colors enliven the story of a young girl on her first long family vacation. Vignette paintings filled with flat colors and staccato patterns evoke the 1950s setting. May, her parents, and her older brother (the one who always wins) set out for a winter vacation in Florida. May is both frightened and excited by the adventure. Khalsa captures this and the delight that a child can take in the smallest details of a new experience. May starts a souvenir collection, coveting motel soap, sugar packs, and postcards. There are also the car games and an undercurrent of sibling rivalry that carry the story along. Khalsa's colors blaze like the southern sun with hot pinks and greens. She packs her pictures with detail. From sight-seeing excursions to Parrot Jungle, penny arcades, and miniature golf courses, readers will relish May's experiences and enjoy remembering her family vacation. (pp. 89-90)

> *Judith Gloyer, in a review of "My Family Vacation," in* School Library Journal, *Vol. 35, No. 3, November, 1988, pp. 89-90.*

Sequels can be problematic. The wells of some authors, like Beatrix Potter, never seem to run dry. If she is known above all for *The tale of Peter Rabbit,* many others, like *Tom Kitten* and *Jemima Puddleduck,* also rank as masterpieces. Other children's writers—L. Frank Baum's name springs immediately to mind—never duplicate their initial achievements. Like Potter and Baum, Canadian author-illustrators Dayal Kaur Khalsa and Stéphane Poulin often retread familiar, proven ground—childhood reminiscences from the 1950's and the escapades of Daniel's cat Josephine. But both Khalsa's *My family vacation* and Poulin's *Could you stop Josephine?* retain the freshness and vigour of their prototypes. Moreover, like most good children's books, they address two audiences—children, who look for a good story and absorbing pictures, and adults, who appreciate irony, satire, and wit.

Khalsa, who died tragically of cancer at age 46, had an uncanny memory for what the 1950's world of an American kid looked like. In her straightforward tale of May and Richie's family trip to Florida, she paints familiar incidents that should strike a responsive chord in many adult readers. As I read *My family vacation,* I chuckled more than once at reminders of my own family's 1959 Florida trip: loving "everything about [the motel]—from the big bouncy beds to the paper covers on the drinking glasses to the writing paper and envelopes in the night-table drawer," avoiding the hotel's social director like the plague, and going to a real nightclub on the last night.

For adults, the book's interest lies in its central irony: the children's innocent enjoyment of Florida kitsch at its worst. The frontispiece sets the tone: May's family sits at the dining room table perusing flashy Florida travel brochures. It is a 1950's suburban interior—tinny four-branch chandelier, comfortably drab furniture. On the wall are reproductions of two Vermeer domestic interiors, a wry reminder of a loftier aesthetic.

Khalsa's brilliant, solid-colour acrylic masses and super-imposed planes transform Floridian poor taste into pure design, elevating even the most kitsch of tourist traps: "El Club Flamingo" is a sweeping horseshoe curve of tiers of round, white tables studded with oval, raspberry-coloured chairbacks, separated by the bold, flat black arch of a room divider crowned with huge, pink flamingos.

The children's innocence redeems this tacky world. May takes simple pleasure in collecting free souvenirs (hotel soaps, feathers from Parrot Jungle, and the "little pink paper umbrellas" from the nightclub). She and Richie enjoy a penny arcade, miniature golf, and a bowling alley "that usually didn't allow children": "But since you two look like big spenders from the North," said the manager, "I'll skip the rules today." The existence of these two innocents abroad is a charmed one. (pp. 105-06)

Khalsa's production, tragically, is over—a great loss to the Canadian picture book world. . . . with its rich content, both literary and pictorial, her completed body of work is an enduring legacy to Canada's, and the world's children. (p. 107)

> *Marjorie Gann, "Two Fine Sequels," in* Canadian Children's Literature, *Vol. 57/58, 1990, pp. 105-07.*

How Pizza Came to Our Town (1989; U.S. edition as *How Pizza Came to Queens*)

Sturdy, ebullient, red-haired May, heroine of four previous books from Khalsa, turns up again in this adventure of broadening culinary horizons. Khalsa has a great gift for turning ordinary childhood events into joyous celebrations of family and community warmth. In this story, Mrs. Pelligrino visits from Italy and feels isolated and disoriented until May and her friends discover the old woman's talent for pizza-making.

This simple story is given depth by Khalsa's mastery of the traditional picture-book form. The illustrations define a world of early '50s suburbia, complete with saddle shoes and roadside diners. In her flat, naive style Khalsa reveals an affection for the shapes of domestic objects: angular kitchen chairs, Mrs. Pelligrino's solid black shoes, glorious yellow disks of pizza dough whirling in the air.

The words function where the pictures cannot, as in the description of May's first whiff of pizza: "It smelled as good as toast and french fries and ketchup and grilled cheese sandwiches and spaghetti all rolled into one." Likewise, the pictures contain gentle little jokes unmentioned in the text. In one, May and her friends stand in a cheese shop delicately holding their noses.

How Pizza Came to Our Town is not a book that gives everything away on a first reading. It's not a script for performance, but a story for quiet and intimate family times, to be enjoyed again and again.

> *Sarah Ellis, "Birthday Cake, Pizza Served Up in New Books," in* Books for Young People, *Vol. 3, No. 2, April, 1989, p. 12.*

Although some children will find the idea of no pizza in America inconceivable, this warm story tells how the delicacy came to one family's home. . . . As in her last book, *My Family Vacation,* Khalsa does a masterful job of capturing the ambience of her 1950s setting. A big, red Cadillac sits in front of a castlelike drive-in, while in a suburban backyard, children play croquet or put on shows. Stylistically, her art is unique, both in the way she mixes clear, bright colors and shadings and in her sense of proportion; for example, little children sit on great big chairs as they watch the pizza cooking through the oven window. A delicious effort in both concept and execution.

Ilene Cooper, in a review of "How Pizza Came to Queens," in Booklist, *Vol. 85, No. 15, April 1, 1989, p. 1386.*

[*How Pizza Came to Queens*] is a straightforward little story, with bright, bold, naïve paintings. Any young pizza lover will relish it, but one wishes that the author had exploited the possibilities a little further.

For example, one of the best illustrations shows a 1950's kitchen with Mrs. Pelligrino and the girls tossing pizza dough into the air. But the author's description of pizza itself rests with the way it smells—"as good as toast and french fries and ketchup and grilled cheese sandwiches and spaghetti all rolled into one." (You may question the details of the comparison.)

Nor does the author describe, in either words or pictures, eating pizza. Didn't someone get the untidy slice—the one whose tomato sauce oozes off, plop, onto the table, taking a gob of mozzarella with it on parachute strings?

"When the pizza was done, they had a party"—just some people from the neighborhood—and somehow, first time out, they all knew just how to eat pizza.

The illustrations are cheerful and bright, though some are not up to the uniformly high standard of *I Want a Dog* and *Tales of a Gambling Grandma.* They depict a very suburban Queens, with not an apartment building in sight. One or two of the paintings are oddly focused—for example, the one showing Mrs. Pelligrino's arrival. The eye is drawn to the character who looms largest: Mrs. Penny, the girls' mother. Then there are the children toiling with the suitcase. Way in the background is the yellow taxi with the checker motif, and standing in front of it, you realize, is Mrs. Pelligrino in her apron, clutching a green package. This, it turns out, is not a present, as the children hope, but a rolling pin, which comes into play when the pizza is finally made.

It is well to remember this picture, because as a symbol of absolute domesticity it may help explain why Mrs. Pelligrino was quite content to stay in Queens; she never once went sightseeing, a fact that will cause no particular distress to younger readers, but may puzzle older ones—not even a trip to the Statue of Liberty?

Incidentally, *pellegrino* is Italian for pilgrim or traveler, and the spelling used in this book is unusual. There is only one in the Queens telephone directory.

Natalie M. Healey, in a review of "How Pizza Came to Queens," in The New York Times Book Review, *September 17, 1989, p. 39.*

Large, vivid illustrations fill each page and Khalsa manages to give the flavour of May's entire community: we see long shots, close shots, mood shots, action shots, and everything looks like a lot of fun, especially eating the pizza. The book encourages cross-cultural and cross-generational understanding, and it calls children's attention to the fact that the library is a place for the solving of mysteries. . . . Like the late Elizabeth Cleaver, Khalsa was a multi-talented author-illustrator whose life was cut short by cancer while she was in her prime. With Khalsa's death earlier this year, Canada has suffered another sad loss. (pp. 116-17)

Mary Rubio, in a review of "How Pizza Came to Our Town," in Canadian Children's Literature, *No. 56, 1989, pp. 116-17.*

Julian (1989)

A young woman tells how the coming of Julian—a bumptious golden retriever acquired to chase the groundhogs out of the vegetable garden—transformed her peaceful existence.

Julian is indeed a chaser: he chases cars and cows as well as the groundhogs; he chases the horse (who likes it), the goat (who escapes), and the resident cats. He calms down some after being rescued from the well he bounces into; and after rescuing the smaller of the two cats, he becomes the fast friend of both.

This episodic story has the feel of remembered incidents involving favorite pets rather than a well-plotted story, though Khalsa reports the incidents with engaging enthusiasm and affection. But—as with her other books—the strength here is in the vibrant illustrations. Forms that recall silk-screen in their simplicity; austere use of beautifully selected detail; compelling design; and a strong sense of place combine to make this, visually at least, one of her most successful books. For both animal and art lovers.

A review of "Julian," in Kirkus Reviews, *Vol. LVII, No. 13, July 1, 1989, p. 992.*

A new picture book from the late Dayal Kaur Khalsa, *Julian,* is a typically handsome Tundra production: deep, rich colours glow on the glossy pages. Julian is an overgrown, over-enthusiastic puppy who must learn to restrain his lolloping energies if he is to make friends with his new owner and her two cats in their cozy country house. Khalsa tells the wry, affectionate story in a surprisingly effective first-person narrative. Her most spectacular success, though, is in the way she deploys her vivid paintings on the page, varying their shape and size to create a lively and often witty visual rhythm. Julian's adventures, culminating in his rescue of a lost kitten, make an irresistibly lovable picture book.

Michele Landsberg, "A Handful of Picture Book Plums," in Quill and Quire, *Vol. 55, No. 10, October, 1989, p. 13.*

Julian, published posthumously, was the last completed work and the second last manuscript produced by Dayal Kaur Khalsa before her death last July. *Julian,* while even more beautiful than its predecessors (can that be possible?), is a slight departure from her earlier works. The story is not told in the third person from the dog's point

From Julian, *written and illustrated by Dayal Kaur Khalsa.*

of view, nor by her familiar character May, but, rather, the narrative is told in the first person by the owner of Julian and the farm. Even though the story is told in an adult voice, a first for Khalsa, the text is eminently suitable for group reading to youngsters. There is a sense of rhythm, appropriate for a storyteller, not often seen in the author's previous books.

> Well, Julian certainly was a good chaser. He chased the cows in the next pasture. . . . And he chased and he chased and he chased the cats all over the place.

Once again, Dayal Kaur Khalsa's illustrations are visually stunning. The rich vibrant colours clashing riotously across the pages are offset by the flat untextured quality of the figures. These two normally opposing elements, highly reminiscent of the Japanese block prints that influenced the Impressionists, work well in harmony under the illustrator's talented vision. Khalsa, in her short working life-time, perfected this technique to create a unique personal trademark.

Another of the author's trademarks was the strong sense of humour evident in the touches of whimsy in her illustrations. Adults and children alike will have great fun in poring over the paintings looking at each successive layer of detail. The chief game in *Julian* is to find Ricky Rainbow, the very small kitten of the story, in the pictures. He is indicated by only a couple of unrelieved black touches of the brush and is often hidden and dwarfed by some other element. Yet his charm is somehow emphasized by his visually and physically diminutive stature.

The last recurring element of the author's that I will only mention here was her growing tendency to illustrate the endpapers. (pp. 109-10)

> *Terri Lyons, "Khalsa's Last Book," in* Canadian Children's Literature, *No. 56, 1989, pp. 109-10.*

Cowboy Dreams (1990)

Khalsa, who died recently, often returned to her past for memories that also have pull for children today. In this vividly told and illustrated story, she recalls her burning desire to be a cowgirl. A real cowgirl, of course, has her own horse, but one doesn't appear to be riding into this child's future. So, she makes do with her bike, Old Paint, and a mechanical horse outside the variety store. Khalsa recounts how she entered a contest to win a horse (she lost), and made a pony of the basement banister when it became too cold to ride Old Paint outdoors. But even more than her ersatz equines, it was mostly the songs—"Home on the Range," "Poor Lonesome Cowboy," "Streets of Laredo"—that swept her away to her world of dreams. Excerpted lines of the songs are illustrated beautifully. In fact, the book is filled with Khalsa's vibrant artwork: from the charming endpapers featuring cowboys riding through the cactus-filled prairie, to the inside of a movie theater where Gene Autry sings from the screen, to a Near-Eastern inspired full-page painting with a costly toy horse in the midst of intricate mosaic patterning ("expensive toys like that were meant only for the children of kings and maharajas"). As always, Khalsa's vision of an earlier, simpler era is distinctively her own. It's one that will be missed.

> *Ilene Cooper, in a review of "Cowboy Dreams," in* Booklist, *Vol. 86, No. 19, June 1, 1990, p. 1899.*

It's a sad privilege to review Dayal Kaur Khalsa's last book, completed a few months before her death from cancer last summer. She was forty-six years old. To those who knew the pain she had to overcome to complete seven books in four years, it is a poignant farewell as she dedicates *Cowboy Dreams*

> To All My Old, Old Saddle Pals.
> There's hardly a trail we didn't roam,
> But the sun is setting in the West,
> And it's time for me to head on home.

Children will be delighted with the colour and humour of *Cowboy Dreams,* in which a little girl longs to own a horse. Based on her own experiences, *Cowboy Dreams* affirms the capacity of children to overcome disappointment through imagination and spunk.

Khalsa was a rare children's book creator in that she was able to come up with original stories with spectacular illustrations. Khalsa's illustrations remind one of East Indian paintings, rich in colour and full of detail.

*Hazel Birt, in a review of "Cowboy Dreams,"
in* CM: A Reviewing Journal of Canadian
Material for Young People, *Vol. 18, No. 4,
July, 1990, p. 181.*

Youthful obsessions are enhanced by that great gift of
early childhood: single-minded stubbornness. Children, it
seems obvious to me, experience a smaller world, with
fewer real distractions beyond themselves, and thus their
ability to focus, to concentrate on a thwarted desire, will
continually amaze adults who expect a certain pragmatic
slackening of want to set in.

In the posthumously published **Cowboy Dreams,** Dayal
Kaur Khalsa, whose delightfully distinctive books such as
Tales of a Gambling Grandma and **How Pizza Came to
Queens** have won many awards, examines one case of this
exasperating juvenile tendency. And, as previously, she
draws readers in with her down-to-earth whimsy, primary
colors and the sort of detail (in both word and picture)
that seems so right and familiar as to make adult readers
wonder if they've ever truly grown up.

"When I was a girl I wanted to be a cowboy" is how the
narrative begins. It certainly doesn't sound at all odd to
one who cherishes a photo of herself, at 5, in a black
Hopalong Cassidy suit. But Khalsa's heroine doesn't stop
at imitative costumes, or even at slapping her thigh and
shouting "Giddyap!" Rather, this very determined little
girl perfects a bowlegged walk, calls her bike "Old Paint"
and practices ambushing every family member down to
and including the cat.

But since every cowboy worth his spurs has a horse to bed
down with out there on the prairie, it's equine monomania
that soon takes over. Yet it's not at all surprising, except
to the sorely disappointed narrator, that her parents aren't
as enthusiastic as she is about the possibility of winning
a horse in a raffle. Just because the hoped-for congratula-
tory letter fails ever to arrive, however, doesn't mean no
mount. Instead, looking for an acceptable substitute—one
that doesn't require stabling—she discovers the basement
bannister, and, with the addition of makeshift stirrups,
reins and saddle (blanket), this becomes her perch.

Again, it's a simple detail, but thanks to Khalsa, the very
act of pretending to have a horse, what it felt like, comes
flooding over me. . . .

The book closes with some snatches of western songs—
"Home on the Range" and "Streets of Laredo" are two
of them—and it is to be hoped that all mothers and fathers
reading **Cowboy Dreams** to their children will be able to
do even partial justice to these haunting American melo-
dies. The large and very bright illustrations are themselves
almost musical, so vibrant are they, and the image of a
black-and-white Gene Autry serenading his own horse up
on a movie theater screen early on in the story is practical-
ly a talking picture in itself, with its poignant evocation
of an innocent age when heroes were neither super nor
mutant and definitely not teen-age.

As might be surmised, **Cowboy Dreams** may appeal to
parents more than to today's youngsters, but Dayal Kaur
Khalsa's empathy with a child's obsessive yearning can be
understood by all ages and belongs to no era in particular.

*Michele Slung, in a review of "Cowboy
Dreams," in* The New York Times Book Review, *August 26, 1990, p. 25.*

In **Cowboy dreams,** as always, Khalsa uses the bright,
opaque colours and naive perspectives that give her work
an engagingly childlike quality. Khalsa's text has the same
dignified simplicity, speaking to children without affecta-
tion and with a quiet sense of humour that allows her to
touch on profound issues without a hint of pretension.

Cowboy dreams is the story of a girl whose one great
dream is to own a horse. Although this desire is never realized, she responds to her frustrations by creating a rich
fantasy world. (p. 86)

Khalsa never forgets the boundaries imposed on dreams.
The girl knows that, because her father is a tailor and not
a wealthy maharaja, she "wasn't going to get that horse."
But looking at paintings of horses, watching old Gene
Autry movies, and singing the cowboy songs that so poignantly evoke her loss and her longing, the girl finds ways
to enter a wider, less restricting world.

Even death, the end of all our dreams, loses its terrifying
finality in Khalsa's hands. On the last page, the girl, following a cowboy mounted on a golden palomino, rides
away on her toy horse, through a mountain scene where
the setting sun blazes and turns a river to a stream of red.
There are images of death here; but they are presented,
through the vivid beauty of the scene, with a sense of quiet
affirmation. The imaginative power that lives in our "cowboy dreams" will carry us over the inevitable endings and
losses.

While confronting her own death, Khalsa created a beautiful work that, like all her other creations, catches us with
its profound whimsy. The last words of **Cowboy dreams**
poignantly convey her affirmation of fantasy and humour;
Khalsa makes her farewell in the true cowboy spirit.

And, you know, every once in a while I find myself humming one of those old sweet songs—and
I feel as bold and brave and free as a cowboy
again. *Giddyap!*

(pp. 86-7)

*Ulrike Walker, in a review of "Cowboy
Dreams," in* Canadian Children's Literature,
No. 63, 1991, pp. 83-7.

Chiyoko Nakatani

1930-1981

Japanese author and illustrator of picture books.

Major works include *The Animals' Lullaby* (written by Alberti Trude, 1966), *The Brave Little Goat of Monsieur Séguin: A Picture Story from Provence* (written by Alphonse Daudet, 1968), *The Day Chiro was Lost* (1969), *Fumio and the Dolphins* (1970), *The Lion and the Bird's Nest* (written by Eriko Kishida, 1973), *The Zoo in My Garden* (1973).

One of Japan's most celebrated authors and illustrators of juvenile literature, Nakatani produced picture books known for their broad appeal to children from a variety of ethnic backgrounds as well as for their unusual quality, consistent charm, and unity of text and illustration. Primarily depicting children and their interactions with animals, Nakatani's stories are known for the economy of her prose and for her illustrations, featuring spare lines and soft, gentle colors. Regarding her technique, Nakatani remarked that "the rhythm of lines (especially pen lines) and the harmony of colors [are] most important." She also illustrated works by a wide range of children's authors, including nineteenth-century French writer Alphonse Daudet and contemporary children's writer Eriko Kishida.

While an art student at the University of Tokyo, Nakatani became interested in the paintings of the French Impressionists. Subsequently, she began working with oil paints to produce textured canvasses, rather than adopting the traditional, smooth, pen-and-ink and color print styles of her native Japan. Her subjective approach, presenting emotion through colors and lines, is also characteristic of French Impressionism. The characters in her first book, *The Animals' Lullaby,* a look at the ways in which animals sleep, are bathed in soft blue tones in order to evoke a sense of nighttime; several reviewers have commented on the beauty of these illustrations. Nakatani is also praised for the expressiveness of her characterizations. *The Lion and the Bird's Nest,* for example, tells of King Jojo, an aging and weary lion who performs a kind and generous act in allowing a bird to build her nest in his crown. Critics observe that the range of emotions Nakatani presents though pictures of Jojo's face and posture allow preschoolers to understand the story without being able to read. *The Day Chiro was Lost,* in which a dog jumps off the back of a truck and becomes lost in the streets of Tokyo, is the first book Nakatani both wrote and illustrated and features detailed illustrations of shops and highways, effectively depicting the bustle and confusion of city life. Nakatani is perhaps best known for her award-winning illustrations accompanying Alphonse Daudet's story *The Brave Little Goat of Monsieur Séguin.* In this story Blanquette, a little goat who seeks adventure and freedom, runs away from her safe pasture and is rescued by her owner after encountering and fighting with a wolf. Here Nakatani depicts the French countryside in warm

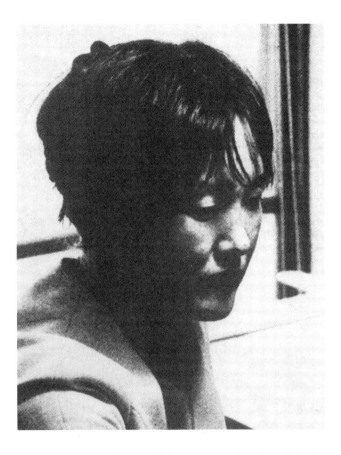

and luminous colors, which contrast sharply with the white goat, emphasizing that character's independence and bravery.

Nakatani's illustrations for the works of other authors are widely praised. Although some critics have suggested that the content of her own stories is too slight to keep a child's attention, most others describe her picture books as heartwarming, expressive, and unique, providing a satisfying reading experience for children. Many have found her work appealing to all ages, and note her lively characters and understated yet luminous double-page spreads as proof of her international appeal. Nakatani received several Japanese awards for picture books as well as the 1968 Spring Festival Award for her illustrations in *The Brave Little Goat of Monsieur Séguin.*

(See also *Something about the Author,* Vols. 40, 55.)

ILLUSTRATOR'S COMMENTARY

[*The following excerpt is from a letter to Grace Allen Hogarth.*]

Of herself and her work, Chiyoko Nakatani writes: "I

graduated from [Tokyo University] in 1952. In 1960, my first picture book, *The Lion and the Bird's Nest,* attracted the attention of Mrs. Bettina Hürlimann, and it was published later by her Atlantis Verlag. In 1963, I was invited by Mr. Paul Faucher (Père Castor) to his villa during my European tour, and I was much impressed by his enthusiasm for children's books. He liked my book *Hippopotamus* and selected it as one of *The Albums of Père Castor.* In 1966, Atlantis Verlag published *The Animals' Lullaby* in Switzerland. In 1968, *The Brave Little Goat* was published in New York. Then (1971) Picture Puffins published *Hippo Boat* and *The Animals' Lullaby.* . . . I began to illustrate children's books with enthusiasm in my twenties when I held after-school classes of painting for children in my home. I wished to give good picture books to children in order to add a good element for their environment. New ideas for picture books spring inside me when I am observing children (especially my beloved nephews) and when I try various methods of creation. And when I try to express these ideas in my illustrations, I consider the rhythm of lines (especially pen lines) and the harmony of colors to be most important. My big problem is how to adopt new movements of modern arts to my picture books without ruining my originality."

> *Grace Allen Hogarth, "Biographies of Illustrators Active 1967-1976: Chiyoko Nakatani," in* Illustrators of Children's Books 1967-1976, *Lee Kingman, Grace Allen Hogarth, Harriet Quimby, eds., The Horn Book, Inc., 1978, p. 146.*

GENERAL COMMENTARY

Elaine Moss

Chiyoko Nakatani was in London for one whole day—her first visit—last spring. She speaks no English. I speak no Japanese. When I was invited to meet her, there seemed to be little point in taking along a notebook, even less a tape recorder. Could there be any communication between us, even if the promised interpreter materialized?

At my suggestion we met at the Puffin Club Exhibition, and when I arrived it didn't take me long to locate Mrs. Nakatani. Over in the corner, hemmed in by polite but eager kids waving pieces of paper she stood, leaning against a bookcase, drawing Chiro the dog (from *The Day Chiro Was Lost*), a lion (from *The Lion and the Bird's Nest*), a hippo (from *The Hippo Boat*), and animal after animal from *The Animals' Lullaby* for Puffineers to take home with them. The Puffineers made their choice of animal known to her by pointing, flapping, grunting, and gesticulating; the artist responded in large, sure, soft line-drawings. There *was* communication—by picture.

This was hopeful. But I still felt daunted as we sat down to tea. I couldn't see myself gesticulating, as the children had, and looking for a picture in reply. And to talk to someone as obviously lively and intelligent as Chiyoko Nakatani through an interpreter would, I thought, be like that party game in which one tries to bite a juicy bun dangling always just beyond one's reach.

How wrong I was. The interpreter, far from being a barrier, succeeded in opening up channels I might not otherwise have explored. Soon the conversation was flowing, and Chiyoko Nakatani and I were bouncing our questions and answers off a delighted "middle-woman".

Now in her forties, Mrs. Nakatani studied art, specializing in oil painting, at Tokyo University. She emphasized the university status of art training in Japan, and was astonished that I was astonished to discover that French Impressionism was the major influence in modern Japanese art: a reversal of roles, for it had been Japanese artifacts that inspired and delighted the nineteenth-century French painters who later became known as the Impressionists. The young Chiyoko was, as the interpreter put it, "taught" by Renoir and Monet. In fact, when visiting Paris ten years ago, she felt totally at home in the studios of the Ecole des Beaux Arts because the curriculum was so similar to that of the Tokyo University Art Department of her student days.

Although art is highly rated in Japan as a university discipline, twenty years ago it was poorly taught in schools, and educationists had not yet woken up to the importance of the picture book, which Chiyoko Nakatani considers to be the child's personal art gallery. Adults, she says, go to museums and exhibitions; the child has his books.

Looked at from this standpoint, the picture book is not "a piece of illustrating"; it is only good enough for the child if it is a considered work of art. When the twenty-year-old Chiyoko began to paint with and for children (she held after-school classes for them in her home), neither publishers nor parents would have been prepared to spend large sums of money on the kind of picture books she then dreamed of.

But times have changed. As the war receded and the modern westernized Japanese state could forge ahead again, the educational climate altered. With the broadening of Japan's horizons (which had begun in pre-war days but been set back a generation by 1945) its need for communication increased. Unlike the Japanese language, pictures are universally understood: they are international currency.

In 1960 Chiyoko Nakatani's first picture book, *The Lion and the Bird's Nest,* with text by Eriko Kishida, was published in Japan by Fukuinkan-Shoten. In it an ageing lion, friendless because of his erstwhile ferocity, agrees to allow a grieving bird, whose eggs have been destroyed, to lay a second batch within the protective circle of his kingly crown. King Lion, as guardian of the weak instead of predator, is no longer lonely. Sturdy pictures—of animals, birds and jungle—pad their way through the pages of this book.

It was *The Lion and the Bird's Nest* which attracted the attention of Bettina Hürlimann when she was in a Tokyo bookshop at the time of the Swiss Exhibition in Japan. She asked to meet Chiyoko Nakatani, and from that meeting sprang *The Animals' Lullaby,* my own favourite of this artist's books. It appears that Bettina Hürlimann, impressed by Chiyoko Nakatani's beautiful oil paintings, was determined to give her a book to illustrate for Atlantis

Verlag, Zurich, the firm of which she is co-founder. Home in Switzerland she discovered the perfect text for the Japanese artist: it was Trude Alberti's poem about animals going to sleep. She sent the text of *The Animals' Lullaby* winging to Tokyo where Chiyoko Nakatani immediately saw its "children's art gallery" potential. When I asked whether it had been difficult to conceive a picture book in which there was no central character to carry the child from page to page, she said, "In this book the atmosphere of peace and rest and sleep is the central character, and the child is lifted over the pages on the waves of sleep, visiting one baby animal after the other as he makes his way to his own cot—and the lullaby his mother sings to him".

If Bettina Hürlimann was Chiyoko Nakatani's European godmother, Paul Faucher (the famous "Père Castor") was her godfather. She met him in Paris during a long European tour (which didn't include England) in 1963. His "Albums" had something in common with the Japanese *Kodomo no Tomo (Children's Friend),* which also presented facts to very young children in pictorial form. M. Faucher saw that through Chiyoko Nakatani he might be able to publish a genuine Japanese sea story illustrated with Japanese paintings of high quality for his young French readers. Mrs. Nakatani went back to Japan fired with enthusiasm: she wrote the story of *Fumio and the Dolphins* and illustrated it lovingly with blue-green seascape, with dolphins leaping against a sunset and with Fumio himself, a boy whose passion for a mother and baby dolphin urges him to lead them out to sea away from the nets of the fishermen. But by the time the artist had finished her picture book, "Père Castor" had died: the book is dedicated to his memory.

Chiyoko Nakatani is not over-interested in the specifically Japanese quality of Japanese picture books. If the story is set in Japan (like *The Day Chiro was Lost,* in which a dog runs bewildered through the streets of a Japanese town and the maze of motorway fly-overs) it will look Japanese; but if it is about a zoo (she can *not* say *Wake up, Hippopotamus!,* however hard she tries) the image is universal. "So long," she says, "as children everywhere feel this picture is lovely, beautiful, comfortable to be with, that is enough." She is more concerned with being internationally understood *now* than with carrying the artistic heritage of Japan (those wonderful picture-story scrolls of the twelfth century) over into purely Japanese modern forms.

Although she reveres the pen-and-ink and colour-print traditions which Europeans, at any rate, associate with Japanese calligraphy and illustration, she is convinced that for children the appeal of the texture produced by oil-colour on canvas is stronger. Having embarked on full-colour picture books, she knows she must, because of the production costs, find publishers in many countries besides her own; and to achieve international status she subjugates local character to universal comprehensibility. It is a sad fact of life, I feel (but Mrs. Nakatani clearly did not agree with me), that in becoming citizens of the world we are being forced to tread only common ground.

Which western picture-book artists appeal to her? Of the Americans she admires Maurice Sendak—whose *Where the Wild Things Are* looks delicious with a Japanese text—

and Roger Duvoisin, with whom she shares a passion for presenting the fable of tolerance in picture-book terms. The Alpine landscapes of Alois Carigiet from Switzerland excite her. Her British favourites are Beatrix Potter who, like Chiyoko Nakatani, would spend many patient hours drawing and painting animals; and Edward Ardizzone because he too loves to paint the sea in all its moods.

Would she, I asked, as a final favour (I had by now taken up a whole hour of her precious day) kindly autograph my copy of *The Animals' Lullaby*? "Hai, hai, hai! In English or Japanese?" Dare I ask for both? It seemed I dared. With infinite care she inscribed the fly-leaf: first with a perpendicular signature and date in Japanese, then with a horizontal *Chiyoko Nakatani*—a perfect piece of composition which will find a permanent place in this child's "personal art gallery." (pp. 135-38)

> *Elaine Moss, "Chiyoko Nakatani," in* Signal, *No. 12, September, 1973, pp. 135-38.*

TITLE COMMENTARY

The Animals' Lullaby (1966)

[The Animals' Lullaby *was written by Alberti Trude.*]

Everybody sleeps—the baby seal beside the sea, the bear cub in the woods, the little beaver in a lodge by the lake, the baby hedgehogs in the green hedgerow, etc.—but no one sings them a lullaby. The baby owl sleeps all day and sits at the window at night . . . "Who is that singing a lullaby?" A mother and father are singing softly to the baby asleep in the cradle, "Sleep, my little one, sleep." In each double-page spread, the daytime alertness and nighttime stillness of a particular animal is caught with affecting simplicity, making an attractive album for the littlest that also beckons them quietly to bed.

> *A review of "The Animals' Lullaby," in* Kirkus Service, *Vol. XXXV, No. 22, November 15, 1967, p. 1363.*

Based on an Icelandic lullaby, this picture book consists of full-page illustrations facing each four- or five-line stanza. The theme of the song (no music given) is that none of the creatures on land or sea have lullabies sung to them, but a human baby has. The line drawings with color wash are delightfully simple yet eloquent. Parents as well as nursery school and kindergarten teachers will find it a happy pre-nap item.

> *Elsie T. Dobbins, in a review of "The Animals' Lullaby," in* School Library Journal, *Vol. 14, No. 6, February, 1968, p. 67.*

[*The following excerpt is by Bettina Hürlimann, an author and critic who discovered the text of* The Animals Lullaby *and sent it to Nakatani to illustrate.*]

One day I received a manuscript of only a few pages by post. It was called *Wenn Tierkinder Schlafen* (*When Baby Animals Sleep*) and was a translation of an Icelandic lullaby by a German teacher who was quite unknown to me. It struck me as a fascinating theme; ever since my child-

Mrs. Hippo likes the rain.
Baby Hippo loves the rain.
Terrapin likes it too.

Yes, it is raining at the zoo.
Cool and gentle rain.
Plip, plop, plip, plop, splish, splash.
It is raining at the zoo.

From The Hippo Boat, *written by Eriko Kishida. Illustrated by Chiyoko Nakatani.*

hood I had worried about how and where animals spent the night.

If I found a good illustrator the text would be just long enough for a picture book. The illustrations had to be sensitive and beautiful, but neither sentimental nor grotesque. Who could do the job?

Then I thought of Chiyoko Nakatani, the young Japanese artist, whom I knew and who had already done a lovely book about a hippopotamus; her hippopotamus child had delighted many children.

But how to make her understand the text? She spoke only Japanese. I made an English translation as well as I could and sent it to my friend Momoko Ishii, a very good Japanese writer. She was delighted, and translated it herself; it looked beautiful in Japanese characters. Chiyoko Nakatani, too, was delighted, and put a wealth of tender feeling into her paintings of the animals playing and sleeping. She painted them in oil, but they had a translucent look, and there was a lot of blue in them as if the nocturnal scenes were flooded with moonlight.

Chiyoko Nakatani's publisher also liked the book, and had it produced at once. As far as I remember, we had the books printed at the same time, but the Japanese edition with its Japanese letters looked especially beautiful. (p. 164)

> *Bettina Hürlimann, "The Sixth House: The House of Patience, 1942 Onward," in her* Seven Houses: My Life with Books, *translated by Anthea Bell, 1976. Reprint by Thomas Y. Crowell Company, 1977, pp. 145-75.*

The Brave Little Goat of Monsieur Séguin: A Picture Story from Provence   (1968)

[The Brave Little Goat of Monsieur Séguin *was written by Alphonse Daudet.*]

"Monsieur Seguin had never been lucky with his goats." All six of them had broken their ropes, run off to the mountain—and had been devoured by a wolf. If only his pretty new goat would be happy and stay with him. But, alas, Blanquette in her turn raced off to the mountain, reveling in her freedom, eating grass and flowers that tasted like nectar, racing up and down the slopes, making friends of the deer, afraid of nothing. Until night came and with it the howl of the hungry wolf. What followed, the bravery of Blanquette, has become a legend in Provence. At least, so we are told in this charming and poetic tale, which has been translated and adapted from a story in *Letters from My Mill*, a collection of short stories by the 19th-century French writer, Alphonse Daudet.

Chiyoko Nakatani was a happy choice for illustrator. A Japanese artist, she studied art also in Paris and Switzerland, and her love and awareness of the French countryside are evident in exquisite illustrations done in warm luminous colors. The wooded hills and flowery fields make a lovely background for a little white goat, who stands out against them sharp and clear, brave and free, utterly endearing.

> *Polly Goodwin, in a review of "The Brave Little Goat of Monsieur Seguin: A Picture Story from Provence," in* Book World—The Washington Post, *May 5, 1968, p. 4.*

Miss Nakatani's pictorial paean to Provence is in perfect harmony with Daudet's bittersweet parable about a little goat who is not happy in an earthly paradise. A luxurious picture book, it raises hopes that pictures and words can be equal partners in 1968.

> *Selma G. Lanes, in a review of "The Brave Little Goat of Monsieur Seguin," in* The New York Times Book Review, *May 5, 1968, p. 55.*

With a softened ending, the famous "M. Séguin's Goat" in Daudet's *Letters from My Mill* has become a charming picture book for the very youngest. The seventh little goat of M. Séguin was no different from the others: Blanquette loved her freedom and could not resist running free among the trees and flowers and herd of chamois on the mountain; she preferred to risk the wolf than to have the safety of her rope. In fresh, inviting panoramas, a Japanese artist who knows well Daudet's Provence has pictured a lovable little goat whose joy in her mountaintop is happily communicated. In the adapted conclusion, the all-night battle with the wolf lasts until the stars go out; M. Séguin's horn sounds faint, then louder, as he arrives in time to rescue his Blanquette.

> *Virginia Haviland, in a review of "The Brave Little Goat of Monsieur Séguin: A Picture Story from Provence," in* The Horn Book Magazine, *Vol. XLIV June, 1968, p. 314.*

Like Monsieur Séguin's six other goats, the little white goat becomes bored and, longing for freedom, scampers up the mountain paying no heed to Monsieur Séguin's warning that the other goats had been devoured by the hungry wolf that waited there. The adventures of the foolish but brave Blanquette are told in a felicitous text and in charming paintings of the frolicking goat and the French countryside. (pp. 1233-34)

> *A review of "The Brave Little Goat of Monsieur Séguin: A Picture Story from Provence," in* The Booklist and Subscription Books Bulletin, *Vol. 64, No. 21, July 1, 1968, pp. 1233-34.*

A brief story from Daudet's classic *Lettres de Mon Moulin,* slightly altered, provides a refreshing text for a picture story book that has genuine suspense, atmosphere, and literary style. The little goat who escapes the security of Monsieur Seguin's pleasant green lawn for the wild freedom of the mountains, where she courageously fights all night with a wolf, makes an appealingly brave and independent heroine. The charm of Provence and the alluring beauty of the mountains are caught in soft, luminous paintings accented by the innocently cavorting white goat. A picture book of unpretentious integrity and style, this should wear well for either reading aloud or storytelling.

> *Nancy Young Orr, in a review of "The Brave Little Goat of Monsieur Seguin: A Picture Story from Provence," in* School Library Journal, *Vol. 15, No. 1, September, 1968, p. 120.*

The Hippo Boat   (1968)

[The Hippo Boat *was written by Eriko Kishida.*]

[The] story of the flood at the zoo, told in ***The Hippo Boat*** is quietly unexciting. The illustrations in themselves are pleasing. The pages are bathed in soft blues, greens and grays; and the animals, who serenely make their escape on the Hippo's back, are simple shapes. (Hippo is especially appealing—sculptural and solid, yet soft and fluid). But there is no urgency in either the pictures or the story. The situation is under control immediately. Soothing for some children, but bland for others.

> *Alice Low, in a review of "The Hippo Boat," in* The New York Times Book Review, *October 27, 1968, p. 42.*

There's a deluge at the zoo, so Mrs. Hippo and her baby play Noah's Ark as they carry all the frightened animals (even the giraffe) to the safety of dry land. The animals are charming, in spare black line, softly washed illustrations, but the choppy, repetitive text prompts depressing thoughts of long-ago reading lessons about the notorious Spot who ran, ran, ran.

> *Joyce Baumholtz, in a review of "The Hippo Boat," in* School Library Journal, *Vol. 15, No. 3, November, 1968, p. 77.*

The charm of the flood story set in a zoo has a simplicity which directs it to the very youngest. Watercolor paintings give to the animals such liveliness and appeal as the artist achieved earlier this year with her ***Brave Little Goat of Monsieur Séguin.*** They portray Mrs. Hippo as a rescuing heroine and her baby as rescuer, too; for both of their broad backs carry a mixed passenger load from rising waters to safe, dry rock.

> *Virginia Haviland, in a review of "The Hippo Boat," in* The Horn Book Magazine, *Vol. XLV, No. 1, February, 1969, p. 42.*

The Day Chiro Was Lost   (1969)

The picture-book is now truly international, and one turns to a contribution from a far-off country with especial enthusiasm, for its merits and for the light it shines on its country of origin. ***The Day Chiro Was Lost*** disappoints on both these counts. Only a very few details show that this scene is Japan, not a city in England or, more probably, America. The careful, painstaking pictures are painted thinly on canvas, the ground texture of which shows, not altogether pleasingly, in each scene. Books which show small children the commonplaces of everyday life are most valuable, but must they be so insipid and lacking in character? (pp. 100-01)

> *A review of "The Day Chiro Was Lost," in* The Junior Bookshelf, *Vol. 33, No. 2, April, 1969, pp. 100-01.*

First published in Japan in 1965, a very simple story about a pet who, on his first ride in the back of a truck, jumps out and is lost, then finds his way home. The theme is appealing but the story is slight; the illustrations are most attractive: a few show intriguing details of open shop fronts, and several are quite stunning double-page spreads of the pattern of city traffic, with its intricate cloverleaf roads and sweeping lines of overpasses.

> *Zena Sutherland, in a review of "The Day Chiro Was Lost," in* Bulletin of the Center for Children's Books, *Vol. 23, No. 2, October, 1969, p. 29.*

In some words and many pictures Chiyoko Nakatani tells the story of a dog, still floppy with puppyhood who gets lost and wanders around the town (Tokyo) getting found again, ***The Day Chiro Was Lost.*** . . . Miss Nakatani's paintings, reproduced so painstakingly that the thread of canvas is still visible, are full of the power of the city, the thunder of traffic, the sweep of dizzying overpasses, the blaze from shopwindows. The bigness and boldness of her pictures, their accuracy, and especially an unfamiliar dog's-eye perspective, make this an unusual picturebook.

A boy finds a dog, shaggy, and white just like the one he has seen so often in cloud formations. He has been expecting it. His parents are sure it must be returned to its rightful owner. The end is comfortingly expected.

> *Pamela Marsh, "Dragons and other Sights," in* The Christian Science Monitor, *November 6, 1969, p. B2.*

A quiet, read-and-show book built around a very slight story. A pet dog, Chiro, goes for a truck ride with his young master and jumps out prematurely in the midst of traffic. After much bewilderment and a few tame adventures (he's frightened by a big, mean dog; meets a friendly little dog he knows, etc.), he finds his way home. Effective coordination between pictures and text supports the loving character of an always smiling Chiro, and the sights and sounds of the big city (Tokyo) are convincingly depicted in the warm colors and varied textures which the author first introduced in her illustrations for **Hippopotamus.**

> *Margaret Riddell, in a review of "The Day Chiro Was Lost," in* School Library Journal, *Vol. 16, No. 5, January, 1970, p. 52.*

A beguiling spaniel-like puppy—with all the friendly curiosity of its kind—jumps from the back of the truck belonging to his young master's father and explores on foot the modern city of Tokyo. It is a small-dog-high view of the heavy traffic, the masses of tramping feet, the complex superstructure of city freeways, of other dogs—and finally, of course, of his own young master again. The pictures, uncrowded but full of lively action and drawn vividly in soft colors, successfully suggest the atmosphere of the huge westernized capital. By the artist of the strikingly different illustrations for **The Brave Little Goat of Monsieur Séguin.**

> *Virginia Haviland, in a review of "The Day Chiro Was Lost," in* The Horn Book Magazine, *Vol. XLVI, No. 1, February, 1970, p. 33.*

Fumio and the Dolphins   (1970)

Textured paper forms a fine background for strong wash pictures; the stippled water and the beautiful design of each picture make the book a joy to look at. The brief story rises from the author's own observation of dolphins in Japan and is dedicated to Père Castor, who would certainly have delighted in the affectionate care shown by two little boys for a dolphin and her newborn young.

> *Margery Fisher, in a review of "Fumio and the Dolphins," in* Growing Point, *Vol. 9, No. 4, October, 1970, p. 1607.*

Fumio and the Dolphins is much less ambitious and more immediately acceptable [than C. Iwasaki's *A Brother for Momoko*]. One can't go far wrong with dolphins, and the neat simple story plays them for all they are worth. The drawings are cruder and less effective than we expect from

Japan but they have charm and a little humour. Children who are baffled by *Momoko* will like this book quite well.

> *A review of "Fumio and the Dolphins," in* The Junior Bookshelf, *Vol. 34, No. 5, October, 1970, p. 285.*

This picture story is the result of the author's observing dolphin fishing at a Japanese seaport. Two boys see a mother dolphin and her baby and feed them from their own catch of fish. When the boys return to the waterfront the next day, they find dolphins being caught. Fearing for their new friends, they go to see if they are safe. The mother dolphin and her baby appear, and the boys lead them far away from the port to the safety of the open sea. The paintings, with their warm, vibrant colors, appealing characters (merry looking dolphins and people who thankfully are not stereotyped Orientals), and rich textures (oil paints on rough canvas) are stronger than the text and will enable preschool children to "read" the story.

> *B. Susan Brown, in a review of "Fumio and the Dolphins: A Pirate Story from Japan," in* School Library Journal, *Vol. 17, No. 7, March, 1971, p. 122.*

The author-illustrator has created a little story of dolphin fishing based on observations made in her own country. Her evocative paintings, printed from a canvas surface, have a strong atmosphere, luminous in color and lively in every scene of action. They bring to life the simple business of small Fumio, who "spent all his time fishing or swimming in the sea" and thus became well acquainted with a certain mother and baby dolphin. The boy feared for their lives when the fleet sailed out to net a school of dolphins; but happily the pair had not been caught and Fumio and his friend Taro managed to lead them to safety beyond the nets.

> *Virginia Haviland, in a review of "Fumio and the Dolphins: A Picture Story from Japan," in* The Horn Book Magazine, *Vol. XLVII, No. 2, April, 1971, p. 159.*

In a Japanese fishing village a boy and his fisherman brother make friends with a dolphin and her baby and, fearing they will be caught in a dolphin drive, lead the dolphins far from shore to safety. The story in this picture book is heartwarming and satisfying, but it is the lovely oil paintings of dolphins, Japanese coast, and dolphin fishing that catch the interest and give the most enjoyment.

> *A review of "Fumio and the Dolphins: A Picture Story from Japan," in* The Booklist, *Vol. 67, No. 18, May 15, 1971, p. 799.*

The Lion and the Bird's Nest   (1973)

[The Lion and the Bird's Nest *was written by Eriko Kishida.*]

Nakatani's economically stylized lion embodies both the jaunty majesty and the appealing vulnerability of Kishida's aging jungle king. Jojo invites a sympathetic bird to lay her eggs in his crown—then spends his last days sitting in the sun and listening to the new birds singing. It's a happy instance of symbiosis, with both words and pictures smartly geared to the youngest read-aloud audience.

> *A review of "The Lion and the Bird's Nest," in* Kirkus Reviews, *Vol. XLI, No. 2, January 15, 1973, p. 59.*

Chiyoko Nakatani's airy illustrations in subdued colors give life to this gentle fable. Young readers or listeners will respond to the sadness of old King Jojo, the lion, who is becoming too worn out to remain a fierce leader. A little bird in need of a safe nesting place arrives, and Jojo's offer of help through the winter and spring brings about a hopeful, satisfying conclusion. The theme of kindness is executed beautifully, and the fantasy makes an engaging addition to picture-book collections.

> *Josette A. Boisse, in a review of "The Lion and the Bird's Nest," in* School Library Journal, *Vol. 19, No. 8, April, 1973, p. 56.*

A fanciful story about an endearing lion, King of the Jungle, of whom all the other animals—unaware of his old age and weakening faculties—are afraid. King Jojo is sad because of his weariness, but a small bird who has lost all her eggs is even unhappier. Yet both are happy when the bird builds a nest in Jojo's crown, where Jojo protects her new eggs until all seven babies have hatched. The fewest words possible relay this fable of kindness repaid: "When they grew old enough to fly, the little birds did not leave Jojo. They stayed near him and looked after him." The oil paintings on canvas—in strong, harmonious colors and with a minimum of line—strongly depict the lion in his various moods and the forest in different lights. As effective as **The Hippo Boat;** for the very youngest. (pp. 258-59)

> *Virginia Haviland, in a review of "The Lion and the Bird's Nest," in* The Horn Book Magazine, *Vol. XLIX, No. 3, June, 1973, pp. 258-59.*

The Zoo in My Garden (1973)

Understatement in pictures is an unexpected pleasure when so many picture books brimming with colour and detail are shouting for attention. Chiyoko Nakatani's brief celebration of the animals of house and garden is not short of colour, but it is colour used with restraint and harmony.

> *A review of "The Zoo in My Garden," in* The Times Literary Supplement, *No. 3734, September 24, 1973, p. 1126.*

"Look, Mother, we have a zoo!"—and prodded by this round-faced boy's example, other children might discover that they too have a dog, a pigeon, sparrows, butterflies, ants and wasps in their gardens (or at least some combination thereof) and maybe also a goldfish, turtle or parrot in the house. Nakatani's achievement here lies more in triggering simple recognition than in stretching the imagination, but the pictures are clear and bright and the text spare enough to encourage the youngest viewers to name the pictured animals and to investigate their own domestic zoos.

> *A review of "The Zoo in My Garden," in* Kirkus Reviews, *Vol. XLI, No. 19, October 1, 1973, p. 1092.*

A delightfully unusual picture book, showing how careful observation of his immediate surroundings can reveal for a small child a zoo of his own in his garden. The slightly off-beat colours, design and delineation which represent the unfamiliar Japanese way of viewing Western life are most attractive.

> *M. Hobbs, in a review of "The Zoo in My Garden," in* The Junior Bookshelf, *Vol. 37, No. 6, December, 1973, p. 383.*

An imaginative interpretation of the term *zoo* introduces familiar fauna and flora—dogs, cats, butterflies, tulips—to the youngest child in clear, expressive pictures accompanied by a simple text. The bright illustrations have a textural quality, thus suggesting tactile as well as visual participation in the exploration of everyday experiences. Al-

But from the top Chiro could see only cars.

From The Day Chiro Was Lost, *written and illustrated by Chiyoko Nakatani.*

though obviously useful as a pedagogical tool for those working with young children, the book is aesthetically appealing and delightful as well.

> *Mary M. Burns, in a review of "The Zoo in My Garden," in* The Horn Book Magazine, *Vol. L, No. 1, February, 1974, p. 39.*

This attempt to make very young children aware of animal life outdoors and indoors is too slight to spark attention. Mentioned are dogs, birds, butterflies, frogs, wasps, cats, and ants living outside and a goldfish, turtle, and parrot inside the house. These uninspiring discoveries hardly constitute a zoo, and four-year-olds will not be helped to explore their environment. The full-color illustrations done in oils are pleasant but they cannot sustain the weak text.

> *Linda Lawson Clark, in a review of "The Zoo in My Garden," in* School Library Journal, *Vol. 20, No. 6, February, 1974, p. 55.*

My Teddy Bear   (1976)

Without extending or elaborating on the experiences a boy and his teddy bear might share, Nakatani simply enumerates a few telling ones—a walk on a nice day, "bits of rice stuck to our faces," and finally bath time for first bear and then his master. As with a similar boy's discovery of *The Zoo in My Garden,* the rewards are subtle but palpable steady eye contact with both bear and his pink-cheeked owner, spiffy oilcloth-textured colors, and not least of all the fact that the boy is quite naturally, unstereotypically Japanese.

> *A review of "My Teddy Bear," in* Kirkus Reviews, *Vol. XLIV, No. 15, August 1, 1976, p. 843.*

This is a very simple story for the very youngest child, and one feels that if the youngest were able to write down a brief account of their daily life with their favourite toy, then this is very likely what they would write. In that sense, therefore, every young child will, to some extent, identify with the little boy in this book. The illustrations have the especial charm we have come to associate with this distinguished Japanese artist; nevertheless, this is a very slight book for the price at which it is published.

> *B. Clark, in a review of "My Teddy Bear," in* The Junior Bookshelf, *Vol. 40, No. 5, October, 1976, p. 266.*

A simple low key book on a boy, his bear and their day together, full of warmth and kept within the confines of the home. The pictures in oil on canvas are soft and full of subtle colors.

> *A review of "My Teddy Bear," in* Book World—The Washington Post, *November 7, 1976, p. 68.*

A teddy bear is to play with, to enjoy walks with, to protect, to share meals with, to give baths to, and especially to take to bed at night. Large full-color illustrations, done in oil on canvas, affectionately show the loving and some-

times humorous (an after-bath bear hanging by his ears to dry) relationship of a boy and his special toy. An appealing story for young listeners who will soon "read" it by the pictures alone.

> *Barbara Elleman, in a review of "My Teddy Bear," in* Booklist, *Vol. 73, No. 6, November 15, 1976, p. 476.*

For very young children just emerging from babyhood, one looks for books made with honesty, insight, and self-effacing artistry. In an inviting square-shaped picture book, comfortably sized for holding and for looking at, a little boy explains how he and his best friend, a big, brownish teddy bear, spend their days and their nights together. Imbued with guileless warmth, simplicity, and love, the bright, expressive paintings and the few essential, well-chosen words are wholly right for a fledgling audience.

> *Ethel L. Heins, in a review of "My Teddy Bear," in* The Horn Book Magazine, *Vol. LII, No. 6, December, 1976, p. 615.*

My Day on the Farm   (1976)

A small boy is taken to visit a farm by his mother, and tells with basic simplicity what happened there. It is an idealised version of events: the yard in which the cows are penned is coloured pleasantly pink instead of realistically squelchy brown, and though a day's length—measured from one milking to the next—is a long time, the narrator never grows tired or bored.

Nor does the reader. The text is too short to weary of it, pedestrian though it may be, and the solid sketches, coloured in with clearly visible brush strokes, are very agreeable. Chiyoko Nakatani has a happy facility when drawing expressions, be her subject the stare on the face of a startled boy or the smug contentment of a dozing cow.

> *R. Baines, in a review of "My Day on the Farm," in* The Junior Bookshelf, *Vol. 40, No. 6, December, 1976, p. 317.*

The small boy who enjoys his teddy bear so appealingly in Nakatani's *My Teddy Bear* is, sans toy, enjoying a visit to a farm. He surveys the many animals, feeds the goats and sheep, watches the piglets having lunch, and finally sees that they all get bedded down for the night. The oil on canvas imparts a three-dimensional quality to the full-color illustrations, magnifying the simple text; and use of the first person lends an immediate touch to the excursion.

> *Barbara Elleman, in a review of "My Day on the Farm," in* Booklist, *Vol. 73, No. 14, March 15, 1977, p. 1093.*

First published in Japan, a direct and simple picture book is illustrated with uncluttered, softly colored paintings. A small boy describes his visit to the farm; all his attention is given to the cows, sheep, goats, and pigs as they play, rest, and eat on a summer day. Slight, but the brevity and the subject should appeal to young children. The text is easy to remember and "read," once the book has been read aloud: "In the next field there were some sheep and three goats. I gave them armfuls of grass to eat. Then I took some vegetables to the pigs." Static but realistic.

> *Zena Sutherland, in a review of "My Day on the Farm," in* Bulletin of the Center for Children's Books, *Vol. 30, No. 9, May, 1977, p. 148.*

A low-key narrative about a little boy's visit to a farm. The boy describes farm activities, animals, and operations in short, simple sentences. The soft, canvas-textured illustrations are large and clear yet invoke the haziness of a hot summer day. A gentle little story for the very young.

> *Alice Ehlert, in a review of "My Day on the Farm," in* School Library Journal, *Vol. 23, No. 9, May, 1977, p. 54.*

Bright, expressive oil-on-canvas paintings, like those which distinguished the author-artist's recent **Teddy Bear,** show a very small boy visiting a farm. He learns about cows being milked and fed. "A young calf came right up to me and said 'Moo.' I said 'Moo' back to her." He also observes sheep and goats, who enjoy the armfuls of grass he brings them, and he watches a fat sow with her eleven piglets. At evening all are ready to sleep, and the little adventure ends: "Good night, everyone. Sleep well!" Complete simplicity, with direct meaning and pictorial charm for very young children.

> *Virginia Haviland, in a review of "My Day on the Farm," in* The Horn Book Magazine, *Vol. LIII, No. 3, June, 1977, p. 302.*

My Treasures (1979)

These simple little books have familiar everyday morals: the basket with its treasure of shells, nuts and small toys is neatly linked to kindness to a new baby, and the animal pets only show themselves at their best to the small boy when he leaves them alone. Chiyoko Nakatani's charming illustrations, in clear colours with canvas texture, incorporating effectively the white of the page and unusual pale blues, violets and pinks, are most attractive, with their carefully selective backgrounds.

> *M. Hobbs, in a review of "My Animal Friends" and "My Treasures," in* The Junior Bookshelf, *Vol. 43, No. 6, December, 1979, p. 319.*

Feeding Babies (1981)

Every baby mammal sucks its mother's milk in a different way—baby hippos suck while they are under water, monkeys pull their mother's teats, kittens push the teats, bears climb on their mother's knees. If you require a set of drawings illustrating these habits—and I am not quite sure that we do—then the drawings of this well-known Japanese artist are as charming as any that we are likely to find. The one that perhaps gives least satisfaction is the rather ordinary picture of a human mother and her baby.

> *B. Clark, in a review of "Feeding Babies," in* The Junior Bookshelf, *Vol. 45, No. 5, October, 1981, p. 189.*

Uri Orlev

1931-

(Born Jerzy Henryk Orlowski) Polish-born Israeli author of fiction.

Major works include *The Island on Bird Street* (1984), *The Man from the Other Side* (1991).

Orlev has achieved international acclaim for stories for older children that draw on his experiences as a child growing up during World War II in the Polish ghettos and Bergen-Belsen concentration camp. He has observed that "What other people call the Holocaust was, for me, my childhood." Praised for the realism, power, and unsentimental quality of his works, Orlev is often acknowledged for his skill as a storyteller and delineator of character as well as for his understanding of children. Orlev began writing as a young boy, composing poetry in his native Polish. After the war, however, he settled in Israel, where he became fluent in Hebrew and began writing fiction in that language. He has written numerous books for children and plays for television and radio, as well as novels and short stories for adults. His first work, the adult novel *The Lead Soldier,* was translated into English in 1979 and met with immediate critical success. Anticipating the concerns of his later fiction, *The Lead Soldier* tells of two boys who survive the horrors of a concentration camp by using their imaginations to produce stories and games that help them confront and contain their anguish. Two of Orlev's novels for children have been translated into English. Considered gripping and vivid depictions of persecution during wartime, *The Island on Bird Street* and *The Man from the Other Side* emphasize the courage, imagination, and strong sense of ethnic identity with which children faced adversity.

The Island on Bird Street features eleven-year-old Alex, a Polish Jew who must live alone in the cellar of a bombed-out house after his father has been relegated to a labor camp. Alex awaits his father's return, and, likening himself to Robinson Crusoe, he tames a mouse to be his pet, ventures out occasionally to procure food through various inventive ways, and even manages to sneak out of the area to play soccer with some children. Orlev provides what is usually considered a realistic chronicle of Alex's adventures and his efforts to survive and thrive both physically and emotionally, in an even tone and simple language often praised by critics. Although he includes instances of violence in *The Island on Bird Street*, as when Alex kills a soldier who attempts to shoot a wounded resistance fighter, Orlev emphasizes Alex's humanity and sense of hope.

Based on the experiences of a journalist Orlev met in Israel, *The Man from the Other Side* is also considered a compelling story of bravery in the face of prejudice. The book is narrated by fourteen-year-old Marek, a Catholic boy in Nazi-occupied Poland, who is an antisemite and helps his stepfather profit by smuggling food through the sewer sys-

tem to sell in the walled Jewish ghettos. When Marek learns that his biological father was Jewish—a communist who changed his name and religion to hide his identity and who eventually died in prison—Marek's perspective as well as his values change; he learns to sympathize with Jews and becomes involved in helping them, narrowly escaping the violence of the Warsaw Ghetto uprising. Orlev's characterizations of Marek, his mother, and his antisemitic stepfather have drawn praise from several commentators as has his sensitive portrayal of a boy confronting his own prejudices and those of his friends and family.

Orlev has received numerous awards for his writings. He was recipient of Israel's Prime Minister Prize in 1972 and 1989. *The Man from the Other Side* was awarded the Mildred L. Batchelder Award in 1992, and Orlev was the first recipient of the Janus Z. Korczak Literary Prize in Poland for *The Island on Bird Street;* this story was also awarded the Silver Pencil Prize, the Mildred L. Batchelder Award, and was named a Jane Addams Children's Book Award Honor Book.

(See also *Something about the Author,* Vol. 58; *Contempo-*

rary Authors, Vol. 101; and *Contemporary Authors New Revision Series,* Vol. 34.)

AUTHOR'S COMMENTARY

[The following excerpt is from Orlev's introduction to The Island on Bird Street.*]*

Think of the city that you live in or the city that is nearest to where you live. Imagine all of your city occupied by a foreign army that has separated part of the inhabitants from the rest: let's say, everyone with black or yellow skin, or everyone with green eyes. And imagine that they are not only separated from everyone else but are imprisoned in one of the city's neighborhoods around which a wall has been built. Naturally, this wall would have to cut down or across certain streets and would sometimes even divide single houses and their yards in two. Inside the walled-off neighborhood everything remains the same: the movie houses, the schools, the nightclubs, the different stores, the hospitals. Yet because of the wall and the guards stationed at its few checkposts that can be crossed only by special permission, supplies have trouble reaching the stores and the peddlers who, young and old, increase in number day by day. (p. vii)

If you were wealthy before the occupation you can still afford to buy what you want or even to visit the nightclubs. Although for that you have to be very rich and to watch out for the night curfew. And if you're brave or desperate enough you can try smuggling food from other parts of the city into your walled quarter. If you're caught, you'll be shot, even if you're only a small boy or girl. If you get away with it, though, you'll make a fortune overnight. Next time perhaps you can hire someone else to do the dirty work for you and not have to risk your own neck. You see, here, the difference between being rich and poor is not just a question of how you live or dress or eat. It is a question of life and death. The rich have food while the poor die of hunger and no one is able to help them.

I can remember my mother refusing to go out into the street because she couldn't stand the sight of all the children begging for bread when she had nothing to give them. Her first worry was for me and my brother, and every slice of bread she gave another child meant one less for us. (p. viii)

One day the occupation authorities decided to get rid of the inhabitants of the walled quarter. To send them far away. Today we know that they were sent to extermination camps. Eventually we who lived there knew too. But not at the very beginning. It was too hard for us to believe that civilized people like the Germans could do such a thing. It was hard to believe it even after witnesses escaped from the camps and told us. The city I lived in was Warsaw and the walled quarter was called the ghetto. That's where I was during World War II. But let's get back to our imaginary city.

Suddenly people begin to disappear from it. They take a small suitcase or a knapsack with them and the rest is left behind. Their homes remain as they were with their furniture, their clothing, their beds, and their books all in place.

The front doors are left unlocked because that is the order that has been given. There's just no one living there. Not even cats or dogs, because there isn't anyone to feed them and they've left for other parts of town.

Another thing you won't find is radios. These were forbidden at the beginning of the occupation. And, of course, television hasn't been invented yet.

The occupying army wants to take whatever is left in the empty houses for itself, and so it leaves the wall standing and keeps the guards stationed at the checkposts. Inside the wall, the ghetto is like a ghost town. Only here and there a few little islands of life are left—factories in which people work for nothing in order to make things for the occupiers: army socks, for instance, or boots, or rope, or brushes. And next to each factory is an apartment building for the workers.

My aunt, my little brother, and I lived in such a building for as long as the workers were allowed to keep children with them. By then my mother was no longer alive. I remember how my aunt used to send me, along with two men we knew, to search for coal in the empty houses that lined the abandoned streets. In those days we still heated our homes with coal in the winter and cooked on coal stoves in the kitchen. And, just like you'll read in this book, I went from building to building through passageways in walls and lofts and ran crouching when I had to cross a street. We were searching for coal, but wherever we went, I searched for children's rooms too, and when the men weren't watching, I entered them and looked for books and stamps for my collection. I couldn't take much because I had to return with a sack of coal on my back; still, each time I managed to come back with a new little treasure-trove that made my brother green with envy. I gave him all the duplicates, of course, and the books, though not before I'd read them first. *Robinson Crusoe* was one of the books I found this way.

Which brings us to our own book, *The Island on Bird Street.* The empty neighborhood you'll read about here is the ghetto. It doesn't have to be the Warsaw Ghetto, because there were other ghettos, too. But in this one also the houses have been emptied of food and people while everything else has stayed the same. Alex, the hero of my story, hides in a ruined house that was bombed out at the beginning of the war, although all the other houses around it are untouched and full of possessions. This house is really not very different from a desert island. And Alex has to wait in it until his father comes. But his father does not come back right away and Alex begins to wonder if he ever will. So he must survive by himself for many months, taking what he needs from other houses the way Robinson Crusoe took what he needed from the wrecks of other ships that were washed up on the beach. The difference is that Alex can't grow his own food, that he has to hide, and that he has no spring to get water from. But Alex can see the rest of the world through a peephole in his hideout, because the ruined house overlooks the wall that seals off the deserted ghetto. Through this hole he sees all the people who aren't shut up as he is, even if they too must live under a cruel occupation. He even sees children going to school every morning—and yet, although they seem so near, they are as far away from him as were the nearest inhabited lands from Robinson Crusoe's island. Alex has no man Friday either; he has only a little white mouse. And, yes, one more thing: Alex has hope. Because he is waiting for his father. (pp. ix-xi)

> *Uri Orlev, in an introduction to his* The Island on Bird Street, *translated by Hillel Halkin, Houghton Mifflin Company, 1984, pp. vii-xi.*

TITLE COMMENTARY

The Island on Bird Street   (1984)

Drawing on his own World War II experiences as a child in the Warsaw ghetto, the author has written a book that offers on one level a first-rate survival story and on another a haunting glimpse of the war's effects on individual people. Alex, an eleven-year-old Jewish boy, escaped the Nazi "selection" by hiding in the cellar of a bombed-out house. He was to wait there for his father to return for him, "even if it took a whole year." Through a combination of resourcefulness and good luck the boy eluded capture, although the Nazis routed scores of other Jews from their carefully camouflaged bunkers and cellars. He foraged for food and supplies in the abandoned buildings and fash-

ioned an ingenious hiding place accessible by a rope ladder. With only his pet mouse for company Alex passed days, weeks, and months into a snowy winter, stoically waiting for his father. From his hiding place he could look out over the ghetto wall to the Polish side of town, wistfully observing the bustling street full of shops, working people, and school children. He learned of a way to pass through to that side, risked capture to play with other children, and even formed a special friendship with a girl. While fully aware of his chances of survival, Alex thought of his experience as an adventure akin to Robinson Crusoe's; and although the tone of the book reflects the boy's cheerful, logical disposition, the loneliness and utter desperation of his situation come through with a piercing clarity. The excellently translated [by Hillel Halkin] book is preceded by an introduction that describes life as it was in the occupied cities of World War II. (pp. 197-98)

> *Kate M. Flanagan, in a review of "The Island on Bird Street," in* The Horn Book Magazine, *Vol. LX, No. 2, April, 1984, pp. 197-98.*

In his introduction to **The Island on Bird Street,** author Uri Orlev notes that while the setting is the Warsaw ghetto in 1943-44, the story could take place just about anywhere. Indeed, the novel is so well told that it transcends

Orlev at his desk.

its setting, becoming an adventure story that any older child could appreciate. . . .

There are drama and wartime violence, such as Alex's killing of a soldier about to shoot a wounded resistance fighter. But the way in which it is handled adds much to the empathy one feels for a youngster caught up in the agony of war. Yet even during the bad times, there are good times, too—be it with a pet white mouse named Snow, an impromptu soccer match with other youngsters, or an ice-skating interlude with a newfound girlfriend.

While stories of adventure and heroism during wartime aren't new, there is something special about this one. Maybe it's because it is based in part on Uri Orlev's own childhood experiences in the Warsaw ghetto during the war, which give an added air of realism to the book. Perhaps it is the sense of humanity with which Orlev endows his hero, to the point where the readers can easily identify with him. Or perhaps it is the thread of hope that runs throughout the book and which Orlev, writing from Jerusalem, emphasizes so strongly in his introduction. Whatever the reason, *The Island on Bird Street* is an exceptionally good book.

> *Randy Shipp, "Thread of Hope in Wartime Story," in* The Christian Science Monitor, *May 4, 1984, p. B4.*

In a fine Holocaust survival story, first published in Israel and based on the author's childhood experience hiding in the Warsaw Ghetto, eleven-year-old Alex builds himself an ingenious secret hideout in the ruins of a bombed building on the edge of an unspecified Polish ghetto. . . . The physical details are fascinating: what he eats, how he keeps warm, how he builds the hideout, the secret passageways that connect the lofts and cellars; all described in quiet, unemotional style. Self-pity is prevented by the very pressure of survival, and by Alex's knowledge of the fate of other Jewish children. But his control snaps after he has been forced to shoot a German soldier; and in the poignant scene of his father's return, Alex realizes how much he has suppressed, especially the terror that his father would not come. (pp. 189-90)

> *Zena Sutherland, in a review of "The Island on Bird Street," in* Bulletin of the Center for Children's Books, *Vol. 37, No. 10, June, 1984, pp. 189-90.*

Encamped in the ruins of 78 Bird Street, Alexander is faced with the challenge of physical and psychological survival. . . . Though a thorough pragmatist, he has enough of child-like imagination to see in himself and his pet mouse an analogy with Robinson Crusoe and Friday, and to think of his hide-out as a desert island. This lingering spirit of fantasy presumably played an important part in the survival of such children in real life. In the context of the book, it enhances the sense that this is, above all, an adventure story.

As such, it is successful. The style is crisp, lively and descriptive (only occasionally marred by touches of translator's hamfistedness), though the description rarely goes beyond the visual mechanism into the subtler evocation of atmosphere; as a child's account it is surprisingly devoid of colours and smells. More worrying is the single ethical dimension which, perhaps unavoidably, dominates the book. The pre-adolescent readership for whom it seems largely intended is unlikely to be properly aware of what exactly was at stake for the Jews under Nazi occupation. In its historical context, the uprising was, of course, heroic, and the everyday shooting and looting dismal, but entirely justifiable, necessities of survival. In the ethos of the adventure story, "settling accounts" with Germans seems a more attractive, and attractively simple, activity. Alexander's courage (he saves the lives of two resistance workers) in using the gun must be offset against his earlier childlike relish of its possibilities. Implicit in the book is a justification of the more militant aspects of modern Israel, to which some parents and teachers may not wish their children to be exposed without historical preparation. And that raises other question: how, when, and if young children should be told exactly what the Nazis did to the Jews.

> *Carol Rumens, "The Spirit of Survival," in* The Times Literary Supplement, *No. 4273, February 22, 1985, p. 214.*

[*The Island on Bird Street* is bleak and] uncompromising, and the author's memories of his own childhood experiences in the Warsaw ghetto, even when couched in the third-person tale of a fictitious boy in an unnamed city, have a stark reality about them. . . . [The] force of the writing, plain and unspectacular as it is, draws us into the tiny, circumscribed world where [Alex] waits as he had promised for his father to return for him. The immediacy of the book is astonishing; with a total lack of sentimentality or exaggeration, the author has taken us right into a boy's mind as in his own way he gathers strength from small successes and holds on to the trust in his father by which he has always lived.

> *Margery Fisher, in a review of "The Island on Bird Street," in* Growing Point, *Vol. 24, No. 1, May, 1985, p. 4435.*

The Man from the Other Side (1991)

AUTHOR'S COMMENTARY

[*The following excerpt is from Orlev's introduction to* The Man from the Other Side.]

While watching the evening news one day early last spring, I saw some shots of the smoking wreckage of a Polish airliner that had crashed near Warsaw. The passengers and crew were all killed. Only later did I find out that Marek was among them.

Marek was a Polish newspaperman I became friendly with when he visited Israel. We met by chance at the home of mutual friends. . . . When we parted in the wee hours of the morning, I said to him, "I have an idea. Why don't I take you on a trip up north? I don't mind taking off a few days from work." He was happy to accept and we shook hands warmly on it. (p. 1)

[During] the days of sightseeing that followed in the Galilee and Golan Heights, our talk ranged back and forth in space and time without a dull moment. I told Marek about Israel, its history and its problems, and he continued to tell me about his childhood, from which emerged a story that intrigued me more and more. In the end we spent four memorable days together, and upon returning to Jerusalem I jotted down some notes with the thought of making a book out of them. Of course, I would have asked for his permission, but he never gave me the chance. Perhaps he read my thoughts. In any case, he phoned and made me promise not to put his story in writing. (p. 2)

A week later he called to say goodbye. He told me about his last days in Israel and reminded me of my vow.

"I can't say I'm happy about it," I said, "but you can count on me to keep my promise. Although only," I joked, "as long as you're alive."

"Agreed!" he laughed. "Now you have a reason to outlive me."

We parted with the resolution to meet again in Warsaw.

But the last laugh was fate's. Barely two months have passed since then and here I am sitting down to write his story. (p. 3)

> *Uri Orlev, "A Word About My Friend Marek," in his* The Man from the Other Side, *translated by Hillel Halkin, Houghton Mifflin Company, 1991, pp. 1-3.*

When Israeli author Orlev, who drew on his own ghetto experiences in **The Island on Bird Street,** met a certain Polish journalist, they found that both had been boys in Warsaw during WW II; Orlev kept "Marek's" extensive confidences secret (including his discovery in 1942 that his father—executed in 1934 as a Communist—was Jewish) until his death in 1987. Now, Orlev shapes Marek's account into a powerful novel about a devout 13-year-old Catholic in a virulently anti-Semitic society, responding to his experiences by coming to champion the Jews walled in near his home.

With stepfather Antony, Marek already knows the ghetto: traveling through sewers, they take food to sell there at high prices, often returning with a baby to hide with the nuns (no charge). Still, Marek is casually anti-Semitic until he helps rob a Jewish escapee and is caught by his mother, who points out that "You sentenced him to death" and reveals her own heritage. Deeply shaken, Marek sets out to make amends. He befriends a man he sees crossing himself the wrong way and ultimately leads him back, underground, to the ghetto, during the heroic ghetto uprising.

Orlev's characters are sobering, believable blends: e.g., Antony dislikes Jews but, knowing Marek's background, wants to adopt him; he turns others' dire needs to profit but has "nothing against human beings." Many others in this richly authentic story are equally complex. Subtle, beautifully crafted, altogether compelling.

> *A review of "The Man from the Other Side," in* Kirkus Reviews, *Vol. LIX, No. 9, May 1, 1991, p. 608.*

A true story of WW II Warsaw, this novel relates events so dramatic as to be cataclysmic. But the voice of its 14-year-old narrator, Marek, would be gripping given any plot, so candid that it tolerates admissions of less-than-exemplary behavior as well as a more-than-exemplary atonement. . . . A survivor of that ghetto, Orlev neither demonizes nor glorifies, whether portraying Poles or Jews, fighters or collaborators. His refusal to exaggerate gives the story unimpeachable impact. (pp. 75-6)

> *A review of "The Man from the Other Side," in* Publishers Weekly, *Vol. 238, No. 24, May 31, 1991, pp. 75-6.*

In future histories of civilization, the twentieth century will be remembered as an era that tested the limits of racism. As masters or servants, the magnitude of death, suffering, and cruelty we and our grandfathers have inflicted on ourselves is unprecedented in recorded history. In the killing fields of Auschwitz and Cambodia, and in the mean streets of Belfast and Palestine, there lurks a common horror that we profess not to understand. We blame our acts of "inhumanity" on madmen and fanatics. We try to distance ourselves—yet we know the truth, that a shadow resides deep within each of us. We ask and cannot answer: "In like situation, what would *I* have done?"

Those who read this book, while they still may not be able to answer the question for themselves, will nevertheless have the benefit of experiencing how it was answered by Marek, a fourteen-year-old boy living outside the Warsaw Ghetto during World War II. (pp. 104-05)

As literature, **The Man from the Other Side** is well written, dramatic, compelling. This book is all the more powerful because it is a true story. But the story's essential power rests in the example it provides of the individual change of heart that is needed to erase prejudice, promote understanding, and foster cooperation and love in human affairs. (p. 105)

> *Dan Dailey, in a review of "The Man from the Other Side," in* The Five Owls, *Vol. V, No. 5, May-June, 1991, pp. 104-05.*

Readers who were caught up in Orlev's World War II ghetto adventure, **The Island on Bird Street,** will not be surprised by the vivid characterization and tight plotting here, but they may not expect the stark realism, which gives this the authenticity of a memoir. . . . Marek's mother, stepfather, grandparents, and friend Jozek are as memorably developed as the boy himself, whose gradual understanding of his stepfather tempers an emergent sense of justice. The sewers through which Marek travels are a naturally apt metaphor for his journey through the underworld of self-knowledge, which involves danger from within as well as without. Neither sensationalized nor sanctified, this young adult Holocaust novel has rather been profoundly considered and patiently crafted. (p. 247)

> *Betsy Hearne, in a review of "The Man from the Other Side," in* Bulletin of the Center for Children's Books, *Vol. 44, No. 10, June, 1991, pp. 246-47.*

Characterizations are vivid and finely drawn, even those

of minor figures such as Marek's empathetic mother who is embarrassed by her countrymen's hatred of Jews; his crude, contradictory stepfather; and his grandparents, who treat Jozek as a family member, all the while hating Jews. This is a story of individual bravery and national shame that highlights just how hopeless was the fate of the Warsaw Jews as they fought alone and heroically against the Nazi war machine.

> *Jack Forman, in a review of "The Man from the Other Side," in* School Library Journal, *Vol. 37, No. 9, September, 1991, p. 283.*

Faith Ringgold

1934-

African-American author and illustrator of picture books.

The following entry presents criticism of Tar Beach.

Ringgold is a celebrated artist best known for her quilts depicting stories from African-American history and culture. Her first children's book, *Tar Beach* (1991) was inspired by her "story quilt" of the same name, and each page of the book is bordered by elaborate patchwork quilt designs. *Tar Beach* relates the experiences and dreams of eight-year-old Cassie Louise Lightfoot, a girl growing up in Harlem in the 1930s. Despite the hardships Cassie, her family, and their neighbors face due to racial discrimination and poverty, they maintain a practical, optimistic outlook on life; the tar-paper roof of their tenement building becomes their "Tar Beach" during the summer months. Cassie's dreams of flying above the rooftops at night symbolize "freedom that real life has taken away" in the words of critic Cathryn A. Camper, and *Tar Beach* is praised for encouraging children to believe that they may overcome societal restrictions and turn deprivation into advantage. Also admired are the work's vibrant, colorful illustrations of city life. These illustrations feature a purposely one-dimensional perspective and primitively rendered figures which resemble, according to Rosellen Brown, "sophisticated versions of what a child herself might paint."

Ringgold's works primarily focus on the concerns of African-American women, and she is generally regarded as a political artist—"that is," in the words of her daughter, Michele Wallace, "an artist who attempts to heighten her viewers' sensitivity to the manmade forces that govern their lives." Her invention of the story quilt, which incorporates sewn material, acrylic paints, and written narration, was inspired by her knowledge of quilting done by female slaves—including Ringgold's great-grandmother—in the antebellum South. The "Tar Beach" quilt has been placed in the permanent collection of the Guggenheim Museum in New York, and Ringgold has recently expressed an interest in discontinuing her story quilting to focus on publishing. She has commented that currently "people buy my paintings as art. Now, if people like my writing, they can get it in a book."

"I started writing stories on quilts because I couldn't get a publisher," says Faith Ringgold. The distinguished contemporary artist, a professor of art at the University of California at San Diego, is a self-described "painter who works in the quilt medium." Her work can be found in the permanent collections of the Metropolitan Museum of Art, the Museum of Modern Art, the Studio Museum of Harlem and the High Museum of Atlanta, as well as in numerous corporate and private collections around the country.

Despite her hard-earned success in the field of modern art,

Ringgold says she found the publishing world much more difficult to break into. "Telling my stories on quilts seemed an excellent opportunity to get my work published without dealing with publishers, editors or anyone else. Anyone who saw my art would automatically get the story as well." Ringgold invented the story-quilt form in 1983, after some 20 years of working as a professional artist in various other media.

A 1988 show at New York's Bernice Steinbaum Gallery (Ringgold's dealer) featured the debut of a story-quilt called "Tar Beach." It was the first in the artist's "Woman on the Bridge" series. Measuring 74″ × 69″, the work incorporates one acrylic painting of an intriguing nighttime scene with a colorful and elaborate quilted border and a semi-autobiographical story written on two canvas panels. An eight-year-old girl talks as she lies on the tarpaper rooftop (or tar beach) of her family's Harlem building in the 1930s. She dreams of flying, wearing the George Washington Bridge "like a giant diamond necklace," claiming buildings that will help her parents with their troubles, staking an ice-cream factory for herself. She is in control and soaring, realizing that "I am free to go wherever I want for the rest of my life," and that "anyone can fly. All you need is somewhere to go that you can't get to any other way."

Ringgold, who has studios in the Sugar Hill section of Harlem and in La Jolla, had returned to California to teach when she got a call from Andrea Cascardi, then an editor at Crown Books for Young Readers. Cascardi had seen a poster of "Tar Beach," had been especially attracted to the remarkably real voice that tells the story, and thought the piece could be developed into a wonderful children's book. After a visit from both Cascardi and John Grandits (then Crown's art director), Ringgold had her first publishing contract.

She soon was immersed in the process of expanding a piece of art originally intended for adults into a 32-page picture book. The job was challenging, the artist says; "scary, but enjoyable." Boosting her confidence was the fact that Crown picked up her story-quilt text virtually unedited. She worked intensively on the all-new paintings in June and July 1990, with Crown rushing production in order to have the book out for Black History Month. The final spread of the book features a reproduction of the original story-quilt and a page of background notes.

Unifying the book's pages are striking fabric borders influenced by African art that were reproduced from transparencies of the original story-quilt. Here Ringgold is working in an art form that has long been part of her family. One of her early influences was her mother, a fashion designer and dressmaker who told stories about her own great-grandmother—a slave in Florida who made quilts as part of her plantation tasks. All the fabrics in "Tar Beach" came from New York stores; all are new (Ringgold never recycles since she doesn't want patches to deteriorate un-

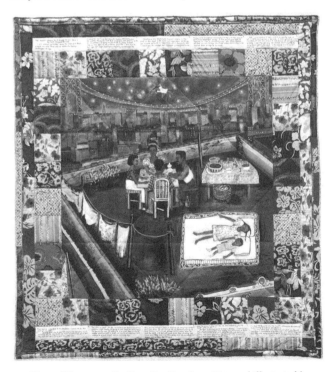

Ringgold's story quilt. From Tar Beach, *written and illustrated by Faith Ringgold.*

equally), and all are selected to evoke the colors and textures of what had originally stimulated this piece: a rooftop scene she views from her Harlem studio.

"Tar Beach"—the story-quilt—now is in the permanent collection of the Solomon R. Guggenheim Museum, currently on loan to a retrospective of Faith Ringgold's 25-year career, which will be touring the country until 1993.

How does Ringgold feel about *Tar Beach,* the book? "So many things have come out of this project that are very inspiring to me. The connection with children, especially, is important." She knows that children respond to her artwork, from receiving their letters and drawings over the years. The chance to reach them in book form is "wonderful." From her own experience, and from having taught art in New York City public schools for 18 years, she knows what a far-reaching influence a book can have. Now she hopes that "kids all over the world love *Tar Beach,* even in places where they have no tar roofs. They still have dreams, don't they?"

Ringgold looks forward to creating more books for children, but currently is working on commissions for Oprah Winfrey (who has called Ringgold "my favorite artist") and for a new elementary school library in Brooklyn. She also is completing her newest set of story-quilts, called "French Collection"—her last story-quilts, Ringgold insists: "I think people buy my paintings as art. Now, if people like my writing, they can get it in a book." (pp. 61-2)

Kathleen Krull "Faith Ringgold: A Quilt Tells a Story," in Publishers Weekly, *Vol. 238, No. 9, February 15, 1991, pp. 61-2.*

To fly! To fly freely over the housetops and through the great glowing chains that hold the bridges up—there isn't a child who doesn't dream of waking up one day with wings.

In Faith Ringgold's first picture book, *Tar Beach,* Cassie Louise Lightfoot is the lucky little girl who gets to float up over the New York City of the 1930's, and wear the George Washington Bridge "like a giant diamond necklace." She lives in Harlem, and the restraints on her life come home to her through her father's pain. He is a construction worker who works on bridges and skyscrapers but he is kept out of the union by racial discrimination and because his own father wasn't a member. Though these details might not make much sense to young children, what will captivate them is the way the lighthearted Lightfoot family threshes pleasure out of their lives in spite of what they can't do and don't have.

In summer they go up to the tar-paper roof of their tenement—Tar Beach!—and there Mom, Dad and the next-door neighbors eat, laugh and tell stories around an old green card table, while Cassie and her little brother lie on a mattress dreaming that the whole city is theirs and there is no one to say no. Cassie imagines herself sailing across all of it, wingless—the sky, the stars and skyscrapers—and it makes her feel rich, "like I owned all that I could see." Best of all, in her flight the bridge her father worked so hard to build is hers. She will fly over the union building that has frustrated his ambitions and made her mother

I will always remember when the stars fell down around me and lifted me up above the George Washington Bridge.

From Tar Beach, *written and illustrated by Faith Ringgold.*

cry, and buy it for him; she'll wing on down to the ice cream factory to make sure her family can have ice cream every night of the endless festive summer of her childhood.

Cassie is making stunning new use of a folk-tale motif of willed flight that we've met before in the Afro-American tradition, in such writers as Toni Morrison and in slave narratives, which gave people a satisfying escape from their deadly restraints, a way to rise above them, literally, into an ineffably beautiful freedom. For a child of the 30's (and for all too many children even now), to be able to say she'll be "free to go wherever I want for the rest of my life" is to speak, by indirection, of all the places she cannot actually expect to go. But Cassie has such perfect confidence that no one would dream of contradicting her when she says generously, "Anyone can fly. All you need is somewhere to go that you can't get to any other way." That's a beguiling promise that turns worse into better, and a deprivation into an advantage. It's a habit of artists as well as poor people.

The painter Faith Ringgold has bound her story to a woman's tradition as well. Having heard that her slave ancestors made quilts as part of their work on the plantations, she began to paint on fabric and then to quilt her images. **Tar Beach** is derived from one of her own quilts, which hangs in the Guggenheim Museum. The paintings made for the book, with quilted borders at the lower edge

of the page, are exuberant and richly colored, sophisticated versions of what a child herself might paint. Cassie flies with amusing bluntness, stiff-limbed; her beloved Tar Beach and the city around it float in a mock-primitive perspectiveless world. And, as a kind of bonus, inside the back cover we are shown the original, dazzling and complex quilt that inspired the story.

It's hard to imagine a child who wouldn't willingly imagine something—a place, a tough spot, a hard life or a high ambition—worth flying out of or into. There's an air of triumph, not the downfall of Icarus but perhaps the swooping power of the eagle or the phoenix, only domesticated in perfect detail, in Ms. Ringgold's vision. Fortunately it's not exclusive: it's not only for African-Americans, or girls, or even—I'll testify—for children.

Rosellen Brown, in a review of "Tar Beach," in The New York Times Book Review, *February 24, 1991, p. 30.*

Vigorous acrylic paintings based on one of the artist's story quilts project the fantasy of eight-year-old Cassie, who dreams of flying above the George Washington Bridge from her nighttime rooftop. Free associating to the bridge, Cassie tells how she was born the day it was finished, how her father worked on its steel girders but couldn't get into the union because he is black, and how her imagined flights will get everything her family needs, from employment to ice cream. Like the folk heroes in Virginia Hamilton's *The People Could Fly,* Cassie eventually initiates someone else, her little brother Be Be, into the magic. Ringgold has met the challenge of transferring images from one medium to another by a skillful adaptation of techniques. Her figures in the picture book art appear larger, the compositions more spacious, and the colors vital but carefully focused for the movement and emphasis of each double spread. A bottom frame of photographed patchwork is separated from the main compositions by a strip of buff canvas that grounds the text and keeps the total effect from becoming too cluttered. This is more evocation than story, but wish fulfillment supported by innovative illustration adds up to striking effects. (pp. 175-76)

> *Betsy Hearne, in a review of "Tar Beach," in* Bulletin of the Center for Children's Books, *Vol. 44, No. 7, March, 1991, pp. 175-76.*

Artist Faith Ringgold's first book is a celebration of the strength and the traditions of black families. Cassie Louise Lightfoot tells the story of how she and her brother liked to sleep up on the roof of their New York apartment building (tar beach) while the grownups played cards. Cassie imagines that the stars lift her up so she can fly over the city and near the twinkling lights of the George Washington Bridge. The bridge, which her father helped build, and the act of flying give Cassie a freedom that real life has taken away. She imagines a job for her father, the luxury of sleeping in late for her mother, and ice cream for dessert every night for her whole family. The book ends with Cassie's empowering message to her little brother, "I have told him it's very easy, anyone can fly. All you need is somewhere to go that you can't get to any other way. The next thing you know, you're flying among the stars."

The book's postscript explains the history of the story's origin and how Ringgold originally sewed the story in a quilt. . . . The vibrant quilt, upon which the illustrations are modeled, is reprinted here. By borrowing symbols from the folk literature of her ancestors and by sewing her story into a historical form of African-American folk art, Ringgold both preserves her cultural heritage and gives it

meaning in the present-day world. This whole book sings with color and life and is a flight of imagination not to be missed.

> *Cathryn A. Camper, in a review of "Tar Beach," in* The Five Owls, *Vol. V, No. 4, March-April, 1991, p. 75.*

Quilt motifs, frequently employed as part of a book's border design, and without any discernible connection to its content, are fast becoming a cliché of contemporary picture-book art. In **Tar Beach** Faith Ringgold has produced a fascinating book, originally created as a story quilt, without compromising the integrity of either art form. She recounts the dream adventure of eight-year-old Cassie Louise Lightfoot, who flies above her apartment-building rooftop, the "tar beach" of the title, looking down on 1939 Harlem. The George Washington Bridge becomes a giant diamond necklace under her magical transformation. She proclaims ownership of the union building that her father, a high-steel worker, is helping to build although he is denied union membership. She envisions picnics on the roof with the neighbors and even takes her little brother along, teaching him to fly as well. "All you need is somewhere to go that you can't get to any other way," she tells him. Part autobiographical, part fictional, this allegorical tale sparkles with symbolic and historical references central to African-American culture. The spectacular artwork, a combination of primitive naive figures in a flattened perspective against a boldly patterned cityscape, resonates with color and texture. The book ends with a photograph of the original quilt. A page of text detailing the various historical, artistic, and personal elements that went into the creation of this work will be of interest to adults. Children will recognize and delight in the universal dream of mastering one's world by flying over it; their curiosity will be aroused by the book's quaint and provocative images. A practical and stunningly beautiful book.

> *Nancy Vasilakis, in a review of "Tar Beach," in* The Horn Book Magazine, *Vol. LXVII, No. 3, May-June, 1991, p. 322.*

Theodore Taylor

1921-

American author of fiction and nonfiction.

Major works include *The Cay* (1969); *Air Raid—Pearl Harbor* (1971); *The Maldonado Miracle* (1973); the Cape Hatteras trilogy: *Teetoncey* (1974), *Teetoncey and Ben O'Neal* (1975), and *The Odyssey of Ben O'Neal* (1977); *The Trouble with Tuck* (1981); *The Hostage* (1987).

Taylor is a celebrated writer whose works—realistic and historical fiction and informational books for middle graders and young adults—are considered notable for their excitement, immediacy, insight, and thought-provoking quality. Best known as the author of *The Cay*, a Robinson-nade for middle graders that has prompted both acclaim and controversy, Taylor reflects his personal background and interest in nature lore, dogs, islands, and the sea in all of his works. Taylor is often praised for the accuracy and vividness of his descriptions of regional details as well as for the environmental consciousness which underscores his books. In addition, he is acknowledged for his respect for and understanding of both young people and animals and is noted for the distinctive approach he brings to the genre of adventure fiction. As a novelist, Taylor usually writes suspenseful stories involving preteen or adolescent protagonists, both male and female, who cope with challenges which often concern their physical survival. Through their experiences, these characters learn independence and self-respect as well as acceptance of other people and cultures. Although he includes instances of suffering and death in his novels, Taylor balances the seriousness of his themes with humor and fast-paced narratives. As a prose stylist, Taylor uses spare, simple language and includes such stylistic features as epilogues and varying points of view. His nonfiction characteristically centers on naval subjects, most frequently the great sea battles of World War II. A recognized naval historian, Taylor presents young adult readers with information on both successful and failed ventures in a colloquial style, often in present tense. Observers frequently note Taylor's thorough research and the fascination of his topics as well as the dramatic quality of his narrative approach.

Taylor's life is intimately connected with his works. Born in North Carolina, he also lived in Tennessee and Virginia as a young man; several of his books are set in the South. After becoming a journalist, Taylor joined the merchant marines in 1942 and also became a member of the naval reserve, experiences which began his extensive international travels. He began his literary career as an author with adult nonfiction on naval subjects, then became a Hollywood press agent and documentary filmmaker; he also worked extensively as a screenwriter on feature films. When his children asked how motion pictures were made, Taylor wrote his first book for the young, *People Who Make Movies* (1967). His next work was his first novel for young people, *The Cay*. Inspired by a wartime newspaper

story about a young boy lost at sea on a raft in the Caribbean and by a boyhood friend of Taylor's whose racism was taught to him by his mother, *The Cay* describes how eleven-year-old Phillip Enright, a bigoted white Virginian, is shipwrecked on a cay, a small island, with the elderly black sailor Timothy as his only companion. Struck on the head by debris during the evacuation of his ship when it is shelled by a German submarine, Phillip loses his sight before landing on the cay; depending on Timothy for his survival, Phillip learns responsibility and understanding through their relationship. Timothy, a kind and resourceful man, sacrifices his life to protect Phillip during a hurricane. After Timothy dies, Phillip is rescued, reunited with his parents, and has his vision restored; at the end of the novel, he vows to return to the cay. Initially acclaimed for his successful evocation of Phillip's enlightenment and the exceptional storytelling in *The Cay*, Taylor began receiving charges of racism in the mid-1970s from both white and black organizations for portraying Timothy in a stereotypical fashion, as a faithful slave who sacrifices his life for his "young bahss." The novel was also viewed negatively for introducing young readers to a colonialist view of life and for using dialect for Timothy's speech. The controversy reached its peak in 1975, when Taylor was asked to return the Jane Addams Children's Book Award he had won for *The Cay* in 1970; the book was also banned from several libraries during this period. Taylor responded that the novel was written without racist intent and that the character of Timothy, which was modeled on an acquaintance of Taylor's and several composites, is a hero, not a stereotype. Currently, *The Cay* is most often recognized as a moving and eloquent initiation story that accurately reflects the period in which it is set.

In addition to *The Cay*, Taylor has written several other works of fiction, notably the Cape Hatteras trilogy, which describes the adventures of Wendy Lynn Appleton, a mute young English girl shipwrecked off the coast of South Carolina in 1898, and her rescuer, Ben O'Neal, an island boy who wants to go to sea. Nicknamed "Teetoncey," or simpleton, by the South Carolina islanders with whom she stays after being rescued, Wendy regains her speech and memory in the second volume of the series, *Teetoncey and Ben O'Neal.* The growing relationship of the protagonists form the basis of the novels, which end with an afterword informing young readers that Wendy and Ben eventually marry and settle in the Outer Banks. Taylor is also the author of two books about Tuck, a golden retriever who loses his sight and learns to rely on a seeing-eye dog, as well as several books which feature Hispanic protagonists. In addition to receiving the Jane Addams Award for *The Cay*, a work which also won a Lewis Carroll Shelf Award in 1970, Taylor received two awards for his body of work, the first from the Southern California Council on Literature for Children and Young People in 1978 and the second from the George G. Stone Center for Children's Books in 1980. He has also received several regional awards, both adult- and child-selected.

(See also *Something about the Author,* Vols. 5, 54; *Something about the Author Autobiography Series,* Vol. 4; *Authors and Artists for Young Adults,* Vol. 2; *Contemporary Authors New Revision Series,* Vols. 9, 25, 38; and *Contemporary Authors,* Vol. 21-24, rev. ed.)

AUTHOR'S COMMENTARY

[The following excerpt is from an interview by Norma Bagnall.]

Theodore Taylor believes that a writer should constantly feed the fires of inspiration "by being on the go, by doing different things, by seeking new experiences." In practicing that philosophy of life and writing, Mr. Taylor has done many different things in many different places. At thirteen he began a newspaper career by becoming a copy boy. He went on to write news and sports stories. He has been manager of a prize fighter. He has been a merchant seaman, an officer in the navy, and a magazine writer. For the movie industry he has done publicity, been a production assistant, and made documentary films. Being on the go has taken him around the world. He has worked in Japan, Taiwan, Hong Kong, as well as in many European countries.

Some of the background for Taylor's novel, *The Cay,* came as a result of living in the Caribbean, mainly in Puer-

to Rico and the Virgin Islands. A question we like to ask an author about his story is, "Did this story really happen?" That was the question put to me by a fourth-grader when he and I had finished reading *The Cay.* I couldn't answer, but I did write to Theodore Taylor and received this reply: "I'm so glad that you enjoyed *The Cay,* and I am pleased that Wes found it a good reading experience. The story is fiction but based partially on fact, and the characters are drawn from real life. In 1955-56, I was researching an adult book on submarine warfare, and I came across an incident involving a small Dutch vessel. I had sailed those waters during the war, and I had also lived in the Caribbean for almost two years after the war. So I knew something about the people. For the character of Phillip, I used a boyhood friend whose mother hated blacks, any blacks. In turn, she tragically transferred that hatred to my friend. I'd known a number of West Indian sailors, one in particular, and they collectively became my Timothy. I combined the incident with the characters and out of that came *The Cay.* Even the cat had a true life counterpart. It is a fictional story against a true background."

That was an early experience I had with *The Cay,* and my first personal experience with Theodore Taylor. Since then I've shared his story with hundreds of children and met the man when he was on the Texas A & M University campus as a guest speaker. It was then that I had the opportunity to ask more questions about *The Cay* and about his other writings.

[Bagnall:] Mr. Taylor, I've talked with many children about *The Cay,* and I have never met a child who did not like the story. Do you have any idea why this is so?

[Taylor:] I've really no idea, but I've wondered about it. It seems to be a universal thing. The book was a best seller in Japan. Now, why? I wouldn't think the Japanese would identify with that story, yet Japanese kids, and Japanese adults too, were really turned on to that book.

[Bagnall:] I think that *The Cay* contains several universal themes; there is a strong theme of people's interdependence; it is also a story of survival. What else do you see in it?

[Taylor:] I set out to write an adventure story, and if anything else came into it that was fine. As I got going, the black and white thing became equal at least with adventure and survival. But I really did not see it as a survival story at first. I write the way I feel and whatever comes of that, well, that's what it is. Partly survival, partly adventure, and perhaps a subtle message about the evils of racial prejudice.

[Bagnall:] Did you feel there was any handling of racial prejudice in *The Maldonado Miracle?*

[Taylor:] Slightly, because again I was trying to deal with a different kind of survival and with national pride. That's one of the reasons I sent the boy back to Mexico. I wanted him to be proud of his own heritage and make his own way in his own country rather than in the United States.

[Bagnall:] Were you disparaging of our cultural values in the United States because of that?

[Taylor:] I don't think so. But sometimes we do think too highly of our own way of life and there is a distortion that comes into that. Like all my stories this one came from a true experience. I was camping in Baja California; my youngest son met a Mexican boy and played with him on the beach. He told us he was going to be smuggled into the Salinas Valley in California where his father was a migrant worker; his mother was dead. I thought, "Wow, a story idea," and that's how that story came about.

[Bagnall:] I think you have some special feeling for that child, maybe for children that age.

[Taylor:] I've been down in that part of the world many times, and I do have some sort of feeling for these kids. I don't know if I am stuck with people that age so far as young people's books are concerned. Somehow I seem to stick with main characters who are between the ages of ten and fourteen; I seem to be able to understand kids that age.

But, another thing I was trying to do with that story was promote self-reliance. I think young people need to learn at an early age the satisfaction of relying on themselves.

[Bagnall:] José seems very young to have the self-reliance called for in that story, but I assume you think it is possible for a youngster to be self-reliant.

[Taylor:] The boy in *The Cay* does the same thing; more so even. On top of that, he is blind. But I have the feeling we should do this kind of story. Ben O'Neal in the Cape Hatteras trilogy does the same thing. In the third book when he finally goes off, he is operating on his own, and he is thirteen.

[Bagnall:] I like Ben O'Neal; he is a very capable and very likeable character. I notice that you killed off the mother of Teetoncey in one paragraph, and with Ben you get him into a boat and into a storm and out of it in about a page and a half. Is that part of your journalistic style?

[Taylor:] No, I think you get kind of a feeling in your head about how long a scene will hold, and you write that scene as long as it will hold; then you say "that's enough of that or the reader will get bored with it, so let's end it right here." You develop that feeling if you've written for a number of years. It's sort of a "gut and head" feeling, how to handle an individual scene. In the second book, towards the end, Ben's mother dies. That was a very tough one because I liked the mother; she was a very strong character, a very strong woman. The feminists have objected to her in some ways, because she was long suffering, but I don't agree at all. She was a heroic woman, very gutsy.

[Bagnall:] What is your background for the Cape Hatteras trilogy?

[Taylor:] When I was a child about ten, my father used to take me to the Outer Banks of North Carolina. They are America's shipwreck banks; over six hundred ships have been destroyed on those shoals since the time of Sir Walter Raleigh. When I first went down there to fish, I was turned on by the things any boy would be turned on by. The little villages had whalebone fences around them, and inside the houses were furnishings from the sea. Things that washed up on those sands were brought into those houses. Many of the timbers used in the construction of the houses came from the sea. There were still the bones of ships upon the sands, and I played among those bones. Throughout my lifetime I went back to the Outer Banks periodically, and I decided to do a story about them and the people on them. I went to the University of North Carolina where they have a large collection of diaries and documents of the Outer Banks. I was looking over all the shipwreck records and came across a true story about a British barkentine that had wrecked in 1898. I was drawn to one individual. There were three passengers, a father, mother, and a little girl. I had always been too cowardly to do a story about a girl, so I took my daughter, Wendy, as a model. That's the easiest thing to do when you are a writer; pick someone you know, put her in the fictional skin and go from there. In the original shipwreck, all got off safely; I doubt that they got their feet wet. Well, that doesn't work in fiction. I wanted the little girl in trouble from the beginning, so the first thing I had to do was kill off her parents. I washed her ashore where Ben O'Neal and his dog could find her; he brought her to his mother who had wanted a girl child. On the Banks it is not unusual for women to resist the sea to the point where they dress their boy children in dresses as long as they can, and this had happened to Ben. So, we have the girl in a catatonic state, Mrs. O'Neal wanting a daughter, and that is what sets up for the story.

[Bagnall:] I see Ben O'Neal as the protagonist in that series of books, although you've said quite a lot about Teetoncey.

[Taylor:] Well, sure he is, but she, well, I've tried to make her grow. I've felt that the strength was always there; it just wasn't evident, and suddenly in that third book she just bursts out on her own. I planned it that way, and it works.

[Bagnall:] Ben is intimidated by her, isn't he?

[Taylor:] Yes, he is by the third book.

[Bagnall:] Don't you think he is from the beginning?

[Taylor:] No; he is not intimidated by her at the beginning. She is a foreign element to him in a certain sense. He doesn't know what to make of her. He doesn't know what to make of girls, period. He talks a good game, but underneath it all he is very uncertain.

[Bagnall:] That's a fairly realistic picture of boys around age twelve though, isn't it?

[Taylor:] Oh yes, I think so, remembering back to where I was then, it is realistic.

[Bagnall:] In your Cape Hatteras trilogy Ben faces problems in growing and developing like any young boy. For example, Ben and his friends went out into the lonely sand dunes to learn to swear. Is that part of your own background?

[Taylor:] Yes, and not only learning how to swear, but learning how to chew tobacco as well. Kids in Virginia and North Carolina did that. Kids in California don't learn how to chew tobacco, but we did, and we got pretty sick doing it.

There is a great deal of difference between the twelve-year-old boy in Laguna Beach and the twelve-year-old boy in Asheville, North Carolina. The boy in Laguna Beach is living in a very sophisticated, a very liberal, town. That is not true of his counterpart in Asheville. I was back in Asheville recently and talked with the kids there. I see a big difference, and I think the kids there are better off.

[Bagnall:] Do you see your proto-1979 Laguna Beach child having a pseudo sophistication?

[Taylor:] That's part of it, and there is real sophistication too. But there is also that yearning, and this is what really touches you, to be that twelve year old in Asheville. These beach kids do not have the opportunity to test their self-reliance the way the Asheville kids do. There are many things in Laguna to entertain kids, and the kids don't have the opportunity to do certain things kids in North Carolina can do. There are no woods there to get lost in, no creeks to wade in or to go after crawdads. They can go to the beach and play in the surf, or go to the tennis court, but most of that is adult supervised. I went down the Catawba River with a group of kids on a raft we had made when I was eleven. My parents knew I was going and they didn't tell me I couldn't. They depended on me to use my head, not to do anything foolish, not to get myself drowned. We were gone about four days. Kids around Laguna Beach would never have that kind of experience; it's an entirely different environment.

[Bagnall:] And so, in your writing you include these ideas that incorporate self-reliance and self-sufficiency.

[Taylor:] Every story I have written is about real people and stems from real-life events. They include kids who have figured out things for themselves because kids like that really exist. I think they serve as models; I *hope* they serve as models, models of self-sufficiency and self-reliance.

[Bagnall:] You think then that children need models?

[Taylor:] Definitely. And I think if they can have peer models they are better off.

[Bagnall:] Some of your work has been criticized as anti-feminist or anti-black. Does that affect how you write?

[Taylor:] I refuse to be intimidated by any organization, because I cannot write with somebody sitting there behind my back. *The Cay* was pretty well worked over. In *Teetoncey and Ben O'Neal* I have a scene in which three or four children are going out to hunt for treasure in the boat. The little girl turns to Ben and says, "Well, what can I do?" He responds, "You can fix the lunch." That's a no-no. Now, as a writer, if I have to be worried about that kind of thing, I can't write. And the only way I can do it, is simply to forget all that stuff and do my story in the hope that as a human being I'll be fair. I try to do that.

I'm proud to write for young people, but when I sit down to write I do not consciously think, "Now, you're writing for young people." I let the story go the way that story should go; the worst thing a writer can do is write down to children. I am just not conscious of whether I am writing for young people or for adults.

But I will probably do other books with characters like Ben O'Neal, José, Phillip, and Teetoncey. They are the kind of peer models children can like and respect; all of them are self-reliant; all are self-sufficient. They find their own way without constant reference to adults. I like that kind of kid; I think kids like that kind too, and if it helps them aim toward self-reliance, then I've done a good job. (pp. 86-91)

> *Norma Bagnall, "Theodore Taylor: His Models of Self-Reliance," in* Language Arts, *Vol. 57, No. 1, January, 1980, pp. 86-91.*

TITLE COMMENTARY

People Who Make Movies   (1967)

A most interesting book, written by a motion picture press agent in a lively colloquial style with occasional errors ("slight of hand") and frequent witticisms. Each chapter is devoted to one job—either one so exalted as the producer or director, or one of lower rank, such as the stuntman or the publicist. The book contains a few anecdotes; they add appeal, but are hardly needed, since the industry has its own glamor which is fully exploited by the author. Mr. Taylor views his associates with wry sympathy, describing their duties, their problems, and the restrictions imposed upon them by time, money, weather, caprice, and their colleagues. A glossary and an index are appended. (pp. 18-19)

> *Zena Sutherland, in a review of "People Who Make Movies," in* Bulletin of the Center for Children's Books, *Vol. 21, No. 1, September, 1967, pp. 18-19.*

Theodore Taylor, press agent for a major Hollywood film company, tells how the producer, director, cameraman, and various studio departments operate in making movies. The author describes each job clearly and shows that, although Hollywood operates on a basically bureaucratic and mechanical assembly line, there is room for the creative flair, the sudden inspiration. This work does not cover the European and independent cinema productions but is otherwise a useful, and frequently fascinating, book on film mechanics.

> *Russell W. Shymansky, in a review of "People Who Make Movies," in* School Library Journal, *Vol. 14, No. 1, September, 1967, p. 138.*

Hollywood is a land of make-believe. But behind its myth are the real-life, dedicated, talented "people who make movies." Going behind the screen, [this book features] the men and women whose sophisticated artistry and cinematic technique can be as interesting as the pictures they create.

In *People Who Make Movies* readers will discover the part played by producer, director, writer, editor, stunt man, grip, gaffer, extra, publicist and all the others responsible for millions of reels each year. Theodore Taylor, a screen publicist, has not simply thumped tubs for them here, he has adhered to the truth and shown the importance of each person's role in moviemaking. Using sprightly anecdotes, he has provided an informative, occasionally funny manual of a complex art and business.

A. H. Weiler, in a review of "People Who Make Movies," in The New York Times Book Review, *September 17, 1967, p. 34.*

The Cay (1969)

[*The first eight excerpts in this entry have been chosen to represent some of the issues which arose during the controversy surrounding* The Cay. *The following excerpt was written by Albert V. Schwartz. At the time this article was published, Schwartz was Assistant Professor of Language Arts at Richmond College in Staten Island, New York. In his essay on* The Cay, *Schwartz charges Taylor with racism.*]

Rather than praise for literary achievement on behalf of "brotherhood," **The Cay** by Theodore Taylor should be castigated as an adventure story for white colonialists to add to their racist mythology. That the major review publications and the five organizations that gave it literary awards—one even for "brotherhood"—so totally misinterpreted **The Cay's** meaning supports the charge that children's book publishing is indeed a racist institution.

The Cay is the story of the initiation of a white upper-middle-class boy into his superior role in a colonialist, sexist, racist society. Colonialist, because the people of Curaçao and most other people of the Caribbean Isles, where the story is set, are "owned" by outside white powers, which is taken for granted by the author as an acceptable way of life. Sexist, because the only woman in the story is a weak, subservient mother, whose very weakness sets in motion the boy's adventures. Racist, because the white boy is master and the Black man is subservient throughout the story. It is incredible that in a book for children today, any writer would be so racially insensitive as to put a Black man in the role of subservience to a white boy—a servant who risks his life for the boy and, in the end, sacrifices his life so the white boy may live.

Specifically, the story is about eleven-year-old Phillip Enright, who is marooned on a small island (a cay) with an elderly West Indian, Timothy (no last name). Phillip, who relates the tale, has been living in the Caribbean because his father is an oil refining expert on loan to the Royal Dutch Shell from a U.S. company.

The first half of the book sets Phillip up as a young Southern cracker. The reader knows from the outset that the boy's bigoted remarks are deliberate and that the author will slap Phillip down. Phillip early in the book declares that his mother was brought up in Virginia and that "she didn't like them." The "them" are Black people. Of the Black Timothy, says Phillip, "[his] smell was different and strong." The Black man's appearance, says Phillip, "is very much like the men I'd seen in jungle pictures. Flat nose and heavy lips." Phillip recoils from the touch of Timothy.

Midway in the book Phillip undergoes a conversion—or so the author would like the reader to believe. This is the "character growth" of young Phillip that is supposed to

contribute to the literature espousing "brotherhood." If Phillip's racist attitudes were to undergo substantive change, were Phillip really to have his consciousness raised and grow in human understanding as a result of his close association with Timothy—all well and good. But this just doesn't happen. All that changes in Phillip's growth is a shift in the direction of his racism.

Binnie Tate in an article dealing with authenticity and the Black experiences in children's books states that, from the Black point of view, "the author fails in his attempt to show Phillip's growth in human understanding."

Phillip's "conversion" stems from loss of eyesight after he is shipwrecked, and he comes to depend on Timothy for help and protection. The conversion comes when Phillip—remember, now, he is blind—lies down next to Timothy and says, "[Timothy] felt neither white or Black." Soon he is saying that Timothy is "kind and strong." Then comes the question: "Timothy, are you still black?"

Elsewhere in this issue of *Interracial Books for Children*, Ray Anthony Shepard contrasts the interpretations of the Black experience by two author/illustrators, one white and the other Black. Mr. Shepard makes the point that the stories of the white author/illustrator are oriented toward the liberal insistence on human similarities and sameness, whereas the Black author/illustrator celebrates the ethnic differences of Blacks.

In this light, consider the implications of Phillip's question to Timothy: "Are you still black?" Phillip is really saying that in order for him to have warm feelings toward a person, that person must be white. Instead of having Timothy answer loud and clear, "No, I am not white, I am Black," he has Timothy disappearing into anonimity.

True to the liberal absurdities of a bygone age, the *New York Times* book review of **The Cay** made this comment on Phillip's question: "Phillip . . . realized that racial consciousness is merely a product of sight." What a racially unaware remark that is!

One thing we are certain about. Phillip won't grow up to march with a Martin Luther King (to whose memory **The Cay** is dedicated). On the contrary, Phillip will return to the Islands and, following in his father's footsteps, he will become a leader in the system that exploits the "natives."

Near story's end, when Phillip has successfully fulfilled his initiation, he puts on a verbal blackface: "Dis b'dat outrageous cay, oh, Timothy?" In the end, the white boy is given control even of the Black man's language!

We will be hearing a lot in the months and years to come about "Black language." One thing Black language is *not* is verbal blackface, and that is the use of apostrophes and abbreviated word forms to stereotype the language of America's non-white minorities and, to some extent, its lower-class whites. The use of apostrophes and abbreviated word forms is a shoddy literary device used to connote inferior status under the guise of authenticity.

We have said very little about the Black servant. At the story's beginning and through to its conclusion, Timothy is very much the invisible man. We know more about him by omission than by commission. We know that he is good, kind, generous, resourceful and happy. We know that he is well schooled in oppression and colonialism. He is very much aware that the system dictates he call a white boy "Young bahss." Only when the white boy no longer is afraid of his servant is Timothy given permission (which is granted, not assumed) to call the white boy by *his* first name. Phillip at eleven knows much history. The considerably older Timothy knows no history. When asked about Africa, Timothy answers: "I 'ave no recollection o' anythin' 'cept dese islands. 'Tis pure outrageous, but I do not remember anythin' 'bout a place called Afre-ca."

Outrageous? Yes. What should outrage all of us is that the book's author, its editor, and its publisher should foist upon our children such an image of a Black man today!

Not only is Timothy denied his color by the act of a white boy's "conversion." He is denied parents, family, children. He is denied all social ties except one, and that single tie is with a white boy, for whom in the end he is denied his life. (pp. 7-8)

Albert V. Schwartz, " 'The Cay': Racism Still Rewarded," in Interracial Books for Children, *Vol. 3, No. 4, 1971, pp. 7-8.*

[*The Cay* was televised in 1974. Prior to the broadcast, the Council on Interracial Books for Children issued a position paper on the television script. The first excerpt which follows is from that position paper; the second excerpt is from a review of the telecast.]

Recognizing the impact of the mass media on the American consciousness and, particularly, its impact on the impressionable minds of young people, we become deeply concerned when they serve as a conduit for racist images and values. (p. 282)

On the surface, it would appear that the media have been responsive to the pressures of minority groups for more frequent and accurate representation of their cultural milieus. Images of Blacks and other minority peoples are no longer absent from the TV screen. They appear in commercials, newscasts, dramatic and comedy programs. However, closer scrutiny reveals that far from being eliminated from TV fare, racist stereotypes and attitudes are being given new life, reinforced and perpetuated in a variety of subtle ways.

Case in point: The forthcoming nationwide telecast of Theodore Taylor's *The Cay.* (pp. 282-83)

The Cay is a two-character story about an 11-year-old white boy and a 70-year-old Black seaman who survive the torpedoing of their boat by Nazis during World War II. The Black male character, called Timothy (no last name), conforms to the traditional stereotype of the faithful slave or retainer who is happy to serve and even sacrifice his life for his "young bahss"—a term which establishes, at the outset, the man's implied inferiority. Timothy's servility and ignorance juxtaposed with the white boy's gentility, self-assurance and erudition clearly evoke the time-worn conception of Blacks as immature, self-negating, unpredictable and, thus, threatening "creatures" and whites as

effectual, commanding and superior beings no matter what their age!

The above conceptions are conveyed 1) by the use of terms like "young bahss" and other self-effacing language by the Black seaman; 2) through the use of dialect by the seaman as compared to the well-spokenness of the boy; 3) by the denial of a second name to Timothy, whereas the boy is identified as Phillip Enright; 4) by dramatic teasers designed to make the viewer wonder about Timothy's intentions toward the boy—a particularly insidious device. On one level, the adapter seems to assign kind and protective qualities to Timothy; on another, dramatic tension is achieved by suggesting that he might be a threat to the child. Hence, elements of suspense are achieved at the expense of Timothy's—and all Blacks'—humanity; 5) by Timothy's embracing the notion of his own uselessness and obsolescence as the boy becomes adjusted to his blindness and can take care of himself; 6) by the death of Timothy which, given the overall complexion of the story, has the ring of a metaphorical statement to the effect that it is for Blacks to serve and die and whites (white civilization) to *be served* and prevail.

Add to these negative features the fact that at least one opportunity was missed to deal with certain issues on a meaningful level. To the boy's query as to why people are different colors, Timothy gives a wholly inadequate reply. Of course, the author and adapter precluded the possibility of enlightening their audiences in this and other matters by making Timothy the ignorant and limited character that he is.

The choice of a work that has been strongly criticized by groups and authoritative individuals raises questions about the standards and procedures used in the selection of TV material, as well as about the judgment of the decision-makers involved. It is further regrettable that the program is being billed as family entertainment and will be telecast in a prime time slot, assuring it the widest possible audience. Clearly, this implies endorsement of the story's images and values by the network and sponsor, which is bound to spur sales of the original book. (pp. 283-84)

The Council on Inter-racial Books for Children in a letter to the editor on October 15, 1974, in Top of the News, *Vol. 31, No. 3, April, 1975, pp. 282-84.*

The Bell System Family Theater's telecast of Russell Thacher's adaptation of *The Cay,* by Theodore Taylor, was shown as scheduled on NBC October 21, 1974, in the midst of sharp criticism leveled against it by an educators' coalition, formed by the CIBC.

The coalition, including representatives from the National Education Association, *Freedomways* magazine, a task force from Teachers College, Columbia University and the CIBC, had challenged the selection for TV adaptation of a book that serves to reinforce and perpetuate racist stereotypes of Black people and other antihumanistic values. . . .

The Cay is about an eleven-year-old white boy named Phillip Enright, played by Alfred Lutter III, and a seventy-year-old West Indian seaman called Timothy (of no last name or fixed address), played by James Earl Jones. . . .

The TV film fails on several levels. A situation that is not inherently racist but, in fact, contains the potential for dramatic tension, suspense and illumination of vital issues, was invested with none of these elements. Rather, the story limps along anemically, missing opportunities and reinforcing discredited stereotypes and ideas as it goes.

Jones, in perhaps the least effective portrayal of his career, mugs, grimaces and infantilizes his way through the role of illiterate Timothy, whose assigned lot is to sustain young Phillip, the latter having been blinded in the shipwreck. Speaking in a heavy dialect of undefined origins, he emotes broadly, at one point reassuring his "young bahss" that the blindness will pass and, at another, ranging about the island in a malaria-induced fit. (Given the weakening effects of malarial fever, we found this towering seizure to be one of several implausible occurrences.) Responding to a curse from Phillip—"you stupid Black trash"—he slaps the boy, then retreats like a child to soothe his wounded feelings by singing a spiritual-like "island" folk tune (shades of the plantation "mammy").

Young Lutter, for his part, expresses the essential emptiness of the character of Phillip, failing to infuse it by his acting with any substance whatsoever.

Phillip's blindness emerges as a symbolic contrivance for peddling the notion that color blindness is the highest state of humanitarian consciousness. "Timothy, are you still Black?" asks Phillip midway in the saga. Yes, ol' Timothy is still Black, but it doesn't matter a jot Phillip supposedly discovers in the course of his experiences on that little cay in the middle of nowhere. In addition to the primitive state of the author's awareness in race matters that this message suggests, he would further seem to be saying that the only way Blacks and whites can interact positively is under such unusual and temporary circumstances as prevail in this story. Back on land, extensive contact is still a no-no.

Then, there is the thorny matter of Timothy's death during a storm. John J. O'Connor, TV critic for *The New York Times,* put it this way in his review of *The Cay:* "Perhaps the time has come for television, in its search for 'tender' racial lessons, to find material in which the black [sic] becomes more than a disposable instrument for educating the white." We would go further. Timothy's death constitutes a devastating allegorical statement to the effect that it is for Blacks to serve and die and for whites (white civilization) to be served, rule and prevail.

The adapter might have approached his task quite differently. He might have chosen to depart from the narrow conceptions of character provided in the original material and wrought them anew. He might have uplifted the "message" of the tale from its current level of underdevelopment to one of some sophistication and enlightenment. He did not, and as a result, vast numbers of whites were given aid and comfort in their prejudices, while Blacks were relegated to their same, old "place."

The telecast may or may not be repeated in the future, but unfortunately we have definitely not heard the last of *The Cay.* Since sales of the book have surely been spurred by the advertising campaign surrounding the telecast and, of course, by the telecast itself, we may expect *The Cay*'s outdated lessons to influence the minds of young children for some time to come.

"White Supremacy Extolled in TV Film of 'The Cay'," in Interracial Books for Children, Vol. 5, No. 6, 1974, p. 9.

[*The following excerpts are taken from statements made at a press conference held by the Council on Interracial Books for Children on 17 October 1974 in response to the upcoming telecast of* The Cay. *In the first excerpt Bertha Jenkinson, the chairperson of the Jane Addams Children's Book Award Committee in 1974, declares that the selection of* The Cay *for the 1970 Jane Addams Award was "a mistake." In the second excerpt, Samuel B. Ethridge, then director of the Civil and Human Rights program for the National Education Association, presents his views.*]

As the present chairperson of the Jane Addams Children's Book Award Committee, I feel that the choice of *The Cay* by Theodore Taylor for our award in 1970 was a mistake. Children's books are not published in a vacuum, and so it is possible that even an interracial committee of "specialists," alert to stereotypes, can lose sight of what is good for children's minds, what they need to fulfill themselves and how best to teach them through reading and visual materials that people are to be respected precisely because of their own special rich heritage. Members of our committee have been subjected to the same layers of prejudice built up by every branch of communications, the family, friends, and the distorted reading materials of our formative years. We need to educate ourselves and involve members of minority groups in decision-making in the creation of children's books at the prepublication stage and at all levels of the publishing process, in teacher education courses, and mass media programming in our schools, radio and television. (pp. 6-7)

Bertha Jenkinson, in an excerpt from Interracial Books for Children Bulletin, Vol. 6, Nos. 3 & 4, 1975, pp. 6-7.

I come not to either bury or to praise *The Cay* but to use it. Certainly any book which has won 11 awards can't be all bad—or could it be? I have read through the book carefully and I have underlined a number of passages which reek with blatant racism or total insensitivity to the social concerns of our time. But I will not take the time to point them out. . . .

As a matter of fact, given the particular storytelling technique, a narrative by an eleven-year-old southern boy who has obviously been taught by both his parents that "those people" were different and not to be trusted, I really don't see how we could have expected any other result. All of the narrative—even direct quotes from Timothy—are interpreted through Phillip.

Only if the author had had the courage to try to get inside of *Timothy's* head to make clear his private and innermost thoughts could he have made the kind of contribution which is demanded of him by the nineteen seventies.

The reader knows vividly what Phillip thinks of Timothy and that he attributes some of Timothy's action to "those people being like that" and some to his being "a dumb old black man." But what does Timothy think of Phillip's behavior? How does he react emotionally to this strange situation? What kinds of past experiences prepare him to make the ultimate sacrifice? Who in his life taught him to love? Readers are robbed of these answers because the author wisely knows that he lacks the experience with Black people necessary to treat this kind of revelation and that he lacks the sensitivity to understand that a Black person has the capability of feeling, thinking, and resolving. This is racism at its "best."

Ten years ago when we talked to book publishers about biased materials, they responded by painting some Dick and Jane characters brown or presented stories in which the presence of minorities is acknowledged. This is Level One. Several years later we began to get books such as *The Cay* in which the races began to relate to each other. This was Level Two. And *The Cay* probably deserves the awards which it received in 1969 when even most American critics were at Level Two.

At Level Three, the characters begin to deal with each other as humans on an emotional level and as social equals. At Level Four, they begin to deal with the culture and life styles and the social institutions which tend to create winners and losers. At Level Four, there are no cultural winners or losers, just mutual acceptance.

We congratulate CIBC for their courage to raise this issue, and the Jane Addams book committee for their recognition that we are moving to higher levels of sensitivity.

> *Samuel B. Ethridge, in an excerpt from* Interracial Books for Children Bulletin, *Vol. 6, Nos. 3 & 4, 1975, p. 7.*

[*The following excerpts are taken from three letters. The first, written to the editor of* Top of the News *on 6 February 1975, is Taylor's response when he was asked by the Jane Addams Committee to return the award given to* The Cay *in 1970. The second excerpt, from a letter originally written on 29 April 1975, responds to Taylor's correspondence. It was written by John Donovan, director of the Children's Book Council. The third excerpt, which answers Donovan's letter, was written by Albert V. Schwartz.*]

Recently, I had the unusual experience of bundling up the 1970 Jane Addams Children's Book Award for my novel, *The Cay,* and returning it to the current selection committee of the Jane Addams Peace and Freedom Association. I did so by choice; not in anger, but with troubling questions. The committee had decided, so many years later, to publicly state that the prestigious award had been a "mistake." Presented this fact, I had little desire to see it on my office wall day after day.

Since 1970, *The Cay* has been under varied attack as "racist", mainly from the Interracial Council on Children's Books, but also from some black organizations; some individual librarians and teachers, white and black. On several occasions, in verbal confrontations with critics, I have attempted to answer the charges. For the most part, I have gone on to other work and remained silent. Obviously, my verbal answers were inadequate and my silence of five years an indication of agreement. The latter is far from the truth.

Charges of "racism" have been largely supported by the "under-lining" of various passages in the book, usually descriptive of the black character, *Timothy;* then the broader contention that the white character, the boy *Phillip,* was not changed by his experience with the 70-year-old West Indian. Needless to say, passages in any book can be underlined and utilized for whatever purpose the reader chooses. That purpose does not always coincide with what the writer had in mind; nor always with the total meaning; nor always with the majority of the readers. However, simplifying the issues here would be unjust.

In my own mind, I did not set out to write a "racist" novel, vintage 1942; harm any human being, black or white; damage the black struggle for human equality. Further, I am not at all convinced that I did write a "racist" novel. The goal was to the contrary. Directed primarily toward the white child (thinking that the black child did not need to be told much about prejudice), I hoped to achieve a subtle plea for better race relations and more understanding. I have reason to believe that I partially achieved that goal, despite acknowledged omissions and commissions; flaws.

I do not have the ability to write fantasy. My stories are taken from fragments of real-life though I do not expect anyone to accept them as more than fiction; nor do I place a greater value on them. The characters of the prejudiced white boy, Phillip, and his prejudiced mother, were taken from real-life. Though I elected to change the circumstances, and add composites, I played with the boy in my own childhood and knew his mother. The character of Timothy was developed from West Indian sailors, primarily one man, but also a composite.

I lived in the Caribbean for a while; sailed it; roamed the area from Haiti to Grenada and Carricou; Curaçao and Aruba to Coco Solo. The descriptions of the places, characters, and generally the events are not from guide books or lectures. From the Ruyterkade schooner market in Curaçao (Venezuelan blacks and Indians mixed bloods, bi and multi-lingual) to carnival day and the *bambola* in Charlotte Amalie, St. Thomas, I was lucky enough to see it, hear it and taste it. I listened and I looked and I asked questions whenever I could.

Between two separate experiences, one in the early forties, another in the early fifties, I met and talked at length with upwards of twenty bona fide West Indian sailors of several nationalities; sailed with one for a short period; fished with others; sat on the decks of several of those schooners and soaked up as much as I could, simply because of an interest in the ships and sailors, with no intention of doing a book a quarter century later. These expert seamen, a unique breed, were probably only amused with me but I was enchanted with the Caribbean sailor/merchants of that day and still am. The idea for *The Cay* evolved from research in 1955 and 1956 for Caribbean chapters in an adult book, published by W. W. Norton, 1958. The story of Phillip and Timothy was not written until 1968, so progression, from concept to completion, was not in undue haste.

This backdrop does not in any way relieve me of the total creative responsibility for the novel and what is in it, good and bad.

Last fall, on the occasion of the Bell Telephone television production of **The Cay,** a disappointing film for which I hold no brief, Mr. Samuel Ethridge, director of Civil and Human Rights for the National Education Association, took me to task for lacking the courage to get inside Timothy's head; to make known his private and innermost thoughts; to show that black people were capable of "feeling, thinking and resolving." Perhaps I cannot read my own work with a sense of fairness and reason; perhaps I am too conditioned to make proper judgment, but I truly believe that Timothy did all three from the first moment on the raft. One does not have true compassion without the ability to feel; one cannot make decisions (and he made many) without the ability to think and resolve.

I do think I clearly understand Mr. Ethridge's well-taken point on the depth of penetration of Timothy's character and his indirect questioning of my qualifications to write the story. Truthfully, I did not stop for a moment to even think about my qualifications, nor about whether I was white or black; whether or not I could step into Timothy's skin. Lengthy deliberations of this sort would lead to a frozen typewriter; fear of ever doing any story. None of us are really equipped to cross that barrier, even to crawling inside a person's skin when they are of the *same* color, but I think we should try.

I had the story in mind for a long time and went about doing it to the best of my ability. I told the story from the viewpoint of the white boy because: (1) Timothy needed no lessons from the white boy about prejudice, survival or anything else. (2) I knew that Timothy would not be introduced until the third chapter and would die before the story ended. I needed a continuing narrator. (3) I felt that a needed intimacy could be gained by first person treatment. (4) I knew much more about the white boy than I did about Timothy.

If a black writer were to handle this same story, or a variation of it, I'm inclined to think that he or she would tell it from the black point-of-view, simply because of that experience. Being white, I told it from the white boy's point-of-view. That being the case, right or wrong, Phillip could only be privy to Timothy's innermost thoughts as they were volunteered. Realistically, I doubt that a 70-year-old Indies schoonerman would share too many innermost thoughts with an 11-year-old white boy. For one thing, it was not the nature of the character, as I saw him, to say much beyond the comments of the moment.

I can be faulted for not doing the story third-person but it never occurred to me to do it that way, enabling deeper penetration into Timothy's character and his life. From the beginning, I was concentrating on what would come out, more or less naturally, once they met on the raft. By so doing, I was hoping to achieve a semblance of reality; dialogue and action as it might happen within the fictional scope.

Space does not permit me to deal individually with each underlined passage that I have seen but those most used to support the disparaging "racist" charge usually include my first description of Timothy, as seen by the racially programmed boy: *He was ugly. His nose was flat and his face was broad; his head a mass of wiry gray hair.* I don't think I am completely insensitive and realize why these words explode on paper for some people, both black and white.

As a matter of story construction and nothing else, I purposely made Timothy facially ugly to enable what I thought would be an important change later on. To be blunt, had I made Timothy beautiful when Phillip awakened on that raft, I could see no valid reason for marked reaction or for the hateful fires of prejudice to be refueled. Timothy's appearance simply reinforced the poison planted by Phillip's mother.

Quite purposely, I strengthened this a few paragraphs on with an even more unattractive description of Timothy. Given the same story circumstance, that of conflict and transformation, I would do it again. Also, quite on purpose, not carelessly, I had Phillip view Timothy as "dumb and old and black and different." Given the lessons of his mother, how else could Phillip view Timothy?

If conflict cannot be dealt with, on its many levels, pap will be the result. If a character cannot truthfully state a visual reaction to another character, one level of conflict is eliminated. If a white writer must view every black as "beautiful, wise, young and the same as every white," there can be no conflict; therefore no understanding which might possibly come out of conflict. If the black writer must say that every white is "beautiful, wise, young and the same as blacks," why bother with the story; why strive for truth?

Terribly trite but true, facially, without getting into yellow, brown or red, we cannot all be Diahann Carroll or O. J. Simpson; Paul Newman or Faye Dunaway. Also worn, but true, human experience, time and time again, is that the facially unattractive person, of any hue, can become quite beautiful as the inner person emerges. I had hoped that Timothy would emerge as a beautiful man. Obviously, for some, I failed.

I have been faulted for the derogatory use of dialect by Timothy, even though most West Indian sailors of 1942 spoke dialect. To me, calypso is the single most pleasing, most musical dialect on earth; a black treasure, I would think. It may jar some white ears, and some black ears, but I would use it again without hesitation. I hope it is never laundered, sanitized and ironed flat on the boards of social change. Everyone will lose.

Much has also been said about my purposely "blinding" Phillip. Why could he not learn his lessons while sighted? In so far as prejudice is concerned, I honestly felt that Phillip was already blind, as was his mother, long before he suffered the injury. I believed that Phillip should dramatically know that much of prejudice is a matter of eyesight (as with ugliness)—my own opinion. Finally, I wanted him to reach the point where "color" made no difference, leading to the line, "Are you still black, Timothy?" I did not want to use a sledgehammer at this tender point of the story. I felt it best to let Phillip say it in his own way. I feel secure that the character of Timothy understood, as do most readers.

It has been charged that I did not really show a change in Phillip; that he remained a total "racist." This can be argued for years, though I hope it won't be. Without preaching a sermon, because I've found that few people listen, including young readers, I attempted to show that change beginning with page 72. And for every so-called "racist" passage, I believe I can underline one which shows the beginning of understanding; the growth of affection; the slow recognition of Timothy's humaneness, wisdom and courage as a distinct and valuable person. Despite novels and movies, people seldom change overnight. The process is slow and difficult but there is always a starting point. So it was, I believed and tried to write it, with Phillip and his superficial knowledge of Timothy.

Of course, I could have written a summary, re-stating every change in Phillip, crossing the bridges, using a sledgehammer as we go off into the sunset. No thanks. For either young readers or adults, I prefer not to bang on anvils. The exercise is annoying, if not useless.

Debating the obnoxious aspects of Phillip's character, his visual reactions, his verbal reactions, before Los Angeles county librarians some years back, an opposing spokesman said, "He (Timothy) would have thrown that boy overboard." I think not. I doubt very much that the compassionate Timothy would have tossed Phillip to the sharks. I am compelled to think that he would, and did, handle it with wisdom and dignity. Had I committed that untruthful "overboard" scene to paper the "racist" charges would be entirely justified. I would have painted a picture of a black man who did not care about human existence; who could not cope with the mindless mouthings of a child.

I do not know how much personal contact the members of the Interracial Council on Children's Books, Mr. Samuel Ethridge, or the Jane Addams committee, have with young readers. My own, gratefully, has been considerable. Since 1970, between visits to schools and libraries, book fairs, and in correspondence with complete strangers, I estimate that I have been enriched by contact with approximately 25,000 young readers, parents, teachers and librarians. In all that time, I have yet to see or learn of an indication much less of a *concrete example* of "racism" promoted by *The Cay;* of even that general type of damage done by *The Cay.* Perhaps the young readers, parents, librarians and teachers were not aware of damage done—subconscious rather than conscious—an evil thing. I do not know. I would like to find out.

However, I do not take much stock in theory and guesses; possibilities and probabilities. I am very much for fact, and in that regard, to be of great and lasting aid to young readers, parents, teachers and librarians, and selfishly, my-

self, I can think of nothing better than for the Interracial Council, the NEA and the Jane Addams committee to join hands and determine, as scientifically as possible, the exact furtherance of "racism" by *The Cay.* I will be glad to turn over boxes of letters containing names and addresses of young readers, parent-readers, teacher-readers, librarian-readers, schools, etc., across the country, cutting through all walks of life, as a start toward this important determination. The correspondence is unsolicited and could provide access to at least one known group of readers. Other new test groups would be needed, of course.

I am taking for granted that we are all talking specifically about "racism" charges against a specific book and not the uneasy issue of a writer being allowed expression on any subject, to any audience. I would hope that in *any* work of fiction *any* black writer could describe a white person as "ugly," as "dumb," as "different," as "racist" or anything else; choose to do what he or she wanted with the white character—girl, boy, woman or man—without fear of reprisal or intimidation from anyone. I would also hope this would equally apply to writers of any color; any ethnic group; that none would be subjected to pressures beyond those of vigorous, honest opinion, be it good or bad; right or wrong; recommendations that the book be read or not read; bought or not bought, as forceful as the critic wishes.

I would also hope that the day never comes when any council, association, book award committee, political group, or government agency, can dictate to a writer; or can punish the writer, directly or indirectly, beyond the above, for words committed to paper.

While I believe in freedom of expression, steadfastly and deeply, "racism" is a grave and frightening charge and if it is proven that *The Cay* is a "racist" work, damaging to young readers, I will, as a parent and grandparent first, and writer second, be very prompt in advocating its immediate removal from every bookshelf—home, school and library.

Meanwhile, as I informed the Jane Addams committee, "I will continue to write stories as I see and feel them, knowing that I will make mistakes forever. I do hope that some small good will be in each one. I will also try very hard, as I have tried in the past, not to harm any human, no matter color. . . ." (pp. 284-88)

> *Theodore Taylor, in a letter to the editor on February 6, 1975, in* Top of the News, *Vol. 31, No. 3, April, 1975, pp. 284-88.*

Dear Ted:

I have read with great interest your letter about *The Cay* in the April issue of *Top of the News*. It seems to me that while the attack on your book by the Council on Interracial Books for Children and other pressure groups has hardly been a trivial one, it has been insulting in the extreme. That you have had to explain yourself seems to me absurd, and I admire the patience and reason you display. The fact is that you wrote a magnificent novel—true and honest as you and your fully realized characters were truthful and honest to themselves.

Taylor with his sisters Mary (left) and Eleanor in 1935.

While realizing that Bertha Jenkinson has been quoted as regretting that *The Cay* received the Addams Award, I find it beyond my understanding that Bertha, whom I have always regarded an eminently sensible and fair-minded person, has been so brainwashed as to utter these thoughts.

The whole affair is deeply regrettable. I hope it will not affect your own thinking about your books. Creative work cannot exist in a climate of censorship and oppression.

I suppose I should mention that these remarks are my own, and don't represent the Children's Book Council's official views. I think it's accurate to say that publishers feel that *their* principal object is to identify good writers, and to nourish their careers.

Yours sincerely,

John Donovan

> *John Donovan, in a letter to Theodore Taylor in 1975, in* Interracial Books for Children Bulletin, *Vol. 6, Nos. 3 & 4, 1975, p. 6.*

Dear John,

I believe I can understand your great upset with Bertha Jenkinson and the Addams Award Committee for changing their minds about the value of *The Cay* after a "pressure group" like the Council on Interracial Books for Children "attacked" the book. I understand because—not long ago—I might have reacted in similar fashion.

It is our feeling that Bertha Jenkinson and her group should be lauded for their courage in openly recognizing racism in past decisions. The last decade has been one of great upheaval in American perceptions. Racial minorities and women have been responsible for many minds opening up, growing, changing. Some white males have been led, through personal grappling with ideas, to a new consciousness about the many manifestations of racism and sexism.

But there are those, like yourself and Theodore Taylor, who stalwartly resist fresh insights and are deeply upset by criticism. You righteously assure Mr. Taylor, "That you have had to explain yourself seems to me absurd." Why absurd? Why are you, I, Taylor or anyone so above the currents of life, so hallowed, that we need not be expected to explain ourselves. Explanation is one method of human communication.

I agree with you when you say that "Creative work cannot exist in a climate of censorship and oppression." Yet it is absurd to me that you do not perceive that a climate which is thoughtfully anti-racist is the opposite of a climate of oppression. What greater oppression can exist than racism? It is also absurd to me that Taylor refuses to recognize that his brand of "well-intentioned" paternalistic racism is offensive to enlightened sensibilities.

I believe that creative *criticism* cannot exist in a "climate of censorship and oppression." And I feel that there are times when you, and some of the prestigious establishment groups with which you are associated, create a climate which stifles anti-racist criticism.

Yours sincerely,

Al Schwartz

P.S. John, I realize your circle of business associates in publishing is indeed wide, but do you *really* believe that " . . . it's accurate to say that publishers feel that their *principal* object is to identify good writers, and to nourish their careers."?

> *Al Schwartz, in a letter to John Donovan in 1975, in* Interracial Books for Children Bulletin, *Vol. 6, Nos. 3 & 4, 1975, p. 6.*

Theodore Taylor dedicated this story "To Dr. King's dream, which can only come true if the very young know and understand." Written with eloquent understatement, this immensely moving novel should do much to help a reader to "know and understand." The narrator is an 11-year-old American boy, Phillip Enright, living on the Caribbean island of Curaçao in 1942 when German submarines were sinking tankers and threatening the refinery where Phillip's father worked to produce oil for the war effort. Phillip's mother insisted on taking the reluctant Phillip back to America and safety, but on the way their freighter was torpedoed, Phillip was separated from his mother and found himself alone on a raft with a huge, ugly, very old Negro, and with a terrible pain in his head. The pain went away, but it left the boy blind, utterly dependent on the illiterate, superstitious but wise West Indian, whom first he resented, even scorned, but whom he came to love and trust.

The weeks man and boy spent on the raft and on a small, uninhabited cay make unforgettable reading. And in Timothy, building a shelter, fishing for food, giving Phillip a course in survival against the day he might be alone, and finally sacrificing his life to protect the boy from a hurricane, the author has created a wonderful human being, whose heart and courage matched his big frame. Phillip, who survived to tell the story, would never forget his friend. Nor will the reader.

> *Polly Goodwin, "Fare for Older Boys," in* Book World—The Washington Post, *May 4, 1969, p. 36.*

Theodore Taylor has skillfully developed the perenially popular castaway plot into a good adventure story, set in the Caribbean in 1942. The castaways are 11-year-old American, Phillip Enright and Timothy, an illiterate West Indian Negro still physically powerful despite his 70-odd years.

Their adventures and relationship gain deeper significance after Phillip, the narrator (a caste-conscious product of neo-colonial white society on Curaçao) becomes blind from injuries received during the shipwreck. He soon realizes that racial consciousness is merely a product of sight: to him Timothy *feels* "neither white nor black." Mr. Taylor has provided an exciting story (though some may be deterred by Timothy's musical West Indian dialect). The idea that all humanity would benefit from this special form of color blindness permeates the whole book—though it is never overtly discussed. The result is a story with a high ethical purpose but no sermon.

> *Charles W. Dorsey, in a review of "The Cay,"* in The New York Times Book Review, *June 29, 1969, p. 26.*

This treatment of the initiation-into-manhood theme is very similar to, and even stronger than, Jones' *Edge of Two Worlds* (Dial, 1968). In both books, the young males undergo physical disaster, a catharctic experience that strips them of security and props of convention. The ensuing boy-to-man metamorphosis is then guided by a primordial Father Nature figure, representing the key to wisdom and survival while also embodying the things most hated and feared by each boy; in *The Cay,* the mentor is a massive, ancient black West Indian, Timothy. Phillip is leaving war-torn Curaçao with his mother, a shrewish racist from Virginia, when their ship is torpedoed. He finds himself on a raft with Timothy (whom he regards according to his upbringing), then goes blind from a head injury. Motivated by both concern and self-interest, Timothy helps the boy grow from petulant apathy to independence, through slaps, stubbornness, and affection. They beach on a deserted island (a cay), and together work at survival. Months later, when Timothy's death follows a hurricane, Phillip is self-sufficient enough to endure till rescued a few weeks after. Returning to Curaçao when operations had restored partial vision, he is deeply changed by the experience and by having known Timothy. Minor flaws—flatness of background characters, predictable ending in

which Phillip plans to return to the cay—are dwarfed by the fully realized setting, the artful, unobtrusive use of dialect, the impact of Timothy. However, the book's essential value lies, not in the obvious themes of maturing or racism, but in the representation of a hauntingly deep love, the poignancy of which is rarely achieved in children's literature.

> *Marilyn Singer, in a review of "The Cay," in* School Library Journal, *Vol. 16, No. 1, September, 1969, p. 162.*

[*The following excerpt is from an essay by Binnie Tate, a librarian at the Los Angeles Public Library. Tate presents the comments of a joint committee of Los Angeles children's librarians—two black and two white—who met to evaluate children's books about the black experience.*]

The Cay by Theodore Taylor, highly praised as a book about interracial understanding, appears on many "Black Experience" lists. One committee member accepted this book as an "excellent survival story." Mr. Taylor fully depicts Philip's revulsion toward Timothy, describing him as old and ugly.

> His face couldn't have been blacker, or his teeth whiter. They made an alabaster trench in his mouth, and his pink-purple lips peeled back over them like the meat of a conch shell. He had a big welt, like a scar, on his left cheek. I knew he was West Indian. I had seen many of them in Willemstad, but he was the biggest one I'd ever seen.

This very real white reaction on Philip's part remains throughout the story as truth. Thus the author fails in his attempt to show Philip's growth in human understanding. Philip's *image* of Timothy remains unchanged, though he supposedly grieves for the man who gave his life for him. (*Edith White: "Timothy's dignity is apparent throughout, but nowhere is there an articulation that his background and culture were germane to his humaneness."*) The author's point of view posits complete acceptance of Timothy's servitude and Philip's condescension. Upon returning to his community and regaining his eyesight, Philip spends a lot of time talking to the black people. Philip states:

> I liked the sound of their voices. Some of them had known old Timothy of Amalie, I felt close to them.

This is the extent of his racial appreciation. This is typical of the books which supposedly show racial understanding.

The black people Philip talked with still had full lips and flat noses. If judged by the aesthetic standards the boy Philip had applied to Timothy, they apparently remained ugly and inferior. (*Tate: "How can this book be acclaimed as an outstanding novel of interracial understanding? Can racial understanding really be so separate from racial appreciation?"*) (p.98)

> *Binnie Tate, "In House and Out House," in* School Library Journal, *Vol. 17, No. 2, October, 1970, pp. 97-100.*

The point of **The Cay** is firmly, almost remorselessly

pressed home and those who prefer to interpret allegory for themselves will find the tone of the book irritating. The best way to approach it is to accept the author's deliberate use of fiction to make one more statement of a stringent problem. Researching on the German submarine attacks in the Caribbean in World War II, he found an account of a Dutch vessel sunk on the way to Panama, with a small boy surviving on a raft. He writes:

> I . . . wondered what might have happened had an adult been with him, a man of the sea, perhaps one with primal instinct.

> So the boy became Phillip Enright, and the old man was Timothy. I blinded Phillip because I wanted him to live in a colourless world. It was not enough for him to leave the island with survival knowledge. Our country may be threatened with complete civil war over race relations. Only the new generations can straighten out this problem. So I wanted young readers to understand that colour is simply a matter of vision in its basic form.

It is perhaps the fault of pressure from publishers and teachers, anxious to *use* books to convey attitudes, that the point is made so unsubtly throughout the story. The book has an appealing Crusoe flavour in the descriptions of how the old negro fishes for langosta, makes a palm-leaf shelter and helps the boy, blinded by a blow, to find his way about and fend for himself. As slowly as the old man's arrangements for survival take shape, Phillip's state of mind changes; where he has recoiled from the coloured man because of his mother's prejudice, he gradually realises how much he depends on the strength and wisdom of someone whose colour is irrelevant. The inevitable ending is tactfully contrived. It only seems a pity that the author's point, which is so important to him, should not have been allowed to *become* important to young readers through their attentive reading.

> *Margery Fisher, in a review of "The Cay," in* Growing Point, *Vol. 9, No. 7, January, 1971, p. 1669.*

Most of the story of **The Cay** takes place on a small, Caribbean island (a cay) over thirty years ago. Here, the author sets up his thesis which is supposed to show the gradual enlightenment of the white, eleven-year-old, racist Phillip. (Islands are very popular for fictional experiments because writers can isolate the factors they wish to deal with.) On this one, Phillip and Timothy, an elderly West Indian, are stranded. We can look at each in turn, to see what happens. Phillip Enright is established as a racist at the beginning. He's repelled by the smell, the appearance and the touch of Timothy. However, he's very dependent upon the experienced seaman for survival and becomes even more so when he goes blind. This is symbolic because the most important aspect of his blindness is that he's colour blind. The reader is clearly meant to date his conversion from this point. As for Timothy, we first meet him as an 'ugly' 'Negro', who's afterwards referred to as a 'black man'. Later we learn from him his first name, which, he says, is the only name he has. A master-servant relationship is immediately set up when the two meet, Timothy calling Phillip 'young bahss'. Later, Phillip asks Timothy to call him

by his first name. Eventually, according to the old literary cliché, found in race, class and sex contexts in about that order of frequency, the 'inferior' gives her/his life for the 'superior': Timothy, in a storm, sacrifices his life protecting Phillip. The author doesn't make very much of his death and this, together with the fact that, unlike Phillip, he doesn't seem to have relatives or friends anywhere, or if he does they don't matter, again gives a sort of isolated, fish-tank effect. At the end we're expected to believe that Phillip is a changed character but it obviously doesn't go very deep.

> *Bob Dixon, "Racism; All Things White and Beautiful: 'The Cay'," in his* Catching Them Young 1: Sex, Race and Class in Children's Fiction, *Pluto Press, 1977, p. 115.*

[*The Cay*] is both a war survival story and one of overcoming prejudice. After the Germans torpedoed the freighter on which Phillip and his mother were traveling from wartime Curaçao to the U.S., Phillip finds himself cast up on a barren little Caribbean Island with an old black man named Timothy. A blow on the head during the wreck had left Phillip blind and completely dependent upon Timothy. Born in Virginia of Southern parents, Phillip was prejudiced toward blacks. Timothy, who has been criticized for being an "Uncle Tom," probably really was one. . . . Both Phillip and Timothy are products and prisoners of their backgrounds. Gradually, Phillip begins to understand and trust the wisdom and selflessness of Timothy. His way of overcoming his prejudice is to make Timothy white in his mind. . . . And following the hurricane in which Timothy bears the brunt of the storm while protecting him, Phillip has to live without him, for Timothy dies. . . . This story of a color-conscious white boy and a self-sacrificing black was not meant to provide a model for today's living; what it does do is present a realistic account of a survival story in the Caribbean in 1942. Similar to *Edge of Two Worlds* by Jones and *Cross-Fire* by Graham, this book suggests human interdependence in time of crisis. It is one of the few stories that details the gradual loss of prejudice. (pp. 509-10)

> *Charlotte S. Huck and Doris Young Kuhn, "Books for Special Interest: 'The Cay'," in their* Children's Literature in the Elementary School, *third edition, Holt, Rinehart and Winston, Inc., 1979, pp. 509-10.*

[*The Cay*] is easily accessible on the printed page to most of the ability range. A portion of a typical page goes like this:

> To the south, the beach sloped gradually out into the water. On the north-side, it was different. There were submerged coral reefs and great shelves. The water became deep very abruptly. Timothy warned against going into the water here because the sharks could swim close to the shore.

Phillip's situation is a classic childhood fantasy, but with two important variants: his outwardly unattractive companion, and his blindness. Blindness at least figures in children's "let's pretend" games, and benign dependability may, for many children, more often be associated with adults of grandparental than parental age. The story's movement towards guided self-reliance is appealing.

The prelude to the "castaway" story, though it occupies only eighteen pages, seems longer and presents questions about how it should be dealt with. Nevertheless, its difficulties enhance the pleasure of release which is afforded by the real disaster and the ensuing crises, and its motif—parental disharmony that comes short of causing Phillip acute unhappiness but which is sufficient to disturb his trust in adults—is perhaps close to most children's experience and is certainly a foil to Phillip's relationship with Timothy on the raft and on the cay. In this relationship lies the appeal of the story and its success as a class-reader.

> From what I could feel and hear, our cay seemed
> a lovely island, and I wished I could see it.

Timothy, whom Phillip had found somewhat intimidating and repellent before he lost his sight, offers him "vision," not only by telling him what things look like, but also by making him develop confidence in his other senses. This subtext to the adventure yarn is quietly impressive, and it extends the book's scope for a mixed-ability class. Much of *The Cay* must be read aloud for full value, particularly because of Timothy's voice and idiom, in which Phillip comes to delight. (pp. 125-26)

> *Stephen Wicks, in a review of "The Cay," in* Children's literature in education, *Vol. 11, No. 3, Autumn, 1980, pp. 124-26.*

Air Raid—Pearl Harbor! The Story of December 7, 1941 (1971)

Unlike Walter Lord's older *Day of Infamy* (1957), this present tense recreation conveys the whys and the hows as well as the moment-to-moment events of the Japanese attack and American response. Informing the particulars of battle here are behind-the-scenes episodes of spying and code-breaking, disingenuous (on both sides) negotiating, and dove-and hawk jousting in Tokyo and Washington. Japanese leaders appear as individuals of varying personalities and persuasions; American decisions betray poor intelligence, poor communication, and an incredible disregard (ascending with rank) for more and more telling evidence; even the approaching bombers, reported by radar observers, are dismissed by their officers as undoubtedly our own planes on maneuvers. Despite an overlush opening picture of tranquil pre-war Hawaii and a superfluous closing eulogy for heroes and scapegoats, readers will remain alert.

> *A review of "Air Raid—Pearl Harbor! The Story of December 7, 1941," in* Kirkus Reviews, *Vol. XXXIX, No. 11, June 1, 1971, p. 598.*

With the scenarist's eye for the effective fadeout, closeup and symbolic detail, Theodore Taylor has presented a vividly credible account of the attack on Pearl Harbor. Like John Toland, in his brilliant *The Rising Sun,* Mr. Taylor has made extensive use of Japanese records and interviews with Japanese survivors which lend his work laudable objectivity. He has dutifully recognized the legitimate inter-

ests of America in the Pacific and the efforts of informed Orientalists like Ambassador Joseph C. Grew to assure peace. But he recognizes no national barriers to truth: Japan's determination to free Asia from what we must admit *was* white Western domination; her desperate need for food and raw materials to feed, clothe and house a nation of 80 million crammed onto home islands smaller, in their sum, than the state of California; her fury over America's and Britain's freezing of her economic assets, and her final decision to repay Commodore Perry's 19th-century gunboat diplomacy in spades. Taylor presents it all with arresting candor.

From the arrival of the Japanese spy ship Taiya Maru at Pearl Harbor in November, 1941, through the unbelievable bureaucratic blunders and diplomatic hypocrisy—on both sides—that led to the holocaust, Taylor's book moves from irony to suspense at a relentless pace. F.D.R.'s statesmanlike last-minute appeal to Hirohito is delayed by hours in the mailing. Gen. George Marshall's eleventh-hour alert—to Pearl Harbor—is sent not by high-speed Navy radio, but by commercial cable, delivered hours after the bombs cripple the Pacific Fleet. Taylor notes that a Japanese destroyer, in a telling irony, is named "Kasumi," or "Mist of Flowers." When the signal for takeoff for Pearl Harbor is given, we are aboard the Japanese flagship itself, as the suicide pilots of the Emperor are anointed with perfume and don the samurai headband. We are with command pilot Mitsuo Fuchida over Pearl Harbor as he gives the order to attack. And we are on the ground, amid the first incredulous cries, as the Arizona snaps in two, taking 1,500 men, in a split second, to the bottom. It is a masterful narrative.

I wish Mr. Taylor had resisted the temptation to assess "blame" for the tragedy. Surely there are too many missing documents, too many rather obvious questions neither asked nor answered. He correctly observes that "Too many, from President Roosevelt on down, were deeply involved in bad judgment and gross negligence." Certainly, too, Admiral Kimmel and General Short the commanders at Pearl Harbor, should have been informed that the Japanese code had been broken and apprised of the intelligence thus gained, nor should they have been made scapegoats. But it is preposterous to quote what Mr. Taylor calls "harsher judgments" that F.D.R. "welcomed the attack because it permitted entry into World War II, a step that even his most ardent critics acknowledge as inevitable." I find it difficult to accept the fact that *any* American President would "welcome" the death of 2,500 of his defenseless countrymen and almost 1,200 wounded.

But perhaps Mr. Taylor cannot really be faulted for entering a "blame" game that has staggered lifelong scholars in the field. His achievement in any case, transcends partisan controversy. He is right on target in reminding us of perhaps the greatest lesson of December 7, 1941: the high cost of our failure to respect a proud and burgeoning nation with legitimate interests and aspirations, with traditions as sacred to its people as America's were to Americans. "To most people," in 1941, Taylor writes, Japan was "a place whose inhabitants make cheap toys and have large front teeth and bad eyesight. They can't pronounce l's, and they say 'prease' instead of 'please.' It [was] a silly, funny place, with kimonos and paper houses, where the people copy articles of merchandise made in the United States or England, and always take off their wooden clogs before entering a home." It was a stereotype that America could ill-afford then, and dare not afford, of any nation, now.

> *William Sullivan, in a review of "Air Raid—Pearl Harbor! The Story of December 7, 1941," in* The New York Times Book Review, *July 11, 1971, p. 8.*

Theodore Taylor spent over a year doing research for a film on Pearl Harbor, visiting Japan and interviewing some of the participants. Gathering momentum in the best suspense-story style, his narrative shuttles between the Japanese plans, the diplomatic and military snarls in Washington, and the composure of the command at Pearl Harbor as it progresses chronologically toward the 7th of December, 1941. Despite imputations of negligence and many instances of error, the fact that Pearl Harbor came as a surprise clearly indicates that it was too complicated an event to assign blame. Vividly written, this combines the values of a documentary with the excitement of a cliff-hanger.

> *Zena Sutherland, in a review of "Air Raid—Pearl Harbor!" in* The Saturday Review, *New York, Vol. LIV, No. 34, August 21, 1971, p. 27.*

[*The following excerpts are from reviews of the revised edition published in 1991.*]

An old standard of the World War II genre makes a new appearance with a slight face-lift. Taylor has revised his account of the attack on Pearl Harbor by basically rewriting the first chapter and changing the entire volume from the present tense to a much easier-to-read past tense. . . . The text gives an in-depth look at the conditions of the time, allowing readers to better understand why this event took place. A listing of the key figures and an author's note are appended. Libraries that do not have the original title should give definite consideration to this one.

> *Eldon Younce, in a review of "Air Raid—Pearl Harbor: The Story of December 7, 1941," in* School Library Journal, *Vol. 37, No. 12, December, 1991, p. 130.*

Taylor's Note at the end of the book gives examples of new sources he has used to update his 1971 nonfiction account of the Japanese attack on Pearl Harbor. This year is the fiftieth anniversary of the attack, and it seems appropriate for a revised version of the book to appear. Although Taylor does not create dialogue for his characters, he does give them characteristics which make them seem more real. For instance, Fuchida was given a headband before he left on his attack plane which "meant that the warrior was ready to die for his country. Tears in his eyes, Fuchida tied it on, and then climbed into his cockpit." "Admiral Yamamota displayed no emotion but asked that the time of attack be carefully checked." This technique successfully draws the reader into the action of the book.

As readers of a documented event such as this, we are challenged to read magazine and newspaper accounts of the time, view movies depicting the event, interview people who were living then, and compare other accounts with this one. It would seem the relations with the Japanese at that time can serve young readers with insights into the world of diplomacy, what is said compared to what was meant by what was said. Instead of just being an account of dramatic events of the past, this book will raise questions about why things happened as they did and if events such as this could still occur.

> *Ruth Cline, in a review of "Air Raid—Pearl Harbor! The Story of December 7, 1941," in* Voice of Youth Advocates, *Vol. 14, No. 6, February, 1992, p. 401.*

The Children's War (1971)

Average historical fiction set on an imaginary Alaskan island at the beginning of World War II, the same period treated in Taylor's superior *The Cay.* Twelve-year-old Dory's father is a Navy radioman, his mother an innocuous hausfrau. Dory befriends old Bakutan, the mysterious local hunter/hermit, goes hunting with the wolf pup and gun he has received for his birthday, and puts up with his spinsterish new teacher who quietly remains a pacifist, even after Pearl Harbor. The story picks up in the final third of the book when the Japanese invade the island and imprison all the men on a neighboring island. Dory and a young friend, Charlotte, guide an Army commando to the prison island, and, for unexplained reasons, the teacher ultimately dies along with the commando in a successful rescue of the prisoners. Though the final section of the book is an exciting, mature presentation of a life-and-death endeavor, the routine characterizations and the slow unfolding of Dory's life on the sparsely populated island will cause reader interest to lag long before the action starts.

> *Margaret A. Dorsey, in a review of "The Children's War," in* School Library Journal, *Vol. 18, No. 4, December, 1971, p. 67.*

Taut, terse novel about 12-year-old Dory Scofield in the Japanese occupation of the Aleutians in 1942. The narrative centers on emotions felt and bonds made and severed; the boy loses his teacher, his zeal for weapons, his childhood. The strongest element is his relationship with an old taciturn Eskimo hunter whom he idolizes, yet in one of several heartbreaking scenes calls, "coward." Like the bond between Phillip and an old West Indian, Timothy, in *The Cay,* the author's previous novel, this friendship is achieved between two cultures and two age levels.

> *A review of "The Children's War," in* The New York Times Book Review, *January 9, 1972, p. 8.*

Dory Scofield loved the Alaskan wilderness where he could hunt and roam freely, and was far from delighted when a school opened in their small town. He resented the teacher, and she knew it. When World War II started, the community was apprehensive, because there was a naval station just off shore. The story flares into action when a paratrooper shows up to scout the station after it has been taken over by the Japanese. Dory, excited and patriotic, wants to help and does, but it is the quiet teacher, whose anti-war sentiments have annoyed him, that risks—and loses—her life to help the paratrooper. The setting is interesting, the characters well-drawn, and the plot strong; it is, however, Dory's change from unthinking ardor to a sober realization of the horror of war that gives the book substance. (pp. 98-9)

> *Zena Sutherland, in a review of "The Children's War," in* Bulletin of the Center for Children's Books, *Vol. 25, No. 6, February, 1972, pp. 98-9.*

The Maldonado Miracle (1973)

His father had already gone to the United States, leaving Jose Maldonado in Mexico and arranging for his illegal entry into the country. Twelve years old, Jose worked at crop-picking until the unwelcome advances of an *americano* man drove him to run off. Injured while attempting to hide, Jose took refuge in a choir loft. And that was how the "miracle" took place, for the blood that dripped down fell on the statue of Christ, and the word spread. Although the focus shifts from Jose to the priest, Father Lebeon, the story holds up well; the priest is a strong character, a man of integrity who doubts the "miracle of San Ramon" that his credulous parishioners and townspeople eager for publicity embrace. Jose, knowing that he can clarify the situation, confesses the truth to Father Lebeon, who is grateful and who helps the boy convince his father that he should go back to Mexico. The treatment of the priest's struggle with his own conscience and of the cupidity of the townspeople is almost at an adult level; Taylor does not write down to his readers. It does weaken the book as an entity to have the shift of emphasis, but the two elements are brought together periodically, and the ending is strong: most books about Mexican migrant workers assume that it is preferable to be in the United States. (pp. 178-79)

> *Zena Sutherland, in a review of "The Maldonado Miracle," in* Bulletin of the Center for Children's Books, *Vol. 26, No. 11, July-August, 1973, pp. 178-79.*

Taylor realistically depicts the plight of migrant workers whose dreams of a better life compel them to resort to illegal means of entering the U.S. and make them prey to the greedy and unscrupulous of both races. However, the episode of the blood-stained cross, with its implication of Mexican credulity and superstition, may prove offensive. (pp.75-6)

> *Ruth Robinson, a review of "The Maldonado Miracle," in* School Library Journal, *Vol. 20, No. 1, September, 1973, pp. 75-6.*

Like all Theodore Taylor's books, [**The Maldonado Miracle**] has a strong, overt message and the characters are chosen and developed to illustrate certain aspects of modern life. Nor does the laconic, almost brusque prose-style encourage any real probing into José's character. It is all

the more remarkable that he does stand out as an individual. The boy who nerved himself to refuse to travel without his dog has the courage it takes to change the plans of a lifetime. Faced with the complexity, the makeshift consolations of the civilized world, he takes the hardest step and the one that he knows is best for him in the long run.

> *Margery Fisher, "Jose Maldonado," in her* Who's Who in Children's Books: A Treasury of the Familiar Characters of Childhood, *Holt, Rinehart and Winston, 1975, p. 162.*

[**The Maldonado Miracle,** is the] story of a twelve-year-old Mexican boy who entered the U.S. illegally to work in the fields. It concludes with an interesting incident at a church, that many believed was a miracle. The author insists in comparing life in the U.S. and Mexico from a purely materialistic point of view: Jose's father " . . . talked about the wonderful things he'd seen in California . . . He'd talked on about having running water, an indoor toilet, electricity, a TV set, a motorbike; maybe even a car". The author also denies any feelings of pride or self-respect to Mexican people: "He told him everything except the fact that he now thought he'd like to have white skin and red hair like Miguel. Speak English and live in a house like that". And, "Giron wore slacks, a yellow jumper, and expensive-looking shoes. Jose was proud to be with him. He looked more 'Americano' than Mexican." (pp. 58-9)

> *Isabel Schon, "Lifestyles: 'The Maldonado Miracle'," in her* A Bicultural Heritage: Themes for the Exploration of Mexican and Mexican-American Culture in Books for Children and Adolescents, *The Scarecrow Press, Inc., 1978, pp. 58-9.*

Rebellion Town: Williamsburg, 1776 (1973)

Taylor spotlights pre-Revolutionary Williamsburg rather in the manner of Phelan's successful present tense reconstructions of highlights of American history, but with somewhat less drama and immediacy as he covers a time span of eleven years and frequently switches, like a nervous camera, from Williamsburg to Philadelphia or Boston (though at other times, anchored in Williamsburg, we feel cut off from the main action), and there is no one central event to unify the pieces. However, the closeup shots of debates and confrontations bring home the significant role of a number of now illustrious Virginians in the early struggle for independence, and the unfolding career of Patrick Henry—bursting in with his maiden speech in the opening episode, providing highly charged radical leadership through the first years, ousted by rivals from the defiant colony's rebel army, occasionally veering toward conservatism as the Revolution gets under way—gives the snowballing movement a human focus.

> *A review of "Rebellion Town: Williamsburg, 1776," in* Kirkus Reviews, *Vol. XVI, No. 23, December 1, 1973, p. 1313.*

Taylor effectively involves readers in a momentous year in Virginia's history—May, 1775 to July, 1776. The people and events which propelled Virginia to independence are accurately and interestingly described. Taylor's skillful narrative and delineation of significant figures (especially Patrick Henry) create suspenseful, fast reading history. Attractively illustrated [by Richard Cuffari] with line drawings, this will have special appeal for Williamsburg buffs and for people planning a visit to colonial Virginia landmarks. A good bibliography and an excellent index are also included. (pp. 111-12)

> *Judith M. Olsen, in a review of "Rebellion Town: Williamsburg, 1776," in* School Library Journal, *Vol. 20, No. 7, March, 1974, pp. 111-12.*

In a carefully researched book that follows the developing resentment and protest against British rule as it was evidenced in Williamsburg, Taylor gives a logical picture of the move toward independence. While the text is not cohesive, there are some moments of drama and a vivid picture of Patrick Henry as he develops from a rustic figure with a gift for oratory to a seasoned legislator who becomes the first governor of the state of Virginia. The book also makes clear how much of our Declaration of Independence (and other, similar documents in other countries) was based on the work of George Mason, whose Declaration of Rights for the Virginia colony was adapted by Thomas Jefferson.

> *Zena Sutherland, in a review of "Rebellion Town: Williamsburg, 1776," in* Bulletin of the Center for Children's Books, *Vol. 27, No. 9, May, 1974, p. 151.*

Teetoncey (1974)

Teetoncey is the North Carolina Banks people's word for little and that's what they name the frail blond girl of ten or eleven who, as sole survivor of an 1898 shipwreck, is washed ashore on "The Graveyard of the Atlantic" and found by Ben, twelve or so, who lives alone with his mother, a sea widow who tried until he was five to raise him as a girl so he wouldn't meet the common fate of the island's male population. Tee is near death and takes a few days to come to; even then she is mute and Ben resents the attention his mother lavishes on this creature the doctor says will probably remain a "vegetable." But he too grows to care for her and at last, one stormy night when Tee is notably restless, Ben's mother forces him to take Tee to the shore where she relives the experience and regains her memory and speech. This prescription ending is a bringdown when we've been prepared for drama and astonishment, but as usual Taylor has the scene and the accents right (the unique landscape, speech and culture of the Outer Banks is intriguing in itself) and his usual skilled handling of an unpromising outline makes it possible to share Ben's involvement with the castaway.

> *A review of "Teetoncey," in* Kirkus Reviews, *Vol. XLII, No. 14, July 15, 1974, p. 744.*

Teetoncey, a dialect word for a simpleton, is the sobriquet given to the nameless heroine of Taylor's latest sea saga. . . . The prologue, which reveals the girl's identity, robs the story of some of its mystery, and there is a dis-

tracting subplot which involves the death of Ben's father during a rescue at sea years before. The island people are well drawn, especially Rachel, the embittered widow, and Ben, who is reluctant to be saddled with the strange girl. However, the situation has been done before, and the thrilling sea rescues and poetic descriptions of island life do not raise this above the level of a "who-is-she?" amnesia story. (pp. 121-22)

> *Roberta Rogow, in a review of "Teetoncey," in* School Library Journal, *Vol. 21, No. 2, October, 1974, pp. 121-22.*

The sea provides much, but exacts high tribute for its provision. While it may look fair and gentle, it is quietly, constantly wearing away the sand and rock. During a storm the sea becomes monstrous—destroying without selection. Men who depend on the sea learn to watch it with respect and suspicion. But there are always the few who are born hearing its siren call, like 11-year-old Ben O'Neal in Theodore Taylor's story set on the Outer Banks of North Carolina 75 years ago. Stumbling into adolescence, Ben wants only to become a seaman. His widowed mother resents the sea for having taken her husband and two other sons [the second of whom went to the Caribean] and fights to keep her last son at home. But then on the beach after a hurricane, Ben rescues Teetoncey, a half-drowned castaway who has suffered loss of memory. The girl eventually becomes the key that unlocks Rachel's pride, enabling her to accept the reality of her husband's death. Teetoncey's presence also help Ben learn to accept his mother's feelings.

In an earlier story, **The Cay,** Mr. Taylor threw readers into the jaws of a hurricane in the Caribbean. In this one we experience two furious Atlantic gales that turn the sea so savage that ships are snapped apart as if they were matchsticks, and the cries of the human sacrifices are lost in the screaming wind and waves. Taylor has us walking the beaches, smelling the salt air and watching the sky for storm signals.

> *Nancy Berkowitz, in a review of "Teetoncey," in* The New York Times Book Review, *October 6, 1974, p. 8.*

Teetoncey and Ben O'Neal (1975)

The second volume in the projected Outer Banks trilogy focuses on the developing relationship between Ben O'Neal and Wendy Lynn Appleton, the girl called *Teetoncey,* sole survivor of the shipwreck in which her parents had perished. In contrast to its predecessor which was told from the standpoint of an omniscient author, the sequel is narrated by Ben reminiscing about the fateful weeks following Teetoncey's recovery of her memory and her reassumption of her identity as a gently bred, well-educated English girl. Like his father and brothers, Ben dreamed of escaping the monotonous confines of the banks to find adventure as a sailor. Prevented from pursuing his dreams by his mother's animosity toward the sea which had claimed both her husband and one of her sons, he sees Teetoncey's coming as a means of escaping his mother—for Rachel O'Neal becomes deeply attached to the orphaned girl and schemes to circumvent her return to England. Teetoncey acquiesces in the plot only too willingly for, as Ben discovers, in the submerged wreck of the ill-fated *Malta Empress* lies a fortune in silver bullion which she hopes to recover. Ben's initial resentment of the girl's growing influence in his mother's life turns gradually to grudging respect and ultimately to affection as they work to find the treasure. Filled with local color and laced with regional expressions, homespun humor, and superstitions, the story evokes the chancy existence at the turn-of-the-century of the sturdy, weather-tuned residents of the Carolina Shoals.

> *Mary M. Burns, in a review of "Teetoncey and Ben O'Neal," in* The Horn Book Magazine, *Vol. LI, No. 6, December, 1975, p. 596.*

Battle in the Arctic Seas: The Story of Convoy PQ 17 (1976)

Convoy PQ 17, a ragtag assortment of converted merchant vessels with an ineffective naval escort assigned to deliver lend-lease arms to Russia in 1942, introduces us to a different brand of heroism from that of Shapiro's *Screaming Eagles*. Much in the manner of his ***Air Raid— Pearl Harbor!*** Taylor splices together a documentary overview of tangled communications, faulty intelligence, and cold-blooded risk-cutting: in the mistaken belief that the German battleship *Tirpitz* was in the area, naval brass ordered the convoy scattered, allowing the helpless tubs to be picked off by enemy bombs and torpedos. Some crews went down fighting while others decided to "sit out" the war in isolated harbors. Taylor zeros in on the unprepossessing courage of Ensign Carroway, a newly mustered South Carolinian who referred to himself (in a diary excerpted here) as the "Great American Chicken," stepped forward to volunteer for a commando raid against a Nazi-held radio station, and was hugely relieved to find that the Russians had done the job for him. The saga explains why SNAFU became a useful addition to military vocabularies, and with the rhetoric of invincibility stripped away, the individual dramas of men like Ensign Carroway take on a significance that a whole platoon of *Screaming Eagles* couldn't claim.

> *A review of "Battle in the Arctic Seas," in* Kirkus Reviews, *Vol. XLIV, No. 18, September 15, 1976, p. 1048.*

Using diary excerpts and present-tense narrative, Taylor sets the scene and charts the converging events that influenced Allied commanders in their decision to abandon protective measures for the convoy. The order for them to "scatter" ensured German attack, and when it came the results were disastrous: Taylor records that never in contemporary military history did a convoy lose as many ships as PQ 17. Reportage of this "bitter military lesson" is succinct yet many-sided; an instructive close-up for the World War II section of your history shelf. (p. 671).

> *Denise M. Wilms, in a review of "Battle in the Arctic Seas: The Story of Convoy PQ 17," in* Booklist, *Vol. 73, No. 9, January 1, 1977, pp. 670-71.*

An engrossing account of a naval disaster of World War II is based on careful research and told with a high sense of drama, its somber events given relief by the diary excerpts of one young officer. The United States, Russia, and Great Britain were joined in a massive effort to deliver much-needed supplies to Russia; the convoy sailed from Iceland with seven million dollars' worth of cargo on a motley collection of ships protected by escort vessels. Some of the chapters are based on German source materials, so that the reader can see the plotting and counterplotting as each of the combatants tries to outdo the other in gathering intelligence and predicting next moves. (pp. 98-9)

> *Zena Sutherland, in a review of "Battle in the Arctic Seas: The Story of Convoy PQ 17," in* Bulletin of the Center for Children's Books, *Vol. 30, No. 6, February, 1977, pp. 98-9.*

The Odyssey of Ben O'Neal (1977)

The final title in Taylor's Cape Hatteras Trilogy *Odyssey . . .* is made in the enjoyable company of realistic and convincing characters. To deliver the news of his mother's death to his older brother, Ben O'Neal, protagonist of ***Teetoncey*** and ***Teetoncey and Ben O'Neal,*** leaves home and signs aboard one of the remaining sailing ships working the South Atlantic Coast in 1899. Of course, the appealing heroine, Teetoncey, reappears in Ben's life as a refugee from the British consul's wrath. Full of wit and wise observations, this historical adventure offers an affectionate, but not nostalgic, glance back to the close of the 19th Century when the sea-faring way of life was beginning to disappear and modern industrialization to take over in America.

> *Michael T. Carollo, in a review of "The Odyssey of Ben O'Neal," in* School Library Journal, *Vol. 23, No. 5, January, 1977, p. 106.*

In the concluding volume of the Cape Hatteras trilogy about Ben O'Neal and Teetoncey, Ben started out as a true innocent in a surprising new world. When he went away to sea after the death of his mother, he was excited and awed by trains, cars, trolleys, and the enormous metropolis of Norfolk, Virginia. Only stubborn determination gave him the courage to apply for the job of steward's boy on the *Christine Conyers,* a square-rigged sailing ship with a fierce captain and a slave driver of a bosun. Ben has another problem, too: He thought the castaway Teetoncey, with her dog Boo, was safely on her way home to London. But he found her hiding at Norfolk because she was refused permission to take the dog home. To his dismay, Teetoncey sailed as a passenger on the *Christine Conyers,* and many machinations were required to extract her from the long arm of the law. Ben concluded, "the lesson to be learned . . . was that you did not pick on female orphans, rich or poor, nor their dogs" and he finally was able to escort her and Boo safely to England. One misses in this volume the sterling, rough-hewn characters of the inhabitants of the Outer Banks. Ben's stubborn honor and homespun goodness are credible, and Teetoncey's wily pursuit of Ben and ability to get what she wants are beguiling. A brief epilogue tells that the two eventually married and returned to the Banks to live. The saga of Ben's experiences at sea is enriched with authentic nautical detail and many humorous episodes; it is an interesting picture of the last days of sail and the emergence of steam.

Ann A. Flowers, in a review of "The Odyssey of Ben O'Neal," in The Horn Book Magazine, *Vol. LIII, No. 3, June, 1977, p. 318.*

The last volume in Taylor's Hatteras Banks triology is the least satisfying, partially because earlier installments involved the reader in the emotional growth of both Ben and Teetoncey through their weathering of crises; this functions only on the level of an adventure story, and an uneven one at that. . . . Taylor is a good prose stylist—but here a weak storyteller. Descriptive passages of the shipping world initially create a vivid sense of mood, time, and place but later slow the pace of unfolding events. In terms of character, Tee is a capable, determined sort. Ben's avowal that "That girl needs someone to look out for her all the way" is belied by her independent behavior; casting him as her protector on a London voyage thus seems patronizing in spite of his budding romantic attachment to her.

Denise M. Wilms, in a review of "The Odyssey of Ben O'Neal," in Booklist, *Vol. 73, No. 19, June 1, 1977, p. 1504.*

A Shepherd Watches, A Shepherd Sings (with Louis Irigaray, 1977)

No one who has dined at any one of the many Basque hotels in western America is likely to forget its family-style service its savory, rich soups, its rich, redolent main dishes of simmered meat, beans, and vegetables. Nor will he have failed to notice those who appear to be the hotel regulars, the Basque shepherds on leave, or looking for work, some of them newly arrived from the Basque provinces of Spain and France. They have a special look about them, an aloofness that asserts indifference to the tourist outsiders; but they also wear an air of subdued confidence, which is often the mark of the resourceful, competent man. This book is their story, an "as told to" narrative rich in character and in detail so cleverly presented that the reader finds himself captivated by its people, its animals, who are much more than simple animals here, and by the demanding, often harsh yet beautiful California pasturelands above hot southern valleys.

Apart from the narrator as a most unusual and sensitive boy, the sheepherders at first appear to us much as they do in their clannish groups in their hotel dining rooms—aloof, taciturn, not much given to joy, fierce when fierceness is called for proud, honorable, sure of their place in this world. Yet the narrator and his writer manage, through suggestive understatement and the judicious use of anecdote, to let us see through the herders' private shells. We glimpse the depth of their loyalty and respect for themselves, their capacity for affection, their struggle against sentimental show. We feel keenly their loneliness, the insecurities, deprivations, and the risks in their job.

The book's title is deceptive, more suited to the dust cover for a recording by yet another folk singer riding the ethnic boom. Ignore the PR title. What we have here is a rich, strong, moving story of people we admire, people whose qualities we envy. Louis Irigaray and Theodore Taylor have produced a marvelous book, touched everywhere by Mr. Irigaray's natural, unpretentious reporting and remembrance. Though he is a principal in the narrative, appearing throughout, he almost always leaves the stage to others. Theodore Taylor too must be congratulated for his part in this work, especially for his skill in maintaining what we willingly accept as the authentic voice of a second-generation Basque boy growing up in the California sheep business. (pp. 212-13)

Robert V. Williams, in a review of "A Shepherd Watches, A Shepherd Sings," in Best Sellers, *Vol. 37, No. 7, October, 1977, pp. 212-13.*

The Battle off Midway Island (1981)

Theodore Taylor has provided readers of any age with a splendid picture of the naval battles that turned the Pacific War around. Wisely, he has chosen to include a description of the Battle of the Coral Sea, a preliminary to Midway. He has also devoted attention to two other aspects of the battle often ignored in longer books. One is the atmosphere in Japanese naval headquarters. The second is the feats of "Hypo," the Combat Intelligence Unit at Pearl Harbor.

Without some knowledge of how intelligence contributed to the Midway victory or about Adm. Isoroku Yamamoto and his overly optimistic, victory-hungry staff, the Midway story is incomplete.

The climax of the battle came at midmorning on June 4, 1942, when, after 35 of the 41 torpedo planes from the American carriers Hornet, Enterprise and Yorktown had been destroyed, the American bombers zeroed in on the Japanese carriers. Fortune favored the brave, and because the Japanese air cover was at a low altitude, where the planes would be better able to deal with another torpedo attack, the air above the carriers was relatively undefended.

At the moment of attack the Japanese carriers were particularly vulnerable. Gas lines were open on their decks, which, in addition, were strewn with instant-contact bombs intended for a strike on Midway itself. The American dive bombers dropped upon the carriers, and the Kaga and the Soryu were wracked by bomb blasts. Fires swept the decks. Unstored bombs exploded. The two carriers were out of the fight.

In this battle, as in all battles, luck played its part, and Mr. Taylor emphasizes that it was luck that enabled American pilots to spot a Japanese destroyer hurrying to rejoin the carriers. Following the destroyer, with their fuel almost exhausted, 33 dive bombers from Enterprise found the carriers and delivered their decisive attack.

The Akagi was the next to go. One bomb penetrated to the hangar below the flight deck, where it detonated loose bombs, creating an explosion that literally lifted the carrier out of the water. Another bomb burst on the flight deck, destroying the bomber and torpedo planes assembled there in preparation for a strike on the American carriers.

Shortly after noon the American carrier Yorktown was hit by three bombs. She came to a stop and later was abandoned.

By this time the Hiryu was the only Japanese carrier left in the battle. Her aircraft had done well against Yorktown, but nevertheless she was doomed. She was soon hit by four 1,000-pound bombs; torpedoes and bombs on her hangar deck began to explode. At nightfall the Pacific was lit by fires on the Akagi, Kaga, Hiryu and Soryu. Japanese naval supremacy in the Pacific was ended.

This is only an outline of the climax of the great battle, which Mr. Taylor describes so colorfully and skillfully. He does not strain for effect; he does not have to. His depiction of the men, the aircraft and the ships makes the action seem as vivid as it was that day when the Navy took its first step on the long road to victory. (pp. 54, 69)

> *Drew Middleton, "Winning in the Pacific," in* The New York Times Book Review, *November 15, 1981, pp. 54, 69.*

In a matter of 120 seconds on the morning of June 4, 1942, the course of the war in the Pacific was reversed. Unlike the attack on Pearl Harbor, where mistakes and slighted intelligence reports allowed the Japanese a surprise attack, the Battle of Midway was a carefully monitored success story for U.S. intelligence. Midway was an incredible victory for the U.S. Navy, and Taylor has written an engrossing account of the battle and the events that led up to it. His account compares favorably with Charles Mercer's *Miracle at Midway* (Putnam, 1977) and is more thorough than Ira Peck's *The Battle of Midway* (Scholastic, 1977). In spite of a slightly irritating use of the present tense by Taylor, the book should satisfy readers.

> *Therese Bigelow, in a review of "The Battle off Midway Island," in* School Library Journal, *Vol. 28, No. 9, May, 1982, p. 75.*

The Trouble with Tuck   (1981)

This sentimental story of a young golden Labrador retriever who loses his sight and learns to rely on a Seeing Eye dog will have built-in appeal to dog lovers. . . . The story's weaknesses include a set of parents too good to be true and some improbable situations, such as the California Companion Dogs for the Blind representative who is deeply affected by Tuck's plight. Taylor's practiced hand manages to steer the story through its soapier elements effectively enough. The fact that a real-life situation such as this did exist provides the story its needed steady base.

> *Denise M. Wilms, in a review of "The Trouble with Tuck," in* Booklist, *Vol. 78, No. 11, February 1, 1982, p. 709.*

[This story of a] California girl and her beautiful dog [is] destined for success. Totally lacking in the self-confidence exuded by her good-looking, carefree older brothers,

Helen was given a golden Labrador puppy by her parents. Her life and her attitudes underwent a visible change; but before he was three years old the dog began to go blind, and Helen was devastated. For months she stubbornly refused to heed the sensible advice of the veterinarian, and the family suffered with the girl, as confining the proud, magnificent animal for his own safety produced only frustrating and disastrous consequences. Helen at thirteen undertook—with ultimate success—the difficult, highly unusual task of training her now resentful and jealous pet to accept the companionship and the guidance of an experienced Seeing-Eye dog. Promotion people may glibly characterize the narrative as moving and heart-warming, but it must be added that Theodore Taylor is too skillful a writer to descend into sentimentality or melodrama.

> *Ethel L. Heins, in a review of "The Trouble with Tuck," in* The Horn Book Magazine, *Vol. LVIII, No. 2, April, 1982, p. 170.*

H. M. S. Hood vs. Bismarck: The Battleship Battle (1982)

Drawing on official records and survivors' accounts, Naval historian Taylor reconstructs the World War II encounter between England's super-dread nought and Nazi Germany's brand-new monster warship in May 1941. Hitler ordered Kapitan Lindemann to evade blockading British ships in the North Sea and to sink Atlantic convoys bringing supplies to England from America. En route, the *Bismarck* was met by *Hood* and an escorting cruiser. A lucky shot hit the *Hood*'s ammunition stores and the ship exploded and sank, with three survivors. Then Prime Minister Churchill himself directed a massive sea hunt, with every available British ship and plane tracking down and sinking the *Bismarck,* in three days. The author's narrative holds the excitement of suspense fiction as the story switches from ship to ship. In the end, the German captain is standing on the sinking prow of his ship, his hand raised in salute.

> *A review of "H. M. S. Hood vs. Bismarck: The Battleship Battle," in* Publishers Weekly, *Vol. 222, No. 3, July 16, 1982, p. 79.*

A veteran naval officer during World War II as well as a practiced author of books for young people follows up his depiction of the drama that took place on Midway Island in 1942 with a chronicle of the events that led to the sinking of the *Bismarck*. . . . Taylor's interpretation of the naval strategy of both sides is brief but vigorous, again featuring the use of present tense (with mixed results) as a device to involve readers more directly in the action. Teens who relished the first book and other World War II buffs—especially those who have followed the war at sea—won't want to miss this fast-paced version of the *Bismarck*'s last days at sea. Bibliography appended. To be indexed. Junior high and high school.

> *Stephanie Zvirin, in a review of "H. M. S. Hood vs. Bismarck: The Battleship Battle," in* Booklist, *Vol. 79, No. 3, October 1, 1982, p. 196.*

Taylor with his mother as a newly-commissioned ensign, USNR, in 1944.

The desperate five-day search for and attack on Germany's greatest battleship was one of the great confrontations of World War II. But despite the book title, the British battle cruiser H.M.S. *Hood,* sunk in four minutes in the first exchange of gunfire, was not the chief participant in the battle. Rather, it was a number of smaller ships and aircraft, struggling against weather, communications difficulties and human errors that finally triumphed over the *Bismarck.* Taylor's moment-by-moment story of the battle is so detailed as to be monotonous. The attempt to give immediacy to the account by using the present tense throughout the book leads to confusion since the events, in the spring of 1941, are past history. Also, there is little attempt to place the naval battle in the overall strategy of the war or to explain, in view of current military capabilities, the limits of World War II weapons. While Taylor's research is evident and admirable, William L. Shirer's *The Sinking of the Bismarck* is more readable, more dramatic and still to be recommended.

> *Shirley Wilton, in a review of "H. M. S. Hood vs. Bismarck: The Battleship Battle," in* School Library Journal, *Vol. 29, No. 3, November, 1982, p. 104.*

Battle in the English Channel (1983)

Another in Taylor's series of books on great sea battles of WW II keeps up with its predecessors in terms of vibrancy and detail. The use of present tense again increases the im-

mediacy of the historical replay, which begins with background and goes on to events surrounding the passage of three of Hitler's major battleships through the English Channel, right under the noses of the British. Taylor's main focus is on German forces as they prepare to confront their enemy, but he also introduces principal British participants in what turned out to be one of the more embarrassing, unfortunate disasters of British naval history. Fascinating and fast-paced stuff that naval-history devotees and WW II buffs will relish. . . . Bibliography and index appended. (pp. 231-32)

> *Stephanie Zvirin, in a review of "Battle in the English Channel," in* Booklist *Vol. 80 No. 3, October 1, 1983, pp. 231-32.*

In 1588 the Spanish Armada was defeated when it sailed into the English Channel; in 1942 a less numerous gathering of enemy ships succeeded in eluding both the Royal Navy and Royal Air Force while en route from France to safe harbor in German waters. The general reaction to this feat was reflected in the London *Times* comment that "nothing more mortifying to the pride of sea power has happened in home waters since the seventeenth century." The humiliating episode is the subject of a skillfully honed documentary written in a journalistic style by a former naval officer, author of ***The Cay*** and the Teetoncey series. Beginning in September 1941 with Grand Admiral Erich Raeder's visit to Adolf Hitler, the book re-creates the circumstances which led to the planning, execution, and successful completion of the daring maneuver and concludes with a brief assessment of its effects, both immediate and long range, on the course of World War II. The conclusion of the book states its central theme: "Operation Fuller failed because of the command structure and not from lack of individual effort on the part of those who had to go out and fight." In the course of his report, to reinforce his thesis the author has included several poignant vignettes of brave men who, knowing how slim were the chances for survival, still flew their missions. And while his attitude toward the incompetent is clear, his admiration for those who exemplified gentlemanly virtues—whether British or German—is equally apparent. Concise, fluent, fast-paced, the book evidences a combination of content and format which appeals to a wide audience.

> *Mary M. Burns, in a review of "Battle in the English Channel," in* The Horn Book Magazine, *Vol. LX, No. 1, February, 1984. p. 79.*

In February, 1942, Hitler launched Operation "Cerberus"—a surprise escape by the German battleships *Gneisenau* and *Scharnhorst* and the heavy cruiser *Prinz Eugen* from Brest up the English Channel on to Germany "right under the nose of the British." The account is well documented and includes a bibliography and an index. However, the map showing the path of the German ships is difficult to read and the black-and-white drawings add nothing to the story. (pp. 127-28)

> *Civia M. Tuteur, in a review of "Battle in the English Channel," in* School Library Journal, *Vol. 30, No. 8, April, 1984, pp. 127-28.*

Sweet Friday Island (1984)

Taylor spins an adventure tale involving a 15-year-old girl and her father, who decide to vacation on a remote, uninhabited island off the Baja Peninsula. Their arrival at the coastal village from which they'll depart for Isla Viernes Dulce (Sweet Friday Island) brings the first intimations of trouble when a storekeeper tries to steer them away from the place with a variety of excuses. The Tolands are not to be deterred, however; come dawn, they leave a misleading note and head straight for the island. Trouble is there, all right. Someone slashes their rubber boat and wreaks havoc with their belongings and supplies. The situation is complicated by Mr. Toland's diabetic condition, which becomes a dangerous liability when his insulin supply disappears. It looks like a madman is loose, and the Tolands are completely at his mercy. Taylor pays much attention to his characters' psychological status. The Tolands' fear is vivid and their moves to defend themselves born of almost tangible panic and desperation. This effective evocation of emotion colors the resolution as well, when the assailant is revealed to be an unbalanced, frightened old man who once killed a *gringo,* and whose family keeps him on the island rather than have him placed in an institution for the criminally insane. The result is a finish that's thoughtful: no one killed but no one left unscathed; and everyone, readers included, are left to ponder the consequences of deliberately decided actions.

> *Denise M. Wilms, in a review of "Sweet Friday Island," in* Booklist, *Vol. 81, No. 3, October 1, 1984, p. 252.*

A close father-daughter relationship takes this novel one notch beyond the typical adventure story. . . . The story starts somewhat slowly, but the drama of the situation will hold even reluctant readers. An added dimension is Sam and Peg's mutual reluctance to solve their problem with a direct, and possibly violent, confrontation. This shows their strength but it also allows their fears to grow. A story that is compelling and suspenseful.

> *Eleanor K. MacDonald, in a review of "Sweet Friday Island," in* School Library Journal, *Vol. 31, No. 3, November, 1984, p. 139.*

It is hard to believe that Theodore Taylor wrote this trite tale about an admirable father who takes his capable daughter on a camping trip. Despite vague warning that the island is unsafe, the two head for the Mexican Isle Viernes Dulce where they are stalked by an unseen cave dweller who destroys their boat, their personal belongings and their peace of mind. Situations are predictable, characters are one dimensional and crises are too easily solved. There is never any doubt as to what will happen and who will rescue whom. The story's very structure is flawed by the author's inability to disclose the island dweller's identity within the bounds of the story. Instead, the unsurprising disclosure is revealed in a postscript chapter which takes place several years after the story ends.

> *Patricia Tomillo, in a review of "Sweet Friday Island," in* Voice of Youth Advocates, *Vol. 7, No. 6, February, 1985, p. 333.*

Rocket Island (1985)

Using the present tense and writing with the same dramatic flare he displayed in his series on great sea battles of World War II, Taylor offers a dynamic account of Germany's post-World War I push to produce rocket weaponry, carried out secretly on the island of Usedom ("Rocket Island") in defiance of the Versailles treaty. While he focuses mainly on the roles of rocket scientist Wernher von Braun and Walter Dornberger, head of the developmental program, Taylor cites the names of numerous individuals related to the research and its outcome as he highlights various stages of weapons production, fitting them into the context of the Second World War, and tracks the response of Allied forces to their discovery of Hitler's backdoor doings. While there are no specific source notes, Taylor has included a bibliography, along with an index. For personal reading and research.

> *Stephanie Zvirin, in a review of "Rocket Island," in* Booklist, *Vol. 82, No. 3, October 1, 1985, p. 215.*

In the late 1920s and early 1930s several young German scientists began working with rocketry. Their early experimentation blossomed into weapons research with the start of World War II. Although their experiments were aimed at perfecting a weapon, most of the top scientists saw that one day their work would bring mankind into space exploration. In the early days, one of the scientists, Wernher von Braun, thought that his work would lay the groundwork, but that he would not live to see man in space. By the end of the war, as he and his companions attempted to escape the Nazis and surrender to the Americans, von Braun knew that he would see that day. Those interested in rocketry and/or World War II books will find the background that will help them understand more difficult and complete books on the two topics. Taylor has provided an easily readable overview of the development of the research facilities at Usedom.

> *Barbara Stiber, in a review of "Rocket Island," in* Voice of Youth Advocates, *Vol. 8, No. 5, December, 1985, p. 336.*

Walking Up a Rainbow: Being the True Version of the Long and Hazardous Journey of Susan D. Carlisle, Mrs. Myrtle Dessery, Drover Bert Pettit, and Cowboy Clay Carmer and Others (1986)

Susan Carlisle begins her story in 1851, when she's thirteen, newly orphaned, and trying to save her property from the skinflint saloon owner who claims her father had owed him $15,000. That's when Susan craftily arranges to go west with a drover (to whom she lies) without telling her guardian (to whom she lies) so that she can make a profit from selling sheep and get money from a West Coast uncle she doesn't know. This is humorous period fiction, set in the 1850's, in the Patricia Beatty mold, with a feisty, determined heroine who loses her property but gets her man (Bashful Cowboy type) in a long, rollicking novel in which everything that can happen does happen as the wagon "Walking Up a Rainbow," takes Susan's party on an arduous journey to the seamiest parts of San Francisco.

Susan writes the first and third parts, the middle section being by the handsome cowboy. All the familiar natural dangers of the trail are here, as well as some incidents (rescue of Susan from a drunken quartet attempting rape, Susan's friendship with a heart-of-gold prostitute) that make this more sophisticated than the Beatty books. The story has lively characters, some of whom seem deliberately typecast to achieve a comic note, and it has variety, pace, and first-person styles that are both convincing and that are in effective contrast. (pp. 178-79)

> *A review of "Walking Up a Rainbow," in* Bulletin of the Center for Children's Books, *Vol. 39, No. 9, May, 1986, pp. 178-79.*

Historical fiction is a rare commodity these days, especially stories that pretend to be nothing more than good, entertaining tales. To his wife's request for "a tall tale about an adventuresome girl," Taylor responds with this story of Susan Carlisle, a feisty 14-year-old Iowa orphan, who, in 1852, embarks on a daring and somewhat foolish venture to raise the money she needs to pay off her dead father's debts and retain her lovely home. . . . Taylor's plot takes Susan on a cross-country "westering" journey full of hardship, adventure, intrigue, danger, and a little romance. That Susan is brave and sharp-witted is a given; fleshing out the story are assorted secondary characters and events, all carefully created with an eye to the realities of the time. Occasionally Taylor overdraws his developments, but there's no getting around the pervasive sense of lickety-split adventure—pages will turn right up to the finish.

> *Denise M. Wilms, in a review of "Walking Up a Rainbow," in* Booklist, *Vol. 82, No. 20, June 15, 1986, p. 1545.*

The story of 14-year-old orphan Susan D. Carlisle and her attempt to foil a villain who has placed a lien on her entire inheritance for a debt of her father's. Susan and her guardian, Indian Myrt Dessery, hire drover Burt Pettit and his absurd crew to drive a herd of sheep that are in her name to California to feed the Forty-Niners. A French-speaking black Moroccan and the "original cowboy" Clay B. Carmer, Susan's hero, are the most notable characters. After getting enough money—partly from the sale of the sheep and partly from gambling—Susan heads home but not in time to meet her deadline. She eventually receives a sort of "love" letter from Clay and heads for New Mexico and perhaps marriage. **Walking Up a Rainbow** is almost exciting and funny, but it falls short. The characters don't quite come alive; the humor isn't quite light enough; the adventures are too serious for the plot (Susan is almost raped at Independence Rock). Susan narrates parts One and Three, and Carmer narrates the middle section, a technique that is somewhat confusing. Also, the story's mood lapses occasionally with explanations "For those of you not familiar with history. . . . " In the book's favor are its realistic descriptions of life on a sheep drive and especially the trip by sea from California down to Panama, overland to the Gulf and home via the Mississippi. Enjoyable despite its flaws.

> *Dorcas Hand, in a review of "Walking Up a*

Rainbow," in School Library Journal, *Vol. 32, No. 10, August, 1986, p. 107.*

The Hostage (1988)

For a few days, a struggling salmon fisherman and his family believe their fortunes will be made by selling a killer whale they have captured to a marine park in southern California.

As far as Jamie Tidd's father is concerned, "Tyrannus" is just another fish, and a dangerous one at that. Trading him for $100,000 seems the chance of a lifetime. Jamie (14), who yearns to escape their backwater in British Columbia, agrees—until his own observations and attractive neighbor Angie (15) begin to convince him that Tyrannus has near-human feelings and a right to rejoin "Desdemona" and "Persephone," who have been faithfully waiting outside the net that confines him. Greenpeace demonstrations, unfriendly media coverage, and a terrifying encounter between Angie and Tyrannus, who briefly holds her in his mouth under the sea, all conspire toward a turnaround; but ultimately Jamie and his Dad make their own decision to free Tyrannus.

Taylor can be relied on to draw his characters well and tell his story with assurance, as he does here. And though he is unmistakably on the side of the whale, he also presents both sides of a controversial issue as well as the irony of the emphasis that media attention gives to some problems at the expense of others. A satisfying adventure, though the image of the title is not perfectly worked out—neither Angie nor Tyrannus serves as a hostage in the strict sense of the idea. (pp. 129-30)

> *A review of "The Hostage," in* Kirkus Reviews, *Vol. LVI, No. 2, January 15, 1988, pp. 129-30.*

Taylor, author of **The Cay** and **Walking Up a Rainbow,** captures Jamie's loneliness, desires, and uncertainty with clarity and insightfulness. The tale itself is simple, but with angles that ought to provoke young minds. Taylor does not, however, succeed in creating credible, supportive secondary characters. Many are either reduced to stereotypes or made too extraordinary. These minor character flaws are, however, easy to overlook in an otherwise enjoyable book that should be popular with YAs.

> *Laurie P. Greener, in a review of "The Hostage," in* Voice of Youth Advocates, *Vol. 11, No. 1, April, 1988, p. 30.*

This splendid tale vibrates with vivid descriptions of the Canadian far west. The writer shares his knowledge of nature, fishing, whales, and people. Kindness and cruelty duel. Danger and tensions are always on his shores.

The relationships in the family are warm, and the people honest, especially about their flaws. The ache in Jamie's heart is genuine. True, boy rescues girl in the tradition of male chauvinism, but this deed does not dim Angie's daring. And boy decides girl is right.

The environmental issue is popular with young people,

though bound to cause conflict in lovers of killer whale performers such as Sea World's Baby Shamu.

Superior writing makes *The Hostage* a joy to read. The novel begins: "There was poetry to the killer whale's world as he swam along, gliding just beneath the surface or rising and falling in the thin band of light. Sky. Wind and sea. A lovely free loneliness."

> *Lucille S. deView, "A Trio of Stories with Heroines Equal to Any Man," in* The Christian Science Monitor, *May 6, 1988, p. B7.*

Sniper (1989)

Left in charge of his parents' wild animal preserve while they travel in Africa, 15-year-old Ben Jepson tries to prove he is capable of the job. But when the chief animal handler is critically injured and a sniper begins to pick off the wild cats, Ben's responsibilities and headaches multiply, especially when he is unable to reach his parents. Even though he does solicit help from the neighbors, law enforcement personnel, and employees on the reserve (who are unfortunately referred to at times simply as "the Latinos" or "the African"), Ben is pretty much on his own when it comes to making decisions about the animals' safety and trying to capture the sniper. Although Ben is concerned that the right decisions will improve his mother's opinion of him, readers will be more involved in the suspense and senselessness of the murders and the unpredictability of the animals. The first two-thirds of the book is taut reading, a mood supported at times by an abrupt sentence structure. The last third is not so gripping. When the main suspect is killed (the murderer and motives are never revealed) and a new suspect bent on revenge is quickly uncovered, the story loses some of its tension. Still, readers will likely stay with the story until the final page, which gives Ben a well-deserved rest from the pressures and losses of the whole harrowing episode.

> *Susan Schuller, in a review of "Sniper," in* School Library Journal, *Vol. 35, No. 15, November, 1989, p. 115.*

This novel commands the reader's attention more for its action and setting than for its characters. Ben Jepson, a teenage boy, remains behind at his family's ranch—a private zoological preserve for big cats—when his parents go off to Africa to research poaching. Shortly after their departure, the ranch hand whom they had left in charge is hospitalized as a result of an accident, and Ben is left to manage affairs on his own, a turn of events that harbors unexpected danger when a sniper begins picking the animals off, one by one. Too stagily constructed to allow for mystery, the plot offers little room for guesswork, and the identity of the sniper is of minor interest. The book's fascination lies, rather, in the author's treatment of and obvious respect for the big cats—the lions, tigers, leopards, and cougars—that populate the novel. These felines with their distinctive habits, personalities, strengths, and weaknesses are described in such careful detail that the reader comes to know them better than most of the human characters, particularly the minor ones, whose characterizations are serviceable rather than profound. Getting to

know the animals as well as we do, we can feel total empathy with Ben's fierce desire to find their killer. An unusual young adult book, this novel will appeal to those who like animal stories and outdoor adventures.

> *Nancy Vasilakis, in a review of "Sniper," in* The Horn Book Magazine, *Vol. LXVI, No. 1, January-February, 1990, p. 72.*

The boy's torment of doubt and fear as he copes with danger and with the difficult business of moving the remaining animals to a safer part of the grounds and his agony as he waits for news of his parents, who are missing in Kenya, give a powerful thrust to a story whose events are strongly related, with a firm background of landscape and the support of technical details of wildlife management. This is a book whose powerful plot is ably handled so that character, taking second place in a sense, is carried on expert timing and an immediacy of place and event.

> *Margery Fisher, in a review of "Sniper," in* Growing Point, *Vol. 29, No. 5, January, 1991, p. 5449.*

Tuck Triumphant (1991)

With her knock-knees and braces, "wilting lily" Helen Ogden never thought she could be an advocate for hard-luck cases. But training Tuck, her blind Labrador, to consent to be led about by Lady Daisy, a German Shepherd guide dog, was a great confidence booster. Now she's facing an even greater challenge: to convince her family to keep the adopted six-year-old Korean boy they have just discovered is deaf. Building upon the events of *The Trouble with Tuck,* Taylor has again succeeded in rallying dog lovers to the cause of the blind hero in this thoughtful yet action-packed sequel. Children are likely to overlook the somewhat obvious plot devices and the occasional unfortunate racial stereotype in exchange for Helen's exhilarating, fierce loyalty for both her dog and her helpless brother.

> *A review of "Tuck Triumphant," in* Publishers Weekly, *Vol. 237, No. 50, December 19, 1990, p. 67.*

Set in the 1950s, Taylor's novel *The Trouble with Tuck* concerns the family who owns Tuck, a dog who goes blind but learns to get around with the help of a seeing-eye dog. This sequel is also narrated by Helen, now 14. In the opening scene, she's distraught because Tuck's missing. That crisis resolved, the story shifts to the next: Helen's family has agreed to adopt a six-year-old Korean boy named Chok-Do, but when they meet him at the airport, they discover that he is deaf. For the rest of the story, they agonize about whether or not to keep him and who will provide the care he needs. Meanwhile, a pit bull attacks and kills Lady Daisy (Tuck's guide dog), and Chok-Do is almost run over by a truck, almost drowned in a drain pipe, almost attacked by a mountain lion, and almost drowned (again) in a swollen mountain stream. While some may find the series of disasters and near-disasters overdone, less critical readers may simply find the story exciting. Taylor handles the characters and their relationships with finesse. While not as focused as its predecessor, the story will satisfy the curiosity of readers who learned to care for the characters in the first book and want to know what happens next. (pp. 1127, 1129)

> *Carolyn Phelan, in a review of "Tuck Triumphant," in* Booklist, *Vol. 87, No. 11, February 1, 1991, pp. 1127, 1129.*

All the details of a deaf-mute are accurate, as are the harrowing, potentially deadly incidents that wouldn't occur if Chok-Do could hear. The dog relationships are very appealing. Helen's character—resolute, brave, open-minded, patient—is an excellent model for readers, and there's enough excitement, carefully spaced, to keep readers interested or to make this a good read-aloud. Not a great book, but a satisfying one.

> *Ellen Ramsay, in a review of "Tuck Triumphant," in* School Library Journal, *Vol. 37, No. 3, March, 1991, p. 196.*

The Weirdo   (1991)

Chip Clewt, known locally as "The Weirdo" because of his appearance, rescues 16-year-old Samantha after she is forced to spend a night alone in the swamp. Their relationship continues to develop after Chip's friend and partner, Ted, mysteriously disappears and Chip assumes leadership of the fight to protect the bears living in the swamp. The controversy intensifies as area hunters, led by Sam's father, demand access to the swamp for hunting, Ted's disappearance remains unresolved, and Sam is torn between her feelings for Chip and her father's stand on the issue. Taylor skillfully combines many elements in this multidimensional tale of suspense and friendship. The rural landscape surrounding the swamp suggests a tranquillity just on the edge of danger, while vivid aural and visual imagery create a setting at once beautiful and foreboding. Interspersed throughout the story, beautifully written entries from Clewt's journal add depth and perspective, but they may be lost on readers anxious to resolve the conflict. References to current personalities and television shows will date this otherwise notable novel.

> *Karen Hutt, in a review of "The Weirdo," in* Booklist, *Vol. 88, No. 8, December 15, 1991, p. 759.*

"Weirdo" is the insulting nickname the townsfolk give Chip Clewt, a 17-year-old boy who had been badly burned in an airplane crash before he came to live with his artist father in the secluded Powhatan Swamp. Now assisting a graduate student observe and tag bears in the swamp in order to protect them, he has aroused the tempers of local hunters. Samantha Sanders, the 16-year-old daughter of one of the most vocal opponents of the hunting ban, meets Chip when she follows a prize hunting dog into the swamp. She gradually comes to understand the issues that concern him, and when the graduate student disappears, she and Chip investigate on their own. A strong friendship develops as the two lonely teenagers solve a murder while lobbying for animal rights. The story is carefully plotted with revealing flashbacks and alternating chapters that

juxtapose Samantha's experiences with Chip's college essays on life in the Powhatan. The language is richly descriptive and the animal research information interesting. Both teenagers come to the realization that self-acceptance is the first stage in loving someone else, and that gives them the courage to make a difference in their environmental stand. A highly readable story that has the elements of romance, mystery, and animal adventure going for it.

> *Yvonne Frey, in a review of "The Weirdo," in* School Library Journal, *Vol. 38, No. 1, January, 1992, p. 137.*

Theodore Taylor weaves strong elements of natural history and human psychology into a long but absorbing suspense story that switches back and forth in point of view as it develops several themes, most notably that of teenage idealism against adult anger and intolerance. Chip grows in self-confidence through his internship with a naturalist studying black bears in the Powhatan and through his developing friendship with Sam. Family dynamics shift as Sam defies her father and as Chip and his father break through walls of reserve. Sam comes to terms with her fears and together with Chip solves the mystery of the two murders. The violence erupting in the disagreement between conservationists and hunters is timely, realistic, and chilling. Taylor's blend of an interesting nature story with a young-adult problem novel is richly rendered, imbued with humor as well as drama. (p. 212)

> *Margaret A. Bush, in a review of "The Weirdo," in* The Horn Book Magazine, *Vol. LXVIII, No. 2, March-April, 1992, pp. 211-12.*

Maria: A Christmas Story   (1992)

Eleven-year-old Maria Gonzaga lives in a small town in California, where every Christmas is celebrated with a parade of gorgeous and elaborate floats. No Mexican-American family or business has ever entered a float in the parade, but Maria, envious and tired of the prattlings of the Anglo girls about their families' floats (" . . . hundreds of white and yellow mums, white and red roses, and hundreds of poinsettias. Everything flowers. Everything. We're calling it 'Winter Garden,' " gushes one of the girls) announces that her family too will be entering a float. Her family is poor and her father strict, so although Maria succeeds in getting her family entered, their meager funds keep them to a simple Nativity scene on an old wooden wagon. In the parade, however, the biblical simplicity unsurprisingly wins out over the gaudier entries, and "it was evident the humble had swept away the grand." This is enough of a fable (it's set "many years ago") that the absence of serious characterization isn't a problem, and Taylor doesn't make villains of the rich folks in order to make heroes of the poor. The San Joaquin Valley location makes for an unusual backdrop to this old-fashioned but still sweet true-meaning-of-Christmas story.

> *Deborah Stevenson, in a review of "Maria: A Christmas Story," in* Bulletin of the Center for Children's Books, *Vol. 46, No. 2, October, 1992, p. 56.*

Much of the tension of the story is centered around wanting the Gonzagas to succeed, hoping alongside them. Readers are certain to trust from the first that a happy ending is in store, but they will not necessarily have predicted its actual outcome. At the last minute, the stubborn ox intended to pull the float refuses, and twenty Mexican-American men come to the rescue.

As the story draws to its satisfying conclusion, it soon becomes evident that "the humble had swept aside the grand." The "simple is best" theme is nothing new; countless other Nativity stories such as *The Little Juggler, The Clown of God,* and *The Silver Whistle* espouse the same truth. Perhaps its Mexican-American characters and setting are what make it decidedly different. Without seeming superfluous, Spanish words are skillfully interwoven throughout the text, lending authenticity.

This affectionate tale of one family's strength is told with clarity and spare language. Their determination to overcome economic and cultural disadvantage makes for a universal story of simplicity, tradition, and belief.

Add to a growing list of books containing strong Hispanic characters this dignified holiday story with its timeless message that begs to be read aloud, cherished Christmas after Christmas. (pp. 38-9)

> *Megan McDonald, in a review of "Maria: A Christmas Story," in* The Five Owls, *Vol. VII, No. 2, November-December, 1992, pp. 38-9.*

Alvin Tresselt

1916-

American author of picture books, reteller, and editor.

Major works include *Rain Drop Splash* (1946), *White Snow, Bright Snow* (1947), *Hide and Seek Fog* (1965), *The Beaver Pond* (1970), *The Dead Tree* (1972).

Tresselt is respected for introducing young children to the natural world in quiet, impressionistic concept books noted for their artistry and sensitivity as well as for the solidity of their information. Referring to Tresselt as "one of the pathbreaking American picture book authors," critic James Cross Giblin comments that Tresselt "helped to establish the patterns of the 'mood' picture book which sought to catch and hold the attention of young listeners and readers by projecting the essence of a familiar experience in vivid yet simple language." Tresselt conveys a sense of nature's patterns and cycles while encouraging his young readers to be aware of their surroundings. Often using nature as a protagonist, he evokes the mood and inherent beauty of the natural world through poetic texts and illustrations by such award-winning artists as Leonard Weisgard, Milton Glaser, and Roger Duvoisin. His partnership with Duvoisin resulted in more than fifteen books, and critics have praised the combined effect of Tresselt's rhythmic prose and Duvoisin's dramatic illustrations; reviewer Ellen Lewis Buell called their series "a notable addition to American picture books." The team's meditations on snow, *White Snow, Bright Snow,* and on fog, *Hide and Seek Fog,* are regarded as classics of children's literature for capturing a child's wonder at these fascinating aspects of weather. Tresselt has also published several retellings of folk tales from around the world, drawing most frequently from Japanese sources. These retellings are considered successful in preserving the sense of the original tales, though they are not as popular as his nature books. Tresselt served as managing editor of *Humpty Dumpty's Magazine* from 1952 to 1965. In this capacity he created an ongoing ecology feature in the magazine, prompted by the same belief that informed many of his writings—that children have a special relationship to the natural world.

Tresselt's career as an author of children's books began with his association in the 1940s with the esteemed children's writer Margaret Wise Brown and the illustrator Leonard Weisgard, who were then in the beginning stages of their own careers. Inspired by Brown's poetic style, Tresselt wrote *Rain Drop Splash,* an account of a drop of water as it ricochets off of the nose of a rabbit and proceeds from puddle to brook to lake, and finally, to the sea. Illustrated by Weisgard, the book was a commercial success, and it led to further explorations into the moods and phases of nature. *White Snow, Bright Snow,* the first collaboration with Duvoisin, chronicles a snowflake as it falls and highlights the differences between child's and adult's reactions to a snowstorm. *Johnny Maple-Leaf* and *Follow*

the Wind similarly trace the various stages and changes in nature. *Hide and Seek Fog,* written in 1965, evokes the mood of a foggy day, providing an amusing look at the children's enthusiasm for playing in the fog, while the adults bemoan the bad weather. With the publication of *The Beaver Pond,* Tresselt's objectives shifted slightly. According to Pamela R. Giller, "While [Tresselt's] early books stressed ecological concerns and the interdependence of living things, his later books use these themes as the basis for deeper exploration, and include more information converted through richer, more complex language." Depicting the state of a beaver pond over several years, the book details the relationship between beavers and other animals in and near the pond. Critics find that Tresselt portrays the interdependence of the natural world with depth and intelligence and without compromising his poetic style. *The Dead Tree,* which is illustrated by Charles Robinson, is another well-known work from the later part of Tresselt's career. The book tells the story of a fallen oak, which provides food and shelter for animals and plants and eventually decays over hundreds of years. Tresselt explains how this process nourishes the forest. *The Dead Tree* was reissued in 1992 as *The Gift of the Tree,* with illustrations by Henri Sorenson.

(See also *Something about the Author,* Vol. 7; *Contemporary Authors,* Vols. 49-52; *Contemporary Authors New Revisions Series,* Vol. 1.)

AUTHOR'S COMMENTARY

[The following excerpt is from a speech which was originally delivered on 19 October 1974.]

I am neither a teacher nor a librarian, so I do not have firsthand knowledge; but I strongly suspect that my books are not for every child. To paraphrase T. S. Eliot, "I am not Dr. Seuss nor was meant to be. Am an attendant lord, one that will do to swell a progress, start a scene or two." Well, I'll settle for that. If I can start a scene or two for a child here and there; if I can begin to open up an aspect of nature, a feeling for weather, a sense of the progress of the seasons; if I can make a child aware of what goes on around him day in and day out—I have successfully gone beyond the book.

My father was very much involved with nature. He loved his garden, he loved the fields and seasons and the secrets of the woods. Unfortunately he died when I was barely three; but he had passed this love on to my considerably older sister, and she in turn gave it to me. Each year we would scratch out a flower bed in the begrudging soil of our backyard. Somehow by midsummer the weeds predominated, but no matter. (p. 261)

At the age of nine I spent a summer on a farm; and I discovered for the first time that nothing smelled better than a barnful of cows and a field that has just been mowed. . . . I came home that fall convinced that I would be a farmer. . . . (pp. 261-62)

Although I was an avid reader, I actually owned very few books. Somehow, library cards in three different libraries kept me well supplied with reading material. (p. 262)

In addition to my love of words for reading, I also loved the sound of words. As a choir boy I remembered how I enjoyed listening to the minister as he read the Lesson and the Epistle from the Bible each Sunday. In the days when *I* went to school we had what were called Opening Exercises. In addition to saluting the flag, the teacher would read one of the psalms. Each teacher, as I went through the grades, had her own repertoire of favorites; and at one time I could recite in my head a dozen or more from memory, just from hearing them read aloud each morning. In a way, children today are the poorer, thanks to the Supreme Court's ruling forbidding this sort of thing. Even though I now classify myself as a God-fearing atheist, the poetry of the Bible read aloud can still move me as almost nothing else can. I like to think that the rolling cadences of that great poetry have a faint but audible echo in my own writing.

Words carry such a heavy freight. We use thousands of them day in and day out in communicating with one another, and we devour them with our eyes in books and newspapers. Yet who knows better than a diplomat threading his way toward a detente, a psychiatrist trying to unravel a patient's knotted ball of words, a child striving to express his worries, what slippery, insecure and treacherous things words can be.

And what of the writer trying to reach a child with words! He has a barrier of bodies to leap before he reaches the child. His manuscript has to get past an editor who in turn must please a publisher and a sales manager. A reviewer must give it a nod so that the purchasers—librarians or parents—know it exists. They in turn must pass judgment, and finally the child for whom the words were intended at last gets a crack at them.

No wonder, then, that children make up their own secret vocabulary for intimate involvement with one another. They learn to communicate among themselves and with themselves, giving words an intimacy and reality far outside Mr. Webster's definitions. The sound to the ear, the feel to the tongue, even the sight to the eye, enhance these words; and outsiders can only guess at what they really mean.

A few from my own remembrance come to mind. There was a Sunday comic I used to read avidly about a character called Boob McNutt. Through some circumstances he found himself, along with various companions, in a place called an *is land.* They had all sorts of crazy adventures there, and I thought that surely no place could be as exciting as this *is land.* I was so disappointed when one day a smarty-pants friend pointed out that it wasn't an *is* land, it was an *i* land where all this took place. In another instance, my mother had spent her early childhood in a city which she called *Tra-east,* and the stories she would recount always had a special glamour because they had taken place in Tra-east. It was such a letdown for me when I learned years later that where she had lived was just plain Trieste. (pp. 262-63)

So how do I know what happens to my words when they finally do get to a child? Does a youngster see what I see when I speak of a melon-yellow moon? When I say that the trees have a tired and rusty look, does a child sense what I am saying about the running down of summer? Does he realize that I am pinpointing the recycling of life with the last sentence of *The Beaver Pond*? All I can do is take my chances.

When I began writing for children it never occurred to me to inhibit my vocabulary. True, I didn't make a point of seeing how many polysyllabics I could use in a given sentence. I merely said what I wanted to say in what I felt were the most appropriate words—terse Anglo-Saxon, or rolling tongue-and-ear- satisfying words that grew first in the rich soil of Latin. I also didn't hesitate to use metaphors and similes that would stretch the text beyond the mere incident or story I was telling. In *It's Time Now* I describe a flower wagon in spring:

> Up one street and down another goes the creaky wagon, carrying daffodils filled with spring sunshine, crimson geraniums, bright as fresh paint, and baskets of pansies with squinchy velvet faces.

I can be totally pragmatic, as in *White Snow Bright Snow:*

> The postman said it looked like snow.

The farmer said it smelled like snow.
The policeman said it felt like snow,
    and his wife said her big toe hurt, and that
    always meant snow.

Or by contrast, completely lyrical, as in *The Dead Tree:*

Now it was the autumn weather, and it was long
and lazy. Yellow-gray and misty mornings, mid-
days filled with false summer warmth, and the
nights pierced with frost.

(p. 263)

I use obscure words if I feel they are right. I speak of leathery oak leaves *moldering* under the snow . . . of squirrels
garnering their winter food. Who knows what obscure or
obvious word the child will understand? If it bothers him,
he will ask; if he understands it in context, fine. If he puts
his own definition to it, he will have a word that will always have a special value, even after he knows for certain
what it really means.

In one instance I unwittingly got myself in a bit of trouble
this way. In the fog book I said the children *spoddled* in
the lazy lapping waves on the beach. Shortly after the
book came out I began getting letters wanting to know
what this word meant. It was a word I had known all my
life. My mother would say, "Stop spoddling in the sink
and finish washing those dishes." Or, "Stop spoddling and
finish your bath." So it seemed a perfect word to use in the
book.

I confidently went to the dictionary, but it wasn't there.
Then I recalled that my mother had grown up in England;
and, thinking it might be a British word, I called a friend
at Oxford University Press—in New York—and asked her
to check the *Oxford English Dictionary.* It wasn't there,
either. Then she checked a dictionary of regional English
words and found *spuddle,* which means: "to dig idly in
dirt—related to spud, a potato; to play with water . . . peculiar to two certain counties in England." My mother
had grown up in an adjoining county, and apparently the
pronunciation had changed slightly when it crossed the
county line.

The payoff, though, was when a British edition of the book
came out. I looked through the copy that was sent me and
noted that naturally some of the spellings had been
changed—*gray* was spelled *grey,* and *vacation* had become
holidays. Then I checked out *spoddle* and found that my
good English word had been changed to *paddled.* Some
time later I met the British editor, and I asked him why.
"Oh," he said, "we thought it was one of your strange
American words." Be that as it may, I hope that some
American children have had their vocabularies enriched
by this strange English word.

Just as I have never written down in my books, always
hoping to take a child a step or two beyond, so too as an
editor I have tried to expose the young reader or listener
to something more. It is better that a child stretch up than
to stoop down. (p. 264)

In sharing with you what going beyond the book means
to me, I must pay a small tribute to someone who was responsible for my getting involved with children's books in
the first place. In the course of growing up I had various

ideas about what I wanted to be when I had completed the
process. One that never crossed my mind was writing
books for children. In my twenties—still with no ideas, although now it was getting a little late in the game—I became good friends with Leonard Weisgard and Margaret
Wise Brown. At the time they were still struggling to gain
real recognition in the field, and I sat in on their many discussions about what was right and wrong with children's
books. I was very impressed with Margaret's forthright
but sensitive and poetic way of writing for children; and
one day I decided to see how simply I could cover the journey of raindrops down to the sea, hewing to essentials,
with just a few peripheral details to flesh it out. (p. 265)

Rain Drop Splash did well enough for [editor Beatrice
Creighton] to start hounding me for another manuscript.
It turned out to be *White Snow Bright Snow,* which happened to win a Caldecott medal for Roger Duvoisin; and
as far as Beatrice was concerned there was no turning
back. Willy-nilly, I found myself a writer of books for children. . . .

Margaret, whom I admired so much as a writer, paid me,
I think, the greatest compliment I have ever received.
After reading *White Snow Bright Snow* she said, simply,
"I wish I had written that." . . .

I consider Margaret Wise Brown one of the most significant influences in contemporary children's literature. She
opened the way not only for me but for many of today's
writers. The concept book, the book of mood and feeling,
the story that embodies a bit of philosophic thought rather
than a moral, owes no small debt to her. I think her book
The Little Island is a masterpiece.

They say a writer writes best about the things that mean
the most to him. Nature in all its aspects has been just that
to me; and coupling this with my love of words I have tried
to pass on my feelings about nature, using words as best
I can. I trust, then, that I have helped a child go beyond
in two areas, helping him to better see and appreciate nature, and at the same time giving him an awareness of
words.

But in a way it is almost presumptuous for me to talk
about how I try to go beyond the book. Any good writer
for children tries to do this. Margaret was a writer who
I think excelled at it. And Sendak, who caused a sensation
when his *Wild Things* first appeared, not to mention his
naked little boy [in *In the Night Kitchen*]; Arnold Lobel,
who so skillfully combines deceptively simple texts with
farm illustrations and a real feeling of relationships in his
Frog and Toad books; Ruth Krauss, with her frequently
zany view of the world; Tana Hoban, with her incredible
photographs, helping a child to see things differently; Lilian Moore, with her small poems, cut and polished like fine
cameos. I'm sure each of you could think of dozens more.
(p. 265)

Alvin Tresselt, "Books and Beyond," in Childhood Education, *Vol. 51, No. 5, March, 1975,
pp. 261-66.*

GENERAL COMMENTARY

Bernard J. Lonsdale and Helen K. Mackintosh

Alvin R. Tresselt's first book was **Rain Drop Splash.** In lyrical prose the sounds, movements, and magic of rain move through the story. . . .

White Snow, Bright Snow portraying the fun of the first snowfall for children and its effect on adults followed **Rain Drop Splash.** The natural quality of the text and the beautiful illustrations by Roger Duvoisin capture the out-of-doors in all its snowy splendor. . . .

Among the many titles that portray the wonders of nature are **Follow the Wind, A Thousand Lights and Fireflies,** and **Under the Trees and Through the Grass.** The magic and the power of the wind are beautifully described through rhythmic text and colorful illustrations [by Roger Duvoisin] that sweep across the pages and give strength to the story in **Follow the Wind.** The lyrical text of **A Thousand Lights and Fireflies** and the color illustrations [by John Moodie] catch the moods of the city and country. Prose glows under Tresselt's pen, and what he does not say with words, Roger Duvoisin says beautifully with pictures in **Under the Trees and Through the Grass.**

The excellence of Tresselt's stories comes across in the way he portrays the out of doors. No mood of nature escapes his pen. His feelings for the wonders of nature are beautifully expressed in rhythmic prose that captures the beauty, excitement, and drama of the natural world.

> *Bernard J. Lonsdale and Helen K. Mackintosh, "Picture-Story Books: Alvin R. Tresselt,"* in their Children Experience Literature, *Random House, 1973, p. 261.*

Zena Sutherland and May Hill Arbuthnot

Midway between the awareness and the theme-plot schools of writing for young children lie the picture stories of Alvin Tresselt. Tresselt constructs his stories about weather and nature in simple, rhythmic prose, and with Roger Duvoisin's pictures, they develop a real sense of drama. **Hide and Seek Fog,** for example, describes how the fog affects sea and seaside activities, and **What Did You Leave Behind?** encourages appreciative observation. These little everyday miracles of the weather are made exciting, something to be watched and enjoyed, never feared. Texts and pictures are full of reassurance and beauty.

> *Zena Sutherland and May Hill Arbuthnot, "Books for Younger Children: Alvin Tresselt,"* in their Children and Books, *seventh edition, Scott, Foresman and Company, 1986, p. 335.*

TITLE COMMENTARY

Rain Drop Splash   (1946)

This odyssey of a raindrop will not only reconcile your child to an inconvenient rainstorm but will also open his eyes to the wonder of the elements. Here he will follow the raindrop's course from the first soft splash against a rabbit's nose, into puddle, into brook, into lake overflowing, to its ultimate meeting with the sea.

It is a rare accomplishment to have encompassed such a vast progress into one small story, perfect of its kind. The text is simple, evocative, the pictures [by Leonard Weisgard] exciting in their detail and fine design, combining to stimulate the imagination of the picture-book age.

> *Ellen Lewis Buell, in a review of "Rain Drop Splash,"* in The New York Times Book Review, *November 10, 1946, p. 4.*

I trust you do not wish your child, even if he lives in a city, to share the anti-social attitude of a city dweller toward wet weather. Perhaps only those who have lived on a farm long enough to feel the relief of waking to the sound of raindrops breaking a six weeks' drought, can have the really right attitude toward rain, but there is no proper excuse for a city slicker's typical opinion that wet weather is bad weather and a rainy day a lost day. A good book to put a little child in the right frame of mind on weather is this combination of few words and many pictures showing a steady rainfall going "drip-drop-splash" until it makes a little pond which spills over into a brook, tumbles into a lake and in time makes its way as a river to the sea. The pictures are large and colored; they show all nature enjoying life-giving rain, from the house plant set on the sill to the green frog on whose back raindrops come down splunk. As it ends, the sun has come out at last and the rain has stopped, but the welcoming earth has used it well.

> *May Lamberton Becker, in a review of "Rain Drop Splash,"* in New York Herald Tribune Weekly Book Review, *December 22, 1946, p. 9.*

White Snow, Bright Snow   (1947)

Never shall I forget the afternoon I came alone in a motor, from far in Westchester to my home on Morningside. For the year's first snowfall went just ahead of us, traveling at the same pace. From estates and suburban gardens, slum tenements and school gates, children came, holding up their hands to catch the flakes in gestures almost ritualistic, performing the spontaneous dance with which generations have greeted the first snow. Had I not seen them I would still have known the first snow was falling: all the way along the air had a joyful humming note that, once heard, is forever recognized.

All this and more one finds in this simple narrative with its introductory poem "Softly, gently in the secret night, down from the North came the quiet white."

> *A review of "White Snow, Bright Snow,"* in New York Herald Tribune Weekly Book Review, *November 16, 1947, p. 8.*

Even grown-ups, to whom snow means discomfort and inconvenience, will see this picture book's beauty with delight. It puts into words the snowflakes' silent fall, the mystery of the snow-filled night, and the glory of the glistening whiteness of the day. Roger Duvoisin's colored pictures and the fun and poetry of the text fit each other perfectly and present to a small child the magic of a soft, white world. (pp. 1692-93)

Gertrude Andrus, in a review of "White Snow, Bright Snow," in Library Journal, *Vol. 72, December 1, 1947, pp. 1692-93.*

A lovely idea, this, of the excitement that snow brings, with all it means to children and not-too-hardened grown-ups, too. There's a lilting sound to the text, and appealing pictures by Roger Duvoisin in soft, misty grey-blues, shocking yellow and bright red. An attractive book, without very much dramatic appeal to children—not the sort of book they want to go back to of their own accord.

A review of "White Snow, Bright Snow," in Virginia Kirkus' Bookshop Service, *Vol. XVI, No. 11, June 15, 1948, p. 281.*

The Wind and Peter (1948)

Our favorite weather man is Alvin Tresselt who, with rare foresight, gave us last fall **White Snow, Bright Snow** and a year ago **Raindrop Splash.** Now, employing a different narrative technique but equal charm, he describes for children of 4 to 7 the moods of the wind. Thus we have the brief story of Peter who liked the wind in all seasons and when there came a hot still day set out to find a breeze. He didn't "talk up a storm," but the results of his search are almost the same.

The tempo of the prose changes sensitively with the temper of the wind.

Ellen Lewis Buell, in a review of "The Wind and Peter," in The New York Times Book Review, *February 22, 1948, p. 31.*

Children are often curious about the wind and in this gentle picture book they may see what it does to the leaves, how it cools the air in summer, how it bites in winter. With Peter they will learn how we should miss the wind if it never blew. As in **Rain Drop Splash** and **White Snow Bright Snow,** Alvin Tresselt aims to give little children an idea of one of the great forces of Nature, but the pictures here [by Garry MacKenzie] are far less striking than in the earlier books. On the other hand, for those who like a personal story, an individual child is introduced.

Alice M. Jordan, in a review of "The Wind and Peter," in The Horn Book Magazine, *Vol. XXIV, No. 4, July, 1948, p. 274.*

Johnny Maple-Leaf (1948)

Beautifully designed, rich in subtle color, [illustrator Roger] Duvoisin's pictures excitingly portray the turn of the seasons in this life-cycle of a maple leaf in the deep woods. They follow the shifting moods of the prose-poem from the electric anticipation of a spring morning, the hush of a spring evening into the full activity of woods life in summer, through the excitement of autumn on to the sleepy peace of the first snow sifting down on fallen leaves. Although the subject is more passive than those of Mr. Tresselt's other books of wind and weather and, therefore, the story has less dynamic thrust, one sees with Johnny Maple-Leaf that "there was always something happening

beneath the tree" and the poetic child of picture-book age will sense the inevitable rightness of the changing year.

Ellen Lewis Buell, in a review of "Johnny Maple-Leaf," in The New York Times Book Review, *December 26, 1948, p. 11.*

From his vantage point at the top of a forest tree, Johnny Maple-Leaf observes the cycle of the seasons, enjoying the woodland dramas that each brings. Author's gently rhythmic story and Roger Duvoisin's brilliantly imaginative pictures complement each other perfectly, one suggesting the poetry of nature, the other supplying details of the teeming life of the deep woods. A beautiful and satisfying book for younger children.

Elizabeth Hodges, in a review of "Johnny Maple-Leaf," in Library Journal, *Vol. 74, No. 1, January 1, 1949, p. 67.*

Bonnie Bess, the Weathervane Horse (1949)

A funny, gay picture story of "the smartest horse in the country," who told her farmer all about the weather. The farmer moved away, and through the long seasons alone, sad things happened to Bonnie Bess, atop the old barn. At last she is in an antique shop, then happily restored to the same barn by a new farmer who also properly appreciates her.

This simple story is cleverly planned to give the many exact details about a farm which nonfarmer children will find new and interesting, and farm children will recognize with pleasure. It makes the work of the weathervane just as clever and important as it is. I would like a bit more wind—surely the wind should blow strongly through such a tale—but that is a very minor criticism, and this is not an imaginary story, just a little record of an item of real Americana.

Louise S. Bechtel, in a review of "Bonnie Bess: The Weathervane Horse," in New York Herald Tribune Weekly Book Review, *May 8, 1949, p. 5.*

Bonnie Bess, the weathervane horse, was subject not only to the four winds of heaven but also to the winds of fate. For a hundred years she had foretold the weather from her perch on a comfortable barn, but when the farmer moved away Bess was left alone and forlorn. The old barn roof caved in and Bess tumbled into a snow bank. She was rescued from that ignominy by an antique dealer and then her story comes full circle. Bess returns to the old barn and again directs the planting and the haying.

If not exactly static, a weathervane is a passive subject and so this little story lacks a certain emotional intensity. Mr. Tresselt does, however, achieve a feeling of satisfaction and some of that happy awareness of the natural world which distinguished his **Raindrop Splash** and **White Snow, Bright Snow.**

Ellen Lewis Buell, "East Wind, West Wind," in The New York Times Book Review, *May 15, 1949, p. 22.*

[The following excerpt is from a review of an edition published in 1970 with illustrations by Erik Blegvad.]

The text of a 1949 publication is given a contemporary note by the illustrations, precise and delicate and tidy. "She's the smartest horse in the country," said the farmer who owned Bess, many years ago. But Bonnie Bess was left atop the barn when the farm was abandoned, and years later retrieved by a junkman. "That's just the weathervane for my barn," said a stalwart young farmer (black) and he bought her. "She's the smartest horse in the county," he says. A neat little tale, with the satisfying element of a cycle completed, but limited for some readers by the quiet tone and the sedate plot.

> *Zena Sutherland, in a review of "Bonnie Bess the Weathervane Horse," in* Bulletin of the Center for Children's Books, *Vol. 24, No. 2, October, 1970, p. 35.*

Sun Up (1949)

This gifted team [Tresselt and illustrator Roger Duvoisin] gives us this season an artistic, sensitive picture book which manages to avoid being just another day on a farm book. The various phases round the clock are suggested in the nuances of coloring in [Roger] Duvoisin's full page illustrations,—pink of dawn across the fields as the cock crows, brilliant white heat of noonday sun, threatening black clouds before a summer thunder storm. Text and pictures are perfectly integrated to create an atmosphere of pastoral simplicity and drowsy summer activity.

> *A review of "Sun Up," in* Virginia Kirkus' Bookshop Service, *Vol. XVII, No. 22, November 15, 1949, p. 623.*

Weather is never a commonplace to the sentient person. Here, as in *White Snow, Bright Snow* and *Johnny Maple-Leaf,* the team of Tresselt and Duvoisin again create an evocative impression of the changing moods of wind and weather. *Sun Up* describes in fluid text and brilliant pictures the course of a summer day as seen and *felt* by a little farm boy. Here is the hot light of a scorching morning, the stillness of noonday, the mounting tension and the blue-black violence of a thunderstorm, and the rain-washed peace at day's end. It is a lovely book which will stir children of 4 to 8 to a sharper realization of existence. And that, after all, is one of the prime purposes of literature.

> *Ellen Lewis Buell, "A Summer Day," in* The New York Times Book Review, *November 27, 1949, p. 26.*

In four previous picture books Mr. Tresselt has written gentle, impressionistic brief texts which describe nature for small children. To the surprise of many, these fairly storyless books have appealed widely. *Sun Up* is more of the same: the little story of one summer day on a farm, a day of rising sun, hot sun for work, a thunderstorm, a rainbow, a beautiful sunset, night. There is a little boy, but he is just a watcher, not a hero. There are farm animals, and naturally the rooster begins and ends it all.

Children will like it because it offers them facts they know

and understand, the quality of poetry coming from the dramatic sequence, not from any very poetic writing. This carping critic does not FEEL the sun in the book, just as she missed the feel of the wind in the weathervane book.

> *Louise S. Bechtel, in a review of "Sun Up," in* New York Herald Tribune Book Review, *January 22, 1950, p. 8.*

[The following excerpts are from reviews of an edition published in 1991 with illustrations by Henri Sorensen.]

Originally published with illustrations by Roger Duvoisin, this title is given new life by a newcomer to the field. Tresselt, in his lyrical prose, presents a day on a farm, a blistering hot day given reprieve by a thundering storm. The farm has been modernized, but the simplicity and serenity of the setting remain. Cows and chickens dot the landscape as a boy and his dog fish by the shadows of a nearby pond. The mood is lazy, as the easy pace of the day is dictated by the weather. Each expansive page glows with a light so pure that readers can almost feel the heat of the pulsing sun and be relieved once the rain arrives, turning the parched, dusty earth into cool mud. Sorensen's naturalistic oil paintings help children feel a part of this special day-by-day world. Kids today might be impatient with such a slow meandering, but they will be rewarded by the immediacy of this world in which animals and people are given equal consideration. (pp. 84-5)

> *Martha Topol, in a review of "Sun Up," in* School Library Journal, *Vol. 37, No. 5, May, 1991, pp. 84-5.*

Using a modern family farm as the setting, Sorensen provides strong, sunlit paintings that sensitively interpret the mood and sense of Tresselt's rhythmic text. A good choice for reading aloud, this will complement the more abundant narrative picture books set on farms.

> *Carolyn Phelan, in a review of "Sun Up," in* Booklist, *Vol. 87, No. 20, June 15, 1991, p. 1975.*

"Hi, Mr. Robin!" (1950)

Waiting for spring is an impatient business, no matter how young or how old you are. In this new book the author and artist of *White Snow, Bright Snow* and *Sun Up* have caught the teasing uncertainty of that time when the little boy thinks (just like you and me) that spring will never come. The robin shows him the secret signs which only the wise know. Even so, there is hope deferred by the late snow, but then comes the first crocus, that poignant moment just before the buds break and, finally, the unbelievable burst of blossom in a new green world. As in other picture books created by the Tresselt-Duvoisin partnership, the text and pictures are perfectly matched. This is the loveliest book they have yet made in praise of the seasons.

> *Ellen Lewis Buell, "Spring Song," in* The New York Times Book Review, *May 28, 1950, p. 22.*

The successful team of *White Snow, Bright Snow* and *Sun*

Up have produced another lovely picture book, this time about the coming of spring in the country. With warm, luminous colors, predominantly green, orange and yellow, Roger Duvoisin has visualized the tremulous and dramatic progress of spring in the earth and sky—the shadowy grey of the first pussy willows in the snow, the white surprise of the first crocus, fresh green and yellows in a mist of rain and the triumphant burst of color under blue sky when the spring has finally come—has all the freshness of childhood impressions. The text, following the coming of spring from the first cheery note of the robin—"it's here, it's here"—to the bird's wise "I told you so" as the little boy shouts "spring is here!"—is atmospheric and lyrical. . . . Captures the mystery and enchantment of the spring spectacle.

> *A review of "Hi, Mister Robin!" in* Virginia Kirkus' Bookshop Service, *Vol. XVIII, No. 11, June 1, 1950, p. 302.*

This alluring title may amuse small children, even though the days of spring have passed. It is, we suppose, the final book in the four companion volumes Mr. Tresselt has written about the seasons. It opens with snow and bare branches, and a small boy asking everyone when spring will come. The robin said it had come, and told the boy to use his eyes, so he found the pussywillows; to use his ears, so he heard the frogs. Then he found one crocus, then the peach buds were sticky. Then at last came a day when everything was in bloom, and the boy told the robin it really was spring.

This very tenuous little story, of watching and waiting, is retold with an enrichment of "looking" in the big color pictures. Mr. Duvoisin combines a love of the atmospheric with ability to make details clear and dramatic for the child. . . . [*"Hi, Mr. Robin!"*] is one of those books of very simple transcription of feelings that we are discovering children before six enjoy. Besides hearing Mr. Tresselt's words, they like to make up their own about all they see in the pictures.

> *Louise S. Bechtel, in a review of "Hi, Mr. Robin!" in* New York Herald Tribune Book Review, *June 4, 1950, p. 10.*

Follow the Wind (1950)

In this new "weather" book by the author of *White Snow, Bright Snow* and *"Hi, Mr. Robin!"* the wind is hero. It is a frolicky wind on a spree. The kite tries to follow it, so do the bird, the cloud and the sailboat. The wind leaves them all behind until in the end, tired of blowing, "it grew gentler and gentler and gentler, and quietly rocked itself to sleep." It is no small feat to have caught in a few words the force and movement, the gentleness and the violence of the wind, as Mr. Tresselt has done.

> *Ellen Lewis Buell, "Frolicky Wind," in* The New York Times Book Review, *November 12, 1950, p. 35.*

The Tresselt-Duvoisin team haven't missed yet and here is another lovely picture book. This is the story of the wind which "blew for days and days", bending the trees, snap-ping up kites, blowing off hats, turning windmills, making rain and hurricanes. Nothing can go to the end of the wind; nothing can stop the wind, but the wind grows tired and gently rocks itself to sleep. The full color pictures [by Roger Duvoisin] gleam with natural colors, the lines twist and turn with movement, and the prose supplies the personality of the wind itself, laughing, crying, singing softly. The uncomplicated, simple story and the quiet, satisfying climax makes this pleasant bedtime reading.

> *A review of "Follow the Wind," in* Virginia Kirkus' Bookshop Service, *Vol. XVIII, No. 24, December 15, 1950, p. 724.*

Autumn Harvest (1951)

With *Autumn Harvest* this author and [illustrator Roger Duvoisin] complete the cycle of seasonal books begun with *White Snow, Bright Snow,* a series which is a notable addition to American picture books. Here they celebrate the autumn as only Americans know it, for nowhere else in the world is it so brilliant and exciting. There is a subtle interplay between text and pictures, which makes one sharply aware of the mellow light of Indian summer, the sharpness of first frost, the smell of bonfires. In a few instances the borders surrounding the pages of text distract the eye from the facing illustrations, but as a whole this book is lovely to look at and to listen to.

> *Ellen Lewis Buell, "American Autumn," in* The New York Times Book Review, *November 11, 1951, p. 40.*

Another evocative picture book by the successful Tresselt-Duvoisin combination, this time dedicated to the pungent excitement of the autumn season. From the first late summer evening song of the katydids through the cooling nights, the harvest of golden wheat, the busy hoarding of the little woodland animals, apple picking, first frosts, brilliant sunlight and flashing leaves, to the bustling gathering of the family at Thanksgiving, the words and pictures catch the startling beauty of Autumn's surplus—sudden contrasts of misty colors and sharp, black tree branches; dazzling light and chilly weather; wide, wide spaces of sky and the coziness of the indoors. Although the prose seems less fluid than in the other books, Mr. Duvoisin's stunning full-color illustrations contribute drama and coherence.

> *A review of "Autumn Harvest," in* Virginia Kirkus' Bookshop Service, *Vol. XIX, No. 22, November 15, 1951, p. 661.*

A Day with Daddy (1953)

A story told in the first person by a girl of about three of the things she does with her Daddy from the time he comes home from work one day, all the next day, until he goes to work again the following day. They do things like making pancakes, going for a walk, reading stories, and mowing the lawn. Very young children (under four) will enjoy the story as a stimulus to telling about what they do with their Daddies, but the older picture-book age will demand more plot.

Mary K. Eakin, in a review of "A Day with Daddy," in Bulletin of the Center for Children's Books, *Vol. VII, No. 2, October, 1953, p. 16.*

A Day With Daddy, one of the better photographic records of childhood. Helen Heller's pictures show a typical suburban day when a little girl has a chance to work and play with her father. Actually, this begins with waiting for Daddy to come home from work. There is the report of the day's fun, the bath, the bedtime story, and the next day is filled with chores and games. With one or two exceptions, the photographs have a spontaneous air and give an effect of intimacy without being embarrassing and the text is childlike, mercifully free from cuteness. This is one of the "here and now" books which children delight in because they can compare the activities with their own experiences.

Ellen Lewis Buell, "Abroad and At Home," in The New York Times Book Review, *January 3, 1954, p. 22.*

Follow the Road   (1953)

A little boy wanders with his rattly red wagon along the fascinating never-ending road, and what he sees Tresselt describes in rhythmic prose. With Roger Duvoisin's pictures, many double-spread, some colored, we, too, see "the wind weave the leaves of the trees in the sunlight" and "the road going past the city, across the railroad tracks, over a river through twisty, pretzel, clover-leaf roads on to the turnpike." Good for developing awareness.

Florence W. Butler, in a review of "Follow the Road," in Library Journal, *Vol. 79, No. 1, January 1, 1954, p. 71.*

The only trouble with Alvin Tresselt and Roger Duvoisin's picture book, **Follow the Road,** is that it is likely to give young stay-at-homes a severe case of wanderlust. It is true that the little boy who sets out to travel the road stops to play, but the reader goes on—through cool woods, little towns, into a great city and out again onto a Superhighway Throughway Turnpike. Along the way you meet or pass a generous assortment of wagons, passenger cars, buses, trucks, even trains, which adds to the illusion of being part of the traffic, as well as giving youngsters a chance to pick out their favorite type of automobile. The rhythmic prose and the finely detailed pictures capture the tantalizing wonder of a road that goes on and on—"over the hills and through the valleys. All over the world."

Ellen Lewis Buell, "Abroad and At Home," in The New York Times Book Review, *January 3, 1954, p. 22.*

A picture book intended to show the un-endingness of roads. A small boy starts traveling down the road in front of his house to see where it goes. He meets a friend and stops to play, but the road goes on. It passes through woods, through farm land, through a small town, and through a large city until it becomes a super-highway. Soon it becomes a country road again and at the end it is back in front of the little boy's house. The idea that roads circle and come back to where they began is not a particularly accurate one to give young children, and the personification of the road in the text makes the idea even more difficult for the young child to grasp.

Mary K. Eakin, in a review of "Follow the Road," in Bulletin of the Children's Book Center, *Vol. VII, No. 9, May, 1954, p. 80.*

I Saw the Sea Come In   (1954)

The first person on the shore one morning "while the soft gray fog still hung in the sky" was Timothy Robbins. Most might think it would be a lonely place then but not Timothy. The sea and sand had a busy beauty all their own. There were feathers and conch shells to be examined, hermit crabs and sandhoppers to capture, and sand castles to build. Far out on the sea, bell buoys bobbled with a "Clink, watch out . . . clank, take care." As the sun burned away the fog, gay beach umbrellas began to dot the sand. Then the high tide came. Timothy didn't mind, though. He was exultant for he had been there first to see the sea come in.

The highly sentient quality in the experiences presented will probably escape younger members of the picture-book age. But for those who are older and have been to the shore its charm will nourish growing tastes for beauty and simple pleasures. Roger Duvoisin's illustrations in line and color complete the book's excellence.

George A. Woods, "Timothy Was First," in The New York Times, *October 17, 1954, p. 44.*

This quiet, imaginative story has long been a favourite in America, and is surely one of the best works to come from the combined efforts of Duvoisin and Tresselt. Its serene charm and simple adventure will appeal to three- to five-year-olds whether they have seen the sea come in or not. The story describes Timothy Robbins's day at the seaside, the shells and animals he finds there, the sandcastles he builds, the sounds of the birds and the foghorn, and the lapping of the waves far out on the shingle. But it all has a special significance to Timothy because he is the first one there, and it is like being an explorer. Gradually the sunbathers arrive, boats appear on the horizon, and the tide begins to come in. But Timothy knows that it is only he, "the very first one", who really *sees* the sea come in. Pictures and text unite to create a powerful atmosphere of the seashore, from calm to crowds to calm again, while an absorbing story line prevents the book from becoming yet another "mood" book.

J. Davies, in a review of "I Saw the Sea Come In," in Children's Book News, *London, Vol. 3, No. 1, January-February, 1968, p. 13.*

Wake Up, Farm!   (1955)

On Mr. Tresselt's populous farm the first heralders of morning are the birds. Then the rooster joins the chorus, followed by the chickens, ducks, hungry pigs, the goose, the turkey, the pigeons, the dog, the bees and the cows.

Early risers, too, but less noisy, are the horse and colt, the sleepy donkey, the sheep and lambs and tabby and her kittens. Just as the sun comes over the hill, the farmer appears with his milk pails. And last of all a little boy awakens in the farmhouse.

This simply written, ruggedly illustrated [by Roger Duvoisin] book will please youngsters familiar with the delights of waking up on a farm and will provide young city dwellers with a good introduction to farm animals, their habits and sound effects.

> *Marjorie Burger, "Dawn on the Farm," in* The New York Times Book Review, *November 13, 1955, p. 47.*

[*The following excerpt is from a review of an edition published in 1991 with a revised text by Tresselt and illustrations by Carolyn Ewing.*]

A new edition of a picture book, first published in 1955, about the earliest morning activities on a modern farm. Tresselt's updated, lyrical text is longer and more sophisticated as hens "flutter" rather than "hop" and the sun prefers to "rise" rather than "come up." In an effort to "enhance its appeal to a new generation of readers," Duvoisin's distinctive drawings (flat colors, economical lines) have been replaced by lush, realistic paintings [by Carolyn Ewing] in colors that are rich and muted. While there's one minor visual flaw (the barn isn't always red), the overall effect is certainly lovely. (pp. 2159-60)

> *Julie Corsaro, in a review of "Wake Up, Farm!" in* Booklist, *Vol. 87, No. 2, August, 1991, pp. 2159-60.*

The Rabbit Story (1957)

In **The Rabbit Story,** Author Alvin Tresselt and Artist Leonard Weisgard, who so effectively combined their talents in **Rain Drop Splash,** now present the first title in a promising new nature series. In this life cycle story of the rabbit, we watch baby rabbits outgrow their nest and, warned of dangers from fox and farmer, learn to make their own way in the world. In particular, we follow Little Rabbit who, caught in a trap, becomes a boy's pet until the wild free life calls her back and she winds up in a snug burrow with babies of her own.

> *Polly Goodwin, in a review of "The Rabbit Story," in* Chicago Sunday Tribune, *April 7, 1957, p. 9.*

It is good to have another book from the team of Tresselt and Weisgard. . . . **The Rabbit Story** is the life cycle of a little wild rabbit and is the first of a new nature series. The text is poetic and charming and the large illustrations are beautifully reproduced in gravure. Every child will welcome the little rabbit who was taught to "Beware the swift-running fox. . . . The hungry weasel. . . . The velvet-winged owl. . . . Be careful . . . watch out!", but who had not been warned about traps and the little boy who was his friend.

> *Mary Peacock Douglas, in a review of "The*

Rabbit Story," in The Saturday Review, *New York, Vol. XL, No. 19, May 11, 1957, p. 62.*

[*The following excerpts are from reviews of an edition published in 1989 with a revised text by Tresselt and illustrations by Carolyn Ewing.*]

A reissue of a pleasant cyclical story with fresh watercolor illustrations [by Carolyn Ewing]. The story of a wild rabbit's birth, early life, capture, domestication, return to the wild, and eventual motherhood is given the timeless feeling of changing seasons through Tresselt's prose. Changes in the text are minor and enhance clarity—for example, "she remembered the wild free life" is changed to "she felt a yearning for the wild free life." More realistic than Weisgard's brown-toned illustrations, Ewing's paintings will have more immediate appeal to today's children. Her newly captured rabbit cowers in her hutch, while Weisgard's merely looks surprised. While there is certainly a plethora of rabbit stories available, few have as naturalistic an approach as this unpretentious story. Its very simplicity and almost soothing tone, however, may limit its use, as the book may be too quiet for most children. It would provide an excellent introduction to life cycles in elementary science, but may not achieve much popularity as either a read-along or a read-aloud unless children have a particular interest in rabbits.

> *Louise L. Sherman, in a review of "The Rabbit Story," in* School Library Journal, *Vol. 36, No. 2, February, 1990, p. 80.*

First published in 1957, **The Rabbit Story** is now embellished with new illustrations and an updated text. It tells the simple story of a year in the life of a wild rabbit, from birth through maturation. It ends when the rabbit gives birth to another generation. Along the way, there is a relatively nonalarming interlude where Little Rabbit is caught by a farmer in his vegetable garden and kept in a cage as a pet. Freedom comes with escape, and Little Rabbit's life continues unaffected by other dangers of the world. This is not a children's scientific text, but rather a tale of growth that any animal-loving child should enjoy. Soft and easy on the eye, Carolyn Ewing's illustrations carry the story along, making all sentences easily understood even by the youngest reader and allowing a child's imagination to enter a small part of the natural world.

> *Katherine Gillen, in a review of "The Rabbit Story," in* Science Books & Films, *Vol. 25, No. 4, March-April, 1990, p. 214.*

Wake Up, City! (1957)

"Under the stars the city sleeps. . . ." Then, slowly, the city begins to wake. Lights come on, the sky brightens, the buses start their rounds, ships come into the dock, trucks are loaded with fresh fruit and vegetables for the market. All over the city people start to work, children start out for school.

Good morning, says Alvin Tresselt in this remarkable picture of the coming alive of a big city. And as he has caught its bigness and busyness in his word pictures, so has Roger Duvoisin painted them in his colorful line drawings. A refreshingly different picture book, which deserves a lasting place in your child's library.

> *Elizabeth Dutton, in a review of "Wake Up, City!" in* Chicago Sunday Tribune, *Part 4, May 12, 1957, p. 7.*

The mood of this picture book is set by the deep blue cloth cover stamped in white with a milkman driving his horse and cart. The night has departed from the city. The first happenings of day occur. A policeman walks his beat, alarm clocks ring, newspapers rustle on the newsstands, toasters pop. There is a smell of coffee in the air. Off to school go the children. It is "good morning." This is a companion to **Wake Up, Farm** by the same collaborators and will be pleasant to read to nursery and kindergarten groups in the city. Children will surely see everyday scenes in a fresh way, perhaps even be inspired to draw their own impressions of the awakening city.

> *Margaret Sherwood Libby, in a review of "Wake Up, City!" in* New York Herald Tribune Book Review, *August 4, 1957, p. 8.*

[*The following excerpts are from reviews of an edition published in 1990 with a revised text by Tresselt and illustrations by Carolyn Ewing.*]

New illustrations [by Carolyn Ewing] interpret again the direct and evocative text, here revised, of a book first published in 1957. Tresselt's description of some of the things that happen when the day starts in a large city are just as applicable now as then; Ewing's paintings add some touches that will please feminists (a policewoman, a woman bus driver—at least, a bus driver who could be a woman) and some that reflect the architectural variety, the bustle of various activities, and the multiracial composition of the urban scene. (pp. 201-02)

> *Zena Sutherland, in a review of "Wake Up, City!" in* Bulletin of the Center for Children's Books, *Vol. 43, No. 8, April, 1990, pp. 201-02.*

Tresselt's classic picture book shows the city from daybreak until the beginning of the nine-to-five work day. Minimal changes to the text reflect changing realities and perceptions: female police officers and bus drivers appear, and mothers are no longer left at home to wash the dishes and make the beds. While some of Duvoisin's illustrations for the original volume captured the flavor of big-city life with inimitable panache, Ewing's watercolors offer a prettier, somewhat more sentimental view that focuses on individuals rather than on the city itself.

> *Carolyn Phelan, in a review of "Wake Up, City!" in* Booklist, *Vol. 86, No. 17, May 1, 1990, p. 1711.*

The Frog in the Well (1958)

The frog as portrayed by [illustrator] Roger Duvoisin in this jolly picture book is the very essence of frogdom—such wonderful long green legs, such a smooth round throat and stomach, such greenness, such stretchability. In a dozen poses, from contemplating a butterfly to standing on his forefeet with his mighty jumpers in the air, he

delights us against bright red end papers. As his story (the old fable, trimmed a bit by Alvin Tresselt, of the frog who thought the well he lived in was the whole world until he explored a little and found what amazing things the world contained) progresses, he is equally beguiling lying prone as he decides that "the world is nothing but moss covered rock with a pool of water at the bottom," climbing in a leggy fashion up, up out of the well to see what the end of the world would be like or singing chug-a-rum in a delightful spring shower. Whether in full color or green, black and white, these wonderfully humorous pictures offer the greatest fun for children from four to eight, although they and the drolly worded little moral fable, with some of the charm of the immortal one of the toad of Albury Heath can hardly fail to please any age.

> *Margaret Sherwood Libby, in a review of "The Frog in the Well," in* New York Herald Tribune Book Review, *November 2, 1958, p. 4.*

An ideal collaboration of author and illustrator has produced something completely gay in this tale of a frog who "had one very strange idea. He thought his well was the whole world!" The prose lines, set like verse, carry descriptions of the frog's world, his reflections, and growing wisdom as he ventures forth into a wider realm. Mr. Duvoisin has captured the cool greenness of the frog's world in the well and, in full color, the springlike world above. The frog himself becomes a real character—mobile in expression and lively in action. The picture-book age and older will find much to attract them here.

> *Virginia Haviland, in a review of "The Frog in the Well," in* The Horn Book Magazine, *Vol. XXXIV, No. 6, December, 1958, p. 464.*

The Smallest Elephant in the World (1959)

This whimsical, nonsense picture book is unlike Tresselt's earlier works. The smallest elephant in the world has a very unhappy time, until he finds a circus and is accepted by the smallest midget in the world. Milton Glaser's modernistic pictures in brilliant red and green tend to overwhelm the story. Text has the quality of a folk tale in the opening pages, but the mixture of realism and fantasy which resolves the story seems not quite consistent. Strong, excellent format. Will probably be liked very much or not at all by both children and adults.

> *Allie Beth Martin, in a review of "The Smallest Elephant in the World," in* Junior Libraries, *Vol. 84, No. 22, November, 1959, p. 32.*

The place for an elephant the size of a house cat might appear to be with house cats. But the Smallest Elephant in the World tries this experiment and turns elsewhere. The reasoning which leads him to his eventual home may not seem too watertight to those strictest of logicians, the 4-8's. But the splashy primary-colored illustrations should go a long way toward making them forgive the inconsistencies of adult thinking.

> *A review of "The Smallest Elephant in the World," in* The Christian Science Monitor, *November 5, 1959, p. 2B.*

The smallest elephant in the world was very unhappy because all the other animals and birds in the Indian jungle laughed at him . . . he was the size of a house cat. So he ran away, and being so small he was not found when he stowed away on a ship. He found a boy named Arnold, but Arnold's mother didn't want even so small an elephant as a pet. She called a circus and they did want him and he found a very happy life there; nobody laughed at a small elephant, even the big elephants. A pleasant bit of nonsense, told in bland, light style.

> *A review of "The Smallest Elephant in the World," in* Bulletin of the Center for Children's Books, *Vol. XIII, No. 7, March, 1960, p. 122.*

Timothy Robbins Climbs the Mountain (1960)

This is an expression of the wonderful sense of release anyone feels, who has been confined by a long winter, when he is able to set forth on a spring day to climb a "little mountain." In glorious colors, the pictures [by Roger Duvoisin]—full-page and doublespread—take the two boys of the story (and the reader) through the woods, along the brook, over the jagged rocks, up to the very top where they have their lunch, "by the side of a wind-twisted tree, with the whole world down below." Early spring is truly in these pages.

> *Ruth Hill Viguers, in a review of "Timothy Robbins Climbs the Mountain," in* The Horn Book Magazine, *Vol. XXXVI, No. 2, April, 1960, p. 126.*

Alvin Tresselt and Roger Duvoisin salute spring and the joys of being outdoors in one of their most beautiful and radiantly colorful picture books. It was not a rocky mountain, nor a little hill, but a mountain right for a boy to climb that lured Timothy Robbins, his dog, and a friend on a bright spring day. And young readers are going to have a wonderful time sharing the boys' discoveries at every turn of the path as it winds along a brook, over the rocks, and thru the woods until it reaches the top where, "by the side of a wind-twisted tree, with the whole world down below, they ate their lunch."

> *Polly Goodwin, in a review of "Timothy Robbins Climbs the Mountain," in* Chicago Sunday Tribune, *Part 4, April 24, 1960, p. 10.*

Timothy and his friend, together with a dog, fishing poles, compass and lunches, hike onward and upward. And like innumerable boys before them, they see animal tracks and flowers, drink spring water and finally stand "nearer to the sun and closer to the clouds . . . with air all around them." It is a quiet adventure, but poignant and exhilarating, just as life is to small boys. (p. 30)

> *George A. Woods, "The World through Multi-Colored Magnifying Glasses," in* The New York Times Book Review, *Part II, May 8, 1960, pp. 30-1.*

Under the Trees and through the Grass (1962)

"Who goes by? / Who goes by in the woods? / Who goes under the trees / and through the whispery grasses? / 'I go by,' says a little raccoon. / 'I go by with my black and white tail.' "

Alvin Tresselt's nature books with their rhythmic texts are known to be among the best of this type that we have. Here, each animal introduces itself and tells some of the things that it does.

> *Alice Dalgliesh, in a review of "Under the Trees and through the Grass," in* Saturday Review, *Vol. XLV, No. 45, November 10, 1962, p. 34.*

The Mitten: An Old Ukrainian Folktale (1964)

The Mitten is a retelling of an old Ukrainian folk tale. A boy loses his mitten in the woods, and magically all the forest animals crawl into it, seeking shelter from the cold. Each episode is just predictable enough to keep the listener at rapt attention, and Alvin Tresselt's writing has great verve.

> *Alberta Eiseman, in a review of "The Mitten," in* The New York Times Book Review, *November 1, 1964, p. 58.*

A rather tepid version of the Ukrainian tale about an accumulation of forest animals that take refuge in a child's lost mitten. The mitten holds a mouse, a rabbit, a fox, a wolf, a bear, a boar, etcetera; it gives way, finally, when a tiny cricket tries to join the other creatures. The illustrations [by Yaroslava] are attractive although not distinguished; the costume detail is appropriate for the story's source, but this adds little to a text that gives no hint of the locale.

> *Zena Sutherland, in a review of "The Mitten," in* Bulletin of the Center for Children's Books, *Vol. XVIII, No. 5, January, 1965, p. 80.*

Hide and Seek Fog (1965)

There is something very special about a fog in its own peculiar movements and in the way it transforms life. The gently poetic text follows the fog in its three day passage in and around a picturesque little resort on Cape Cod, and expresses the reactions of the people to this heavy weather. The paintings [by Roger Duvoisin] capture perfectly the three dimensional mist and its motion. The return to the normal life in the bright, cheerful village plays up the unique qualities of the phenomenon. The mood of the fog has been skillfully evoked by the author and illustrator who teamed up on the award-winning **White Snow, Bright Snow** and many other excellent picture books.

> *A review of "Hide and Seek Fog," in* Kirkus Reviews, *Vol. XXXIII, No. 3, February 1, 1965, p. 105.*

The inviting title and book jacket picture of children at play on a hazy shore will beckon each child who spies this book. He won't be disappointed when he listens to this poetic mood piece describing a New England village as it waits for a long and heavy fog to pass. He will feel the chill and dampness as he studies Roger Duvoisin's exquisite water colors. . . . The text falters occasionally but not enough to mar the feeling of suspended motion throughout the village. " . . . the fog twisted about the cottages like slow-motion smoke. It dulled the rusty scraping of the beach grass. It muffled the chattery talk of the low tide waves." There are several fine picture books about the atmosphere along the New England coast. This takes its place among them and has a quality all its own. (pp. 956-57)

> *Patricia H. Allen, in a review of "Hide and Seek Fog," in* Library Journal, *Vol. 90, No. 4, February 15, 1965, pp. 956-57.*

The fog rolls in over ocean and bay sending fishermen, sailors, and vacationers back to their docks, moorings, and cottages. Laden with moisture and apprehension, it shrouds the town for three days, permeating spirits as well as atmosphere. While grownups grumble, children play. Childhood's response to the unusual, the unknown, is given sensitive and spontaneous expression. Mr. Tresselt's poetic prose, characteristic of his other stories describing seasonal experiences, is simple, direct, friendly. [Roger] Duvoisin's illustrations, however, are a departure from his previous work for children. As shadowy shapes and muted shades move, haunting and ephemeral, through floating, "cotton-wool" mist, who can say what surprises lie in wait beyond the gray haze? Another distinguished achievement by the author-illustrator team.

> *Priscilla L. Moulton, in a review of "Hide and Seek Fog," in* The Horn Book Magazine, *Vol. XLI, No. 2, April, 1965, p. 164.*

The perfect partnership of author and artist that made **White Snow, Bright Snow** memorable has been productive again in **Hide and Seek Fog.** Alvin Tresselt's description of the fog drifting in, stopping all activities in a seaside village, has the rhythm and gentle motion of the mist, and Roger Duvoisin's pictures fairly drip with moisture yet show that luminousness that gives fog such an eerie effect. Mood-picture books are very popular—with the grownups, anyway—but rarely do they add, as here, a bit of genuine life to their mature, impressionistic descriptions. One feels that children will be able to imagine themselves dodging around these misty streets.

> *A review of "Hide and Seek Fog," in* Book Week—The Sunday Herald Tribune, *May 9, 1965, p. 28.*

Lovely, lovely illustrations for a read-aloud story about a three day fog at Cape Cod. The text, very direct and simple, describes the fog rolling in and the suspension of most outdoor activities, the ennui of the adults and the fun for the children. Although straightforward, the text has phrases that are happily exact: "On the beach, the sand was suddenly cold and sticky." The misty and luminous pastels of the illustrations would be attractive even if they were not evocative, but they give almost tangibly the clammy aura of fog. (pp. 51-2)

> *Zena Sutherland, in a review of "Hide and*

Seek Fog," in Bulletin of the Center for Children's Books, *Vol. 19, No. 3, November, 1965, pp. 51-2.*

A Thousand Lights and Fireflies (1965)

The thousand lights of the title are city lights. The fireflies are country lights. The text is a series of comparisons between city and country conditions. The author seems to have intended to show that whether people are in the city or the country, both groups have children who like to keep pets or fly kites; that the adults like to potter around with flowers. The illustrations [by John Moodie] are distinctive, but the comparisons and some of the pictures combine to a total effect of menace for anything associated with the city. For instance, the city birds are tank-like pigeons in black; country birds stream in color against an endless sky. Or, city horses carry policemen; country horses run in pastures and win prizes at horse shows. Or country noises are chirpings and water gurgling; city noises are "the machine-gun blast of a jackhammer, the shriek of a fire engine . . . " The text is a misleading mood piece and the book is a showcase for the artist who has a masterful command of color and whose impressionistic technique conveys a powerful sense of movement.

> *A review of "A Thousand Lights and Fireflies," in* Virginia Kirkus' Service, *Vol. XXXIII, No. 8, April 15, 1965, p. 431.*

No story to this one, but plenty of good color effects in very modern pictures, with pleasant-sounding words. As a comparison between city and country, however, this would seem only to confuse. Houses in the country do not "sit apart so they can look at one another." "A city sky is caught between tall buildings" will not mean much to a child. Perhaps it would be better to go back to some of Alvin Tresselt's far more successful descriptive books such as **Raindrop Splash!** and **White Snow, Bright Snow.** And, going back only a very short distance, there is this season's fine book **Hide and Seek Fog. . . .**

> *A review of "A Thousand Lights and Fireflies," in* Saturday Review, *Vol. XLVIII, No. 20, May 15, 1965, p. 44.*

A read-aloud picture book that is beautifully illustrated with pictures in bold colors, somewhat in Wildsmith's style. . . . The text is simple, pleasantly written, not unusual in theme but appealing. It contrasts patterns in city and in country, then points out some aspect of living in which there is a similarity, repeating this three-part pattern throughout.

> *Zena Sutherland, in a review of "A Thousand Lights and Fireflies," in* Bulletin of the Center for Children's Books, *Vol. 19, No. 4, December, 1965, p. 70.*

The World in the Candy Egg (1967)

Not since Pamela Bianco looked inside a spun-sugar egg has anyone done justice to the enchanted existence behind the glass window, and seldom has there been an equally evocative Easter book. There's no story—there doesn't need to be—just the candy egg sitting on the toyshop shelf as each of the other toys takes a look, as each watches the "secret world, magic world, spun of sugar and light." The shepherd chases crows in the cornfield, two kittens tumble on the doorstep, the cool brook bubbles in the window, the shepherd trips on his stick, until . . . the shopkeeper packs the egg in a box: then it is dark in the egg and nothing happens for a long time. Then suddenly the wrappings crackle . . . a little girl picks up the egg and peeks inside . . . "And there was everyone busy working again." In a gaily colored combination of painting and collage, Roger Duvoisin conjures up a crowded store and a pretty pastorale inside the egg. A few of the scenes are overcrowded and overcolored, a few of the figures are awkwardly placed, but never mind—it's a delightful book.

> *A review of "The World in the Easter Egg," in* Kirkus Reviews, *Vol. XXXV, No. 1, January 1, 1967, p. 2.*

All the warmth and color of springtime are in the exuberant illustrations of this Easter picture book for the very young; the miniature scene in the candy egg is filled with sun and flowers, and the egg itself is set in the merry jumble of a toyshop shelf. Alvin Tresselt describes in a gay, simple style the toys gazing into the tiny panorama; the egg is then boxed, and a quiet suspension of activity ends when a delighted child unwraps her gift and sees the magic world in the candy egg.

> *Zena Sutherland, in a review of "The World in the Candy Egg," in* Saturday Review, *Vol. L, No. 7, February 18, 1967, p. 41.*

It is [the] love of the tiny that makes **The World in the Candy Egg** so appealing. The world of course is the frankly idyllic one glimpsed through the window of a chocolate egg. "Little world, tiny world, where everything's snug and tight." All the toy animals peer in on this springtime of a world and tell what they see in Alvin Tresselt's cozy, one-eye-on-the-adult verse. But sweetness, especially at bedtime, is welcomingly soothing. . . .

> *Pamela Marsh, "Scaled for Lilliput," in* The Christian Science Monitor, *May 4, 1967, p. B2.*

The Tears of the Dragon   (1967)

[*The Tears of the Dragon was originally written in Japanese by Hirosuke Hamada; the English-language version is by Tresselt.*]

[This is] an unconvincing fantasy from Japan. For many years the people in a Japanese village lived in fear of a wicked dragon which no one had seen but which, reportedly, lived in a mountain cave above the village. Unlike the adults and the other children, Akito did not accept the terrible stories about the dragon. Since no one could really enlighten him he decided to go find out, and invite it to his birthday celebration. After a difficult climb and a search that lasted into a second day, Akito found a dragon that wept so copiously at his kind invitation a great river was formed. As the dragon with Akito on its back floated

down to the valley and approached the village, the monster changed into a dragon boat which the whole village could enjoy instead of fear. Exquisite illustrations [by Chihiro Iwasaki] in soft watercolor fail to save the stilted, choppy text.

> *Marjorie Schmidt, in a review of "The Tears of the Dragon," in* School Library Journal, *Vol. 14, No. 4, December, 1967, p. 61.*

Akito alone is unafraid of the monstrous dragon, who all of the villagers believe lives in the craggy mountains nearby. So sorry is the boy for the dragon he decides to invite him to his birthday party. Akito's adventures in the mountains constitute the remainder of the tale. The story first appeared in this country as a picture story, *The Dragon's Tears.* By comparison, the less colloquial, more poetic style of Alvin Tresselt is nearer to the fairytale tradition.

> *Marian Marx, in a review of "The Tears of the Dragon," in* The Horn Book Magazine, *Vol. XLIV, No. 2, April, 1968, p. 170.*

The Legend of the Willow Plate   (with Nancy Cleaver, 1968)

First spun by the dynasty poets in the days of the emperors, this ancient Chinese legend is the tale of two lovers: a mandarin's daughter elopes with his secretary, who has wooed her under a willow tree with lovely lyrics. When they are discovered, the gods transform them into doves so that they can flutter out of reach and soar "free and happy, high in the blue skies of China." In the late 18th century a Staffordshire potter, Thomas Minton, borrowed the theme for his now classic blue-and-white willow-ware. In turn, his porcelain pattern has inspired the authors to set down the old tale for a new generation of children who may have admired the scene on a willow plate and wondered about its meaning. In graceful prose as polished as fine jade, they have given it a fresh, appealing interpretation. Further embroidered by Joseph Low in illustrations drawn with blithe, impressionistic strokes and glowing jewel-toned washes, the story has come full cycle, a marriage of traditional and modern artistry.

> *Margaret F. O'Connell, in a review of "The Legend of the Willow Plate," in* The New York Times Book Review, *April 14, 1968, p. 20.*

Simplicity, beauty, and dignity—elements inherent in the tale itself—mark this retelling of the Chinese legend of the willow plate. . . . Harmony is achieved by the illustrations, decorative and outlined in blue to evoke the willow-plate design. Action and added colors in subtle tones bring alive the events of the story. (pp. 317-18)

> *Marion Marx, in a review of "The Legend of the Willow Plate," in* The Horn Book Magazine, *Vol. XLIV, June, 1968, pp. 317-18.*

A charming picture-book version of a popular legend of unknown origin which interprets the dramatic Chinese scene depicted on the famous blue-and-white willow pattern dinnerware first manufactured in England around

1780. The tragic love story of the lovely, highborn Koong-se and the poor peasant poet Chang is retold with grace and simplicity and illustrated with soft-hued pictures which accentuate the Oriental setting.

> *A review of "The Legend of the Willow Plate," in The Booklist and Subscription Books Bulletin, Vol. 64, No. 19, June 1, 1968, p. 1145.*

The Crane Maiden (1968)

[The Crane Maiden *was originally written in Japanese by Miyoko Matsutani; the English-language version is by Tresselt.*]

Luminous watercolor illustrations [by Chihiro Iwasaki] give added dimension to the old Japanese tale about a crane who takes human form to repay the kindness of a man who had freed her from a trap. In some variations she appears as his wife, but in this version the crane becomes a lovely young girl, who comes to live as their daughter with the kindly old couple. When she realizes their poverty, she weaves, in strictest secrecy, a length of rare brocade for them to sell. However, when the old woman disobeys the girl's command never to watch her at work, the spell is broken and the crane must leave forever. The details of Tsuru-san's life with the old pair are elaborated just enough so that the telling remains graceful. Glowing double-page illustrations reinforce the story's fairy-tale quality and are a lyrical accompaniment to the fine storytelling.

> *Margaret A. Dorsey, in a review of "The Crane Maiden," in School Library Journal, Vol. 14, No. 9, May, 1968, p. 73.*

Lafcadio Hearn did it first and then Yei Ozaki at the turn of the century—masterfully adapted Japanese folktales for Western children. The majority of those who have followed have not been true to the literary and scholarly demands of re-creating a folktale. Alas for the tale that does not receive the master's touch; it becomes a mere glimmer of its real self.

Such is the case with this translation of **The Crane Maiden,** one of Japan's most compelling folktales. In this version of the story a beautiful white crane assumes human shape and becomes the daughter of a poor woodcutter. She weaves a rare bolt of material for the old man and his wife with the admonition that they do not peek while she is at the loom. When the wife betrays her by looking, the crane disappears into the sky.

Originally published in Japan, **The Crane Maiden** has been translated into stiff and literal English that loses the poetry of the story. The maiden greets her new family in the morning with: "If you will wash your hands we may eat breakfast, for the porridge is cooked and ready"; and she attracts the neighborhood children because "she was such a delight to be with." The illustrations are enchanting, however, bold and fanciful, revealing much of the magic of an important tale that deserves a better treatment.

> *Betty Jean Lifton, in a review of "The Crane*

Maiden," in The New York Times Book Review, August 11, 1968, p. 18.

How Rabbit Tricked His Friends (1969)

[How Rabbit Tricked His Friends *was originally written in Japanese by Mieko Maeda; the English-language version is by Tresselt.*]

A Japanese version of the rabbit and the tar baby, a story loved in this country from the moment Joel Chandler Harris put pen to paper to write his "Uncle Remus" stories, is a welcome version, thanks to the fluid and colorful illustrations [by Yasuo Segawa] and its lively text. (We can thank Alvin Tresselt for *that*.)

> *A review of "How Rabbit Tricked His Friends," in Publishers Weekly, Vol. 195, No. 6, February 10, 1969, p. 75.*

Mieko Maeda recast the American Uncle Remus story characters in a Japanese tale; in Alvin Tresselt's translation of the Japanese adaptation, readers will find that, instead of just Brer Bear and Brer Fox conspiring to catch that smart-alecky Brer Rabbit, their counterparts are joined by four other animals—Lion, Wolf, Monkey and Elephant. It hasn't rained for months, and the seven animals are perishing of thirst in a drought. When Elephant remembers having seen a man get water from a hole in the ground, he and the other friends join in the digging—except for clever, lazy Rabbit, who doesn't want to dirty his fur. Water appears, and the six industrious ones vow to guard the pool against Rabbit, who nevertheless outsmarts them. So, to catch him, they construct a tar baby—and from there the ensuing antics parallel the episodes in the Uncle Remus story. The book should have included more explanatory material on the origin of the tale doesn't specify if the American tale (was the basis of this version or whether there was a parallel Japanese folk story), but the end product, with its fun-enhancing water colors [by Yasuo Segawa], is an enjoyable variant of a tested favorite.

> *Susanne Gilles, in a review of "How Rabbit Tricked His Friends," in School Library Journal, Vol. 15, No. 8, April, 1969, p. 103.*

It's Time Now! (1969)

Because of the felicitous union of text and [Roger Duvoisin's] illustrations a time-worn theme seems new and fresh in this attractive picture book. Tresselt's descriptive text and Duvoisin's pictures in full color vividly convey a sense of the changing seasons in the city and expressively portray urban scenes and activities characteristic of each season. (pp. 59-60)

> *Ruth P. Bull, in a review of "It's Time Now!" in The Booklist, Vol. 66, No. 1, September 1, 1969, pp. 59-60.*

A quiet book that beautifully describes a year of seasons in the city. . . . The pervading mood of the book is one of great happiness, with text and pictures contributing to the overall effect. While it is refreshing to find this approach today in a book with an urban setting, assumptions like: fall is the "Time to go shopping for a new pair of shoes, new pants, new dresses."; or "At noontime the streets shimmer in the midday heat. 'Now is the time . . . for a day at the beach.' " may be disturbing for many urban children and misleading for rural children.

> *Barbara S. Miller, in a review of "It's Time Now!" in* School Library Journal, *Vol. 16, No. 3, November, 1969, p. 113.*

The seasons of the year pictured in terms of a child's life: it has all been done before and well done but this is one of those themes to which every artist is entitled to add his own interpretation. Here the artist produces one of his most attractive picture books, having chosen the life of a child in an American city, with the textual concession to the British child, "suddenly it's Hallowe'en and Guy Fawkes". The eye travels with pleasure over the pastel shades of spring, the festoons of coloured lights round the park bandstand in high summer, the swirling snow at the year's end culminating in the glowing Christmas tree in the winter streets, underlining the author's contention that "now comes the best time". The carping sociologist will find that the artist shows the sad fact that while small white and coloured children play together in the park, as they grow up they segregate: an artist must paint what he sees. If this saddens the adult, it is neither here nor there for the child who cannot fail to take the greatest delight in the procession of pictures though he probably will tend to ignore the text—he can more easily supply his own. Texts like this probably give more pleasure to adults and older children above the picture book stage. (pp. 100-01)

> *C. Martin, in a review of "It's Time Now!" in* The Junior Bookshelf, *Vol. 35, No. 2, April, 1971, pp. 100-01.*

The Fisherman under the Sea (1969)

[The Fisherman under the Sea *was originally written in Japanese by Miyoko Matsutani; the English-language version is by Tresselt.*]

The tale of Taro, a young fisherman, who rescues a turtle and finds it's really the daughter of the king of the sea, is charmingly related in this English-language version of a Japanese folk tale. Taro is taken to the undersea kingdom where he marries the princess and lives happily for a long while. However, he begins to long for his earthly home, and goes back for a visit; the princess gives him a box which, if opened, will prevent him from returning to her. On land, Taro finds that a great many years have passed. Puzzled, he opens the box, hoping for an answer to his confusion, and immediately becomes an old man—his own life had been enclosed in the box to ensure his perpetual youth—and now he can't return to his beautiful underwater princess. The lovely, softly shaded color illustrations [by Chihiro Iwasaki] give the illusion of underwater scenes and enhance the gentle, simple story.

> *Estelle Schulman, in a review of "The Fisherman under the Sea," in* School Library Journal, *Vol. 16, No. 1, September, 1969, p. 104.*

In return for an act of kindness a young fisherman is taken to the Dragon Palace beneath the sea where he marries the beautiful princess and lives happily until the desire to see his parents and his village leads him to an unhappy fate. The ancient Japanese legend is retold and illustrated with the grace and beauty which marked *The Crane Maiden,* by the same author and illustrator. (pp. 138-39)

> *A review of "The Fisherman under the Sea," in* The Booklist, *Vol. 66, No. 2, September 15, 1969, pp. 138-39.*

The Rolling Rice Ball (1969)

[The Rolling Rice Ball *was originally written in Japanese by Junichi Yoda; the English-language version is by Tresselt.*]

This version of a Japanese folktale (the origins of which are not fully documented in the book) transcends the barriers of nationality and time while maintaining an Oriental feeling. One day, an old woodcutter comes upon fantastic adventure while having his noon meal. One of his rice balls falls into a hole in the ground and is lost. Upon hearing a voice singing in the hole, the woodcutter drops in two more rice balls, meets a mouse, and is soon transported to a strange underground world. For his patience and generosity, he is handsomely rewarded. A neighbor, learning of such good fortune, desires the same and meets disaster. Bold, highly expressive watercolors [by Saburo Watanabe] embellish the tale and will attract individual children as well as program leaders seeking picture books with group impact.

> *Josette A. Boissé, in a review of "The Rolling Rice Ball," in* School Library Journal, *Vol. 17, No. 1, September, 1970, p. 155.*

Gengoroh and the Thunder God (1970)

[Gengoroh and the Thunder God *was originally written in Japanese by Miyoko Matsutani; the English-language version is by Tresselt.*]

A magic drum, which has won him renown and wealth, sends Gengoroh's nose shooting to the heavens where it is used as an anchor on a bridge across the Milky Way. Reverse magic indeed shortens the nose, but because it is so firmly anchored, the Japanese boy is drawn up to the end of it where he is freed by the thunder god whose assistant he becomes. The story line of the folktale is here confused by too many events, but it's redeemed by the humor of the situations, the smooth quality of the text, and the playful, light-filled color illustrations [by Yasuo Segawa] which enliven every page.

> *Margaret Riddell, in a review of "Gengoroh and the Thunder God," in* Library Journal, *Vol. 95, No. 13, July, 1970, p. 2529.*

The Beaver Pond (1970)

The clear, simple language and animated illustrations

[Roger Duvoisin's] take readers full cycle—from stream to beaver-made pond and back to stream. As the beavers build their dam, the stream gradually becomes a pond: reeds grow along the shore; ducks and kingfishers fish; raccoons and other life make their home there. Life at the pond undergoes natural seasonal changes. Over the years, the beavers become too numerous for the pond so they go further downstream to make a new one, and their old dam is washed away by the force of a spring flood. Beautifully illustrated with full-color paintings and a few black line drawings, the commendable book gives some insight into nature's plan that can be understood and appreciated by listening and viewing audiences as well as by young independent readers.

> *Eleanor Glaser, in a review of "The Beaver Pond," in* School Library Journal, *Vol. 17, No. 3, November, 1970, p. 103.*

The Beaver Pond traces the birth, life, and death of a pond, built, as you have guessed, by beavers. The theme is ecology and the relationship of beavers to the other animals that come to live on or near the pond. Even though the beavers move, the pond is still used by many other forms of life until the old dam gives way and once again the stream runs free. Even at this point the story does not end, but new life grows in the rich soil that was once the pond bottom. **The Beaver Pond** is a well-written, well-illustrated book that will be enjoyed by the adult reading the story to the preschooler as much as the child will enjoy it.

> *Ryan B. Walden, in a review of "The Beaver Pond," in* Appraisal: Children's Science Books, *Vol. 4, No. 2, Spring, 1971, p. 32.*

Similar in design to many other nature stories produced by the same team. The graphic and handsome full-page (and nearly full-page) color illustrations are printed on somewhat shiny paper, which robs them of a little of their charm; but for a child's examination the scenes add immensely to an understanding of the interplay between beaver activity and wildlife scenery. The story describes changing seasons for beaver, fish, birds, and other creatures in and around a pond created by the beavers' dam—until "As the years passed the pond grew smaller / and more shallow /. . . . the pond grew too small for all the beavers. / So . . . off went the beavers / down the stream / to find a new place for their home." Spring torrents freed the stream, and a green meadow sprang up where there was once a pond, while the beavers farther down "had already built / a new strong dam, / and a new pond sparkled in the sunlight." An apt introduction to ecology for the picture-book age.

> *Virginia Haviland, in a review of "The Beaver Pond," in* The Horn Book Magazine, *Vol. XLVII, No. 2, April, 1971, p. 163.*

Between cheerful painted scenes, the short sentences tell how a family of beavers uses a dam to hold water where they can find food and live in a sturdy lodge. But silt in the stream gradually reduces the size of the pond until the beavers desert, the dam falls into disrepair, then breaks and lets the water cut a channel again much as it was be-

fore the beavers came. Fitted into this story of succession is a pleasant and adequate account of other animals and plants that live in the area because of the activity of the beavers. The reader (or the child that is read to) gets a feeling for the ecological relations without realizing that this is more than an interesting story about the outdoor world.

> *A review of "The Beaver Pond," in* Science Books: A Quarterly Review, *Vol. 7, No. 1, May, 1971, p. 51.*

The Ogre and His Bride   (1971)

[The Ogre and His Bride *was originally written in Japanese by Nami Kishi; the English-language version is by Tresselt.*]

The ugly little ogre in this Japanese Beauty and the Beast tale deserves all the sympathy. In exchange for making it rain and saving the crops, the lonely ogre asks for one of the farmer's daughters in marriage. The youngest becomes his bride and "The ogre was very kind to Kaiko, and she was not unhappy living . . . with him." Despite this, Kaiko retraces her steps in the spring, is welcomed back by her family, and the poor ogre is tricked into leaving without her. The illustrations [by Shosuke Fukuda] combine cartoon-like figures with murky backgrounds; they and the questionable story line make a poor frame for Tresselt's fine writing.

> *Dorothy Gunzenhauser, in a review of "The Ogre and His Bride," in* School Library Journal, *Vol. 18, No. 1, September, 1971, p. 151.*

Wonder-Fish from the Sea   (1971)

[Wonder-Fish from the Sea *was originally written in German by Josef Guggenmos; the English-language version is by Tresselt.*]

This strange, mystical story is a visual treat with [Irmgard Lucht's] unusual use of leaf prints and soft greens, browns and oranges. The story starts slowly, but a mood is set as the leaves are evocatively described. They unfold, with only the wind and rain for companions. Then birds come and build their nests in "the friendly secret shadows of the leaves." The leaves listen as the birds tell of their travels to faraway places. Then the wind tells the leaves about one place the birds never mention—the sea. One day, a secret message passing from tree to tree causes the leaves to "let go of the twigs and branches," be caught up in the wind and brought by it to the sea where magically they become leaf-fish. Two such dandelion fish spawn and their eggs later hatch into many tiny fish. A fisherman decides to catch some, but when he lifts his nets full of "the wonder-fish of the sea," he finds that they are nothing but forest leaves. Beautifully illustrated, sensitively told, this story will be best enjoyed if it is introduced and read to children by an appreciative adult.

> *Eleanor Glaser, in a review of "Wonder-Fish from the Sea," in* School Library Journal, *Vol. 18, No. 1, September, 1971, p. 2357.*

Lum Fu and the Golden Mountain (1971)

[Lum Fu and the Golden Mountain *was originally written in Japanese by Hisako Kimishima; the English-language version is by Tresselt.*]

Another in a series of Japanese folktales skillfully translated by Alvin Tresselt and including the original illustrations. Lum Fu is fortunate enough to arrive on the scene when the god of the mountain has spread his gold coins under the full summer moon. Given three coins, then another three, Lum Fu's greed leads him to involve his whole family in seeking more and more—and eventually to lose all, even his original six coins and the basket of grass he was gathering for his animals. The illustrations [by Daihachi Ohta] are strikingly colorful and, though the tale is highly moral, it is convincing and gently humorous in true folk fashion.

> *Margaret Riddell, in a review of "Lum Fu and the Golden Mountain," in* School Library Journal, *Vol. 18, No. 16, September, 1971, p. 2906.*

Stories from the Bible (1971)

Dutifully reverent—including pseudo-archaic transpositions of verb and subject—prose transcriptions of a few of the best known Old Testament stories are accompanied by well designed, but forbidding, brown and black lithographs [by Lynd Ward]. The result is an oversized volume which exudes Sunday School sanctity but considerably diminishes the stature of the material. Tresselt offers neither the simplified language of Sholem Asch's *In the Beginning* (1966) nor the expanded narratives of Walter de la Mare's *Stories From the Bible*. In short, whatever you're looking for in biblical adaptations, you will find it better done elsewhere.

> *A review of "Stories from the Bible," in* Kirkus Reviews, *Vol. XXXIX, No. 20, October 15, 1971, p. 1129.*

With such an experienced and well-known author and illustrator as Alvin Tresselt and Lynd Ward, it is disappointing to note this book, an adaptation of 12 Old Testament Bible stories, is a seemingly forced rewriting of the material from which it was taken. The black and brown lithograph illustrations, although bold and dynamic, are too somber in appearance for the intended audience.

> *A review of "Stories from the Bible," in* Publishers Weekly, *Vol. 200, No. 19, November 8, 1971, p. 49.*

No more could be asked of an Old Testament adaptation than that it retain the poetic quality and drama of the stories, and be appropriately written for its audience. When this is combined with illustrations that not only share the spirit of reverence but have their own powerful beauty as well, the result is impressive. Oversize pages lend dignity to Lynd Ward's lithographs and provide a handsome setting for Alvin Tresselt's sensitive rendering of some favorite stories.

> *Zena Sutherland, in a review of "Stories from*

the Bible," in Saturday Review, *Vol. LV, No. 3, January 15, 1972, p. 47.*

The Hare and the Bear and Other Stories (1971)

[The Hare and the Bear and Other Stories *was originally written in Japanese by Yasue Maiyagawa; the English-language version is by Tresselt.*]

Mr. Hare is the anti-hero of these three Japanese stories translated by Alvin Tresselt. In the first story, Mr. Hare gets the most mileage out of his sore foot after Mr. Bear inadvertently steps on it. Kindhearted Bear gives Hare bed and board, but no matter what he does it isn't enough, until visiting Mr. Fox suggests an operation that sends Mr. Hare scurrying. The second story begins with an old car which is being refurbished by Mr. Elephant and Mr. Hippo with much advice and no labor from Mr. Hare, and ends with a car wreck and Mr. Hare hopping away again. In the last story our hero, who has become an artist, makes a fool out of a jackass who fancies that he looks fierce and cannot accept the true to-life portrait Mr. Hare paints of him. The episodes are fast-paced, and young children should enjoy the humor in both the text and the bright, attractive watercolor illustrations [by Yoshiharu Suzuki]. (pp. 57-8)

> *Gail Abbott, in a review of "The Hare and the Bear and Other Stories," in* School Library Journal, *Vol. 18, No. 6, February, 1972, pp. 57-8.*

The Dead Tree (1972; also published as *The Gift of the Tree*)

With surgical thoroughness, this occasionally lugubrious labor of love probes the process of decay as it advances through a moribund, then lifeless, oak during "hundreds of years" until it disappears into a "brown ghost of richer loam." Without ever forcing analogies, Tresselt makes clear that the dying of a single tree plays a vital role in the woodland life cycle of countless creatures, that death is never final in the larger scheme of things. Again, there is a special child somewhere waiting for Tresselt's quiet message. One can only be grateful that there are publishers around willing to chance finding him.

> *Selma G. Lanes, "Afterwords," in* Book World—Chicago Tribune, *May 7, 1972, p. 15.*

Illustrated with handsome pictures [by Charles Robinson] in soft-hued water colors, this gives much the same story that is in *Who Lives in This Log?* by Ross . . . , but the text is far superior. Alvin Tresselt has the ability to give accurate information simply while using prose that has a poetic quality. The illustrations echo and amplify the mood of woodland stillness that is a background for the busy procession of creatures and plants that use a fallen tree for food and shelter. The text follows the tree's life from full maturity to its return to the rich humus of the forest floor.

> *Zena Sutherland, in a review of "The Dead*

Tree," in Bulletin of the Center for Children's Books, *Vol. 26, No. 2, October, 1972, p. 33.*

The regeneration of life in nature is beautifully celebrated in this picture book, in which the accuracy of observation is enriched by perceptive interpretation. The text is set against lovely watercolor illustrations, each doublespread depicting some aspect of the changing life of the tree.

> *Beryl Robinson, in a review of "The Dead Tree," in* The Horn Book Magazine, *Vol. 49, No. 2, April, 1973, p. 136.*

[*The following excerpts are from reviews of* The Gift of the Tree, *published in 1992 with illustrations by Henri Sorensen.*]

With a new title, larger format, and expansive new illustrations, a reissue of **The Dead Tree,** the prolific author's 1972 account of the natural end of an oak's long life: rotting wood attracts insects and then leaves holes that become homes for other creatures; after the tree falls, it continues to nurture and provides homes for the forest wildlife until "there remained only a brown ghost of richer loam where the proud tree had come to rest." Sorensen, a Danish painter who also reillustrated Tresselt's **Sun Up,** contributes sun-dappled, impressionistic illustrations that beautifully reflect an evocative text that's a reminder that just 20 years ago young children could be expected to take words like "garner" and "moldered" in their stride. One of the best of a spate of spring books designed to encourage the treasuring of trees.

> *A review of "The Gift of the Tree," in* Kirkus Reviews, *Vol. LX, No. 4, February 15, 1992, p. 260.*

New illustrations breathe freshness into this book originally published as **The Dead Tree.** It stands as a tribute to the mighty oak tree, focusing on its majesty in maturity, through gradual decline to final decay. The interdependence of plant and animal life is clearly evident, including both those that seek its shelter and those that hasten the decaying process to prepare the soil for new life. The original text stands the test of time, reaching its audience with power and emotion as it directs attention to the forces of nature at work. The writing style encourages the young to develop a sensitivity to all aspects of nature without lecturing. Illustrations stretch from cover to cover across double-page spreads to immerse readers in a forest setting. Seasons and years fade one into another through impressionistic woodland scenes that form the background for the oak and various animals that appear in realistic form. Color tones reflect the seasons, as they are softly muted in fall and winter; more vivid in spring and summer. These illustrations are far more vibrant than those in the previous edition. A perfect choice to use with Romanova's *Once There Was a Tree* (Dial, 1985) and Hiscock's *The Big Tree* (Atheneum, 1991) to promote a full understanding of the natural cycle of trees, ever changing, ever renewing.

> *Diane Nunn, in a review of "The Gift of the*

Tree," in School Library Journal, *Vol. 38, No. 6, June, 1992, p. 111.*

What Did You Leave Behind? (1978)

The suggestion here is that from any sensory experience—a day at the beach, a parade, a romp in the snow—we bring back not only souvenirs (a shell, a balloon, a "cherry-red nose") but also impressions. And that, of course, is inarguable: in book after book from **White Snow, Bright Snow** onward, Tresselt and [illustrator Roger] Duvoisin gave us, implicitly, the impressions of just such experiences. But the vehicle was their word-and-picture art: the book was a creative simulation-cum-evocation of the experience as a tangible and intangible whole. Here, instead, we're fed dollops of imagery—"Did you leave the thunder-crash of great waves, stumbling and spilling on the smooth wet sand?"—and asked, after the fact, to embrace it as personal, lasting experience. The difference is that between lyric poetry that speaks to the reader and the teacher who drums in its meaning.

> *A review of "What Did You Leave Behind?" in* Kirkus Reviews, *Vol. XLVI, No. 6, March 15, 1978, p. 369.*

Remarkably vibrant and lovely paintings from Duvoisin's gifted hands accompany Tresselt's poetic text, inducements to observation and thought. Taking young readers on several outings, the book reminds them gently that they have brought home mementos: from the seashore, shells and sand in their shoes; from a parade, a "sassy balloon" and a proud flag; from a fair, toys they have won and other souvenirs. But, he asks, have they really left behind the sounds, sights, smells or feelings connected with all the excursions. The author and illustrator have collaborated on several outstanding picture books, and here is one of their most attractive.

> *A review of "What Did You Leave Behind?" in* Publishers Weekly, *Vol. 213, No. 13, March 27, 1978, p. 72.*

Both members of a familiar team are at their best here, Duvoisin's brilliant colors and skilled compositions especially effective in outdoor scenes, and Tresselt's clear, poetic text evocative. In a series of settings (the beach, a parade, a winter's day) Tresselt reminds children that one retains more than the physical evidence of beauty or pleasure, that in addition to the snow, or sand, or wildflowers, or a balloon, one remembers "the hot scent of wild roses, the cool tingle of the salt spray" . . . the music echoing in your ears . . . the sound of marching feet . . . the sunlight coming down all speckled through the new green of young leaves. A pleasure to look at, the book encourages, with no didacticism, the joy of heightened observation.

> *Zena Sutherland, in a review of "What Did You Leave Behind?" in* Bulletin of the Center for Children's Books, *Vol. 32, No. 2, October, 1978, p. 37.*

Children's
Literature
Review

CUMULATIVE INDEX TO AUTHORS

This index lists all author entries in *Children's Literature Review* and includes cross-references to them in other Gale sources. References in the index are identified as follows:

Author Index

CUMULATIVE INDEX TO NATIONALITIES

Gantos, Jack 18
Geisel, Theodor Seuss 1
George, Jean Craighead 1
Gibbons, Gail 8
Giblin, James Cross 29
Giovanni, Nikki 6
Glubok, Shirley 1
Goble, Paul 21
Goffstein, M. B. 3
Gordon, Sheila 27
Graham, Lorenz B. 10
Gramatky, Hardie 22
Greene, Bette 2
Greenfield, Eloise 4
Guy, Rosa 13
Haley, Gale E. 21
Hamilton, Virginia 1, 11
Hansen, Joyce 21
Haskins, James 3
Hautzig, Esther R. 22
Haywood, Carolyn 22
Henkes, Kevin 23
Henry, Marguerite 4
Hentoff, Nat 1
Highwater, Jamake 17
Hinton, S. E. 3, 23
Hoban, Russell 3
Hoban, Tana 13
Hoberman, Mary Ann 22
Hogrogian, Nonny 2
Howe, James 9
Hughes, Langston 17
Hunt, Irene 1
Hunter, Kristin 3
Hurmence, Belinda 25
Hyde, Margaret O. 23
Isadora, Rachel 7
Jackson, Jesse 28
Jarrell, Randall 6
Jeffers, Susan 30
Jonas, Ann 12
Jordan, June 10
Joyce, William 26
Keats, Ezra Jack 1
Kellogg, Steven 6
Kennedy, X. J. 27
Kerr, M. E. 29
Kherdian, David 24
Klein, Norma 2, 19
Konigsburg, E. L. 1
Kotzwinkle, William 6
Krementz, Jill 5
Kuskin, Karla 4
Langstaff, John 3
Lasky, Kathryn 11
Lauber, Patricia 16
Lawson, Robert 2
Le Guin, Ursula K. 3, 28
Leaf, Munro 25
L'Engle, Madeleine 1, 14
Lenski, Lois 26
LeShan, Eda J. 6
Lester, Julius 2
Lionni, Leo 7
Lipsyte, Robert 23
Livingston, Myra Cohn 7
Lobel, Arnold 5
Locker, Thomas 14
Lowry, Lois 6
MacLachlan, Patricia 14
Manley, Seon 3
Marshall, James 21

Mathis, Sharon Bell 3
Mayer, Mercer 11
Mazer, Harry 16
Mazer, Norma Fox 23
McCloskey, Robert 7
McClung, Robert M. 11
McCord, David 9
McDermott, Gerald 9
McHargue, Georgess 2
McKinley, Robin 10
McKissack, Patricia C. 23
Meltzer, Milton 13
Merriam, Eve 14
Milne, Lorus J. 22
Milne, Margery J. 22
Mohr, Nicholasa 22
Monjo, F. N. 2
Moore, Lilian 15
Mukerji, Dhan Gopal 10
Munsch, Robert N. 19
Myers, Walter Dean 4, 16
Naylor, Phyllis Reynolds 17
Ness, Evaline 6
Nixon, Joan Lowery 24
O'Brien, Robert C. 2
O'Dell, Scott 1, 16
Oneal, Zibby 13
Parish, Peggy 22
Pascal, Francine 25
Patent, Dorothy Hinshaw 19
Paterson, Katherine 7
Paulsen, Gary 19
Peck, Richard 15
Peet, Bill 12
Petersham, Maud 24
Petersham, Miska 24
Petry, Ann 12
Pfeffer, Susan Beth 11
Pierce, Meredith Ann 20
Pike, Christopher 29
Pinkwater, D. Manus 4
Politi, Leo 29
Prelutsky, Jack 13
Pringle, Laurence 4
Provensen, Alice 11
Provensen, Martin 11
Pyle, Howard 22
Raskin, Ellen 1, 12
Rau, Margaret 8
Reiss, Johanna 19
Rey, H. A. 5
Rey, Margret 5
Ringgold, Faith 30
Rockwell, Thomas 6
Rodgers, Mary 20
Rylant, Cynthia 15
Sachar, Louis 28
Sachs, Marilyn 2
Salinger, J. D. 18
Sanchez, Sonia 18
Sattler, Helen Roney 24
Say, Allen 22
Scarry, Richard 3
Schwartz, Alvin 3
Schwartz, Amy 25
Scieszka, Jon 27
Scott, Jack Denton 20
Sebestyen, Ouida 17
Selden, George 8
Selsam, Millicent E. 1
Sendak, Maurice 1, 17
Seredy, Kate 10

Seuss, Dr. 9
Showers, Paul 6
Shulevitz, Uri 5
Silverstein, Alvin 25
Silverstein, Shel 5
Silverstein, Virginia B. 25
Simon, Seymour 9
Singer, Isaac Bashevis 1
Sleator, William 29
Slote, Alfred 4
Smucker, Barbara 10
Sneve, Virginia Driving Hawk 2
Sobol, Donald J. 4
Speare, Elizabeth George 8
Spier, Peter 5
Spinelli, Jerry 26
Steig, William 2, 15
Steptoe, John 2, 12
Sterling, Dorothy 1
Stevenson, James 17
Strasser, Todd 11
Suhl, Yuri 2
Tarry, Ellen 26
Taylor, Mildred D. 9
Taylor, Theodore 30
Thomas, Ianthe 8
Thomas, Joyce Carol 19
Thompson, Julian F. 24
Thompson, Kay 22
Tobias, Tobi 4
Tresselt, Alvin 30
Tudor, Tasha 13
Tunis, Edwin 2
Uchida, Yoshiko 6
Van Allsburg, Chris 5, 13
Viorst, Judith 3
Voigt, Cynthia 13
Walter, Mildred Pitts 15
Watson, Clyde 3
Weiss, Harvey 4
Wells, Rosemary 16
Wersba, Barbara 3
White, E. B. 1, 21
White, Robb 3
Wibberley, Leonard 3
Wilder, Laura Ingalls 2
Wilkinson, Brenda 20
Willard, Nancy 5
Williams, Jay 8
Williams, Vera B. 9
Wojciechowska, Maia 1
Wood, Audrey 26
Wood, Don 26
Worth, Valerie 21
Yarbrough, Camille 29
Yashima, Taro 4
Yep, Laurence 3, 17
Yolen, Jane 4
Yorinks, Arthur 20
Young, Ed 27
Zim, Herbert S. 2
Zindel, Paul 3
Zolotow, Charlotte 2

AUSTRALIAN
Baker, Jeannie 28
Base, Graeme 22
Chauncy, Nan 6
Clark, Mavis Thorpe 30
Fox, Mem 23
Hilton, Nette 25
Klein, Robin 21

Lindsay, Norman **8**
Mattingley, Christobel **24**
Ormerod, Jan **20**
Ottley, Reginald **16**
Phipson, Joan **5**
Southall, Ivan **2**
Spence, Eleanor **26**
Thiele, Colin **27**
Travers, P. L. **2**
Wrightson, Patricia **4, 14**

AUSTRIAN
Bemelmans, Ludwig **6**
Nostlinger, Christine **12**

BELGIAN
Herge **6**
Vincent, Gabrielle **13**

CANADIAN
Blades, Ann **15**
Burnford, Sheila **2**
Cleaver, Elizabeth **13**
Cox, Palmer **24**
Doyle, Brian **22**
Gay, Marie-Louise **27**
Houston, James **3**
Hughes, Monica **9**
Khalsa, Dayal Kaur **30**
Korman, Gordon **25**
Kurelek, William **2**
Lee, Dennis **3**
Little, Jean **4**
Lunn, Janet **18**
Major, Kevin **11**
Markoosie **23**
Milne, Lorus J. **22**
Montgomery, L. M. **8**
Mowat, Farley **20**
Munsch, Robert N. **19**
Pearson, Kit **26**
Poulin, Stephane **28**
Richler, Mordecai **17**
Smucker, Barbara **10**
Stren, Patti **5**
Wynne-Jones, Tim **21**

CHILEAN
Krahn, Fernando **3**

CHINESE
Young, Ed **27**

CZECHOSLOVAKIAN
Sasek, M. **4**

DANISH
Andersen, Hans Christian **6**
Bodker, Cecil **23**
Drescher, Henrik **20**
Haugaard, Erik Christian **11**
Nielsen, Kay **16**

DUTCH
Biegel, Paul **27**
Bruna, Dick **7**
DeJong, Meindert **1**
Haar, Jaap ter **15**
Lionni, Leo **7**
Reiss, Johanna **19**
Schmidt, Annie M. G. **22**
Spier, Peter **5**

ENGLISH
Adams, Richard **20**
Ahlberg, Allan **18**
Ahlberg, Janet **18**
Aiken, Joan **1, 19**
Alcock, Vivien **26**
Ardizzone, Edward **3**
Ashley, Bernard **4**
Awdry, W. V. **23**
Baker, Jeannie **28**
Banner, Angela **24**
Base, Graeme **22**
Bawden, Nina **2**
Bianco, Margery Williams **19**
Biro, Val **28**
Bond, Michael **1**
Boston, L. M. **3**
Briggs, Raymond **10**
Brooke, L. Leslie **20**
Browne, Anthony **19**
Burnett, Frances Hodgson **24**
Burningham, John **9**
Burton, Hester **1**
Caldecott, Randolph **14**
Carroll, Lewis **2, 18**
Causley, Charles **30**
Chauncy, Nan **6**
Christopher, John **2**
Clarke, Pauline **28**
Cooper, Susan **4**
Corbett, W. J. **19**
Cresswell, Helen **18**
Cross, Gillian **28**
Dahl, Roald **1, 7**
de la Mare, Walter **23**
Dickinson, Peter **29**
Doherty, Berlie **21**
Farmer, Penelope **8**
Fine, Anne **25**
Gardam, Jane **12**
Garfield, Leon **21**
Garner, Alan **20**
Gerrard, Roy **23**
Goble, Paul **21**
Godden, Rumer **20**
Goodall, John S. **25**
Grahame, Kenneth **5**
Greenaway, Kate **6**
Handford, Martin **22**
Harris, Rosemary **30**
Hill, Eric **13**
Howker, Janni **14**
Hughes, Monica **9**
Hughes, Shirley **15**
Hughes, Ted **3**
Hutchins, Pat **20**
Jacques, Brian **21**
Jones, Diana Wynne **23**
Kemp, Gene **29**
Lear, Edward **1**
Lewis, C. S. **3, 27**
Lively, Penelope **7**
Lofting, Hugh **19**
Macaulay, David **3, 14**
Mark, Jan **11**
Mayne, William **25**
Milne, A. A. **1, 26**
Naidoo, Beverley **29**
Nesbit, E. **3**
Norton, Mary **6**
Oakley, Graham **7**
Ottley, Reginald **16**

Oxenbury, Helen **22**
Pearce, Philippa **9**
Peyton, K. M. **3**
Pienkowski, Jan **6**
Potter, Beatrix **1, 19**
Pullman, Philip **20**
Ransome, Arthur **8**
Reid Banks, Lynne **24**
Serraillier, Ian **2**
Sewell, Anna **17**
Sharp, Margery **27**
Shepard, E. H. **27**
Simmonds, Posy **23**
Streatfeild, Noel **17**
Sutcliff, Rosemary **1**
Tenniel, Sir John **18**
Townsend, John Rowe **2**
Travers, P. L. **2**
Treece, Henry **2**
Walsh, Jill Paton **2**
Westall, Robert **13**
Wildsmith, Brian **2**
Willard, Barbara **2**
Williams, Kit **4**

FILIPINO
Aruego, Jose **5**

FINNISH
Jansson, Tove **2**

FRENCH
Ayme, Marcel **25**
Berna, Paul **19**
Brunhoff, Jean de **4**
Brunhoff, Laurent de **4**
Guillot, Rene **22**
Saint-Exupery, Antoine de **10**
Ungerer, Tomi **3**

GERMAN
Benary-Isbert, Margot **12**
d'Aulaire, Edgar Parin **21**
Ende, Michael **14**
Hartling, Peter **29**
Heine, Helme **18**
Janosch **26**
Kastner, Erich **4**
Kruss, James **9**
Rey, H. A. **5**
Rey, Margret **5**
Richter, Hans Peter **21**
Zimnik, Reiner **3**

GREEK
Aesop **14**
Zei, Alki **6**

HUNGARIAN
Biro, Val **28**
Galdone, Paul **16**
Seredy, Kate **10**

INDIAN
Mukerji, Dhan Gopal **10**

IRISH
Bunting, Eve **28**
Dillon, Eilis **26**
Lewis, C. S. **3, 27**
O'Shea, Pat **18**

Nationality Index

CUMULATIVE INDEX TO TITLES

233

Title Index

Title Index

Title Index

Title Index

Title Index

Title Index

ISBN 0-8103-5703-8

CLR 30

90000

9 780810 357037